Frommer's

W9-AJN-130

Hong Kong
8th Edition

by Beth Reiber

Here's what the critics say about Frommer's:

"Amazingly easy to use. Very portable, very complete."
—*Booklist*

"Detailed, accurate, and easy-to-read information for all price ranges."
—*Glamour Magazine*

"Hotel information is close to encyclopedic."
—*Des Moines Sunday Register*

"Frommer's Guides have a way of giving you a real feel for a place."
—*Knight Ridder Newspapers*

WILEY

Wiley Publishing, Inc.

About the Author

Beth Reiber worked for several years in Germany as a freelance travel writer writing for major U.S. newspapers and in Tokyo as editor of the *Far East Traveler*. Now a freelance travel writer residing in Lawrence, Kansas, with her two sons, she's the author of several Frommer's guides, including *Frommer's Japan* and *Frommer's Tokyo*, and is a contributor to *Frommer's Europe from $85 a Day*, *Frommer's USA*, and *Frommer's China*.

Published by:

Wiley Publishing, Inc.

111 River St.
Hoboken, NJ 07030-5774

ISBN 0-7645-7669-0

Editor: Kendra L. Falkenstein
Production Editor: Ian Skinnari
Cartographer: Nicholas Trotter
Photo Editor: Richard Fox
Production by Wiley Indianapolis Composition Services

Front cover photo: Hong Kong: Street scene with man on cellphone
Back cover photo: Dragon-boat races in Aberdeen harbor

For information on our other products and services or to obtain technical support, please contact our Customer Care Department within the U.S. at 800/762-2974, outside the U.S. at 317/572-3993 or fax 317/572-4002.

Wiley also publishes its books in a variety of electronic formats. Some content that appears in print may not be available in electronic formats.

Manufactured in the United States of America

5   4   3   2   1

Contents

List of Maps

Acknowledgments

I would like to thank some fine and very special people who graciously extended their help in the preparation of this book: Diana Budiman, Cynthia Leung, and Eliza Cheng of the Hong Kong Tourist Association; and Teresa Costa Gomes of the Macau Government Tourist Office. A special thanks goes to my sons, Matthias and Johannes, for putting up with my long absences ever since they can remember.

An Invitation to the Reader

In researching this book, we discovered many wonderful places—hotels, restaurants, shops, and more. We're sure you'll find others. Please tell us about them, so we can share the information with your fellow travelers in upcoming editions. If you were disappointed with a recommendation, we'd love to know that, too. Please write to:

Frommer's Hong Kong, 8th Edition
Wiley Publishing, Inc. • 111 River St. • Hoboken, NJ 07030-5774

An Additional Note

Please be advised that travel information is subject to change at any time—and this is especially true of prices. We therefore suggest that you write or call ahead for confirmation when making your travel plans. The authors, editors, and publisher cannot be held responsible for the experiences of readers while traveling. Your safety is important to us, however, so we encourage you to stay alert and be aware of your surroundings. Keep a close eye on cameras, purses, and wallets, all favorite targets of thieves and pickpockets.

Other Great Guides for Your Trip:

Suzy Gershman's Born to Shop Hong Kong, Shanghai & Beijing
Frommer's China
Frommer's Shanghai
Frommer's Beijing
Frommer's Southeast Asia

Frommer's Star Ratings, Icons & Abbreviations

Every hotel, restaurant, and attraction listing in this guide has been ranked for quality, value, service, amenities, and special features using a **star-rating system.** In country, state, and regional guides, we also rate towns and regions to help you narrow down your choices and budget your time accordingly. Hotels and restaurants are rated on a scale of zero (recommended) to three stars (exceptional). Attractions, shopping, nightlife, towns, and regions are rated according to the following scale: zero stars (recommended), one star (highly recommended), two stars (very highly recommended), and three stars (must-see).

In addition to the star-rating system, we also use **seven feature icons** that point you to the great deals, in-the-yknow advice, and unique experiences that separate travelers from tourists. Throughout the book, look for:

Finds	Special finds—those places only insiders know about
Fun Fact	Fun facts—details that make travelers more informed and their trips more fun
Kids	Best bets for kids and advice for the whole family
Moments	Special moments—those experiences that memories are made of
Overrated	Places or experiences not worth your time or money
Tips	Insider tips—great ways to save time and money
Value	Great values—where to get the best deals

The following **abbreviations** are used for credit cards:

AE	American Express	DISC	Discover	V	Visa
DC	Diners Club	MC	MasterCard		

Frommers.com

Now that you have the guidebook to a great trip, visit our website at **www.frommers.com** for travel information on more than 3,000 destinations. With features updated regularly, we give you instant access to the most current trip-planning information available. At Frommers.com, you'll also find the best prices on airfares, accommodations, and car rentals—and you can even book travel online through our travel booking partners. At Frommers.com, you'll also find the following:

- Online updates to our most popular guidebooks
- Vacation sweepstakes and contest giveaways
- Newsletter highlighting the hottest travel trends
- Online travel message boards with featured travel discussions

What's New in Hong Kong

Here are the latest openings, offerings, changes, and events in Hong Kong.

PLANNING YOUR TRIP Due to the 2003 SARS (Severe Acute Respiratory Syndrome) outbreak that sickened 1,755 people and claimed 299 lives in Hong Kong, all incoming passengers arriving by plane, train, and boat are scanned for fever. Travelers are advised to avoid traveling with a fever and should consider flu shots if traveling during flu season.

Note, too, that since the terrorist attacks of September 11, 2001, some airlines (like Northwest and United) allow check-in services at Hong Kong Station and Kowloon Station but others (like Continental) don't.

For complete information on planning your trip, see chapter 2.

GETTING TO KNOW HONG KONG The new KCR East Tsim Sha Tsui Station, opened at the end of 2004 at the tip of Kowloon in Tsim Sha Tsui East, provides a convenient link between the MTR subway system and the KCR **East Rail** with service to the New Territories and China. There's also a new **West Rail** linking West Kowloon with Tuen Mun in the northwestern part of the New Territories.

For complete information on getting to know Hong Kong, see chapter 3.

WHERE TO STAY Relaxed restrictions for tourists from selected cities in mainland China, freeing them from mandatory group tours and allowing them to travel to Hong Kong on their own, have brought a flood of visitors to Hong Kong's medium-priced hotels.

While bargains do exist, especially on the Internet, it's prudent to make reservations far in advance and then keep checking for updated bargains.

The Great Eagle Hotel has changed its name to **Langham Hotel,** 8 Peking Rd. (© **800/223-6800** in the U.S. and Canada), a reflection of its association with the historic Langham Hotel in London.

Hong Kong's hippest new hotel is **Jia,** 1–5 Irving St., Causeway Bay (© **852/3196 9000**), a 57-room boutique hotel created by design guru Philippe Starck and featuring oh-so-cool stylish rooms bathed in white and divided into distinct, high-tech living areas.

For complete information on Hong Kong's hotels, see chapter 4.

WHERE TO DINE Several long-time restaurants have sadly closed, most notably the old-fashioned **Great Shanghai.** More than likely they just couldn't compete with the spate of trendy new restaurants that have upped the ante in decor, cuisine, and breathtaking views. Among the best new arrivals, top on a short list is **Hutong,** 1 Peking Rd., Tsim Sha Tsui (© **852/3428 8342**), serving creative North Chinese fare in a dark dining hall that spotlights the stunning views from its 28th-floor perch.

On the other side of the harbor, Times Square in Causeway Bay turns up the heat with the addition of two very popular venues to its top-floor dining mecca: **Ramas Greens** (© **852/ 3101 0656**), which dishes out

East-Meets-West fusion cuisine in a contemporary but cozy dining hall, and **Wasabisabi** (© 852/2506 0009), a chic Japanese restaurant that looks like it was airlifted straight from Tokyo and with a very cool bar for après–dinner drinks.

For complete information on Hong Kong's restaurants, see chapter 5.

EXPLORING HONG KONG Hong Kong has never rested on past laurels when it comes to attractions. To increase its tourism appeal, every night the city now stages the **Symphony of Lights,** an 18-minute multimedia light and laser show projected from 18 buildings on Hong Kong Island. The best place to take in the show is from the Tsim Sha Tsui waterfront, which honors Hong Kong's most famous movie personalities with its new **Avenue of Stars,** where embedded plaques pay tribute to Bruce Lee, Jackie Chan, and other film greats.

In the works is **Hong Kong Disneyland,** slated to open by late 2005/early 2006 on reclaimed land on Lantau island. This and other upcoming tourist attractions are the subject of a modest yet fascinating museum, **The Hong Kong Planning and Infrastructure Exhibition Gallery,** 3 Edinburgh Place, Central (© 852/3101 6516), which gives an unparalleled glimpse into Hong Kong's future. Visitors can "stroll" Hong Kong's waterfront via a three-dimensional panorama, "fly" over Sha Tin and other budding satellite towns, and view eye-popping models of all existing and planned infrastructure projects throughout Hong Kong.

For complete information on exploring Hong Kong, see chapters 6 and 7.

HONG KONG SHOPPING Central has revved up its shopping appeal with the opening of **ifc mall,** located next to Hong Kong Station. It offers more than 200 high-end boutiques and restaurants, some of the latter with uninterrupted harbor views.

For more information on shopping in Hong Kong, see chapter 8.

HONG KONG AFTER DARK You could lose sleep trying to keep up with Hong Kong's ever-expanding nightlife scene, but there's no chance of dozing off at **Aqua Spirit,** which hovers above Tsim Sha Tsui on the 30th floor, 1 Peking Rd. (© 852/3427 2288), with fabulous views of the city. Other new hot spots include **Dragon-i,** 60 Wyndham St., Central (© 852/3110 1222), a popular watering hole for Hong Kong's beautiful people, and **Klong Bar & Grill,** 54–62 Lockhart Rd., Wan Chai (© 852/2217 8330), an upmarket venue that lets its hair down on weekends.

Bottoms Up, Hong Kong's most famous topless bar, has moved from its staid Tsim Sha Tsui location to raunchier Wan Chai at 37–39 Lockhart Rd. (© 852/2721 4509).

For complete information on Hong Kong's nightlife, see chapter 9.

MACAU A new **TurboJET Sea Express ferry service** now operates directly between Hong Kong International Airport and Macau. Travelers who wish to take advantage of this great convenience should check into the Air/Sea Transfer Desk *before* passing through customs.

In Macau, there's a new **Macau Tourist Hotline** at © 853/333000.

Macau's most ambitious tourism project of the new century is **Fisherman's Wharf,** a huge complex on reclaimed land that includes shops, restaurants, bars, a disco, an amusement park, and even an "active" volcano. Meanwhile, Macau's reputation as Asia's gambling mecca continues with the opening of themed, Las Vegas–style casinos like **Pharaoh's Palace,** Avenida da Amizade (© 853/788111), and **Sands Macau,** beside Fisherman's Wharf (© 853/883388).

For complete information on Macau, see chapter 11.

The Best of Hong Kong

Every time I come to Hong Kong, I feel as though I've wandered onto a movie set. Maybe I'm an incurable romantic, but when I stand at the railing of the famous Star Ferry as it glides across the harbor, ride a rickety old tram as it winds its way across Hong Kong Island, or marvel anew at the stunning views afforded from atop Victoria Peak, I can't help but think I must have somehow landed in the middle of an epic drama where the past has melted into the present. So many images float by—wooden boats bobbing up and down in the harbor beside huge ocean liners; crumbling tenements next to ultramodern high-rises; squalid alleys behind luxury hotels; old Chinese people pushing wheelbarrows as Rolls-Royces glide by; market vendors selling chicken feet and dried squid while talking on cellular phones.

In fact, one of the most striking characteristics of Hong Kong is this interweaving of seeming contradictions and the interplay of the exotic and the technically advanced. There are as many skyscrapers here as you're likely to see anywhere, but they're built with bamboo scaffolding. Historic trams rumble through Central, while below ground is one of the most efficient subways in the world, complete with the world's first "contactless" tickets, cards that are waved over a scanner. The city has what are arguably some of the best and most sophisticated restaurants in the world, but it also has *dai pai dong*, street-side food stalls. Hong Kong is home to one of the world's largest shopping malls, but there are also lively street markets virtually everywhere.

Because of these dazzling contrasts, Hong Kong offers visitors something unique—the chance to experience a vibrant Chinese city without sacrificing the comforts of home. To be sure, much of Hong Kong's Western fabric comes from the legacy left by the British, who ruled the colony until 1997, when it was handed back to China as a Special Administrative Region (thus the SAR abbreviation you'll see there and throughout this book). British influence is still evident everywhere, from Hong Kong's school system to its free-market economy, from its rugby teams to its double-decker buses, and from English pubs and tea in the afternoon to (my favorite) orderly queues. But though the city was molded by the British, it has always been, at its heart, Chinese, with Chinese medicine shops, street vendors, lively dim sum restaurants, old men taking their caged birds for walks in the park, and colorful festivals. Indeed, for the casual visitor, Hong Kong seems little changed since the 1997 handover. No doubt some visitors remain oblivious to even the most visible sign of that change: the replacement of the Union Jack and old flag of the Crown Colony of Hong Kong with the red, starred flag of China and the new red Hong Kong flag with its emblem of the bauhinia flower.

Hong Kong was founded as a place to conduct business and to trade, and it continues to serve that purpose both aggressively and successfully. The world's fourth-largest banking and financial center in terms of external assets, Hong

Hong Kong Region

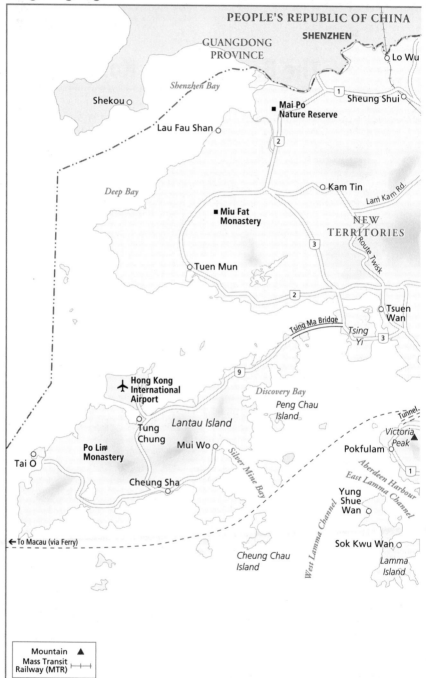

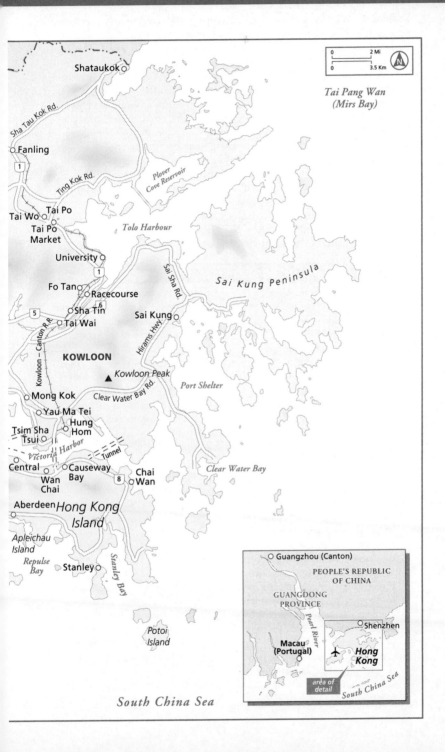

Shataukok

Tai Pang Wan
(Mirs Bay)

Sha Tau Kok Rd.

Fanling

1

Ting Kok Rd.

Plover
Cove Reservoir

Tai Po
Tai Wo
Tai Po
Market

Tolo Harbour

University

1

Sai Sha Rd.

Sai Kung Peninsula

Fo Tan
Racecourse
6
Sha Tin
Tai Wai

5

Sai Kung

Kowloon – Canton R.R.

Hirams Hwy.

KOWLOON

Kowloon Peak

Port Shelter

Mong Kok

Clear Water Bay Rd.

Yau Ma Tei
Hung
Hom
Tsim Sha
Tsui

Victoria Harbor

Tunnel

Central
Causeway
Bay

Clear Water Bay

Wan
Chai

8

Chai
Wan

Aberdeen Hong Kong
Island

Apleichau
Island

Repulse
Bay

Stanley

Stanley Bay

Potoi
Island

South China Sea

Guangzhou (Canton)

PEOPLE'S REPUBLIC
OF CHINA

GUANGDONG
PROVINCE

Pearl River

Shenzhen

Macau
(Portugal)

Hong
Kong

area of
detail

South China Sea

0   2 Mi
0   3.5 Km

Kong is the "Wall Street of Asia," with banking, international insurance, advertising, and publishing among its biggest industries. Hong Kong also boasts the world's eighth-largest trading economy, and is one of the world's leading exporters of toys, garments, and watches.

Little wonder, then, that as a duty-free port, Hong Kong attracts approximately 14 million visitors a year, making tourism one of its leading industries despite a devastating downturn in tourism in 2003 due to an outbreak of Severe Acute Respiratory Syndrome (SARS). Shopping is one of the main reasons people come here, and at first glance, the city does seem rather like one huge department store. But there's much more to Hong Kong than shopping. There's also wining, dining, and sightseeing, as well as isolated places to get away from it all.

For those who wish to journey farther afield, Macau, a former Portuguese colony handed back to China in 1999, is just an hour's boat ride away; and vast China itself lies just beyond Hong Kong's border, making it the perfect gateway for trips to Guangzhou, Shanghai, Beijing, and beyond.

The more you search for in Hong Kong, the more you'll find. Before long, you, too, may find yourself swept up in the drama.

1 Frommer's Favorite Hong Kong Experiences

- **Dining on Dim Sum:** A great way to start your day, nothing conveys a sense of Chinese life more vividly than a visit to a crowded, lively Cantonese restaurant for breakfast or lunch, where trolleys of dim sum in bamboo steamers are wheeled from customer to customer. Simply peer into the passing bamboo baskets and choose what appears the most tempting. See section 7 of chapter 5, beginning on p. 153, for more on Hong Kong's dim sum restaurants.

- **Getting Up Early to Watch Tai Chi:** Before breakfast, head to one of Hong Kong's many parks to watch people going through the slow, graceful motions of tai chi, or shadow boxing. For the best viewing, go to Kowloon Park, Hong Kong Park, Victoria Park, or the Zoological and Botanical Gardens (see section 4 of chapter 6, beginning on p. 170, for more on these parks and gardens). You can even participate in free practice sessions, held 3 mornings a week on the Tsim Sha Tsui waterfront promenade. See p. 179.

- **Riding the Star Ferry:** To reacquaint myself with the city, one of the first things I do on each return trip is to hop aboard the Star Ferry for one of the most dramatic—and cheapest—5-minute boat rides in the world. Hong Kong's harbor is one of the world's busiest, and beyond it rises one of earth's most breathtaking skylines. See p. 55.

- **Taking a Tram:** Take a double-decker tram ride from one end of Hong Kong Island to the other for an unparalleled view of life in the crowded city as you pass skyscrapers, street markets, traditional Chinese shops, and department stores. See p. 54.

- **Gazing upon Hong Kong from Victoria Peak:** You don't know Hong Kong until you've seen it from here. Take the tram to Victoria Peak, famous for its views of Central, the harbor, Kowloon, and undulating hills beyond, followed by a 1-hour circular hike and a meal with a view. Don't miss the nighttime view, one of the most spectacular and romantic in the world. See p. 47.

- **Visiting a Tailor:** Nothing beats the thrill of having something custom-made to fit you perfectly. If this is your dream, make a trek to a tailor one of your first priorities so that you'll have time for several fittings. See p. 220.
- **Bargain-Hunting in Stanley:** Stall after stall of casual wear, silk clothing, tennis shoes, accessories, and souvenirs and crafts imported from China make this a shopper's paradise. And after a day of bargaining, I like to recuperate in one of Stanley's trendy yet casual restaurants. See p. 218.
- **Window-Shopping on Nathan Road:** Open-fronted clothing boutiques, jewelry stores, camera shops, tailors, tourists from around the world, international cuisine, huge neon signs, and whirling traffic combine to make this boulevard Hong Kong's most famous shopping street. See p. 198.
- **Shopping at Shanghai Tang:** This 1930s-style Chinese department store is oh-so-chic, with lime-green- or fuchsia-colored jackets, Mao watches, 1930s reproduction home decor, and more. The shopping bag that comes with your purchase is a bonus—just way too cool—and the shop's free postcards are also pretty fab. See p. 212.
- **Browsing for Chinese Souvenirs:** In addition to Shanghai Tang and Stanley Market, many Chinese emporiums sell vases, vase stands, porcelain figurines, chinaware, calligraphy brushes, birdcages, jade, silk jackets, teas, and various Chinese crafts and products. See chapter 8.
- **Strolling Tsim Sha Tsui's Waterfront:** There's a pedestrian promenade that stretches from the Star Ferry eastward along Tsim Sha Tsui and Tsim Sha Tsui East, providing close-up views of the

harbor and Hong Kong Island with its skyscrapers. After dark, this is a wonderful romantic stroll, with the lights of Hong Kong Island shimmering across the water. And every evening at 8pm, Hong Kong puts on a spectacular laser and light show projected from skyscrapers on Hong Kong Island. The best place to see this colorful extravaganza? On the Tsim Sha Tsui waterfront alongside the Hong Kong Cultural Centre. See p. 198.
- **Hearing the Birds Sing at Yuen Po Street Bird Garden:** See pampered birds at this unusual garden, brought by their owners so they can sing and communicate with other birds on their daily outing. Vendors sell wooden birdcages, porcelain bird dishes, and other paraphernalia. See p. 171.
- **Paying Respects at the Big Buddha:** Laze on the open aft deck during the 50-minute ferry ride to Lantau island (and enjoy great views of the harbor and skyline along the way), followed by a hair-raising bus ride over lush hills to see the world's largest, seated, outdoor bronze Buddha, located at the Po Lin Monastery. Complete your pilgrimage with a vegetarian meal at the monastery. See the "Lantau" section of chapter 10, beginning on p. 246.
- **Hiking Across Lamma:** An excursion to this outlying island will do your soul good. Start with the 35-minute ferry trip, followed by a 90-minute hike across the island, perhaps some swimming at a beach, and finally a meal of fresh seafood at an open-air waterfront restaurant. See the "Lamma" section of chapter 10, beginning on p. 252.
- **Expanding Your Cultural Horizons at the Hong Kong Museum**

of Art: Hong Kong's most important art museum is a must-see for its vast collection of Chinese antiquities, including ceramics, jade, and lacquerware, as well as its gallery of old paintings depicting Hong Kong through the ages and its changing exhibition of contemporary Hong Kong art—all against the dramatic backdrop of Hong Kong's harbor outside its windows. See p. 162.

- **Reliving the Past at the Hong Kong Museum of History:** For a quick 101 course on Hong Kong history, make a visit to the Hong Kong Museum of History one of your first priorities. A life-size diorama of a Neolithic settlement, replicas of fishing boats and traditional houses, ethnic clothing, re-created street scenes, displays of colorful festivals, and the Chinese take on the opium wars are just some of the visual feasts awaiting visitors. If you see only one museum during your stay, this should be it. See p. 164.
- **Having Your Fortune Told:** Want to know about your future love life, marriage, family, or career? Consult one of Hong Kong's many fortune-tellers; those who speak English can be found at Man Mo Temple in the Western District, or Wong Tai Sin temple and the Tin Hau Temple near the Temple Street Night Market. See p. 169, 170, and 200, respectively.
- **Exploring the Western District:** Produce, bolts of cloth, live snakes, ginseng, dried seafood, Chinese herbs and medicines, a historic temple, a museum dedicated to Chinese and Western medicine, and antiques and collectibles are just some of the things you'll see while strolling through one of Hong Kong's most fascinating neighborhoods. See p. 48.

- **Browsing Antiques Shops on Hollywood Road:** Whether you have thousands of dollars to spend on Ming dynasty heirlooms or just a couple of bucks for a snuff bottle, there's something for everyone in the dozens of antiques shops lining this famous Hong Kong Island road and from outdoor vendor stalls on nearby Cat Street. A sightseeing bonus is Man Mo Temple (p. 194), Hong Kong's oldest temple, on Hollywood Road. See the "Antiques & Collectibles" section of chapter 8, beginning on p. 208.
- **Hopping Aboard the Central/ Mid-Levels Escalator:** Hop aboard the world's longest covered people mover as it snakes its way uphill in a series of escalators. You can hop off at one of 29 exits to enjoy a drink or meal at one of the many establishments along its link, or take it to the top for a 20-minute ride. See p. 58.
- **Meeting the People:** Learn about pearls, Chinese antiques, *feng shui* (geomancy), tai chi (shadow boxing), and other cultural traditions on free, 1-hour tours and lectures given by local experts. Stop by one of the Hong Kong Tourism Board's Visitor Information & Services Centres for the *Cultural Kaleidoscope* brochure outlining HKTB's "Meet the People" program. See chapter 3's "Visitor Information" section, beginning on p. 43, for more information on the Hong Kong Tourism Board.
- **Taking High Tea at a Posh Hotel:** The British rulers may be gone, but their legacy lives on in the afternoon tea. Virtually all upper-class hotels offer afternoon tea, but my favorites are those offered by The Peninsula and Hotel InterContinental. Come for afternoon tea, nibble on finger sandwiches, and gaze away. See p. 156.

- **Betting on the Horses:** Join thousands of spectators (between Sept and May) at Hong Kong's favorite sporting event. The city boasts two sophisticated racing tracks, and if you need help in wagering bets, consider joining a special tour of the races. See the "Spectator Sports" section of chapter 6, beginning on p. 180.

- **Regressing to Childhood at Ocean Park:** Southeast Asia's largest oceanarium and fun park boasts one of the world's longest and fastest roller coasters among its many thrill rides; a great cable-car ride with breathtaking views of the South China Sea; playgrounds just for kids; and a theater with seats that move with the action on the screen. If it's wildlife you're wild about, you'll find the world's largest reef aquarium, a shark tank with an underwater pedestrian tunnel, a fascinating collection of weird and wonderful goldfish, an aviary and butterfly dome, panda bears, and a dolphin and killer-whale show. A must for kids of all ages. See p. 174.

- **Escaping to the New Territories:** The New Territories is a vast area stretching from the densely populated area of Kowloon to the Chinese border. Almost half of Hong Kong's population is housed here in huge satellite towns, but pockets of rural life and preserved country parks remain. One of the best things to do is follow a self-guided hike that will take you past traditional Chinese homes, temples, and other buildings in a small village. See p. 237.

- **Imbibing at Happy Hour at a British Pub:** End a busy day of sightseeing and shopping by rubbing elbows with Hong Kong's working population as they take advantage of happy-hour prices in British pubs throughout the city. Most pubs and bars offer a happy hour that can stretch on for hours, with two drinks for the price of one or drinks at reduced prices. See "The Bar, Pub & Lounge Scene" section of chapter 9, beginning on p. 228, for more on Hong Kong's pubs and bars.

- **Celebrating Sundown with a Cocktail:** Many hotel lounges offer spectacular views of the city as well as live music. As the sun disappears, watch the city explode in neon. See "The Bar, Pub & Lounge Scene" section of chapter 9, beginning on p. 228, for venues with especially good views.

- **Stuffing Yourself at a Buffet Spread:** If you have a big appetite or like variety in your meal, there's no better bargain than Hong Kong's countless all-you-can-eat buffet spreads. Almost all hotels offer buffet lunches and dinners; other restaurants may feature buffets for lunch. Many offer an assortment of international fare, from Japanese sushi and Chinese dishes to pasta and carveries. See chapter 5.

- **Relaxing at an Open-Air Seafood Restaurant:** Get rid of stress by relaxing over a meal of fresh seafood at one of Hong Kong's rural waterfront seafood restaurants. Favorite places include Lamma island and Sai Kung in the New Territories. See p. 253 and 245.

- **Eating Your Way Through China:** There's no better place in the world to sample regional Chinese cuisine than Hong Kong, where you can eat everything from the ubiquitous Cantonese food to Sichuan, Shanghainese, Hunanese, Beijing, Chiu Chow, and Pekingese dishes. See chapter 5.

- **Dining with a View:** Enjoy Chinese or Western cuisine at one of

Hong Kong's many restaurants that offer spectacular views of either Kowloon (with its glowing neon lights) or Hong Kong Island (with its skyscrapers and Victoria Peak). In fact, Hong Kong boasts so many restaurants with views, the dilemma will be in the choosing. The absolute winners? Those atop Victoria Peak. See "Victoria Peak" in the "Around Hong Kong Island" section of chapter 5, beginning on p. 149.

- **Spending Time at the Temple Street Night Market:** Highlights include shopping for casual clothing, music, toys, and accessories; enjoying a meal at a *dai pai dong* (roadside food stall); watching amateur street musicians; and having your fortune told. See p. 236.
- **Listening to the World's Largest Professional Chinese Orchestra:** Established more than 25 years ago, the 80-member Hong Kong Chinese Orchestra is the world's largest, playing traditional and modern Chinese instruments in orchestrations that combine

Chinese and Western musical elements. See p. 224.

- **Partying Till Dawn at Lan Kwai Fong:** It's standing-room only at bars and pubs in Central's most famous nightlife district, where the action spills out onto the street and continues till dawn. Other burgeoning nightlife districts include SoHo, Knutsford Terrace, and Wan Chai. See chapter 9.
- **Zipping Over to Macau:** Macau, a Portuguese colony until it was handed back to the Chinese in 1999, is just an hour away by jetfoil and offers a fascinating blend of Chinese and Mediterranean lifestyles, evident in its spicy cuisine, colorful architecture, temples, churches, and handful of special-interest museums. Although you can "do" Macau in a day, I strongly urge you to spend at least a couple days in this tiny outpost. You'll save money doing so, too—Macau's hotels and restaurants cost a fraction of their Hong Kong counterparts. See chapter 11.

2 Best Hotel Bets

Choosing a favorite hotel in Hong Kong can be a bit overwhelming, if not impossible, because the choices are so vast and there are so many competitors. Few cities offer such a large number of first-rate hotels, and few places can compete with the service that has made the Hong Kong hotel industry legendary. With apologies to the rest, here are my personal favorites. For full details on Hong Kong's hotels, see chapter 4.

- **Best Historic Hotel:** This category has no competition: **The Peninsula,** Salisbury Road, Tsim Sha Tsui (✆ **800/462-7899**), Hong Kong's oldest hotel, has long been the grand old hotel of Hong Kong. Built in 1928 and

boasting the most ornate lobby in Hong Kong, it retains the atmosphere of a colonial past, even down to its restaurants, Gaddi's and The Verandah, both of which have changed little over the decades. Even its new tower, with high-tech rooms and a trendy rooftop restaurant, only adds to the general aura. See p. 71.

- **Best for Business Travelers:** If you can afford it, spring for a room at **The Ritz-Carlton,** 3 Connaught Rd., Central District (✆ **800/241-3333**), conveniently located right in the heart of Central's financial district. Small and intimate and filled with art and antiques, it seems more like an expensive apartment complex than a hotel; it offers rooms with sweeping harbor views; excellent service; a state-of-the-art business center; and a health club with a heated outdoor swimming pool. For those who like to stay connected, there are also rooms that come with a computer hooked up to the Internet, a fax, printer, and scanner. For even more pampering, executive floors offer special privileges, including a private lounge with complimentary snacks and drinks throughout the day. And for busy executives with no time for shopping, the hotel even offers personal shoppers. See p. 74.

- **Best for Business Travelers Paying Their Own Way:** The **Best Western Rosedale on the Park,** 8 Shelter St., Causeway Bay (© 800/528-1234), is making waves with its complimentary broadband Internet service and cordless phones in each room, in-house mobile phones that keep you connected even if you step out of your room, free drinks in your fridge, and—in case you left your laptop at home—a lounge with computers hooked to the Internet. Best of all, you won't go broke staying here. See p. 92.

- **Best for a Romantic Getaway:** Go to Macau, where the **Westin Resort Macau,** Estrada de Hac Sa on Colôane Island (© 800/228-3000), has the perfect and most idyllic setting for those who want to get away from it all, with large rooms (each with private terrace) overlooking the sea, landscaped grounds, indoor and outdoor pools, and a nearby beach for moonlit walks. See p. 270.

- **Best Trendy Hotel:** Design guru Philippe Starck is the mastermind behind **Jia,** 1–5 Irving St., Causeway Bay (© 852/3196 9000), a 57-room boutique hotel featuring whimsical furniture in its lobby but minimalist, high-tech decor and gadgets in its rooms. A slew of freebies (such as Internet broadband access and Continental breakfast), rooms that are divided into distinct living, dining, and working areas, and monthly rates make this a shoo-in for fashion-conscious travelers ready to burrow in. See p. 85.

- **Best Lobby for Pretending That You're Rich:** The Peninsula has long been the favorite lobby for people-watching (no Japanese tourist misses it), but there's nothing that quite matches the overt extravagance of the **Grand Hyatt,** 1 Harbour Rd., Wan Chai (© 800/233-1234), which flaunts space and is decorated like a 1930s Art Deco ocean liner. Just walking down the curved staircase can make you feel like Greta Garbo. See p. 76.

- **Best Budget Hotel:** The overwhelming number-one choice has long been **The Salisbury YMCA,** Salisbury Road, Tsim Sha Tsui (© 800/537-8483), with a fantastic location right next to the prestigious (and very expensive) Peninsula and just a short walk from the Star Ferry. Rooms are simple but offer virtually everything (from cable TVs to wireless Internet access and coffeemakers); some even have stunning harbor views. Throw in two inexpensive restaurants, a health club, and laundry facilities, and you have more than enough to satisfy budget-minded vacationers who don't want to sacrifice convenience. See p. 98.

- **Best for Families:** Again, the number-one choice for families in terms of price, facilities, and location is **The Salisbury YMCA** (see address and telephone above). It offers large suites great for families (and even views of the famous Victoria Harbour and Hong Kong Island), an inexpensive cafeteria serving buffet meals, two indoor swimming pools (including a children's pool), a play area on the fourth-floor terrace, and babysitting. See p. 98.

- **Best Service:** Other hotels may be just as good, but probably none can match the professional, unobtrusive service offered by **The Peninsula** (see address and telephone above); it has one of the highest staff-to-guest ratios in Hong Kong. See p. 71.
- **Best Location:** The **Mandarin Oriental,** 5 Connaught Rd., Central (℃ **800/526-6566**), a longtime landmark in the heart of Central, is just a few minutes' walk away from the Star Ferry, trams, MTR, and Hong Kong Station with service to the airport. It's the best place to stay if you want to rub elbows with professionals who actually live and work in Hong Kong, but even better are its rooms with harbor views, which boast balconies and binoculars, making this also a good location for would-be spies pretending they're characters in a John Le Carré novel. See p. 72.
- **Best Health Club:** Most of Hong Kong's deluxe hotels boast state-of-the-art health clubs. But what I like most about the health club at the **Hotel InterContinental Hong Kong,** 18 Salisbury Rd., Tsim Sha Tsui (℃ **800/327-0200**), is that it's open 24 hours a day, so you can work out when it fits your schedule. There's also an outdoor, filled-to-the-brim horizonless Jacuzzi that gives the illusion of flowing into the harbor, and a state-of-the-art spa that

observes architectural rules for *feng shui* (geomancy) and specializes in jetlag relief and Oriental treatments. And to top it off, this hotel even offers free tai chi classes for its guests. See p. 71.

- **Best Hotel Pool:** The **Grand Hyatt** (see address and telephone above) and **Renaissance Harbour View Hotel Hong Kong,** 1 Harbour Rd., Wan Chai (℃ **800/228-9898**), share one of Hong Kong's largest outdoor pools, surrounded by a lush, landscaped garden and with views of the harbor. See p. 76 and 85.
- **Best Views:** Most of Hong Kong's deluxe hotels boast harbor views, making this category the toughest. However, in my opinion, the best harbor views are from the Kowloon side, where you can feast your eyes not only on the boats plying the water but also on Hong Kong Island with its stunning architecture, Victoria Peak, and, at night, the shimmering of neon lights and laser-light extravaganza of Hong Kong's nightly Symphony of Lights. And no hotel is as close to the water as the **Hotel InterContinental Hong Kong** (see address and telephone above), built right over the harbor; as many as 70% of its rooms command sweeping views of the water and boast floor-to-ceiling and wall-to-wall windows, making the most of one of the world's most breathtaking city views. See p. 71.
- **Best for Those Addicted to the Internet:** The **Grand Hyatt** (see address and telephone above) offers rooms with cordless keyboards that access the Internet and e-mail through an interactive TV at speeds 50 times faster than a conventional modem; views of the harbor are a bonus. The moderately priced **Kowloon Hotel,**

19–21 Nathan Rd., Tsim Sha Tsui (© **800/262-9467**), impresses with its sophisticated "interactive telecenter," allowing access to the Internet, interfacing with a fax machine (which also acts as a printer), and even containing video games. Best of all: Internet access is free. See p. 76 and 89, respectively.

- **Best for Art Lovers:** The **Island Shangri-La Hong Kong,** Pacific Place, Central (© **800/942-5050**), is a gorgeous hotel with more than 700 Viennese chandeliers, lush Tai Ping carpets, flower arrangements, and more than 500 paintings and artworks. But the clincher is the 16-story-high Chinese painting in the hotel atrium, drawn by 40 artists from Beijing and believed to be the largest landscape painting in the world. See p. 84.
- **Best for Ex-Pat Wannabes:** Mid-Levels has long been a favorite residential area for ex-pats living and working in Hong Kong. **Bishop Lei International House,** 4 Robinson Rd., Mid-Levels (© **852/2868 0828**), is located about halfway up Victoria Peak, with great views from its smallish rooms. Nearby ethnic restaurants and neighborhood bars abound, but for a real taste of Mid-Levels living, travel the escalator that local residents use to get to and from their jobs in Central. See p. 91.
- **Best Hotel for Dining:** Hong Kong boasts some of the best hotel restaurants in the world, but for an all-around winner, **The Peninsula** (see address and telephone above) offers a variety of restaurants that never disappoint, from the longtime favorite Gaddi's, serving traditional French cuisine, to the over-the-top Felix, designed by Philippe Starck, as well as restaurants serving Cantonese, Swiss, and Japanese food. See p. 71.

3 Best Dining Bets

I'm convinced Hong Kong has some of the best restaurants in the world—which makes it extremely difficult to choose the best of the best. Nevertheless, the following are my personal favorites. For full details on Hong Kong's restaurants, see chapter 5.

- **Best Spot for a Romantic Dinner:** With views of Hong Kong's fabled harbor, live piano music, French cuisine, and one of Hong Kong's best wine lists, **Petrus,** Island Shangri-La Hotel, Supreme Court Road, Central (© **852/ 2820 8590**), sets the mood for a special evening à deux. You'll want to linger for some time here, savoring the Mediterranean-influenced food, the castle-like ambience, the view, and each other. See p. 132.
- **Best Spot for a Business Lunch:** Since 1963, business travelers have favored the **Mandarin Grill,** Mandarin Oriental Hotel, 5 Connaught Rd., Central (© **852/ 2522 0111**), conveniently located in the heart of Hong Kong's financial and business district. It offers drawing-room comfort and high-powered food, a winning combination for clinching those business deals. And since no children are allowed except for Sunday brunch, business deals won't have to compete with toddler theatrics. See p. 130.
- **Best Spot for a Celebration:** An elegant, colonial-age setting, attentive service, dependably good French haute cuisine, and an

extensive wine list make **Gaddi's,** The Peninsula hotel, Salisbury Road, Tsim Sha Tsui (✆ **852/ 2315 3171**), a natural for a splurge or special celebration. If, however, your idea of a celebration is more exuberant and youthful, you can do no better than **M at the Fringe,** 2 Lower Albert Rd., Central (✆ **852/2877 4000**), a Hong Kong favorite for its quirky interior, artsy crowd, and always excellent creative cuisine. See p. 135.

- **Best Decor:** The avant-garde **Felix,** in The Peninsula hotel, Salisbury Road, Tsim Sha Tsui (✆ **852/2315 3188**), was designed by Philippe Starck. In addition to providing Hong Kong's most unusual, innovative setting, the restaurant offers stunning views, one of the world's smallest discos, and slightly exhibitionist bathrooms. Wear your trendiest duds— you, too, will be part of the display. See p. 116.

- **Best View:** In a town famous for its views, you might as well go to the very top, where the curved facade of **Cafe Deco,** Peak Galleria, Victoria Peak (✆ **852/2849 5111**), offers Hong Kong's best panorama, along with live jazz in the evening and moderately priced—though occasionally mediocre—international cuisine. Reserve a harbor-view window seat a couple of weeks in advance; what you're really paying for here is the unparalleled view. See p. 149.

- **Best Wine List:** Not only does **SPOON by Alain Ducasse,** Hotel InterContinental Hong Kong, Salisbury Road, Tsim Sha Tsui (✆ **852/2313 2256**), offer great harbor views, excellent contemporary French cuisine, and impeccable service, but it also boasts a selection of 3,000 bottles of wine, on view at the restaurant's entrance. See p. 113.

- **Best Cantonese Cuisine:** With some of the world's best Cantonese restaurants located in Hong Kong, this is obviously a tough call, but you can't go wrong at the very sophisticated and classy **Yan Toh Heen,** Hotel InterContinental Hong Kong, Salisbury Road, Tsim Sha Tsui (✆ **852/ 2721 1211**), where the emphasis is on stark simplicity, a view of the harbor, and traditional and creative dishes that border on Chinese nouvelle cuisine. See p. 118.

- **Best Chinese for the Uninitiated:** If you're unfamiliar with Chinese food beyond sweet-and-sour pork and feel—perhaps reluctantly— that Hong Kong is the place to widen your horizons, **Shang Palace,** Kowloon Shangri-La Hotel, 64 Mody Rd., Tsim Sha Tsui East (✆ **852/2733 8754**), is a good introduction to the almost limitless variety of Cantonese food, all listed on an English menu. It's also a good place to try dim sum for the first time. The helpful staff is happy to make recommendations. The elaborately decorated lacquered walls and Chinese lanterns all fit the fantasy of a Chinese restaurant in Asia. See p. 118.

- **Best Chinese Hot Spot:** Make reservations early for **Hutong,** on the 28th floor of an office building at 1 Peking Road, Tsim Sha Tsui (✆ **852/3428 8342**). This place is as hip as a Chinese restaurant can be, with fantastic views over Hong Kong, a darkened interior with splashes of red lighting, and innovative northern Chinese cuisine. Dining here will want to make you live forever, if only to see what can possibly top this; this being Hong Kong, something eventually will. See p. 122.

- **Best Dim Sum Experience:** The quaint ceiling fans, spittoons, and wooden booths evoke a 1930s ambience at **Luk Yu Tea House,** 24–26 Stanley St., Central (© **852/2523 5464**). First opened in 1933, it's one of Hong Kong's oldest restaurants, famous for its dim sum and filled daily with regular customers. It's hard to find an empty seat here but worth the effort. See p. 139.

- **Best American Cuisine:** There's no better place in town for a Caesar salad than **Napa,** Kowloon Shangri-La Hotel, 64 Mody Rd., Tsim Sha Tsui East (© **852/2733 8752**), where you can follow your salad with Californian cuisine that includes pastas and seafood. The great harbor views make it a perfect place for a relaxed lunch or dinner. See p. 117.

- **Best French Cuisine: Petrus,** Island Shangri-La (see "Best Spot for a Romantic Dinner," above) is the top French restaurant in more ways than one: It's located on the 56th floor and offers breathtaking harbor views. Decorated like a French castle, it features contemporary French creations and one of Hong Kong's most definitive wine lists, delivered by a professional and discreet staff. See p. 132.

- **Best Italian Cuisine:** There are a lot of contenders in this category, but the harbor views, airy palatial setting, and traditional northern Italian home-style cooking combine to make **Grissini,** Grand Hyatt Hong Kong Hotel, 1 Harbour Rd., Wan Chai (© **852/2588 1234**), a favorite choice for lunch or dinner. See p. 143.

- **Best Western/Asian Fusion Cuisine:** Trendy restaurants utilizing Western and Asian ingredients to create new dishes are the vogue in Hong Kong, but few carry it off as masterfully as **Vong,** Mandarin Oriental Hotel, 5 Connaught Rd., Central (© **852/2522 0111**), offering what is arguably the best interpretation of Franco-Asian cuisine in this part of the hemisphere (same owner/chef as the Vong in New York City), as well as great views of the harbor and a nattily dressed crowd. See p. 133.

- **Best Seafood:** Huge decorative seafood tanks and views of Victoria Harbour provide the perfect setting for a memorable seafood dinner at **Yü,** Hotel InterContinental Hong Kong, Salisbury Road, Tsim Sha Tsui (© **852/2721 1211**). Lobster, crabs, prawns, abalone, mussels, and fish are kept alive until the decisive moment. Chefs prepare your food according to your wishes; there are also imported oysters and a sushi bar. See p. 114.

- **Best Buffet Spread:** Lots of hotels offer buffets, but none can match the sheer extravagance and chic atmosphere of **café TOO,** Island Shangri-La Hotel, Supreme Court Road, Central (© **852/2820 8571,** ext. 8571). Overlooking the greenery of Hong Kong Park and sporting a hip, contemporary look, it features open kitchens and seven "stations" of food presentations spread throughout the restaurant, eliminating the assembly-line atmosphere inherent in most buffet restaurants. The danger? The temptation to try every delectable dish on display. See p. 136.

- **Best Steaks:** Juicy U.S. prime Midwestern beef, broiled to perfection, is the forte of American chain **Ruth's Chris Steak House,** 68 Mody Rd., Tsim Sha Tsui East (© **852/2366 6000**) and 89 Queensway, Central (© **852/2522 9090**), along with side dishes of mashed potatoes, sautéed spinach, and Caesar salad. This place is guaranteed to satisfy the cravings of the most dedicated carnivore. See p. 117.

- **Best Burgers and Beer: Dan Ryan's Chicago Grill,** with two locations both sides of the harbor at 88 Queensway, Central (© **852/2845 4600**), and Ocean Terminal (© **852/2735 6111**), offers casual dining, good burgers (and other good American food), and drinks throughout the day; its Kowloon branch even provides a view of the busy harbor. See p. 120.

- **Best Pizza:** Located in Hong Kong's prime nightlife district, **Baci Pizza,** 1 Lan Kwai Fong, Central (© **852/2840 0153**), is a small casual pizzeria offering delicious, wafer-thin pizzas at reasonable prices, as well as pastas. See p. 142.

- **Best Outdoor Dining:** Atop Victoria Peak, away from the constant drone of Hong Kong's traffic, is the delightful **Peak Lookout,** 121 Peak Rd., Victoria Peak (© **852/2849 1000**), which serves international cuisine. From an outdoor terrace surrounded by lush foliage, you can actually hear the birds sing. Some tables provide views of Hong Kong Island's southern coast. Musicians entertain nightly with oldies but goldies. See p. 150.

- **Best for Families:** **Mövenpick Marché,** Peak Tower, Victoria Peak (© **852/2849 2000**), is a cafeteria offering something for everyone (pizza and pasta for the kids, international fare and drinks for the parents), along with great views of Hong Kong. It's also one of the few restaurants that actually acknowledge the existence of kids, with a children's corner complete with a toddler slide, toys, crayons, and other diversions. For older kids, there's a Ripley's Believe It or Not! Odditorium, Madame Tussaud's, and a motion-simulation theater in the same building on the Peak. See p. 150.

- **Best Place to Chill Out:** If the stress of travel and the noise and crowds of Hong Kong have pushed you to the breaking point, take a ferry to one of the open-air seafood restaurants on the waterfront of Sok Kwu Wan village on Lamma island, where you can dine on fresh seafood, drink a beer or two, and regain perspective. For even more relaxation, hike to one of the island's beaches. See p. 252.

- **Best Afternoon Tea:** For that most British institution, no place is more famous than the golden-age and unparalleled **Peninsula Hotel Lobby,** Salisbury Road, Tsim Sha Tsui (© **852/2920 2888**), where you can nibble on delicate finger sandwiches and scones, watch the parade of people, and listen to live classical music being played from an upstairs balcony. See p. 156.

- **Best Sunday Brunch:** You'll be spoiled forever—or at least for the rest of the day—if you begin Sunday morning at **The Verandah,** 109 Repulse Bay Rd., Repulse Bay (© **852/2812 2722**), complete with a three-piece band. Wonderfully reminiscent of the colonial era, it features Hong Kong's most famous Sunday spread, with main courses like eggs Benedict from a menu, a carving of the day, pasta cooked to order, sushi, dim sum, and more. If ever there were a place that inspired champagne for breakfast, this is it. See p. 151.

- **Best Desserts:** I was born without a sweet tooth, but even I was tempted when the dessert cart was wheeled out at the end of a memorable dinner at **Sabatini,** Royal Garden hotel, 69 Mody Rd., Tsim Sha Tsui East (© **852/2733 2000**). The sinfully rich creations were all lovingly described and looked equally delicious. In the end, I went for the tiramisu, and I can't imagine the meal without it. See p. 118.

Planning Your Trip to Hong Kong

2

Much of the anxiety associated with travel comes from a fear of the unknown—not knowing what to expect can give even seasoned travelers butterflies. This chapter will help you prepare for your trip to Hong Kong—but don't stop here. Reading through the other chapters before leaving will also help you in your planning. Just learning that Hong Kong has hiking trails and beaches, for example, may prompt you to pack your hiking boots or swimsuit. However, keep in mind that information given here may change during the lifetime of this book.

1 Visitor Information

The **Hong Kong Tourism Board (HKTB)** offers a wealth of free information for travelers. See "Orientation" in chapter 3 for a complete listing of tourist offices in Hong Kong itself and a rundown of available booklets and brochures.

HKTB ONLINE

You can have a virtual visit to Hong Kong by visiting HKTB's home page at **www.discoverhongkong.com**. The site provides a comprehensive overview of Hong Kong—maps of the region, major attractions, a detailed weekly calendar of performing arts and festivals, listings for hotels and restaurants, and guided tours. It even provides e-ticketing service so you can book shows, events, and concerts online before your arrival.

OVERSEAS

Although the information stocked by HKTB offices abroad is sometimes not as up-to-date or as thorough as that available in Hong Kong itself or through the Internet (see above), it's worth contacting a local HKTB office before leaving home for general information and a map.

In the **United States:** General information can be obtained by calling © **800/282-4582.** HKTB offices are located at 115 E. 54th St., Second Floor, New York, NY 10022-4512 (© **212/421-3382;** fax 212/421-8428; nycwwo@hktb.com); 10940 Wilshire Blvd., Suite 2050, Los Angeles, CA 90024-3915 (© **310/208-4582;** fax 310/208-1869; laxwwo@hktb.com); and 130 Montgomery St., San Francisco, CA 94104 (© **415/781-4587;** fax 415/392-2964; sfowwo@hktb.com).

In **Canada:** Hong Kong Trade Centre, 9 Temperance St., Toronto, ON, Canada M5H 1Y6 (© **416/366-2389;** fax 416/366-1098; yyzwwp@hktb.com). There's also a toll-free number: © **800/563-4582.**

In the **United Kingdom:** 6 Grafton St., London W1S 4EQ, England (© **20/7533-7100;** fax 20/7533-7111; lonwwo@hktb.com).

In **Australia:** Hong Kong House, Level 4, 80 Druitt St., Sydney, NSW 2000, Australia (© **02/9283-3083;** fax 02/9283-3383; sydwwo@hktb.com).

2 Entry Requirements & Customs

ENTRY REQUIREMENTS

The only document most tourists need to enter the Hong Kong Special Administrative Region (SAR) is a passport, valid for at least 1 month beyond the planned departure date from Hong Kong. Americans, Australians, New Zealanders, Canadians, and other British Commonwealth citizens can stay for 90 days without a visa, while citizens of the United Kingdom can stay for 180 days without a visa. Immigration officers may also ask arriving visitors for proof of onward travel or a return ticket (unless they are in transit to mainland China or Macau) and that they have adequate funds for their stay in Hong Kong (generally, a confirmed hotel reservation and a credit card will suffice).

Once in Hong Kong, visitors must carry photo identification at all times, such as a passport or driver's license. Safeguard your passport in an inconspicuous, inaccessible place like a money belt. If you lose it, visit the nearest consulate of your native country as soon as possible for a replacement. As an extra safety precaution, it's a good idea to photocopy your passport.

If you plan to make an excursion to mainland China, you'll need a visa, which can easily be obtained in Hong Kong. Applications require one photo and generally take 3 working days to process (see section 3 of chapter 10, beginning on p. 255, for information on obtaining a visa to China).

CUSTOMS

ENTERING HONG KONG   Visitors 18 and older are allowed to bring into the SAR duty-free a 1-liter (34-oz.) bottle of alcohol and 200 cigarettes (or 50 cigars or 250g of tobacco). For more information, go to www.info.gov.hk/customs.

WHAT YOU CAN TAKE HOME   Returning **U.S. citizens** who have been away for at least 48 hours are allowed to bring back, once every 30 days, $800 worth of merchandise duty-free including (for those 21 and older) 1 liter of wine or spirits. You'll be charged a flat rate of duty on the next $1,000 worth of purchases. Any

---

Destination: Hong Kong—Red Alert Checklist

- Have you photocopied your passport, credit cards, plane tickets, and other important documents, leaving one copy at home with friends or family?
- To check in at an airline kiosk with an e-ticket, do you have the credit card you bought your ticket with or a frequent-flier card?
- If you purchased traveler's checks, have you recorded the check numbers and stored the documentation separately from the checks?
- Do you have your credit card personal identification numbers? Do you know your daily withdrawal limit?
- Do you have a safe, accessible place to store money?
- Did you bring ID cards, such as a student ID, that could entitle you to discounts?
- Did you bring emergency drug prescriptions and extra glasses and/or contact lenses?
- Did you leave a copy of your itinerary with someone at home?

dollar amount beyond that is dutiable at whatever rates apply. On mailed gifts, the duty-free limit is $200. Be sure to have your receipts or purchases handy to expedite the declaration process.

To avoid having to pay duty on foreign-made personal items you owned before you left on your trip, bring along a bill of sale, insurance policy, jeweler's appraisal, or receipts of purchase. Or you can register items that can be readily identified by a permanently affixed serial number or marking—think laptop computers, cameras, and CD players—with Customs before you leave. Take the items to the nearest Customs office or register them with Customs at the airport from which you're departing. You'll receive, at no cost, a Certificate of Registration, which allows duty-free entry for the life of the item.

With some exceptions, you cannot bring fresh fruits and vegetables into the United States. For specifics on what you can bring back, download the invaluable free pamphlet *Know Before You Go* online at **www.cbp.gov**. (Click on "Travel," and then click on "Know Before You Go! Online Brochure.") Or contact the **U.S. Customs & Border Protection (CBP),** 1300 Pennsylvania Ave., NW, Washington, DC 20229 (© 877/287-8667) and request the pamphlet.

For a clear summary of **Canadian** rules, write for the booklet *I Declare,* issued by the **Canada Border Services Agency** (© 800/461-9999 in Canada, or 204/983-3500; www.cbsa-asfc.gc.ca). Canada allows its citizens a C$750 exemption, and you're allowed to bring back duty-free one carton of cigarettes, 1 can of tobacco, 40 imperial ounces of liquor, and 50 cigars. In addition, you're allowed to mail gifts to Canada valued at less than C$60 a day, provided they're unsolicited and don't contain alcohol or tobacco (write on the package "Unsolicited gift, under

$60 value"). *Note:* The $750 exemption can only be used once a year and only after an absence of 7 days.

U.K. citizens returning from **a non-EU country** have a customs allowance of: 200 cigarettes; 50 cigars; 250 grams of smoking tobacco; 2 liters of still table wine; 1 liter of spirits or strong liqueurs (over 22% volume) or 2 liters of fortified wine, sparkling wine or other liqueurs; 60cc (ml) perfume; 250cc (ml) of toilet water; and £145 worth of all other goods, including gifts and souvenirs. People under 17 cannot have the tobacco or alcohol allowance. For more information, contact HM Customs & Excise at © **0845/010-9000** (from outside the U.K., 020/8929-0152), or consult their website at www.hmce.gov.uk.

The duty-free allowance in **Australia** is A$400 or, for those under 18, A$200. Citizens can bring in 250 cigarettes or 250 grams of loose tobacco, and 1,125 milliliters of alcohol. A helpful brochure available from Australian consulates or Customs offices is *Know Before You Go.* For more information, call the **Australian Customs Service** at © **1300/363-263,** or log on to www.customs.gov.au.

The duty-free allowance for **New Zealand** is NZ$700. Citizens over 17 can bring in 200 cigarettes, 50 cigars, or 250 grams of tobacco (or a mixture of all three if their combined weight doesn't exceed 250g); plus 4.5 liters of wine and beer, or 1.125 liters of liquor. New Zealand currency does not carry import or export restrictions. Most questions are answered in a free pamphlet available at New Zealand consulates and Customs offices: *New Zealand Customs Guide for Travellers, Notice no. 4.* For more information, contact **New Zealand Customs,** The Customhouse, 17–21 Whitmore St., Box 2218, Wellington (© **04/473-6099** or 0800/428-786; www.customs.govt.nz).

3 Money

According to figures released by the Hong Kong Tourism Board, North Americans spend an average of HK$2,816 (US$366) per day on hotels and meals. While Hong Kong may seem expensive compared to many other Asian cities, bargains abound, especially when it comes to off-season hotel rates, meals at local Chinese restaurants, public transportation, and museum admissions. With a long history of tourism—and shopping—Hong Kong is well equipped to meet visitors' money demands.

CURRENCY

The basic unit of currency is the **Hong Kong dollar (HK$),** which is divided into 100 cents. Since 1983, when negotiations between Britain and China concerning Hong Kong's future sent public confidence and the value of the Hong Kong dollar into a nose dive, the Hong Kong dollar has been officially pegged to the U.S. dollar at a rate of 7.8 (which means that US$1 equals HK$7.8), giving the Hong Kong currency greater stability.

Three banks, the Hongkong and Shanghai Banking Corporation (HSBC), the Bank of China, and the Standard Chartered Bank, all issue their own colorful notes, in denominations of HK$10, HK$20, HK$50, HK$100, HK$500, and HK$1,000. The government also issues a $10 note. As for coins, they're issued by the government in bronze for HK10¢, HK20¢, and HK50¢ pieces; in silver for HK$1, HK$2, and HK$5; and in nickel and bronze for HK$10.

At any rate, throughout the SAR, you'll see the dollar sign ("$"), which of course refers to Hong Kong dollars, not U.S. dollars. To prevent confusion, this guide identifies Hong Kong dollars with the symbol "HK$" (followed in parentheses by the U.S. dollar conversion). Although the official conversion rate is pegged at 7.8, you'll receive slightly less at banks, hotels, and currency exchange offices. During my last trip, I encountered exchange rates ranging from 7.75 (at a Hang Seng bank) to 7.02 (at a currency exchange office). Banks offer the best exchange rates but charge a commission (worth it if you're exchanging large amounts of money); American Express offices have slightly lower exchange rates but do not charge a commission on American Express traveler's checks. If possible, avoid changing money at hotels and currency exchange offices, which generally offer the worst rates.

For the matter of convenience, all conversions in this book are based on HK$7.70 to US$1 (and then rounded off to the nearest nickel on amounts less than US$10 and to the nearest dollar on amounts more than US$10). If the exchange rate changes drastically—that is, it is no longer pegged to the U.S. dollar—plan your budget accordingly.

ATMs

There are ATMs (automated teller machines) throughout Hong Kong, making a credit or debit card the most convenient way to obtain cash since it eliminates the hassle of exchanging money only during banking hours. Holders of MasterCard and Visa can use ATMs at the airport and various convenient locations around the city, including the Star Ferry concourses in Kowloon and Central, all major MTR (subway) stations, and major banks such as the Hongkong and Shanghai Banking Corporation (which has 24-hr. machines). American Express cardholders have access to Jetco ATM and can withdraw local currency or traveler's checks at the Express Cash machines at both American Express offices (see "Fast Facts: Hong Kong" in chapter 3).

The Hong Kong Dollar, the British Pound & the U.S. Dollar

For American Readers Although the official conversion rate is pegged at HK7.80, at this writing, 1 U.S. dollar equals approximately HK$7.70 at banks and exchange offices (or HK$1 = US13¢), and this was the rate of exchange used to calculate the U.S. dollar values given in this book (rounded off to the nearest nickel for prices less than US$10 and to the nearest dollar for prices more than US$10). While stable since it was pegged to the U.S. dollar, this exchange rate may not be the same when you travel to Hong Kong. Therefore, the following table should be used only as a guide.

For British Readers At this writing, £1 equals approximately HK$14 (or HK$1= 7 pence), and this was the rate of exchange used to calculate the pound values in the table below.

HK$	US$	UK£	HK$	US$	UK£
0.25	0.03	0.02	150	19.48	10.52
0.50	0.06	0.04	200	25.97	14.02
1.00	0.13	0.07	250	32.47	17.53
2.00	0.26	0.14	300	38.96	21.03
3.00	0.39	0.21	350	45.45	24.53
4.00	0.52	0.28	400	51.95	28.03
5.00	0.65	0.35	450	58.44	31.53
6.00	0.78	0.42	500	64.94	35.03
7.00	0.91	0.49	550	71.43	38.54
8.00	1.04	0.56	600	77.92	42.05
9.00	1.17	0.63	650	84.42	45.55
10.00	1.30	0.70	700	90.91	49.05
15.00	1.95	1.05	750	97.40	52.56
20.00	2.60	1.40	800	103.90	56.08
25.00	3.25	1.75	850	110.39	59.57
30.00	3.90	2.10	900	116.88	63.07
35.00	4.55	2.45	1,000	129.87	70.08
40.00	5.19	2.80	1,250	162.34	87.59
45.00	5.84	3.15	1,500	194.80	105.11
50.00	6.49	3.50	1,750	227.27	122.66
75.00	9.74	5.25	2,000	259.74	140.18
100.00	13.00	7.01	2,250	292.21	157.72

The **Cirrus** (© **800/424-7787;** www.mastercard.com) and **PLUS** (© **800/843-7587;** www.visa.com) networks span the globe; look at the back of your bank card to see which network you're on. Before leaving home, be sure you know your personal identification number (PIN) and your daily withdrawal limit. However, keep in mind that many banks impose a fee every time a card is used at a different bank's ATM, and that fee can be higher for international transactions (up to $5 or more) than for domestic ones (where they're rarely more than $1.50). On top of this, the bank from which you withdraw cash may charge its own fee. For international withdrawal fees, ask your bank.

CREDIT CARDS

Credit cards are a safe way to carry money, provide a convenient record of all your expenses, and generally offer relatively good exchange rates. Although many of the smaller shops in Hong Kong will give better prices if you pay in cash with local currency, most shops accept international credit cards, although some of the smaller ones do not. Look for credit card signs displayed on the front door or near the cash register. Readily accepted credit cards include American Express, Visa, and MasterCard. Note, however, that shops have to pay an extra fee for transactions that take place with a credit card—and they will try to pass on that expense to you. Keep this in mind if you're bargaining (see section 1 in chapter 8, "Shopping"), and make sure the shopkeeper knows whether you're going to pay with cash or plastic. All major hotels and better restaurants accept credit cards, but budget restaurants often don't. If you do pay with a credit card, check to make sure that "HK" appears before the dollar sign given for the total amount. In addition, keep in mind that when you use your credit card abroad, most banks assess a 2% fee above the 1% fee charged by Visa or MasterCard or American Express for currency conversion on credit charges.

But credit cards still may be the smartest way to go when you factor in things like exorbitant ATM fees and higher traveler's check exchange rates (and service fees).

TRAVELER'S CHECKS

These days, traveler's checks are something of an anachronism, since Hong Kong has plenty of 24-hour ATMs. However, since you're likely to be charged an ATM withdrawal fee if the bank is not your own, if you wish to exchange money every day or two to avoid carrying around large amounts of cash, you might be better off with traveler's checks, which will be replaced if lost or stolen. Traveler's checks can be readily exchanged for Hong Kong dollars at banks, hotels, and currency-exchange offices (banks provide the most favorable rates). Traveler's checks also command a slightly better exchange rate than cash. Although Thomas Cook and other agencies can issue traveler's checks in Hong Kong currency, I don't think this offers any advantage. For one thing, Hong Kong shops, restaurants, and hotels are not as willing as their U.S. counterparts to accept traveler's checks for payment. Secondly, you can use leftover traveler's checks in U.S. dollars (or your own national currency) for future trips, but leftover traveler's checks in Hong Kong dollars must either be reconverted (not financially advantageous, because you lose money with each conversion) or saved for future trips to Hong Kong. You'll need your passport to exchange traveler's checks.

4 When to Go

Hong Kong's peak tourist season used to be in the spring and fall, but now tourists come to Hong Kong virtually year-round, especially from neighboring mainland China. It's best, therefore, to make hotel reservations in advance, particularly if you're arriving during the Chinese New Year or one of the festivals described below. In addition, major conventions and trade fairs can also tie up the city's best hotels, particularly in spring (Mar–Apr) and

autumn (Oct–Nov); check www.
discoverhongkong.com for an updated
calendar. If you're on a budget, keep in
mind that many Hong Kong hotels
offer package deals and cheaper rates in
summer and winter.

CLIMATE
Because of its subtropical location,
Hong Kong's weather is generally mild
in winter and uncomfortably hot and
humid in summer, with an average
annual rainfall of 89 inches. The most
pleasant time of year is late September
to early December, when skies are
clear and sunny, temperatures are in
the 70s (21°C–26°C), and the humidity drops to 70%. January and February are the coldest months, with
temperatures often in the 50s
(10°C–5°C), but it's still a pleasant
time of year. You'll want a jacket during this time. In spring (Mar–May),
the temperature can range between

60°F and 80°F (16°C–27°C) and the
humidity rises to about 84%, with fog
and rain fairly common. That means
you'll need a raincoat and there may
not be much of a view from the cloud-
enveloped Victoria Peak. By May, it
can also be quite hot and muggy.

By summer (late May to mid-Sept),
temperatures are often in the 90s
(32°C–37°C), humidity can be 90%
or more, and there's little or no relief,
even at night. If you're visiting the SAR
this time of year, you'd be prudent to
carry a hat, sunblock, sunglasses, and
plenty of bottled water with you wherever you go. You'll also want a light
jacket for air-conditioned rooms and
an umbrella. This is when Hong Kong
receives the most rain; it's also typhoon
season. However, Hong Kong has a
very good warning system, so there's
no need to worry about the dangers of
a tropical storm.

Hong Kong's Average Monthly Temperatures & Days of Rain

	Jan	Feb	Mar	Apr	May	June	July	Aug	Sept	Oct	Nov	Dec
Temp. (F°)	59	59	64	72	77	80	84	84	80	77	70	64
Temp. (C°)	15	15	18	22	25	27	29	29	27	25	21	18
Days of Rain	5.6	8.9	10.1	11.1	14.9	14.2	17.5	17.3	14.4	8.6	5.9	3.9

HOLIDAYS
Hong Kong has 17 public holidays a
year, including some of the festivals
described below. The majority are
Chinese and are therefore celebrated
according to the lunar calendar, with
different dates each year. Since most
shops, restaurants, and attractions
remain open except during the Chinese New Year, the holidays should
not cause any inconvenience to visitors. Banks, however, are closed. *Note:*
If a holiday falls on a Sunday, Monday
becomes a public holiday. New Year
and Easter are always 3-day holidays,
excluding Sundays.

**Public holidays for 2005 and
2006** are: New Year's Day (Jan 1),
Lunar New Year (Feb 9–Feb 11, 2005;
Jan 29–Feb 1, 2006), Easter (Good
Friday through Easter Monday; Easter
Sunday: Mar 27, 2005; Apr 16, 2006),
Ching Ming Festival (Apr 5, 2005;
Apr 5, 2006), Labour Day (May 2,
2005; May 1, 2006), Buddha's Birth-
day (May 16, 2005; May 5, 2006),
Tuen Ng Festival (Dragon Boat Festi-
val; June 11, 2005; May 11, 2006),
Establishment Day of the Special
Administrative Region (Hong Kong's
return to China; July 1), day following
Mid-Autumn Festival (Sept 19, 2005;
Oct 6, 2006), National Day (Oct 1),
Chung Yeung Festival (Oct 11, 2005;
Oct 11, 2006), Christmas (Dec 25–
27, 2005; Dec 25–26, 2006).

HONG KONG CALENDAR OF EVENTS

If you're lucky, your trip might coincide with one of Hong Kong's colorful festivals. The only time shops and offices close at festival time is during the Chinese New Year, though some in Tsim Sha Tsui remain open to cater to tourists.

Below are the most popular events, including Chinese festivals and festivals of the arts. Your best source for additional information on all of these events is the **Hong Kong Tourism Board** (© 852/2508 1234 in Hong Kong), which can provide detailed information on where events are being staged and how to get there. For several of the festivals, HKTB even offers organized tours, which is one of the best ways to secure front-row seats without battling the crowds.

January/February

Chinese New Year. The most important Chinese holiday, this is a 3-day affair, a time for visiting friends and relatives, settling debts, doing a thorough housecleaning, consulting fortune-tellers, and worshipping ancestors. Strips of red paper with greetings of wealth, good fortune, and longevity are pasted on doors, and families visit temples. Most shops (except those in tourist areas) close down for at least 2 or 3 days; streets and building facades are decorated with elaborate light displays; flower markets sell peach trees, chrysanthemums, and other good-luck flowers; a parade winds its way along the waterfront, usually on the first day; and a dazzling display of fireworks lights up the harbor, usually on the second day of the holiday. Since this festival is largely a family affair (much like the Christian Christmas), it holds little interest for the tourist. In fact, if you're planning a side trip into China, this would be the worst time to go, since all routes to the mainland are clogged with Hong Kong Chinese returning home to visit relatives. Late January or early February (Feb 9–11, 2005; Jan 29–Feb 1, 2006).

February/March

Hong Kong Arts Festival. This is a 3-week-long celebration with performances by world-renowned orchestras, pop and jazz ensembles, opera, dance, and theater companies (including experimental theater and Chinese operas), and with ethnic music and art exhibitions. For a schedule of events, venues, and ticket information, call © 852/2824 2430 or HKTB at © 852/2508 1234, or visit the website www.hk.artsfestival.org. February/March.

March

Hong Kong Sevens Rugby Tournament, Hong Kong Stadium. Known as "The Sevens," this is one of Hong Kong's most popular, and one of Asia's largest, sporting events, with more than 20 teams from around the world competing for the Cup Championship. A 3-day pass costs HK$750 (US$98). Contact the Hong Kong Rugby Football Union at © 852/2504 8311 or www.hksevens.com.hk. Fourth weekend in March.

March/April

Ching Ming Festival, all Chinese cemeteries (especially in Aberdeen, Happy Valley, Chai Wan, and Cheung Chau island). A Confucian festival to honor the dead, observed by sweeping ancestral graves, burning incense, offering food and flowers, and picnicking among the graves. Contact HKTB at © 852/2508 1234. Fourth or fifth day of the Third Moon, March/April (Apr 5, 2005; Apr 5, 2006).

April

Tin Hau Festival, all Tin Hau temples, especially in Joss House Bay and Yuen Long. One of Hong Kong's most colorful festivals, this celebrates the birth of Tin Hau, goddess of the sea and Hong Kong's most popular deity among fishing folk. The celebration stems from a legendary fisherman's daughter who could supposedly calm stormy seas and protect fishermen. To pay her tribute, fishing boats are decorated with colorful flags, there are parades and lion dances, and family shrines are carried to shore to be blessed by Taoist priests. Contact HKTB, which organizes special tours of the events, at 🕿 **852/2508 1234.** Twenty-third day of the Third Moon (usually Apr) (May 1, 2005; Apr 1, 2006).

Hong Kong International Film Festival, Hong Kong Arts Centre, Hong Kong Cultural Centre, City Hall, and other venues around town. More than 300 films from more than 40 countries are featured at this 2-week event, including new releases, documentaries, and archival films. Tickets cost HK$55 (US$7.15). For more information, call 🕿 **852/2970 3300,** or check www.hkiff.org.hk. Two weeks in April.

April/May

Cheung Chau Bun Festival, Pak Tai Temple, Cheung Chau island. Unique to Hong Kong, this week-long affair is thought to appease restless ghosts and spirits. Originally held to placate the unfortunate souls of those murdered by pirates, it features a street parade of lions and dragons and Chinese opera, as well as floats with children seemingly suspended in the air, held up by cleverly concealed wires. The end of the festival is heralded by three bun-covered scaffolds erected in front of the Pak Tai Temple. These buns supposedly bring good luck to those who receive them. HKTB organizes tours of the parade; call 🕿 **852/2508 1234.** Usually late April or early May (May 15, 2005; May 5, 2006).

Buddha's Birthday, Buddhist temples throughout Hong Kong. Worshippers flock to pay respect to Siddhartha Sakyamuni, founder of Buddhism, and to bathe Buddha statues. The Po Lin Monastery on Lantau island is one of the most popular destinations on this day. Contact the HKTB at 🕿 **852/2508 1234.** Ninth day of the Fourth Moon, usually either in April or May (May 15, 2005; May 5, 2006).

June

Dragon Boat Races (Tuen Ng Festival). Races of long, narrow boats, gaily painted and powered by oarsmen who row to the beat of drums. It originated in ancient China, where legend held that an imperial adviser drowned himself in a Hunan river to protest government corruption. His faithful followers, wishing to recover his body, supposedly raced out into the river in boats, beating their paddles on the surface of the water and throwing rice to distract sea creatures from his body. There are two different races: approximately 500 local Hong Kong teams compete on Tuen Ng Festival Day in May or June, with races held at Stanley, Aberdeen, Chai Wan, Yau Ma Tei, Tai Po, and outlying islands. An international competition is held—usually a week later, along the waterfront in Tsim Sha Tsui East. Contact HKTB at 🕿 **852/2508 1234.** Fifth day of the Fifth Moon (June 11, 2005; May 11, 2006) for local races; contact HKTB for international races.

August

Yue Lan Festival (Festival of the Hungry Ghosts). Released from the underworld, ghosts are believed to roam the earth for 1 lunar month each year. Religious ceremonies, street performances, and offerings of food and paper replicas of life's necessities are burned to appease the spirits of discontented ghosts (those who were murdered, died without proper funeral rites, or are without descendants to care for them), in an attempt to prevent the unhappy souls from seeking vengeance on humans. Contact HKTB for various venues (popular venues are King George V Memorial Park in Kowloon and Moreton Terrace Playground in Causeway Bay) at © **852/2508 1234.** Fourteenth day of the Seventh Moon (Aug 19, 2005; Aug 8, 2006).

September/October
Mid-Autumn Festival, Victoria Park, Kowloon Park, and Victoria Peak. Held in early autumn, this major festival (sometimes referred to as the Moon Festival) celebrates the harvest and the brightest moon of the year. In honor of the event, local people light lanterns in the shapes of fish, flowers, and even ships and planes, gaze at the moon, and eat mooncakes (sweet rolls with sesame seeds, duck eggs, and ground lotus seeds). The mooncakes commemorate the 14th-century uprising against the Mongols, when written messages calling for the revolt were concealed in cakes smuggled to the rebels. Today the Urban Council organizes lantern carnivals in parks on both Hong Kong Island and Kowloon, where you can join the Chinese for strolls among hundreds of lanterns, making this one of Hong Kong's most charming and picturesque festivals. Contact HKTB at © **852/2807 6177.** Fifteenth day of the Eighth Moon, either in September or October (Sept 18, 2005; Oct 6, 2006).

October
Chung Yueng Festival, all Chinese cemeteries. The second time of year when ancestral graves are swept and offerings are made. Ninth day of the Ninth Moon (Oct 11, 2005; Oct 11, 2006).

5 Travel Insurance

Check your existing insurance policies and credit card coverage before you buy travel insurance. You may already be covered for lost luggage, canceled tickets, or medical expenses. The cost of travel insurance varies widely, depending on the cost and length of your trip, your age and health, and the type of trip you're taking, but expect to pay between 5% and 8% of the vacation itself.

TRIP-CANCELLATION INSUR-ANCE Trip-cancellation insurance helps you get your money back if you have to back out of a trip, if you have to go home early, or if your travel supplier goes bankrupt. Allowed reasons for cancellation can range from sickness to natural disasters to the State Department declaring your destination unsafe for travel. (Insurers usually won't cover vague fears, though, as many travelers discovered who tried to cancel their trips in October 2001 because they were wary of flying.) In this unstable world, trip-cancellation insurance is a good buy if you're getting tickets well in advance—who knows what the state of the world, or of your airline, will be in 9 months? Insurance policy details vary, so read the fine print—and especially make sure that your airline or cruise line is on the list of carriers covered in case of bankruptcy. A good resource is **"Travel Guard Alerts,"** a list of companies considered high-risk by Travel Guard International (see website below). Protect yourself further by paying for the insurance with a credit card—by law, consumers can get their money back on goods and services not received if they report the loss within 60 days after the charge is listed on their credit card statement.

For information, contact one of the following recommended insurers:

Access America (© 866/807-3982; www.accessamerica.com); **Travel Guard International** (© 800/826-4919; www.travelguard.com); **Travel Insured International** (© 800/243-3174; www.travelinsured.com); and **Travelex Insurance Services** (© 888/457-4602; www.travelex insurance.com).

MEDICAL INSURANCE For travel overseas, most health insurance policies (including Medicare and Medicaid) do not provide coverage, and the ones that do often require you to pay for services up front and reimburse you only after you return home. Even if your plan does cover overseas treatment, most out-of-country hospitals make you pay your bills up front and send you a refund only after you've returned home and filed the necessary paperwork with your insurance company. If you require additional medical insurance, try **MEDEX Assistance** (© 410/453-6300; www.medexassist.com) or **Travel Assistance International** (© 800/821-2828; www.travelassistance.com; for general information on services, call the company's Worldwide Assistance Services, Inc., at © 800/777-8710).

LOST-LUGGAGE INSURANCE On domestic flights, checked baggage is covered up to $2,500 per ticketed passenger. On international flights (including U.S. portions of international trips), coverage is limited to approximately $9.07 per pound, up to approximately $635 per checked bag. If you plan to check items more valuable than the standard liability, see if your valuables are covered by your homeowner's policy, get baggage insurance as part of your comprehensive travel-insurance package, or buy Travel Guard's "BagTrak" product. Don't buy insurance at the airport, as it's usually overpriced. Be sure to pack any valuables or irreplaceable items in your carry-on luggage, as many valuables (including money and electronics) aren't covered by airline policies.

If your luggage is lost, immediately file a lost-luggage claim at the airport, detailing the luggage contents. For most airlines, you must report delayed, damaged, or lost baggage within 4 hours of arrival. The airlines are required to deliver luggage, once found, directly to your house, hotel, or destination free of charge.

6 Health & Safety

STAYING HEALTHY
The two major health concerns for travelers to Hong Kong the past few years have been SARS and avian flu. At the time of going to press, neither pose a threat for those going to the SAR (yes, its name is an unfortunate coincidence). Hong Kong has culled its entire poultry population several times since the first reported avian flu outbreak in 1997, and importation from mainland China is immediately halted whenever any outbreaks occur there. As for SARS, since the 2003 outbreak that sickened 1,755 people in Hong Kong and killed 299 of them,

Hong Kong has monitored passengers arriving by air, boat, and train by taking their temperatures. Passengers with pneumonia or fever, as well as those arriving from infected areas, are kept under close monitoring or isolation. To avoid being unnecessarily detained, don't travel with a fever. As an extra precaution, you might wish to have a flu shot before departing for Hong Kong.

Otherwise, no shots or inoculations are required for entry to the SAR, but you will need proof of a vaccination against cholera if you have been in an infected area during the 14 days preceding your arrival. Check with your travel agent or call the Hong Kong Tourist Authority if you are traveling through Asia before reaching Hong Kong. Also, the United States **Centers for Disease Control and Prevention** (© 800/311-3435; www. cdc.gov) provides up-to-date information on health hazards by region or country and offers tips on food safety.

Prescriptions can be filled at Hong Kong pharmacies only if they're issued by a local doctor. To avoid the hassle, be sure to bring more prescriptions than you think you'll need, clearly labeled in their original packages; pack prescription medications in your carry-on luggage. It's also a good idea to carry copies of your prescriptions in case you run out, including generic names in case a local pharmacist is unfamiliar with the brand name. Over-the-counter items are easy to obtain, though name brands may be different from those back home, and some ingredients allowed elsewhere may be forbidden in Hong Kong (and vice versa).

If you're traveling during the hot and humid summer months, limit your exposure to the sun, especially during the first few days of your trip and particularly from 11am to 2pm. Use a sunscreen with a high protection factor. To avoid dehydration, you should also carry a water bottle, especially when hiking. Another concern when hiking in the New Territories or the islands is snakes. I've never seen one, but of Hong Kong's 49 native species, nine are venomous.

Generally, you're safe eating anywhere in Hong Kong, even at roadside food stalls. Stay clear of local oysters and shellfish, however, and remember that many restaurants outside the major hotels and tourist areas use MSG in their dishes as a matter of course, especially fast-food restaurants and Chinese kitchens that import products from the mainland. Water is safe to drink except in rural areas, where you should drink bottled water.

If you get sick, you may want to contact the concierge at your hotel—some upper-range hotels have in-house doctors or clinics. Otherwise, your embassy in Hong Kong can provide a list of area doctors who speak English. You can also contact the **International Association for Medical Assistance to Travellers (IAMAT)** (© 716/754-4883, or, in Canada, 416/652-0137; www.iamat.org), an organization that lists many local English-speaking doctors and also posts the latest developments in global SARS and avian flu outbreaks. Otherwise, if you can't find a doctor who can help you right away, try the emergency room at the local hospital. Many emergency rooms have walk-in-clinics for cases that are not life-threatening. See "Fast Facts," p. 58, for a list of hospitals and emergency numbers.

STAYING SAFE

Hong Kong is relatively safe for the visitor, especially if you use common sense and stick to such well-traveled nighttime areas as Tsim Sha Tsui, Lan Kwai Fong, or Causeway Bay. On the other hand, the main thing you must guard against is pickpockets. They often work in groups to pick men's pockets or slit open a woman's purse, quickly taking the valuables and then relaying them on to accomplices who disappear in the crowd. Favored places are Tsim Sha Tsui, Causeway Bay, and Wan Chai. You should also be on guard on crowded public conveyances such as the MTR. To be on the safe side, keep your valuables in your hotel's safe-deposit box. If you need to carry your passport or large amounts of money, conceal everything in a money belt. Don't leave your passport in your hotel room unless it's in a safe or safe-deposit box.

7 Specialized Travel Resources

TRAVELERS WITH DISABILITIES

Hong Kong can be a nightmare for travelers with disabilities. City sidewalks—especially in Central and Kowloon—can be so jam-packed that getting around on crutches or in a wheelchair is exceedingly difficult. Moreover, to cross busy thoroughfares it's often necessary to climb stairs to a pedestrian bridge or use an underground tunnel. Also, most shops are a step or two up from the street, due to flooding during rainstorms.

As for transportation, taxis are probably the most convenient mode of transportation, especially since they can load and unload passengers with disabilities in restricted zones under certain conditions and do not charge extra for carrying wheelchairs and crutches. Otherwise, the MTR (subway) has wheelchair access (elevators, ramps, or other aids) at major stations, as well as tactile pathways leading to platforms and exits for the visually impaired. Ferries are accessible to wheelchair users on the lower deck, and approximately 30% of buses are wheelchair accessible. More information is available from the **Transport Department,** Floor 41, Immigration Tower, 7 Gloucester Road, Wan Chai (✆ **852/2804 2660;** www.info. gov.hk/td/index.html), which publishes a booklet called *A Guide to Public Transport for People with Disabilities,* which can also be downloaded online. Other good sources include the **Social Welfare Department's** website, www. cyberable.net, for information on public transportation and reserved car parking, as well as an accessibility guide for the disabled; and the **Hong Kong Council of Social Services'** access guide for disabled visitors, with information on hotels, consulates, museums, restaurants, shopping malls, performing venues and more through its website, www.hkcss.org.hk.

Organizations that offer assistance to disabled travelers include **MossRehab** (www.mossresourcenet.org), which provides a library of accessible-travel resources online; **SATH (Society for Accessible Travel & Hospitality)** (✆ 212/447-7284; www.sath.org; annual membership fees: $45 adults, $30 seniors and students), which offers a wealth of travel resources for all types of disabilities and informed recommendations on destinations, access guides, travel agents, tour operators, vehicle rentals, and companion services; and the **American Foundation for the Blind (AFB)** (✆ **800/232-5463;** www.afb.org), a referral resource for the blind or visually impaired that includes information on traveling with Seeing Eye dogs.

GAY & LESBIAN TRAVELERS

There are only a handful of openly gay establishments in Hong Kong—the gay community is not a vocal one, and information in English is hard to come by. **The International Gay & Lesbian Travel Association (IGLTA)** (✆ **800/ 448-8550** or 954/776-2626; www. iglta.org) is the trade association for the gay and lesbian travel industry and offers an online directory of gay- and lesbian-friendly travel businesses; go to their website and click on "Members."

The following travel guides are available at most travel bookstores and gay and lesbian bookstores, or you can order them from **Giovanni's Room** bookstore, 1145 Pine St., Philadelphia, PA 19107 (✆ **215/923-2960;** www.giovannisroom.com): *Out and About* (✆ **800/929-2268;** www.out andabout.com), which offers guidebooks and a newsletter ($20/year; 10 issues) packed with solid information on the global gay and lesbian scene; and *Spartacus International Gay Guide* (Bruno Gmünder Verlag; www.spartacusworld.com/gayguide) and *Odysseus: The International*

Gay Travel Planner (Odysseus Enterprises Ltd.), both good, annual English-language guidebooks focused on gay men.

SENIOR TRAVEL

Seniors receive half-price or free admission to most museums in Hong Kong. In addition, seniors can ride the cross-harbor ferry free of charge and receive reduced fares for ferries to the outlying islands, the trams (including the Peak Tram), and the subway system. Some discounts are available to seniors older than 60; others for seniors older than 65. In any case, seniors should carry identification for proof of age and should keep in mind that there are many stairs to climb in Hong Kong, including overhead pedestrian bridges and in subway stations. In addition, remember that it is *very* hot and humid in summer.

Before leaving home, consider becoming a member of the **AARP** (formerly known as the American Association of Retired Persons), 601 E St. NW, Washington, DC 20049 (© **888/687-2277;** www.aarp.org), which brings such benefits as *AARP: The Magazine* and a monthly newsletter. Anyone 50 and older can join.

If you want something more than the average vacation or guided tour, **Elderhostel** (© **877/426-8056;** www. elderhostel.org) arranges study programs for those aged 55 and over (and a spouse or companion of any age) in more than 80 countries around the world. Most courses abroad, which include seminars, lectures, and field trips, last 2 to 4 weeks and many include airfare, accommodations in student dormitories or modest inns, meals, and tuition.

FAMILY TRAVEL

Hong Kong is a great place for older kids, since many of the attractions are geared toward them and even offer discounts for children, sometimes as much as 50%. In addition, public transportation is half price for children. As for very young children, keep in mind that there are many stairs to climb, particularly in Central with its elevated walkways, and in subway stations. Also, young children may not be welcome at finer restaurants.

As for hotels, many allow children under a certain age (usually 12 but sometimes up to 18) to stay free of charge in their parent's room. Generally, only one child is allowed, or there's a maximum limit of three persons per room, and there's no extra charge only when no extra bed is required. Baby cots are usually available free of charge, and most hotels also offer babysitting.

To locate those accommodations, restaurants, and attractions that are particularly kid-friendly, refer to the "Kids" icon throughout this guide.

FOR STUDENTS

Students receive a slight discount to most museums in Hong Kong, but major attractions like Ocean Park do not offer discounts.

Before you leave home, you'd be wise to arm yourself with an **International Student Identity Card (ISIC),** which offers substantial savings on plane tickets and entrance fees. It also provides you with basic health and life insurance and a 24-hour help line. The card is available for $22 from **STA Travel** (© **800/781-4040** in North America; www.sta.com or www.statravel.com), the biggest student travel agency in the world. If you're no longer a student but are still under 26, you can get an **International Youth Travel Card (IYTC)** for the same price from the same people, which entitles you to some discounts (but not on museum admissions).

In Hong Kong, **STA Travel,** 1703 Silvercord Rd., Tsim Sha Tsui (© **852/ 2736 1618;** www.1hkst.com/statravel), can help with cheap flights, accommodations, cruises, and rail passes to other destinations. It's open Monday through

Friday from 9am to 6pm and Saturday from 9am to 1pm.

FOR SINGLES

You shouldn't have any problems as a single traveler to Hong Kong. Almost every time I've come here, I've traveled alone. The biggest problem is one of expense, since many hotels charge the same for both double and single occupancy. The other problem is with Chinese food—it's best when enjoyed with a group. Try fixed-price meals or all-you-can-eat buffets when dining alone, or join one of the organized tours where meals are often included.

Female travelers may also want to check out the award-winning website Journeywoman (www.journeywoman.com), a "real life" women's travel information network where you can sign up for a free e-mail newsletter and get advice on everything from etiquette and dress to safety. They have a special section called "GirlTalk Hong Kong," which carries tips on accommodations, restaurants, shopping, things to do, what to wear, and details of venues where solo female travelers will feel at home, submitted by women who have traveled to Hong Kong. You might also want to get the travel guide *Safety and Security for Women Who Travel* by Sheila Swan and Peter Laufer (Travelers' Tales, Inc.), offering common-sense tips on safe travel.

8 Planning Your Trip Online

SURFING FOR AIRFARES

The "big three" online travel agencies, **Expedia.com, Travelocity.com,** and **Orbitz.com** sell most of the air tickets bought on the Internet. (Canadian travelers should try expedia.ca and Travelocity.ca; U.K. residents can go for expedia.co.uk and opodo.co.uk.) Each has different business deals with the airlines and may offer different fares on the same flights, so it's wise to shop around. Expedia and Travelocity will also send you **e-mail notification** when a cheap fare becomes available to your favorite destination.

Also remember to check **airline websites.** Even with major airlines you can often shave a few bucks from a fare by booking directly through the airline and avoiding a travel agency's transaction fee. But you'll get these discounts only by **booking online:** Most airlines now offer online-only fares that even their phone agents know nothing about. For the websites of airlines that fly to Hong Kong, go to "Getting There," p. 34.

SURFING FOR HOTELS

Shopping online for hotels is generally done one of two ways: by booking through the hotel's own website or through an independent booking agency. These Internet hotel agencies have multiplied in mind-boggling numbers of late, competing for the business of millions of consumers surfing for accommodations around the world. This competitiveness can be a boon to consumers who have the patience and time to shop and compare the online sites for good deals— but shop they must, for prices can vary considerably from site to site. And keep in mind that hotels at the top of a site's listing may be there for no other reason than that they paid money to get the placement.

Expedia.com offers a long list of special deals and "virtual tours" or photos of available rooms, so you can see what you're paying for (a feature that helps counter the claims that the best rooms are often held back from bargain booking websites). **Travelocity** posts unvarnished customer reviews and ranks its properties according to the AAA rating system. Also reliable are **Hotels.com** and **Quikbook.com.** An excellent free program, **TravelAxe** (www.travelaxe.net), can help you search multiple hotel sites at once, even ones you may never have heard of—and conveniently lists the total price of the room, including the taxes and service charges. Other good sources include **Asiatravel.com, Asia-hotels.com,** and **Planetholiday.com,** but be sure to compare rates with those

at **Hkha.com.hk** (website of the Hong Kong Hotels Association) and individual hotel websites to make sure you're getting a good deal. It's a good idea to **get a confirmation number** and **make a printout** of any online booking transaction.

9 The 21st-Century Traveler

INTERNET ACCESS AWAY FROM HOME

Travelers have any number of ways to check their e-mail and access the Internet on the road. Of course, using your own laptop gives you the most flexibility, but if you don't have one you can still access your e-mail from cybercafes.

WITHOUT YOUR OWN COMPUTER

Cybercafes are growing in number, though they are still few and far between. In addition to the list provided under "Internet Access" under "Fast Facts: Hong Kong" in chapter 3, check **www.cybercaptive.com** and **www.cybercafe.com** for an updated list. In any case, avoid **hotel business centers** unless you're willing to pay exorbitant rates.

To retrieve your e-mail, ask your **Internet Service Provider (ISP)** if it has a Web-based interface tied to your existing e-mail account. If your ISP doesn't have such an interface, you can use the free **mail2web** service (www.mail2web.com) to view and reply to your home e-mail. For more flexibility, you may want to open a free, Web-based e-mail account with **Yahoo! Mail** (http://mail.yahoo.com). (Microsoft's Hotmail is another popular option, but Hotmail has severe spam problems.) Your home ISP may be able to forward your e-mail to the Web-based account automatically.

If you need to access files on your office computer, look into a service called **GoToMyPC** (www.gotomypc.com). The service provides a Web-based interface for you to access and

manipulate a distant PC from anywhere—even a cybercafe—provided your "target" PC is on and has an always-on connection to the Internet. The service offers top-quality security, but if you're worried about hackers, use your own laptop rather than a cybercafe computer to access the GoToMyPC system.

WITH YOUR OWN COMPUTER

Wi-fi (wireless fidelity) is the buzzword in computer access, and more and more hotels, cafes, and retailers are signing on as wireless "hotspots" where you can get high-speed connection without cable wires, networking hardware, or phone line (see below). Many laptops sold the past year have built-in wi-fi capability (an 802.11b wireless Ethernet connection). Mac owners have their own networking technology, Apple AirPort. For those with older computers, an 802.11b/**Wi-Fi card** (around $50) can be plugged into your laptop.

Hotels in Hong Kong that do not offer wi-fi generally have high-speed dataports. **Call your hotel in advance** to see what your options are.

In addition, major Internet Service Providers (ISP) have **local access numbers** around the world, allowing you to go online by simply placing a local call. Check your ISP's website or call its toll-free number and ask how you can use your current account away from home, and how much it will cost.

If you're traveling outside the reach of your ISP, the **iPass** network has dial-up numbers in most of the world's countries. You'll have to sign up with an iPass provider, who will then tell you how to set up your computer for your destination(s). For a list of iPass providers, go to www.ipass.com and click on "Individual Purchase." One solid provider is **i2roam** (www.i2roam. com; ✆ **866/811-6209** or 920/ 235-0475).

Wherever you go, bring a **connection kit** of the right power and phone adapters, a spare phone cord, and a spare Ethernet network cable—or find out whether your hotel supplies them to guests.

USING A CELLPHONE

The three letters that define much of the world's **wireless capabilities** are GSM (Global System for Mobiles), a big, seamless network that makes for easy cross-border cellphone use throughout Europe and dozens of other countries worldwide, including Hong Kong. In the U.S., T-Mobile, AT&T Wireless, and Cingular use this quasi-universal system; in Canada, Microcell and some Rogers customers are GSM, and all Europeans and most Australians use GSM.

Using your own mobile phone in Hong Kong is easy, as most of the telephone systems used around the world (such as GSM 900, PCS 1800, and CDMA) are operational in Hong Kong. If your cellphone is on a GSM system, and you have a world-capable multiband phone such as many Sony Ericsson, Motorola, or Samsung models, you can make and receive calls in Hong Kong. Mobile operators in Hong Kong have roaming agreements with most overseas operators, enabling visitors to use their own phone in Hong Kong. Just call your wireless operator and ask for "international roaming" to be activated on your account. Unfortunately, per-minute charges can be high, so be sure to ask about pricing before you leave.

That's why it's important to buy an "unlocked" world phone from the get-go. Many cellphone operators sell "locked" phones that restrict you from using any other removable computer memory phone chip (called a **SIM card**) card other than the ones they supply. Having an unlocked phone allows you to install a cheap, prepaid SIM card, found at retailers throughout Hong Kong. (Show your phone to the salesperson; not all phones work on all networks.) **CSL** is a well-known local company that offers a variety of phone services, including a prepaid SIM Card (✆ **852/179 179;** http:// prepaid.hkcsl.com) that costs as low as HK$88 ($11) and allows 293 minutes of local calls, with local calls costing HK$.30 (4¢) a minute. It's sold at **1010 Centres** throughout Hong Kong, including Central Square, 1–13 D'Aguilar St., Central (✆ **852/2918 1010**), open daily 9am to 11pm; and at Canton Plaza, 82–84 Canton Rd., Tsim Sha Tsui (✆ **852/2910 1010**), open daily 7am to 11pm. You'll get a local phone number and lower calling rates. Getting an already locked phone unlocked can be a complicated process, but it can be done; just call your cellular operator and say you'll be going abroad for several months and want to use the phone with a local provider.

Renting a phone is also an option. **CSL** offers rental phones (✆ **852/ 2883 3938**) beginning at HK$35 ($4.55) per day, plus a HK$180 ($24) SIM card and a HK$300 ($39) deposit. You can rent from the locations given above or at Hong Kong International Airport, shop E32 in the arrival hall, open daily 7am to 11pm. Avoid renting a phone from hotel business centers; at the Peninsula, you'll pay as much as HK$400 ($52) per day, plus HK$5 (65¢) per minute.

You may wish to rent a phone before leaving home. That way you can give loved ones and business associates your new number, make sure the phone works, and take the phone

Online Traveler's Toolbox

Veteran travelers usually carry some essential items to make their trips easier. Following is a selection of handy online tools to bookmark and use:

- **Airplane Seating and Food.** Find out which seats to reserve and which to avoid (and more) on all major domestic airlines at www.seat guru.com. And check out the type of meal (with photos) you'll likely be served on airlines around the world at www.airlinemeals.com.
- **Foreign Languages for Travelers** (www.travlang.com). Learn basic terms in more than 70 languages and click on any underlined phrase to hear what it sounds like.
- **Intellicast** (www.intellicast.com) and **Weather.com** (www.weather. com). Gives weather forecasts for all 50 states and for cities around the world.
- **Subway Navigator** (www.subwaynavigator.com). Download subway maps and get savvy advice on using subway systems in dozens of major cities around the world.
- **Time and Date** (www.timeanddate.com). See what time (and day) it is anywhere in the world.
- **Travel Warnings** (http://travel.state.gov/travel_warnings.html, www. fco.gov.uk/travel, www.voyage.gc.ca, www.dfat.gov.au/consular/ advice). These sites report on places where health concerns or unrest might threaten American, British, Canadian, and Australian travelers. Generally, U.S. warnings are the most paranoid; Australian warnings are the most relaxed.
- **Universal Currency Converter** (www.xe.com/ucc). See what your dollar or pound is worth in more than 100 other countries.
- **Visa ATM Locator** (www.visa.com), for locations of PLUS ATMs worldwide, or **MasterCard ATM Locator** (www.mastercard.com), for locations of Cirrus ATMs worldwide.

wherever you go—especially helpful for overseas trips through several countries, where local phone-rental agencies often bill in local currency and may not let you take the phone to another country.

Two good wireless rental companies are **InTouch USA** (© **800/872-7626;** www.intouchglobal.com) and **Road-Post** (© **888/290-1606** or 905/272-5665; www.roadpost.com). Give them your itinerary, and they'll tell you what wireless products you need. InTouch will also, for free, advise you on whether your existing phone will work overseas.

10 Getting There

With more than 40 airlines and half a dozen cruise lines serving Hong Kong from around the world, it's certainly not difficult to get there. Your itinerary, the amount of time you have, and your pocketbook will probably dictate how you travel. Below are some pointers to get you headed in the right direction.

BY PLANE
THE MAJOR AIRLINES Airlines that fly nonstop between North

America and Hong Kong include **Air Canada** (✆ **888/247-2262;** www.air canada.com), with daily flights from Vancouver; **Cathay Pacific Airways** (✆ **800/233-2742;** www.cathaypacific.com), Hong Kong's own airline with daily service from Los Angeles, San Francisco, New York, and Vancouver; **Continental Airlines** (✆ **800/231-0856;** www.continental.com), with flights most days of the week from New York; **Singapore Airlines** (✆ **800/742-3333;** www.singaporeair.com), with daily service from San Francisco; and **United Airlines** (✆ **800/538-2929;** www.united.com), with daily service from San Francisco and Chicago. Other airlines flying between North America and Hong Kong with stops en route include **Northwest Airlines** (✆ **800/447-4747;** www.nwa.com), **Japan Airlines** (✆ **800/525-3663;** www.japan air.com), **Korean Air** (✆ **800/438-5000;** www.koreanair.com), and **Philippine Airlines** (✆ **800/435-9725;** philippineairlines.com).

From the United Kingdom, **Cathay Pacific** (✆ **020/8834 8888**), **British Airways** (✆ **0870/850 9850;** www.britishairways.com), and **Virgin Atlantic Airways** (✆ **0870/380 2007;** www.virgin-atlantic.com) offer daily nonstop service from London to Hong Kong. From Australia, both Cathay Pacific (✆ **131747**) and **Qantas** (✆ **131313;** www.qantas.com.au) offer daily nonstop service from Sydney and Melbourne. From New Zealand, **Cathay Pacific** (✆ **0508/800454**) offers daily nonstop service from Auckland.

AIRFARES

Regardless of how you buy your ticket, there are certain regulations you should know about airfare pricing. While first-class, business-class, and regular economy fares (those with no restrictions) are the same year-round to Hong Kong, the cheapest fares (including Advance Purchase Excursion fares) usually vary according to the season. The most expensive time to go is during the peak season (June–Aug) and the last couple of weeks in December. The lowest fares are available mid-January through March. Fares in between these two extremes, known as the shoulder season, are available in April and May and again from September to mid-January. To complicate matters, each season also has different rates for both weekday and weekend flights. There are also special promotional fares.

Because the flight to Hong Kong is such a long one (almost 16 hours from Chicago, 12 hours from London, and 9 hours from Sydney), you may wish to splurge for a roomier seat and upgraded service, including special counters for check-in, private lounges at the airport, and better meals, as well as a higher ticket price when choosing your carrier. You should also consider a mileage program, since this round-trip flight will earn you a lot of miles.

Flying for Less: Tips for Getting the Best Airfare

Passengers within the same airplane cabin are rarely paying the same fare. Travelers who need to purchase tickets or change their itinerary at the last minute pay the premium rate. Here are some ways to keep your costs down:

- Passengers who can book their ticket **long in advance,** who can **stay over Saturday night,** or who **fly midweek** or **at less-trafficked hours** may pay a fraction of the full fare.
- You can also save on airfares by keeping an eye out in local newspapers for **promotional specials** or **fare wars,** when airlines lower prices on their most popular routes. You rarely see fare wars offered for peak travel times, but if you can travel in the off-months, you may snag a bargain.
- Search **the Internet** for cheap fares (see "Planning Your Trip Online," above).

- **Consolidators,** also known as bucket shops, are great sources for international tickets, though they usually can't beat the Internet on fares within North America. Start by looking in Sunday newspaper travel sections; U.S. travelers should focus on the *New York Times, Los Angeles Times,* and *Miami Herald.* For less-developed destinations, small travel agents who cater to immigrant communities in large cities often have the best deals. *Beware:* Bucket shop tickets are usually nonrefundable or rigged with stiff cancellation penalties, often as high as 50% to 75% of the ticket price, and some put you on charter airlines, which may leave at inconvenient times and experience delays. Several reliable consolidators are worldwide and available on the Net. **STA Travel** is now the world's leader in student travel, thanks to their purchase of Council Travel. It also offers good fares for travelers of all ages. **FlyCheap** (© **800/FLY-CHEAP;** www.1800flycheap.com) is owned by package-holiday megalith MyTravel and so has especially good access to fares for sunny destinations. **Air Tickets Direct** (© **800/778-3447;** www.airtickets direct.com) is based in Montreal and leverages the currently weak Canadian dollar for low fares; it'll also book trips to places that U.S. travel agents won't touch, such as Cuba.
- Join **frequent-flier clubs.** Accrue enough miles, and you'll be rewarded with free flights and elite status.

HOW TO HAVE AN (ALMOST) FIRST-CLASS EXPERIENCE IN COACH

Anyone who has traveled in coach or economy class in recent years can attest to the frustrating reality of cramped seating. But with a little savvy and advance planning, you can make an otherwise unpleasant coach experience almost bearable.

- Your choice of airline and airplane will definitely affect your leg room. Find more details at www.seatguru. com, which has extensive details about almost every seat on six major U.S. airlines. For international airlines, research firm Skytrax has posted a list of average seat pitches at www.airlinequality.com.
- Emergency exit seats and bulkhead seats typically have the most legroom. Emergency exit seats are usually held back to be assigned the day of a flight (to ensure that the seat is filled by someone ablebodied); it's worth getting to the ticket counter early to snag one of these spots for a long flight. Many passengers find that bulkhead seating (the row facing the wall at the front of the cabin) offers more legroom, but keep in mind that bulkheads are where airlines often put baby bassinets, so you may be sitting next to an infant.
- To have two seats for yourself in a three seat row, try for an aisle seat in a center section toward the back of coach. If you're traveling with a companion, book an aisle and a window seat. Middle seats are usually booked last, so chances are good you'll end up with three seats to yourselves. And in the case that a third passenger is assigned the middle seat, they'll probably be more than happy to trade for a window or an aisle.
- To sleep, avoid the last row of any section or a row in front of an emergency exit, as these seats are the least likely to recline. Avoid seats near highly trafficked toilet areas. Avoid seats in the back of many jets—these can be narrower than those in the rest of coach class. You also may want to reserve a window seat so that you can rest your head and avoid being bumped in the aisle.

- Get up, walk around, and stretch every 60 to 90 minutes to keep your blood flowing. This helps avoid **deep vein thrombosis,** or "economy-class syndrome," a potentially deadly condition that can be caused by sitting in cramped conditions for too long. Other preventative measures include drinking lots of water and avoiding alcohol (see next bullet).

- Drink water before, during, and after your flight to combat the lack of humidity in airplane cabins—which can be drier than the Sahara. Bring a bottle of water on board. Avoid alcohol, which will dehydrate you.

- If you're flying with kids, don't forget to carry on toys, books, pacifiers, and chewing gum to help them relieve ear pressure buildup during ascent and descent. Let each child pack his or her own backpack with favorite toys.

COPING WITH JET LAG

A major consideration for visitors flying to Hong Kong, especially on long flights from North America, is jet lag. To minimize its adverse effects—primarily fatigue and slow adjustment to your new time zone—avoid drinking carbonated drinks, coffee, or alcohol during the flight. In addition, eat light and healthy meals high in vegetable and cereal content and drink plenty of water the day before, during, and the day after your flight to prevent dehydration. Exercise during the flight by walking around the cabin and by flexing your arms, hands, legs, and feet. It also helps to set your watch (and your mental clock) to Hong Kong's time zone as soon as you board the plane.

Once you reach Hong Kong, schedule your day according to local time. Put in a normal day, even if you're tired. I find it useful to take melatonin 2 hours before bedtime. A natural, sleep-inducing hormone, it's thought that melatonin will trick your body into thinking night has fallen earlier and help you adjust to a new time zone. But **don't sleep longer than you normally would** to try to "catch up."

If you follow these instructions, your body should be back to normal within a couple of days.

ARRIVING AT HONG KONG INTERNATIONAL AIRPORT

No one who ever flew into Hong Kong's former Kai Tak Airport could quite forget the experience of landing in one of the world's most densely populated cities. The runway extended out into the bay, past apartments so close you could almost reach out and touch the laundry fluttering from the bamboo poles.

But Kai Tak, which ranked as the world's third busiest airport in 1996, was retired in 1998. Taking its place is the **Hong Kong International Airport** (© 852/2181 0000; www.hongkongairport.com), four times the size of Kai Tak. Situated just north of Lantau island on Chek Lap Kok island and reclaimed land, about 32km (20 miles) from Hong Kong's central business district, the new, state-of-the-art airport is one of the world's most user-friendly. Two runways operate 24 hours a day, and a baggage-handling system delivers bags in approximately 10 minutes.

After Customs, visitors find themselves in the arrivals hall. One of the first things you should do is stop by one of three **Hong Kong Tourism Board (HKTB)** counters, where you can pick up a map of the city, sightseeing brochures, and a wealth of other information, as well as get directions to your hotel. They're open during peak hours, generally daily from 7am to 11pm. iCyberLink computers provide access to Discoverhongkong.com 24 hours a day.

Also in the arrivals hall is the counter of the **Hong Kong Hotel Association** (www.hkha.com.hk), where you can book a room in one of its 60-some member hotels without paying a service fee; open daily 6am to midnight. Note that while they do not have information on rock-bottom establishments, they can book rooms in several low-priced lodgings and the YMCAs.

If you plan on traveling to Macau some time during your stay in Hong Kong, stop by the **Macau tourist information counter,** also in the arrivals lobby at AO6; it's open daily from 9am to 1pm, 1:30 to 6pm, and 6:30 to 10pm. However, if you are traveling directly to Macau from Hong Kong International Airport via the new Ferry Transfer service, do not pass through immigration. Rather, purchase tickets at the Ferry Transfer desk near the transfer area E1 and proceed directly to the ferry pier (see chapter 11, "Macau," for more information).

You can **exchange money** at the arrivals hall, but since the rate here is rather unfavorable, it's best to exchange only what you need to get into town—about US$50 should do it.

If you need to leave luggage at the airport, there is a **luggage-storage counter** on the departure floor.

GETTING INTO TOWN FROM THE AIRPORT

The quickest way to get to downtown Hong Kong is via the sleek **Airport Express Line** (© 852/2881 8888; www.mtr.com.hk), which is straight ahead after passing Customs and entering the arrivals hall. Trains run every 12 minutes between 6am and 1am and take 20 minutes to reach Kowloon Station (off Jordan St. at the old Jordan Ferry Pier and near hotels in Tsim Sha Tsui and Yau Ma Tei) and 23 minutes to reach Hong Kong Station, on Hong Kong Island in the Central District (just west of the Star Ferry terminus). Fares are HK$90 (US$12) to Kowloon and HK$100 (US$13) to Central; round-trip tickets are HK$160 (US$21) and HK$180 (US$23), respectively. Or, if you're in

Hong Kong only 3 days, consider purchasing the Tourist Transport Pass for HK$300 (US$39), which allows unlimited travel by public transportation for 3 days and includes the trip from and to the airport (see "Getting Around" in chapter 3 for more information and other ticket options). From both Kowloon and Hong Kong stations, free shuttle bus service transfers passengers to most major hotels, departing every 12 to 24 minutes between 6:18am and 11:10pm.

In addition to the Airport Express, there are also dedicated airport buses that connect the airport with major downtown Hong Kong areas. Easiest if you have lots of luggage—but most expensive—is the **Airport Shuttle** (© 852/2735 7823), which provides door-to-door service between the airport and major hotels. Tickets, available at a counter in the airport arrivals hall, cost HK$120 (US$16), with buses departing every 30 minutes. It takes about 30 to 40 minutes to reach Tsim Sha Tsui, depending on the traffic.

Slower, with more stops, are **Cityflyer Airbuses** (© 852/2873 0818; www.citybus.com.hk), also with ticket counters in the arrivals hall (if you pay onboard, you must have exact fare). Most important for tourists are Airbus A21, which travels through Mong Kok, Yau Ma Tei, Jordan, and down Nathan Road through Tsim Sha Tsui on its way to the KCR East Rail Hung Hom Station; and Airbus A11, which travels to Hong Kong Island. Buses depart every 10 to 30 minutes, with fares costing HK$33 (US$4.30) to Kowloon and HK$40 to HK$45 (US$5.20–US$5.85) to Central and Causeway Bay.

The easiest way to travel from the airport, of course, is to simply jump in a **taxi,** since taxis are quite cheap in Hong Kong but expensive for the long haul from the airport. Depending on traffic and your final destination, a taxi to Tsim Sha Tsui costs approximately

HK$300 (US$39) and takes 30 to 45 minutes, while a taxi to the Central District will cost about HK$365 (US$47) and will take 35 to 50 minutes. There's also an extra luggage charge of HK$5 (US65¢) per piece of baggage.

NOTES ON DEPARTING   Passengers flying Cathay Pacific, Virgin, and a handful of other airlines are offered the extra benefit of being allowed to check in for return flights at one of two satellite stations—at Hong Kong Station in Central and at Kowloon Station, both served by the Airport Express Line (see above). Both allow you advance check-in any time from 24 hours to 90 minutes before your flight: You'll get your boarding pass, and your bags will be transferred to the airport. Note, however, that since the 9/11 terrorist attacks, some U.S.-bound flights do not allow check-in at satellite stations. At the time of going to press, Cathay Pacific and Continental did not allow check in at Hong Kong and Kowloon stations, while Northwest and United did (call your airline to inquire about its policy). In any case, there is a left-luggage service at both stations, useful if your flight is later in the day and you want to do some sightseeing before heading for the airport.

If you travel directly to the airport and go through check-in there, plan on arriving about 2 hours before departure. Although most tickets now include airport departure tax in their price, you may be required to pay the tax (HK$120/US$16) if yours does not. At any rate, passengers waiting for flights can browse at the Hong Kong Sky Mall, with more than 100 outlets offering merchandise and food.

BY TRAIN
It's unlikely you'll arrive in the SAR by train, unless, of course, you're traveling via China. The Beijing-Kowloon Railway provides a direct link between the two cities in approximately 26 hours and costs HK$1,191 (US$155) for a bed in a deluxe, two-bed cabin, HK$934 (US$121) for a "soft bed" in a four-bed cabin, and HK$601 (US$78) for a "hard bed" in a six-bed cabin, one-way. Service is also available from Shanghai in a little more than 23 hours, costing HK$508 to HK$1,039 (US$66–US$135) one-way, and from Guangzhou (formerly Canton), costing HK$190 to HK$230 (US$25–US$30) and taking approximately 2 hours.

In any case, the end terminus for train travel to Hong Kong is the new East Tsim Sha Tsui Station, with an underground pedestrian passageway linking it to the nearest MTR subway station in Tsim Sha Tsui and its many hotels.

BY SHIP
Some 30 international cruise ships make Hong Kong a port of call each year. The SAR's main docking facility is Ocean Terminal, located in the heart of Tsim Sha Tsui and part of a massive shopping complex which includes 700 shops and 50 restaurants. Just a stone's throw away is the Star Ferry with service to Hong Kong Island.

11 Escorted Tours, Package Deals & Special-Interest Vacations
Before searching for the lowest airfare, you may want to consider booking your flight as part of an escorted tour or package tour.

PACKAGE TOURS
Package tours are not the same thing as escorted tours. With a package tour, you travel independently but pay a group rate. Package tours are simply a way to buy airfare, accommodations, and other elements of your trip (such as airport transfers or city tours) at the same time and often at discounted prices—kind of like one-stop

shopping. Packages are sold in bulk to tour operators—who resell them to the public at a cost that usually undercuts standard rates.

Package tours can vary by leaps and bounds. Some offer a better class of hotels than others. Some offer the same hotels for lower prices. Some offer flights on scheduled airlines, while others book charters. Some limit your choice of accommodations and travel days. You are often required to make a large payment up front. On the plus side, packages can save you money, offering group prices but allowing for independent travel. Some even let you to add on a few guided excursions or escorted day trips (also at prices lower than if you booked them yourself) without booking an entirely escorted tour.

Before you invest in a package tour, get some answers. Ask about the **accommodations choices** and prices for each. Then look up the hotels' reviews in this guide and check their rates online for your specific dates of travel. Be sure to find out what **type of room** you get. If you need a certain type of room, ask for it; don't take whatever is thrown your way. Request a nonsmoking room, a quiet room, a room with a view, or whatever you fancy.

One good source of package deals is the Hong Kong Tourism Board's website at Discoverhongkong.com, which lists the latest deals from various tour companies. Another good source is the airlines themselves. From the U.S., **United Airlines** offers the most options with its **United Vacations** (© 800/917-9246; www.uv-asia.com), with a variety of escorted and independent package deals to Hong Kong and other Asian destinations.

Travel packages are also listed in the travel section of major Sunday newspapers. Or check ads in national travel magazines such as *Arthur Frommer's Budget Travel Magazine, Travel &* *Leisure, National Geographic Traveler,* and *Condé Nast Traveler.*

As for tour companies specializing in Asia, two of the largest are **Pacific Delight Tours** (© 800/221-7179; www.pacificdelighttours.com) and **Pacific Bestour** (© 888/666-6202; www.bestour.com).

ESCORTED TOURS

If you're the kind of traveler who doesn't like leaving such arrangements as accommodations, transportation, and itinerary to chance, you may wish to join an escorted group tour with a group leader. If you book an escorted tour, most everything is paid for up front, so you deal with fewer money issues. They allow you to enjoy the maximum number of sites in the shortest time, with the least amount of hassle, as all the details are arranged by others.

On the downside, an escorted tour often requires a big deposit up front, and lodging and dining choices are pre-determined. You'll get little opportunity for serendipitous interactions with locals. Escorted tours can be jam-packed with activities, leaving little room for individual sightseeing, whim, or adventure. They also often focus only on the heavily touristed sites, so you may miss out on lesser-known gems.

Before you invest in an escorted tour, ask about the **cancellation policy:** Is a deposit required? Can they cancel the trip if they don't get enough people? Do you get a refund if they cancel? If *you* cancel? How late can you cancel if you are unable to go? When do you pay in full? *Note:* If you choose an escorted tour, think strongly about purchasing trip-cancellation insurance, especially if the tour operator asks you to pay up front. See the section on "Travel Insurance," p. 26.

You'll also want to get a complete **schedule** of the trip to find out how much sightseeing is planned each day and whether enough time has been allotted for relaxing or wandering solo.

The **size** of the group is also important to know up front. Generally, the smaller the group, the more flexible the itinerary, and the less time you'll spend waiting for people to get on and off the bus. Find out the **demographics** of the group as well. What is the age range? What is the gender breakdown? Is this mostly a trip for couples or singles?

Discuss what is included in the **price.** You may have to pay for transportation to and from the airport. A box lunch may be included in an excursion, but drinks might cost extra. Tips may not be included. Find out if you will be charged if you decide to opt out of certain activities or meals.

Among the many companies offering group tours are **Pacific Delight Tours** and **Pacific Bestour** (see "Package Tours," above), which offer trips primarily to China but include stops in Hong Kong, as well as **General Tours** (✆ **800/221-2216;** www.generaltours.com) and **China Focus Travel** (✆ **800/868-7244;** www.chinafocustravel.com).

Luxury **cruise liners** are also a common sight in Hong Kong's harbor, anchored conveniently right next to the territory's largest shopping mall at Ocean Terminal on the Kowloon side.

Cruise lines with ports of call in Hong Kong include **Cunard** (✆ **800/7-CUNARD;** www.cunard.com), **Holland America** (✆ **877/724-5425;** www.hollandamerica.com), **Orient Lines** (✆ **800/333-7300;** www.orientlines.com), and **Princess Cruises** (✆ **800/PRINCESS;** www.princesscruises.com). More information on package tours and cruises can be obtained from your travel agent.

COOKING VACATIONS

If cooking is your passion, you might consider joining one of nine 5-day cooking classes conducted by The Peninsula, one of Hong Kong's premier hotels. Up to 15 participants participating in The Peninsula Academy Culinary Experience enjoy a dinner with the chef, morning cooking demonstrations, a daily breakfast, afternoon tea, airport transfers in a Rolls-Royce, and upgrades to a junior suite. The price of the package is HK$16,600 (US$2,158) for one person or HK$20,600 (US$2,678) for two persons sharing a room. For more information, including the various cooking classes available, call ✆ **852/2315 3150** (fax 852/2315 3147; academy.pen@peninsula.com).

12 Recommended Reading

If you want to read something about Hong Kong before setting out on your trip, a good place to start is *Fragrant Harbour: A Short History of Hong Kong* (Greenwood, 1977) by G. B. Endacott and A. Hinton, which is out of print but may be available at your library or online. This book gives a thorough historical account of the colony's early beginnings to the mid-1960s; or *A Borrowed Place* (Kodansha, 1993) by Frank Welsh, which paints a more academic picture of Hong Kong's history from its ignoble beginning through the early 1990s. Likewise, *The Hong Kong Story* (Oxford University Press, 1997) by Caroline Courtauld and May Holdsworth presents Hong Kong's history from the beginning to the 1997 handover, complete with illustrations. Life in Hong Kong during the opium trade is chronicled in Nigel Cameron's *The Cultured Pearl* (Oxford University Press, 1978), while life in the infamous Walled City is the subject of Greg Girard and Ian Lambot's *City of Darkness: Life in Kowloon Walled City* (Watermark Publications, 2003), complete with photographs of a life now vanished. Even though it remains slightly dated, one of my favorite books is Jan Morris's *Hong Kong: Epilogue to an Empire* (Vintage, 1997), which traces the evolution of the British colony from its birth during the Opium Wars to just before the handover. This book gives a unique perspective on the workings of the former colony and imparts an astonishing wealth of information, making it fascinating armchair reading. Also insightful is Christopher Patten's *East and West: China, Power, and the Future of Asia* (Times Books, 1998), reflections from Hong Kong's last governor concerning the years leading up to the handover, negotiations with the Chinese, and his struggle to assure Hong Kong's residents certain democratic rights.

I love looking at pictures of old Hong Kong, and especially fascinating is Nigel Cameron's *An Illustrated History of Hong Kong* (Oxford University Press, 1991), with photographs that show Hong Kong of yore and vividly illustrate how much the city has changed. An even more thorough pictorial history is presented in *Old Hong Kong* (FormAsia Books Ltd., 2002), edited by Trea Wiltshire and covering Hong Kong from 1860 through the June 1997 handover.

For an intimate view of Hong Kong, a recommended book is *Hong Kong: Borrowed Place, Borrowed Time* (Praeger, 1968) by Richard Hughes, a foreign correspondent who lived in Hong Kong for several decades and was said to have been the inspiration for several characters in John Le Carré's novels. Similarly, another exceptional—though hard to find—read is Austin Coates's *Myself a Mandarin* (Heinemann, 1977), which gives a passionate firsthand account of the author's experiences working as a Special Magistrate in Hong Kong's New Territories. A great accompaniment to any guidebook is *Travelers' Tales Hong Kong* (Travelers' Tales Inc., 1996), an anthology edited by James O'Reilly and filled with personal accounts and essays by well-known writers about life in Hong Kong. Likewise, *Hong Kong: Somewhere Between Heaven and Earth*

(Oxford University Press, 1996), edited by Barbara-Sue White, is a collection of poems, short stories, novel excerpts, letters, speeches, and diaries with ties to Hong Kong, written by both Chinese and people of other nationalities from all walks of life—soldiers, doctors, politicians, writers, and others, from Queen Victoria to Jules Verne and ranging from historic accounts dating from the Song dynasty to the present day.

Fictional accounts that depict the character of Hong Kong are Richard Mason's *The World of Suzie Wong* (World Pub., 1957) and Han Suyin's *A Many-Splendored Thing* (Little Brown, 1952), an autobiographical account of life in Hong Kong shortly after the Chinese revolution in the late 1940s and early 1950s. James Clavell's *Tai-Pan* (Atheneum, 1966) is a novel about Hong Kong's beginnings; *Noble House* (Delacorte Press, 1981) is its sequel. John Le Carré's *The Honourable Schoolboy* (G. K. Hall, 1977) details the activities of George Smiley, acting head of the British Secret Service in Hong Kong. *The Monkey King,* by Timothy Mo (Faber & Faber, 1988), is a hilarious account of a Macau native who marries into a dysfunctional Cantonese family in 1950s Hong Kong. More recent is Paul Theroux's *Kowloon Tong* (Houghton Mifflin, 1997), the story of a British expatriate born and raised in Hong Kong but who lives as an outsider, never learning Chinese and failing to understand what's at stake when he's offered a large sum of money by a Chinese mainlander for his family business just before the handover. *Fragrant Harbor* (Putnam, 2002) by John Lanchester is a historical novel that brings to life Hong Kong from the 1930s to the present, as seen through the eyes of an Englishman in love with a Chinese woman and spying for the Empire during the Japanese occupation.

3

Getting to Know Hong Kong

Hong Kong is an easy city to get to know: It's surprisingly compact, with most streets clearly marked in English. And not only is public transportation well organized and a breeze to use, but the Star Ferry and the trams themselves are also sightseeing attractions. In general, however, walking is the best way to go, particularly in the narrow, fascinating lanes and alleys where vehicles can't go. This chapter describes the layout of the city, explains how best to get around it, gives practical advice, and tells you where to turn for additional information.

1 Orientation

For information on getting to the city from the airport, see "Getting There" in chapter 2.

VISITOR INFORMATION

The **Hong Kong Tourism Board (HKTB)** is an excellent source for tourist information. Before your trip you can check its website at **www.discover hongkong.com**.

There are three HKTB counters in the arrivals hall of the Hong Kong International Airport, open daily from 7am to 11pm.

In town, there are two HKTB Visitor Information & Services Centres, one located on each side of the harbor. On the Kowloon side, there's a convenient office in Tsim Sha Tsui, right in the Star Ferry concourse, open daily from 8am to 6pm.

On Hong Kong Island, the larger, main HKTB Visitor Information Centre is located in the Central District at 99 Queen's Rd. Central, also open daily from 8am to 6pm. It's rather inconvenient, however—about a 10-minute walk west of the Star Ferry pier and Central MTR station.

If you have a question about Hong Kong, you can call the English-speaking **HKTB Visitor Hotline** (© 852/2508 1234), available daily from 8am to 6pm. After hours a telephone-answering device will take your call and a member of HKTB will contact you the next day at your hotel.

The HKTB publishes a large assortment of free, excellent literature about Hong Kong. *Visitor's Kit* is a booklet that gives a brief rundown of Hong Kong's major tourist attractions and information on shopping, while *Hong Kong Museums & Heritage* is useful for its information on how to reach Hong Kong's museums and attractions using public transportation. Be sure, too, to pick up HKTB's free map, providing close-ups of Tsim Sha Tsui, the Central District, Wan Chai, and Causeway Bay. There are also brochures outlining various organized tours. In addition, invaluable leaflets are available showing the major bus routes throughout Hong Kong, including Hong Kong Island, Kowloon, and the New Territories. If you plan to visit any of the outlying islands, be sure to get the current ferry schedules at HKTB as well.

To find out what's going on during your stay in Hong Kong, pick up HKTB's free weekly leaflet *What's On—Hong Kong,* which tells what's happening in theater, music, and the arts, including concerts and special exhibitions in museums. *HK Magazine,* distributed free at restaurants, bars, and other outlets around town (and aimed at a young expat readership), is a weekly that lists what's going on at the city's theaters and other venues, including plays, concerts, exhibitions, the cinema, and events in Hong Kong's alternative scene. *Where Hong Kong, CityLife,* and *bc* are other magazines published monthly with information on Hong Kong. *Where Hong Kong* and *CityLife* are distributed to rooms in major hotels and are also available at HKTB offices. *bc* is distributed to bookstores and restaurants. All of the above are free.

CITY LAYOUT

The Hong Kong Special Administrative Region (SAR) is located at the southeastern tip of the People's Republic of China, some 1,996km (1,237 miles) south of Beijing; it lies just south of the Tropic of Cancer at about the same latitude as Mexico City, the Bahamas, and Hawaii. Most people who have never been to Asia probably think of Hong Kong as an island—and they'd be right if it were 1842. But not long after the colony was first established on Hong Kong Island, the British felt the need to expand, which they did by acquiring more land across Victoria Harbour on the Chinese mainland. Today, Hong Kong Island is just a small part of the SAR, which covers 1,100 sq. km (425 sq. miles) and measures 49km (30 miles) north to south and 72.5km (45 miles) east to west—much of it mountainous.

Hong Kong can be divided into four distinct parts: Hong Kong Island, Kowloon Peninsula, New Territories, and the outlying islands. On **Hong Kong Island** are the Central District (Hong Kong's main financial and business district and usually referred to simply as Central), the Western District, Wan Chai, and Causeway Bay, all on the island's north side. Hong Kong Island is the home to such major attractions as Hong Kong Park, Victoria Peak, Stanley Market, Ocean Park, and the Zoological and Botanical Gardens.

Across Victoria Harbour, at the tip of **Kowloon Peninsula,** is Tsim Sha Tsui and its many hotels, restaurants, museums, and shops, as well as Tsim Sha Tsui East, and the Yau Ma Tei and Mong Kok districts.

The **New Territories** are by far the largest area, stretching north of Kowloon all the way to the Chinese border. Once a vast area of peaceful little villages, fields, and duck farms, the New Territories in the past few decades have witnessed a remarkable mushrooming of satellite towns with huge public-housing projects. Sha Tin, with a population approaching almost 700,000 and home of one of Hong Kong's two horse-racing tracks, is the largest; in all, the New Territories house approximately half of the SAR's population. And yet, much of the New Territories remains open and uninhabited. Close to 70% of Hong Kong's total land mass is rural, with 23 country parks and 14 nature reserves accounting for more than 40% of Hong Kong's land area. The fact that Hong Kong is more than just a city surprises many first-time visitors.

As for Hong Kong's 260 **outlying islands,** most are barren and uninhabited; those that aren't lend themselves to excellent exploration into Hong Kong's past. Lantau, Lamma, and Cheung Chau are three of the region's best known and most easily accessible islands, where a gentler, slower, and more peaceful life prevails. Lantau, boasting the world's largest seated bronze Buddha (located at a monastery noted for its vegetarian meals), is the most popular destination. Lamma is famous

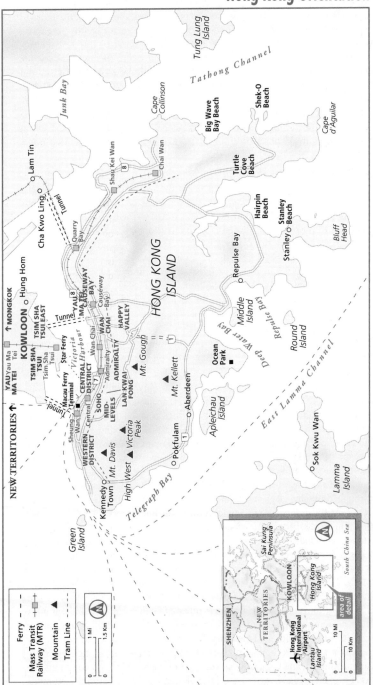

for its open-air waterfront seafood restaurants, beaches, pleasant hiking trail, and expat community, while Cheung Chau makes for a pleasant half-day excursion with its lively traditional village, boat population, and beach.

For the visitor, however, most hotels, restaurants, and points of interest are concentrated in the following areas: **Tsim Sha Tsui, Tsim Sha Tsui East,** and **Yau Ma Tei** on the Kowloon side; and **Central District, Wan Chai,** and **Causeway Bay** on Hong Kong Island. Because these areas are so compact, the city must rank as Asia's most accessible and navigable city. I'd argue that Hong Kong is also the most stunning, given the ferries, cargo ships, fishing boats, and ocean liners bustling in Victoria Harbour, juxtaposed against many peaks that punctuate the cityscape.

MAIN ARTERIES & STREETS   Hong Kong Island's Central District is larger now than it was originally, thanks to massive land reclamation. **Queen's Road,** now several blocks inland, used to mark the waterfront, as did **Des Voeux Road** and **Connaught Road** in subsequent years. Today they serve as busy thoroughfares through Central, since the steep incline up Victoria Peak follows close on their heels. From the Central District, **Hennessy Road** and **Gloucester Road** lead east through Wan Chai to Causeway Bay.

It wasn't until 1972 that the first **cross-harbor tunnel** was built, connecting Causeway Bay on Hong Kong Island with Tsim Sha Tsui East in Kowloon. In 1989 a second tunnel was completed under Victoria Harbour; a third tunnel was completed in conjunction with Hong Kong's new International Airport.

On the Kowloon side, the most important artery is **Nathan Road,** which stretches north up the spine of Kowloon Peninsula and is lined with hotels and shops. **Salisbury Road** runs east and west at the tip of Tsim Sha Tsui from the Star Ferry through Tsim Sha Tsui East along the waterfront. Also on the waterfront is a promenade affording great nighttime views of neon-lit Hong Kong Island.

FINDING AN ADDRESS   With a good map, you should have no problem finding an address. Streets are labeled in English (though signs are sometimes lacking in more congested areas like the Western District and Yau Ma Tei) and building numbers progress consecutively. For the most part, streets that run east to west (such as Des Voeux Rd. Central, Hennessy Rd., Lockhart Rd., and Salisbury Rd.) all have the even-numbered buildings on the north side of the street and the odd-numbered ones on the south. From Central, roads running through Wan Chai all the way west to Causeway Bay start with the lowest numbers near Central, with the highest-numbered buildings ending at Causeway Bay. On Nathan Road, Kowloon's most important thoroughfare, the lowest-numbered buildings are at the southern tip near the harbor; the numbers increase consecutively, with the evens on the east and the odds to the west.

Remember that the floors inside buildings follow the British system of numbering. What Americans call the first floor, therefore, is called the ground floor in Hong Kong; the American second floor is numbered the first floor. In addition, if you're trying to find a specific office or factory outlet in a big building, it's useful to know that number 714 means it's on the seventh floor in Room 14, while 2312 means Room 12 on the 23rd floor.

STREET MAPS   You can get a free map of the SAR, which shows the major roads and streets of Tsim Sha Tsui, Yau Ma Tei, Mong Kok, the Central District, the Western District, Wan Chai, and Causeway Bay, from the HKTB (see "Visitor Information" above). It should be adequate for locating most hotels, restaurants, shops, and bars mentioned in this book. There are also free giveaway maps available at most hotels. If you want to explore Hong Kong in more detail, you can purchase an entire book with maps of the city region and areas in the New Territories called *Hong Kong Guidebook,* available at bookstores (see "Fast Facts," later in this chapter), but you probably won't need this.

NEIGHBORHOODS IN BRIEF

Hong Kong Island

Central District This is where the story of Hong Kong all began, when a small port and community were established on the north end of the island by the British in the 1840s. Named "Victoria" in honor of the British queen, the community quickly grew into one of Asia's most important financial and business districts, with godowns (waterfront warehouses) lining the harbor. Today the area known as the Central District but usually referred to simply as "Central" remains Hong Kong's nerve center for banking, business, and administration. If there is a heart of Hong Kong, it surely lies here, but there are few traces remaining of its colonial past.

The Central District boasts glass and steel high-rises representing some of Hong Kong's most innovative architecture, a couple of the city's posh hotels, expensive shopping centers filled with designer shops, office buildings, and restaurants and bars catering to Hong Kong's white-collar workers, primarily in the nightlife district known as Lan Kwai Fong. Although hotel choices in Central are limited to only a few upper-range hotels, staying here makes you feel like a resident yourself, as you rub elbows with the well-dressed professional crowd who work in Central's office buildings. Banks are so important to the Central District that their impact is highly visible—the Hongkong and Shanghai Bank, designed by British architect Norman Foster, and the Bank of China Tower, designed by I. M. Pei, are just two examples of the modern architecture that has dramatically transformed the Central District's skyline since the 1980s. Hong Kong's tallest building is the new 88-story International Finance Centre, which towers above Hong Kong Station and the ifc mall shopping complex near the Star Ferry.

Yet Central is also packed with traditional Chinese restaurants, outdoor markets, and the neon signs of family-run businesses. Rickety old trams—certainly one of Hong Kong's most endearing sights—chug their way straight through Central. There are also oases of greenery at Chater Garden—popular with office workers for a lunchtime break, the Botanical Gardens, and Hong Kong Park with its museum of teaware, housed in Hong Kong's oldest colonial-age building.

Lan Kwai Fong Named after an L-shaped street in Central, this is Hong Kong's premier nightlife-and-entertainment district, occupying not only Lan Kwai Fong but also neighboring streets like D'Aguilar, Wyndham, and other hillside streets. Filled with restaurants and bars in all price categories but popular mostly with people in their 20s and 30s, it's an entertaining place to spend an evening.

Victoria Peak Hong Kong's most famous mountaintop, Victoria Peak has long been Hong Kong's most exclusive address. Cooler than the steamy streets of Central below, Victoria Peak, often called simply The Peak, was the exclusive domain of the British and other Europeans—even nannies had to have the governor's permission to go there, and the only way up was by sedan carried by coolies or by hiking. Today, Victoria Peak is much easier reached by the Peak Tram and affords Hong Kong's best views of Central, Victoria Harbour, and Kowloon. In fact, the view is nothing short of stunning. Also on The Peak are several attractions, some good restaurants, and multimillion-dollar mansions, glimpses of which can be had on a circular 1-hour walk around The Peak.

Mid-Levels Located above Central on the slope of Victoria Peak, the Mid-Levels has long been a popular residential area for Hong Kong's yuppies and expatriate community. Though not as posh as the villas on The Peak, its swank apartment buildings, grand sweeping views, lush vegetation, and slightly cooler temperatures make it a much-sought-after address. To serve the army of white-collar workers who commute down to Central every day, the world's longest escalator links the Mid-Levels with Central, an ambitious project with 20-some escalators and moving sidewalks (all free) stretching a half mile (you can board and exit as you wish).

SoHo This relatively new dining-and-nightlife district, flanking the Hillside Escalator Link that connects Central with the Mid-Levels, is popular with area residents and those seeking a quieter, saner alternative to the crowds of Lan Kwai Fong. Dubbed SoHo for the region "south of Hollywood Road," it has since blossomed into an ever-growing neighborhood of cafe-bars and intimate restaurants specializing in ethnic and innovative cuisine, making SoHo the most exciting addition to Hong Kong's culinary and nightlife map. Most establishments center on Elgin, Shelley, and Staunton streets.

Western District Located west of the bustling Central District, the Western District is a fascinating neighborhood of Chinese shops and enterprises and is one of the oldest, most traditional areas on Hong Kong Island. Since it's one of my own personal favorites, I've spent days wandering its narrow streets and inspecting shops selling traditional herbs, ginseng, medicines, dried fish, antiques, and other Chinese products. The Western District is also famous for Hollywood Road, long popular for its many antiques and curio shops, and for Man Mo Temple, one of Hong Kong's oldest temples. Unfortunately, modernization has taken its toll, and more of the old Western District seems to have vanished every time I visit, replaced by new high-rises and other projects. One of these projects is the Hillside Escalator Link, which snakes through Western as it connects the Mid-Levels with Central.

Admiralty Actually part of the Central District, Admiralty is located just below Hong Kong Park, centered around an MTR subway station of the same name. It consists primarily of tall office buildings and Pacific Place, a classy shopping complex flanked by three deluxe hotels.

Wan Chai Located east of Central, few places in Hong Kong have changed as dramatically or noticeably as Wan Chai. It became notorious after World War II for its sleazy bars, easy women, tattoo parlors, and sailors on shore leave looking for a good time. Richard Mason's 1957 novel *The World of Suzie Wong* describes this bygone era of Wan Chai; during the Vietnam War, it also served as a popular destination for American servicemen on R & R. Although a somewhat raunchy nightlife remains along Lockhart, Jaffe, and Luard roads, most of Wan Chai has slowly become respectable (and almost unrecognizable) the past few decades with the addition of new, mostly business-style hotels, more high-rises, the Hong Kong Arts Centre, the Academy for Performing Arts, and the huge Hong Kong Convention and Exhibition Centre, a familiar sight on the Wan Chai waterfront with its curved roof and glass facade.

Causeway Bay Just east of Wan Chai, Causeway Bay is popular as a shopping destination, since shops stay open late and several department stores have branches here. The whole area was once a bay until land reclamation turned the water into soil several decades ago. Now it's a busy area of Japanese department stores; clothing, shoe, and accessory boutiques; street markets; and restaurants. On its eastern perimeter is the large Victoria Park.

Happy Valley Once a swampland, Happy Valley's main claim to fame is its racetrack, built in 1846—the oldest racetrack in Asia outside of China.

Aberdeen On the south side of Hong Kong Island, Aberdeen was once a fishing village but is now studded with high-rises and housing projects. However, it is still known for its hundreds of sampans, junks, boat people, and huge floating restaurant. Just to the east, in Deep Water Bay, is Ocean Park with its impressive aquarium and amusement rides.

Stanley Once a fishing village, Stanley is now a lively center for discount markets selling everything from silk suits to name-brand shoes, casual wear, and souvenirs. It's located on the quiet south side of Hong Kong Island and boasts a popular public beach, a residential area popular with Chinese and foreigners alike, and, most recently, a growing number of trendy restaurants strung along a waterfront promenade.

Kowloon Peninsula

Kowloon North of Hong Kong Island, across Victoria Harbour, is the Kowloon Peninsula. Kowloon gets its name from *Gau Lung*, which means "nine dragons." Legend has it that about 800 years ago, a boy emperor named Ping counted eight hills here and remarked that there must be eight resident dragons, since dragons were known to inhabit hills. (The ninth "dragon" was the emperor himself.)

Today the hills of Kowloon provide a dramatic backdrop for one of the world's most stunning cityscapes. Kowloon Peninsula is generally considered the area south of these hills, which means it also encompasses a very small part of the New Territories. However, "Kowloon" is most often used to describe its southernmost tip, the 12 sq. km (4¾ sq. miles) that were ceded to Britain "in perpetuity" in 1860. Its northern border is Boundary Street, which separates it from the New Territories; included in this area are the districts Tsim Sha Tsui, Tsim Sha Tsui East, Yau Ma Tei, and Mong Kok. Once open countryside, Kowloon has practically disappeared under the dense spread of hotels, shops, restaurants, and housing and industrial projects. It has also grown due to land reclamation.

Tsim Sha Tsui At the southern tip of Kowloon Peninsula is Tsim Sha Tsui (also spelled "Tsimshatsui"), which, after Central, rates as Hong Kong's most important area. This is where most tourists stay and spend their money, since it has the greatest concentration of hotels, restaurants, and shops in Hong Kong. In fact, some of my acquaintances living in Hong Kong avoid Tsim Sha Tsui like the plague, calling it the "tourist ghetto." On the other hand, Tsim Sha Tsui does boast the Space Museum, a new cultural center for the performing arts, a great art museum, Kowloon Park, one of the world's largest shopping malls, a nice selection of international restaurants, a jumping nightlife, and Nathan Road, appropriately nicknamed the "golden mile of shopping." Although you'd be foolish to spend all your time in Tsim Sha Tsui, you'd also be foolish to miss it.

Tsim Sha Tsui East Not surprisingly, this neighborhood is east of Tsim Sha Tsui. Built entirely on reclaimed land, the area has become increasingly important, home to a rash of expensive hotels, entertainment centers, shopping and restaurant complexes, science and history museums, and the new KCR East Tsim Sha Tsui Station, providing direct train service to mainland China and connected to the Tsim Sha Tsui MTR station via underground pedestrian passageway. A hover-ferry service also connects Tsim Sha Tsui East with Central.

Yau Ma Tei If you get on the subway in Tsim Sha Tsui and ride two stations to the north (or walk for about 25 min. straight up Nathan Rd.), you'll reach the Yau Ma Tei district (also spelled "Yaumatei"), located on Kowloon Peninsula just north of Tsim Sha Tsui. Like the Western District, Yau Ma Tei is very Chinese, with an interesting produce market, a jade market, and the fascinating Temple Street Night Market. There are also several modestly priced hotels here, making this a good alternative to tourist-oriented Tsim Sha Tsui.

Mong Kok On Kowloon Peninsula north of Yau Ma Tei, Mong Kok is a residential and industrial area, home of the Bird Market, the Ladies' Market on Tung Choi Street, and countless shops catering to Chinese. Its northern border, Boundary Street, marks the beginning of the New Territories.

2 Getting Around

If you've just been to Tokyo or Bangkok, Hong Kong will probably bring a rush of relief. For one thing, English is everywhere—on street signs, on buses, in the subways. In addition, the city of Hong Kong is so compact, and its public transportation system so efficient and extensive, that it's no problem at all zipping from Tsim Sha Tsui to Causeway Bay or vice versa for a meal or some shopping. Even the novice traveler should have no problem getting around. Transportation is also extremely cheap. Just remember that cars drive on the left side of the street, English-style, so be careful when stepping off the curb.

BY PUBLIC TRANSPORTATION

Each mode of transportation in the SAR—bus, ferry, tram, and train/subway—has its own fare system and therefore requires a new ticket each time you transfer from one mode of transport to another. However, if you're going to be in Hong Kong for a few days, consider purchasing the **Octopus.** This electronic smart card allows users to hop on and off trains, trams, subways, and most (but not all) buses and ferries without worrying about purchasing tickets each time or fumbling for exact change. It also gives a slight discount over regular fares—a regular HK$14 (US$1.80) fare, for example, costs HK$13 (US$1.70) using an Octopus. Sold at all MTR subway stations, train stations, and some ferry piers, the Octopus costs a minimum of HK$150 (US$20), including a HK$50 (US$6.50) refundable deposit, and can be reloaded in HK$50 (US$7.50) and HK$100 (US$13) units. Children and seniors pay HK$70 (US$9.10) for the card, including deposit. Alternatively, you can also buy an Octopus good for 3 days of unlimited travel for HK$300 (US$39), including the trip from and to the airport on the Airport Express Line.

To use the Octopus, simply sweep the card across a special pad at the entry gate (you'll notice that most commuters don't even bother removing the card from their wallets or purses); the fare is automatically deducted. The Octopus is valid for all MTR subways, the Kowloon-Canton Railway trains (which serve the New Territories), the Airport Express Line (which runs between the airport and Kowloon and Central), all trams (including the Peak Tram), buses, some minibuses, the Star Ferry, and most ferries to outlying islands. In addition, the Octopus can be used for purchases at all 7-Eleven convenience stores and even

> ### (Tips) Public Transport Tips
>
> Keep in mind that transportation on buses and trams requires the **exact fare.** It's therefore imperative to have lots of loose change with you wherever you go. Even though ferries and subways will give change, you'll find it more convenient if you have exact change, especially during rush hours. Alternatively, and especially if you're in Hong Kong for more than a couple of days, consider purchasing a stored-value **Octopus** card, good for travel on subways, the Kowloon-Canton Railway trains, the Airport Express Line, trams (including the Peak Tram), buses, some minibuses, the Star Ferry, and most ferries to outlying islands.

to make phone calls at selected public telephones. At the end of your Hong Kong stay, be sure to turn in the Octopus card for a refund of your deposit and any unused value stored in the card. For information, call the Octopus Hotline at © **852/2266 2266** or check its website at www.octopuscards.com.

BY SUBWAY   The Star Ferry and trams are so popular and at times so crowded that it's hard to imagine what they must have been like before Hong Kong's subway system was constructed to relieve the human crunch. Hong Kong's **Mass Transit Railway (MTR)** is modern, efficient, clean, and easy to use, and it's also much faster than the older modes of transportation (and sometimes even taxis). Take note, however, that there are no public toilets at any of the stations or on the trains, and that smoking, drinking, and eating are prohibited. The MTR operates daily from 6am to 1am. For general inquiries, call the MTR 24-hour Hotline at © **852/2881 8888** or check its website at www.mtr.com.hk.

Built primarily to transport commuters in the New Territories to and from work and running under the harbor to link Kowloon with Hong Kong Island, the MTR serves more than 2.4 million passengers a day. You'll probably want to avoid rush hours, unless you enjoy feeling like a sardine in a can. There are only five lines, each color-coded, with the next station displayed above each compartment door and announced in English, so you shouldn't have any problem finding your way around. Stations are named for the areas they serve: Go to Central MTR station if you're looking for an address in the Central District, to Mong Kok MTR station if you're looking for a place in Mong Kok, Kowloon. Probably the most important line for tourists is the **red-coded Tsuen Wan Line,** which starts in Central on Hong Kong Island, goes underneath Victoria Harbour to Tsim Sha Tsui, and then runs north the length of Nathan Road, with stops at Jordan, Yau Ma Tei, and Mong Kok stations before heading northwest to the satellite town of Tsuen Wan in the New Territories. The **blue-coded Island Line,** with 14 stations, operates on the north side of Hong Kong Island from Sheung Wan (where you'll find the Macau Ferry Pier) east to Chai Wan, passing through Central, Wan Chai, and Causeway Bay. The other three lines, used mainly by commuters, are the **Kwun Tong Line,** which arches from Yau Ma Tei eastward to the New Territories; the **Tseung Kwan O Line,** which runs from North Point on Hong Kong Island and then goes under the harbor before connecting with the Kwun Tong Line; and the **Tung Chung Line,** which mirrors the Airport Express Line as it runs from Hong Kong Station in Central to Kowloon Station and onward to Tung Chung on Lantau island. Additionally, the **Airport Express Line,** serving airport passengers, runs between Hong Kong Station in Central and Hong Kong International Airport, with a stop at Kowloon Station.

Single-ticket, one-way fares range from HK$4 to HK$26 (US50¢–US$3.40) depending on the distance, but the most expensive ride is the trip underneath the harbor, which costs HK$9 (US$1.15) from Tsim Sha Tsui to Central (still cheap, but outrageous when compared to the Star Ferry's fare of HK$1.70/US20¢ for second class or HK$2.20/US30¢ for first class). Fares for seniors 65 and older and children ages 3 to 11 range from HK$3 to HK$13 (US40¢–US$1.70). Fares are indicated by giving your destination on a touch screen above all vending machines, which accept HK$10, HK$5, HK$2, HK$1, and HK50¢ coins and HK$10 and HK$20 notes and give back change.

In any case, your ticket is plastic, the size of a credit card, and you feed it into a slot at the turnstile. It disappears and then shoots up at the other end of the turnstile. *Be sure to save your ticket*—at the end of your journey, you will again insert your ticket into the turnstile (only this time you won't get it back unless it's an Octopus). Since these tickets are used again and again and have a magnetized strip, be careful not to bend or damage them.

As mentioned above, if you think you're going to be doing a lot of traveling on public transportation, consider buying the Octopus, which saves you from having to buy another ticket each time you ride and gives a negligible discount. Alternatively, there's a 1-day tourist MTR pass available for HK$50 (US$6.50).

BY TRAIN   In addition to the MTR and Airport Express Line, there are three other rail lines in Hong Kong, operated by the **Kowloon-Canton Railway (KCR) Corporation** (✆ **852/2602 7799;** www.kcrc.com.hk), which also operates long-distance through trains to mainland China. Most useful for visitors is the **East Rail,** which travels from the KCR East Tsim Sha Tsui Station in Kowloon up to Sheung Shui in the New Territories. That is, Sheung Shui is where you must get off if you don't have a visa to go onward to China. If you do have a visa, you can continue to the border station of Lo Wu and travel onward all the way through China—and even Russia and Europe if you want to, ending up in London. There are two different kinds of trains on this line: the express through-train to Guangzhou, Shanghai, and Beijing; and the local commuter service for those going to towns in the New Territories.

At any rate, if you're taking the East Rail commuter train, you'll make stops at Hung Hom, Mong Kok, Kowloon Tong, Tai Wai, Sha Tin, Fo Tan, Sha Tin Racecourse (on horse-racing days only), University, Tai Po Market, Tai Wo, and Fanling before reaching Sheung Shui. The whole trip from Kowloon to Sheung Shui takes only a half hour, so it's the easiest and fastest way to see part of the New Territories. It's also convenient, with trains running every 3 to 8 minutes daily from approximately 5:30am to midnight. Finally, it's also cheap, costing HK$9 (US$1.15) for ordinary (second) class and HK$18 (US$2.35) for first class if you go all the way to Sheung Shui. Fares to Lo Wu cost HK$33 (US$4.30) and HK$66 (US$8.50), respectively. Seniors 65 and older and children aged 3 through 11 pay half fare; those under 3 travel free. If you're curious about the New Territories, its scenery, and satellite towns, this is a fast, cheap, and painless way to see it.

In addition to the East Rail, there's also a new **West Rail,** which links Sham Shui Po in West Kowloon with Tuen Mun in the northwestern part of the New Territories in 30 minutes, with fares ranging from HK$4.50 to HK$13 (US60¢–US$1.70). Extending from the western end of the West Rail is a feeder **Light Rail** transit system, which connects towns in the northwestern New Territories. It's not likely you'll use it, but fares for this range from HK$3.70 to HK$5.80 (US50¢–US75¢). Trains run from about 6am to midnight.

Understanding the Deluge: Tropical Storm Warnings

It's not likely you'll experience a tropical storm during your stay in Hong Kong, but if you do, consider it part of your Asian experience. Called typhoons in this part of the world (after the Cantonese *dai fung*, which translates as "big wind") and hurricanes in the West, these severe tropical storms generally vent their fury from May to November and are especially prevalent in September. There's no need to worry that a storm may sneak up on you unawares—storms are tracked and monitored and are rated according to their strength. Their approach dominates local news, but even if you don't read the newspapers or listen to the evening news, there are other tell-tale signs of a coming typhoon—MTR stations, hotel lobbies, and businesses post notices, and shopkeepers cover their windows with storm shutters.

Whenever a severe tropical rainstorm or typhoon is approaching Hong Kong, an alert is broadcast continuously on TV and the radio to keep you informed of the storm's movements. To keep people better informed of the severity of a storm, a system of numbers has been developed that begins at Typhoon Signal No. 1, continues to Typhoon Signal No. 3, and then jumps to Typhoon Signal No. 8 and up. (There used to be numbers in between, but these were dropped when the long range proved too confusing.)

Typhoon Signal No. 1 goes up when a tropical storm that could escalate into a typhoon has moved within an 800km (496-mile) radius of Hong Kong. Although public transportation and organized tours and outdoor activities continue as scheduled, this signal indicates that the public should be on alert. Most locals, however, are rather indifferent to a No. 1, especially since this condition can last for several days, with little physical indication of an approaching storm.

Typhoon Signal No. 3 is given when the winds have escalated, accompanied, perhaps, by heavy rains. By this time, organized guided tours and harbor cruises have generally been suspended. Visitors should check with authorities before venturing on day trips to the outlying islands or Macau. Some businesses may close, as employees head for home while public transportation is still running.

Typhoon Signal No. 8 indicates that the gale has reached Hong Kong. Banks, offices, museums, and most shops and restaurants close, and road, ferry, and air transport are suspended. You should never take a Signal No. 8 lightly, but rather, remain in your hotel and celebrate with a typhoon party, which is pretty much what everyone else does. There's nothing like a tropical storm to set the adrenaline running.

Full details of Hong Kong's typhoon warning system can be found in the local telephone directory. For information during a storm, listen to TV or radio broadcasts or call the Hong Kong Observatory at © 852/ 2835 1473 or check its website at www.weather.gov.hk.

BY BUS Hong Kong buses are a delight—especially the British-style double-deckers. They're good for traveling to places where other forms of public transport don't go, such as to the southern part of Hong Kong Island like Stanley or up into parts of Kowloon and the New Territories. Bus numbers containing an "X" are for express buses, with limited stops. Depending on the route, buses run from about 6am to midnight, with fares ranging from HK$1.20 to HK$45 (US15¢–US$5.85); the fare is halved for children under 12 and seniors over 65. Air-conditioned buses cost more than non-air-conditioned buses. (There aren't many buses that are not air conditioned nowadays, but they still exist in rural areas like Lantau. It says air conditioned on the bus; if it's not air conditioned, the bus won't say anything.) *You must have the exact fare,* which you deposit into a box as you get on. Make sure, therefore, that you always carry a lot of spare change, or buy an Octopus card. Drivers often don't speak English, so you may want to have someone at your hotel write down your destination in Chinese, particularly if you're traveling in the New Territories. And with the exception of congested areas like Central or Tsim Sha Tsui, you must flag down a bus to make it stop, especially in the New Territories or on an island.

Hong Kong's buses are operated by three companies: **New World First Bus** (© **852/2136 8888;** www.nwfb.com.hk), which operates mainly on Hong Kong Island; **Kowloon Motor Bus** (KMB; © **852/2745 4466;** www.kmb. com.hk), operating in Kowloon and the New Territories; and the common yellow buses run by **Citybus** (© **852/2873 0818;** www.citybus.com.hk), operating on Hong Kong Island, Kowloon, and in the New Territories. There are two major bus terminals, located at or near both ends of the Star Ferry. On Hong Kong Island, most buses depart from Exchange Square in the Central District or from bus stops in front of the Outlying Islands Ferry Piers. Some buses also depart from Admiralty Station. In Kowloon, buses depart from in front of the Star Ferry concourse in Tsim Sha Tsui.

The HKTB has individual leaflets for Hong Kong Island, Kowloon, and the New Territories that show bus routes to most of the major tourist spots, indicating where you can catch buses, their frequency and fares, and where to get off. Keep in mind that buses can get very crowded at rush hours and that some buses look pretty ancient—which can make the winding trip to Stanley in a double-decker bus a bone-rattling and exciting experience.

BY TRAM Tram lines are found only on Hong Kong Island. Established in 1904 along what used to be the waterfront, these are old, narrow, double-decker affairs that clank their way 16km (10 miles) in a straight line slowly along the northern edge of the island from Kennedy Town in the west to Shau Kei Wan in the east, with one branch making a detour to Happy Valley. Passing through the Central District, Wan Chai, and Causeway Bay on Des Voeux Road, Queensway Road, and Hennessy Road, they can't be beat for atmosphere and are easy to ride since most of them go only on one line (those branching off to Happy Valley are clearly marked). In the zeal to modernize Central, it's a wonder that these trams have survived at all. Ever since the advent of the subway, there's been talk of getting rid of these ancient trams, but this has raised a storm of protest. Since their future is uncertain, be sure to ride them while you can. They are easily one of the most nostalgic forms of transportation in Hong Kong.

Enter the trams from the back and go immediately up the winding stairs to the top deck. The best seats in the house are those in the front row, where you have an unparalleled view of Hong Kong: laundry hanging from second-story windows, signs swinging over the street, markets twisting down side alleys, crowded sidewalks, and people darting in front of the tram you'd swear couldn't have made it. Riding the tram is one of the cheapest ways of touring Hong Kong Island's northern side, and the fare is the same no matter how far you go. Once you've had enough, simply go downstairs to the front of the tram and deposit the exact fare of HK$2 (US25¢) into a little tin box next to the bus driver as you exit. Children and seniors pay half fare. If you don't have the exact amount, don't panic—no one will arrest you for overpaying a few cents. You can also use the Octopus card. Trams run daily from about 6am to 1am.

In addition to the old-fashioned trams, there's also the **Peak Tram,** a funicular that transports passengers to one of Hong Kong's star attractions: Victoria Peak and its incomparable views. Its lower terminus is on Garden Road in Central, which you can reach via a HK$3.20 (US40¢) shuttle bus departing from the Star Ferry concourse (next to City Hall) at 10- to 20-minute intervals daily from 10am to 11:45pm (to 8pm on Sun and public holidays). The tram itself runs every 15 minutes from 7am to midnight, with round-trip tickets costing HK$30 (US$3.90) for adults and HK$9 (US$1.15) for children. You can also use an Octopus card.

BY STAR FERRY   A trip across Victoria Harbour on one of the white-and-green ferries of the **Star Ferry Company** (✆ **852/2367 7065;** www.starferry.com.hk) is one of the most celebrated rides in the world. Carrying passengers back and forth between Hong Kong Island and Kowloon ever since 1898, these boats have come to symbolize Hong Kong itself and are almost always featured in travel articles on Hong Kong Island. They all incorporate the word "star" in their names, like *Night Star, Twinkling Star,* or *Meridien Star.*

The Star Ferry is very easy to ride. Simply drop your coins into a slot on the ancient-looking turnstile, follow the crowd in front of you down the ramp, walk over the gangway, and find a seat on one of the polished wooden benches. A whistle will blow, a man in a sailor uniform will haul up the gangway, and you're off, dodging fishing boats, tugboats, and barges as you make your way across the harbor. Businesspeople who live in Hong Kong are easy to spot—they're usually buried behind their newspapers; visitors, on the other hand, tend to crowd around the railing, cameras in hand.

The whole trip is much too short, about 7 minutes total from loading pier to unloading dock, with the ride across the harbor taking about 5 minutes. But that 5-minute ride is one of the best in the world, and it's also one of the cheapest. It costs only HK$1.70 (US20¢) for ordinary (second) class; if you really want to splurge, it's only HK$2.20 (US30¢) for first class. First class is located on the upper deck, and it has its own entryway and gangway (follow the signs in the ferry concourse); if it's raining or cold, first class is preferable because there are glass windows in the bow. Otherwise I find ordinary class much more colorful and entertaining because it's the one the locals use and the view of the harbor is often better.

Star Ferries ply the waters daily from 6:30am to 11:30pm between Hong Kong Island's Central District and the tip of Kowloon's Tsim Sha Tsui. Ferries depart every 4 to 5 minutes, except for early in the morning or late at night, when they leave every 10 minutes.

BY OTHER FERRIES   Besides the Star Ferry, there are also many ferries to other parts of the city. Ferries from the Central District, for example, also go back and forth to Kowloon's Hung Hom from 7am to 7pm for HK$5.30 (US70¢). There's hover-ferry service between Central and Tsim Sha Tsui East (near the Grand Stanford Hotel), running at 20-minute intervals between 7:40am and 8:20pm and costing HK$4.50 (US60¢). From Wan Chai, there's ferry service to Tsim Sha Tsui, running from 7:30am to 11pm and costing HK$2.20 (US30¢), and to Hung Hom, available from 7am to 7pm and costing HK$5.30 (US70¢).

In addition to ferries crossing the harbor between Kowloon and Hong Kong Island, a large fleet serves the many outlying islands and the northern part of the mainland. If you want to go to one of the outlying islands, you'll find that most of these ferries depart from the Outlying Islands Ferry Piers stretching west of the Star Ferry terminus in Central. The latest schedules and fares are available from the Hong Kong Tourism Board (HKTB). One thing to keep in mind is that on the weekends the fares are higher and the ferries are unbelievably crowded with locals who want to escape the city, so it's best to travel on a weekday. Even so, the most you'll ever pay for a ferry, even on deluxe class on a weekend, is HK$31 (US$4). You can use the Octopus card on most ferries. See chapter 10, "Side Trips from Hong Kong," for more information on ferries to specific islands.

BY TAXI

REGULAR TAXIS   As a rule, taxi drivers in Hong Kong are strictly controlled and are fairly honest. If they're free to pick up passengers, a red FOR HIRE flag will be raised in the windshield during the day and a lighted TAXI sign will be on the roof at night. You can hail them from the street, though there are some restricted areas, especially in Central. In addition, taxis are not allowed to stop on roads with a single yellow line between 7am and 7pm; they are not allowed to stop at all on roads with a double yellow line. Probably the easiest place to pick up a taxi is on side streets, at a taxi stand (located at all bus terminals), or at a hotel. Taxis are generally abundant anytime except when it's raining, during rush hour (about 5–8pm), during shift change (usually around 4pm), and on horse-racing days from September to May. Since many drivers do not speak English, it's a good idea to have your destination written in Chinese.

Taxis on Hong Kong Island and Kowloon are red. Fares start at HK$15 (US$1.95) for the first 2km (1¼ miles), then are HK$1.40 (US18¢) for each additional 200m (about 656 ft.). Waiting time, incorporated in the meter, is HK$1.40 (US20¢) per minute, luggage costs an extra HK$5 (US65¢) per piece, and taxis ordered by phone add a HK$5 (US65¢) surcharge. Extra charges, which include the driver's return trip, are also permitted for trips through tunnels: HK$20 (US$2.60) for the Cross-Harbour Tunnel, HK$30 (US$3.90) for the Eastern Harbour Crossing, HK$45 (US$5.85) for the Western Harbour Tunnel, and HK$5 (US65¢) for the Aberdeen Tunnel. Note, too, that there's an additional charge per bird or animal you might want to bring with you in the taxi. For a tip, simply round off your bill to the nearest HK$1 or add a HK$1. Although taxi drivers can service both sides of Victoria Harbour, they tend to stick to a certain neighborhood and often aren't familiar with anything outside their area.

Taxis in the New Territories are green, with fares starting at HK$13 (US$1.60) at flag-fall. They cover only the New Territories and are not allowed to transport you back into Kowloon.

If you have a complaint about a taxi driver, call the police hotline (✆ **852/ 2527 7177**), but make sure you have the taxi's license number. The driver's name, photograph, and car number are displayed on the dashboard.

MINIBUSES   These small, 16-passenger buses are the poor person's taxis; although they are quite useful for the locals, they're a bit confusing for tourists. For one thing, although the destination may be written in both Chinese and English, you almost need a magnifying glass to read the English, and by then the vehicle has probably already whizzed by. Even if you can read the English, you may not know the bus's route or where it's going.

There are two types of vehicles, distinguishable by color. The green-and-yellow public "light buses" (though also called minibuses) follow fixed routes, have numbers, and charge fixed rates ranging from HK$2 to HK$20 (US25¢–US$2.60), depending on the distance, and require the exact fare as you enter (many also accept Octopus cards). The most useful ones on Hong Kong Island are probably those that depart from the Star Ferry concourse for Bowen Road and Ocean Park, as well as those that travel from Central's Lung Wui Road to Victoria Peak or from Causeway Bay to Stanley.

The red-and-yellow **minibuses** are a lot more confusing, because they have no fixed route and will stop when you hail them from the street (except for some restricted areas in Central). However, they're useful for traveling along Nathan Road or between Central and Causeway Bay. Fares range from HK$2 to HK$23 (US25¢–US$2.90), depending on the distance and demand (higher fares are charged on rainy days, race days, or cross-harbor trips), and you pay as you exit. Just yell when you want to get off.

BY CAR

Rental cars are not advisable in Hong Kong and hardly anyone uses them, even businesspeople. For one thing, nothing is so far away that you can't get there easily, quickly, and cheaply by taxi or public transport. In addition, there probably won't be any place to park once you get to your destination. If you want a chauffeur-driven car, most major hotels have their own private fleet—you can even rent an air-conditioned limousine. If you're still determined to rent a car or plan to take a driving tour of the New Territories, self-drive firms—such as Avis and Hertz—have branches here, along with a couple of dozen local firms. Your hotel concierge should be able to make arrangements; expect to pay about HK$850 (US$111) for 1 day. A valid driver's license is required, and, remember, traffic flows on the left-hand side of the street. You can reach Avis by calling **© 852/2881 8291** and Hertz at **© 852/2525 2838.**

BY RICKSHAW

Rickshaws hit the streets of Hong Kong in the 1870s and were once the most common form of transport in the colony. Now, however, they are almost a thing of the past—no new licenses are being issued. A couple of ancient-looking men sometimes hang around the Star Ferry terminal in the Central District, but they're usually either snoozing or reading the paper. I've never once seen them hauling a customer. Rather, they make money by charging up to HK$50 (US$6.50) for tourists who want to take their pictures. If you do want to take a ride, they'll charge up to HK$100 (US$13) to take you around the block, clearly the most expensive form of transportation in Hong Kong, and by their appearance, that's probably about as far as they can go. But whether you're just taking a photograph or going for a ride, negotiate the price first.

ON FOOT

One of the great things about Hong Kong is that you can explore virtually the entire city proper on foot. You can walk from the Central District all the way through Wan Chai to Causeway Bay in about an hour or so, while the half-hour walk up Nathan Road to Yau Ma Tei is recommended to all visitors. Unfortunately, land reclamation has been carried out so ambitiously, it may even be possible one day to walk from Hong Kong Island to Kowloon.

In the Central District, there are mazes of covered, elevated walkways to separate pedestrians from traffic, connecting office buildings, shopping complexes, and hotels. In fact, some roads have no pedestrians because they're all using overhead passageways. You can, for example, walk from the Star Ferry concourse to the Prince's Building, Alexandra House, and Landmark all via covered bridges. Likewise, you can walk from the Star Ferry concourse all the way to the Macau Ferry Pier via a walkway. These walkways can be confusing, though signs direct pedestrians to major buildings. Tourists will probably find streets easier to navigate if using a map, but walkways are convenient when it rains and are safer, since the walkways separate pedestrians from traffic.

There's also an interesting "people-mover," the free Central/Mid-Levels Escalator between Central on Des Voeux Road Central and the Mid-Levels on Victoria Peak. It's a series of moving walkways and escalators that snake their way through the Central District up the steep slope of the Peak. Constructed in the hope of alleviating traffic congestion for commuters who live in the Mid-Levels (about halfway up the Peak), the combination escalator/walkway has a total length of just less than .75km (½ mile) and transports approximately 27,000 people a day, moving downward in the morning until 10am and then reversing uphill the rest of the day to accommodate those returning home. There are many entrances/exits, so commuters can get on and off as they like.

FAST FACTS: Hong Kong

Your hotel concierge or guest relations manager is usually a valuable source of information. The Hong Kong Tourism Board (HKTB) is also well equipped and eager to help visitors and answer their questions.

American Express There are two American Express offices, one located on each side of Victoria Harbour. On Hong Kong Island, you'll find American Express on the first floor of the Henley Building, 5 Queen's Rd. Central, in the Central District (© **852/2110 2008**). In Tsim Sha Tsui, it's at 48 Cameron Rd. (© **852/2926 1606**). Both offices are open Monday to Friday from 9am to 5pm and Saturday from 9am to 12:30pm. American Express cardholders can withdraw local currency and traveler's checks 24 hours a day at automated-teller machines (ATMs) at both locations, as well as at Jetco ATMs throughout Hong Kong, as long as you know your personal identification number.

Area Code The international country code for Hong Kong is 852.

Bookstores There are lots of English-language bookstores, particularly in Central and Tsim Sha Tsui. Ask your hotel concierge for the one nearest you. Otherwise, one of the largest is **Pageone**, with two locations, at Shop 3002, Zone A, Harbour City, Canton Road, Tsim Sha Tsui (© **852/2730 6080**), open daily from 10am to 8pm; and in Basement One of Times Square, 1 Matheson St., Causeway Bay (© **852/2917 7252**), open Sunday to Thursday 10:30am to 10pm and Friday and Saturday 10:30am to 11pm. Both carry books on Hong Kong and China, as well as English-language novels, nonfiction, and magazines. A small but convenient **Dymocks** bookstore is located in the Star Ferry concourse in Central (© **852/2522 1012**), open Monday to Saturday 8am to 10:30pm and Sunday 9am to 10:30pm.

Business Hours Although open hours can vary among banks, banking hours are generally Monday to Friday from 9am to 4:30pm and Saturday from 9am to 12:30pm. Keep in mind, however, that some banks stop their transactions—including foreign currency exchange—an hour before closing time.

Most business offices are open Monday to Friday from 9am to 5pm, with lunch hour from 1 to 2pm; Saturday business hours are generally 9am to 1pm.

Most shops are open 7 days a week. Shops in the Central District are generally open from 10am to 7pm; in Causeway Bay and Wan Chai, 10am to 9:30pm; and in Tsim Sha Tsui, 10am to 9 or 10pm (and some even later than that). As for bars, most stay open until at least 2am; some stay open until the crack of dawn.

Currency See "Money," p. 20.

Currency Exchange When exchanging money in Hong Kong, you'll get the best rate at banks. The exchange rate can vary among banks, however, so it may pay to shop around if you're exchanging a large amount. Some banks, for example, offer a better exchange rate but charge a commission of about HK$50 to HK$60 (US$6.50–US$7.80); others many not charge commission but have lower rates. Most charge a commission on traveler's checks (unless, of course, you're cashing American Express checks at an American Express office), but the exchange rate is usually better for traveler's checks than cash. The three main banks in Hong Kong are the **Hongkong and Shanghai Banking Corporation** (usually shortened to Hongkong Bank or HSBC), 29 Queen's Rd., Central (℃ **852/2847 7222**); **Standard Chartered Bank,** 4 Des Voeux Rd., Central (℃ **852/2820 3984** or 852/2820 3333); and **Bank of China,** 1 Garden Rd., Central (℃ **852/2826 6888**). Major banks are open Monday to Friday from 9am to 4:30pm and Saturday from 9am to 12:30pm. The **Hang Seng Bank,** which I find offers good exchange rates (but does charge a commission of about HK$60/US$7.80), has branches virtually everywhere, including a convenient location next to Kowloon Hotel at 4 Hankow Rd., Tsim Sha Tsui (℃ **852/2198 0575**).

Hotels give a slightly less favorable exchange rate but are convenient because they're open at night and on weekends. Money changers are found in the tourist areas, especially along Nathan Road in Tsim Sha Tsui. Avoid them if you can. They often charge a commission or a "changing fee," or give a much lower rate. Check exactly how much you'll get in return before handing over your money. If you exchange money at Hong Kong International Airport, change only what you need to get into town—US$50 should be enough—because the exchange rate here is lower than what you'll get at banks in town.

There are also ATMs throughout Hong Kong, including MTR subway stations and the Star Ferry concourse in both Tsim Sha Tsui and Central. The Hongkong and Shanghai Banking Corporation and Hang Seng Banks have ATMs open 24 hours for Visa and MasterCard holders and Plus and Cirrus members can use just about any machine. American Express cardholders have access to Jetco ATMs and card machines located at both American Express offices (see "American Express," above).

Dentists/Doctors Most first-class hotels have medical clinics with registered nurses, as well as doctors, on duty at specified hours or on call 24 hours for emergencies. Otherwise, the concierge can refer you to a doctor or dentist. See chapter 4 for hotels with in-house physicians. The U.S. consulate can also provide information on English-speaking doctors. If it's an emergency, dial © **999** (a free call) or contact one of the recommendations under "Hospitals," below.

Drugstores There are no 24-hour drugstores in Hong Kong, so if you need something urgently in the middle of the night, you should contact one of the hospitals listed below. One of the best-known pharmacies in Hong Kong is **Watson's,** which dates back to the 1880s. Today, there are more than 90 Watson's drugstores in Hong Kong, most of them open from 9am to 10pm. Ask the concierge at your hotel for the location of a Watson's or drugstore nearest you.

Electricity The electricity used in Hong Kong is 220 volts, alternating current (AC), 50 cycles (in the U.S. it's 110 volts and 60 cycles). Most hotels are equipped to fit shavers of different plugs and voltages, but for other gadgets, you'll need transformers and plug adapters (Hong Kong outlets take plugs with three rectangular prongs). Most laptop computers nowadays are equipped to deal with both 110 and 220 volts, though you'll still need a prong adapter (ask your hotel whether they have one you can use—they often do).

Embassies/Consulates If you need to contact a consulate about an application for a visa, a lost passport, tourist information, or an emergency, telephone first to find out the hours of the various sections. The visa section, for example, may be open only during certain hours of the day.

The **American Consulate,** 26 Garden Rd., Central District (© **852/2523 9011;** 852/2841 2211 for the American Citizens Service; www.hongkong. usconsulate.gov), is open Monday to Friday from 8:30am to 12:30pm and 1:30 to 5:30pm. The **Canadian Consulate,** 11th–14th floor of Tower One, Exchange Square, 8 Connaught Place, Central District (© **852/2810 4321;** www.dfait-maeci.gc.ca/hongkong), is open Monday to Friday from 8:30am to 12:30pm and 1:30 to 5pm; closed Wednesday afternoon. Its passport section is open Monday to Friday from 9am to noon.

The **British Consulate,** at 1 Supreme Court Rd., Central District (© **852/ 2901 3000;** 852/2901 3222 for passport inquiries; www.britishconsulate. org.hk), is open Monday to Friday from 8:45am to 3pm.

The **Australian Consulate** is on the 23rd and 24th floors of Harbour Centre, 25 Harbour Rd., Wan Chai, on Hong Kong Island (© **852/2827 8881;** www.australia.org.hk), and is open Monday to Friday from 9am to 5pm. The **New Zealand Consulate** is on the 65th floor of Central Plaza, 18 Harbour Rd., Wan Chai (© **852/2525 5044;** www.nzembassy.com/hongkong), and is open Monday to Friday from 8:30am to 1pm and 2 to 5pm.

For information on visa applications to mainland **China,** contact a tour operator such as China Travel Service (see "China" in chapter 10).

Emergencies All emergency calls are free—just dial © **999** for police, fire, or ambulance.

Holidays See "When to Go" in chapter 2 for a list of Hong Kong's holidays and festivals.

Hospitals The following hospitals can help you around the clock: Queen Mary Hospital, 102 Pokfulam Rd., Hong Kong Island (✆ **852/2855 3111**); and Queen Elizabeth Hospital, 30 Gascoigne Rd., Kowloon (✆ **852/ 2958 8888**).

Hot Lines The Hong Kong Tourism Board's hot line is ✆ **852/2508 1234**, with service available daily from 8am to 6pm. The Police Crime Hotline (including complaints against taxi drivers) is ✆ **852/2527 7177**.

Information See "Visitor Information" earlier in this chapter.

Internet Access All upper-range and most medium-priced hotels in Hong Kong are equipped with high-speed dataports that allow guests to use laptop computers. In some hotels, Internet access is available upon purchase of an Internet access card for about HK$100 (US$13), valid for anywhere from 100 minutes to unlimited use for 5 days, depending on the hotel (in general, the more expensive the hotel, the more expensive its Internet rates). Other hotels, especially those with keyboards that use the TV as computer, charge a flat rate per day. In addition, many hotels offer business centers as well, most equipped with computers and Internet access (fees are usually charged).

Outside hotels, **Shadowman,** 7 Lock Rd., Tsim Sha Tsui (✆ **852/2366 5262**), across from the Hyatt Regency, is a small cybercafe with a half-dozen computers, providing free Internet access for 20 minutes with the purchase of a drink or food and charging HK$10 (US$1.30) per 15 minutes beyond that. It's open Monday to Saturday from 8am to midnight and Sunday from 9am to 11pm. **Itfans,** 12–13 Jubilee St., Central (near the Hong Kong Tourism Board's Visitor Information Centre), is open daily 8am to 5am with 100 computers, charging HK$20 (US$2.60) an hour Monday through Thursday and HK$22 (US$2.85) per hour Friday to Sunday and holidays, plus a HK$10 (US$1.30) membership fee. In addition, **Pacific Coffee** is a chain of coffee shops, several with a couple of computers that customers can access for free (you'll probably have to wait in line), including shop 1022 in the International Finance Center (IFC), above Hong Kong Station in Central (✆ **852/2868 5100**), open Monday to Saturday from 7am to 10pm and Sunday from 8:30am to 9pm; and in the Peak Tower on Victoria Peak (✆ **852/2849 6608**), open Monday to Thursday from 8am to 10:30pm and Friday to Sunday from 8am to 11pm. Another place with free Internet access is **Computer City,** on the second floor of Star House across from the Star Ferry concourse in Tsim Sha Tsui, where six computers provide Internet access daily from 10am to 8pm, but you have to stand to use them.

Languages Before the 1997 handover, English and Cantonese were Hong Kong's two official languages. Now, however, English and "Chinese" are listed as the two official languages. There is no one Chinese language, however. While most Hong Kong Chinese speak Cantonese, that's a foreign language in Beijing, where the official language is Mandarin (*Putonghua*). In reality, Mandarin has also become the official language of the SAR and is being taught in Hong Kong schools. At any rate, while Mandarin and Cantonese differ widely, they use the same characters for writing. Therefore, while a Hong Kong Chinese and a mainland Chinese may not be able to communicate orally, they can read each other's newspapers. Chinese characters number in the tens of thousands; knowledge of at least 1,500 characters is necessary to read a newspaper. Chinese is difficult to learn primarily because of the tonal variations. Western ears may find these differences in pronunciation almost impossible to detect, but a slight change in tone changes the whole meaning. One thing you'll notice, however, is that Chinese is spoken loudly—whispering does not seem to be part of the language.

Despite the fact that English is an official language and is spoken in hotels and tourist shops, few Chinese outside these areas understand it. Bus drivers, taxi drivers, and waiters in many Chinese restaurants do not speak English and will simply shrug their shoulders to your query. To avoid confusion, have someone in your hotel write out your destination in Chinese so that you can show it to your taxi or bus driver. Most Chinese restaurants in tourist areas—and all those listed in this book—have English menus. If you need assistance, try asking younger Chinese, since it's more likely that they will have studied English in school.

Laundry All expensive and medium-range hotels in Hong Kong provide laundry service. Several of the hotels in the medium and budget ranges have laundry facilities. If you don't want to use the facilities at your hotel, ask someone at your hotel or a local shopkeeper where the nearest laundry is.

Liquor Laws The drinking (and smoking) age in Hong Kong is 18. The hours for bars vary according to the district, though those around Lan Kwai Fong and Tsim Sha Tsui stay open the longest, often till dawn.

Lost & Found Be sure to tell all of your credit card companies the minute you discover your wallet has been lost or stolen and file a report at the nearest police precinct. Your credit card company or insurer may require a police report number or record of the loss. Most credit card companies have an emergency toll-free number to call if your card is lost or stolen; they may be able to wire you a cash advance immediately or deliver an emergency credit card in a day or two. Visa's Hong Kong emergency number is © 852/2810 8033. American Express cardholders and traveler's check holders should call © 852/2811 6122. MasterCard holders should call © 852/2511 6387. If you need emergency cash over the weekend when all banks and American Express offices are closed, you can have money wired to you via **Western Union** (© 800/325-6000 from the U.S.; www.westernunion.com).

Luggage Storage/Lockers The best and most convenient place to store luggage is at your hotel, even if you plan on traveling to Macau or China for a couple of days. Otherwise, there are luggage-checking services ("left-luggage") at Hong Kong International Airport, Hong Kong Station, the Macau Ferry Terminal on Hong Kong Island, and the China Hong Kong Terminal on Canton Road, Tsim Sha Tsui.

Mail Most hotels have stamps and can mail your letters for you. Otherwise, there are plenty of post offices throughout the SAR. Most are open Monday to Friday from 9:30am to 5pm and Saturday from 9:30am to 1pm. The main post office is on Hong Kong Island at 2 Connaught Place, in the Central District near the Star Ferry concourse (© 852/2921 2222), where you'll find stamps sold on the first floor (what those from the U.S. would call the second floor). If you don't know where you'll be staying in Hong

Kong, you can have your mail sent here "Poste Restante." The post office will hold mail for 2 months; when you come to collect it, be sure to bring along your passport for identification. On the Kowloon side, the main post office is at 10 Middle Rd., which is 1 block north of Salisbury Road (© **852/2366 4111**). Both are open Monday to Saturday from 8am to 6pm and Sunday from 9am to 2pm.

Mailboxes are a bright orange-red in Hong Kong. Airmail letters up to 20g and postcards cost HK$3 (US40¢) to the United States or Europe. You can count on airmail letters to take about 5 to 7 days, sometimes longer, to reach the United States.

To mail a package via surface mail to the United States, it costs HK$251 (US$33) for a package weighing 5 kilos (11 lb.) and HK$441 (US$53) for a package weighing 10 kilos (22 lb.). A 5-kilo package sent airmail will cost HK$419 (US$54), a 10-kilo package HK$799 (US$104). Post offices sell boxes called Postpak that are handy for mailing items home; they come in four sizes costing HK$14 (US$1.75) to HK$35 (US$4.55). For general inquiries, call © **852/2921 2222.**

Newspapers The *South China Morning Post* and *The Standard* are the two local English-language daily newspapers. For a different perspective, you might also want to pick up the *China Daily,* from Beijing. The *Asian Wall Street Journal, Financial Times, International Herald Tribune,* and *USA Today International* are also available.

Pharmacies See "Drugstores" above.

Police You can reach the police for an emergency by dialing © **999,** the same number as for a fire or an ambulance. This is a free call. There's also a crime hot line (© **852/2527 7177**), a 24-hour service that also handles complaints against taxis. For general police inquiries, call © **852/2860 2000**). If calling from a private phone, these calls are all free (*all* local calls are free in Hong Kong). However, you'll be charged the regular rates if calling from a public phone or hotel room (see "Telephone," below).

Post Office See "Mail" above.

Safety See "Health & Safety," in chapter 2.

Taxes Hotels will add a 10% service charge and a 3% government tax to your bill. Restaurants and bars will automatically add a 10% service charge, but there is no tax. There's an airport departure tax of HK$120 (US$16) for adults and children older than 12, but this is usually—though not always—included in your ticket price. If you're taking the boat to Macau, you must pay a Hong Kong departure tax of HK$19 (US$2.45), which is already included in the price of your boat ticket.

Telephone The international country code for Hong Kong is 852. There-fore, to **call Hong Kong** from the United States:
1. Dial the international access code: 011.
2. Dial the country code: 852.
3. Then dial the number. So the whole number you'd dial would be 011-852/0000 0000.

To make international calls: To make international calls from Hong Kong, first dial © **001** and then the country code (U.S. or Canada 1, U.K. 44, Ireland 353, Australia 61, New Zealand 64). Next dial the area code and number. For example, if you wanted to call the British Embassy in Washington, D.C., you would dial 001-1-202-588-7800.

For free directory assistance in English: Dial © **1081** if you're looking for a number inside Hong Kong, and dial © **10013** for numbers to all other countries.

For collect calls: To make a collect call from any public or private phone in Hong Kong, dial © **10010.**

In Hong Kong, local calls made from homes, offices, shops, restaurants, and some hotel lobbies are free, so don't feel shy about asking to use the phone. From hotel lobbies and public phone booths, a local call costs HK$1 (US15¢) for each 5 minutes; from hotel rooms, about HK$4 to HK$5 (US50¢–US65¢).

Most hotels in Hong Kong offer direct dialing. Otherwise, long-distance calls can be made from specially marked International Dialing Direct (IDD) public phones. The most convenient method of making international calls is to use an Octopus card (see "Getting Around," earlier in this chapter). Alternatively, a PCCW Hello PhoneCard, which comes in denominations ranging from HK$50 to HK$300 (US$6.50–US$39), is available at HKTB information offices, 7-Eleven convenience stores, machines located beside telephones, and other locations around Hong Kong. Simply insert the card into the slot and dial. There are also prepaid phone cards available for HK$100 (US$13) at Watson's drug stores. You can also charge your telephone call to a major credit card by using 1 of about 100 credit card phones in major shopping locations.

You can also make cashless international calls from any telephone in Hong Kong by using Home Direct, which gives you immediate and direct access to an operator in the country you're calling. Calls can then be charged collect or charged to an overseas telephone card, making it cheaper than a regular international call from Hong Kong. Some designated Home Direct telephones in Hong Kong, located at the airport, Ocean Terminal in Tsim Sha Tsui, and other locations, even allow you to talk with an operator in your country with the push of a button. Home Direct numbers from Hong Kong are © **800 96 0161** for Australia, © **800 96 1100** for Canada, © **800 96 0064** for New Zealand, and © **800 96 0044** for the United Kingdom. For the United States, dial © **800 96 1111** or 800 93 2266 for AT&T, © **800 96 1121** for MCI, and © **800 96 1877** for Sprint. For more information on dial access numbers for Home Direct, phone locations, where PhoneCards can be purchased and operated, time zones, or other matters pertaining to international calls, call © **10013.**

Television There are two English-language TV channels, TVB Pearl and ATV World, broadcasting weekday mornings, evenings, and all day weekends and holidays, with a choice of local programs and shows imported from America, Australia, and Britain. In addition, all first-class and most moderate hotels have satellite television (with imported American, Australian, and British programming, a sports channel, BBC and CNN news channels, and MTV) or cable TV (BBC). Generally, satellite provides more channels, though services can vary depending on how many programs a hotel is signed up for (in general, the cheaper hotel, the fewer channels available). Many hotels also offer in-house pay movies and may also subscribe to the Hongkong Channel, which features short, 5-minute features on Hong Kong's history, transportation networks, traditional customs and festivals, cultural events, shopping tips, and other information.

Time Zone Hong Kong is 8 hours ahead of Greenwich mean time, 13 hours ahead of New York, 14 hours ahead of Chicago, and 16 hours ahead of Los Angeles. Since Hong Kong does not have a daylight saving time, subtract 1 hour from the above times if you're calling the United States in the summer. Because Hong Kong is on the other side of the International date line, you lose 1 day when traveling from the West to Asia. Don't worry—you gain it back when you return, which means that you arrive back home the same day you left Hong Kong.

Tipping Even though restaurants and bars will automatically add a 10% service charge to your bill, you're still expected to leave small change for the waiter. A general rule of thumb is to leave 5%, but in most Chinese restaurants where meals are usually inexpensive, it's acceptable to leave change up to HK$5 (US65¢). In the finest restaurants, you should leave 10%. If you're paying by credit card, pay a cash tip, since gratuity put on a credit card is likely to go to the restaurant and not the staff.

You're also expected to tip taxi drivers, bellhops, barbers, and beauticians. For taxi drivers, simply round up your bill to the nearest HK$1 or add a HK$1 (US15¢) tip. Tip people who cut your hair 5% or 10%, and give bellhops HK$10 to HK$20 (US$1.30–US$2.60), depending on the number of your bags. If you use a public restroom with an attendant, you may be expected to leave a small gratuity—HK$2 (US25¢) should be enough. In addition, chambermaids and room attendants are usually given about 2% of the room charge.

Toilets The best places to track down public facilities in Hong Kong are its many hotels. Fast-food restaurants and shopping malls are other good bets. There may be an attendant on hand, who will expect a small tip of about HK$2 (US25¢). Note that there are no public facilities at any of the MTR subway stations. Hotels and tourist sites usually have Western toilets, but you may encounter Chinese toilets on ferries and in rural areas. To use them, squat facing the hood.

Water It's considered safe to drink urban tap water, though most people prefer bottled water, which is widely available. In summer it's wise to carry bottled water with you. Some hotels have their own purification systems. I always drink the water and have never gotten ill. If you travel into rural Hong Kong or China, however, drink only bottled water.

Weather If you want to check the day's temperature and humidity level or the 2-day forecast, dial ✆ **18501** or 187 8066. Both are in English and both are free. Otherwise, if a storm is brewing and you're worried about a typhoon, tune in to one of the radio or television stations described above.

4

Where to Stay in Hong Kong

For many years, hotel managers in Hong Kong were in the enviable position of having too many guests and not enough rooms to accommodate them. High demand and low supply caused hotel prices to skyrocket in the 1980s and most of the 1990s—many hotels raised their rates a whopping 15% to 20% a year, and to keep up with the demand, new hotels mushroomed. In December 1985 there were 18,180 hotel rooms in Hong Kong; by the end of 1997, the number had swelled to an incredible 33,425.

But then came the 1997 handover, the Asian financial crisis, and more recently, a general decline in long-distance travel following the September 11, 2001, terrorist attacks in the United States, followed by the 2003 outbreak of Severe Acute Respiratory Syndrome (SARS), which transformed Hong Kong into a virtual ghost town.

But while long-distance tourism in Hong Kong is still down, overall tourism is way, way up—thanks to a huge influx of mainland Chinese who, because of relaxed visa regulations, are filling lower-end and medium-ranged hotels. Increased demand has caused hotel rates to rise. Still, bargains abound, especially on the Internet (see "Planning Your Trip Online" on p. 31). Additionally, upper-end hotels may offer special packages, including weekend getaways, off-season incentives, and upgrades while lower-end hotels may offer special promotional rates in the off season.

But hotels are still not cheap in the SAR, especially when compared with those in many other Asian cities.

Rather, prices are similar to what you'd pay in major U.S. and European cities, and while US$150 might get you the best room in town in Topeka, Kansas, in Hong Kong it will get you a small, undistinguished box not unlike a highway motel room. In other words, except for the cost of getting to Hong Kong, your biggest expenditure is going to be for a place to stay.

You should always book rooms well in advance, especially if you have a particular hotel, location, or price category in mind. The SAR's biggest hotel crunches traditionally occur twice a year, during Hong Kong's most clement weather: in March and April and again in October and November. In addition, major trade fairs at Hong Kong's expanded convention center can wreak havoc on travelers who arrive without reservations—on one of my visits, all of Hong Kong's hotels were fully booked. Unsurprisingly, prices are highest during peak season and major trade fairs. While bargains are abundant during the off seasons, many hotels use their published rack rates during peak season and major trade fairs.

As for trends in the hotel industry, Hong Kong's biggest markets nowadays are business travelers and tourists from mainland China. This translates into crowded elevators and lobbies in the moderately priced hotels that Chinese frequent. Hotels catering to executive-level business travelers, meanwhile, have beefed up business services, from state-of-the-art business centers to in-room high-speed Internet connections or TVs

Choosing a Place to Stay

No one area in this compact city is really a more convenient location than any other. Public transportation is efficient and easy to use, and the attractions are spread throughout the city. However, most visitors do stay in Tsim Sha Tsui, on the Kowloon side, simply because that's where you'll find the greatest concentration of hotels, as well as shops and restaurants. Business travelers often prefer the Central District, while those who want to avoid the tourist crowds may like the hotels strung along the waterfront of Wan Chai and Causeway Bay. Yau Ma Tei and Mong Kok, situated on the Kowloon Peninsula north of Tsim Sha Tsui, are great places to stay if you want to be surrounded by Chinese stores and locals, with hardly a souvenir shop in sight. See "Neighborhoods in Brief," beginning on p. 47, for more information on these neighborhoods.

with keyboards that double as computers for Internet access.

Hotels have also improved services and in-room amenities, so that even moderately priced rooms nowadays have hair dryers, room safes, and often cable or satellite TVs with in-house pay movies, as well as coffee/tea-making facilities. No-smoking floors are common in virtually all hotels now except for some of the inexpensive ones. Most hotels also have tour desks or can book tours for you through the concierge or front desk.

Unless otherwise stated, all hotels in this book have air-conditioning (a must in Hong Kong), private bathroom, telephones with international direct dialing, and usually a minibar or empty fridge you can stock yourself. Room service (either 24 hr. or until the wee hours of the morning), babysitting, and same-day laundry service are standard features of very expensive to moderate hotels, as are Western and Asian restaurants and business centers. Many also offer health clubs with swimming pools free for guests (though a few charge extra for their use).

Some hotels even differentiate among their guests, charging health-club fees, for example, for those who book through a travel agent but not for those who pay rack rates (the maximum quoted rates). Guests booking through travel agents may also receive fewer amenities. Note that while many hotels allow children under a specific age to room free with parents, there are restrictions. Some allow only one child, while others allow a maximum of three people in a room. Virtually all will charge extra if an extra bed is required.

It's nearly impossible to predict what might happen in the next few years. In 1997, it was expected that some 40 new hotels would open by the year 2000, pushing the number of rooms to 48,172. Instead, 36,438 rooms were available, with 50,000 expected by the end of 2005 (showing that hotel building fell far short from what was anticipated by 2000, but that there is a building boom going on now). Only one thing is certain: If the tourists continue to pour into Hong Kong, hotels will continue to happily raise their rates.

PRICE CATEGORIES

The hotel prices listed in this book are the rack rates, which you might end up paying if you come during peak season (Chinese New Year, Mar/Apr, Oct/Nov). Otherwise, you can probably get a room for much less. It's *imperative*, therefore, to shop around and ask about special packages, upgrades, or promotional fares

Tips Ways to Save on Your Hotel Room

The **rack rate** is the maximum rate that a hotel charges for a room. Although a few deluxe hotels stick to their published rack rates year-round and most hotels charge rack rates during peak travel times in spring and autumn and during major fairs and conventions, you can probably strike a better bargain.

- **Ask about special rates or other discounts.** Always ask whether a room less expensive than the first one quoted is available. Hong Kong hotels usually have a variety of rates based on room amenities, views, and other factors. Find out the hotel policy on children— do kids stay free in the room or is there a special rate?

- **Dial direct.** When booking a room, compare the rates offered by the hotel's local line with that of the toll-free number. A hotel makes nothing on a room that stays empty, so the local hotel reservation desk may be willing to offer a special rate unavailable elsewhere.

- **Book online.** Many hotels offer Internet-only discounts on their own websites. Cheaper rates are also available through room suppliers on the Internet (see "Planning Your Trip Online," beginning on p. 31), so be sure to shop around.

- **Remember the law of supply and demand.** Avoid high-season stays whenever you can: Planning your vacation just a week before or after official peak season (generally spring and autumn) can mean big savings. Many hotels offer promotional fares throughout the summer. Business hotels may offer discounts over the weekend.

- **Look into group or long-stay discounts.** If you come as part of a large group, you should be able to negotiate a bargain rate, since the hotel can then guarantee occupancy in a number of rooms. Likewise, if you're planning a long stay (at least 5 days), you might qualify for a discount.

- **Avoid excess charges.** Find out whether your hotel imposes a surcharge on local and long-distance calls. A pay phone, however inconvenient, may save you money. And don't be tempted by the room's minibar offerings: Most hotels charge through the nose for water, soda, and snacks.

- **Consider a suite.** If you are traveling with your family or another couple, you can pack more people into a suite (which usually comes with a sofa bed), and thereby reduce your per-person rate. Remember that some places charge for extra guests.

- **If traveling with children, try to find a hotel that allows children to stay free** in their parent's room. There's an age limit (generally anywhere from 12–18 years of age), there's sometimes a maximum of three people to a room, and children are usually free only if no extra bed is required.

- **Book an efficiency.** A room with a kitchenette allows you to shop for groceries and cook your own meals. This is a big money saver, especially for families on long stays.

when making reservations, particularly in the off season. Although I've included toll-free numbers for the United States and Canada for many of the listings below, I also recommend contacting the hotels directly to inquire about rates and special deals, and checking websites for deals that might be offered only through the Internet. During a summer promotional, for example, the Regal Airport Hotel and Regal Kowloon Hotel recently offered rooms for 70% off the rack rates, while the Mandarin Oriental offered a room that usually costs HK$2,950 (US$383) for one person for HK$1,802 (US$234) for two. The Renaissance Harbour View Hotel Hong Kong, with rack rates that begin at HK$2,302 (US$299), offers the same rooms for HK$886 (US$115) in the off season.

Generally speaking, the price of a room in Hong Kong depends upon its view and height rather than upon its size. Not surprisingly, the best and most expensive rooms are those with a sweeping view of Victoria Harbour, as well as those on the higher floors. Is a harbor view worth it? Emphatically, yes. Hong Kong's harbor, with watercraft activity ranging from cruise ships and barges to fishing boats and the Star Ferry, is one of the most fascinating in the world; the city's high-rises and mountains are icing on the cake. Waking in the morning and opening your curtains to this famous scene is a thrill. Hotels know it, which is why they charge an arm and a leg for the privilege. There are, however, a few moderately priced accommodations that offer harbor views, though these, too, represent their most expensive rooms.

In any case, don't be shy about asking what price categories are available and what the differences are among them. Keep in mind that the difference in price between a room facing inland and a room facing the harbor can be staggering, with various price categories in between. There are, for example, "partial" or "side" harbor views, which means you can glimpse the harbor looking sideways from your window or between tall buildings. Double rooms that range from HK$2,000 to HK$3,000 (US$260–US$390), for example, may include five different categories, beginning with a "standard" room on a lower floor facing inland and then increasing in cost to those on upper floors facing inland, those with side harbor views, those on lower floors facing the harbor, and, most expensive, "deluxe" rooms on higher floors with full harbor views. To save money, consider requesting the highest room available in the category you choose. If "standard" rooms, for example, run up to the 8th floor and deluxe rooms are on floors 9 to 20, you'll save money by asking for a standard room on floor 8. If

Landing the Best Room

Somebody has to get the best room in the house. It might as well be you. You can start by joining the hotel's frequent-guest program, which may make you eligible for upgrades. Always ask about a corner room. They're often larger and quieter, with more windows and light, and they often cost the same as standard rooms. When you make your reservation, ask if the hotel is renovating; if it is, request a room away from the construction. Ask about nonsmoking rooms, rooms with views, rooms with twin, queen-, or king-size beds. If you're a light sleeper, request a quiet room away from vending machines, elevators, restaurants, bars, and discos. Ask for a room that has been most recently renovated or redecorated. If you aren't happy with your room when you arrive, ask for another one. Most lodgings will be willing to accommodate you.

(Tips) **Best Hotel Bets**

See chapter 1 for a list of my hotel favorites—the best for business travelers, the best for a romantic getaway, and more.

---

you decide to spring for a full harbor view, be sure to ask for it when making your reservation, and request the highest floor available.

For moderately priced or inexpensive lodgings, few of which offer any kind of view at all, rates are usually based on height, decor, and sometimes size, and it's prudent to inquire whether there's a difference in price between twin and double rooms; some hotels charge more for two beds in a room (more sheets to wash, I guess).

In any case, the wide range of prices listed below for double rooms in each of the listings reflects the various categories available. In moderately priced and inexpensive lodgings, single rates are also usually available, but more expensive hotels often charge the same for double or single occupancy.

All of Hong Kong's expensive hotels, most of the moderately priced hotels, and a few of the inexpensive hotels are members of the Hong Kong Hotels Association (HKHA; www.hkha.com.hk), though not every hotel named in this chapter is. The advantage of staying at a member hotel is that if you have a complaint, you can lodge it directly with the Hong Kong Tourism Board. Furthermore, the HKHA maintains a counter at Hong Kong International Airport where you can reserve a room at one of its member hotels at no extra charge.

The hotels in this chapter are arranged first by price and then by geographical location. The categories are based on rates for a double room (excluding tax and service) as follows: **Very Expensive,** HK$3,000 (US$390) and up; **Expensive,** HK$2,000 to HK$2,999 (US$260–US$389); **Moderate,** HK$1,000 to HK$1,999 (US$130–US$259); and **Inexpensive,** less than HK$1,000 (US$130).

Keep in mind that prices given in this book are for room rates only—a 10% service charge and 3% government tax will be added to your final bill. Since a 13% increase can really add up, be sure to take it into account when choosing your hotel.

1 Very Expensive

Hong Kong's top hotels are among the best in the world, with unparalleled service, state-of-the-art business and health-club facilities, guest rooms equipped with just about everything you can imagine, some of the city's best restaurants, and views of famous Victoria Harbour. They also offer the convenience of a concierge or guest-relations staff, on hand to help with everything from theater tickets to restaurant and tour reservations. Among other extras are turndown service, 24-hour room service, welcoming tea brought to your room shortly after your arrival, free newspaper delivered to your room, and many in-room conveniences and amenities, including voice mail and bedside controls that regulate everything from do-not-disturb lights to the opening of the curtains (it's great to wake up in the morning and have the city appear before you with a mere push of a button). Many also offer executive floors, a "hotel-within-a-hotel" concept catering primarily to business executives with such added services as express check-in and checkout; use of a private executive lounge serving complimentary breakfasts, snacks, and drinks; free services that may include complimentary pressing service or free use of the business center; and an executive-floor concierge or attendant who can take care of such details as restaurant reservations, theater bookings, or transportation arrangements.

KOWLOON

Hotel InterContinental Hong Kong (formerly The Regent Hong Kong) ★★★   It was no small shock when this famous property became the flagship InterContinental in 2001, but management took great pains to assure continuity, maintaining the same staff, calling in the hotel's original design team to create a more contemporary look, and even employing masters of *feng shui* (geomancy) to insure architectural harmony with nature. While some may rue the demise of The Regent's fabled fleet of Daimler limousines, the InterContinental has thankfully shed the former hotel's exclusivity that bordered on the snobbish. With half its guests hailing from North America, the InterContinental seems more relaxed and more egalitarian than its predecessor ever did. And it still has what made this property so beloved in the first place: what may well be the best views of Victoria Harbour from Tsim Sha Tsui. In fact, you can't get much closer to the water than this—built in 1981 of polished rose granite and rising 17 stories, the hotel is located on the water's edge on a projection of reclaimed land.

Great views are trademarks of its unfussy lobby with its soaring glass facade and most of its rooms, 70% of which command sweeping views of the harbor with floor-to-ceiling and wall-to-wall windows (the remaining—and less expensive— rooms face the outdoor swimming pool and landscaped sun terrace). Even the outdoor pool's sun terrace and whirlpools overlook the harbor. Notable features of the hotel are its high-rated restaurants; spacious bathrooms (each fitted in Italian marble with a sunken bathtub, separate shower, and adjoining walk-in closets); an air purification system in all guest rooms; a state-of-the-art spa renowned for its jet-lag and Oriental healing treatments; free tai chi classes for hotel guests; and wireless broadband that enables guests to access the Internet even from poolside.

18 Salisbury Rd., Tsim Sha Tsui, Kowloon, Hong Kong. ✆ **800/327-0200** in the U.S. and Canada, or 852/2721 1211. Fax 852/2739 4546. www.hongkong-ic.intercontinental.com. 514 units. HK$3,100–HK$3,700 (US$403–US$481) single or double; HK$500 (US$65) extra for Club Floors; from HK$5,500 (US$714) junior suite. Children under 18 stay free in parent's room. AE, DC, MC, V. MTR: Tsim Sha Tsui. **Amenities:** 5 restaurants (French, Cantonese, seafood, steaks, Continental); bar; lounge; outdoor pool and whirlpools overlooking Victoria Harbour; fitness room (open 24 hr.); spa; concierge; limousine service; business center; upscale shopping arcade; 24-hr. room service; massage; babysitting; same-day laundry/dry-cleaning service; executive-level rooms; house doctor. *In room:* A/C, satellite TV w/keyboard for Internet access and on-demand pay movies, wireless broadband service, minibar, coffeemaker, hair dryer, safe, bathroom scale, complimentary welcoming tea, fruit, and bottled water.

The Peninsula ★★★   This is Hong Kong's most famous hotel, *the* place to stay if you are an incurable romantic, have a penchant for the historical, and can afford its high prices. Built in 1928, it exudes elegance from its white-gloved doormen to one of the largest limousine fleets of Rolls-Royces in the world. Its lobby, reminiscent of a Parisian palace with high gilded ceilings, pillars, and palms, has long been Hong Kong's foremost spot for afternoon tea and people-watching. Its restaurants are also among the city's best, and service throughout the hotel is sterling. After The Peninsula lost its fabled view of the harbor following construction of the unsightly Space Museum on reclaimed land across the street, it remedied the problem in 1993 with a magnificent 32-story tower providing fantastic harbor views from guest rooms and its top-floor restaurant Felix, designed by Philippe Starck. For the cultural minded, The Peninsula offers classes on everything from tai chi to cooking. I absolutely love this place.

Spacious rooms, so wonderfully equipped that even jaded travelers are likely to be impressed—are all equipped with a silent fax machine with a personalized phone number; free high-speed Internet access; headphones for both radio and TV; extremely focused bedside reading lights designed to keep sleeping partners happy; telephones and control panels on both sides of gigantic beds; a display panel showing outdoor temperature and humidity; and a box in the closet where attendants can place your morning newspaper or take your dirty shoes for complimentary cleaning. Each huge bathroom is equipped with its own TV, hands-free phone (which automatically mutes the TV or radio and digitally filters the sound of running water), mood lighting, separate bathtub and shower stall, and two sinks, both with a magnifying mirror. It may be worth the extra money to spring for a stunning harbor view in the tower, since views facing the back are a disappointment and those in the older part of the hotel are marred by the Space Museum. Both the Star Ferry and MTR are just a short walk away.

Salisbury Rd., Tsim Sha Tsui, Kowloon, Hong Kong. (②) 800/462-7899 in the U.S. and Canada, or 852/2920 2888. Fax 852/2722 4170. www.peninsula.com. 300 units. HK$3,000–HK$4,900 (US$390–US$637) single or double; from HK$5,600 (US$727) suite. AE, DC, MC, V. MTR: Tsim Sha Tsui. **Amenities:** 6 restaurants (French, Pacific Rim crossover, Continental, Swiss, Cantonese, Japanese); 2 bars; lounge; gorgeous indoor pool with sun terrace overlooking the harbor; health club; spa; concierge; limousine service; business center; designer-brand shopping arcade; salon; 24-hr. room service; massage; babysitting; same-day laundry/dry-cleaning service; in-house nurse, practice music room with grand piano. *In room:* A/C, cable/satellite TV w/CD/DVD player (free CDs and DVDs available), fax, high-speed dataport, minibar, hair dryer, safe, bathroom scale, complimentary welcoming tea, fruit, and bottled water.

CENTRAL DISTRICT

In addition to the recommendations here, consider the **Four Seasons Hong Kong,** 8 Finance Rd., Central (② **800/819-5053** in the U.S. and Canada or 852/3196 8888; www.fourseasons.com/hongkong), scheduled to open by summer 2005 next to the ifc mall near the Star Ferry. With 396 luxurious rooms, Chinese, French, and Japanese restaurants, a health club with a heated outdoor pool, and a 24-hour business center, it seems poised to become one of Central's leading hotels. Opening later in 2005 is the **Landmark Mandarin Oriental,** which will be a 114-room boutique hotel in the Landmark shopping complex.

Mandarin Oriental ★★   With so many newer hotels on Hong Kong Island, the Mandarin, a 25-story landmark built in 1963, seems like a familiar old-timer. Truth be told, it's starting to look like an old-timer as well, with an exterior that is increasingly showing its age and verging on the shabby and a lobby that seems dated. Still, the Mandarin is famed for its service and is consistently rated as one of the top hotels in the world. Because of its great location in the heart of Hong Kong's business district (just a 2-min. walk from the Star Ferry), it attracts mostly a business clientele. For tourists, one advantage to staying in Central is that you're surrounded mostly by people who actually live and work in Hong Kong, as opposed to Tsim Sha Tsui, which is crowded largely with other tourists. The Mandarin's restaurants are among the best in Hong Kong,

---

Did You Know?

The Hong Kong Housing Authority is one of the world's largest public landlords. More than one-third of Hong Kong's population lives in public rental housing, and the world's largest public housing project is in Hong Kong.

Where to Stay in Kowloon

Anne Black Guest House **1**
Booth Lodge **4**
BP International House **12**
Caritas Bianchi Lodge **3**
Chungking Mansion **29**
Dorset Seaview Hotel **6**
Eaton Hotel **7**
Empire Hotel Kowloon **14**
Guangdong Hotel **20**
Holiday Inn Golden Mile **30**
Hotel InterContinental
  Hong Kong **26**
Hyatt Regency Hong Kong **31**
Imperial Hotel **28**
InterContinental Grand
  Stanford **23**
Kimberley Hotel **16**
Kowloon Hotel **32**
Kowloon Shangri-La,
  Hong Kong **24**
Langham Hotel
  (formerly Great Eagle) **36**
Majestic Hotel **9**

The Marco Polo Gateway **37**
The Marco Polo Hongkong
  Hotel **35**
The Marco Polo Prince **18**
Miramar **17**
Nathan Hotel **8**
New Kings Hotel **5**
New World Renaissance
  Hotel **25**
The Peninsula **33**
Pruton Prudential Hotel **10**
Ramada Hotel Kowloon **19**
Regal Kowloon Hotel **22**
Royal Garden **21**
The Salisbury YMCA **34**
Shamrock Hotel **11**
Sheraton Hong Kong
  Hotel & Towers **27**
Stanford Hillview Hotel **13**
YMCA International
  House **2**

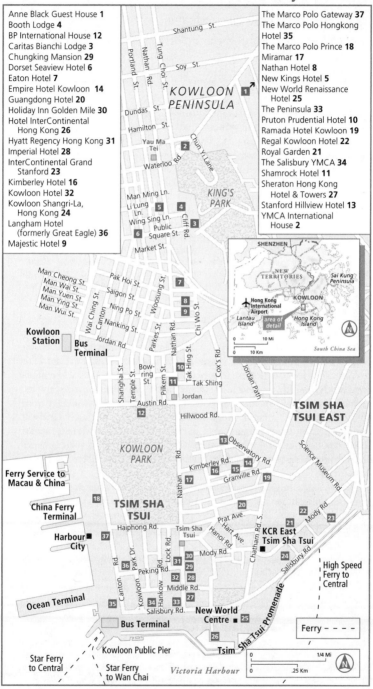

Fun Fact **You've Got to Be Kidding!**

The Chinnery, a bar in the Mandarin Oriental hotel with more than 100 single-malt whiskies, remained off-limits to women until, incredibly enough, 1990.

---

but its indoor pool is disappointingly small. Rooms, on the small side and decorated in an Asian theme with an understated elegance, come mostly with balconies (rare in Hong Kong and, admittedly, a bit noisy) and face either the harbor or inland—those facing the harbor even come with binoculars. Rooms feature all the amenities and facilities you could possibly want, including purified tap water for drinking, but if you are still in need of something, the staff will make every effort to fulfill your wishes.

5 Connaught Rd., Central, Hong Kong. ℂ 800/526-6566 in the U.S. and Canada, or 852/2522 0111. Fax 852/ 2810 6190. www.mandarinoriental.com. 541 units. HK$2,950–HK$4,200 (US$383–US$545) single; HK$3,200–HK$4,450 (US$416–US$578) double; from HK$5,500 (US$714) suite. AE, DC, MC, V. MTR: Central. **Amenities:** 4 restaurants (Continental, Franco-Asian, Cantonese, coffee shop); 3 bars; lounge; indoor pool; health club (open 24 hr.); spa; sauna; concierge; tour desk; limousine service; business center; shopping arcade; salon; 24-hr. room service; babysitting; same-day laundry/dry-cleaning service; Cuban-style cigar divan. *In room:* A/C, satellite TV w/keyboard for Internet access and on-demand pay movies, high-speed dataport, minibar, hair dryer, safe, bathroom scale, complimentary welcoming tea, fruit, and shoeshine.

The Ritz-Carlton ★★★ *Kids*   Opened in 1993, the Ritz-Carlton occupies a smart-looking 25-story building in the heart of the Central District not far from the waterfront and Star Ferry. It follows the Ritz-Carlton tradition of excellent service and fine dining and has an extensive collection of 18th- and 19th-century artwork and antiques. Its lobby is subdued and intimate, resembling more closely a wealthy person's home than a public place, with the reception desk tucked away in an alcove. All in all, the hotel, with its hushed, home-away-from-home atmosphere, is a far cry from the crowds at Hong Kong's more plebeian megahotels. Even the restaurants seem discreetly hidden, most without views so as to discourage outside traffic. If you revel in personalized service—from butler-drawn baths to 24-hour technology butlers and personal shoppers—this is the place for you.

The low-key atmosphere prevails upstairs as well; since there are only 10 to 12 rooms on each floor, it seems more like an upscale apartment complex than a hotel, which obviously appeals to its overwhelmingly business clientele, many of whom are long-staying guests. Yet the hotel doesn't overlook its wee guests either, installing safety devices such as electric outlet plugs for families with preschoolers. The rooms are rather neutral in tone with an understated elegance, with half facing the harbor and offering great views; even those that face inland provide a nice view of the lush Chater Garden and The Peak. Marble bathrooms feature two sinks and separate toilet areas; flowers are a nice touch. Two floors are designed with business travelers in mind, complete with computers hooked up to the Internet, faxes, printers, and scanners.

3 Connaught Rd., Central, Hong Kong. ℂ 800/241-3333 in the U.S. and Canada, or 852/2877 6666. Fax 852/ 2877 6778. www.ritzcarlton.com. 216 units. HK$3,200–HK$3,600 (US$416–US$467) single or double; HK$3,800–HK$4,200 (US$493–US$545) Ritz-Carlton Club executive floor; from HK$7,800 (US$1,013) suite. Children under 13 stay free in parent's room (maximum 3 persons per room). AE, DC, MC, V. MTR: Central. **Amenities:** 5 restaurants (Italian, Cantonese, Shanghainese, Japanese, Continental); lounge; heated outdoor pool; health club; Jacuzzi; sauna; concierge; limousine service; business center; 24-hr. room service; massage

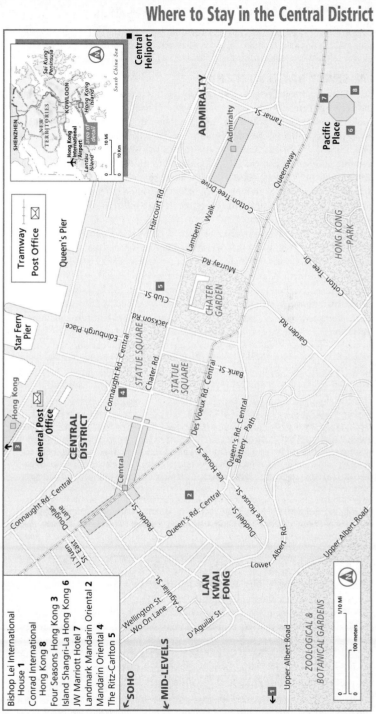

Bishop Lei International House **1**
Conrad International Hong Kong **8**
Four Seasons Hong Kong **3**
Island Shangri-La Hong Kong **6**
JW Marriott Hotel **7**
Landmark Mandarin Oriental **2**
Mandarin Oriental **4**
The Ritz-Carlton **5**

Tramway
Post Office ⊠

(including in-room); babysitting; same-day laundry/dry-cleaning service; executive-level rooms. *In room:* A/C, cable/satellite TV w/pay movies on demand, high-speed dataport, minibar, coffeemaker, iron/ironing board, hair dryer, safe, bathroom scale, complimentary welcome tea, fruit, bottled water, and shoeshine.

CAUSEWAY BAY & WAN CHAI

Grand Hyatt Hong Kong ★★★ *(Kids)*   In a city with so many first-class hotels and such stiff competition, sooner or later a hotel had to exceed all the others in opulence and grandeur. Walking into the lobby of the Hyatt International's Asian flagship hotel is like walking into the Bavarian castle of a modern-day King Ludwig, a lobby so palatial in design that the word "understatement" has certainly never crossed its threshold. Decorated to resemble the salon of a 1930s Art Deco luxury ocean liner, it literally flaunts space, with huge black granite columns, massive flower arrangements, palm trees, bubbling fountains, and furniture and statuettes reminiscent of that era. It's not the kind of place you want to be seen on a bad hair day.

Located on the waterfront adjacent to the Convention Centre and only a 5-minute walk from the Wan Chai Star Ferry pier that delivers passengers to Tsim Sha Tsui, it offers smart-looking, contemporary rooms, soothingly decorated to ease stress and invite relaxation. Pluses are the specially made beds with Egyptian cotton sheets, sliding clothes rack in the closet, cordless keyboards to access the Internet through an interactive TV, coffee-table books, and marble bathrooms complete with 18-karat-gold fixtures and separate bathtub and shower areas. Some 75% of the rooms provide a full harbor view, while the rest have a view of the free-form pool (Hong Kong's largest outdoor hotel pool) and garden with partial glimpses of the harbor. With all this hotel has to offer, little wonder former President Clinton chose the hotel's presidential suite during his 1998 visit (you, too, can stay there for "just" HK$25,900/US$3,364 a night).

1 Harbour Rd., Wan Chai, Hong Kong. © **800/233-1234** in the U.S. and Canada, or 852/2588 1234. Fax 852/2802 0677. www.hongkong.grand.hyatt.com. 572 units. HK$3,600–HK$4,400 (US$467–US$571) single; HK$3,850–HK$4,650 (US$500–US$604) double; HK$4,350–HK$4,750 (US$566–US$617) Regency Club executive-floor double; from HK$5,800 (US$753) suite. Children under 12 stay free in parent's room (maximum 3 persons per room). AE, DC, MC, V. MTR: Wan Chai. **Amenities:** 4 restaurants (Italian, Cantonese, Continental, Japanese); lounge; champagne bar; huge outdoor heated pool (shared with adjacent Renaissance Harbour View Hotel and open year-round); children's splash pool and playground; golf-driving range; 2 outdoor tennis courts; health club; jogging track; concierge; tour desk; limousine service; business center; salon; 24-hr. room service; babysitting; same-day laundry/dry-cleaning service; executive-level rooms; free shuttle to Central, Causeway Bay, and Admiralty. *In room:* A/C, satellite TV w/cordless keyboard for Internet access and on-demand pay movies, fax, high-speed dataport, minibar, coffeemaker, hair dryer, safe, bathroom scale, complimentary fruit and bottled water.

2 Expensive

Many expensive hotels offer almost as much as Hong Kong's very expensive hotels, though only a handful have great views of Victoria Harbour. In this category, you can expect a guest-relations/concierge desk, 24-hour room service, health clubs, business centers, same-day laundry service, and comfortable rooms with hair dryers, cable or satellite TVs with in-room movies, voice mail, and coffee/tea-making facilities. But since this category of hotels sometimes caters to tour groups, they can also be noisier, with less personalized service than deluxe hotels. On the other hand, many also have executive floors for business travelers.

KOWLOON

Holiday Inn Golden Mile   Named after the "golden mile of shopping" on Nathan Road, this Holiday Inn, built in 1975 but renovated many times over

Where to Stay in Causeway Bay & Wan Chai

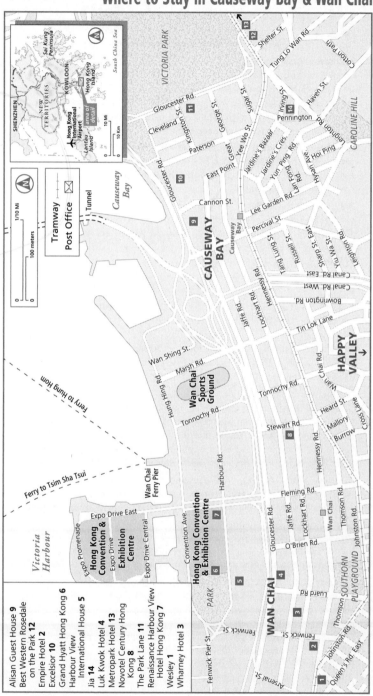

Alisan Guest House **9**
Best Western Rosedale on the Park **2**
Empire Hotel **2**
Excelsior **10**
Grand Hyatt Hong Kong **6**
Harbour View International House **5**
Jia **14**
Luk Kwok Hotel **4**
Metropark Hotel **13**
Novotel Century Hong Kong **8**
The Park Lane **11**
Renaissance Harbour View Hotel Hong Kong **7**
Wesley **1**
Wharney Hotel **3**

VICTORIA PARK

CAROLINE HILL

Gloucester Rd.
Cleveland St.
Kingston St.
George St.
Sugar St.
Yee Wo St.
Paterson
East Point
Jardine's Bazaar
Jardine's Cres.
Irving St.
Pennington
Haven St.
Hysan Ave.
Wan Hoi Ping
Leighton Rd.
Cannon St.
Lee Garden Rd.
Percival St.
Causeway Bay
Tang Lung St.
Russell St.
Sharp St. East
Lan Fong Rd.
Yun Ping Rd.

CAUSEWAY BAY

Gloucester Rd.

Jaffe Rd.
Lockhart Rd.
Hennessy Rd.
Canal Rd. West
Canal Rd. East
Bowrington Rd.
Tin Lok Lane

HAPPY VALLEY →

Wan Shing St.
Marsh Rd.
Hung Hing Rd.

Wan Chai Sports Ground

Tonnochy Rd.
Tonnochy Rd.
Heard St.
Wan Chai Rd.
Mallory
Burrow
Cross Lane

Stewart Rd.
Hennessy Rd.

Ferry to Hung Hom

Ferry to Tsim Sha Tsui

Wan Chai Ferry Pier

Harbour Rd.

Victoria Harbour

Expo Promenade
Expo Drive East
Expo Drive
Hong Kong Convention & Exhibition Centre
Expo Drive Central
Convention Ave.

Hong Kong Convention & Exhibition Centre

Fleming Rd.
Gloucester Rd.
Jaffe Rd.
Lockhart Rd.
O'Brien Rd.
Thomson Rd.
Johnston Rd.
Thomson Rd.

PARK

WAN CHAI

Fenwick Pier St.
Fenwick St.
Fenwick St.
Luard Rd.
Arsenal St.
Johnston Rd.
Queen's Rd. East

SOUTHORN PLAYGROUND

Causeway Bay

Tunnel

SHENZHEN
NEW TERRITORIES
KOWLOON
Sai Kung Peninsula
Hong Kong Island
South China Sea
Hong Kong International Airport
Lantau Island
area of detail

0 10 Km
0 10 Mi

Tramway
Post Office

0 100 meters
0 1/10 Mi

Shelter St.
Tung Lo Wan Rd.
Cotton Path
Leighton Rd.

(Kids) Family-Friendly Hotels

BP International House (p. 87)   This inexpensive hotel offers "Family Rooms" with bunk beds that sleep four for HK$1,540 (US$200). Parents will appreciate the convenience of a laundry room. But best of all is the adjacent Kowloon Park, with its indoor and outdoor public swimming pools, children's playground, lake with flamingos and other birds, and plenty of romping space for active bodies.

Grand Hyatt/Renaissance Harbour View (p. 76 and 85)   These two hotels share one of Hong Kong's largest outdoor swimming pools, as well as a splash pool for smaller children and a playground. Both hotels also offer babysitting.

Pruton Prudential Hotel (p. 90)   Not only can one child under 12 years old stay free in their parent's room, but there's no charge for an extra bed either (a rarity in Hong Kong). Other pluses at this hotel are the rooftop pool and their babysitting services.

Regal Airport Hotel (p. 86)   You won't want to stay at the airport unless you have to, but this hotel has the best-equipped children's recreation room I've seen in Hong Kong, complete with toys, books, and slides that appeal to children 3 to 9 years old, as well as table tennis, air hockey, darts, electronic games, and other games that appeal to teenagers and adults. It's open Monday to Saturday 11am to 9:30pm and Sunday and holidays from 9:30am to 9:30pm. Staff is on hand to supervise, though there is no babysitting there per se; the hotel does offer babysitting in the privacy of your hotel room.

The Ritz-Carlton (p. 74)   For toddlers used to only the best, this first-class hotel ensures their safety by installing precautionary devices upon check-in, including electrical-outlet plugs, water temperature controls and tub spout covers, locking lids for waste baskets, night lights, and more. And just in case, parents receive a first-aid kit with Band-Aids, diaper rash ointment, and other items.

Salisbury YMCA (p. 98)   The overwhelming choice for families in terms of price, facilities, and location (just a short walk to both the Star Ferry and the MTR), this Salisbury Road establishment offers large suites suitable for families, an inexpensive cafeteria serving buffet meals, two indoor swimming pools (including a children's pool), an indoor climbing wall, and a bookstore with a children's corner where tots can try out games and books before parents fork over the cash. Babysitting is also available.

from top to bottom, has a great location right in the heart of bustling Tsim Sha Tsui, about a 6-minute walk from the Star Ferry. The MTR is right across the street, too. Maybe that's why it's popular with tour groups, mainly from North America and China, which can make the lobby rather crowded, noisy, and bothersome. Rooms are spotless, modern, and fairly large for Tsim Sha Tsui, featuring either a king-size bed or two double beds. Although boasting floor-to-ceiling windows, views are blocked by adjacent buildings; those facing the unsightly

Chungking Mansion are glazed (believe me, it's better this way). Those facing Mody Road are brighter but noisier; try to get a room on a high floor. All in all, this is a functional hotel in a convenient location.

50 Nathan Rd., Tsim Sha Tsui, Kowloon, Hong Kong. © 800/465-4329 in the U.S. and Canada, or 852/2369 3111. Fax 852/2369 8016. www.goldenmile-hk.holiday-inn.com. 600 units. HK$2,100–HK$2,650 (US$273–US$344) single; HK$2,500–HK$2,750 (US$325–US$357) twin; HK$3,150 (US$409) Executive Club double; from HK$5,800 (US$753) suite. Up to 2 children under 19 stay free in parent's room. AE, DC, MC, V. MTR: Tsim Sha Tsui. **Amenities:** 3 restaurants (modern European, international buffet, Cantonese); bar; heated rooftop pool open year-round; health club; sauna; concierge; tour desk; limousine service; business center; shopping arcade; salon; 24-hr. room service; massage; babysitting; same-day laundry/dry-cleaning service; executive-level rooms; house doctor. *In room:* A/C, satellite/cable TV w/pay movies, high-speed dataport (some rooms), minibar, coffeemaker, hair dryer, safe, complimentary bottled water.

Hyatt Regency Hong Kong ★★ *Value* Established in 1969 as Hyatt's first property in Asia, this hotel occupies prime real estate on Nathan Road but unfortunately does not offer any harbor-view rooms or a swimming pool. However, it is the only Hong Kong hotel to offer floating rates that change according to season and demand (reflected in the price range below), making it a very good value in the off season (but for my money, in peak season, I'd rather spend it at a hotel with views of famous Victoria Harbour). It boasts a convenient location in the midst of Nathan Road's so-called "golden mile of shopping," just a 5-minute walk from the Star Ferry and a 1-minute walk from the Tsim Sha Tsui MTR subway station. It has undergone extensive renovation through the decades as tastes have changed, getting rid of its flamboyant red-and-gold lobby so popular in the 1970s in favor of a subdued, more sophisticated marble-and-teakwood reception area decorated with Chinese antiques. Among my favorites in this hotel: a Chinese fortune-teller, palm, and face reader in residence in the lobby, and the fabulous late-night dessert buffet at Nathan's Restaurant and Bar. As for rooms, the lacquered Chinese chests housing the TVs and Chinese brush paintings on the walls represent hints of local culture. Rooms facing Nathan Road are equipped with double-glazed windows and insulated walls to reduce outside noise.

67 Nathan Rd., Tsim Sha Tsui, Kowloon, Hong Kong. © 800/233-1234 in the U.S. and Canada, or 852/2311 1234. Fax 852/2739 8701. www.hongkong.regency.hyatt.com. 723 units. HK$880–HK$2,100 (US$114–US$273) single; HK$1,080–HK$2,300 (US$140–US$299) double; HK$350 (US$45) supplement for Regency Club; from HK$1,000 (US$130) supplement for suite. Children under 13 stay free in parent's room (maximum 3 persons per room). AE, DC, MC, V. MTR: Tsim Sha Tsui. **Amenities:** 4 restaurants (Continental, Cantonese, international, coffee shop w/wireless connection); 2 bars; small exercise room (Club guests only); access to nearby health club; concierge; tour desk; limousine service; business center; shopping arcade; salon; 24-hr. room service; babysitting; same-day laundry/dry-cleaning service; executive-level rooms; house nurse. *In room:* A/C, satellite/cable TV w/pay on-demand movies, high-speed dataport, minibar, coffeemaker, hair dryer, safe.

InterContinental Grand Stanford ★★ This older hotel has seen lots of renovations and upgrades that have lifted it from its previous mundane existence into one of Tsim Sha Tsui East's top hotels. It's located right on the waterfront, near the hover-ferry service to Central and the new KCR station, and boasts a lively, high-ceilinged lobby with a café perfect for watching the never-ending stream of international guests. I also like the rooftop swimming pool, which is heated and open year-round and affords great city views. Rooms are more homey than most hotel accommodations, with such added details as trim work bordering the ceiling, large mirrors above TV consoles, good bedside lights, plants on desks, lit magnifying mirrors that reveal flaws you never knew you had, and good harbor views through floor-to-ceiling windows of half the rooms (because of a highway that runs alongside the harbor, be sure to request a room on a high floor). If you can't afford a full harbor view, "side harbor views" are almost as good, due to the hotel's undulating V-shaped facade; unfortunately, the windows of the least expensive rooms open rather unceremoniously onto a windowless wall. Probably the biggest drawback is the 10-minute walk to Tsim Sha Tsui, but it does offer hotel guests a free shuttle service to several locations in Tsim Sha Tsui every 30 to 45 minutes.

70 Mody Rd., Tsim Sha Tsui East, Kowloon, Hong Kong. ⓒ 800/327-0200 in the U.S. and Canada, or 852/2721 5161. Fax 852/2732 2233. www.hongkong.intercontinental.com. 579 units. HK$2,500–HK$3,300 (US$325–US$429) single or double; HK$3,000–HK$3,800 (US$390–US$494) executive-floor; from HK$4,000 (US$519) suite. Children under 18 stay free in parent's room. AE, DC, MC, V. MTR: Tsim Sha Tsui. **Amenities:** 4 restaurants (Continental, international, Cantonese, Italian); bar; lounge; outdoor heated pool; health club (open 24 hr.); spa; concierge; tour desk; limousine service; business center; salon; 24-hr. room service; massage (including in-room); babysitting; same-day laundry/dry-cleaning service; executive-level rooms; doctor and dentist on call; free shuttle service to Tsim Sha Tsui. *In room:* A/C, satellite TV w/pay on-demand pay movies and CD/DVD player, high-speed dataport, minibar, coffeemaker, hair dryer, safe, bathroom scale, complimentary bottled water.

Kowloon Shangri-La, Hong Kong ★★★ (Finds)
The 21-story Kowloon Shangri-La, on the waterfront of Tsim Sha Tsui East, is a popular choice for business travelers, the majority of whom are American. The well-trained staff provides sterling service, which is probably one reason why repeat guests make up more than 40% of hotel occupancy. The two-story lobby is one of the most spacious in Hong Kong, with an expansive white Carrara marble floor, massive Viennese crystal chandeliers, a fountain, and Chinese landscape murals. The hotel, just a minute's walk from the hover-ferry pier with service to Central, is a bit of a hike to Tsim Sha Tsui (luckily, there's free shuttle service every 45 minutes). Rooms, offering either harbor views or rather mundane "garden views" (a popular euphemism for windows that face inland), are large and luxuriously appointed, with ceiling-to-floor bay windows and either a king-size bed or two double beds. If you pay rack rates, additional benefits include free airport transfer, free laundry and dry-cleaning service, free American or continental breakfast, free local telephone calls and Internet access, and a late 6pm checkout.

64 Mody Rd., Tsim Sha Tsui East, Kowloon, Hong Kong. ⓒ 800/942-5050 in the U.S. and Canada, or 852/2721 2111. Fax 852/2723 8686. www.shangri-la.com. 725 units. HK$2,450–HK$3,600 (US$318–US$468) single; HK$2,650–HK$3,800 (US$344–US$494) double; HK$400 (US$52) Horizon Club executive-floor supplement; from HK$4,300 (US$558) suite. Children under 18 stay free in parent's room. AE, DC, MC, V. MTR: Tsim Sha Tsui. **Amenities:** 6 restaurants (French, Californian, Cantonese, Japanese, international buffet, deli); tapas bar; lounge; small indoor pool; health club; Jacuzzi; sauna; concierge; limousine service; business center (open 24 hr.); salon; 24-hr. room service; massage (including in-room); babysitting; same-day laundry/ dry-cleaning service; executive-level rooms; house doctor; free shuttle service to Tsim Sha Tsui. *In room:* A/C, satellite TV w/pay movies, high-speed dataport, minibar, coffeemaker, hair dryer, safe, iron/ironing board, complimentary welcoming tea and shoeshine.

Langham Hotel (formerly Great Eagle) ★★
This 16-story hotel, an affiliate of the historic Langham Hotel in London (and more than half the hotel guests are from North America and Europe), is located a couple of blocks inland from the harbor, just a few minutes' walk from the Star Ferry and the huge Harbour City shopping complex, giving it a very convenient location. Unfortunately, none of its rooms have harbor views. Its lobby, bathed in warm gold tones, exudes a classic Italian atmosphere, with chandeliers, marble floor, a hand-painted dome ceiling, and glass art by American artist Dale Chihuly. It bills itself as an "intelligent" hotel, with bedside control panels that allow guests to operate lights, adjust air-conditioning levels, select a TV or radio program, call up messages or the hotel bill on the television screen, and switch on a "Do Not Disturb" light that automatically disconnects the door chime (I found the

light controls a bit too confusing for my own intelligence, however). As an added safety precaution, staff keys are programmed for specific times only, thereby barring anyone from entering rooms after a shift ends. What's more, a printer records all hotel employee use, indicating when each key was used, where, and by whom. As if that weren't enough, the rooms are also equipped with electronic safes. Contemporary rooms are small but comfortable, with marble bathrooms sporting separate showers and tubs and mist-free mirrors.

8 Peking Rd., Tsim Sha Tsui, Kowloon, Hong Kong. © 800/223-6800 in the U.S. and Canada, or 852/2375 1133. Fax 852/2375 6611. www.langhamhotels.com. 487 units. HK$2,200–HK$2,600 (US$286–US$338) single; HK$2,400–HK$2,800 (US$312–US$364) double; HK$3,400–HK$3,600 (US$442–US$467) Concierge Club executive-floor double; from HK$6,000 (US$779) suite. Children under 13 stay free in parent's room. AE, DC, MC, V. MTR: Tsim Sha Tsui. **Amenities:** 4 restaurants (Cantonese, seafood, international buffet, American deli); lounge; rooftop outdoor pool and Jacuzzi; health club (open 24 hr.); sauna; concierge; limousine service; business center; shopping arcade; 24-hr. room service; massage; babysitting; same-day laundry/dry-cleaning service; executive-level rooms; doctor on call. *In room:* A/C, satellite TV w/keyboard for Internet access (most rooms) and pay movies, high-speed dataport, minibar, coffeemaker, hair dryer, safe.

The Marco Polo Gateway   One of three Marco Polo hotels on Canton Road (see other hotels, below), this property, for the money, does not offer as much as others in its price range. With a small and simple lobby, it's located in the Harbour City shopping complex with its many choices in restaurants and shops, just a 5-minute walk from the Star Ferry. Its comfortable, good-size rooms are priced according to the floor, with the more expensive rooms on the 12th to 16th floors. If noise bothers you, ask for a room away from Canton Road, though these face another building and tend to be dark. Otherwise, only 13 of its highest-priced deluxe rooms have views of a side harbor where the cruise ships dock (not the famous Victoria Harbour), so these should be booked in advance. Business travelers appreciate the desks with large workspaces. Although this hotel has no pool or fitness room of its own, guests can use facilities at the companion Marco Polo Hongkong Hotel down the street. Personally, I'd try other hotels with more services and facilities before reserving a room here.

Harbour City, Canton Rd., Tsim Sha Tsui, Kowloon, Hong Kong. © 800/448-8355 in the U.S. and Canada, or 852/2113 0888. Fax 852/2113 0022. www.marcopolohotels.com. 431 units. HK$1,950–HK$2,200 (US$253–US$286) single; HK$2,050–HK$2,300 (US$266–US$299) double; from HK$3,450 (US$448) suite. 1 child under 14 can stay free in parent's room. AE, DC, MC, V. MTR: Tsim Sha Tsui. **Amenities:** Restaurant (French); coffee shop; bar; access to outdoor pool, exercise room, and spa at sister hotel; tour desk; limousine service; business center; shopping arcade; room service 6am–midnight; babysitting; same-day laundry/dry-cleaning service; executive-level rooms; doctor on call. *In room:* A/C, cable TV w/pay movies, high-speed dataport, minibar, coffeemaker, hair dryer, safe.

The Marco Polo Hongkong Hotel   A member of the Marco Polo Hotel group and the best of three Marco Polo properties lining this street (see above and below), this hotel is as close as you can get to the Star Ferry and is connected via air-conditioned walkway to the largest shopping complex in Asia, Harbour City. It is also close to the China Hong Kong Terminal with departures for Macau and Shenzhen. Built in the 1960s and well maintained, it has a marble lobby that is spacious and comfortable but often overcrowded. Guest rooms, decorated in bold color schemes, are far from luxurious but are quite large and are mostly so-called "Hollywood" twins (two twin beds pushed together) with a sitting area, large working desks, and walk-in closet. The lowest-price rooms face the small courtyard swimming pool and other guest rooms and can be quite dark, while the most expensive rooms boast unparalleled views of harbor activity, including the ocean liners that dock right next door as well as evening sunsets.

Harbour City, 3 Canton Rd., Tsim Sha Tsui, Kowloon, Hong Kong. ✆ **800/448-8355** in the U.S. and Canada, or 852/2113 0088. Fax 852/2113 0011. www.marcopolohotels.com. 664 units. HK$2,300–HK$3,530 (US$299–US$459) single; HK$2,400–HK$3,630 (US$312–US$472) double; HK$3,200–HK$4,270 (US$416–US$555) Continental Club executive-floor double; from HK$4,660 (US$605) suite. 1 child under 14 can stay free in parent's room. AE, DC, MC, V. MTR: Tsim Sha Tsui. **Amenities:** 5 restaurants (Continental, Japanese, Chiu Chow, American, coffee shop); lounge; small heated outdoor pool (open year-round); exercise room; spa; concierge; tour desk; limousine service; business center; shopping arcade; salon; 24-hr. room service; babysitting; same-day laundry/dry-cleaning service; executive-level rooms; doctor on call. *In room:* A/C, cable TV w/pay on-demand movies, high-speed dataport, minibar, coffeemaker, hair dryer, safe.

The Marco Polo Prince   The third in a row of Marco Polo hotels on Canton Road (and therefore a slightly longer walk to and from the Star Ferry), the Prince Hotel is also situated in the huge Harbour City shopping complex and caters to business travelers (mostly Japanese) and tour groups. Opened in 1984 but recently renovated (thankfully, its tiny lobby was expanded to help alleviate the front-desk crunch), it's a small hotel with equally small, simple rooms that feature either twin or queen-size beds, large working desks, and surprisingly roomy bathrooms with lots of counter space. The lowest-priced rooms are on the lower floors (and are used mainly by tour groups); only four of its deluxe rooms have views of a side harbor. Again, guests staying here can use the outdoor pool and fitness room at The Marco Polo Hongkong Hotel (see above), though it's a hike.

Harbour City, Canton Rd., Tsim Sha Tsui, Kowloon, Hong Kong. ✆ **800/448-8355** in the U.S. and Canada, or 852/2113 1888. Fax 852/2113 0066. www.marcopolohotels.com. 393 units. HK$1,950–HK$2,200 (US$253–US$286) single; HK$2,050–HK$2,300 (US$266–US$299) double; HK$2,650 (US$344) Continental Club double; from HK$3,950 (US$402) suite. 1 child under 14 can stay free in parent's room. AE, DC, MC, V. MTR: Tsim Sha Tsui. **Amenities:** Restaurant (Asian buffet); lounge; access to outdoor pool, fitness room, and spa at sister hotel; tour desk; limousine service; business center; shopping arcade; 24-hr. room service; babysitting; same-day laundry/dry-cleaning service; executive-level rooms; doctor on call. *In room:* A/C, cable TV w/pay on-demand movies, high-speed dataport, minibar, coffeemaker, hair dryer, safe.

Royal Garden ★★ *Finds*   A small hotel with a lot of architectural surprises, the Royal Garden has always been one of my favorites. It features a cool, sleek lobby and a 15-story inner atrium, a concept adapted from the traditional Chinese inner garden. Plants hang down from balconies ringing the soaring space, glass-enclosed elevators glide up the wall, a piano sits on an island in the middle of a pool, and the sound of rushing water adds freshness and coolness to the atmosphere. A wonderful 25m-long (82 ft.) rooftop swimming pool is uncovered in summer, covered, and heated in winter. Off the lobby is a very interesting martini bar, and its Italian restaurant, Sabatini, is one of Hong Kong's best. All in all, it's the kind of hotel that invites exploration. The rooms, the most expensive of which have partial harbor views between two buildings ("partial harbor view" means either that other buildings are obstructing part of your view or that your windows do not squarely face the water), are smartly decorated with a mix of colonial-style and modern furniture and feature a chilled, purified water tap in the bathroom. Although a slight hike to the action of Tsim Sha Tsui, it's only a minute's walk to the hover-ferry pier with service to Central.

69 Mody Rd., Tsim Sha Tsui East, Kowloon, Hong Kong. ✆ **800/448-8355** or 852/2721 5215. Fax 852/2369 9976. www.rghk.com.hk. 422 units. HK$2,100–HK$2,600 (US$273–US$338) single; HK$2,250–HK$2,750 (US$292–US$357) double; HK$2,950–HK$3,150 (US$383–US$409) Crown Club executive-floor double; from HK$3,850 (US$500) suite. 1 child under 12 can stay free in parent's room. AE, DC, MC, V. MTR: Tsim Sha Tsui. **Amenities:** 6 restaurants (Italian, Cantonese, Pekingese, Japanese, Continental, international buffet); bar; lounge; heated rooftop outdoor/indoor pool and Jacuzzi; putting green; lighted outdoor tennis court; exercise room; sauna; concierge; limousine service; business center; shopping arcade; 24-hr. room service; massage; babysitting; same-day laundry/dry-cleaning service; executive-level rooms. *In room:* A/C, satellite TV w/keyboard for Internet access and on-demand pay movies, high-speed dataport, minibar, coffeemaker, hair dryer, safe.

Sheraton Hong Kong Hotel & Towers ★★   The 30-some-year-old Sheraton has one of the most envied locations in Hong Kong—near the waterfront
on the corner of Nathan Road and Salisbury Road—and is an easy walk to the
subway and Star Ferry. In fact, it's such a choice spot that for years rumors
buzzed that the Sheraton would close down to make way for a more lucrative
office building. Instead, the Sheraton underwent massive renovations that
upgraded its facilities and image (and increased its room rates). Its lobby, previously plagued by overcrowding from locals who used it as a convenient waiting
place to meet friends, was moved to the second floor to discourage foot traffic
and was updated with a sleek, contemporary look graced by Asian motifs and
subdued lighting. A plus is the outdoor rooftop swimming pool, heated in winter, offering a spectacular view and more privacy than pools lower to the ground.
Guest rooms are decorated in neutral brown, which seems to be the rage nowadays and range from those facing an inner courtyard (the cheapest) to those facing the harbor with great views even from bathrooms. In between are those that
overlook surrounding Tsim Sha Tsui, some of which face Nathan Road and even
provide sideways glimpses of the harbor. Still, located between The Peninsula
and InterContinental, it plays second fiddle to both in terms of reputation,
class—and, luckily, price. Americans account for one-third of the guests here.

20 Nathan Rd., Tsim Sha Tsui, Kowloon, Hong Kong. ℂ **800/325-3535** in the U.S. and Canada, or 852/2369
1111. Fax 852/2739 8707. www.sheraton.com/hongkong. 780 units. HK$2,500–HK$3,200 (US$325–US$416)
single, HK$2,700–HK$3,400 (US$351–US$442) double; Tower executive-floor rooms HK$3,400–HK$4,100
(US$442–US$532) single, HK$3,600–HK$4,300 (US$468–US$558) double; from HK$4,000 (US$519) suite.
AE, DC, MC, V. MTR: Tsim Sha Tsui. **Amenities:** 5 restaurants (American, oysters/seafood, Japanese,
Cantonese, international); bar; 2 lounges; outdoor heated rooftop swimming pool and Jacuzzi; health club;
spa; concierge; tour desk; limousine service; business center; shopping arcade; salon; 24-hr. room service;
massage; babysitting; same-day laundry/dry-cleaning service; executive-level rooms; house doctor. *In room:*
A/C, satellite TV w/keyboard for Internet access and pay movies, high-speed dataport, minibar, coffeemaker,
hair dryer, safe, iron/ironing board, bathroom scale.

CENTRAL DISTRICT

Conrad International Hong Kong ★★★   The 61-story Conrad, built in
1990, is one of a trio of exclusive hotels perched on a hillside above Pacific Place,
an upscale shopping center located about halfway between the Central District
and Wan Chai. One of the conveniences of staying here is that Pacific Place
abounds in very good restaurants, greatly expanding dining options without having to venture far. Hong Kong Park is also just steps away, and the MTR can be
reached without stepping outside. The Conrad's facilities appeal to both businesspeople (who make up 70% of the hotel's clientele, the majority of whom are
American or European) and well-heeled leisure travelers. Although the architecture is contemporary, the hotel's classic furnishings and interior design soften the
modern effect, giving it a cozy atmosphere with wood paneling, polished granite,
and comfortable furniture. I especially like the lighthearted touch of the larger-
than-life butterflies and wildflowers on the murals of the massive lobby pillars.
Large-size rooms feature windows that extend the width of the room, offering
views of either The Peak or the harbor (harbor-view rooms, of course, are better
and cost more, though some so-called "city view" rooms offer a partial harbor
view through buildings), and spacious bathrooms with separate shower and bathtub facilities. On a playful note, the bathrooms even feature a floating duck or
other toy for a bit of fun in the bathroom, while a stuffed bear is placed on beds
at turndown. In short, this is a great choice for business or pleasure.

Pacific Place, 88 Queensway, Central, Hong Kong. ℂ **800/445-8667** in the U.S. and Canada, or 852/2521
3838. Fax 852/2521 3888. www.conradhotels.com. 513 units. HK$2,850–HK$3,350 (US$370–US$435) single

or double; HK$3,550–HK$3,850 (US$461–US$500) executive-floor; from HK$5,700 (US$740) suite. Children under 18 stay free in parent's room (maximum 3 persons per room). AE, DC, MC, V. MTR: Admiralty. **Amenities:** 4 restaurants (Italian, Cantonese, French, international); bar; lounge; heated outdoor pool; state-of-the art health club; Jacuzzi; sauna; concierge; limousine service; business center; shopping arcade; 24-hr. room service; massage; babysitting; same-day laundry/dry-cleaning service; executive-level rooms; house doctor. *In room:* A/C, cable/satellite TV w/pay on-demand movies, high-speed dataport, minibar, coffeemaker, hair dryer, safe, iron/ironing board, bathroom scale, complimentary welcoming tea, fruit, and bottled water.

Island Shangri-La Hong Kong ★★★ *(Finds* Hong Kong Island's tallest hotel (measured from sea level) offers the ultimate in extravagance and luxury, rivaling the grand hotels in Paris or London: It's one of my favorite hotels in the world. More than 700 Viennese chandeliers, lush Tai Ping carpets, artistic flower arrangements, and more than 500 paintings and artworks adorn the hotel. The 17-story atrium, which stretches from the 39th to the 56th floors, features a marvelous 16-story-high Chinese painting, drawn by 40 artists from Beijing and believed to be the largest landscape painting in the world. Also in the atrium are a private lounge open only to hotel guests and a two-story old-world–style library. The hotel itself is enhanced by the connecting Pacific Place shopping center, with its many options in dining; across the street is Hong Kong Park. Upon arrival, guests are personally escorted to their rooms (all of which ring the 17-story atrium) by a guest-relations officer, who also explains the rooms' features. Rooms, among the largest in Hong Kong and the largest on Hong Kong Island, face either The Peak or spectacular Victoria Harbour and feature marble-topped desks, Chinese lacquerware TV cabinets, and silk bedspreads. Oversize bathrooms are equipped with two sinks and separate tub and shower areas (harbor-view rooms only), bidet, TVs, and even jewelry boxes. Fresh flowers are another nice touch. Guests paying rack rates receive such additional services as free transportation from and to the airport, free laundry and dry cleaning throughout their stay, complimentary American or continental breakfast, free local telephone calls and Internet access, and 6pm late checkout.

Pacific Place, Supreme Court Rd., Central, Hong Kong. © 800/942-5050 in the U.S. and Canada, or 852/2877 3838. Fax 852/2521 8742. www.shangri-la.com. 565 units. HK$2,400–HK$3,700 (US$312–US$481) single; HK$2,600–HK$3,900 (US$338–US$506) double; from HK$5,800 (US$753) suite. Children under 18 stay free in parent's room. AE, DC, MC, V. MTR: Admiralty. **Amenities:** 5 restaurants (French, lobster/seafood, Cantonese, Japanese, buffet); lounge; outdoor heated pool big enough for swimming laps; health club (open 24 hr.); spa; Jacuzzi; sauna; steam bath; concierge; tour desk; limousine service; business center (open 24 hr.); adjoining shopping arcade; salon; 24-hr. room service; massage; babysitting; same-day laundry/dry-cleaning service; executive-level rooms; medical clinic; free shuttle to Queen's Pier in Central and Convention Centre. *In room:* A/C, satellite TV w/pay on-demand movies, fax/printer/scanner, high-speed dataport, minibar, coffeemaker, hair dryer, safe, bathroom scale, complimentary welcoming tea, and fruit.

JW Marriott Hotel ★★ *(Value* The 27-story Marriott, which opened in 1989 as the first of three hotels at Pacific Place, is overshadowed by the more luxurious Conrad and Island Shangri-La (see above). Its lobby, while not as grandiose as others in this category, is nonetheless the only one of Pacific Place's hotels to offer views of the harbor from its lounge (though recent construction has robbed the lounge of its once grandiose panorama). Best of all, its harbor-view rooms are the cheapest of the three, making it a good value. Rooms, though small, are all designed with right-angled "saw-toothed" windows to maximize views of the harbor or Peak and are outfitted with colorful, hand-painted bedspreads, large marbled bathrooms with separate tub and shower areas, oversize desks equipped with office supplies, and two queen-size or a king-size bed. On the downside, rooms facing the harbor are subject to the slight din of traffic; since rates are the same, request a room on a high floor.

Pacific Place, 88 Queensway, Central, Hong Kong. ©️ **800/228-9290** in the U.S. and Canada, or 852/2810 8366. Fax 852/2845 0737. www.marriotthotels.com. 602 units. HK$2,090–HK$3,400 (US$271–US$442) single or double; HK$3,400–HK$3,3,800 (US$442–US$494) executive-floor single or double; from HK$6,000 (US$780) suite. A/C, DC, MC, V. MTR: Admiralty. **Amenities:** 3 restaurants (Cantonese, Californian, coffee shop); lounge; outdoor heated pool open year-round; health club (open 24 hr.); Jacuzzi; sauna; steam room; concierge; limousine service; business center (open 24 hr.); shopping arcade; 24-hr. room service; massage; babysitting; same-day laundry/dry-cleaning service; executive-level rooms; house doctor. *In room:* A/C, satellite TV w/pay on-demand movies, high-speed dataport, minibar, coffeemaker, hair dryer, iron/ironing board, safe, bathroom scale, complimentary welcoming tea, fruit, and bottled water.

CAUSEWAY BAY & WAN CHAI

Jia ★★ *Finds*   Travelers who are allergic to ugly hotel rooms will want to head straight to Hong Kong's hippest boutique hotel, opened in 2004 by a Singaporean 20-something entrepreneur and designed by Philippe Starck. From the moment guests step into the low-key lobby with its teak wood floors, white sheer curtains, and whimsical furniture and are greeted by staff in chic Shanghai-Tang-designed uniforms, they know this is no ordinary place of abode. Stylish rooms, bathed in white and divided into living, dining, and working areas, feature kitchens and home theater units consisting of flat-panel TVs, DVD players, and surround sound. Guests enjoy free local telephone calls, free broadband Internet access, complimentary Continental breakfast, complimentary cocktail hour, and free access to a local gym. I wouldn't be surprised if some people check in and never leave. Studios (380 sq. ft) and one- and two-bedroom suites are available.

1–5 Irving St., Causeway Bay, Hong Kong. ©️ **852/3196 9000.** Fax 852/3196 9001. www.jiahongkong.com. 57 units. HK$2,000 (US$260) single or double; from HK$3,000 (US$390) suite. Monthly rates available. Rates include Continental breakfast. AE, DC, MC, V. MTR: Causeway Bay. **Amenities:** Restaurant (Asian); bar; free access to nearby health club; rooftop Jacuzzi; sun deck; 24-hr. room service; self-service laundry; same-day laundry/dry-cleaning service. *In room:* A/C, satellite/cable TV w/DVD player, kitchen, hair dryer, safe, iron/ironing board.

The Park Lane ★   Although it's inland, I've always liked the location of this hotel—across from huge Victoria Park and close to many area restaurants, shops, and department stores. First opened in 1974 and attracting primarily business travelers, this 28-story hotel has undergone extensive renovation; now its lobby has a more modern, brighter look and deluxe guest rooms sport fun, contemporary furnishings like glass-topped desks and coffee tables and even glass-bowled sinks. Rooms vary in price according to floor level, decor, and view—the best are those facing Victoria Park (where you can watch people practicing tai chi in the morning), with the harbor beyond. Standard rooms, on the other hand, have uninspiring views and are rather ordinary. On the downside, the lobby gets a lot of street traffic from area shoppers, making it difficult to attract individual attention from the overworked staff. Be sure to book at least one meal at the top-floor Riva, with sweeping views of Victoria Park and the harbor.

310 Gloucester Rd., Causeway Bay, Hong Kong. ©️ **800/457-4000** in the U.S. and Canada, or 852/2293 8888. Fax 852/2576 7853. www.parklane.com.hk. 792 units. HK$2,000–HK$3,100 (US$260–US$402) single or double; HK$3,300–HK$3,800 (US$429–US$494) Premier Club executive rooms; from HK$5,000 (US$649) suite. Children under 12 stay free in parent's room (maximum 3 persons per room). AE, DC, MC, V. MTR: Causeway Bay. **Amenities:** 3 restaurants (Continental, international, American); bar; lounge; health club; Jacuzzi; sauna; concierge; tour desk; limousine service; business center; shopping arcade; salon; 24-hr. room service; massage; babysitting; same-day laundry/dry-cleaning service; executive-level rooms; house doctor. *In room:* A/C, satellite/cable TV w/pay movies, dataport, minibar, coffeemaker, hair dryer, safe, complimentary bottled water.

Renaissance Harbour View Hotel Hong Kong ★ *Kids* *Value*   This large, 43-story hotel sits beside the Convention and Exhibition Centre on the Wan Chai waterfront, separated from the Grand Hyatt (p. 76) by Hong Kong's largest outdoor hotel swimming pool and a garden, shared by the two hotels. Just a couple of minutes' walk from the Wan Chai Star Ferry that delivers passengers to Tsim Sha Tsui and Hung Hom, it provides some of the same facilities and advantages as the Hyatt, but at a lower price; obviously, it caters largely to those attending functions at the convention center, which can make it quite busy, as well as business travelers. Its expansive, white-marbled lobby is airy with views of the harbor, and more than 65% of the rooms also boast outstanding views of the water.

1 Harbour Rd., Wan Chai, Hong Kong. © 800/228-9898 in the U.S. and Canada, or 852/2802 8888. Fax 852/ 2802 8833. www.renaissancehotels.com. 862 units. HK$2,300–HK$2,700 (US$299–US$351) single or double; HK$2,700–HK$3,000 (US$351–US$390) Renaissance Club executive floor; from HK$3,600 (US$468) suite. AE, DC, MC, V. MTR: Wan Chai. **Amenities:** 3 restaurants (Continental, Cantonese, coffee shop); lounge; dance club; huge outdoor pool; children's splash pool and playground; golf-driving range; 2 lighted outdoor tennis courts; health club; Jacuzzi; jogging trail; concierge; limousine service; business center; 24-hr. room service; babysitting; same-day laundry/dry-cleaning service; executive-level rooms; house doctor. *In room:* A/C, cable TV w/pay on-demand movies, fax, high-speed dataport, minibar, coffeemaker, hair dryer, safe.

AT THE AIRPORT

Regal Airport Hotel 🐾 *Kids*   Opened in autumn 1998 as Hong Kong's largest hotel and the only hotel at Hong Kong International Airport, this Regal chain hotel is only a 5-minute walk from the airport via covered walkway and is convenient for those with early-morning flights. Standout facilities include a cafe offering Asian and Western fare unique for its rotating art gallery, which moves through the restaurant on tracks, and a very good children's recreation room with games ranging from slides, toys, and books for youngsters to air hockey, table tennis, and electronic games for teenagers. Otherwise, because central Hong Kong is only a 20-minute train ride away, I think you're much better off staying in town, near the shops, restaurants, sights, and street-life vitality that make Hong Kong unique. In addition, even though the hotel makes a conscious effort to brighten its interior with lots of mirrors and glass, including a glass dome over the lobby and gleaming black floors that reflect light, it can't seem to escape its airport connection, and the futuristic decor (including a flying-saucer–shaped stage for live music in the lobby), reminds me of a spaceship. Guest rooms are quite large and soundproof, with modern furniture in eye-popping colors of purple, red, or lime green; all but the cheapest also have TVs with keyboards for Internet access and electronic games.

9 Cheong Tat Rd., Chek Lap Kok, Hong Kong. © 800/222-8888 in the U.S. and Canada, or 852/2286 8888. Fax 852/2286 8686. www.regalhotel.com. 1,100 units. HK$2,000–HK$2,800 (US$260–US$364) single or double; HK$2,950 (US$383) Regal Class; HK$3,500 (US$455) Regal Club; from HK$5,000 (US$649) suite. Children under 12 stay free in parent's room (maximum 3 persons per room). AE, DC, MC, V. Airport Express Liner: Hong Kong International Airport. **Amenities:** 5 restaurants (Cantonese, Shanghainese, Japanese, international, steaks); lounge; indoor and outdoor pools; health club and spa; children's recreation room; concierge; limousine service; business center (open 24 hr.); shopping arcade; salon; 24-hr. room service; babysitting; same-day laundry/dry-cleaning service; executive-level rooms; house doctor. *In room:* A/C, satellite TV w/keyboard for Internet connection, games, and pay movies, minibar, coffeemaker, hair dryer, safe.

3 Moderate

Since tour groups have long been a mainstay of tourism in Hong Kong, you're most likely to encounter them at the moderately (and inexpensively) priced hotels, which account for the majority of hotels in Hong Kong. And with increased tourism from mainland China filling rooms in this category, it's imperative to book early. As for rooms, they tend to be rather small compared to American hotel rooms, with generally unexciting views, but usually have such amenities as hair dryers, minibars or empty refrigerators you can stock yourself, and instant coffee, as well as room service, bellhops, no-smoking floors, tour desks, and sometimes a swimming pool and/or fitness room. Since harbor views are usually not available, rates are generally based on height/floor number and decor and sometimes on size.

KOWLOON

BP International House ⚑ _Kids_   The word "House" in this accommodation's name is misleading, since it is actually a 25-story modern hotel, with a spacious but utilitarian lobby catering mainly to tour groups, school excursions, and budget-conscious business travelers, which gives it a dormitory-like atmosphere. Built in 1993 at the north end of Kowloon Park, it's just a stone's throw from the park's indoor and outdoor public swimming pools and a short walk to a playground, making it good for families. The park's many paths also make it popular with joggers. The guest rooms, located on the 14th to 25th floors, are clean, pleasant, and modern. Although located inland, the best and priciest rooms on higher floors offer good views of the harbor (with height limitations in Kowloon now gone, however, due to the relocation of the airport, you can expect that taller buildings will someday eclipse those views). Business travelers usually opt for one of the Corporate Rooms on the top five floors. There are also very simple "Family Rooms" equipped with bunk beds that sleep four for HK$1,540 (US$200).

8 Austin Rd., Tsim Sha Tsui, Kowloon, Hong Kong. ☏ 800/223-5652 in the U.S. and Canada, or 852/2376 1111. Fax 852/2376 1333. www.bpih.com.hk. 535 units. HK$990–HK$1,450 (US$129–US$188) single; HK$1,100–HK$1,500 (US$143–US$195) double; HK$1,600–HK$1,800 (US$208–US$234) Corporate double room; from HK$3,100 (US$403) suite. Children under 13 stay free in parent's room. Rates include buffet breakfast. AE, DC, MC, V. MTR: Jordan. **Amenities:** Coffee shop; lounge; babysitting; coin-op laundry; laundry/dry-cleaning service; executive-level rooms. _In room:_ A/C, satellite TV w/pay movies.

Dorsett Seaview Hotel   This 19-story brick hotel looks slightly out of place amidst the hustle and bustle of this Chinese neighborhood, just a stone's throw from a famous Tin Hau (Goddess of the Sea) Temple and Temple Street's famous Night Market. Catering mainly to visitors from the mainland and Southeast Asia, it has a tiny lobby (often packed) and, best of all, a cocktail lounge on the top floor offering views of a harbor (not the famous Victoria Harbour, but a working harbor nonetheless). Narrow corridors lead to the smallest rooms I've seen in Hong Kong, so miniature that TVs are mounted to the wall to save space. It reminds me of a Japanese business hotel, functional and clean but so small you can almost reach out and touch all four walls. At any rate, since rooms lack the convenience of a desk or large closet space, there's virtually no place to unpack or put your luggage. It's basically just a place to rest your weary bones; as for those Night Market bargains you just purchased, you'll have to either stow them under your bed or sleep with them. Nevertheless, this hotel gets recommended for its superb, colorful location.

268 Shanghai St., Yau Ma Tei, Kowloon, Hong Kong. ☏ 852/2782 0882. Fax 852/2781 8800. www. dorsettseaview.com.hk. 268 units. HK$880–HK$1,280 (US$114–US$166) single; HK$1,280–HK$1,580 (US$166–US$205) double; from HK$2,400 (US$312) suite. AE, DC, MC, V. MTR: Yau Ma Tei. **Amenities:** Restaurant (Continental); lounge; tour desk; small business center; room service 7am–4pm; babysitting; same-day laundry/dry-cleaning service; doctor on call. _In room:_ A/C, TV w/pay movies, minibar, coffeemaker (but no coffee), hair dryer.

Eaton Hotel ⚑⚑ _Finds_   This hotel has more class and more facilities than most other hotels in this group, making it one of my top picks. A handsome brick 21-story hotel, located above a shopping complex not far from the Temple Street

Night Market, it features one of the longest hotel escalators I've seen—it takes guests straight up to the fourth-floor lobby, where a cheerful and efficient staff awaits your arrival. The lobby lounge (offering wireless Internet connection) is bright and cheerful, with a four-story glass-enclosed atrium that overlooks a garden terrace with a water cascade, where you can sit outside with drinks in nice weather. Other pluses are the small but nicely done rooftop pool with sunning terrace and the icemakers on every floor (which means you don't have to call room service and which are somewhat of a rarity in Hong Kong). Guest rooms are small but welcoming, with all the basic creature comforts. I especially like the innovatively designed (and highest-priced) deluxe rooms, with curved floor-to-ceiling windows giving views of a distant harbor.

380 Nathan Rd., Yau Ma Tei, Kowloon, Hong Kong. © 800/223-5652 in the U.S. and Canada, or 852/2782 1818. Fax 852/2782 5563. www.eaton-hotel.com. 460 units. HK$1,730–HK$2,230 (US$225–US$290) single or double; HK$2,530 (US$329) executive room. AE, DC, MC, V. MTR: Jordan. **Amenities:** 3 restaurants (Cantonese, Asian/Western, coffee shop); bar; lounge; small outdoor pool; exercise room; concierge; business center; shopping arcade; room service 7am–2:30am; babysitting; same-day laundry/dry-cleaning service; *In room:* A/C, satellite TV w/pay on-demand movies, high-speed dataport, minibar, coffeemaker, hair dryer, safe.

Empire Hotel Kowloon

Opened in 2002, this is one of Kowloon's newest hotels, giving it a contemporary, upbeat edge over competitors. Rooms, occupying the 8th through 26th floors of a round, hollow, glass-sheathed tower, boast wall-to-wall and floor-to-ceiling windows, though only those above the 17th floor have distant harbor views. Glass-topped desks and bowl-shaped basins rise above ordinary hotel furnishings in more deluxe rooms, but the dim, bedside-reading lamps will ruin your eyes. Unlike most Hong Kong hotels, showers here greatly outnumber tubs. There's a pool, but it's at the bottom of the pit-like tower, rendering it grossly uninviting. Still, this hotel, popular with Japanese guests, is a welcome addition to Kowloon's medium-priced accommodations.

62 Kimberley Rd., Tsim Sha Tsui, Kowloon, Hong Kong. © 800/830-6144 in the U.S. and Canada, or 852/2685 3000. Fax 852/2685 3685. www.asiastandard.com. 315 units. HK$1,400–HK$2,200 (US$182–US$286) single or double; from HK$2,800 (US$364) suite. Children under 12 stay free in parent's room. AE, DC, MC, V. MTR: Tsim Sha Tsui. **Amenities:** 2 restaurants (Japanese, buffet); bar; outdoor pool; exercise room; sauna; limousine service; business center; room service 7am–11pm; babysitting; same-day laundry/dry-cleaning service. *In room:* A/C, cable TV w/keyboard for Internet access and pay movies, high-speed dataport, minibar, hair dryer, safe.

Imperial Hotel

Location, location, location—that's the best thing this hotel has going for it. It's located right on Nathan Road between the Sheraton and Holiday Inn and near the MTR station. Otherwise, it doesn't offer much in terms of service, and its standard rooms are tiny and motel-like; some even have pink bathrooms. Its cheaper rooms face the back of Chungking Mansion, notorious for its cheap and often uninviting rooms, laundry strung everywhere, and garbage piled up below, apparently tossed unconcernedly from the windows above. You won't know this, however, as newly added glazed windows now hide the formerly enlightening view. It's an improvement with a price: Rooms are now rather gloomy and claustrophobic and the cheapest are quite small. If you can, spring for a deluxe room that faces Nathan Road, although keep in mind that these rooms are subject to the noise of traffic; those on the top floors are high enough to offer glimpses of the harbor. Because of its cheap prices, this hotel attracts a mixed international clientele, many of whom look like they wish they were elsewhere. It is a rather grim place, but the location is ideal.

30–34 Nathan Rd., Tsim Sha Tsui, Kowloon, Hong Kong. © 800/44-UTELL in the U.S. and Canada, or 852/2366 2201. Fax 852/2311 2360. www.imperialhotel.com.hk. 225 units. HK$950–HK$1,700 (US$123–US$221) single; HK$1,100–HK$2,000 (US$143–US$260) double. 1 child under 12 can stay free in parent's room. AE, DC, MC, V. MTR: Tsim Sha Tsui. **Amenities:** Restaurant (Italian); Irish pub; tour desk; babysitting; same-day laundry/dry-cleaning service. *In room:* A/C, cable TV w/pay on-demand movies, minibar, coffeemaker (but no coffee), hair dryer.

Kimberley Hotel   The 20-story Kimberley Hotel, on the northern edge of Tsim Sha Tsui, about a 15-minute walk from the Star Ferry, opened in 1991 and was long one of the favorites for its moderate prices, location, and facilities. However, it is now starting to show its age, a bit worn around the edges and with outdated decor. It's clearly time for a face-lift (at press time, some rooms had received new carpets and wallpaper). Still, it does a thriving business attracting both the tourist and business trade, including many Japanese and tour groups. Guest rooms, constructed with V-shaped windows that let in more sunlight and allow for more panoramic—though not scenic—views, are rather small and plain but come with all the basics. The most expensive rooms are on higher floors and are larger, but even these are rather small. The suites represent an especially good deal since they occupy the top three floors and are equipped with kitchenettes and a lounging/dining area, making them ideal for long-term guests and families.

28 Kimberley Rd., Tsim Sha Tsui, Kowloon, Hong Kong. (C) 800/876-5278 in the U.S., or 852/2723 3888. Fax 852/2723 1318. www.kimberley.com.hk. 546 units. HK$1,100–HK$1,750 (US$143–US$227) single; HK$1,200–HK$1,850 (US$156–US$240) double; from HK$2,150 (US$279) suite. AE, DC, V. MTR: Tsim Sha Tsui. **Amenities:** 3 restaurants (Cantonese, Japanese, coffee shop); lounge; golf cages; fitness room; spa; sauna; tour desk; business center; shopping arcade; salon; room service 6am–midnight; massage; babysitting; same-day laundry/dry-cleaning service. *In room:* A/C, satellite TV w/pay movies, dataport, minibar, coffeemaker, hair dryer.

Kowloon Hotel ★★   If you like high-tech hotels but don't want to pay a fortune, this is the place for you. The Kowloon is a modern glass-walled structure right behind The Peninsula; they are both under the same management. Its location is great, just a few minutes' walk from the Star Ferry. I also like the fact that the lobby has a Satellite Newspaper KiOSK offering the latest editions of 131 newspapers from 54 countries, as well as a computerized street directory for consulates, points of interest, and other addresses, with a printout in both English and Chinese to instruct taxi drivers. The hotel also has a very good pizzeria. But its main selling point is that it has long offered the most technically advanced rooms in its price category (it even offered them long before upper-priced hotels jumped on the Internet bandwagon). Every room boasts an interactive telecenter (a multisystem TV linked to a central computer), which allows free access to the Internet and contains video games. The telecenter also interfaces with in-room fax machines that double as printers; guests receive private fax numbers and personalized e-mail addresses. The downside of the hotel: rooms are minuscule and are plagued by traffic noise. Although they have V-shaped bay windows, allowing unobstructed views up and down the street, The Peninsula's tower has robbed harbor views from all but the most expensive rooms.

19–21 Nathan Rd., Tsim Sha Tsui, Kowloon, Hong Kong. (C) 800/262-9467 in the U.S., or 852/2929 2888. Fax 852/2739 9811. www.thekowloonhotel.com. 736 units. HK$1,300–HK$2,550 (US$169–US$331) single; HK$1,400–HK$2,650 (US$182–US$344) double; from HK$3,700 (US$480) suite. AE, DC, MC, V. MTR: Tsim Sha Tsui. **Amenities:** 3 restaurants (Italian, Cantonese, international buffet); bar; access to nearby YMCA pool and health club (fee charged); tour desk; limousine service; business center; shopping arcade; salon; room service 6am–2am; babysitting; same-day laundry/dry-cleaning service. *In room:* A/C, satellite TV w/access to Internet, fax, free high-speed dataport, minibar, coffeemaker, hair dryer, safe.

Miramar   Across from Kowloon Park, the Miramar is strategically located in the midst of a shopping area, including the Park Lane shopping arcade and Miramar Shopping Centre. An older hotel once known for its showy exterior and glitzy gold-colored decor, this 50-some-year-old property toned down its public areas during a major renovation some years back; the last trace of the Miramar's former flashy self can only be seen in its stained-glass windows in the lobby's atrium ceiling. Since it caters largely to Asian tour groups, all but 22 of the rooms are twins and doubles. They're quite roomy though rather standard, with some of the higher-floor deluxe rooms offering views of Kowloon Park.

118–130 Nathan Rd., Tsim Sha Tsui, Kowloon, Hong Kong. ✆ 800/44-UTELL in the U.S., or 852/2368 1111. Fax 852/2369 1788. www.miramarhk.com. 525 units. HK$1,200–HK$2,000 (US$156–US$260) single or double; HK$2,600–HK$2,800 (US$338–US$364) Miramar Club executive floor; from HK$3,800 (US$494) suite. Children under 12 stay free in parent's room. AE, DC, MC, V. MTR: Tsim Sha Tsui. **Amenities:** 5 restaurants (2 Cantonese, Sichuan, East-meets-West fusion, coffee shop); bar; indoor pool; exercise room; sauna; concierge; tour desk; limousine service; business center; shopping arcade; room service 7am–12:30am; massage; babysitting; same-day laundry/dry-cleaning service. *In room:* A/C, satellite TV w/pay on-demand movies and keyboard for Internet access, minibar, hair dryer, safe.

New World Renaissance Hotel   This hotel is tucked inside the New World Centre shopping complex, which contains more than 50 shops and boutiques. Modern in both decor and technology, this 20-some-year-old hotel nevertheless suggests an Asian atmosphere with its large flower arrangements and sleek black furniture, but I find the windowless lobby slightly claustrophobic. Furthermore, despite its prime location right on the waterfront near the InterContinental (p. 71), oddly enough, only one restaurant provides harbor views, and none of its rooms face the water. Rather, all rooms face Salisbury Road or the pool (which is quieter), with a few offering partial glimpses of the water. Otherwise, the rooms are comfortable enough, with modern Asian decor and all the usual amenities, including separate tub and shower areas in deluxe rooms.

22 Salisbury Rd., Tsim Sha Tsui, Kowloon, Hong Kong. ✆ 800/421 8188 in the U.S. and Canada, or 852/2369 4111. Fax 852/2369 9387. www.renaissancehotels.com/hkgnw. 549 units. HK$1,700–HK$2,000 (US$221–US$260) single or double; HK$2,300 (US$299) Renaissance Club executive floor; from HK$3,300 (US$429) suite. AE, DC, MC, V. MTR: Tsim Sha Tsui. **Amenities:** 3 restaurants (Euro-Asian, Cantonese, coffee shop); lounge; outdoor pool; health club; limousine service; business center (open 24 hr.); shopping arcade; salon; 24-hr. room service; babysitting; same-day laundry/dry-cleaning service; executive-level rooms. *In room:* A/C, cable TV w/pay movies, fax, high-speed dataport, minibar, coffeemaker, hair dryer, safe.

Pruton Prudential Hotel ✿ *Kids*   This 1991 hotel, at the northern end of Tsim Sha Tsui, towers 17 stories above a six-level shopping complex and the MTR Jordan station, providing easy and direct access to the rest of Hong Kong. About a 20-minute walk from the Star Ferry and only minutes from the Temple Street Night Market, Jade Market, and a Tin Hau (Goddess of the Sea) temple, it offers smartly decorated rooms with sleek furniture, artwork, and Japanese moving panels framing the windows. The rates are based on the view and height, with the cheapest rooms on lower floors. If possible, avoid those facing the back and nondescript buildings. Deluxe rooms feature floor-to-ceiling bay windows, some with a partial glimpse of the harbor in the distance. Although the hotel itself has only a coffee shop and a bar, there are several other restaurants within the shopping complex. Another plus is the 18m-long (60 ft.) rooftop pool. Families take note: Unlike most hotels, there's no charge for one extra bed for children under 12 years old.

222 Nathan Rd. (entrance on Tak Shing St.), Tsim Sha Tsui, Kowloon, Hong Kong. ✆ 852/2311 8222. Fax 852/2311 4760. www.prutonhotel.com. 431 units. HK$1,000–HK$1,700 (US$130–US$221) single or double; HK$2,000 (US$260) Executive Club floor; from HK$2,700 (US$351) suite. 1 child under 12 stays free in parent's room. AE, DC, MC, V. MTR: Jordan. **Amenities:** Restaurant (coffee shop); bar; outdoor pool; exercise room; tour desk; limousine service; business center (open 24 hr.); shopping arcade; salon; room service 6:30am–1am; babysitting; same-day laundry/dry-cleaning service. *In room:* A/C, satellite/cable TV w/pay movies, wireless/high-speed dataport, minibar, coffeemaker (but no coffee), hair dryer, safe.

Ramada Hotel Kowloon   Popular with Asian business travelers, this no-nonsense, Chinese-owned hotel offers simple, clean rooms and not much else in terms of facilities or services. Even its so-called business center has only one computer. Its location on Chatham Road, across the street from the science and history museums, is not as convenient as other business hotels in this category, though it is within walking distance of the MTR (about 8 min.), Star Ferry (about 15 min.), and hover ferry with service to Central (about 10 min.). The cheapest rooms are small and have glazed windows, while the highest-priced rooms, which have extras including a room safe, free bottled water, and instant coffee, face Chatham Road and have the best views but can be noisy. In short, there's nothing exciting about this hotel, but it will suffice if more desirable and convenient properties are full.

73–75 Chatham Rd. S., Tsim Sha Tsui, Kowloon, Hong Kong. ℭ 800/854 7854 in the U.S. or 852/2311 1100. Fax 852/2311 6000. www.ramadahongkong.com. 205 units. HK$1,300–HK$2,050 (US$169–US$266) single or double; from HK$2,800 (US$364) suite. 1 child under 12 can stay free in parent's room. AE, DC, MC, V. MTR: Tsim Sha Tsui. **Amenities:** Coffee shop; bar; limousine service; tiny business center; babysitting; laundry/dry-cleaning service. *In room:* A/C, cable TV w/pay movies, minibar, coffeemaker (coffee supplied only in more expensive rooms), hair dryer, safe (some rooms).

Regal Kowloon Hotel ⚞   The 15-story Regal Kowloon offers more services and is more attractive than many hotels in its price range, with a lobby that blends East and West with reproduction 18th-century French antiques and Louis XV–style furniture standing alongside Chinese works of art. Recent renovations have brought an unfortunate choice in hallway carpeting, and the guest rooms, all soundproof, are rather middle of the road but perfectly adequate, with the exception of good bedside reading lights. The cheapest rooms face another building, provide no view whatsoever, and tend to be dark. The more expensive rooms face a garden; some even have a glimpse of the harbor between buildings. Business travelers may opt for Regal Class rooms, while Regal Club executive floors go a step further with added services and amenities (like broadband Internet access). The most moderately priced of several hotels in Tsim Sha Tsui East, it's only a minute's walk to the hover-ferry service to Central.

71 Mody Rd., Tsim Sha Tsui East, Kowloon, Hong Kong. ℭ 800/222-8888 in the U.S. and Canada, or 852/2722 1818. Fax 852/2369 6950. www.regalkowloon.com. 592 units. HK$1,800–HK$2,400 (US$234–US$312) single or double; from HK$2,700 (US$351) Regal Class; from HK$3,200 (US$416) Regal Club; from HK$5,000 (US$649) suite. 2 children under 12 can stay free in parent's room. AE, DC, MC, V. MTR: Tsim Sha Tsui. **Amenities:** 3 restaurants (American, Cantonese, coffee shop); bar; lounge; exercise room; tour desk; limousine service; business center; shopping arcade; salon; 24-hr. room service; babysitting; same-day laundry/dry-cleaning service; executive-level rooms; house doctor. *In room:* A/C, satellite TV w/pay movies, dataport, minibar, coffeemaker, hair dryer, safe.

MID-LEVELS

Bishop Lei International House ⚞⚞ *Finds*   If you want to pretend that you live in Hong Kong, in a residential area popular with ex-pats and abounding in charming neighborhood restaurants and bars, this is the place for you. Located in the Mid-Levels, about halfway up Victoria Peak, at the top of the Central/Mid-Levels Escalator that delivers residents to jobs in Central in the morning and then reverses to bring them back home again later in the day, it is not as convenient as other hotels, but it has its certain charm. In addition, the hotel makes up for its out-of-the-way location with free shuttle service to Central; a half-dozen city buses also stop outside its door. Opened in 1996 and managed by the Catholic Diocese of Hong Kong, it offers tiny standard rooms (with even tinier bathrooms, most equipped with showers instead of tubs) that have large windows letting in lots of sunshine. Unfortunately, these face inland. If you can, spring for a more expensive room facing the harbor. Since they're so high up, views are fantastic. Harbor-view rooms also have the advantage of a video player (video-rental shops are located nearby), appealing to the hotel's many long-staying business travelers (long-term packages available). In any case, in acknowledgement that rooms are small, there's a reading room for relaxation, the coffee shop has an outdoor terrace, and surprising for a hotel this size, it also has a small pool and exercise room. If the frenetic pace of Hong Kong sets you on edge, you'll find this a nice retreat.

4 Robinson Rd., Mid-Levels, Hong Kong. ✆ 852/2868 0828. Fax 852/2868 1551. www.bishopleihtl.com.hk. 203 units. HK$1,080 (US$140) single; HK$1,280–HK$1,680 (US$166–US$218) double; from HK$1,880 (US$244) suite. 1 child under 12 can stay free in parent's room. AE, DC, MC, V. Bus: 3B, 12, 12M, 23, 23A, and 40 to Robinson Rd. **Amenities:** Coffee shop; small outdoor pool; small exercise room; business center; 24-hr. room service; babysitting; same-day laundry/dry-cleaning service; free shuttle bus to Central. *In room:* A/C, cable TV, high-speed dataport, minibar, coffeemaker, hair dryer, safe.

CAUSEWAY BAY & WAN CHAI

Best Western Rosedale on the Park ★★★ *Finds*   This hotel across the street from Victoria Park has lots going for it, not least of which is that it opened in 2001, giving it a more contemporary, high-tech edge over older properties in the area. Targeting corporate accounts, it sweetens the deal with several innovative incentives, including complimentary broadband Internet service in each room, cordless phones, in-house mobile phones that allow you to receive calls if you're out of your room (but inside the hotel), free drinks in the fridge upon check in, and a lounge with computers and Internet access. Only 13 rooms on each floor give it a boutique hotel-like atmosphere. Rooms are small but have everything you need, though note that the least expensive "superior" rooms are on lower floors and face another building. Some rooms on the 31st-floor executive level have side views of the harbor (you have to be standing at the window to see it), but the best deal are the junior suites with microwaves and kitchen utensils, making them a good bet for long-staying guests.

8 Shelter St., Causeway Bay, Hong Kong. ✆ 800/528-1234 in the U.S. and Canada, or 852/2127 8888. Fax 852/2127 3333. www.rosedale.com.hk. 274 units. HK$1,180–HK$1,280 (US$153–US$166) single; HK$1,280–HK$1,380 (US$166–US$179) double; HK$1,580 (US$205) executive double; from HK$1,980 (US$257) suite. Weekly and monthly rates available. Children under 18 can stay free in parent's room. AE, DC, MC, V. MTR: Causeway Bay. **Amenities:** 3 restaurants (2 Cantonese, Western); lounge; small fitness room; business center; room service (7am–1am); babysitting; same-day laundry/dry-cleaning service. *In room:* A/C, cable TV w/pay on-demand movies, high-speed dataport, fridge, coffeemaker, hair dryer, iron/ironing board, safe, complimentary soda, beer, and bottled water.

Empire Hotel ★ *Value*   Nicely situated in the heart of Wan Chai and popular with midlevel business travelers for its convenience to Central, this business hotel offers good value, with many of the same amenities, services, and facilities found at higher-priced hotels, including a rooftop outdoor swimming pool large enough for swimming laps and a highly recommended Shanghainese restaurant called Wu Kong (p. 126). Narrow hallways may provide a challenge to the claustrophobic, while rooms, with rates based on size (none provide a view of the harbor), are also small but comfortable and pleasant, each equipped with a Data View Information System, which allows guests to receive messages on their television sets, check flight schedules, check information (on stocks, finance, or shopping), play video games, and view the hotel services directory (but it does not provide Internet access). The top five floors, comprised of Empire Plus rooms, are geared toward business travelers with such extras as wall-mounted TVs (leaving more desk space), fax machines, and a magnetic whiteboard.

33 Hennessy Rd., Wan Chai, Hong Kong. ℭ 800/830-6144 in the U.S. and Canada, or 852/2866 9111. Fax 852/2861 3121. www.asiastandard.com. 360 units. HK$1,400–HK$1,600 (US$182–US$208) single or double; HK$2,000 (US$260) Empire Plus room; from HK$2,200 (US$264) suite. AE, DC, MC, V. MTR: Wan Chai. **Amenities:** 3 restaurants (Shanghainese, steak, coffee shop); lounge; outdoor pool; exercise room; sauna; concierge; tour desk; limousine service; business center; room service 7am–11pm; massage; babysitting; same-day laundry/dry-cleaning service. *In room:* A/C, satellite TV w/pay movies, high-speed dataport, minibar, coffeemaker, safe.

Excelsior ℛ Located on the waterfront near a lively shopping area, the Excelsior, built in 1973, belongs to the Mandarin Oriental group of hotels but is relatively moderately priced. However, because up to 20% of the people staying here belong to tour groups, the lobby is often overcrowded and buzzing with activity, sometimes making it difficult to get front-desk service or find an empty seat. The elevators are also crowded. On the plus side, this is a good place to stay if you like to jog, since it's close to 20-hectare (50-acre) Victoria Park, Hong Kong's largest city park. In addition, the hotel offers free guided tours to the nearby Noon Day Gun, which fires every day at . . . well . . . noon, and its top-floor ToTT'S Asian Grill & Bar (p. 144) offers spectacular harbor views, outrageous decor, and great East-meets-West cuisine. Most rooms are the same small size with the same decor and tend to be crowded. Those that command a view of the harbor with the Hong Kong Yacht Club and Kowloon on the other side are the most expensive and the largest; slightly cheaper are those with side harbor views or views of the park, while the cheapest face inland toward the city. Wireless connections are available in all hotel public areas, including restaurants and guest rooms.

281 Gloucester Rd., Causeway Bay, Hong Kong. ℭ 800/526-6566 in the U.S. and Canada, or 852/2894 8888. Fax 852/2895 6459. www.excelsiorhongkong.com. 884 units. HK$1,900–HK$2,700 (US$247–US$351) single or double; HK$2,300–HK$3,100 (US$299–US$403) Executive Floor; from HK$3,800 (US$494) suite. AE, DC, MC, V. MTR: Causeway Bay. **Amenities:** 4 restaurants (Pacific Rim fusion, Cantonese, Italian, international buffet); bar; lounge; 2 indoor tennis courts; exercise room; sauna; steam room; concierge; tour desk; business center; salon; 24-hr. room service; babysitting; same-day laundry/dry-cleaning service; executive-level rooms. *In room:* A/C, satellite TV w/pay-on-demand movies, high-speed dataport, minibar, coffeemaker, hair dryer, iron/ironing board, safe.

Harbour View International House ℛ *(Value* Opened in 1986, this YMCA occupies a prime spot on the Wan Chai waterfront, right next to the Hong Kong Arts Centre and not far from the convention center. Rooms, all twin or double beds, are rather stylish for a YMCA, attracting guests mostly from mainland China and North America. Best of all, more than half the rooms face the harbor with V-shaped windows, making this the cheapest place on Hong Kong Island with great views. Rooms that face inland are even cheaper.

4 Harbour Rd., Wan Chai, Hong Kong. ℭ 852/2802 0111. Fax 852/2802 9063. www.harbour.ymca.org.hk. 320 units. HK$1,200–HK$1,750 (US$156–US$228) single or double. Children under 12 stay free in parent's room. AE, DC, MC, V. MTR: Wan Chai. **Amenities:** Restaurant (Chinese/Western); lounge; tour desk; room service 7am–11:30pm; babysitting; laundry/dry-cleaning service. *In room:* A/C, cable TV, wireless Internet access, minibar.

Luk Kwok Hotel ℛ The Luk Kwok was originally built in the 1930s on what was then the waterfront; seven stories high, at the time it was the tallest building in Wan Chai. It achieved its greatest fame, however, for its role in Richard Mason's fictional *The World of Suzie Wong*, when Wan Chai was the domain of prostitutes and sailors. How things have changed since then! After a complete demolition, the Luk Kwok reopened in 1990 as a totally new and remodeled larger hotel, slightly antiseptic, and appealing mainly to business travelers, probably because of its lack of facilities (exercise room, pool, etc.). Now located some 2 blocks inland due to land reclamation, not far from the Hong Kong Convention and Exhibition Centre, the new hotel is high-tech and modern, with a granite-and-marble lobby and updated rooms. The hotel's two restaurants are on the first floor, while the next 17 floors are used for a parking garage and offices. Guest rooms, located on the 19th to 29th floors, are a cut above those in other area business hotels, larger in size (though standard rooms are a bit cramped), and equipped with all the necessities, including large counter space in the bathroom. The addition of plants in every bathroom is a nice touch, and some rooms even have a glimpse of the harbor between buildings. I also like the small cocktail lounge open only to hotel guests.

72 Gloucester Rd., Wan Chai, Hong Kong. ℂ 800/44-UTELL in the U.S. and Canada, or 852/2866 2166. Fax 852/2866 2622. www.lukkwokhotel.com. 195 units. HK$1,450–HK$1,800 (US$188–US$234) single; HK$1,600–HK$1,950 (US$208–US$253) double; HK$2,300–HK$2,400 (US$299–US$312) executive-floor double; from HK$3,600 (US$468) suite. AE, DC, MC, V. MTR: Wan Chai. **Amenities:** 2 restaurants (Cantonese, international); lounge; exercise room; concierge; tour desk; limousine service; business center; 24-hr. room service; babysitting; same-day laundry/dry-cleaning service; executive-level rooms; house doctor. *In room:* A/C, satellite TV w/pay-on-demand movies, high-speed dataport, minibar, coffeemaker, hair dryer, safe.

Metropark Hotel ⭐⭐ *Value*   Although not as centrally located as my other picks in Causeway Bay, this new hotel has some compelling advantages that put it near the top of the list (and in any case, the MTR and tram lines are just outside the door and the hotel provides a free shuttle bus to the shopping district in Causeway Bay). For one thing, it's cheerier and more colorful than most hotels, with a contemporary and fun design that extends through the lobby and into the rooms, the most expensive of which have great views over Victoria Park to the harbor (the cheapest rooms face another building). In addition, it has all the facilities most travelers need, including free broadband Internet service and a rooftop pool complete with great views and—this is a Hong Kong first—underwater music (closed in winter). Unfortunately, bathrooms are small, with showers instead of tubs and limited counter space, but in-room vanities provide extra place to stow stuff. In short, this is a welcome addition to Causeway Bay, despite its unlikely location.

148 Tung Lo Wan Rd., Causeway Bay, Hong Kong. ℂ 800/223-5652 in the U.S. and Canada, or 852/2600 1000. Fax 852/2600 1111. www.metroparkhotel.com. 266 units. HK$1,500–HK$1,800 (US$195–US$234) single/double; from HK$2,600 (US$338) suite. AE, DC, MC, V. MTR: Tin Hau. **Amenities:** Restaurant (coffee shop); bar; outdoor pool; exercise room; Jacuzzi; sauna; tour desk; business center; 24-hr. room service; same-day laundry/dry-cleaning service; free shuttle to Causeway Bay. *In room:* A/C, cable TV w/pay on-demand movies, high-speed dataport, minibar, coffeemaker, hair dryer, safe.

Novotel Century Hong Kong   Opened in 1992, this gleaming white 23-story hotel is a 7-minute walk via covered walkway from the Hong Kong Convention and Exhibition Centre and the Wan Chai Star Ferry terminus with service to Tsim Sha Tsui and Hung Hom. Its airy, smart-looking two-story lobby has floor-to-ceiling windows overlooking a busy intersection and is plagued by the constant hum of traffic, but since there are very few seats available, you probably won't spend much time here anyway. Narrow corridors lead to minuscule rooms, which are mercifully equipped with double-paned windows as well as touch pads on phones for controlling lights, the TV, and other functions. A few of the most expensive doubles offer a partial harbor view between buildings, as do some of the rooms on the Royal Club executive floor, but standard rooms face other buildings. Probably the best thing about this hotel is its facilities, including a wading pool.

238 Jaffe Rd., Wan Chai, Hong Kong. ✆ **800/221-4542** in the U.S. and Canada, or 852/2598 8888. Fax 852/2598 8866. www.accorhotels.com/asia. 516 units. HK$1,600–HK$1,900 (US$208–US$247) single/double; HK$2,205 (US$286) Royal Club executive-floor double; from HK$3,800 (US$494) suite. AE, DC, MC, V. MTR: Wan Chai. **Amenities:** 3 restaurants (Shanghainese, Italian, coffee shop); 2 lounges; outdoor pool; wading pool; putting green; exercise room; sauna; tour desk; limousine service; business center; 24-hr. room service; babysitting; same-day laundry/dry-cleaning service. *In room:* A/C, cable TV w/pay movies, wireless Internet access, minibar, coffeemaker, hair dryer, safe.

Wharney Hotel   This business hotel is often plagued by tour groups (mainly from mainland China) but is conveniently situated in the heart of Wan Chai. It offers small but adequate accommodations divided into five categories of rooms, based on decor and floor level. The best rooms are located on higher floors in a newer addition with an updated contemporary look, but there are no views. Standard rooms are run-of-the-mill and small. Pluses include its varied facilities, including a waiting lounge for hotel guests whose flights leave later in the day, complete with sofas, magazines, and light refreshments.

57–73 Lockhart Rd., Wan Chai, Hong Kong. ✆ **852/2861 1000.** Fax 852/2529 5133. www.wharney.com. 358 units. HK$1,000–HK$1,600 (US$130–US$208) single or double; from HK$2,400 (US$312) suite. 1 child under 12 can stay free in parent's room. AE, DC, MC, V. MTR: Wan Chai. **Amenities:** 2 restaurants (Asian/Western buffet, Cantonese); bar; outdoor pool; exercise room; steam room; sauna; limousine service; business center; room service 6:30am–10:30pm; babysitting; same-day laundry/dry-cleaning service. *In room:* A/C, TV w/pay movies, minibar, coffeemaker, hair dryer.

4 Inexpensive

Unfortunately, Hong Kong has more expensive hotels than it does budget accommodations. Hotels in this category generally offer small, functional rooms with a bathroom and air-conditioning but usually have few services or facilities. Some budget accommodations also offer rooms without private bathroom at cheaper prices (if no mention is made here of rooms without bathroom, you can assume all rooms have bathrooms). Always inquire whether there's a difference in price between rooms with twin beds and those with double beds. If possible, try to *see* a room before committing yourself, since some may be better than others in terms of traffic noise, view, condition, and size. For the most part, however, you shouldn't have any problems with the inexpensive hotels recommended here.

KOWLOON

Anne Black Guest House (YWCA)   This 20-story YWCA, built in 1972 and rather inconveniently located atop a hill about a 10-minute walk from the nearest MTR station, welcomes both men and women in its spotless rooms, most of which are twins with unstocked refrigerator, hair dryer, and private toilet and shower. Six twin rooms have sinks but no bathrooms or refrigerators, so if you're on a budget be sure to book these rooms far in advance. The sixth floor has a communal fridge and microwave. The rooms are fairly plain in a no-nonsense dormitory kind of way; those that face the front offer slightly better views of the surrounding neighborhood. Ask for a room on a higher floor. The staff is friendly, making this a good choice despite its out-of-the-way location.

5 Man Fuk Rd., Kowloon, Hong Kong. © 852/2713 9211. Fax 852/2761 1269. www.ywca.org.hk. 169 units, 127 with bathroom. HK$440 (US$57) single without bathroom, HK$580 (US$75) single with bathroom; HK$580 (US$75) twin without bathroom, HK$780–HK$880 (US$101–US$114) twin with bathroom. Monthly rates available. AE, MC, V. MTR: Yau Ma Tei. **Amenities:** Coffee shop (Western/Cantonese); business center; coin-op laundry. *In room:* A/C, TV, fridge (some rooms), coffeemaker (but no coffee), hair dryer (some rooms).

Booth Lodge ✦✦ *Finds*   About a 30-minute walk to the Star Ferry, but close to the Jade Market, Temple Street Night Market, and Ladies' Market, and only a 2-minute walk from the Yau Ma Tei MTR station, Booth Lodge is located just off Nathan Road on the seventh floor of the Salvation Army building. It has a comfortable lobby and an adjacent coffee shop offering very reasonably priced lunch and dinner buffets with Chinese, Japanese, and Western selections, but best is the restaurant's outdoor brick terrace overlooking a wooded hillside, where buffet barbecues are held in peak season. Rooms, all twins or doubles and either standard rooms or larger deluxe rooms, are spotlessly clean. Some face the madness of Nathan Road, but those facing the hillside are quieter. If you're looking for inexpensive yet reliable lodging in a convenient location, this is a good bet. A bonus: Local telephone calls are free.

11 Wing Sing Lane, Yau Ma Tei, Kowloon, Hong Kong. © 852/2771 9266. Fax 852/2385 1140. www. boothlodge.salvation.org.hk. 53 units. HK$620–HK$1,500 (US$81–US$195) single or double. Rates include buffet breakfast. AE, MC, V. MTR: Yau Ma Tei. **Amenities:** Coffee shop; tour desk; laundry/dry-cleaning service. *In room:* A/C, satellite TV, fridge, hair dryer.

Caritas Bianchi Lodge *Value*   Just down the street from Booth Lodge and also convenient to the jade and night markets and Yau Ma Tei MTR station, this accommodation is not as homey as Booth Lodge and has as much personality as a college dormitory. However, most of the year it charges only two-thirds or less of the rack rates given below, making it a bargain that can't be beat. Most of its very simple rooms, with large desks and closets, face toward the back of the hotel, offering a view of a wooded cliff and a small park, certainly a nicer vista than most hotels can boast. Try to get a room on a higher floor. This establishment, under management of the Roman Catholic Church's social welfare bureau and popular with long-staying guests for its monthly rates, is a good choice for single travelers, including women.

4 Cliff Rd., Yau Ma Tei, Kowloon, Hong Kong. © 852/2388 1111. Fax 852/2770 6669. cblresv@bianchi-lodge. com. 90 units. HK$720 (US$94) single; HK$820–HK$1,200 (US$107–US$156) double. Rates include buffet breakfast. Monthly rates available. AE, DC, MC, V. MTR: Yau Ma Tei. **Amenities:** Restaurant (Western/Chinese); tour desk; room service 7am–9pm; laundry/dry-cleaning service. *In room:* A/C, satellite TV, minibar.

Guangdong Hotel   The Guangdong, owned by mainland Chinese and popular with both Asian business travelers and Chinese tour groups, has one of the most convenient locations among inexpensive lodgings: It's located in the heart of Tsim Sha Tsui, about a 10-minute walk from the Star Ferry and only minutes from the Tsim Sha Tsui MTR station. Its marble lobby is spacious and bare, reflecting the latest look in Hong Kong's hotels when it was built in the late 1980s. Its rooms are very small but clean and pleasant enough, with room rates based primarily on floor level. None of the rooms here offer views; most face other buildings. The cheapest "economy" rooms are on the lowest floors and are for one person only. Otherwise, prices are the same whether it's single or double occupancy. If you want to be away from the din of traffic, splurge for a larger deluxe room on a higher floor, which has the added benefit of a safe.

18 Prat Ave., Tsim Sha Tsui, Kowloon, Hong Kong. © 852/2739 3311. Fax 852/2721 1137. http://gdhk. gdhotels.net. 245 units. HK$850 (US$110) single; HK$950–HK$1,300 (US$123–US$169) single or double; from

HK$2,200 (US$286) suite. 1 child under 12 can stay free in parent's room. AE, DC, MC, V. MTR: Tsim Sha Tsui. **Amenities:** 2 restaurants (Cantonese, coffee shop); lounge; small fitness room; limousine service; business center; room service 7:30am–10pm; massage; babysitting; same-day laundry/dry-cleaning service; doctor on call. *In room:* A/C, satellite TV w/pay on-demand movies, wireless Internet access, minibar, hair dryer.

Majestic Hotel ⟨⟩   This modern brick hotel, located in the colorful Yau Ma Tei district, with its main entrance on Saigon Street, is just a few minutes' walk from the Jordan subway station and the Temple Street Night Market. Built in 1992, it rises above the Majestic Centre complex, which includes a shopping arcade and food court. The hotel offers good-size rooms, with a desk, sitting area, and large windows (but unfortunately no exciting views). The cheapest rooms occupy the lower floors and face another building, while the most expensive rooms are on higher floors and have city views. Unlike most hotels in Hong Kong, the Majestic offers ice machines on every floor, saving a call to room service, and offers more facilities and services than most in its price range.

348 Nathan Rd., Yau Ma Tei, Kowloon, Hong Kong. ⓒ 852/2781 1333. Fax 852/2781 1773. www.majestic hotel.com.hk. 387 units. HK$950–HK$1,850 (US$123–US$240) single or double; from HK$3,000 (US$390) suite. 1 child under 12 can stay free in parent's room. AE, DC, MC, V. MTR: Jordan. **Amenities:** Restaurant (international buffet); bar; tour desk; business center; shopping arcade; room service (6am–midnight); babysitting; same-day laundry/dry-cleaning, doctor on call. *In room:* A/C, satellite TV w/pay movies, wireless Internet access, minibar, coffeemaker, hair dryer, safe.

Nathan Hotel   Almost 40 years old, this is a no-frills hotel with one exception: Since it dates from an earlier era when land was less expensive, its rooms and bathrooms are quite large compared with those in most Hong Kong hotels. Also, as in earlier days, there are attendants on duty on each floor around the clock (as had previously been the custom at all Hong Kong hotels). Otherwise, rooms are very basic in decor and tend to be dark, an annoyance exacerbated by the lack of a good bedside reading light. Since all rooms are basically the same, the rates below reflect the season rather than room type. In any case, the hotel attracts business travelers mainly from mainland China and other Asian countries, though its location near the Temple Street Night Market and Jordan MTR station make it a good choice for leisure travelers as well. It's located north of Tsim Sha Tsui, about a 20-minute walk from the Star Ferry.

378 Nathan Rd. (main entrance on Pak Hoi St.) Yau Ma Tei, Kowloon, Hong Kong. ⓒ **852/2388 5141.** Fax 852/ 2770 4262. www.nathanhotel.com. 185 units. HK$500–HK$950 (US$65–US$123) single; HK$600–HK$1,300 (US$78–US$169) twin. AE, DC, MC, V. MTR: Jordan. **Amenities:** Restaurant (Cantonese/Western); exercise room; tour desk; limousine service; business center; room service 7am–11pm; babysitting; same-day laundry/ dry-cleaning service. *In room:* A/C, cable TV, high-speed dataport, minibar.

New Kings Hotel *Value*   This 30-year-old property underwent extensive renovation in 1997 and reopened as a completely new hotel, with rates that are only slightly higher than before, making it a good value. It also usually offers discounted prices to its rack rates below, so be sure to ask when making a reservation. Located near the jade and night markets and a Tin Hau (Goddess of the Sea) temple, it doesn't have any facilities other than a tiny reception area. Rooms are rather plain and the tiled bathrooms lack counter space. There are only six rooms on each floor, a good thing since corridors are barely wide enough for one person. Expect to wait for the hotel's one elevator. This is a good choice only for budget travelers on the go, since you probably wouldn't want to spend much time here anyway.

473 Nathan Rd. (entrance on Wing Sing Lane), Yau Ma Tei, Kowloon, Hong Kong. ⓒ **852/2780 1281.** Fax 852/ 2782 1833. newkings@netvigator.com. 72 units. HK$550–HK$600 (US$72–US$78) single; HK$650–HK$750 (US$85–US$98) twin. AE, MC, V. MTR: Yau Ma Tei. *In room:* A/C, TV, fridge, safe.

The Salisbury YMCA ⭐⭐⭐ *(Kids)*   For decades, the overwhelming number-one choice among low-cost accommodations has been the YMCA on Salisbury Road, which has the good fortune of being right next to The Peninsula hotel on the waterfront, just a 2-minute walk from both the Star Ferry and Tsim Sha Tsui subway station. Welcoming families as well as individual men and women, it has 19 single rooms (none with harbor view) and more than 250 doubles and twins (the most expensive provide great harbor views), as well as suites with and without harbor views that are great for families. Although simple in decor, these rooms are on a par with those at more expensively priced hotels in terms of in-room amenities.

For budget travelers, there are seven dormitory-style rooms, each with two bunk beds, individual reading lights, private bathroom, and lockers, available only to visitors who have been in Hong Kong fewer than 10 days. Great for families is its sports facility boasting two indoor swimming pools (one a lap pool, the other a children's pool, both free for all hotel guests except those in dormitory) and a fitness gym, two squash courts, and indoor climbing wall (fees charged). A ground-floor bookstore has a children's corner, with games and books kids can try out free before buying. Needless to say, the Salisbury is so popular that you should make reservations in advance, especially if booking for April or October. Although expensive for a YMCA, the location and facilities are worth the price; here you have Tsim Sha Tsui's cheapest rooms with harbor views—it's highly recommended.

Salisbury Rd., Tsim Sha Tsui, Kowloon, Hong Kong. ℂ **800/537-8483** in the U.S. and Canada, or 852/2268 7000 (852/2268 7888 for reservations). Fax 852/2739 9315. www.ymcahk.org.hk. 368 units. HK$700 (US$91) single; HK$800–HK$1,000 (US$104–US$130) double; from HK$1,300 (US$169) suite. Dormitory bed HK$210 (US$27). AE, DC, MC, V. MTR: Tsim Sha Tsui. **Amenities:** 2 restaurants (international buffet, international cafeteria); 2 indoor pools; exercise room; Jacuzzi; sauna; squash courts; badminton; climbing wall; tour desk; salon; room service 7am–11pm; massage; babysitting; coin-op laundry; laundry/dry-cleaning service; bookstore. *In room:* A/C, satellite/cable TV, wireless Internet access, minibar, coffeemaker, hair dryer, safe.

Shamrock Hotel   A pioneer member of HKHA and catering mainly to visitors from China, the Shamrock was built in the early 1950s and, despite recent lobby renovations that added marble floors and walls and artwork from Beijing, I don't think it's changed much since then. The most remarkable thing about this hotel is its lobby—although tiny, the ceiling is covered with about a half-dozen small chandeliers. The guest rooms are unexciting, clean, simple, and small, though high ceilings (with small chandeliers) give the rooms something of a spacious feeling. Some of the cheapest rooms are without windows—Dracula might feel at home, but you might want to spring for some sunshine. It's about a 20-minute walk from the Star Ferry, just north of Kowloon Park and not far from the Temple Street Night Market.

223 Nathan Rd., Yau Ma Tei, Kowloon, Hong Kong. ℂ **852/2735 2271.** Fax 852/2736 7354. www.shamrock hotel.com.hk. 157 units. HK$550–HK$1,250 (US$71–US$162) single; HK$750–HK$1,450 (US$97–US$188) double. AE, DC, MC, V. MTR: Jordan. **Amenities:** Restaurant (Western); limousine service; business center; laundry/dry-cleaning service. *In room:* A/C, satellite TV w/pay movies, high-speed dataport, minibar, coffeemaker (but no coffee), hair dryer, safe.

Stanford Hillview Hotel ⭐ *(Finds)*   This small, intimate hotel, built in 1991, is near the heart of Tsim Sha Tsui and yet it's a world away from it, located on top of a hill in the shade of some huge banyan trees, next to the Royal Observatory with its colonial building and greenery. Knutsford Terrace, an alley with trendy bars and restaurants, is just a couple of minutes' walk away. Its lobby is quiet and subdued (quite a contrast to most Hong Kong hotels) and its staff is friendly and accommodating. The most expensive rooms are on higher floors (ask for one that faces the Observatory), while the cheapest rates below are for four economy rooms on the second floor. All rooms are fairly basic and small. Still, this is a very civilized place, but be prepared for the uphill hike to the hotel.

13–17 Observatory Rd., Tsim Sha Tsui, Kowloon, Hong Kong. (C) **800/858-8471** in the U.S. and Canada, or 852/2722 7822. Fax 852/2723 3718. www.stanfordhillview.com. 163 units. HK$880–HK$1,580 (US$114–US$205) single or double. AE, DC, MC, V. MTR: Tsim Sha Tsui. **Amenities:** Restaurant (international buffet); lounge; outdoor golf-driving nets; small exercise room; business center; 24-hr. room service; babysitting; same-day laundry/dry cleaning. *In room:* A/C, cable TV w/pay movies, Wireless Internet access, minibar, coffeemaker, hair dryer.

YMCA International House   Located just off Nathan Road, only a minute's walk from the MTR station, this YMCA renovated its old building and added a 25-story tower a few years back, transforming itself into a smart-looking establishment that can rival many of the more expensively priced hotels in terms of facilities. However, located halfway up Kowloon Peninsula, far from the action of Tsim Sha Tsui, it plays second fiddle to The Salisbury YMCA in terms of convenience and views. The cheapest rooms occupy the older building, while the new tower rooms are similar in decor and comfort to modestly priced hotel rooms anywhere in the city and even boast wireless Internet access. Ask for a room on a top floor, where it's brighter and you can look out over the city.

23 Waterloo Rd., Yau Ma Tei, Kowloon, Hong Kong. (C) **852/2771 9111.** Fax 852/2388 5926; reservation fax 852/2771 5238. www.ymcaintlhousehk.org. 427 units. HK$680–HK$1,800 (US$88–US$153) single or twin. AE, DC, MC, V. MTR: Yau Ma Tei. **Amenities:** Restaurant (Western); lounge; indoor pool (free to Y guests); tennis and squash courts; fitness room (fee charged); sauna; tour desk; business center; laundry/dry-cleaning service. *In room:* A/C, cable TV, minibar, coffeemaker (but no coffee), hair dryer, safe.

CAUSEWAY BAY & WAN CHAI

Wesley   This simple business hotel opened in 1992 on the former site of the famous Soldiers' & Sailors' Home, a Hong Kong landmark for more than a century. In keeping with Hong Kong's unofficial preferred decorating style, its small lobby is sparsely furnished; facilities and services are also limited—it reminds me of business hotels in Japan. All rooms are small, with V-shaped windows; rates are based on bed configurations, floor level, and, to a small degree, room size: the cheaper rooms are on lower floors and are furnished with twin beds; the most expensive are slightly larger, with king-size beds, a small sitting area, and microwaves. Rooms facing the front of the hotel are noisier. The bathrooms are only large enough for one person, and the closets aren't tall enough to hang dresses. Even its "business center" is the size of a closet. Pluses: It's located on the tramline and is only a few minutes' walk from the Pacific Place shopping center.

22 Hennessy Rd., Wan Chai, Hong Kong. (C) **852/2866 6688.** Fax 852/2866 6633. www.hanglung.com. 251 units. HK$700–HK$1,800 (US$91–US$234) single or double. 1 child under 12 can stay free in parent's room. AE, DC, MC, V. MTR: Admiralty or Wan Chai. **Amenities:** Restaurant (Cantonese); tour desk; limousine service; business center; babysitting; same-day laundry/dry-cleaning service; doctor on call. *In room:* A/C, satellite TV, minibar, coffeemaker, hair dryer.

5 Rock-Bottom Accommodations (Guesthouses & Youth Hostels)

GUESTHOUSES

Hong Kong's cheapest accommodations aren't hotels and aren't recommended for visitors who expect cleanliness and comfort. Rather, these accommodations, usually called "guesthouses," attract a young backpacking crowd, many of whom are traveling through Asia and are interested only in a bed at the lowest price. They also attract laborers, mostly men from Asia, Africa, and the Middle East. At any rate, some guesthouses offer rooms with a private bathroom; others are nothing more than rooms filled with bunk beds. Of Hong Kong's rock-bottom establishments, none is more notorious than **Chungking Mansion.** Although it occupies a prime spot at 40 Nathan Road, between the Holiday Inn Golden Mile and the Sheraton in Tsim Sha Tsui, Chungking Mansion is easy to overlook; there's no big sign heralding its existence. In fact, its ground floor is one huge maze of inexpensive shops.

But above all those shops are five towering concrete blocks, each served by its own tiny elevator and known collectively as Chungking Mansion. Inside are hundreds of little businesses, apartments, guesthouses, eateries, and sweatshops. Some of the guesthouses are passable; many are not.

I stayed at Chungking Mansion on my first trip to Hong Kong in 1983, living in a neon-colored cell that was furnished with two sagging beds, a night table, and closet. In the shared bathroom down the hall lived the biggest spider I have ever seen, a hairy thing that nevertheless behaved itself whenever I was there—it never moved an inch the whole time I took a shower, and when I returned each evening, it was always motionless in another part of the room. I figured that it survived only by being unobtrusive, and I wouldn't be surprised if its progeny is still there. I shared my room with another woman and we paid US$5 each.

Chungking Mansion has changed a lot since then. Whereas most guesthouses were once borderline squalor, today many have cleaned up their act in a bid for the tourists' dollars. Still, Chungking is not the kind of place you'd want to recommend to anyone uninitiated in the seamier side of travel. The views from many room windows are more insightful than some guests might like—the backside of the building and mountains of trash down below. Even worse are the ancient-looking elevators filled to capacity with human cargo; you might want to stick to the stairs. In any case, sometimes the elevators don't work at all, making it a long hike up the dozen flights of stairs to the top floors. But the most compelling argument for avoiding Chungking Mansion is one of safety— it could be a towering inferno waiting to happen. However, for some budget travelers, it's a viable alternative to Hong Kong's high-priced hotels. And you certainly can't beat it for location.

If you insist on staying here, see my recommendation below. Chungking Mansion contains approximately 100 guesthouses, divided into five separate blocks, from A Block to E Block. For the less daring, A Block is the best, since its elevator is closest to the front entrance of the building. The other elevators are farther back in the shopping arcade, which can be a little disconcerting at night when the shops are all closed and the corridors are deserted. I recommend that you begin your search in Block A. I also recommend that you stay on lower floors. If guesthouses here are full or you want to save money, check the guesthouses toward the back of the building in the other blocks. But no matter what the block, never leave any valuables in your room.

CHUNGKING MANSION

Chungking House   This is the best-known guesthouse in Chungking Mansion, due primarily to its location in A Block, with front desks and lobbies on both the fourth and fifth floors. Rooms are dreary, dark, and depressing, with wood paneling, worn carpets, and ancient tiled bathrooms (ask for a "deluxe" room facing Nathan Road; though noisier, they are brighter and a tad more cheerful). The staff tends to be unconcerned and gruff. Still, you might want to try this place first before tackling the elevator or stairs to check out the guesthouses on the upper floors.

A Block, 4th and 5th floors, Chungking Mansion, 40 Nathan Rd., Tsim Sha Tsui, Kowloon, Hong Kong. ℂ **852/2366 5362.** Fax 852/2721 3570. chungkinghouse@yahoo.com.hk. 75 units. HK$250–HK$300 (US$32–US$39) single; HK$320–HK$440 (US$42–US$57) double/twin. No credit cards. MTR: Tsim Sha Tsui. *In room:* A/C, TV.

NON-CHUNGKING MANSION GUESTHOUSE

Alisan Guest House   If Chungking Mansion is your idea of a horror house, this guesthouse, on the other side of the harbor, just around the corner from the Excelsior hotel (p. 93), is a good alternative and has been in business since 1987. Located in a typical residential building, it's owned by English-speaking Tommy Hou, who spends about 15 minutes with each of his mostly Western guests to give advice on sightseeing in Hong Kong. Rooms, scattered on several floors, are small but clean. The best rooms are the triples located on the third floor. However, though these rooms face and have views of the harbor, they also look out onto a busy highway, running between the guest house and the harbor, which can make these rooms slightly noisy due to traffic. Mr. Hou offers free tea, a communal microwave and fridge, and use of his office computer for those who wish to check their e-mail.

Flat A, 5th floor, Hoi To Court, 275 Gloucester Rd. (entrance on Cannon St.), Causeway, Hong Kong. ℂ **852/2838 0762** or 852/2574 8066. Fax 852/2838 4351. http://home.hkstar.com/~alisangh. 21 units. HK$280–HK$350 (US$36–US$45) single; HK$320–HK$380 (US$42–US$49) double/twin; HK$390–HK$480 (US$51–US$62) triple. No credit cards. MTR: Causeway Bay. *In room:* A/C, TV.

YOUTH HOSTELS AND DORMITORY BEDS

If you don't mind giving up your privacy, the best rock-bottom accommodations in town are the dormitory beds available at The Salisbury YMCA (p. 98) for HK$210 (US$27). Otherwise, Hong Kong's cheapest accommodations are at hostels. There are seven youth hostels in Hong Kong, including its islands and territories, and they offer the cheapest rates around. However, most are not conveniently located—indeed, some require a ferry ride and/or a 45-minute hike from the nearest bus stop, as they are located in country parks.

If you don't have a youth hostel card, you can still stay at a youth hostel by paying an extra HK$30 (US$3.90) per night. After 6 nights, nonmembers are eligible for member status and subsequently pay overnight charges at members' rates.

The most conveniently located youth hostel is the 169-bed **Jockey Club Mt. Davis Youth Hostel** (Mau Wui Hall), on the top of Mount Davis on Hong Kong Island (ℂ **852/2817 5715;** www.yha.org.hk). It charges HK$65 (US$8.45) per night for a dormitory bed for those aged 18 and over. There are also a few private rooms, with a double costing HK$150 (US$19) and a triple costing HK$225 (US$29). Facilities include a communal kitchen and coin-op laundry room. To reach it, take the Ma Mui Hall Shuttle Bus, which departs from the Macau Ferry Terminal (MTR: Sheung Wan) daily at 9:30am and 4:30, 7, 9, and 10:30pm. A taxi from Central costs approximately HK$60 to HK$70 (US$7.80–US$9.10). The hostel itself is open daily from 7am to 11pm.

There are six other youth hostels on some of the outlying islands and in the New Territories; most charge HK$45 (US$5.85) for dormitory beds for those 18 and older. Check-in is from 4pm. There are kitchens and washing facilities, as well as campsites. Since these hostels are not easily accessible, they are recommended only for the adventurous traveler. Of these, the **S.G. Davis Hostel,** on Lantau island near the Po Lin Monastery with its giant Buddha (© **852/2985 5610;** www.yha.org.hk), is the easiest to reach from the airport. For more information on Hong Kong's youth hostels, contact the **Hong Kong Youth Hostels Association** (© **852/2788 1638;** www.yha.org.hk). The Hong Kong Tourist Association also has a flyer on youth hostels.

5

Where to Dine in Hong Kong

Dining is one of *the* things to do in Hong Kong. Half the population dines in the city's 11,000 eateries every day. Not only is the food excellent, but the range of culinary possibilities is nothing short of staggering. Hong Kong also has what may well be the greatest concentration of Chinese restaurants in the world. In a few short days, you can take a culinary tour of virtually every major region of China, dining on Cantonese, Sichuan, Shanghainese, Pekingese, Chiu Chow, and other Chinese specialties. Some restaurants are huge, bustling, family affairs, countless others are mere holes in the wall, and a few of the trendiest are Shanghai chic, remakes of 1930s salons and opium dens or are strikingly modern affairs with sweeping views of the city.

But dining in the SAR is by no means limited to Chinese restaurants. Although various national cuisines have long been popular, particularly French, Italian, Thai, and Indian, ethnic restaurants have literally exploded onto the culinary scene in the past decade, offering even greater diversity from tapas and tacos to sushi. Japanese food is especially the rage among locals, and you'll find Japanese offerings on virtually every international buffet spread in Hong Kong, along with sushi delivered via conveyor belts in an ever-growing number of sushi bars.

I'm convinced that you can eat as well in Hong Kong as in any other city in the world. And no matter where you eat or how much you spend, it's sure to be an adventure of the senses. Little wonder, then, that a common greeting among Chinese in Hong Kong translates literally as "Have you eaten?" In Hong Kong, eating is the most important order of the day.

By far, Hong Kong's most well known, exclusive restaurants, both Chinese and Western, have long been located in the hotels. That's not surprising when you realize that first-class hotels are accustomed to catering to well-traveled visitors who demand high quality in service, cuisine, and decor.

In a welcome trend, however, enterprising, ambitious, and talented chefs have been opening establishments in ever-greater numbers, often in modest but imaginative surroundings or in swanky digs on top floors of highrises. These include ethnic restaurants as well as eateries offering innovative dishes, with limited but intriguing menus. A cluster of these restaurants has even created a whole new dining enclave, located on the steep hill alongside the Central/Mid-Levels Escalator that connects Central with the Mid-Levels. Dubbed "SoHo" for the region "south of Hollywood Road," it has blossomed into an ever-growing dining and nightlife district, making it Hong Kong's most exciting addition to the culinary scene.

Other welcome trends are the inclusion of vegetarian and healthy foods on many menus, and the growing popularity of crossover, East-meets-West fusion cuisine, which capitalizes on ingredients and flavors from both sides of the Pacific Rim in the creation of innovative dishes.

/ **Tips** **Ways to Save on Your Hong Kong Meals**

Wherever you decide to eat, remember that a 10% service charge will
be added to your food-and-beverage bill (see "Fast Facts" on p. 65 for
more information on tipping in Hong Kong). There is no tax, however.
You can save a few Hong Kong dollars when eating out by keeping the
following tips in mind:

- **Eat your big meal at lunch.** Most Asian (excluding Chinese) and
  Western restaurants offer special fixed-price lunches that are much
  cheaper than evening meals; their menus often include an appetizer, main course, and side dishes. Don't neglect expensive restaurants just because you assume they're out of your price range. If you
  feel like splurging, lunch is the way to go. For example, you can eat
  lunch at Gaddi's (one of Hong Kong's most famous restaurants) for
  HK$340 (US$44) per person (dinner would be at least double that).

- **Jump on the buffet bandwagon.** Buffet spreads are another great
  Hong Kong tradition. Almost all hotels offer buffets, often for
  breakfast, lunch, and dinner; independent restaurants are more
  likely to feature buffets at lunch. Some include a variety of both
  Asian and Continental dishes, a real bonus for lone diners who want
  to sample a variety of cuisines at a reasonable cost. If you have a
  hearty appetite, buffets are one of the best bargains in town.

- **Eat an early or late dinner to take advantage of special fixed-price
  meals.** A few restaurants offer early-bird or late-night specials. If
  you dine before 7pm at trendy Felix, for example, a three-course
  meal costs only HK$340 (US$44) as opposed to the HK$800 (US$104)
  usually spent for dinner a la carte.

- **If you want to imbibe, stick with beer.** Wine is especially expensive
  in Hong Kong. The estimated meal prices for the restaurants presented in this chapter do not include wine, since you could easily
  spend a fortune on drinks alone. To keep costs down, try the two
  most popular brands of beer: **San Miguel** (Filipino) and **Tsingtao**
  (Chinese). And speaking of beer, many bars and pubs mentioned in
  chapter 9, "Hong Kong After Dark," also serve food.

- **Go the dim sum route.** Dim sum, served mainly in Cantonese restaurants, is another way to economize on breakfast or lunch. Dim sum
  are usually served four to a basket or plate; three baskets are usually
  filling enough for me, which means I can have breakfast or lunch for
  less than HK$100 (US$13).

The restaurants listed below are
grouped first according to location
(the most popular areas are Kowloon,
the Central District, and Causeway
Bay/Wan Chai) and then according to
price. Those in the **Very Expensive**
category ($$$$) will cost more than
HK$600 (US$78) for dinner without
drinks (some restaurants average
HK$1,000/US$130 or more per
person). In the **Expensive** category
($$$), dinners average HK$400 to
HK$599 (US$52–US$78). **Moderate**
restaurants ($$) serve meals ranging

from HK$200 to HK$399 (US$26–US$52), while **Inexpensive** restaurants ($) offer meals for less than HK$200 (US$26). Keep in mind, however, that these guidelines are approximations only.

I should add that Chinese restaurants often have very long menus, sometimes listing more than 100 dishes. The most expensive dishes will invariably be such delicacies as bird's nest (bird's nest is a real nest, created by glutinous secretions of small swifts or swallows to build their nests), shark's fin, or abalone, for which the sky's the limit. In specifying price ranges for "main courses" under each Chinese establishment below, therefore, I excluded both these delicacies and the inexpensive rice and noodle dishes. In most cases, "main courses" refers to meat and vegetable combinations. Remember, since the price range is large, you can eat cheaply even at moderately priced restaurants by choosing wisely. Remember, too, that in Chinese restaurants it's customary to order one main dish for each diner, plus one extra to share.

The usual lunch hour in the SAR is from 1 to 2pm, when thousands of office workers pour into the city's more popular restaurants. Try to eat before or after the lunch rush hour, especially in Central, unless you plan on an expensive restaurant and have a reservation.

Unless stated otherwise, the open hours given below are exactly that—the hours a restaurant remains physically open but not necessarily the hours it serves food. The last orders are almost always taken at least a half hour before closing. Restaurants that are open for lunch from noon to 3pm, for example, will probably stop taking orders at 2:30pm. To avoid disappointment, call beforehand to make a reservation or arrive well ahead of closing time.

As for dress codes, unless otherwise stated, many upper-end restaurants have done away with the jacket-and-tie requirement. Rather, "smart casual" or business casual is nowadays appropriate for most of the fancier places, meaning that men should wear long-sleeved shirts and that jeans and sport shoes are inappropriate.

1 A Taste of Hong Kong
MEALS & DINING CUSTOMS

Traditionally speaking, Chinese restaurants tend to be noisy and crowded affairs, the patrons much more interested in food than in decor. They range from simple diners where the only adornment is likely to be Formica-topped tables, to very elaborate affairs with Chinese lanterns, splashes of red and gold, and painted screens. In the 1980s, a new kind of Chinese restaurant exploded onto the scene—trendy, chic, and minimalist, many in Art Deco style, and catering to Hong Kong's young and upwardly mobile.

In any case, Chinese restaurants are places for social gatherings; since Hong Kong apartments are usually too small to entertain friends and family, the whole gang simply heads for their favorite restaurant.

The Chinese usually dine in large groups; the more, the merrier. The basic rule is to order one dish per person, plus one extra dish or a soup, with all dishes placed in the center of the table and shared by everyone. The more people in your party, therefore, the more dishes are ordered and the more fun you'll have. Dishes usually come in two or three different sizes, so ask your waiter which size is sufficient for your group.

You shouldn't have any problem ordering, since many Chinese restaurants have English menus. If you want to be correct about it, though, a well-balanced meal should contain the five basic tastes of Chinese cuisine—acid, hot, bitter, sweet, and salty. The texture should vary as well, ranging from crisp and tender to dry and saucy. The proper order is to begin with a cold dish, followed by dishes of fish or seafood, meat (pork, beef, or poultry), vegetables, soup, and noodles or rice. Some dishes are steamed, while others may be fried, boiled, or roasted. Many of the dishes are accompanied by sauces, the most common being soy sauce, chili sauce, and hot mustard.

Because most Chinese restaurants cater to groups and Chinese food is best enjoyed if there are a variety of dishes, lone diners are at a distinct disadvantage when it comes to Chinese cuisine. Some modern restaurants, however, make life easier by offering fixed-price meals. An alternative is to dine at hotel buffets that offer Chinese and international dishes.

At any rate, at a Chinese restaurant, the beginning of your meal is heralded by a round of hot towels, a wonderful custom you'll soon grow addicted to and wish would be adopted by restaurants in your home country. Your eating utensils, of course, will be chopsticks, which have been around for 3,000 years and are perfect for picking up bite-size morsels. If you're eating rice, pick up the bowl and scoop the rice directly into your mouth with your chopsticks.

Keep in mind, however, that there are several superstitions associated with chopsticks. If, for example, you find an uneven pair at your table setting, it means you are going to miss a boat, plane, or train. Dropping chopsticks means you will have bad luck; laying them across each other is also considered a bad omen, except in dim sum restaurants where your waiter may cross them to show that your bill has been settled. You can do the same to signal the waiter that you've finished your meal and wish to pay the bill. When dining in a group, avoid ordering seven dishes, since seven dishes are considered food for ghosts, not humans.

As for dining etiquette, it's considered perfectly acceptable to slurp soup, since this indicates an appreciation of the food and also helps cool the soup so it doesn't burn the tongue. Toothpicks are also acceptable for use at the table during and after meals—they can even be used to spear foods too slippery or elusive for chopsticks, such as button mushrooms and jellyfish slices. As in most Asian countries, good manners call for covering your mouth with one hand while you dislodge food particles from your teeth.

A final custom you may see in Chinese restaurants is that of finger tapping—customers often tap three fingers on the table as a sign of thanks to the person pouring the tea.

THE CUISINE

Chinese cooking has evolved over the course of several thousand years, dictated often by a population too numerous to feed. The prospect of famine meant that nothing should be wasted, and the scarcity of fuel meant that food should be cooked as economically as possible; thus, it was chopped into small pieces and quickly stir-fried. Food needed to be as fresh as possible to avoid spoiling. Among the many regional Chinese cuisines, the most common ones found in Hong Kong are from Canton, Beijing (or Peking), Shanghai, Sichuan, and Chiu Chow (Swatow).

Of course, there are many other dishes and styles of cuisine besides those outlined below. It's said that the Chinese will eat anything that swims, flies, or crawls; although that may not be entirely true, if you're adventurous enough, you may want to try such delicacies as snake soup, pig's brain, bird's-nest soup (derived from the saliva of swallows), Shanghai freshwater hairy crabs (available only in autumn), tiny rice birds that are roasted and eaten whole, or eel heads simmered with Chinese herbs. One of the more common—albeit strange—items found on most Chinese menus is *bèche-de-mer,* which translates as sea cucumber but which is actually nothing more than a sea slug.

Words of warning: According to government authorities, you're safe eating anywhere in the SAR, even at roadside food stalls. However, don't eat local oysters—there have been too many instances of oyster poisoning. Eat oysters only if they're imported from, say, Australia. The good restaurants will clearly stipulate on the menu that their oysters are imported. Some expats, warning of cholera, also steer clear of local shellfish and fish caught from local waters. Nowadays, restaurants catering largely to tourists offer fresh seafood caught outside Hong Kong's waters.

Hong Kong has also been ravaged by several outbreaks of avian flu since 1997, resulting in mass poultry cullings. Naturally, chicken dishes disappear from menus during outbreaks, importation from mainland China ceases during outbreaks there, and increased vigilance by local authorities has helped quell the transfer of the flu to humans (6 out of 18 people infected in 1997 died). In addition, vaccinations for poultry are being tested that might eradicate the flu. I still eat chicken in Hong Kong, but whether you choose to is up to you.

Watch your reaction to monosodium glutamate (MSG), which is used to enhance the flavor in Chinese cooking. Some people react strongly to this salt, reporting bouts of nausea, headaches, and a bloated feeling. Fortunately, an awareness of the detrimental side effects of MSG has long prompted most Chinese upper- and medium-range restaurants, especially those in hotels, to stop using it altogether. However, fast Chinese food is likely to be full of MSG, as are dishes prepared using products imported from China, where MSG is used as a matter of course.

CANTONESE FOOD

The majority of Chinese restaurants in Hong Kong are Cantonese; this is not surprising since most Hong Kong Chinese are originally from Canton Province (now called Guangdong). It's also the most common style of Chinese cooking around the world and probably the one with which you're most familiar. Among Chinese, Cantonese cuisine is considered the finest, and many Chinese emperors employed Cantonese chefs in their kitchens.

Cantonese food, which is noted for fast cooking at high temperatures (usually either steamed or stir-fried), is known for its fresh, delicate flavors. Little oil and few spices are used so that the natural flavors of the various ingredients prevail, and the Cantonese are sticklers for freshness (traditionalists may shop twice a day at the market). If you're concerned about cholesterol, Cantonese food is preferable. On the other hand, those with active taste buds may find it rather bland.

Since the Cantonese eat so much seafood, your best choice in a Cantonese restaurant is fish. I love steamed whole fish prepared with fresh ginger and spring onions, but equally good are slices of garoupa (a local fish), pomfret, red mullet, sole, and bream. It's considered bad luck to turn a fish over on your plate (it represents a boat capsizing), so the proper thing to do is to eat the top part of the fish, lift the bone in the air and then extract the bottom layer of meat with your chopsticks. Other popular seafood choices include shrimp and prawns, abalone, squid, scallops, crab, and sea cucumber. Shark's-fin soup is an expensive delicacy.

Other Cantonese specialties include roast goose, duck, and pigeon; pan-fried lemon chicken; stir-fried minced quail and bamboo shoots rolled in lettuce and eaten with the fingers; *congee* (thick rice porridge); crabmeat; sweet corn soup; and sweet-and-sour pork.

Another popular Cantonese dish is dim sum, which means "light snack" but whose Chinese characters literally translate as "to touch the heart." Dating back to the 10th century, dim sum is eaten for breakfast and lunch and with after-noon tea; in Hong Kong it is especially popular for Sunday family outings. It consists primarily of finely chopped meat, seafood, and vegetables wrapped in thin dough and then either steamed, fried, boiled, or braised. Dim sum can range from steamed dumplings to meatballs, fried spring rolls, and spareribs.

Many Cantonese restaurants offer dim sum from about 7:30am until 4pm, traditionally served from trolleys wheeled between the tables but nowadays just as often available from a written menu. The trolleys are piled high with steaming bamboo baskets, so ask the server to let you peek inside. If you like what you see, simply nod your head. There are nearly 100 different kinds of dim sum, but some of my favorites are *shiu mai* (steamed minced pork and shrimp dumplings), *har gau* (steamed shrimp dumplings), *cha siu bau* (barbecued pork buns), *au yuk* (steamed minced beef balls), *fun gwor* (steamed rice-flour dumplings filled with pork, shrimp, and bamboo shoots), and *tsuen guen* (deep-fried spring rolls filled with shredded pork, chicken, mushrooms, bamboo shoots, and bean sprouts). A serving of dim sum usually consists of two to four pieces on a plate and averages about HK$20 to HK$30 (US$2.60–US$3.90) per plate. Your bill is calculated at the end of the meal by the number of plates on your table or by a card stamped each time you order a dish.

Since I can usually manage only three dishes, dim sum is one of the cheapest meals I eat in Hong Kong and is also the best when I'm dining alone. I often have it for breakfast with lots of tea (the actual term is *yum cha,* traditionally meant as an early breakfast of dim sum and Chinese tea). But it's more than just the price that draws me to traditional dim sum restaurants—they are noisy, chaotic, and the perfect place to read a newspaper or gossip. No one should go to Hong Kong without visiting a dim sum restaurant at least once.

For a light snack or late-night meal, try *congee,* which is a rice porridge popular for breakfast and usually topped with a meat, fish, or vegetable. Many of Hong Kong's countless, cheapest restaurants specialize in *congee,* as well as noodles in soup, the most famous of which is probably *wun tun meen,* noodle soup with shrimp dumplings.

PEKINGESE FOOD

Many Pekingese dishes originated in the imperial courts of the emperors and empresses and were served at elaborate banquets. This theatrical flamboyance is still evident today in the making of Pekingese noodles and the smashing of the clay around "beggar's chicken." Because of its northern source, the food of Peking (or Beijing) tends to be rather substantial (to keep the body warm), and it is richer than Cantonese food. Liberal amounts of peppers, garlic, ginger, leeks, and coriander are used. Noodles and dumplings are more common than rice, and roasting is the preferred method of cooking.

Most famous among Peking-style dishes is Peking duck (or Beijing duck), but unfortunately, a minimum of six persons is usually required for this elaborate dish. The most prized part is the crisp skin, which comes from air-drying the bird and then coating it with a mixture of syrup and soy sauce before roasting.

It's served by wrapping the crisp skin and meat in thin pancakes together with spring onion, radish, and sweet plum sauce.

Another popular dish prepared with fanfare is beggar's chicken: A whole chicken is stuffed with mushrooms, pickled Chinese cabbage, herbs, and onions, wrapped in lotus leaves, sealed in clay, and then baked all day. The guest of honor usually breaks open the hard clay with a mallet, revealing a tender feast more fit for a king than a beggar.

For do-it-yourself dining, try the Mongolian hot pot, where diners gather around a common pot in a scene reminiscent of campfires on the Mongolian steppes. One version calls for wafer-thin slices of meat, usually mutton, to be dipped in a clear stock and then eaten with a spicy sauce. Another variety calls for a sizzling griddle, over which thin-sliced meat, cabbage, bean sprouts, onions, and other vegetables are barbecued in a matter of seconds.

SHANGHAINESE FOOD

A big, bustling city, Shanghai incorporates the food of several surrounding regions and cities, making it the most diverse cuisine in China. Because of the cold winters in Shanghai, its food is heavier, richer, sweeter, and oilier than Cantonese or Pekingese food, seasoned with sugar, soy sauce, and Shaoxing wine. In addition, because of hot summers, which can spoil food quickly, specialties include pickled or preserved vegetables, fish, shrimp, and mushrooms. Some dishes are rather heavy on the garlic, and portions tend to be enormous. The dishes are often stewed, braised, or fried.

The most popular Shanghainese delicacy in Hong Kong is freshwater hairy crab (a crab with long, hairy-looking legs), flown in from Shanghai in autumn, steamed, and eaten with the hands. Other Shanghainese dishes include "yellow fish," (usually marinated in wine lees), braised eel with huge chunks of garlic, "drunken chicken" (chicken marinated in Chinese wine), sautéed shrimp in spicy tomato sauce over crispy rice, and sautéed shredded beef and green pepper. As for the famous hundred-year-old egg, it's actually only several months old, with a limey, pickled-ginger taste. Breads, noodles, and dumplings are favored over rice in this region's cuisine.

SICHUAN FOOD

This is my favorite Chinese cuisine, because it's the spiciest, hottest, and most fiery style of cooking. The fact that its spiciness recalls Thailand, India, and Malaysia is no coincidence, since this huge province shares a border with Burma and Tibet.

The culprit is the Sichuan chile, fried to release its explosiveness. Seasoning also includes chile-bean paste, peppercorns, garlic, ginger, coriander, and other spices. Foods are simmered and smoked rather than stir-fried. The most famous Sichuan dish is smoked duck, which is seasoned with peppercorns, ginger, cinnamon, orange peel, and coriander; marinated in rice wine; then steamed; and then smoked over a charcoal fire of camphor wood and tea leaves.

Other specialties include pan-fried prawns in spicy sauce, sour-and-peppery soup, sautéed diced chicken in chili-bean sauce, and dry-fried spicy string beans. Most Sichuan menus indicate which dishes are spicy.

CHIU CHOW FOOD

Chiu Chow refers to the people, dialect, and food of the Swatow area in southeastern Canton. Chiu Chow chefs pride themselves on their talents for vegetable carvings—those incredible birds, flowers, and other adornments that are a part of every Chiu Chow banquet.

Influenced by Cantonese cooking, Chiu Chow food is rich in protein, light, and tasty. Seafood, ducks, and geese are favorites, while sauces, often sweet and using tangerine or sweet beans for flavor, are liberally applied. A meal begins with a cup of *kwun yum* tea, popularly called Iron Buddha and probably the world's strongest and most bitter tea. It's supposed to cleanse the system and stimulate the taste buds. Drink some of this stuff and you'll be humming for hours.

Two very expensive Chiu Chow delicacies are shark's fin and bird's nests. Other common menu items include steamed lobster, deep-fried shrimp balls, sautéed slices of whelk, fried goose blood, goose doused in soy sauce, stuffed eel wrapped in pickled cabbage, and crispy fried *chuenjew* leaves, which literally melt in the mouth. While not greasy, the food does favor strong, earthy tastes.

DRINKS

Tea is often provided regardless of whether you ask for it, often at a small charge. Grown in China for more than 2,000 years, tea is believed to help clear the palate and aid digestion. There are three main types: green or unfermented tea; black *bo lay* fermented tea (the most popular in Hong Kong); and *oolong*, or semifermented tea. These three teas can be further subdivided into a wide variety of specific types, with taste varying according to the region, climate, and soil. At any rate, if you want more tea at a restaurant, simply cock the lid of the teapot half open and someone will come around to refill it. Afterwards, tap three fingers on the table as a sign of thanks.

If you want something a bit stronger than tea, there are **Chinese wines.** Although there are Chinese red and white wines made from grapes, most Chinese wines aren't really wines in the Western sense of the word. Rather, they are spirits distilled from rice, millet, and other grains, as well as from herbs and flowers. Popular Chinese wines include *siu hing*, a mild rice wine that resembles a medium-dry sherry, which goes well with all kinds of Chinese food, and is best served warm; *go leung* and *mao toi*, fiery drinks made from millet with a 70% alcohol content; and *ng ka pay*, a sweet herbal wine favored for its medicinal properties, especially against rheumatism. These wines can be cheap or expensive, depending on what you order, and remember that Chinese rarely drink outside of bars.

As for **beer,** there's Tsingtao from mainland China, first brewed years ago by Germans and made from sparkling mineral water. San Miguel is also very popular. One thing to keep in mind, however, is that excess drinking is frowned upon by the Chinese, who often don't drink anything stronger than tea in restaurants. In fact, one waiter told me that Westerners spend much more in restaurants than Chinese simply because Westerners drink alcoholic beverages.

2 Restaurants by Cuisine

Fook Lam Moon ★★★ (Kowloon,
Wan Chai, $$$, p. 153)

Happy Garden Noodles & Congee
Kitchen (Kowloon, $, p. 128)

Jade Garden Restaurant (Kowloon,
Causeway Bay, $$, p. 123)

Jumbo Kingdom ★ (Aberdeen, $$,
p. 152)

Luk Yu Tea House ★★★ (Central,
$$, p. 155)

Man Wah ★★★ (Central, $$$,
p. 135)

One Harbour Road ★★ (Wan
Chai, $$$$, p. 144)

Shang Palace ★★★ (Kowloon,
$$$, p. 154)

The Square ★★ (Central, $$,
p. 140)

Super Star Seafood Restaurant ★
(Kowloon, Central, Wan Chai,
Causeway Bay, $$, p. 154)

Tsui Hang Village Restaurant
(Kowloon, Central, $$, p. 125)

Yan Toh Heen ★★★ (Kowloon,
$$$, p. 155)

Yung Kee ★★ (Central, $$, p. 141)

Zen Chinese ★★ (Central, $$,
p. 141)

CHIU CHOW

City Chiuchow Restaurant
(Kowloon, $$, p. 153)

Golden Island Bird's Nest
(Kowloon, $$, p. 121)

CONTINENTAL

Avenue Restaurant & Bar ★★
(Kowloon, $$, p. 119)

Hugo's ★★ (Kowloon, $$$, p. 117)

Jimmy's Kitchen ★★ (Kowloon,
Central, $$, p. 138)

M at the Fringe ★★★ (Central,
$$$, p. 135)

Mandarin Grill ★★★ (Central,
$$$$, p. 130)

Post 97 ★ (Central, $$, p. 139)

Riva ★★ (Causeway Bay, $$$,
p. 144)

Sammy's Kitchen (Western District, $, p. 152)

The Verandah ★★★ (Repulse Bay,
$$$, p. 151)

DIM SUM

See "Dim Sum," on p. 153

FRENCH

BB's Bistro (Kowloon, $$, p. 119)

Cafe des Artistes ★★ (Central,
$$$, p. 134)

Gaddi's ★★★ (Kowloon, $$$$,
p. 113)

Le Parisien (Central, $$, p. 138)

Le Tire Bouchon ★★ (Central, $$,
p. 138)

Petrus ★★★ (Central, $$$$,
p. 132)

SPOON by Alain Ducasse ★★★
(Kowloon, $$$$, p. 113)

FUSION

Felix ★★★ (Kowloon, $$$, p. 116)

Ramas Greens ★★ (Causeway Bay,
$$, p. 147)

ToTT'S Asian Grill & Bar ★★★
(Causeway Bay, $$$, p. 144)

Vong ★★★ (Central, $$$$,
p. 133)

HUNANESE

Hunan Garden ★★ (Central, $$$,
p. 134)

INDIAN

The Ashoka (Central, $, p. 142)

Banana Leaf Curry House ★★
(Kowloon, Causeway Bay, $,
p. 126)

Gaylord ★★ (Kowloon, $$, p. 121)

Koh-I-Noor ★ (Kowloon, Central,
$, p. 128)

The Viceroy ★★ (Wan Chai, $$,
p. 147)

Woodlands (Kowloon, $, p. 130)

INDONESIAN

Bebek Bengil 3 ★★ (Wan Chai,
$$, p. 146)

INTERNATIONAL

Cafe Deco ★ (Victoria Peak, $$,
p. 149)

café TOO ★★★ (Central, $$,
p. 136)

The Greenery (Kowloon, $$,
p. 122)

Harbour Side ✹ (Kowloon, $$, p. 122)

Lucy's ✹ (Stanley, $$, p. 151)

Mövenpick Marché ✹ (Victoria Peak, $, p. 150)

Open Kitchen ✹✹ (Wan Chai, $, p. 112)

The Peak Lookout ✹✹ (Victoria Peak, $$, p. 150)

The Salisbury (Kowloon, $, p. 129)

ToTT'S Asian Grill & Bar ✹✹✹ (Causeway Bay, $$$, p. 144)

ITALIAN/PIZZA

Baci ✹✹ (Central, $$$, p. 133)

Baci Pizza ✹ (Central, $, p. 142)

Fat Angelo's ✹ (Kowloon, Central, Causeway Bay, $, p. 126)

Gaia Ristorante ✹ (Central, $$$, p. 134)

Grappa's ✹ (Central, $$, p. 137)

Grissini ✹✹✹ (Wan Chai, $$$$, p. 143)

Nicholini's ✹✹✹ (Central, $$$$, p. 130)

The Pizzeria ✹✹ (Kowloon, $$, p. 124)

Sabatini ✹✹✹ (Kowloon, $$$, p. 118)

San Marzano Pizza (Central, $, p. 143)

Spaghetti House (Kowloon, Yau Ma Tei, Mong Kok, Central, Wan Chai, Causeway Bay, $, p. 129)

Tutto Bene ✹ (Kowloon, $$, p. 125)

Va Bene ✹✹✹ (Central, $$$, p. 135)

JAPANESE

Genki Sushi (Kowloon, Central, Wan Chai, Causeway Bay, $, p. 127)

Hanagushi ✹ (Central, $$, p. 137)

Osaka (Kowloon, $$, p. 123)

Tokio Joe ✹ (Central, $$, p. 140)

Unkai ✹✹ (Kowloon, $$$$, p. 114)

Wasabisabi ✹✹ (Causeway Bay, $$, p. 147)

KOREAN

Sorabol ✹ (Kowloon, Causeway Bay, $, p. 149)

MALAYSIAN

Banana Leaf Curry House ✹✹ (Kowloon, Causeway Bay, $, p. 126)

MEXICAN

¡Caramba! (Central, $, p. 142)

NORTHERN CHINESE

Hutong ✹✹✹ (Kowloon, $$, p. 154)

PEKINGESE

American Restaurant (Wan Chai, $, p. 148)

Peking Garden ✹ (Kowloon, Central, Causeway Bay, $$, p. 123)

Spring Deer Restaurant ✹ (Kowloon, $$, p. 124)

SANDWICHES

Main Street Deli ✹✹ (Kowloon, $, p. 128)

Pret A Manger (Kowloon, Central, Causeway Bay, $, p. 143)

SEAFOOD

Dot Cod Seafood Restaurant & Oyster Bar (Central, $$, p. 136)

Super Star Seafood Restaurant ✹ (Kowloon, Central, Wan Chai, Causeway Bay, $$, p. 125)

Yü ✹✹✹ (Kowloon, $$$$, p. 114)

SHANGHAINESE

Shanghai Garden (Central, $$, p. 139)

Wu Kong ✹✹ (Kowloon, Causeway Bay, $$, p. 126)

SOUTHEAST ASIAN

Chilli N Spice ✹ (Stanley, Causeway Bay, $, p. 151)

SPANISH

El Cid Spanish Restaurant ✹ (Kowloon, Causeway Bay, Stanley, $$, p. 121)

STEAKS
Ruth's Chris Steak House ⭐⭐
(Kowloon, Central, $$$, p. 117)

SICHUAN
Red Pepper ⭐⭐ (Causeway Bay,
$$, p. 147)
Sichuan Garden ⭐ (Central, $$,
p. 139)

THAI
Banana Leaf Curry House ⭐⭐
(Kowloon, Causeway Bay, $,
p. 126)
Chili Club (Wan Chai, $, p. 148)

Chilli N Spice ⭐ (Stanley,
Causeway Bay, $, p. 151)
Thai Lemongrass ⭐⭐ (Central,
$$, p. 140)

VEGETARIAN
Bo Kong ⭐ (Causeway Bay, $,
p. 148)
Woodlands (Kowloon, $, p. 130)

VIETNAMESE
Golden Bull (Causeway Bay, $$,
p. 146)
Indochine 1929 ⭐⭐ (Central, $$,
p. 137)

3 Kowloon
VERY EXPENSIVE

Gaddi's ⭐⭐⭐ FRENCH   Opened in 1953 and named after a former general manager of The Peninsula, Gaddi's was long considered the best European restaurant in Hong Kong. Although that reputation has since been challenged by the birth of many other superb restaurants, the service is still excellent, the waiters are professional, and the food—classically French but with inventive, European influences—is always beyond reproof. Gaddi's is still a legend in Asia, the epitome of old Hong Kong. Its atmosphere, intended to evoke the hotel's original 1928 neoclassical architecture, is that of an elegant European dining room blended with the best of Asia, with crystal-and-silver chandeliers from Paris, Tai Ping carpet, and a Chinese coromandel screen dating from 1670. As for the food, it's French haute cuisine at its finest, with a changing menu that reflects the seasons in France and utilizes the highest-quality products imported from various countries. Examples of past dishes are baby Pyrenean lamb, roasted in wild honey and lavender, with small goat cheese potato fritters and pan-fried scorpion fish medallions and green asparagus with reduced fish sauce, olive oil crushed potatoes, and hollandaise sauce. The wine cellar is among the best and largest in Hong Kong, with a collection of rare vintages—but who could blame you if you get carried away and splurge on champagne? There's live, discreet music at night and a small dance floor.

In The Peninsula hotel, Salisbury Rd., Tsim Sha Tsui. ✆ 852/2315 3171. www.peninsula.com. Reservations recommended at lunch, required at dinner. Jacket required for men at dinner. Main courses HK$390–HK$440 (US$51–US$57); fixed-price lunch HK$340 (US$44); fixed-price dinner HK$720–HK$1,050 (US$94–US$136). AE, DC, MC, V. Daily noon–3pm and 7–11pm. MTR: Tsim Sha Tsui.

SPOON by Alain Ducasse ⭐⭐⭐ FRENCH   Dinner at this sophisticated venue is more than just a meal—it's an experience. From the moment you walk past the restaurant's "wine cellar," with approximately 3,000 bottles of both New and Old World selections on display, you know that this is a place of superlatives. The focal point of the dining room is the ceiling, where 550 hand-blown Murano glass spoons are lined up like a landing strip, directing one's attention to the open kitchen and to the stunning harbor view just beyond the massive windows. The restaurant is so low and close to the water that dining here is almost like being on a junk—albeit a very luxurious one. The menu, featuring the contemporary cuisine inspired by Chef and Restaurateur Alain Ducasse,

---

(*Moments* **Dining Behind the Scenes**

If you've ever wondered what a kitchen is like during the hustle and bustle of meal times, you'll have your chance to experience it firsthand by participating in Gaddi's Chef Table at The Peninsula hotel. Seating only four (with a minimum of two persons), it offers a fascinating front-row view of Gaddi's kitchen action, a tour of The Peninsula's massive kitchens, and includes three-course lunches for HK$688 (US$89) or five-course and 10-course dinners for HK$1,288 and HK$1,888 (US$167 and US$245) per person. For Chinese food enthusiasts, a similar dining experience is offered by The Peninsula's Spring Moon Chef's Table, with a six-course Cantonese dinner costing HK$11,000 (US$143). For reservations, contact The Peninsula at *(C)* **852/2920 2888** or by e-mail at dining.pen@peninsula.com.

---

gives diners the freedom to mix and match food and cooking styles by selecting an entrée (the steak is among the best I've had), its sauce, and accompanying vegetables. You might, therefore, pair roasted warm salmon with a béarnaise reduction, served with spinach and Swiss chard. Or, your entire group may opt for the Sexy Spoon, a special menu created for your table for HK$750 (US$97) per person.

In the Hotel InterContinental Hong Kong, Salisbury Rd., Tsim Sha Tsui. *(C)* **852/2313 2256.** www.hongkong-ic.intercontinental.com. Reservations necessary. Main courses HK$240–HK$375 (US$31–US$49). AE, DC, MC, V. Daily 6pm–midnight. MTR: Tsim Sha Tsui.

Unkai ✹✹ JAPANESE   The Hong Kong branch of a well-known group of restaurants in Japan, Unkai might well be the best Japanese restaurant in town. With chefs from Osaka (known for its food), it caters to discerning Japanese, who make up a large proportion of the Sheraton's guests, with a variety of authentic dishes. True to Japanese form, the elegance of the restaurant is subtly understated, an aesthetic that is also carried into the food presentation. Foremost, of course, are the *kaiseki* courses, artfully arranged dishes that change according to the season. These are the most expensive fixed-price meals on the menu, but they are so huge that two can share; otherwise, a vegetarian *kaiseki* meal is available for HK$350 (US$46). There's also tempura (meat and vegetables coated in batter and then deep-fried), *teppanyaki* (grilled foods), and sushi counters. Since ordering a la carte can be expensive and bewildering due to the many choices, order a fixed-price meal (called a "course" on the menu) or come for lunch, when you have a choice of several fixed-price menus, including sushi, tempura, and teppanyaki courses and an *obento* lunch box. The *obento* is especially charming, a small lacquered chest with dishes of food in each of the drawers.

In the Sheraton Hong Kong Hotel and Towers. 20 Nathan Rd., Tsim Sha Tsui. *(C)* **852/2369 1111,** ext. 2. Reservations recommended. *Kaiseki* fixed-price meals HK$500–HK$795 (US$65–US$103); *teppanyaki* fixed-price meals HK$780–HK$990 (US$101–US$129); fixed-price lunch HK$145–HK$350 (US$19–US$45). AE, DC, MC, V. Daily noon–2:30pm and 6:30–10:30pm. MTR: Tsim Sha Tsui.

Yü ✹✹✹ SEAFOOD   There's no mistaking what this restaurant serves—it's all right there in front of you, swimming blissfully in part of a 12m (40-ft.) "bubble wall," unaware that their days are numbered. On the other side of the restaurant spreads a stunning view of Victoria Harbour. Located in the swank InterContinental but trendily low-key, Yü offers a nice concept—fresh seafood for cautious diners reluctant to tempt fate by ordering locally caught fish in

Where to Dine in Kowloon

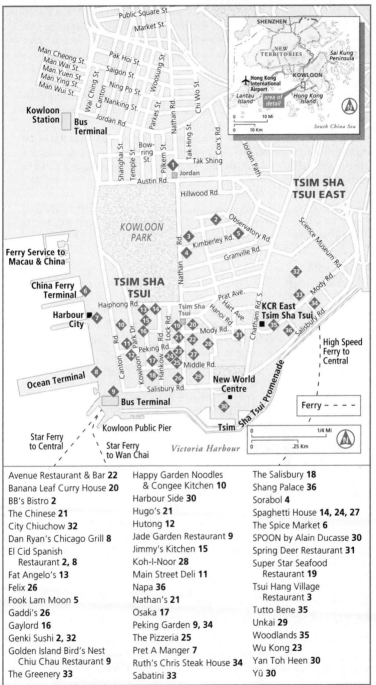

Avenue Restaurant & Bar **22**
Banana Leaf Curry House **20**
BB's Bistro **2**
The Chinese **21**
City Chiuchow **32**
Dan Ryan's Chicago Grill **8**
El Cid Spanish
    Restaurant **2, 8**
Fat Angelo's **13**
Felix **26**
Fook Lam Moon **5**
Gaddi's **26**
Gaylord **16**
Genki Sushi **2, 32**
Golden Island Bird's Nest
    Chiu Chau Restaurant **9**
The Greenery **33**

Happy Garden Noodles
    & Congee Kitchen **10**
Harbour Side **30**
Hugo's **21**
Hutong **12**
Jade Garden Restaurant **9**
Jimmy's Kitchen **15**
Koh-I-Noor **28**
Main Street Deli **11**
Napa **36**
Nathan's **21**
Osaka **17**
Peking Garden **9, 34**
The Pizzeria **25**
Pret A Manger **7**
Ruth's Chris Steak House **34**
Sabatini **33**

The Salisbury **18**
Shang Palace **36**
Sorabol **4**
Spaghetti House **14, 24, 27**
The Spice Market **6**
SPOON by Alain Ducasse **30**
Spring Deer Restaurant **31**
Super Star Seafood
    Restaurant **19**
Tsui Hang Village
    Restaurant **3**
Tutto Bene **35**
Unkai **29**
Woodlands **35**
Wu Kong **23**
Yan Toh Heen **30**
Yü **30**

115

Hong Kong's cheaper, noisier, and more colorful seaside restaurants favored by Hong Kong Chinese. Of course, you also pay a mountain more to eat here, but from the looks of things, there are plenty of takers. All the seafood, including a variety of garoupa, trout, other fish, lobsters, crabs, prawns, abalone, mussels, and oysters, are kept alive in tanks until the moment they're ordered and can be prepared in a variety of both Asian and Western ways, including grilled, poached, sautéed, or steamed. Many diners, however, stick to the imported oysters or begin their meals with the signature Seafood Mountain—fresh seafood laid on a mountain of ice, including oysters, prawns, mussels, scallops, crab, and lobster, served with six different sauces. Sautéed lobster with black beans and fine noodles is the restaurant's signature dish. There's also sushi, and, surprisingly, vegetarian choices. But the real dilemma, in my opinion, is in choosing whether to dine here or in the InterContinental's other top restaurant, SPOON. So many restaurants, so little time . . .

In the Hotel InterContinental Hong Kong, Salisbury Rd., Tsim Sha Tsui. ⓒ 852/2721 1211. www.hongkong-ic.intercontinental.com. Reservations necessary (request a window seat). Main courses HK$220–HK$420 (US$29–US$55); fixed-price lunch HK$195–HK$250 (US$25–US$32); fixed-price dinner HK$650 (US$84). AE, DC, MC, V. Mon–Sat noon–3pm; daily 6–11pm. MTR: Tsim Sha Tsui.

EXPENSIVE

Felix ★★★ *Value* PACIFIC RIM FUSION   Located on the top floor of The Peninsula's tower addition, this strikingly avant-garde restaurant comes as something of a shock in the otherwise staid and traditionally conservative hotel. But what else can you expect from a restaurant designed by Philippe Starck? Your first hint that Felix is not your ordinary dining experience begins with the elevator's wavy walls, which suggest a voyage to the world beyond, and continues inside the restaurant with its huge aluminum wall and two glass facades that curve seductively to reveal stunning views of Kowloon and Hong Kong Island. Two eye-catching zinc cylinders vaguely resemble gigantic snails and contain a cocoon-cozy bar and what may be one of the world's tiniest discos, complete with a heat-sensitive floor that illuminates dancers' movements. There are other bars atop one of the cocoons and on a stage at one end of the restaurant.

The dining area itself is rather—what can I say—stark, and even the view from the windows tends to take second place in this self-conscious, people-watching setting (you, however, should reserve a window seat on the Hong Kong side). The food, featuring Pacific Rim ingredients brought together in East-meets-West combinations, rarely disappoints. You might start with hot California rolls with crabmeat, avocado, and sake soy, followed by teriyaki-grilled giant prawns or the Mongolian-style barbecued rack of lamb. Bargain hunters can save bundles by dining early (before 7pm) and opting for the early-bird, three-course fixed-price dinner for HK$340 (US$44) including a glass of wine. You can also come just for a drink.

In The Peninsula hotel, Salisbury Rd., Tsim Sha Tsui. ⓒ 852/2315 3188. www.peninsula.com. Reservations required. Main courses HK$220–HK$310 (US$29–US$40). AE, DC, MC, V. Daily 6pm–2am (last order 10:30pm). MTR: Tsim Sha Tsui.

Fook Lam Moon ★★★ CANTONESE   Upon entering this restaurant (look for the shrine to the kitchen god at the entrance), you immediately feel as if you've stepped back a couple of decades to a Hong Kong that has all but vanished. The decor is outdated and, unless you're a regular, the waiters are indifferent. Yet for almost 50 years this has remained *the* place to go for exotic dishes, including shark's fin, bird's nest, and abalone, served in a variety of ways, as well as more down-to-earth dishes such as fried crispy chicken and pan-fried lobster bars. Shark's fin, however, is the obvious number-one choice, with 12 different renditions listed on the menu. If you feel like splurging, prices for half a bowl of shark's fin with crabmeat or shredded chicken begin at HK$300 (US$39). If you are not careful, you could end up spending a small fortune (if you go for the exotic dishes, count on at least HK$1,000/US$130 per person), but whatever you order, it's apt to be memorable. Indeed, some Hong Kong old-timers swear this restaurant serves the best Cantonese food in the world, and it's a favorite of local movers and shakers. Unlike many Chinese restaurants, this establishment provides both small (for two to four diners) and large tables.

There's another branch in Wan Chai at 35–45 Johnston Rd. (② **852/2866 0663;** MTR: Wan Chai), with the same hours.

53–59 Kimberley Rd., Tsim Sha Tsui. ② **852/2366 0286.** www.fooklammoon-grp.com. Reservations recommended for dinner. Main dishes HK$100–HK$190 (US$13–US$24). AE, DC, MC, V. Daily 11:30am–2:30pm and 6–11:30pm. MTR: Tsim Sha Tsui.

Hugo's 🏮🏮 CONTINENTAL   Opened in 1969, this was the Hyatt's first Hugo's in Asia (and one of the few of the Hugo's, what used to be a worldwide Hyatt trademark restaurant, still remaining). The rather masculine and slightly grim medieval-themed decor features antique swords and armor on the walls and booths with iron partitions, little changed over the past decades (indeed, loyal patrons throw a fit if the hotel even hints at a makeover). Popular with the locals and visiting businesspeople, it's a good choice for power lunches and a lively place for dinner, with Filipino musicians serenading evening diners. With an open charcoal grill, its specialty is U.S. prime rib of beef and Angus sirloin steak, as well as seafood flown in from around the world. Appetizers and salads are brought to your table on a carousel wagon; many dishes are also prepared tableside. The menu changes twice a year, but if the cognac flambéed lobster bisque or tiger prawns braised in mild pepper sauce and served with red caviar pilaf (house specialties) are on the menu, I recommend them. The desserts are always spectacular, and the wine list is extensive.

In the Hyatt Regency, 67 Nathan Rd., Tsim Sha Tsui. ② **852/2311 1234,** ext. 2877. www.hongkong.regency. hyatt.com. Reservations recommended. Main courses HK$268–HK$438 (US$35–US$57); fixed-price lunch HK$255–HK$275 (US$33–US$36); fixed-price dinner HK$555 (US$72); Sun brunch HK$388 (US$58). AE, DC, MC, V. Mon–Sat noon–3pm; Sun 11:30am–3pm; daily 7–11pm. MTR: Tsim Sha Tsui.

Napa 🏮🏮 AMERICAN/CALIFORNIAN   Located on the top floor of the Kowloon Shangri-La Hotel and boasting great harbor views, this smart-looking restaurant is so upbeat it could make an optimist of even the most travel-weary diner. Crisply decorated with light-colored woods, modern art, and Art Deco–style fixtures (check out the naughty lamps in the bay windows), it offers what may well be the best Caesar salad in town, served in a Parmesan basket with sourdough croutons. Main dishes include steaks and seafood, such as a crispy sea bass. For lighter appetites, there's also a limited selection of pastas, while the fixed-price lunch includes both appetizer and dessert buffets. The wine list features 80 whites and reds from dozens of Californian wineries.

In the Kowloon Shangri-La Hotel, 64 Mody Rd., Tsim Sha Tsui East. ② **852/2733 8752.** www.shangri-la. com. Reservations are not necessary for lunch but are a good idea for dinner. Pastas HK$130–HK$180 (US$17–US$24); main courses HK$220–HK$340 (US$29–US$44); fixed-price lunch HK$218 (US$28). AE, DC, MC, V. Daily noon–3pm and 6:30pm–midnight. MTR: Tsim Sha Tsui.

Ruth's Chris Steak House 🏮🏮 STEAKS/AMERICAN   Craving a big, juicy steak? This well-known American chain fits the bill with its U.S. prime

Midwestern beef, available in cuts of filet, rib-eye, strip, porterhouse, T-bone, and veal in various sizes, broiled to exact specifications and served sizzling. Other entrees include tuna, chicken, lamb chops, and lobster; side dishes, which cost extra, range from mashed potatoes with roasted garlic to fresh sautéed spinach and Caesar salad. Less expensive fare for lunch includes sandwiches in addition to steak.

There's another branch in the Lippo Centre, 89 Queensway, Central (© **852/ 2522 9090;** MTR: Admiralty), open the same hours.

Empire Centre (opposite Regal Kowloon Hotel), 68 Mody Rd., Tsim Sha Tsui East. © **852/2366 6000.** www. ruthschris.com. Reservations recommended for dinner. Main courses HK$240–HK$550 (US$31–US$71); fixed-price dinner HK$520–HK$750 (US$68–US$97). AE, DC, MC, V. Daily noon–3pm and 5:30–11pm. MTR: Tsim Sha Tsui.

Sabatini ✿✿✿ *(Finds* ITALIAN   In 1954, three Sabatini brothers opened their first restaurant in Rome; their success led them to open branches in Japan and, in 1992, Hong Kong. The dining hall is rustic and cozy yet refined, with a terra-cotta tile floor, wooden ceiling, and traditional Roman murals, giving it a more casual and relaxed ambience than most hotel Italian restaurants in the same price range. Its menu is a faithful replica of the original Roman fare (along with chef specialties), with liberal doses of olive oil, garlic, and peppers and featuring such popular dishes as Dover sole with Prosecco, green and black olives, and herbed lemon butter, and veal with morel sauce. The pasta is all handmade, and the antipasti buffet is so delicious it's tempting to fill up just on its selections, but don't forget to leave room for the tiramisu. The list of mostly Italian wines is seemingly endless. Evenings feature guitar music; lunch is popular for its reasonable fixed-price menus. The service is cheerful and polished.

In the Royal Garden hotel, 69 Mody Rd., Tsim Sha Tsui East. © **852/2733 2000.** www.rghk.com.hk. Reservations required. Main courses HK$250–HK$385 (US$32–US$50); fixed-price lunch Mon–Sat HK$125–HK$250 (US$16–US$32); Sun and holiday buffet HK$280 (US$36). AE, DC, MC, V. Daily noon–2:30pm and 6–11pm. MTR: Tsim Sha Tsui.

Shang Palace ✿✿✿ CANTONESE   While many Chinese restaurants have ditched traditional red and gold for a more contemporary look, this remains one of Hong Kong's most traditionally and elaborately decorated restaurants, with walls of carved red lacquerware and Chinese lanterns hanging from the ceiling. All in all, it fits every expectation of how an "authentic" Chinese restaurant should look. If your experience of Chinese food is limited to chop suey, this is a comfortable and memorable place to go, though you also can't go wrong if you're a Chinese-food connoisseur. The dinner menu is quite extensive, with an emphasis on seafood but also serving chicken, duck, pigeon, beef, and pork, Cantonese-style. Consider starting with the shark's-fin soup, followed by pan-fried scallops with minced shrimp in black bean sauce or the deep-fried crispy chicken. If cost is no object, you might consider bird's nest with bamboo fungus, which runs HK$438 (US$57) or more. Otherwise, expect to spend about HK$500 (US$65) per person for a royal feast. Lunch is more economical and always includes a dozen or more varieties of dim sum.

In the Shangri-La Hotel, 64 Mody Rd., Tsim Sha Tsui East. © **852/2733 8754.** www.shangri-la.com. Reservations recommended. Main dishes HK$125–HK$290 (US$16–US$38). AE, DC, MC, V. Mon–Sat noon–3pm; Sun and holidays 10:30am–3pm; daily 6:30–11pm. MTR: Tsim Sha Tsui.

Yan Toh Heen ✿✿✿ CANTONESE   With a name that translates loosely as an "Elegant dining establishment to enjoy the beautiful view," this great restaurant envelopes diners in a sophisticated, hushed environment, with large windows treating diners to a view of famous Victoria Harbour. The decor emphasizes the beauty of stark simplicity, with bonsai trees and flower arrangements that change with the lunar calendar; the restaurant is famous for its beautiful jade table settings (each setting is valued at approximately HK$8,000/US$1,039!). Dishes are traditional Cantonese, as well as imaginative creations that border on Chinese nouvelle cuisine. The menu changes with each lunar month but always includes seafood, the restaurant's signature barbecued suckling pig and Peking duck, seasonal vegetables, and a wide selection of desserts. The restaurant is also known for its dim sum. Since most diners follow the Chinese custom of ordering several dishes and then sharing, the average dinner bill without wine here is HK$1,000 (US$130) for two.

In the InterContinental Hong Kong, 18 Salisbury Rd., Tsim Sha Tsui. ℭ 852/2721 1211. www.hongkong-ic.intercontinental.com. Reservations recommended (request a window seat). Main dishes HK$155–HK$290 (US$20–US$38); fixed-price lunch HK$168 (US$22). AE, DC, MC, V. Mon–Sat noon–3pm; Sun and holidays 11:30am–3:30pm; daily 6–11pm. MTR: Tsim Sha Tsui.

MODERATE

In addition to the choices here, a good standby for Continental cuisine is the Tsim Sha Tsui branch of **Jimmy's Kitchen,** covered in the Central dining section (p. 138).

Avenue Restaurant & Bar 𝈁𝈁 (Value CONTINENTAL   The contemporary, upscale setting of this airy restaurant with its modern artwork, white-washed walls, palm trees, and greenhouselike dining area, together with its menu of modern European food, live jazz from 8pm, and excellent service, could easily mislead one into thinking that this trendy establishment is much more expensive than it is, making it a very good value. It also overlooks Nathan Road, giving an unparalleled view of Hong Kong's bustling street life. The a la carte dinner menu offers an extensive selection tailored to various budgets and tastes, including a whole page devoted to vegetarian dishes that are as delicious as the regular entrees. You might wish to start with an appetizer of crab and avocado with lemon mayonnaise, followed by sautéed sole with spinach, new potatoes, poached egg, and grain mustard sauce. For dessert, try the chocolate soufflé or the crème brûlée. For lunch, only fixed-price meals are available.

In the Holiday Inn Golden Mile, 50 Nathan Rd., Tsim Sha Tsui. ℭ 852/2315 1118. www.goldenmile-hk. holiday-inn.com. Reservations recommended weekend evenings. Main courses HK$168–HK$238 (US$22–US$31); fixed-price lunch HK$160–HK$188 (US$21–US$24); fixed-price dinner HK$318–HK$358 (US$41–US$47); Sun brunch HK$338 (US$44). AE, DC, MC, V. Mon–Sat noon–2:30pm; Sun 11:30am–2:30pm; Mon–Sat 6–10:30pm (last order). MTR: Tsim Sha Tsui.

BB's Bistro FRENCH   This is a good choice for casual dining on Knutsford Terrace, a tucked-away pedestrian lane lined with bars and restaurants at the north end of Tsim Sha Tsui. You can choose to sit outside and watch the human parade, or settle in the simple, dark restaurant at one of the booths or tables. The cuisine ranges from classic French recipes to more interesting creations, including a delicious goat's cheese with mustard sauce, *coq au vin* (chicken stew in a Burgundy wine sauce), pan-fried seabass coated with couscous and a puree of fresh tomato sauce, braised wild rabbit stew, and grilled venison with chestnut sauce and a dash of Cognac. The cheerful service is a bit slow but not deliberately so, making this a good bet only when you won't be ruffled by a languorous—or should we say French?—and carefree dinner. Lunchtime is

faster and more economical, with pastas costing HK$52 (US$6.75) and meat
and fish dishes HK$62 (US$8.05).

13–13a Knutsford Terrace, Tsim Sha Tsui. © 852/2316 2212. www.mhihk.com. Reservations recommended.
Main courses HK$128–HK$218 (US$17–US$28). AE, DC, MC, V. Mon–Sat noon–3pm; daily 6pm–1am. MTR:
Tsim Sha Tsui.

The Chinese 🌟🌟 *Finds* CANTONESE   Decorated in stark black and white
with a blend of Art Deco and modern Chinese, this trend-setting place was
Hong Kong's first Chinese restaurant to ignore the traditional red and gold. It
remains one of the city's most refined Cantonese restaurants, with a small and
intimate dining room reminiscent of Chinese teahouses of the 1920s, complete
with traditional booth seating, which provides intimacy. The innovative menu
combining Chinese ingredients with Western presentation changes with the seasons, but if available, the shark's fin served in papaya, deep-fried crispy chicken,
minced pigeon with butter lettuce, drunken shrimp, and honey barbecued pork
are all equally delicious. Another great deal is the special dim sum available for
lunch, costing HK$28 to HK$48 (US$3.65–US$6.25) per basket.

In the Hyatt Regency, 67 Nathan Rd., Tsim Sha Tsui. © 852/2311 1234, ext. 2881. www.hongkong.regency.
hyatt.com. Reservations recommended for dinner. Main dishes HK$110–HK$220 (US$14–US$29); fixed-price
lunch HK$320 (US$42); fixed-price dinner HK$360–HK$740 (US$47–US$96). AE, DC, MC, V. Mon–Sat
11:30am–3pm; Sun 10:30am–3pm; daily 6:30–11:30pm. MTR: Tsim Sha Tsui.

City Chiuchow Restaurant CHIU CHOW   Riding the crest of a wave of a
newfound popularity for Chiu Chow food, this spacious restaurant overlooks
gardens leading down to a major promenade in Tsim Sha Tsui East. Seating 500,
it features a big tank with fish swimming about, soon to end up on the chopping block. Famous dishes here include Chiu Chow shark's-fin soup, much
thicker and stronger tasting than the Cantonese version; double-boiled shark's-
fin-and-chicken soup, not as strong but equally popular; sliced soy goose; fried
chicken with a black spicy sauce; and seafood dishes, including lobster. I particularly recommend the cold sliced lobster in a special honey sauce—it's not on
the menu but it's available year-round. Dim sum is also served. And don't forget
to try the Iron Buddha tea, a specialty of Chiuchow's, a tea that is so strong it
will knock your socks off—and may keep you awake all night.

E. Ocean Centre, 98 Granville Rd., Tsim Sha Tsui East. © 852/2723 6226. Main dishes HK$62–HK$120
(US$8.05–US$16). AE, DC, MC, V. Daily 11am–11pm. MTR: Tsim Sha Tsui.

Dan Ryan's Chicago Grill 🌟 *Kids* AMERICAN   Located in the huge Ocean
Terminal complex at its southernmost end, where cruise ships dock, this casual
restaurant serves real American food, with portions big enough to satisfy a hungry cowboy. The decor is Anywhere, U.S.A., but with a difference—since it's
located right by the Star Ferry, the Chicago Grill offers views of the famous
harbor from a few select seats. The lunch menu is substantial, including such
classic American favorites as buffalo chicken wings, potato skins, nachos, New
England clam chowder, barbecued ribs, steaks, spaghetti, lasagna, chili, great
hamburgers (a hit with kids), and large deli sandwiches. There are also lunch
specials, available Monday to Friday, beginning at HK$65 (US$8.45). The dinner menu is confined mainly to barbecued steaks, chops, fish, and pasta. Admittedly, most dishes here are a bit pricey, but if you're hungering for the real thing,
you might consider it a lifesaver. You can also come just for a drink at its bar,
and there are also English-language newspapers for customer perusal.

Travel Tip: He who finds the best hotel deal has more to spend on facials involving knobbly vegetables.

Hello, the Roaming Gnome here. I've been nabbed from the garden and taken round the world. The people who took me are so terribly clever. They find the best offerings on Travelocity. For very little cha-ching. And that means I get to be pampered and exfoliated till I'm pink as a bunny's doodah.

travelocity®

1-888-TRAVELOCITY / travelocity.com / America Online Keyword: Travel

Plan your vacation

- flights, hotels, car rentals
- cruises & vacation packages
- destination guides
- fare alerts
- go to yahoo.com, click travel

© 2003 Yahoo! Inc.

powered by

There's another Dan Ryan's at Pacific Place in Admiralty, 88 Queensway (© **852/2845 4600;** MTR: Admiralty), open Monday to Friday from 11am to midnight, Saturday from 9am to 2am, and Sunday from 9am to midnight.

200 Ocean Terminal, Harbour City, Tsim Sha Tsui. © **852/2735 6111.** www.danryans.com/dans. Main courses HK$60–HK$240 (US$7.80–US$32) before 6pm, HK$95–HK$450 (US$12–US$58) after 6pm. AE, DC, MC, V. Mon–Fri 11am–midnight; Sat–Sun 10am–midnight. MTR: Tsim Sha Tsui.

El Cid Spanish Restaurant *Value* SPANISH   This cheerful restaurant was one of the first to open on Knutsford Terrace, a narrow lane lined with bars and restaurants on the northern edge of Tsim Sha Tsui. Recommended are the stuffed baby squid with ink sauce, seafood paella, and codfish with clams in a green sauce; there are also soups and salads. But probably the best thing to do is select from the several dozen tapas on the menu, which can make for wonderful nibbling or out-and-out feasts. Choices include stewed eggplant with herbs and spicy tomato sauce, garlic prawns in olive oil, chorizo, and lamb spareribs with tomato and pine nuts.

There are other El Cid branches at Shop G315 Harbour City, Tsim Sha Tsui (© **852/2721 2181;** MTR: Tsim Sha Tsui), open daily noon to 11pm; 9–11 Cleveland St., Causeway Bay (© **852/2576 8650;** MTR: Causeway Bay), open daily noon to midnight; and Shop 102 in the historic Murray House (with great sea views from its delightful terrace), Stanley Plaza, Stanley (© **852/2899 0858**), open Monday to Thursday noon to 11:30pm, Friday noon to midnight, Saturday 11am to midnight, and Sunday 11am to 11pm.

12 and 14 Knutsford Terrace, Tsim Sha Tsui. © **852/2312 1898.** www.kingparrot.com. Main courses HK$135–HK$180 (US$18–US$23); tapas HK$40–HK$60 (US$5.20–US$7.80); fixed-price lunch HK$95 (US$12); fixed-price dinner HK$200 (US$26). AE, DC, MC, V. Daily noon–2:30pm and 6pm–midnight. MTR: Tsim Sha Tsui.

Gaylord ★★ *Value* INDIAN   This long-established, first-floor restaurant in the heart of Tsim Sha Tsui is classy and comfortable, with private booths and overstuffed sofas. It's popular for its authentic North Indian classics, including tandoori, lamb curry cooked in North Indian spices and herbs, chicken cooked in hot fiery vindaloo curry, prawns cooked with green pepper and spices, and fish with potatoes and tomatoes. There are a dozen vegetarian dishes, and the lunchtime buffet, served every day until 2:30pm except Sundays and public holidays, is a winner. There are also fixed-price dinners, along with a dinner buffet available until 9:30pm for only HK$128 (US$17).

23–25 Ashley Rd., Tsim Sha Tsui. © **852/2376 1001.** Main dishes HK$78–HK$198 (US$10–US$26); lunch buffet HK$88 (US$11); fixed-price dinner HK$150–HK$210 (US$19–US$27). AE, DC, MC, V. Daily noon–2:30pm and 6:30–11pm. MTR: Tsim Sha Tsui.

Golden Island Bird's Nest Chiu Chau Restaurant CHIU CHOW   This Chiu Chow restaurant is conveniently located right in front of the Star Ferry terminus. As the prices below indicate, you can eat quite cheaply here if you order only one dish per person, but you'll pay more if you choose the house specialty—bird's nest, prepared 14 different ways and available as a soup, entree, and even dessert. This was Hong Kong's first restaurant to offer bird's nest as a specialty; although the prices for this dish have risen dramatically over the past few years, here it costs around HK$380 (US$49)—expensive, but less than what you'd pay elsewhere. Anyway, I would suggest that you try at least one of the bird's-nest dishes, along with such Chiu Chow preparations as oyster omelets, prawn balls, or roast soy goose, topping it all off with a thimble-size cup of Chiu Chow tea, which is believed to aid in digestion.

Star House (2nd floor), 3 Salisbury Rd., Tsim Sha Tsui. © 852/2736 6228. Main dishes HK$60–HK$150 (US$7.80–US$20). AE, MC, V. Daily 11am–3pm and 5:30–11:30pm. MTR: Tsim Sha Tsui.

Hutong ★★★ *Finds* NORTHERN CHINESE   A hutong is an ancient alley or lane, common in Beijing's courtyard neighborhoods. This stunning restaurant, however, is about as far from a real hutong as one can get, since it's located on the 28th floor of a strikingly modern highrise. Still, the restaurant is to be commended for its down-to-earth yet dramatic setting, with red lanterns providing the only splash of color against a dark, muted interior and with fantastic views of Hong Kong. Indeed, everything about this place is a class act. The cuisine, which is northern Chinese in origin but uses new ingredients and combinations to create its own trademark dishes, is so enticing it's hard to know what to recommend. I love the drunken raw crab (an appetizer marinated three days in Chinese wine), the crispy deboned lamb ribs, crispy soft-shelled crab with Sichuan red chili, and the lotus root with wild mushroom. Even the pig throat with scallions and cilantro is a whole lot better than it sounds. In short, Hutong raises the bar in chic Chinese restaurants, winning hands down in cuisine, presentation, atmosphere, view, and service. Note that there's a minimum charge of HK$300 (US$39) per person for dinner. Dim sum is available for lunch.

1 Peking Rd. (28th floor), Tsim Sha Tsui. © 852/3428 8342. www.aqua.com.hk. Reservations required for dinner. Main dishes HK$118–HK$288 (US$15–US$37); fixed-price lunch HK$388–HK$468 (US$50–US$61). AE, DC, MC, V. Daily noon–3pm and 6–11:30pm. MTR: Tsim Sha Tsui.

The Greenery INTERNATIONAL   If you're looking for a quick, filling feast in Tsim Sha Tsui East, look no further than the lunch or dinner buffets offered in this popular, open restaurant, located in the hotel's 15-story atrium. The sounds of piano music, a waterfall, and multitudes of hungry diners make eating a rather noisy affair, but the food is good and varied, ranging from Chinese and Japanese to Western fare, from salads and vegetables to ribs and fish, and an efficient staff keeps water glasses filled and used plates whisked away.

In the Royal Garden Hotel, 69 Mody Rd., Tsim Sha Tsui East. © 852/2721 5215. www.rghk.com.hk. Lunch buffet HK$155 (US$20); dinner buffet HK$258 (US$34) Sun–Thurs, HK$278 (US$36) Fri–Sat. AE, DC, MC, V. Daily noon–2:30pm and 6:30–9:30pm. MTR: Tsim Sha Tsui.

Harbour Side ★ INTERNATIONAL   Although located in the elegant InterContinental, this is an informal dining hall, rather plain and bare with a brick floor, wooden chairs, and manicured topiaries, but it's bright and airy because of its three-story-high wall of glass facing the harbor and its clever use of mirrors. It offers nonstop all-day dining and views of people walking along the waterfront promenade. Its open kitchen emphasizes a variety of choices, including salads, pastas, pizzas, sandwiches, seafood, and steak, prepared in imaginative ways. How about the Ahi tuna roll as an appetizer, which comes with king crabmeat salad, wasabi vinaigrette, and artichoke crisps? For a main course you might choose traditional fish and chips, the Spanish paella, or the grilled Boston lobster. Or, if you stick to one of the sandwiches, pizzas, or pasta dishes, you can dine for less than HK$160 (US$21). On Sundays there's a champagne brunch from 11am to 3pm costing HK$325 (US$42) for adults and half price for children.

In the Hotel InterContinental Hong Kong, Salisbury Rd., Tsim Sha Tsui. © 852/2721 1211. www.hongkong-ic.intercontinental.com. Main courses HK$130–HK$350 (US$17–US$45). AE, DC, MC, V. Daily 6am–midnight. MTR: Tsim Sha Tsui.

Jade Garden Restaurant CANTONESE   Jade Garden is part of a chain of restaurants owned by the Maxim's Group, a company that has long been wildly successful throughout Hong Kong and is popular with large Chinese families (other establishments in the group include Sichuan Garden, Shanghai Garden, Chiu Chow Garden, and Peking Garden; the latter one also has a branch in Star House). Jade Garden is the place to go if you don't know much about Chinese food, feel that you should try it, but still aren't very keen on the idea. A plus is the view of the harbor afforded by some of the window-side tables. As in most Cantonese restaurants, lunch is dim sum served from trolleys pushed through the aisles (there's also a dim sum menu). If you'd rather come for dinner, you might consider drunken shrimp boiled in Chinese rice wine, deep-fried boneless chicken with lemon sauce, stir-fried minced pigeon served with lettuce leaves, glazed pork loin, or, if you feel like splurging, barbecued Peking duck, which costs HK$290 (US$38).

Jade Garden has another branch 1 Hysan Ave., Causeway Bay (© 852/2577 9332), open daily from 7:30am to midnight.

Star House (4th floor), 3 Salisbury Rd., Tsim Sha Tsui. © 852/2730 6888. Main dishes HK$60–HK$140 (US$7.80–US$18). AE, DC, MC, V. Mon–Sat 11am–5pm and 5:30pm–midnight; Sun and holidays 10am–midnight. MTR: Tsim Sha Tsui.

Osaka JAPANESE   Japanese in the know have long headed to this reasonably priced, second-floor establishment, Hong Kong's oldest Japanese restaurant, having been open for more than 30 years. Simple and uncluttered, it's divided into several dining areas, where you can feast on higher-priced *kaiseki* meals (called Table D'Hote on the menu and consisting of a complete meal of many dishes), sukiyaki or *shabu-shabu* (one-pot meals featuring beef and vegetables you cook at your own table), or sushi. If you're on a budget, order one of the noodle dishes such as *tempura udon* (breaded prawn on noodles), the *tonkatsu* (fried pork cutlet), fried fish, or barbecued eel; or come for lunch. For a splurge, on the ground floor is a teppanyaki corner, with fixed-price meals of steak and seafood costing HK$380 to HK$500 (US$49–US$65).

14 Ashley Rd., Tsim Sha Tsui. © 852/2376 3323. Most main dishes HK$70–HK$100 (US$9.10–US$13); sukiyaki or *shabu-shabu* HK$210–HK$390 (US$27–US$51); *kaiseki* courses HK$350–HK$380 (US$45–US$49); fixed-price lunch HK$63–HK$90 (US$8.20–US$12). AE, DC, MC, V. Daily noon–3pm and 6–11pm. MTR: Tsim Sha Tsui.

Peking Garden ✿ PEKINGESE   Another Maxim's Group of restaurants, Peking Garden specializes in Pekingese and northern Chinese dishes, including stir-fried Pekingese noodles with shredded pork, braised prawns in red wine sauce, Hunan ham with lotus seed in honey sauce, and beggar's chicken for HK$320 (US$42; order it 24 hr. in advance). Try to be here during its nightly presentation of handmade noodles at 8 or 8:30pm. It's located in the Star House right in front of the Star Ferry.

You'll find other branches at the Empire Centre, 68 Mody Rd., Tsim Sha Tsui East (© 852/2721 8868; MTR: Tsim Sha Tsui); first and second basements of Alexandra House, 6 Ice House St., Central (© 852/2526 6456; MTR: Central); Shop 003 in Pacific Place, 88 Queensway in Central (© 852/2845 8452; MTR: Admiralty); and Hennessy Centre, 500 Hennessy Rd., Causeway Bay (© 852/2577 7231; MTR: Causeway Bay); all have the same open hours.

Star House (3rd floor), 3 Salisbury Rd., Tsim Sha Tsui. © 852/2735 8211. Main dishes HK$86–HK$188 (US$11–US$24). AE, DC, MC, V. Mon–Sat 11:30am–3pm; Sun 11am–3pm; daily 5:30–11:30pm. MTR: Tsim Sha Tsui.

The Pizzeria ★★ *Value* ITALIAN   Located on the second floor of the Kowloon Hotel (just behind The Peninsula), this casual and bustling dining hall with large windows is one of my favorite places in Tsim Sha Tsui for a relaxed meal at good prices, especially when I want great pizza or pasta and don't feel like getting dressed up (you won't however, want to wear shorts; it's a white-tablecloth kind of place even at lunch). Despite its name, this restaurant specializes in pasta, with an a la carte menu that changes often but has included such mouthwatering choices as homemade fettuccine with lobster and spinach in tomato cream sauce and penne pasta with smoked chicken and porcini mushrooms in creamy herb sauce. There are also five different kinds of pizza, and main courses have included baked Mandarin fish fillets in foil with fennel, morels, walnuts, and lemon, and roast quail with bacon, sage, and crispy chickpea roll. Save room for dessert—they're all delicious. For the budget-conscious, lunch is a great time to come, when a trip through the antipasto and salad bar, choice of main dish (meat, pasta, or pizza), and dessert and coffee, are all available at a great price. Incidentally, to reach The Pizzeria, you have to walk through the Window Café, which specializes in international buffets.

In the Kowloon Hotel, 19–21 Nathan Rd., Tsim Sha Tsui. © 852/2929 2888, ext. 3322. www.thekowloon hotel.com. Reservations recommended. Pasta and pizza HK$135–HK$160 (US$18–US$21); main courses HK$190–HK$215 (US$25–US$28); lunch buffet HK$190 (US$25) Mon–Fri, HK$210 (US$27) Sat–Sun. AE, DC, MC, V. Daily 11am–3pm and 6–11pm. MTR: Tsim Sha Tsui.

The Spice Market ASIAN   Accessible from both the Marco Polo Prince Hotel and the third floor of the Gateway shopping mall, this dark and cozy restaurant specializes in buffets offering diners a culinary adventure throughout Asia. There are Chinese noodles; Indian curries; and Chinese, Thai, Vietnamese, and Singaporean favorites. Included are steamed fish, chili crab, satays, Korean barbecue, soups, salads, appetizers, and desserts. True to its name, many of the foods are spicy. While none of the dishes are outstanding, most of them are good; with so many choices, you'll probably end up eating more than you should.

In the Marco Polo Prince Hotel, 23 Canton Rd., Tsim Sha Tsui. © 852/2113 6046. www.marcopolohotels. com. Lunch buffet HK$128 (US$17) Mon–Fri, HK$138 (US$18) Sat–Sun and holidays; dinner buffet HK$248 (US$26) Sun–Thurs, HK$268 (US$35) Fri–Sat and holidays. AE, DC, MC, V. Daily noon–2:30pm and 6:30–10pm. MTR: Tsim Sha Tsui.

Spring Deer Restaurant ★ *Finds* PEKINGESE   A long-time favorite in Hong Kong, this 30-some-year-old restaurant offers excellent Pekingese food at reasonable prices. Spring Deer is cheerful and very accessible to foreigners, but don't expect anything fancy; in fact, your tablecloth may have holes in it, but it will be clean—and the place is usually packed with groups of loyal fans. This is one of the best places to come if you want to try its specialty—honey-glazed Peking duck, which costs HK$280 (US$36) and is good for two to four persons. Since you'll probably have to wait 40 minutes for the duck if you order it during peak time (7:30–9:30pm), it's best to arrive either before or after the rush. Chicken dishes are also well liked, including the deep-fried chicken and walnuts in soy sauce, and the handmade noodles are excellent. Other recommendations include the hot-and-sour soup, freshwater shrimp, and stewed ham and cabbage. Most dishes come in small, medium, and large sizes; the small dishes are suitable for two people. Remember, you'll want to order one dish apiece, plus an additional one to share. Unfortunately, since Spring Deer is crowded with groups, the lone diner is apt to be neglected in the shuffle; it's best to come here only if there are at least two of you.

42 Mody Rd., Tsim Sha Tsui. © 852/2366 4012. Reservations recommended. Small dishes HK$50–HK$90 (US$6.50–US$12). AE, MC, V. Daily 11:30am–3pm and 6–11pm. MTR: Tsim Sha Tsui.

Super Star Seafood Restaurant ⭐ CANTONESE/SEAFOOD Walk past the tanks filled with fish, lobsters, prawns, and crabs up to this lively Cantonese restaurant on the first floor. It's very popular with local Chinese, many of whom consider it one of Hong Kong's top Cantonese restaurants. Its menu includes pictures of major dishes; as its name implies, the restaurant specializes in fresh seafood (though the menu does offer more than seafood). Recommended are the deep-fried stuffed crab claws, sliced sole with spice and chili, baked lobster with minced spinach, and fish in season. Prices for seafood vary with the season and depend on the size of the creature you desire. If you want a specific fish or something else in the tank, simply point, but be sure to ask the price first. Stone fish is popular with the Chinese and is the restaurant's specialty. It's a rather ugly fish, and poisonous to boot if not prepared correctly. If this is what you want, you'll have to wait an hour for it to cook. Dim sum, served until 5pm, starts at HK$15 (US$1.95) per plate.

There are other branches: in Tsim Sha Tsui's Harbour City, 21 Canton Rd. (© **852/2628 0336;** MTR: Tsim Sha Tsui); in Central at 19–27 Wyndham St. (© **852/2525 9238;** MTR: Central); in Wan Chai on the first floor of the Shui On Centre, 8 Harbour Rd. (© **852/2628 0989**); and in Causeway Bay on the 10th floor of Times Square, 1 Matheson St. (© **852/2628 0886**). Call for individual open hours.

83–97 Nathan Rd., Tsim Sha Tsui. © 852/2628 0339. Main dishes HK$70–HK$168 (US$9.10–US$22); fixed-price menu HK$260–HK$300 (US$34–US$39). AE, DC, MC, V. Mon–Fri 10:30am–4:30pm; Sat–Sun 9:30am–4:30pm; daily 5–11pm. MTR: Tsim Sha Tsui.

Tsui Hang Village Restaurant CANTONESE Tsui Hang is named after the home village of Dr. Sun Yat-sen (a Chinese revolutionary leader and statesman who lived from 1866–1925). Located across the street from the Miramar Hotel on the ground floor of a sparkling shopping complex called Miramar Plaza, it's a bright, clean, and modern place with a white jade statue of the Goddess of Mercy at its entrance. This restaurant specializes in its own Cantonese original creations but also serves traditional, home-style Chinese cooking. Dishes you might want to try include braised superior shark's fin and chicken soup in casserole, deep-fried minced shrimp balls with crisp almond, sautéed minced pigeon with lettuce, barbecued Peking duck, deep-fried crispy chicken with green onion, or roast goose. Dim sum, served during lunch and afternoon teatime, Monday to Saturday from 11:30am to 5pm and Sunday from 10am to 5pm, is priced from HK$18 to HK$38 (US$2.35–US$4.95) per plate.

There's another Tsui Hang Village in Central on the second floor of the New World Tower, 16–18 Queen's Rd., Central (© **852/2524 2012;** MTR: Central), open Monday to Friday from 11am to 3pm and 5:30 to 11:30pm, Saturday from 11am to 11:30pm, and Sunday from 10am to 11:30pm.

Miramar Plaza, 132–134 Nathan Rd., Tsim Sha Tsui. © 852/2376 2882. www.miramar-group.com. Main dishes HK$78–HK$260 (US$10–US$34). AE, DC, MC, V. Mon–Sat 11:30am–11:30pm; Sun 10am–11:30pm. MTR: Tsim Sha Tsui.

Tutto Bene ⭐ ITALIAN Located on the northern edge of Tsim Sha Tsui, on a tiny narrow lane known for its bars and restaurants, this small but popular eatery is often packed. Tight indoor quarters prevent it from being even remotely romantic (unless you speak some obscure language, your neighbor is going to hear every word you say); try for one of the few outdoor tables. Prices seem a bit high (about HK$400/US$52 per person without drinks), but the imaginative Italian food, spiced with Asian ingredients, has clearly won over a faithful clientele. Start with the buffalo mozzarella with fresh tomatoes and basil dressing. The antipasto platter is so huge that two can share. For a main course, consider the veal scaloppine served with poached white asparagus and a white wine lemon tarragon reduction or the grilled tiger prawns with shiitake mushrooms and Italian parsley butter. This is a good choice for Italian food if you wish to dine outside a hotel but don't mind paying hotel restaurant prices.

7 Knutsford Terrace, Tsim Sha Tsui. © 852/2316 2116. www.mhihk.com. Reservations recommended. Main courses HK$198–HK$245 (US$26–US$32). AE, DC, MC, V. Sun–Thurs 6pm–1am; Fri–Sat 6pm–1:30am. MTR: Tsim Sha Tsui.

Wu Kong ★★ SHANGHAINESE   This basement restaurant, in the heart of Tsim Sha Tsui, just off Nathan Road, is often packed during mealtimes with locals who come for the good food at excellent prices. More upscale than many Shanghainese restaurants, with its stark-white walls and pond with goldfish in the foyer, it serves a variety of shark's-fin dishes, as well as the usual sautéed fresh prawns, braised shredded eels, braised eggplant with hot garlic sauce, stuffed bean curd, and other dishes common to Shanghai. Other selections include cold pigeon in wine sauce (its signature appetizer), Peking duck, crispy duck, and sautéed sliced duck. If you've had your fill of the more readily available and popular Cantonese and Sichuan food and are ready to experiment with other types of Chinese cuisine, this is an excellent place to start.

There's another branch on the 12th floor of Food Forum, Times Square, 1 Matheson St., Causeway Bay (© **852/2506 1018;** MTR: Causeway Bay), open Monday to Friday from 11:30am to 3pm and 5:30 to 11:30pm, and Saturday and Sunday from 11:30am to 11:30pm; and in the Empire Hotel, 33 Hennessy Rd. (© **852/2527 1383**), open daily 11:30am to 3pm and 6 to 11:30pm.

27 Nathan Rd. (entrance on Peking Rd.), Tsim Sha Tsui. © **852/2366 7244.** www.wukong.com.hk. Main dishes HK$68–HK$180 (US$8.85–US$23). AE, DC, MC, V. Daily 11:30am–3pm and 5:30–11:15pm. MTR: Tsim Sha Tsui.

INEXPENSIVE

Pret A Manger, reviewed in the Central dining section below (p. 143), has a branch in Harbour City and is popular for its inexpensive sandwiches. **Sorabol** (p. 149) is a Korean restaurant described in the Wan Chai/Causeway Bay section.

Banana Leaf Curry House ★★ MALAYSIAN/INDIAN/THAI   This fast-growing local chain has a good idea—more than 100 choices, including chicken, mutton, beef, seafood, and vegetables, cooked in several varieties of curry; and a gimmick—dishes are presented on banana leaves. Add to that the brisk, efficient service and reasonable prices, and you've got the makings of a winner for cheap Malaysian, Thai, South Indian, and other Asian food. You might want to start with chicken satay and peanut sauce or samosas with yogurt sauce. Main dishes run the gamut from Hainan chicken and Malaysian curry crab to vegetarian selections; the dilemma is in making a choice. Tables are crowded and the atmosphere is like a school cafeteria, but that's the nature of the place.

There's a convenient branch at 440 Jaffe Rd., Causeway Bay (© **852/2573 8187;** MTR: Causeway Bay), open daily 11am to 3pm and 6 to 11:30pm.

Golden Crown Ct. (3rd floor), 68 Nathan Rd., Tsim Sha Tsui. © 852/2721 4821. Main dishes HK$54–HK$128 (US$7–US$17). AE, V. Daily 11am–3pm and 6–11:30pm. MTR: Tsim Sha Tsui.

Fat Angelo's ★ Value ITALIAN   With its checkered tablecloths, black-and-white family photographs (all hanging crooked on purpose?), wainscoting, half-size curtains, ceiling fans, and other decor reminiscent of a New World Italian restaurant from the first half of the 20th century, this chain offers good value with its hearty, American renditions of Italian food, including pastas ranging from traditional spaghetti marinara to fettuccine with salmon and main courses that include rosemary roasted chicken, grilled salmon with pesto, and eggplant Parmesan, all of which come with salad and homemade bread. All pastas and main dishes come in two sizes to accommodate the Chinese penchant for sharing, with small dishes large enough for two to share. If you're a lone diner, you can request a half portion of the small dish. In any case, the emphasis here is on quantity, not quality, though the food isn't bad. And they really pack 'em in; this place is bustling, loud, and slightly chaotic. It's sometimes hard to flag down your waitress, but they're cheerful in a we're-all-in-this-together disaster kind of way. All in all, this place is good for a fun outing with a group.

There are two branches on the other side of the harbor, in the Elizabeth House, 250 Gloucester Rd. in Causeway Bay (© **852/2574 6263;** MTR: Causeway Bay), and 49A-C Elgin St., Central (© **852/2973 6808;** MTR: Central), both open noon to midnight.

33 Ashley Rd., Tsim Sha Tsui. © **852/2730 4788.** www.fatangelos.com. Reservations recommended. Small pastas HK$88–HK$165 (US$11–US$21); small main courses HK$125–HK$188 (US$16–US$24); fixed-price lunch (Mon–Fri only) HK$38–HK$68 (US$4.95–US$8.85). AE, DC, MC, V. Daily noon–midnight. MTR: Tsim Sha Tsui.

Genki Sushi JAPANESE   Taking advantage of Hong Kong's surge in popularity of everything Japanese, this simple and always-crowded establishment offers plates of sushi, which circle around the counter via a conveyor belt. Customers, seated at the counter, simply reach out and take whatever they want. The color-coded plates vary in price and include traditional selections such as tuna and shrimp sushi, along with more unusual combinations like corn sushi, crab salad sushi, and California handrolls (seaweed rolled around rice, crab, and avocado). During lunch and dinner, there's often a line of customers waiting at the door (when I don't want to wait, I go straight inside and order takeout to bring back to my hotel). While the food is too generic to pass in Japan, this place is as good as it gets for rock-bottom sushi prices in Hong Kong.

Other branches can be found in Shop G36 on the ground floor of Chuang's London Plaza, 219 Nathan Rd., Jordan (© **852/2736 0019;** MTR: Jordan); on the ground floor of the Far East Finance Centre, 16 Harcourt Rd., Central (© **852/2865 2933;** MTR: Admiralty); Shop B222 in the second basement of Times Square, 1 Matheson St., Causeway Bay (© **852/2506 9366;** MTR: Causeway Bay); Shop P211A, Podium 2, World Trade Centre, Causeway Bay (© **852/2890 2600;** MTR: Causeway Bay); and Shop A, on the ground floor

---

⌒Value Late-Night Munchies

If you find yourself with irresistible cravings late at night (or even for a late dinner), head straight to **Nathan's** in the Hyatt Regency, 67 Nathan Rd. in Tsim Sha Tsui (© **852/2311 1234;** MTR: Tsim Sha Tsui), where you can have your fill of a sumptuous dessert buffet every night from 8 to 11pm. Thirty-some desserts, six main courses, and two soups make this a steal at only HK$118 (US$15) Sunday to Thursday and HK$138 (US$18) Friday, Saturday, and holidays.

> **Fun Fact Did You Know?**
> Many restaurants and shops have tiny red shrines, complete with incense
> and miniature deities of the Earth God or Door God, at their doors to pro-
> tect them from evil spirits, along with offerings of fruit or flowers.

of the CRE Building, 303 Hennessy Rd., Wan Chai (© **852/2802 7018;** MTR:
Wan Chai); all with the same open hours given below.

Shops G7–9, East Ocean Centre, 98 Granville Rd., Tsim Sha Tsui East. © **852/2722 6689.** www.
genkisushi.com.sg. Main dishes HK$9–HK$35 (US$1.15–US$4.55). AE, DC, MC, V. Daily 11:30am–11:30pm.
MTR: Tsim Sha Tsui.

Happy Garden Noodles & Congee Kitchen _Value_ CANTONESE   If you've
passed all those hole-in-the-wall Chinese restaurants, knowing that they're often
much cheaper than establishments catering to tourists but hesitating to enter
because no one speaks English, this is the place for you. Small, clean, bright (too
bright) lighting, and with old-fashioned booth seating, a high ceiling, and
lacquered stools, it has an English menu and specializes in noodle dishes
and _congee_ (a rice porridge traditionally eaten for breakfast or a late-night snack
and usually flavored with meat, fish, or vegetables). Approximately 40 different
kinds of _congee_ are available as well as a wide variety of noodle dishes, from
braised and stir-fried noodles to shrimp wonton noodles and noodles in soup
with barbecued pork. Although congee may not sound exciting, it's actually one
of my favorite snack foods and can be very satisfying. Located about a 4-minute
walk from the Star Ferry, this restaurant is especially good for a quick and inexpensive meal after visiting neighborhood bars.

72 Canton Rd., Tsim Sha Tsui. © **852/2377 2604.** Main dishes HK$28–HK$85 (US$3.65–US$11). No credit
cards. Daily 7am–1am. MTR: Tsim Sha Tsui.

Koh-I-Noor ✦ INDIAN   Don't let the dinginess of the Peninsula Apartments
building deter you from trying this restaurant. Located up on the first floor, it's
modern and clean, with spotless tablecloths and a pleasant pink color scheme.
What's more, service is prompt and courteous and the food is great and reasonably priced; the specialties here are North Indian tandoori and fresh seafood. It
takes its name from a renowned diamond mined in central India years ago. The
restaurant is especially proud of its king prawns, but there are also chicken,
lamb, and vegetable curries; my favorites include the samosas, crab with
coconut, and the Gosht vindaloo—a spicy mix of lamb and potatoes. There's
mashed eggplant with onions and tomatoes; _palak paneer_ (Indian cottage cheese
with spinach); garlic-flavored nan (Indian flat bread) or nan stuffed with cheese,
potatoes, or other ingredients. All of it is good and recommendable.
    There's also a branch on the other side of the harbor in the Lan Kwai Fong
nightlife district, on the first floor of the California Entertainment Building, 34
D'Aguilar St., Central (© **852/2877 9706;** MTR: Central), with the same hours.

Peninsula Apartments, 16C Mody Rd., Tsim Sha Tsui. © **852/2368 3065.** www.lankwaifong.com. Curries
HK$62–HK$150 (US$8.05–US$19); tandoori HK$70–HK$125 (US$9.10–US$16); buffet lunch (Mon–Fri only)
HK$48 (US$6.25) for vegetarian, HK$68 (US$8.85) with meat. AE, DC, MC, V. Daily 11:30am–2:30pm and
6–11:30pm. MTR: Tsim Sha Tsui.

Main Street Deli ✦✦ _Finds_ AMERICAN/SANDWICHES   Hong Kong's
first traditional New York–style deli comes as close as you can get to the real

thing—its chef trained at the 2nd Avenue Deli in the Big Apple and the authentic ingredients are flown in from New York. The tiled floor, open kitchen and deli case, strung sausages, and wood furniture add to the ambience, but the chandeliers left over from a previous restaurant seem woefully out of place. Still, serious deli lovers will find plenty to love, including latkes, matzo ball soup, salads, pizza, pasta, burgers, and a large selection of three-decker and hot deli sandwiches, including a Reuben, the restaurant's signature sandwich. This is a lifesaver for those in desperate need of comfort food. Portions are so generous that the restaurant has instituted the doggy bag, a previously unknown concept in Hong Kong. Don't forget to save room for the cheesecake.

In the Langham Hotel, 8 Peking Rd., Tsim Sha Tsui. ℂ 852/2375 1133, ext. 7883. www.langhamhotels.com. Sandwiches HK$98–HK$118 (US$13–US$15). AE, DC, MC, V. Daily 10am–11pm. MTR: Tsim Sha Tsui.

The Salisbury *Value* INTERNATIONAL One of the cheapest places for a filling meal in Tsim Sha Tsui is the YMCA's main restaurant, a bright and cheerful dining hall located on the fourth floor of the south tower. It serves both Western and Asian food, with an a la carte menu offering sandwiches, pasta, and Asian dishes. Best, however, are the lunch and dinner buffets. The lunch buffet includes a roast-beef wagon, as well as other meat dishes, soups, salads, and desserts, while the dinner buffet includes many more entrees plus unlimited soda or beer. A rare plus for seniors: They get a discount off the lunch buffet. Any group of two or more (no matter their age) get discounts off the dinner buffet. Another rarity: The entire restaurant is nonsmoking. If the prices here are too high, there's a cheaper ground-floor cafeteria, the Mall Cafe, which offers sandwiches and daily specials.

In the Salisbury YMCA, 41 Salisbury Rd., Tsim Sha Tsui. ℂ 852/2268 7818. www.ymcahk.org.hk. Lunch buffet HK$98 (US$13); Sun brunch buffet HK$140 (US$18); dinner buffet HK$218 (US$28). AE, DC, MC, V. Mon–Sat noon–2:30pm; Sun 11:30am–2:30pm; daily 6:15–9:30pm. MTR: Tsim Sha Tsui.

Spaghetti House *Kids* ITALIAN The Spaghetti House chain has a total of 23 branches throughout Hong Kong—and there will probably be more by the time you read this. They're popular with families, young Chinese couples on dates, and foreigners who have had their fill of Chinese food and crave something familiar but cheap. Spaghetti and pizza cooked American-style or with Asian ingredients are the specialties here, and the decor and atmosphere resemble those of an American pizza parlor. There are more than a half-dozen varieties of spaghetti with both Western and Asian toppings, as well as pizzas (in two sizes). Although the food is only average in quality, the quantity more than makes up for it; most orders can be taken out.

Two branches in Tsim Sha Tsui, accessible via the Tsim Sha Tsui MTR station, are located at 57 Peking Rd. (ℂ 852/2367 1683) and 38 Haiphong Rd. (ℂ 852/2376 1015). Other convenient locations include 221 Nathan Rd., Yau Ma Tei (ℂ 852/2377 2005; MTR: Jordan); 594 Nathan Rd., Mong Kok (ℂ 852/2388 4379; MTR: Mong Kok); 10 Stanley St., Central (ℂ 852/2523 1372; MTR: Central); Shop 2004 in the International Finance Centre above Hong Kong Station, Central (ℂ 852/2147 5543); 68 Hennessy Rd., Wan Chai (ℂ 852/2529 0901; MTR: Wan Chai); Shop 8, PJ Plaza, Paterson St., Causeway Bay (ℂ 852/2895 2928; MTR: Causeway Bay); and Shop P113, World Trade Centre, Causeway Bay (ℂ 852/2972 2143l; MTR: Causeway Bay). All Spaghetti Houses have the same hours.

30–34 Nathan Rd., Tsim Sha Tsui. ℂ 852/2721 6703. www.spaghettihouse.com. Individual-size pizza and pasta HK$48–HK$88 (US$6.25–US$11). AE, DC, MC, V. Daily 11am–11pm. MTR: Tsim Sha Tsui.

Woodlands _Value_ INDIAN/VEGETARIAN   The focus of this very simple dining room, looking slightly out of place on the ground floor of the Mirror Tower building in Tsim Sha Tsui East, is clearly on the food—vegetarian dishes from southern India, along with some selections from northern India. Best are the thali fixed-price meals, served on a round metal plate commonly used in India and including Indian bread, rice, and tiny portions of various dishes. Strangely, although the restaurant specializes in food from southern India, the North Indian thali is tastier than its southern counterpart. Alcoholic drinks are not served, but there are fruit juices, milk shakes, Indian teas, and _lassi_ (a yogurt shake).

Mirror Tower, 61 Mody Rd., Tsim Sha Tsui East. ℂ 852/2369 3718. Main dishes HK$35–HK$48 (US$4.55–US$6.25); fixed-price thali meals HK$55–HK$70 (US$7.15–US$9.10). AE, DC, MC, V. Daily noon–3:30pm and 6:30–11pm. MTR: Tsim Sha Tsui.

4 Central District

VERY EXPENSIVE

Mandarin Grill ★★★ _Kids_ CONTINENTAL   Decorated in dark green with details of gold, this is the Mandarin's most popular all-purpose restaurant, offering everything from breakfast and Sunday brunch to steaks and seafood. But since this is the Mandarin, it caters to a well-heeled clientele, and the proper dress is smart casual. Children under 12 years of age are not allowed with the exception of Sunday brunch (when they're accommodated with a special kids' menu and can eat for free if they're under 1m/31/4 ft. tall). U.S. beef is featured, as well as U.S. veal, Australian lamb, a wide selection of seafood, including lobster available in a variety of styles, and a whole page dedicated to vegetarian selections. Especially recommended is lobster bisque with cognac and tarragon; sautéed veal kidneys in spicy Dijon-mustard sauce served with creamed potatoes; whole Dover sole; and prime beef tenderloin with goose liver, truffle, and red-wine reduction. If you can't decide, order the mixed grill, which comes with beef, pork, veal, and lamb. The wine list is extensive, with more than 400 varieties available, and service is impeccable. The restaurant caters to a business crowd during the day, but evenings are more romantic, with live piano music.

In the Mandarin Oriental Hotel, 5 Connaught Rd., Central. ℂ 852/2522 0111, ext. 4020. www.mandarin oriental.com. Reservations required. Main courses HK$265–HK$440 (US$34–US$57). AE, DC, MC, V. Daily 7–11am; noon–3pm; and 6:30–11pm. MTR: Central.

Nicholini's ★★★ NORTHERN ITALIAN   Most of Hong Kong's Italian restaurants seem to fall into one of two categories—high-brow and sophisticated, or rustic and trattoria-like. This one is neither and yet both, combining elegance and lightheartedness in keeping with the Conrad Hotel's overall playful style. Dress is casual to smart casual (though no jeans or tennis shoes are allowed), and the dining room bathes patrons in soothing colors of celadon green, pink, aquamarine, yellow, and plum rose. If you're a fan of Murano glass, be sure to check out the collection at the front of the restaurant. The cuisine here is northern Italian, combined with inventiveness—some claim it's the best Italian restaurant in Hong Kong. Entrees range from pan-fried sea bass with caramelized vegetables in caviar sauce to veal shank ossobuco in a vegetable orange-flavored sauce served with saffron risotto. Pasta—like the favorite angel hair pasta with Maine lobster, fresh tomato, and basil—is available as either a side dish or a main course. For dessert, the Chef's Special Dessert Sampler solves the dilemma for those who want it all. The wine list, mainly Italian but also with

Where to Dine in the Central District

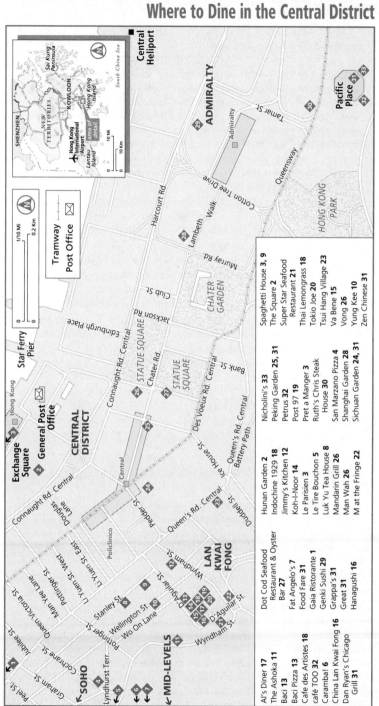

Al's Diner 17
The Ashoka 11
Baci 13
Baci Pizza 13
Cafe des Artistes 18
café TOO 32
Carambal 6
China Lan Kwai Fong 16
Dan Ryan's Chicago Grill 31

Dot Cod Seafood Restaurant & Oyster Bar 27
Fat Angelo's 7
Food Fare 31
Gaia Ristorante 1
Genki Sushi 29
Grappa's 31
Great 31
Hanagushi 16

Hunan Garden 2
Indochine 1929 18
Jimmy's Kitchen 12
Koh-I-Noor 14
Le Parisien 3
Le Tire Bouchon 5
Luk Yu Tea House 8
Mandarin Grill 26
Man Wah 26
M at the Fringe 22

Nicholini's 33
Peking Garden 25, 31
Petrus 32
Post 97 19
Pret a Manger 3
Ruth's Chris Steak House 30
San Marzano Pizza 4
Shanghai Garden 28
Sichuan Garden 24, 31

Spaghetti House 3, 9
The Square 2
Super Star Seafood Restaurant 21
Thai Lemongrass 18
Tokio Joe 20
Tsui Hang Village 23
Va Bene 15
Vong 26
Yung Kee 10
Zen Chinese 31

Kids Family-Friendly Restaurants

Al's Diner (p. 142)   This may be the perfect antidote for restless teenagers who are threatening mutiny if they don't see any "real food" soon. It's located in Central's nightlife district (which might perk your teenager's interest) and offers burgers, hot dogs, sandwiches, sundaes, ice-cream floats, and banana splits. The jukebox is a good diversion, too, but make sure you come during the day or early evening, since the house specialty, vodka jelly shots, attracts a wild crowd at night that may provide a bit more excitement than your teenager might be ready for.

Dan Ryan's Chicago Grill (p. 120)   These two restaurant/bars serve the best burgers in town, as well as huge deli sandwiches. There are plenty of other American dishes as well, and the setting looks just like home.

Mandarin Grill (p. 130)   For little ones who expect only the best, treat them to Sunday brunch at the comfortable but upscale Mandarin Grill, which boasts a children's menu filled with standby favorites. Thumbs up to the fact that children under 1m (3¼ ft.) tall eat absolutely free. During the rest of the week, however, children under 12 are not allowed.

Mövenpick Marché (p. 150)   If one of the best views of Hong Kong and inexpensive prices for self-serve international dishes don't impress your youngsters, this restaurant's children's corner surely will, with a toddler slide, toys, crayons, and other diversions. For older kids, there's a Ripley's Believe It or Not! Odditorium, Madame Tussaud's, and a motion-simulation theater in the same building on The Peak.

Spaghetti House (p. 129)   Locations all over town and low prices make this family chain a winner. There are more than a half dozen different kinds of spaghetti, as well as a wide range of pizza. Just like pizza parlors back home.

international selections, is extensive but pricey, and the service is beyond reproach. Too bad this restaurant doesn't have a view.

In the Conrad Hotel, Pacific Place, 88 Queensway Rd., Central. ℂ 852/2521 3838 ext. 8210. www.conrad hotels.com. Reservations recommended. Main courses HK$270–HK$360 (US$35–US$47); fixed-price dinner HK$538–HK$789 (US$70–US$102); fixed-price lunch HK$228–HK$338 (US$30–US$44). AE, DC, MC, V. Daily noon–3pm and 6:30–11pm. MTR: Central.

Petrus ★★★ (Finds FRENCH   Simply put, the views from this 56th-floor restaurant are breathtaking. In fact, they are probably the best of any hotel restaurant on the Hong Kong side; the only place with a better view is atop Victoria Peak. If you can bear to take your eyes off the windows, you'll find the restaurant decorated like a French castle, with the obligatory crystal chandeliers, black marble and gilded columns, statues, thick draperies, Impressionist paintings, murals gracing dome-shaped ceilings, and a pianist playing softly in the background.

The cuisine emphasizes contemporary Mediterranean/French seasonal ingredients, spiced sparingly to complement the dishes' natural aroma and flavor. The menu changes often but has included such intriguing choices as goose liver terrine with dried fruits and mixed nuts served with black radish salad and Port wine reduction; black-truffle soup with duck liver confit ravioli; roast Bresse pigeon served with baby artichoke, bacon, carrots, and mushrooms; and roast Boston lobster served with vegetables, fennel, morels, and anis star cream sauce. Probably the best way to sample the continuously new creations is with one of the fixed-price meals. As expected, the wine list—particularly Bordeaux—is among the best in Hong Kong, if not the world. With the impressive blend of great views, refined ambience, excellent cuisine, tables spaced far enough apart for intimacy, and professional staff, this restaurant is a top choice for a splurge, romantic dinner, or special celebration.

In the Island Shangri-La (56th floor), Pacific Place, Supreme Court Rd., Central. © 852/2820 8590. www. shangri-la.com. Reservations recommended. Jacket required. Main courses HK$320–HK$530 (US$42–US$69); fixed-price lunch HK$310–HK$350 (US$40–US$45); fixed-price dinner HK$800–HK$950 (US$104–US$123). AE, DC, MC, V. Mon–Sat noon–3pm; daily 6:30–11pm. MTR: Admiralty.

Vong ★★★ FRANCO-ASIAN CROSSOVER Chef Jean-Georges Vongerichten, who made a name for himself with several well-known New York establishments, set Hong Kong abuzz when he opened his much-talked-about restaurant on the 25th floor of the Mandarin Oriental Hotel in 1997. Although newcomers have since stolen the spotlight, this black-and-gold venue, which matches Petrus for its spectacular views of the harbor, still serves what may well be the best interpretation of East-meets-West Franco-Asian cuisine this side of the hemisphere, with exquisite combinations that can set taste buds dancing with excitement. All main courses are tempting—perhaps you'll choose the spiny lobster with Thai herbs, the steamed sea bass and carrot confit with cumin seed and coriander, or the chicken marinated in lemongrass with sweet rice steamed in banana leaf.

If choosing only one dish causes anguish, order the five-course Tasting Menu for HK$548 (US$71) per person, though you'll have to convince everyone else at your table to do the same, since it's available only if the entire table chooses it. At lunchtime you can save money by ordering one of the Black Plate or White Plate menus, which comes with six exquisitely prepared items for HK$268 (US$35). My lunch plate contained a crab spring roll, raw tuna and vegetables rolled in rice paper, prawn satays, lobster wrapped in daikon, curry chicken satays, and crunchy cress salad. The only complaint is that Vong is so popular and busy that its activity and noise level can be like an outdoor market, making it a good place for people-watching but not for a romantic tête-à-tête. Children younger than 12 are not allowed.

In the Mandarin Oriental Hotel (25th floor), 5 Connaught Rd., Central. © 852/2522 0111, ext. 4028. www. mandarinoriental.com. Reservations required. Main courses HK$228–HK$338 (US$30–US$44); fixed-price lunch HK$268–HK$288 (US$35–US$37). AE, DC, MC, V. Mon–Fri noon–3pm; daily 6pm–midnight. MTR: Central.

EXPENSIVE

In addition to the restaurants here, **Ruth's Chris Steak House,** reviewed in the Kowloon section above (p. 117), has a branch near Pacific Place.

Baci ★★ ITALIAN   On the second floor, above a less expensive pizzeria under the same ownership, this smart-looking restaurant with a crisp, white, minimalist interior boasts a friendly staff and authentic Italian cuisine. Ingredients are flown fresh from Italy, and the pasta is homemade. Recommended are the sautéed thin sliced veal with mushroom and Marsala-wine sauce and the pan-fried salmon with crispy potatoes and vegetables in a light mustard sauce. You can also order pizza, which comes with a crispy-thin and delicious crust. There's also a small bar, with windows that open to the madness of Lan Kwai Fong below.

1 Lan Kwai Fong (2nd floor), Central. 🕐 852/2801 5885. www.lankwaifong.com. Reservations recommended. Pizza HK$98–HK$145 (US$13–US$19); main courses HK$185–HK$248 (US$24–US$32); fixed-price lunch HK$150 (US$19). AE, DC, MC, V. Mon–Sat noon–2:30pm; Mon–Thurs 7–11pm; Fri–Sat 7–11:30pm; Sun 6:30–10:30pm. MTR: Central.

Cafe des Artistes ★★ FRENCH   This upscale restaurant is in the heart of Lan Kwai Fong yet remains aloof, removed from the surrounding madness by its subdued setting and white sheer drapes. Dining here imparts a feeling of being above it all, but the real draw is the cuisine from southern France, expertly rendered by the chef into classic culinary masterpieces. The homemade goose-liver terrine is not to be missed; other recommended dishes include the oven-roasted black Angus beef with red wine sauce, shallot confit, black pepper, thyme, rosemary, and gratin potatoes, and oven-roasted duck breast with chestnut mash, duck leg confit, and sautéed spinach. Be sure to save room for desserts like the restaurant's legendary passion fruit soufflé with fresh pulp.

California Tower (ground floor), 30–32 D'Aguilar St., Central. 🕐 852/2526 3880. www.lankwaifong.com. Main courses HK$180–HK$200 (US$23–US$26); fixed-price lunch HK$150–HK$185 (US$21–US$24); fixed-price dinner HK$395 (US$51). AE, DC, MC, V. Mon–Sat noon–2:30pm; Sun–Thurs 7–10:30pm; Fri–Sat 7–11pm. MTR: Central.

Gaia Ristorante ★ _Finds_ ITALIAN   If you can't beat 'em, join 'em. That's the way I feel about all the new construction encroaching on the quaint Western District. This restaurant, ensconced in the colossal Grand Millennium Plaza building on the border between the Central and Western districts, has won me over with what is arguably Central's best terrace, surrounded by lush trees and bushes that create the illusion of dining in a park. The contemporary interior is also inviting, with glass windows overlooking the terrace and a blindingly red bar off to one side. Of course, none of this would matter if the food didn't hold up, which it does. It's hard to resist such temptations as the scallop-stuffed ravioli with porcini mushroom and marinated pumpkin, the grilled lobster with tarragon, barley and caviar salad, or the char-grilled black angus beef with myrtle and raisin. The wine list is heavy on Italian imports.

Grand Millennium Plaza (look for the advertising screen), 181 Queen's Road Central, Central. 🕐 852/2167 8200. www.gaiaristorante.com. Reservations necessary. Pizza and pasta HK$138–HK$198 (US$18–US$26); main dishes HK$238–HK$328 (US$31–US$43); fixed-price lunch HK$198 (US$26). AE, DC, MC, V. Daily noon–3pm and 6pm–midnight. MTR: Sheung Wan.

Hunan Garden ★★ _Finds_ HUNANESE   Although the chile-rich cuisine of Hunan province is quite popular in Taiwan, this has long been one of the few Hunan restaurants in Hong Kong. It's puzzling, because Hunanese food is very spicy, and one would think that with the booming popularity of Thai and Sichuan food in the SAR Hunanese food would eventually catch on. In any case, this restaurant does a thriving business, especially for lunch due to its location next to Hong Kong Station (terminus of the Airport Express Line) and ifc mall. It's a great restaurant, both in decor and food and even has live Chinese music nightly. It's decorated in hot pink and green, and the motif is clearly lotus (Hunan province is famous for its lotus). The dining area is spacious, with tables spread luxuriously far apart. But the real treat is the food. The chefs were trained in both Hunan province and Taiwan and they don't tone down the spiciness of their authentic dishes. Start your meal with one of the soups like the Hunan minced-chicken soup, a clear soup base with ginger and mousse of chicken, served piping hot in a length of bamboo. If you like hot-and-spicy foods, you'll love the braised bean curd with shredded meat and chili, developed by one of Hunan province's most famous chefs. Other recommended dishes include the honey-glazed Hunan ham served in pancakes and fried chicken with chile and garlic. As a special treat, try one of the Hunanese wines.

The Forum (3rd floor), Exchange Square, Central. © 852/2868 2880. Reservations recommended, especially for lunch. Main dishes HK$72–HK$158 (US$9.35–US$21). AE, DC, MC, V. Daily 11:30am–3pm and 5:30–11:30pm. MTR: Central.

M at the Fringe ★★★ *Finds* CONTINENTAL   For a memorable, unusual dining experience, head for this delightful restaurant, located on the upper floor of a former dairy farm building, which is also home of the Fringe Club's theater (p. 225). This has long been a local favorite, with a meal here a treat in more ways than one—the artsy furnishings are a feast for the eyes, while the food, influenced by cuisines along the Mediterranean, is to die for. The handwritten menu changes every 3 months but is always creative and always includes lamb and vegetarian selections. An example of the former is a salt-encased, slowly baked leg of lamb with celery root and potato gratin, French beans, and baby carrots. For dessert, don't pass up the Pavlova.

2 Lower Albert Rd., Central. © 852/2877 4000. www.m-atthefringe.com. Reservations strongly recommended. Main courses HK$208–HK$228 (US$27–US$30). AE, MC, V. Mon–Fri noon–2:30pm; Mon–Sat 7–10:30pm; Sun 7–10pm. MTR: Central.

Man Wah ★★★ CANTONESE   Man Wah has long been one of the most elegant and sophisticated Chinese restaurants in Hong Kong. Traditionally decorated with local rosewood, wood carvings, lanterns that resemble birdcages, and painted silk portraits of Mandarins; and featuring gold tablecloths, exquisite Naruma bone chinaware, 24-carat gold cutlery, fresh flowers, and candles on every table—it's about as romantic as you can get. Unfortunately, although it's located on the 25th floor, only a few tables offer good views of the harbor, so be sure to request a harborside seat when making your reservation. And with a seating capacity of only 62, reservations here are a must.

Although the Cantonese menu changes seasonally, signature dishes usually available include the steamed crab claws with ginger and Chinese rice wine, sautéed filet of sole with green vegetables in a black-bean sauce (complete with a wonderful carving of a dragon fashioned from carrots), anything with shark's fin, and beggar's chicken (order in advance) with its dramatic presentation and costing HK$460 (US$60). Also, if available, the spicy-and-sour soup is divine—piquant and full of noodles, tofu, and mushrooms. Note that the fixed-price menu requires a minimum of two persons and that children under 6 are not allowed except for lunch on weekends.

In the Mandarin Oriental Hotel, 5 Connaught Rd., Central. © 852/2522 0111, ext. 4025. www.mandarin oriental.com. Reservations required. Main dishes HK$98–HK$338 (US$13–US$44); fixed-price meal HK$488–HK$688 (US$63–US$89). AE, DC, MC, V. Daily noon–3pm and 6:30–11pm. MTR: Central.

Va Bene ★★★ ITALIAN   This stylish, upscale Italian restaurant, in the middle of Central's Lan Kwai Fong nightlife district, strives for the simplicity of a rustic Italian villa with its sponged, mustard-hued walls, a sky-blue ceiling, and rows of terra-cotta pots serving as the main decorations. With consistently creative and excellent, mostly northern Italian food, it's extremely popular with Hong Kong's well-heeled expat community, making it a lively and boisterous—though cramped—spot for a meal. Perhaps you'll want to start with wafer-thin carpaccio, followed by homemade beetroot fettuccini with scallops, black truffle, and asparagus. As a main course, you can choose from a number of veal, beef, and seafood offerings, including pan-fried John Dory (a white Australian fish) served with a tomato-potato tart in an olive and capers butter sauce, or roasted chicken breast with spinach and veal mousse on a bed of creamy potatoes. Good Italian wines, great desserts, and attentive service round out the meal; expect to spend about HK$600 (US$78) per person, without wine.

58–62 D'Aguilar St., Central. ℂ 852/2845 5577. www.lankwaifong.com. Reservations required. Pasta HK$188–HK$228 (US$24–US$30); main courses HK$198–HK$288 (US$26–US$37); fixed-price lunch HK$140 (US$18). AE, DC, MC, V. Mon–Fri noon–2:30pm; Sun–Thurs 7–11pm; Fri–Sat 7pm–midnight. MTR: Central.

MODERATE

Several moderately priced restaurants already covered in the Tsim Sha Tsui section have branches in Central: **Dan Ryan's Chicago Grill** (p. 120), located in Pacific Place and offering American classics; **Peking Garden** (p. 123), with two locations in Central and serving food from Peking; **Tsui Hang Village Restaurant** (p. 125), serving Cantonese fare; and **Super Star Seafood Restaurant** (p. 125), known for its Cantonese seafood and dim sum.

café TOO ✦✦✦ *Finds* INTERNATIONAL   Leave it to the Island Shangri-La to take a common dining concept and turn it into a feasting extravaganza. Quite simply, this is the most interesting buffet I've seen in Hong Kong. Light and airy with windows overlooking the lush greenery of Hong Kong Park, contemporary decor, and a well-trained staff dressed in hip traditional Chinese jackets and vests, this restaurant features open kitchens and seven "stations" of food presentations spread throughout the room, thereby dispelling the assembly-line atmosphere of most buffets and giving it a theatrical touch. Browse the appetizer-and-salad table, a cold seafood counter with sushi, fresh oysters, crab, and other delights, a Chinese section with dim sum and main courses, Western hot entrees, pastas that are prepared to order and run the gamut from Chinese to Italian, and Asian dishes from Thai curries to Indian tandoori. But don't fill up, because the dessert table is the crowning glory. The wine list, too, is very impressive. Come here after shopping in Pacific Place or visiting the park's Museum of Tea Ware.

In the Island Shangri-La Hotel, Pacific Place, Supreme Court Rd., Central. ℂ **852/2820 8571**, ext. 8571. www.shangri-la.com. Reservations recommended. Lunch buffet HK$235 (US$31) Mon–Sat, HK$275 (US$36) Sun and holidays; dinner buffet HK$325 (US$42) Mon–Thurs, HK$355 (US$46) Fri–Sun and holidays. AE, DC, MC, V. Mon–Fri noon–2:30pm and 6:30–9:30pm; Sat–Sun noon–3pm and 7–10pm. MTR: Admiralty.

China Lan Kwai Fong ✦✦ CANTONESE   This retro-style restaurant is trendy Lan Kwai Fong's classiest Chinese restaurant, decorated with antiques, hanging lanterns, ceiling fans, and giant bird cages. While the emphasis is on Cantonese food, it offers specialties from other regions as well, including Shanghai, Beijing, and Sichuan. Prawns, for example, are available in six variations, from stir-fried with chiles (Sichuan) to sautéed with black beans and green pepper (Cantonese). Garoupa comes fresh from the restaurant's own tanks. Peking duck (costing HK$380/US$49) is also available.

17–22 Lan Kwai Fong, Central. ℂ **852/2536 0968**. www.lankwaifong.com. Reservations recommended. Main dishes HK$88–HK$138 (US$11–US$18); fixed-price lunch HK$108 (US$14). AE, DC, MC, V. Daily noon–3pm and 6pm–midnight. MTR: Central.

Dot Cod Seafood Restaurant & Oyster Bar SEAFOOD   The Hong Kong Cricket Club owns this basement restaurant (HKCC members get a 30% discount), its location chosen for nostalgic reasons: until the 1960s the club practiced in nearby Chater Garden. Decorated in a nautical theme and popular for power breakfasts and lunches, it takes its name from the popular choice of cod in its menu but is also a play on the dot.com era. You might start with shucked oysters or the prawn cocktail, followed by such signature dishes as the cod fish and chips or smoked haddock. Check the website for monthly specials like the "B.Y.O. Bottle" Monday and Tuesday evenings, when corkage fees are waived for bottles of wine you bring to the restaurant.

Prince's Building, 10 Chater (entrance on Statue Square), Central. ℂ **852/2810 6988**. www.dotcod.com. Reservations recommended. Main dishes HK$158–HK$278 (US$21–US$36). AE, DC, MC, V. Daily 7:30am–midnight. MTR: Central.

Grappa's ✿ ITALIAN   If you like to eat pizza or pasta to the accompaniment of noise, commotion, and lots of people parading past, this is the place for you. Grappa's is decorated like a trattoria, but with big glass windows overlooking the shops of Pacific Place—you can't escape the fact that this place is not a sidewalk cafe but is in a mall. The open kitchen, while providing some diversion, adds to the noise. Still, this is certainly the best place for Italian food anywhere in the area, even though it is strictly standard fare. Homemade bread, served with olive oil and fresh Parmesan, is brought swiftly to every table (and replenished if desired); it is so delicious that you may be tempted to eat your fill before the meal arrives, especially if the place is full and service is slow. The salads are good here, as are the dozen or so authentic Italian pizzas and the even larger selection of homemade pastas. The entrees lean toward the tried and true, from veal-shank stew in Barolo red-wine sauce to roasted lamb chops with rosemary. The Italian wines here are affordable.

Pacific Place, 88 Queensway, Central. ℂ **852/2868 0086**. Reservations recommended. Pizza and pasta HK$90–HK$150 (US$12–US$19); main courses HK$118–HK$280 (US$15–US$36); fixed-price lunch HK$155 (US$20). AE, DC, MC, V. Daily 11:30am–10:30pm (last order). MTR: Admiralty.

Hanagushi ✿ JAPANESE   The only thing missing at this traditionally styled Japanese restaurant, with its gleaming woods, tansu chests, woodblock prints, and waitresses decked out in provincial Japanese clothing, are tatami mats. Unfortunately, the tables are so closely packed here that you'd think you were in a Tokyo subway. The restaurant specializes in yakitori, morsels of food barbecued on a stick, with 46 different kinds available and costing HK$20 to HK$95 (US$2.60–US$12) for a pair. My favorites include asparagus, chicken meatballs, quail eggs, green pepper with minced chicken, and gingko nuts. You can also order fixed-price meals of yakitori, including a vegetarian version and yakitori meals that also include tempura or sashimi. Grilled fish, *udon* noodles, and other typical Japanese fare are also available, along with a dozen different kinds of sake to wash it all down.

17–22 Lan Kwai Fong (1st floor), Central. ℂ **852/2521 0868**. www.lankwaifong.com. Yakitori, tempura, sashimi, and vegetarian yakitori fixed-price meals HK$200–HK$480 (US$26–US$62). AE, DC, MC, V. Mon–Sat 11:30am–3pm and 6–11:30pm. MTR: Central.

Indochine 1929 ✿✿ VIETNAMESE   Designed to resemble a breezy, 1920s veranda from Vietnam's French colonial era, this Lan Kwai Fong eatery serves delicious Indochinese cuisine to a consciously trendy crowd. Start with the signature spring rolls stuffed with shrimp, pork, and herbs or the hot-and-sour fish soup. Other specialties are the fish prepared Hanoi style, with dill, turmeric, rice vermicelli, and peanuts; the salt-and-pepper soft-shell crabs; the beef tenderloin with tomato; and grilled eggplant with scallion oil and soy sauce. If you've never had Vietnamese food, this restaurant with a knowledgeable staff and laid-back atmosphere should make you an instant convert.

California Tower (2nd floor), 30–32 D'Aguilar, Central. © 852/2869 7399. www.lankwaifong.com. Reservations recommended. Main dishes HK$125–HK$260 (US$16–US$34); fixed-price lunch HK$85–HK$148 (US$11–US$19). AE, DC, MC, V. Mon–Sat noon–2:30pm; daily 6:30–11pm. MTR: Central.

Jimmy's Kitchen ★★ CONTINENTAL   This restaurant opened in 1928, a replica of a similar American-owned restaurant in Shanghai. Now one of Hong Kong's oldest Western restaurants, Jimmy's Kitchen has had several homes before moving in the 1960s to its present site. Some of its waiters are descendants from the original staff. The atmosphere reminds me of an American steakhouse, with white tablecloths, dark-wood paneling, and elevator music, but it's a favorite with older foreigners living in Hong Kong and serves dependably good, unpretentious European food. The daily specials are written on a blackboard, and an extensive a la carte menu offers salads and soups, steaks, chicken, Indian curries, and a seafood selection that includes sole, scallops, and the local garoupa. It's also a good place for corned beef and cabbage, beef Stroganoff, and hearty German fare, including Wiener schnitzel (breaded veal), pig's knuckle, and Knockwurst sausage.

There's another branch at 29 Ashley Rd., Tsim Sha Tsui (© **852/2376 0327**), open daily from noon to 11pm.

1 Wyndham St., Central. © 852/2526 5293. www.jimmys.com. Main courses HK$116–HK$268 (US$15–US$35); fixed-price lunch HK$88–HK$158 (US$11–US$21). AE, DC, MC, V. Daily 11:30am–3pm and 6–11pm. MTR: Central.

Le Parisien *Value* FRENCH   Outside of hotels, this is the only French restaurant with a view of the harbor, and its convenient location in the new ifc mall next to Hong Kong Station makes it a popular venue for well-attired business professionals. The friendly staff delivers fixed-price lunches that provide a choice of main dish and accompaniments. Dinner entrees are limited to seven or eight choices, which can include the likes of roasted cod scented with coffee beans and served with couscous together with fresh coriander and asparagus; roasted spring chicken; or pan-fried Dover sole. Or, with views of ferries arriving and departing from their piers, this is also a dreamy place for afternoon tea, available from 3 to 5pm daily, or for a drink at the small bar (happy hour is from 5–8pm daily).

Ifc mall, Shop 2076 (Level 2), Central. © 852/2805 5293. Reservations recommended. Main courses HK$175–HK$230 (US$13–US$22); fixed-price lunch HK$140–HK$165 (US$18–US$21). AE, DC, MC, V. Mon–Fri 11:30am–2:30pm; Sat 11:30am–3pm; daily 6–11pm. MTR: Central.

Le Tire Bouchon ★★ *Finds* FRENCH   This dark, cozy restaurant near the Central/Mid-Levels Escalator was first established in 1986 and claims to be Hong Kong's oldest independent restaurant with a French chef. It sports a Parisian, casual atmosphere and serves classic French food heavy on the sauces. You might wish to start with escargots with garlic and parsley butter, moving on to beef filet in port wine and shallot sauce, fresh duck liver, or steak with black peppercorn sauce. Fatten up even more on any of the sumptuous desserts, and indulge in one of the 190-some bottles of French wines from the restaurant's climatically controlled cellar. You probably wouldn't want to eat like this every day, but you certainly won't regret it while you're here.

48 Graham St., Central. © 852/2523 5459. www.hkdining.com. Reservations recommended. Main courses HK$155–HK$210 (US$20–US$27); fixed-price lunch HK$178–HK$198 (US$23–US$26). AE, DC, MC, V. Mon–Sat noon–2:30pm and 6:30–10:30pm. MTR: Central.

Luk Yu Tea House ★★★ CANTONESE   Luk Yu, first opened in 1933, is the most famous teahouse remaining in Hong Kong. In fact, unless you have a time machine, you can't get any closer to old Hong Kong than this wonderful Art Deco–era Cantonese restaurant, with its ceiling fans, spittoons, individual wooden booths for couples, marble tabletops, wood paneling, and stained-glass windows. It's also one of the best places to try a few Chinese teas, including *bo lai* (a fermented black tea, which is the most common tea in Hong Kong; also spelled bo lay), jasmine, *lung ching* (a green tea), and *sui sin* (narcissus or daffodil).

But Luk Yu is most famous for its dim sum, served from 7am to 5:30pm. The problem for foreigners, however, is that the place is always packed with regulars who have their own special places to sit, and the staff is sometimes surly to new-comers. In addition, if you come after 11am, dim sum is no longer served by trolley but from an English menu with pictures but no prices, which could end up being quite expensive unless you ask before ordering. If you want to come during the day (certainly when Luk Yu is most colorful), try to bring along a Chinese friend. Otherwise, consider coming for dinner when it's not nearly so hectic and there's an English menu listing more than 200 items, including all the Cantonese favorites, though you'll be surrounded mostly by tourists.

24–26 Stanley St., Central. ✆ 852/2523 5464. Main dishes HK$100–HK$220 (US$13–US$29); dim sum HK$25–HK$55 (US$3.25–US$7.15). MC, V. Daily 7am–10pm. MTR: Central.

Post 97 ★ *Value* CONTINENTAL   This is one of the old-timers in Lan Kwai Fong, opened in 1982 (its name is a cheeky reference to the handover), but it's every bit as popular as it was before all the surrounding competition moved in. That proves it must be doing something right, which it is—down-to-earth good food, reasonable prices, cheerful staff, and a comfortable, laid-back atmosphere where diners feel at home. Catering to area businesspeople during the day and to night revelers in the evening, it offers an all-day menu that includes breakfast items like eggs Benedict (free coffee refills until 11:30am), salads, and lighter fare, adding more entrees for dinner such as beef tenderloin, Moroccan spiced spring chicken, and mixed seafood grill. Fixed-price meals are an especially good deal, allowing you to choose from the regular menu.

9 Lan Kwai Fong, Central. ✆ 852/2186 1817. www.lankwaifong.com. Main dishes HK$155–HK$170 (US$20–US$22); fixed-price lunch HK$140–HK$160 (US$18–US$21); fixed-price dinner HK$220–HK$250 (US$29–US$32). AE, DC, MC, V. Sun–Thurs 9:30am–1am; Fri–Sat 9:30am–3am. MTR: Central.

Shanghai Garden SHANGHAINESE   This upscale restaurant (part of the Maxim's group of restaurants) does a good job in presentation and cuisine. Since Shanghai does not have its own cuisine, the dishes served here are from Peking, Nanking, Sichuan, Hangchow, and Wuxi, as well as a few from Shanghai. The menu is extensive, including Chinese spinach and fish puff soup or shark's-fin soup, such cold dishes as crispy shredded eel or fried spicy fish, and such main courses as sautéed prawns, beggar's chicken (which costs HK$250/US$32 and must be ordered in advance), sautéed beef with spring onion, braised pig with vegetables, fried noodles Shanghai-style, and Peking duck (HK$250/US$32). This place, pleasantly and soothingly decorated, does a roaring business, especially for lunch.

Hutchinson House (1st floor), Murray Rd., Central. ✆ 852/2524 8181. Reservations recommended. Main dishes HK$68–HK$150 (US$8.85–US$19). AE, DC, MC, V. Daily 11:30am–3pm and 5:30–11pm. MTR: Central.

Sichuan Garden ★ SICHUAN   Another Maxim's restaurant, the Sichuan Garden is in the chic Landmark Building. The atmosphere is bright, spotless, and elegantly simple, the food excellent, and the service attentive. It's quite popular and almost always crowded, especially at lunch. The hot-and-spicy dishes are clearly marked on the 80-item menu to help the uninitiated, though those who appreciate fiery food will find that dishes here are only mildly hot. Recommended are the hot-and-sour soup, fried prawns in chili sauce, shredded pork in hot garlic sauce, bean curd with minced beef in a pungent sauce, smoked duck, and pigeon smoked in camphor wood and tea leaves. I ordered the pigeon and found it quite good, but I was not prepared to have the head brought out as well.

There's another Sichuan Garden in the Pacific Place mall at Shop 004, 88 Queensway, Central (© **852/2845 8433;** MTR: Admiralty), open Monday to Saturday from 11:30am to 3pm and 5:30 to 11:30pm, and Sunday from 11am to 3pm and 5:30 to 11:30pm.

Gloucester Tower (3rd floor), Landmark Building, Des Voeux Rd., Central. © **852/2521 4433.** Reservations recommended. Main dishes HK$78–HK$160 (US$10–US$21). AE, DC, MC, V. Daily 11:30am–3pm and 5:30–11pm. MTR: Central.

The Square 😾😾 CANTONESE   Opened in 2000 to capture some of the increased traffic in this area due to Hong Kong Station next door, this smartly decorated restaurant features flowers on each table, cabinets filled with Chinese antiques, and, from a few lucky tables in the smoking section, a view of the Star Ferry as it comes and goes from the Central pier. On weekday evenings, a trio performs live music of popular tunes. The menu includes both traditional dishes and original creations. Recommended are the roasted duck, homemade crispy chicken, minced pigeon with lettuce leaves, barbecued pork in honey sauce, and Peking duck (HK$300/US$39). Dim sum is also available for lunch on weekends and holidays, with only a limited number served on weekdays.

Exchange Square II, Central. © **852/2525 1163.** Reservations required for lunch, recommended for dinner. Main dishes HK$80–HK$168 (US$10–US$22); fixed-price lunch HK$198–HK$268 (US$26–US$35). AE, DC, MC, V. Daily 11am–3pm and 6–11pm. MTR: Central.

Thai Lemongrass 😾😾 THAI   Rattan furniture, fake banana trees, and calm statues of Buddha set the mood in this upscale Thai restaurant in Lan Kwai Fong. The menu, drawing from regional cuisines from throughout Thailand and prepared by Thai chefs, includes such favorites as soft-shell crab with chili and garlic on fried basil leaves; chili crabs; and roast duck in red curry with grapes and aubergine. Unlike most Thai restaurants in Hong Kong, which often serve a watered-down version of Thai food, this one serves the real thing.

30–32 D'Aguilar St., Central. © **852/2905 1688.** www.lankwaifong.com. Main dishes HK$110–HK$215 (US$14–US$28); fixed-price lunch HK$98 (US$13). AE, DC, MC, V. Mon–Sat noon–2:30pm; Mon–Thurs 6:30–11pm; Fri–Sat 6:30–11:30pm; Sun and holidays 6–10:30pm. MTR: Central.

Tokio Joe 😾 JAPANESE   As its quirky name suggests, this is a hip sushi bar catering to Lan Kwai Fong's youthful nighttime revelers. Dimly lit even for lunch, it offers sushi (raw seafood on vinegared rice) and sashimi (raw seafood) a la carte, as well as combination platters. A platter of assorted sashimi large enough for two people to share as an appetizer costs HK$490 (US$64); sushi combinations run from HK$150 to HK$360 (US$20–US$47). Unique, however, are the California-style roll creations, like the deep-fried soft-shell crab with avocado, cucumber, crab roe, and mayonnaise, or the roll with crabmeat, asparagus, sliced fish, mushroom, and egg. Probably the best deal is one of the set lunches, featuring sashimi, tempura, or a box lunch. As the menu states, this restaurant has a "slightly irreverent, innovative, and casual approach to the Japanese culinary experience." Luckily, it succeeds.

16 Lan Kwai Fong, Central. © 852/2525 1889. www.lankwaifong.com. Sushi a la carte HK$40–HK$65 (US$5.20–US$8.45); fixed-price lunch HK$110–HK$190 (US$14–US$25). AE, DC, MC, V. Mon–Sat noon–2:30pm; daily 6:30–11pm. MTR: Central.

Yung Kee ★★ CANTONESE   Popular for decades, Yung Kee started out in 1942 as a small shop selling roast goose, which did so well that it soon expanded into a very successful Cantonese enterprise. Through the years, it has won numerous food awards and is the only restaurant in Hong Kong ever to be included in *Fortune* magazine's top 15 restaurants of the world (although, it must be added, the award was in 1968). Its specialty is still roast goose with plum sauce, cooked to perfection with tender meat on the inside and crispy skin on the outside and available only for dinner (A half bird, enough for 5 or 6 people, costs HK$160/US$21; note that goose is pulled from the menu any time there's an avian flu scare). Other specialties include roasted suckling pig or duck, cold steamed chicken, barbecued pork, bean curd combined with prawns, sautéed filet of garoupa, any of the fresh seafood, and thousand-year-old eggs. Dining is on one of the upper three floors, but if all you want is a bowl of *congee* or takeout, join the office workers who pour in for a quick meal on the informal ground floor. This place is very Chinese, and unless you order the roast goose, you can dine here for as little as HK$300 (US$39) per person.

32–40 Wellington St., Central. © 852/2522 1624. www.lankwaifong.com. Main dishes HK$68–HK$180 (US$8.85–US$23). AE, DC, MC, V. Daily 11am–11:30pm. MTR: Central.

Zen Chinese ★★ CANTONESE   Both its name and its appearance leave no doubt that this is no ordinary Cantonese restaurant. Indeed, it became an instant trendsetter when it opened in 1989, eschewing the traditional flashy decor favored by most Chinese restaurants in favor of an austere Zen Buddhist style, with a concrete ceiling, double-layered white tablecloths, fresh flowers on each table, and an open dining hall that allowed customers to see and be seen. To offset the simplicity and starkness of the room, a succession of large glass bowls running the length of the restaurant are suspended from the ceiling, creating a never-ending cascade as water trickles from one red bowl to the next; some think the arrangement looks like a dragon.

As for the food, there is a wide variety of Cantonese specialties that border on the nouvelle. Try the shark's-fin soup with minced chicken, sautéed prawns with dried chili and walnuts, or sautéed crab in an earthen pot. Unlike those of most Chinese restaurants, the wine list is rather extensive, though alcohol will greatly add to your bill. With most dishes averaging HK$90 to HK$130 (US$12–US$17), you can easily dine here for less than HK$400 (US$52) if you abstain. For lunch, you can eat even more cheaply, with dim sum available for HK$30 to HK$55 (US$3.90–US$7.15) a plate.

Shop 001, Pacific Place, 88 Queensway, Central. © 852/2845 4555. Reservations recommended. Main dishes HK$90–HK$180 (US$10–US$23). AE, DC, MC, V. Mon–Fri 11:30am–3pm; Sat 11:30am–5pm; Sun 10:30am–5pm; daily 5:30–11pm. MTR: Admiralty.

INEXPENSIVE

Several inexpensive restaurants reviewed in the previous Tsim Sha Tsui section have branches in Central: **Fat Angelo's** (p. 126) is renowned for its massive portions of American-style Italian food; **Genki Sushi** (p. 127) offers conveyor-belt sushi at low prices; **Koh-I-Noor** (p. 128) is recommended for Indian curries; and **Spaghetti House** (p. 129) is a popular family restaurant.

In addition, many restaurants in the moderate category above offer lunches that even the budget-conscious can afford. Be sure, too, to check the section on "Dim Sum," later in this chapter.

Finally, another good place for a casual, inexpensive meal is the **Food Fare** food court in Pacific Place, 88 Queensway, in Central (take the MTR to Admiralty), where various counters offer Chinese, Thai, Korean, and Japanese food, as well as sandwiches and pasta, daily from 7:30am to 10pm. Also in Pacific Place is **Great,** a gourmet grocery store in the basement of Seibu department store, with counters selling noodles, pizza, burgers, and Asian food. It's open Sunday to Friday 10am to 10pm and Saturday 9am to 10pm. You can dine at both places for around HK$100 (US$13).

Al's Diner *(Kids)* AMERICAN   This is one of the cheapest places for a late-night meal if you're carousing in Central's nightlife district around Lan Kwai Fong. Although it may not win any culinary awards, this informal diner, decorated in 1950s Americana style, definitely hits the spot with burgers, hot dogs, sandwiches, chili, meatloaf, macaroni and cheese, milk shakes, ice-cream floats, banana splits, and breakfast served anytime. With food like this, it's a good, inexpensive bet if you have children in tow. Be aware, however, that this place really packs 'em in during the late hours, when the place pulsates with a DJ, people eating jello shots (jello laced with vodka), and revelers dancing on the table weekend nights.

39 D'Aguilar St., Central. (C) 852/2869 1869. www.lankwaifong.com. Main courses HK$75–HK$158 (US$9.75–US$21). AE, DC, MC, V. Mon–Sat 11:30am–1am, Sun 11:30am–midnight. MTR: Central.

The Ashoka *(Value)* INDIAN   Within walking distance of Central up on winding Wyndham Street, The Ashoka is just one of several Indian restaurants in the area but is among the best known and most popular. Opened in 1973, it claims to be the oldest Indian restaurant on Hong Kong Island. It's extremely tiny and crowded (only 60 seats), so be prepared to sit practically in your neighbor's lap. It's worth it, since the food, mainly northern Indian, is great, the service is enthusiastic, and the prices are even better, with ridiculously cheap fixed-price meals—there are two menus available, a vegetarian and a tandoori, available daily for both lunch and dinner. If you order a la carte, you will find such house specialties as fish or chicken *tikka* (marinated in yogurt and then baked), chicken green masala (chicken served with green chili and tomatoes in a spicy green sauce), and creative vegetarian selections.

57–59 Wyndham St., Central. (C) 852/2524 9623 or 852/2525 5719. www.lankwaifong.com. Main dishes HK$68–HK$76 (US$8.85–US$9.85); fixed-price lunch HK$70 (US$9.10); fixed-price dinner HK$108 (US$14). AE, DC, MC, V. Daily noon–2:30pm and 6–10:30pm. MTR: Central.

Baci Pizza *(*★*)* ITALIAN   This tiny, casual, welcoming pizzeria offers good durum or homemade pasta and various kinds of wafer-thin pizza, including a "four seasons" pizza with cheese, mushrooms, black olives, ham, and artichokes, and a pizza with four cheeses—Gorgonzola, Parmesan, mozzarella, and fontina.

1 Lan Kwai Fong (1st floor), Central. (C) 852/2840 0153. www.lankwaifong.com. Pizzas and pastas HK$90–HK$185 (US$12–US$24). AE, DC, MC, V. Mon–Sat noon–2:30pm; Mon–Thurs 7–11pm; Fri–Sat 7–11:30pm. MTR: Central.

¡Caramba! MEXICAN   Located in the heart of Hong Kong's popular SoHo dining-and-nightlife district and easily accessible via the Mid-Levels escalator, this very narrow Mexican restaurant opened in 1997 as one of the first on the street. Now there are many other ethnic restaurants here, including those serving Cuban, Greek, Italian, and French cuisine. ¡Caramba! offers hearty dishes of tacos, burritos, enchiladas, chimichangas, fajitas, and fresh fish of the day, all served with side dishes of black beans and rice. Of all the Mexican restaurants in Hong Kong, this is probably the best. Tables are too close together for intimate discussions, but after a few margaritas, who cares? On weekends and holidays, brunch is offered until 6pm for HK$99 (US$13), including one drink. *¡Ay caramba!*

26–30 Elgin St., Central. © 852/2530 9963. www.caramba.com.hk. Reservations recommended. Platters with side dishes HK$110–HK$148 (US$14–US$19); Mon–Fri lunch buffet HK$68 (US$8.85). AE, DC, MC, V. Daily noon–midnight. MTR: Central.

Pret A Manger SANDWICHES   Located in the ifc mall at Hong Kong Station, this London import has met with resounding success, providing ready-made salads, juices, cakes, wraps, and sandwiches to busy office workers. All food is made fresh daily without the use of chemicals, additives, and preservatives. What doesn't sell is given away at the end of the day to charities. Sandwiches include familiars like BLTs and clubs, as well as more exotic offerings like Thai chicken and tandoori fish. Although it's mainly for takeout, there are a few tables for dining in. Other branches are located in the AIA Plaza, 18 Hysan Ave., Causeway Bay (© **852/2808 4402;** MTR: Causeway Bay); in the Central MTR Station (© **852/2537 9230**); and in Shop 2122, Harbour City, Tsim Sha Tsui (© **852/2375 0422**).

Shop 1003B, Level 1, ifc mall, 1 Harbour View St., Central. © 852/2295 0405. www.pret.com. Sandwiches HK$18–HK$36 (US$2.35–US$4.70). No credit cards. Mon–Fri 7:30am–7pm; Sat 8am–6:30pm; Sun 10am–6:30pm. MTR: Central.

San Marzano Pizza PIZZA   This glass-walled eatery, on a busy intersection where Lynhurst Terrace, Cochrane, and Gage streets all converge (and in the shadow of the Mid-Levels escalator), is a noisy place for a meal, mainly because there's nothing to break up the acoustics. However, it does diners a favor by devoting the ground floor to nonsmokers and the upper floor to indulgers. The pizza is great, ranging the ordinary (such as the American Pizza with pepperoni, mozzarella, and tomato) to the unusual (like the Peking Duck Pizza with duck, hoisin sauce, chili, spring onion, and mozzarella).

21 Lynhurst Terrace, Central © 852/2850 7898. www.pizzaexpress.com.hk. Pizza HK$78–HK$99 (US$10–US$13). AE, MC, V. Daily noon–midnight. MTR: Central.

5 Causeway Bay & Wan Chai
VERY EXPENSIVE

Grissini ✦✦✦ ITALIAN   This stylish, airy Italian restaurant echoes the palatial setting of the Grand Hyatt Hotel, with a tall ceiling, parquet floors, slick black furniture, and ceiling-to-floor windows offering a spectacular view of the harbor—day and night. Dining is on two levels, giving everyone a ringside seat. The changing menu, which offers some of the best Northern Italian fare in town, always includes the *antipasto misto*, a selection of appetizers. If you're really hungry, you might want to follow it with one of the pasta or risotto dishes, such as the pheasant ravioli with vegetable sauce or the marjoram risotto with scallops and pork cheeks. Main dishes have included grilled lobster with bell peppers, capers, garlic, and basil, and baked duck breast with chestnuts, foie gras, and blueberry sauce. At lunch there is lighter fare and more choices of pasta and risotto, but whether for lunch or dinner, you can't go wrong dining here.

In the Grand Hyatt Hong Kong Hotel, 1 Harbour Rd., Wan Chai. ☎ **852/2588 1234**, ext. 7313. www.hong kong.grand.hyatt.com. Reservations recommended. Main courses HK$280–HK$380 (US$36–US$49); fixed-price dinner HK$650 (US$84); fixed-price lunch (Mon–Fri only) HK$210–HK$275 (US$27–US$36); Sun brunch HK$350 (US$45). AE, DC, MC, V. Daily noon–2:30pm and 7–11pm. MTR: Wan Chai.

One Harbour Road ✿✿ CANTONESE   For elegant Chinese dining in Wan Chai, head to the lobby of the Grand Hyatt Hotel, where a glass bubble elevator will deliver you directly to this eighth-floor restaurant. Designed to resemble the terrace of an elegant 1930s taipan mansion, it's bright and airy, with split-level dining offering views of the harbor. A profusion of plants, a large lotus pond, and the sound of running water give the illusion of outdoor dining; tables spread far apart provide privacy. The extensive Cantonese menu, adapted to Western tastes but wonderful just the same, offers the usual shark's-fin specialties, abalone, bird's nest, Peking duck (order in advance), beggar's chicken (order in advance), and roast goose (which costs substantially more than the prices given below). Specialties include wok-fried scallops with summer squash and fungus, casserole of beef brisket in curry sauce, and wok-fried shredded beef with mushroom in chili sauce. There are also fixed-price lunch and dinner menus, which, unfortunately for lone diners, require a minimum order for two people.

In the Grand Hyatt Hong Kong Hotel, 1 Harbour Rd., Wan Chai. ☎ **852/2588 1234**, ext. 7338. www.hong kong.grand.hyatt.com. Reservations recommended. Main dishes HK$145–HK$250 (US$19–US$32); fixed-price dinner HK$630 (US$82); fixed-price lunch HK$300–HK$470 (US$39–US$61). AE, DC, MC, V. Daily noon–2:30pm and 6:30–10:30pm. MTR: Wan Chai.

EXPENSIVE

Fook Lam Moon (p. 152), famous for its exotic Cantonese fare and already covered in the Tsim Sha Tsui dining section above, also has a branch in Wan Chai.

Riva ✿✿ CONTINENTAL   Using its location high over Victoria Park to full advantage, this restaurant boasts a dark and subdued interior with sweeping views beyond the park to the harbor, making this a great choice for a romantic dinner. The menu is eclectic, with the Australian chef taking inspiration from southern Europe, blending it with Australian seafood and ingredients, and adding Asian touches. The results are surprising creations like spiced kangaroo with spinach-filled ricotta cannelloni on bell pepper and roasted corn salsa. There are, however, also more traditional dishes such as the ossobucco with penne pasta or the roasted rack of lamb. Lunch features a buffet table for appetizers and desserts and a choice of a main dish from a menu. While diners who prefer the tried and true will find enough on the menu to satisfy, this restaurant is especially recommended for those who like culinary adventures.

In the Park Lane Hotel (27th floor), 310 Gloucester Rd., Causeway Bay. ☎ **852/2293 8888**. www.parklane. com.hk. Reservations recommended. Main courses HK$198–HK$318 (US$26–US$41); fixed-price lunch HK$210 (US$27); Sun brunch HK$230 (US$30). AE, DC, MC, V. Daily noon–2:45pm and 6–10:45pm (last order). MTR: Causeway Bay.

ToTT's Asian Grill & Bar ✿✿✿ INTERNATIONAL/FUSION   This flashy restaurant seems to suffer from an identity crisis: gigantic Chinese paint brushes at the entrance and a blood-red interior with zebra-striped chairs. I don't know whether I'm in Africa or China until I look at the fabulous view from the restaurant's 34th-floor perch. This is Hong Kong at its most eclectic, funky self, and though the setting seems contrived, the restaurant itself is relaxed, fun, and

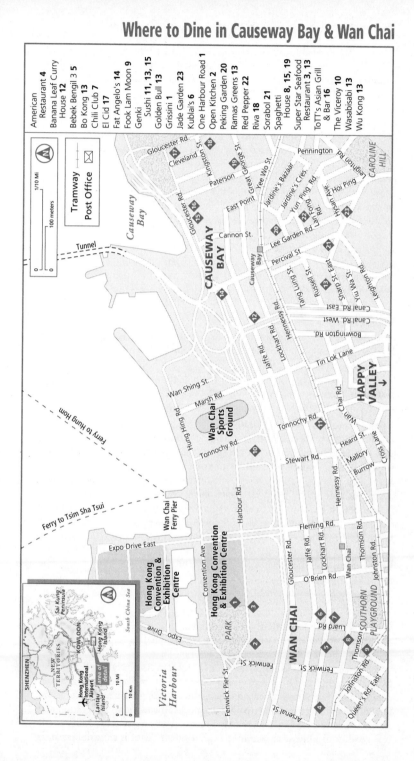

American Restaurant **4**
Banana Leaf Curry House **12**
Bebek Bengil 3 **5**
Bo Kong **13**
Chili Club **7**
El Cid **17**
Fat Angelo's **14**
Fook Lam Moon **9**
Genki Sushi **11, 13, 15**
Golden Bull **13**
Grissini **1**
Jade Garden **23**
Kublai's **6**
One Harbour Road **1**
Open Kitchen **2**
Peking Garden **20**
Ramas Greens **13**
Red Pepper **22**
Riva **18**
Sorabol **21**
Spaghetti House **8, 15, 19**
Super Star Seafood Restaurant **3, 13**
ToTT's Asian Grill & Bar **16**
The Viceroy **10**
Wasabisabi **13**
Wu Kong **13**

highly recommended for its innovative and varied East-meets-West fusion cuisine. Come early for a drink in the restaurant's bar (happy hour 5–8pm), or retire there after dinner for live music and dancing Monday through Saturday nights from 10pm.

There's also an outdoor terrace where you can take your drinks with you to enjoy the view. A glass-enclosed kitchen reveals food being prepared in woks, over charcoal grills, and in tandoori ovens. There's also a sushi bar. The menu is diverse in cuisine and price, allowing diners to eat moderately priced dishes like grilled Thai marinated chicken on red curry angel-hair pasta, or go all out on tandoori-roasted salmon filet on basil whipped potatoes and crisp vegetable chips. Grilled items, from Boston lobster to Angus fillet mignon, come with a choice of a half-dozen interesting sauces, including lemongrass-infused Hollandaise and mango-bourbon barbecue dip. This place is a good choice for those who want dining and entertainment in one spot, as well as for those entertaining first-time visitors to Hong Kong.

In the Excelsior Hotel, 281 Gloucester Rd., Causeway Bay. ⓒ 852/2837 6786. www.excelsiorhongkong.com. Reservations recommended for dinner (request a window seat). Main courses HK$168–HK$338 (US$22–US$44); fixed-price lunch (Mon–Fri only) HK$198 (US$26), Sun brunch HK$298 (US$39). AE, DC, MC, V. Mon–Fri noon–3pm; Sun 11:30am–3pm; Mon–Sat 6:30–11pm; Sun 6:30–10pm. MTR: Causeway Bay.

MODERATE

Several restaurants already covered in the Kowloon dining section, above, have branches in Wan Chai or Causeway Bay: **Wu Kong** (p. 126), which specializes in cuisine from Shanghai; **El Cid** (p. 121), excellent for tapas and Spanish cuisine; **Jade Garden** (p. 123), good for Cantonese food and dim sum; **Peking Garden** (p. 123), which serves Pekingese food; and **Super Star Seafood Restaurant** (p. 125), serving Cantonese dishes, seafood, and dim sum.

Bebek Bengil 3 🌟🌟 *Finds* INDONESIAN   Located in an unlikely modern building in the heart of Wan Chai's nightlife district, this classy Balinese restaurant is so soothingly decorated it transports you immediately from Hong Kong to Bali, making a meal here almost transcendental. Teak furniture, terracotta floors, low lighting, Balinese music, and one of Wan Chai's few outdoor decks make this a delightful place for satays, duck liver pate, Balinese crispy duck (marinated 36 hr. in a secret recipe of Indonesian spices), and steamed whole snapper in banana leaf. To wash it all down, recommended drinks include the Dirty Duck Martini or a refreshing Lemongrass Lime Soda. This restaurant, popular with politicians, diplomats, and celebrities, is the third in the Bebek Bengil chain, with the other two located in Ubud, Bali.

The Broadway (5th floor), 54–62 Lockhart Rd., Wan Chai. ⓒ 852/2217 8000. www.elite-concepts.com. Reservations required. Main dishes HK$90–HK$160 (US$12–US$21). AE, DC, MC, V. Daily 6pm–midnight. MTR: Wan Chai.

Golden Bull VIETNAMESE   This restaurant is a good choice for both the novice and connoisseur of Vietnamese food. If you're not familiar with Vietnamese cuisine, you might want to try the Golden Bull Platter for HK$150 (US$20), which is actually an appetizer plate with a variety of dishes, including spring rolls, fish balls, and satay. Otherwise, typical Vietnamese items include hot-and-sour prawns, roast pig, various noodle dishes, barbecued fish Vietnamese style, grilled jumbo prawns in garlic butter, barbecued chicken in red bean curd sauce, and seafood. If there are two of you, the fixed-price dinner for two (HK$338/US$44) is a good deal. Otherwise, the lunch menu offers Vietnamese snacks such as various rolls of steamed pork or beef, cellophane noodles, vermicelli, and *congee*, most in the HK$40 to HK$50 (US$5.20–US$6.50) price range.

Times Square (11th floor), 1 Matheson St., Causeway Bay. © 852/2506 1028. Main dishes HK$66–HK$185 (US$8.55–US$24). AE, DC, MC, V. Daily noon–11:30pm. MTR: Causeway Bay.

Ramas Greens ✦✦ FUSION   There are so many fusion, East-Meets-West restaurants in Hong Kong that it's hard to keep track. This one, open since 2002, has proven its staying power by continuing to attract a trendy crowd, who lounge on sofas and comfy chairs below sheer curtains hanging from the ceiling. The changing menu runs the gamut from pizza and pasta to Indian tandoori, curries, vegetarian selections, Asian dishes, and fusion cuisine. You might, for example, start with the Shanghainese duck breast salad, followed by seared halibut with a mint yogurt sauce or the stir-fried Boston lobster in lemongrass, ginger, and chili sauce. Desserts are divine, even those with uninviting names like the Frozen Black Pepper Yogurt Sandwiches filled with Aceto Strawberry: Somehow it works. Stick around after dinner, when the restaurant transforms into a bar after 11pm.

Times Square (11th floor), 1 Matheson St., Causeway Bay. © 852/3101 0656. www.ramasgreens.com. Main dishes HK$128–HK$208 (US$17–US$27); fixed-price lunch HK$78–HK$108 (US$10–US$14). AE, DC, MC, V. Sun–Thurs noon–1am; Fri–Sat noon–2am (last order 11pm). MTR: Causeway Bay.

Red Pepper ✦✦ SICHUAN   Open since 1970, the Red Pepper has a large following among the city's expatriates, many of whom seem to come so often that they know everyone in the place. It's a very relaxing, small restaurant, with a rather quaint decor of carved dragons on the ceiling and Chinese lanterns. Specialties include fried prawns with chili sauce on a sizzling platter, sour-pepper soup, fried garoupa with sweet-and-sour sauce, smoked duck marinated with oranges, and shredded chicken with hot garlic sauce and dry-fried string beans. Most dishes are available in two sizes, with the small dishes suitable for two people. Litchi tea is a good accompaniment.

7 Lan Fong Rd., Causeway Bay. © 852/2577 3811. Reservations recommended, especially at dinner. Small dishes HK$85–HK$130 (US$11–US$17). AE, DC, MC, V. Daily 11:30am–11:15pm (last order). MTR: Causeway Bay.

The Viceroy ✦✦ *Finds* INDIAN   Under the same management as the long-popular Gaylord in Tsim Sha Tsui, this contemporary restaurant has something its sister establishment doesn't—outdoor seating on a terrace with great views of the harbor, Wan Chai waterfront, and Kowloon. In the evening, the experience is almost magical, making it a good choice for a romantic dinner. On days when the weather doesn't cooperate (too cold, too hot, or rainy), indoor dining is a good second choice, with large windows offering the same views. Although the innovative menu changes often, tandoori dishes may range from lamb and prawns to lobster. In addition to curries and dishes like roast chicken in yogurt and spices, there are also a fair number of vegetarian dishes, from potatoes cooked with curry leaves to yellow lentils with spinach. The lunch buffet, offered weekdays only, is a steal.

Sun Hung Kai Centre (2nd floor), 30 Harbour Rd., Wan Chai. © 852/2827 7777. www.harilela.com.hk. Main dishes HK$62–HK$148 (US$8.05–US$19); lunch buffet (Mon–Fri only) HK$108 (US$14). AE, DC, MC, V. Daily noon–3pm and 6–11pm. MTR: Wan Chai.

Wasabisabi ✦✦ JAPANESE   This stunning restaurant looks like it was airlifted straight out of Tokyo, and like that huge metropolis, it's easy to get lost here. Luckily, staff is on hand to lead diners past the mirrors and corridors that make this place a confusing maze, to the dark and cozy dining room, where palm leaves and ostrich feathers form a simple but memorable backdrop behind the sushi bar. The menu lists all the usual sashimi (raw seafood), sushi (raw seafood on vinegared rice), and temaki (handrolled sushi), from tuna and prawns to anago (sea eel), but there are also the Japanese chef's own creations like the avocado and smoked-eel temaki. The extensive menu also offers grilled dishes (like grilled salmon), tempura (food that is battered and then deep-fried), and rice and noodle dishes. The restaurant's bar, open until 2am on weekends, is a good, happening place for an after-dinner drink.

Times Square (13th floor), 1 Matheson St., Causeway Bay. © 852/2506 0009. www.aqua.com.hk. Sushi (2 pieces) HK$40–HK$140 (US$5.20–US$18); main dishes HK$75–HK$188 (US$9.75–US$24). DC, MC, V. Daily noon–3pm and 6pm–midnight. MTR: Causeway Bay.

INEXPENSIVE

The **Banana Leaf Curry House, Fat Angelo's, Genki Sushi,** and **Spaghetti House,** reviewed in the Tsim Sha Tsui section, all have branches in Wan Chai or Causeway Bay. See p. 126, 126, 127, and 129, respectively.

In addition to the recommendations below, be sure to go through the moderate section above for inexpensive buffet and fixed-price lunches; also see the "Dim Sum" section later in this chapter.

American Restaurant PEKINGESE Despite its name, the American Restaurant serves hearty Pekingese food and has been doing so since it opened right after World War II. Recently renovated and often filled with noisy, celebratory patrons, it has an English menu listing almost 200 dishes (the small-size dishes are good for two or three people), but the perennial favorites have always been barbecued Peking duck (HK$275/US$36), beggar's chicken (which must be ordered a day in advance and costs HK$350/US$45), sizzling prawns, and the sizzling beef hot plate. Of these, Peking duck remains the most popular and should be shared by two or more people. Otherwise, the staff is happy to make recommendations.

20 Lockhart Rd., Wan Chai. © 852/2527 1000 or 852/2527 7277. Small dishes HK$50–HK$108 (US$6.50–US$14). AE, DC, MC, V. Daily 11am–11pm (last order). MTR: Wan Chai.

Bo Kong ★ *Finds* VEGETARIAN A bit too bright for comfort but soothingly decorated, this pleasant restaurant, located in the Food Forum of Times Square with a dozen other restaurants and with branches in Canada, offers Chinese vegetarian fare that is so cleverly prepared, you'd swear it contained meat. There is braised vegetarian "shark's fin," vegetarian sashimi, an appetizer plate of "cold cuts" that looks like meat but isn't, deep-fried vegetarian "chicken," vegetarian "prawns" in taro nest, and vegetarian "ham" rolled with bean-curd skin. There are also noodle, rice, and *congee* dishes. Neither smoking nor the consumption of alcohol is allowed here.

Times Square (12th floor), 1 Matheson St., Causeway Bay. © 852/2506 3377. Main dishes HK$60–HK$98 (US$7.80–US$13). AE, MC, V. Daily 11am–10:30pm. MTR: Causeway Bay.

Chili Club *Value* THAI This simple upstairs restaurant wastes no money on decor. In fact, the only hint that you're in Asia comes from the rattan chairs and that the service is indifferent at best. But the seafood, curries, and noodles, which include all the Thai favorites, are as spicy as this national cuisine should be. What's more, the price is right, making this one of Hong Kong's best dining values. Try to get a seat near the window, where you can watch the action on the street below, and, if possible, avoid the lunchtime rush.

88 Lockhart Rd., Wan Chai. © 852/2527 2872. Main dishes HK$50–HK$150 (US$6.50–US$19). AE, MC, V. Daily noon–3pm and 6–10:30pm. MTR: Wan Chai.

Kublai's *Value* ASIAN   This very popular restaurant allows diners to select their own ingredients for one-dish meals that are then stir fried by short-order cooks. All-you-can-eat lunches and dinners give choices of vegetables (spinach, cabbage, corn, mushrooms, and more), meats (pork, beef, shrimp, chicken, fish), and sauces (chili, peanut, sesame oil, oyster, black bean, and curry), along with side orders of soup and salad with dinner or a soda with lunch. Needless to say, the ease of dining here, coupled with reasonable prices, make it a hit with foreigners. Arrive early or late to get a window seat above Wan Chai. Otherwise, you'll dine elbow to elbow at long tables. Mercifully, lighting is low.

One Capital Place (3rd floor), 18 Luard Rd. (entrance on Jaffe Rd., behind Delaney's Irish Pub), Wan Chai. ℂ 852/2529 9117. All-you-can eat dinner HK$158 (US$21); all-you-can-eat lunch HK$68 (US$8.85). AE, DC, MC, V. Daily noon–10:30pm. MTR: Wan Chai.

Open Kitchen ★★ *Finds* INTERNATIONAL   This self-serve cafeteria, near the convention center and Grand Hyatt Hotel, is bright with natural lighting and gets my vote as the best place in Wan Chai for an inexpensive and quick meal. Not only does it offer a good selection of food at very reasonable prices, but it also boasts a view of the harbor and even has a tiny outdoor terrace. True to its name, chefs working in an open kitchen prepare everything from lamb chops and tandoori chicken to grilled salmon and curries. Diners can also choose from four or five kinds of pasta, along with a choice of sauce. Lighter fare includes a salad bar, soups, and sandwiches. You can also come just for a drink (I often see people writing postcards or reading a book here in the afternoon), but the minimum charge per person is HK$20 (US$2.60).

Hong Kong Arts Centre (6th floor), 2 Harbour Rd., Wan Chai. ℂ 852/2827 2923. Main courses HK$70–HK$110 (US$9.10–US$14). AE, MC, V. Daily 11am–9pm. MTR: Wan Chai.

Sorabol ★ KOREAN   This is the Hong Kong branch of a successful Korean chain. Popular with local Chinese and Koreans, it can be quite noisy and busy, but partitions between tables lend some privacy. My own personal favorites are the beef strips of *bulgogi* or the *kalbi* (beef strips marinated in a spicy sauce and then barbecued at your own grill). Barbecued fixed-price meals come with side dishes of kimchee (spicy cabbage) and vegetables. Another popular dish is the Mongolian hotpot with vegetables for HK$158 (US$20). You'll do your own barbecuing at smokeless grills at your table, which can be great fun, somewhat like an indoor cookout. In any case, the army of knowledgeable staff keeps things running smoothly and is happy to help the novice barbecuer. There's also a branch in Tsim Sha Tsui on the fourth floor of the Miramar Shopping Centre at 132 Nathan Rd. (ℂ 852/2375 2882), open the same hours.

Lee Theatre Plaza (17th floor), 99 Percival St. (across from Times Square), Causeway Bay. ℂ 852/2881 6823. www.sorabol.com.hk. Barbecued fixed-price meals HK$115–HK$130 (US$15–US$17); fixed-price lunches (Mon–Fri only) HK$40–HK$90 (US$5.20–US$12); Sat–Sun lunch buffet HK$98 (US$13). AE, DC, MC, V. Daily 11am–11:30pm. MTR: Wan Chai.

6 Around Hong Kong Island

VICTORIA PEAK
MODERATE

Cafe Deco ★ *Overrated* INTERNATIONAL   No expense was spared, it seems, in designing this chic, airy restaurant with its wood inlaid floor, authentic Art Deco trimmings (many imported from the U.S. and Europe), and open kitchen serving cuisines of China, Japan, Thailand, India, the U.S., and Italy. In the evening (except Sun), diners are treated to live jazz. All this is secondary, however, to the restaurant's real attraction—the best view in town of Hong Kong. That alone is reason enough for dining here, though some of the view has been stolen with the completion of the Peak Tower's viewing platform. To assure a ringside window seat, be sure to make reservations for the second floor at least 2 weeks in advance, emphasizing that you don't want your view obstructed by the Peak Tower, or opt for one of the 16 outdoor tables, which are often easier to get. The food, designed to appeal to visitors from around the world, is as trendy as the restaurant, with an eclectic mix of international dishes and ingredients, including tandoori kebabs and dishes, Asian noodles, sushi, grilled steaks and chops, pizzas, create-your-own pastas, soups, sandwiches, salads, and burgers. The salads are generous enough for two to share (the house salad is exceptionally good), but main dishes occasionally fall short of expectations. I suppose what you're really paying for here is the view.

Peak Galleria, Victoria Peak. (C) 852/2849 5111. Reservations recommended for dinner (request window seat with view). Pizzas and pastas HK$98–HK$168 (US$13–US$22); main courses HK$108–HK$248 (US$14–US$32); fixed-price lunch (Mon–Fri only) HK$128 (US$17); Sun brunch HK$250 (US$33). AE, DC, MC, V. Mon–Fri 11:30am–11pm; Sat–Sun 9:30am–11pm (last order). Peak tram.

The Peak Lookout 🖈🖈 INTERNATIONAL   Although it's on The Peak, located across the street from the Peak tram terminus, there are only limited views of the South China Sea from the Peak Lookout's terrace. And yet, it has long been a Hong Kong favorite. A former tram station, it's a delightful place for a meal, with exposed granite walls, tall timber-trussed ceiling, open fireplace, wooden floor, and a greenhouselike room that extends into the garden. You can also sit outdoors amid the lush growth where you can actually hear birds singing—one of the best outdoor dining opportunities in Hong Kong on a glorious day (be sure to request a table outdoors if that's what you want). Musicians entertain nightly with oldies but goldies. The menu is eclectic, offering soups (from minestrone to the classic Thai seafood soup Tom Yam Goong), sandwiches, and a combination of American, Chinese, Indian, and Southeast Asian dishes, including tandoori chicken *tikka*, Thai noodles, penne with prawns, grilled steaks and salmon, and curries like Thai green chicken curry with coconut milk.

121 Peak Rd., Victoria Peak. (C) 852/2849 1000. Reservations required for dinner and all weekend meals. Main courses HK$125–HK$238 (US$16–US$31). AE, DC, MC, V. Mon–Thurs 10:30am–11:30pm; Fri 10:30am–1am; Sat 8:30am–1am; Sun 8:30am–11:30pm. Peak tram.

INEXPENSIVE

Mövenpick Marché 🖈 *Kids* INTERNATIONAL   This Swiss chain has been very successful in Europe with its "marketplace" concept in self-service dining, and with the international crowds that visit The Peak, it does quite well here, too. For one thing, it's located in the Peak Tower and offers great views over Hong Kong. In addition, its food is reasonably priced and varied enough to please even fickle palates, the staff is efficient and friendly, and there's even a children's corner, with a small slide, toys, crayons, and other diversions, making it a good place for families. Upon entering, you'll be given a card, which is stamped each time you add a dish to your tray. There are various counters offering different foods, including salads, pizza, pasta, vegetables, sushi, Chinese dishes, and entrees ranging from grilled pork chops and roasted spring chicken to king prawns and sole. You can choose as much or as little as you like, but good dining deals are the three-course fixed-price lunches available weekdays only, the dinner buffets, and the 50% discounts available every evening after 10pm. The two-floor restaurant is divided into various themed rooms, each representing a different country, some with better views than others.

Peak Tower (levels 6 and 7), 128 Peak Rd., Victoria Peak. © 852/2849 2000. Main courses HK$65–HK$80 (US$8.45–US$10); fixed-price lunch Mon–Fri HK$88 (US$11); Sat–Sun brunch HK$208 (US$27); dinner buffet HK$288 (US$37) Mon–Thurs, HK$308 (US$40) Fri–Sun and holidays. AE, DC, MC, V. Mon–Fri 11am–11pm; Sat–Sun 9am–11pm. Peak tram.

REPULSE BAY
EXPENSIVE

The Verandah ★★★ *Finds* CONTINENTAL   Unless you like beaches (there's a popular one here at Repulse Bay), this wonderful, veranda-like restaurant is the only reason to venture to this destination on Hong Kong Island's south side, though you do pass it by on your way to Stanley. A throwback to Hong Kong's colonial days in a setting reminiscent of an exclusive private club, it boasts a stylish yet relaxed atmosphere, with tall ceilings and whirling fans, starched tablecloths and flowers, and windows open wide toward manicured lawns and the sea. If you can, book a table more than a week in advance and arrive starving at its famous Sunday brunch. Otherwise, from the regular menu, you might wish to start with tandoori grilled foie gras, followed by angel-hair pasta in a vanilla lobster foam and garnished with crabmeat and sautéed salmon. For a main course, you might choose fennel-stuffed Dover sole wrapped in black radish with fennel broth, or prime U.S. beef in a potato ring with cabernet sauvignon sauce. There are also vegetarian dishes. In any case, with its excellent service, great food, and wonderful ambience, this is a very civilized place; you'll want to linger.

109 Repulse Bay Rd., Repulse Bay. © 852/2812 2722. www.therepulsebay.com. Reservations required. Main courses HK$268–HK$290 (US$35–US$38); fixed-price dinner HK$478–HK$540 (US$62–US$70); fixed-price lunch HK$218–HK$238 (US$28–US$31); Sun brunch HK$328 (US$43). AE, DC, MC, V. Tues–Sat noon–2:30pm; Sun 11am–2:30pm; daily 6:30–10:30pm. Bus: 6, 6A, 6X, 260, or 973.

STANLEY

In addition to the restaurants described here, **El Cid** (p. 121), already described in the Tsim Sha Tsui section and located in the Murray House, offers a dreamy view of the sea from its outside terrace, a live band Tuesday through Sunday evenings, and an expansive menu of tapas and Spanish food.

MODERATE

Lucy's ★ *Finds* INTERNATIONAL   This tiny, cozy, casual restaurant, snuggled in the ground floor of an older building just off Stanley market (look for the stairs to the right of the Delifrance bakery), is a friendly neighborhood restaurant, attracting expats who live in Stanley rather than hordes of tourists (maybe because it lacks a view of the sea). Its limited menu changes often to reflect what's available and in season, with past entrees ranging from sea bass with orange vinaigrette and artichoke, almond and herb couscous, to beef filet with sweet potato and ginger mash, bok choy, and sesame dressing. Most diners, however, opt for one of the daily specials, which are almost always right on, making sure to save room for the restaurant's famed desserts.

64 Stanley Main St., Stanley. © 852/2813 9055. Reservations required weekends. Main courses HK$150–HK$190 (US$19–US$25); fixed-price dinner (Sun–Thurs only) HK$190–HK$230 (US$25–US$30); fixed-price lunch HK$120–HK$150 (US$16–US$19). MC, V. Mon–Fri noon–3pm and 7–10pm; Sat–Sun noon–4pm; Sat 6:30–10pm; Sun 6:30–9:30pm. Bus: 6, 6A, 6X, 260, or 973.

INEXPENSIVE

Chilli N Spice ★ *Value* THAI/SOUTHEAST ASIAN   Located in the historic Murray House, a massive, colonnaded stone structure built in Central in 1843, dismantled, and rebuilt here stone for stone, this restaurant boasts views of the sea from its outdoor terrace and serves mostly traditional Thai food as well as popular Southeast Asian dishes. You might wish to start with pork and corn in a pastry shell or Indonesian satays. For a main course, I recommend the Singaporean-style fried curry crab; the tiger prawns with lemongrass, dried chile, and garlic; or the Indonesian curry chicken. This is both a relaxing place to end a day of shopping as well as being an affordable option, with most dinners costing around HK$200 (US$26).

There's another branch at 13–15 Cleveland St., Causeway Bay (© **852/2504 3930;** MTR: Causeway Bay), open daily noon to midnight.

Shop 101, Murray House, Stanley Plaza, Stanley. © 852/2899 0147. www.kingparrot.com. Main courses HK$50–HK$130 (US$6.50–US$17). AE, DC, MC, V. Mon–Fri noon–11:30pm; Sat–Sun 11am–11:30pm. Bus: 6, 6A, 6X, 260, or 973.

ABERDEEN
MODERATE
Jumbo Kingdom ☆ *Overrated* CANTONESE   No doubt you've heard about Hong Kong's floating restaurant in Aberdeen, in operation for more than a quarter of a century and claiming to be the largest floating restaurant in the world. Although often included in Hong Kong's organized nighttime tours, the restaurant was steadily loosing out to newer, more authentic, and more affordable restaurants, prompting it to reinvent itself in 2004 as the Jumbo Kingdom, a complex housing a restaurant, retail shops, and an exhibit on the history of Chinese fishing communities. Only time will tell whether the ploy will work. At any rate, if you've always wanted to eat in a floating restaurant, simply take the bus to Aberdeen and then board one of the Jumbo Kingdom's own free shuttle boats, with departures every few minutes. The restaurant, which underwent a complete overhaul that rid it of its opulent golds and reds and transformed it into a slick, contemporary venue, specializes in fresh seafood but also offers roasted goose, Peking duck (HK$280/US$36), and changing seasonal dishes. Dim sum is available from an English menu (from trolleys on Sun and holidays) until 4pm—certainly the least expensive way to enjoy the floating restaurant experience.

Aberdeen Harbour, Hong Kong Island. © 852/2553 9111. www.jumbo.com.hk. Main dishes HK$80–HK$400 (US$10–US$52); dim sum HK$14–HK$26 (US$1.80–US$3.40). Table charge HK$8 (US$1.05) per person. AE, MC, V. Mon–Sat 10:30am–10:30pm; Sun 7:30am–10:30pm. Bus: 7 or 70 from Central to Aberdeen, then the restaurant's private boat.

WESTERN DISTRICT
INEXPENSIVE
Sammy's Kitchen CONTINENTAL   There are few choices for Western food in the Western District, making Sammy's Kitchen, recognizable by the sign in the shape of a cow outside its door, your best bet. A simple and unpretentious place, it offers reasonably priced, rather mediocre meals, but the service is friendly and welcoming. Owner/chef Sammy Yip has been cooking professionally for more than 50 years (including stints at The Peninsula and Mandarin Oriental hotels) and opened this restaurant on his own in 1970. Sammy, whose children have joined him in the family business, speaks English well and is happy to see foreign visitors. There are actually two menus, based on two different concepts. One is cheaper and quicker, available all day and offering rather plain dishes like spring chicken, lamb chops, and noodle and fried rice dishes; they're priced from HK$55 to HK$100 (US$7.15–US$13). In the evening, another, more expensive menu is also available (with entrees ranging from HK$80/US$10–HK$240/US$31), cooked by Sammy himself and served in the separate, more formal Grill Room.

This menu includes fresh seafood, imported steaks, and such specialties as veal with Parmesan and Marsala, chicken with special pepper sauce flaming with cognac, filet mignon, and roasted Siberian blabby rib of lamb with herbs. You can bring your own bottle of wine for a HK$70 (US$9.10) corkage fee.

204–206 Queen's Rd. W., Sheung Wan. © 852/2548 8400. Main courses HK$35–HK$240 (US$4.55–US$31); fixed-price lunch HK$35–HK$100 (US$4.55–US$13). AE, DC, MC, V. Daily 8am–11:30pm. MTR: Sheung Wan.

7 Dim Sum

Everyone should try a dim sum meal at least once, as much for the atmosphere as for the food. It's eaten primarily for breakfast or lunch, or as an afternoon snack with tea. On weekends, restaurants offering dim sum (mostly Cantonese restaurants) are packed with local families. On weekdays, they're popular with shoppers and businesspeople. Prices are low and you order only as much as you want. Simply look over the steaming baskets being pushed around by trolley and choose what appeals to you. Fancier restaurants, particularly those in hotels, offer dim sum from an English menu rather than carts; they claim that since the food is cooked to order, it is fresher, but the prices are also higher. In most restaurants that offer dim sum, one pays by the basket, and each basket usually contains two to four items of dim sum; the average price is about HK$20 to HK$30 (US$2.60–US$3.90). The prices given below, unless otherwise specified, are per basket; expect to spend HK$60 to HK$100 (US$7.80–US$13) per person for a light meal.

You'll find most of the restaurants below also described earlier in this chapter, so they obviously serve more than dim sum. However, since dim sum is such a special Chinese tradition, they are emphasized again below. You may also notice that a restaurant listed in this section may have a different amount of stars than what was given previously in an above listing. This is not a mistake: A restaurant that might be ho hum in all-round meals can be a standout in dim sum.

However, since dim sum is fairly predictable, with the most common dishes covered in the cuisine section at the beginning of the chapter, I've only made specific food recommendations below when the dishes are different and/or are standouts from the usual choices.

KOWLOON

The Chinese ★★ CANTONESE   A refined, modern, and fancy setting for dim sum, with correspondingly high prices. There are no trolleys here, but there's a dim sum menu with about 20 different offerings.

In the Hyatt Regency Hotel, 67 Nathan Rd., Tsim Sha Tsui. © 852/2311 1234, ext. 2881. www.hongkong. regency.hyatt.com. Dim sum HK$28–HK$48 (US$3.65–US$6.25). AE, DC, MC, V. Mon–Sat 11:30am–2:45pm and Sun 10:30am–2:45pm, for dim sum. MTR: Tsim Sha Tsui.

City Chiuchow Restaurant CHIU CHOW   Although it's a Chiu Chow restaurant, this place serves its own dim sum, which is not too surprising if you consider that Chiu Chow food has been greatly influenced by Cantonese food.

East Ocean Centre, 98 Granville Rd., Tsim Sha Tsui East. © 852/2723 6226. Dim sum HK$16–HK$25 (US$2.10–US$3.25). AE, DC, MC, V. Daily 11am–4pm for dim sum. MTR: Tsim Sha Tsui.

Fook Lam Moon ★★★ CANTONESE   This is a Hong Kong old-timer, with an atmosphere that is reminiscent of an earlier era. There aren't any trolleys here, however—just a Chinese menu. Ask an English-speaking waiter for translations.

53–59 Kimberley Rd., Tsim Sha Tsui. © 852/2366 0286. www.fooklammoon-grp.com. Dim sum HK$30–HK$60 (US$3.90–US$7.80). AE, DC, MC, V. Daily 11:30am–2:30pm, for dim sum. MTR: Tsim Sha Tsui.

Hutong ★★★ CANTONESE   Great views of the harbor and creative dim sum is what you get at this hip venue. Expect the likes of steamed lamb dumpling instead of pork, with about eight different kinds of dim sum that change monthly. This place is pricey, but worth it.

1 Peking Rd. (28th floor), Tsim Sha Tsui. ℂ 852/3428 8342. www.aqua.com.hk. Dim sum HK$68–HK$88 (US$8.85–US$11). AE, DC, MC, V. Mon–Sat 11am–3pm, Sun and holidays 10am–3pm, for dim sum. MTR: Tsim Sha Tsui.

Jade Garden Chinese Restaurant CANTONESE   An easy place for the uninitiated, this Cantonese chain is tourist-friendly and conveniently situated across from the Star Ferry terminus. It offers views of Victoria Harbour and trolleys of dim sum, as well as an English menu. You can save money by dining after 2:30pm on weekdays, when most dim sum costs only HK$11 (US$1.45). There's another branch at 25–31 Carnarvon Rd. (ℂ **852/2369 8311;** MTR: Tsim Sha Tsui), serving dim sum daily from 7:30am to 5pm.

Star House (4th floor), 3 Salisbury Rd., Tsim Sha Tsui. ℂ 852/2730 6888. Dim sum HK$16–HK$36 (US$2.10–US$4.70). AE, DC, MC, V. Mon–Sat 11am–5pm, Sun and holidays 10am–5pm, for dim sum. MTR: Tsim Sha Tsui.

Serenade Chinese Restaurant ★ (Finds CANONTESE   This is my top choice for inexpensive dim sum with a view in Tsim Sha Tsui. Located up on the first floor of the Hong Kong Cultural Centre, next to the Star Ferry, it offers views of Victoria Harbour and dim sum served from trolleys. Bright and cheerful, it's more upmarket than some but more casual than hotel restaurants.

Hong Kong Cultural Centre (1st floor), Restaurant Block, Salisbury Rd., Tsim Sha Tsui. ℂ 852/2722 0932. Dim sum HK$28–HK$40 (US$3.65–US$5.20). AE, DC, MC, V. Mon–Fri 11am–4:30pm, Sat–Sun and holidays 9am–4:30pm, for dim sum. MTR: Tsim Sha Tsui.

Shang Palace ★★ CANTONESE   One of Kowloon's most elaborate Chinese restaurants comes complete with red-lacquered walls and Chinese lanterns hanging from the ceiling. Because it provides a menu in English, this is a great place to try dim sum for the first time, not to mention the fact that its dim sum is among the best in town—a bit more expensive, but worth it. Choose your dim sum from the menu, which changes every 2 weeks and always includes more than a dozen varieties.

In the Shangri-La Hotel, 64 Mody Rd., Tsim Sha Tsui East. ℂ 852/2733 8754. Dim sum HK$30–HK$38 (US$3.90–US$4.95). AE, DC, MC, V. Mon–Sat noon–3pm, Sun and holidays 10:30am–3pm, for dim sum. MTR: Tsim Sha Tsui.

Spring Moon ★★★ CANTONESE   As you'd expect from a restaurant in the venerable Peninsula hotel, this is a very refined and civilized place for the humble dim sum, with an English menu that lists more than a dozen dim sum and more than two dozen varieties of Chinese teas available for lunch. In addition, from 3 to 4:30pm, there's a Chinese version of the British afternoon tea, with a fixed-price menu for dim sum and tea (HK$165/US$21). The restaurant is decorated in an Art Deco style reminiscent of how the restaurant would have looked in 1928, the year The Peninsula opened, with cuisine that changes with the season.

In The Peninsula hotel, Salisbury Rd., Tsim Sha Tsui. ℂ 852/2920 2888. www.peninsula.com. Dim sum HK$38 (US$4.95). AE, DC, MC, V. Daily 11:30am–2:30pm, for dim sum. MTR: Tsim Sha Tsui.

Super Star Seafood Restaurant (Finds CANTONESE/SEAFOOD   This lively and popular seafood restaurant, filled with locals, is one of Tsim Sha Tsui's best places for trying authentic dim sum in a typical Chinese setting. There's no English menu, so you'll just have to look at the offerings on the various trolleys.

83–97 Nathan Rd., Tsim Sha Tsui. © 852/2366 0878. Dim sum HK$15–HK$38 (US$1.95–US$4.95). AE, DC, MC, V. Mon–Fri 10:30am–4:30pm, Sat–Sun 9:30am–4:30pm, for dim sum. MTR: Tsim Sha Tsui.

Tsui Hang Village Restaurant CANTONESE   Tsui Hang Village, a modern restaurant located in a shopping complex across from the Miramar Hotel, offers inexpensive plates of dim sum. There's a branch across the harbor on the second floor of the New World Tower, 16–18 Queen's Rd., Central (© **852/ 2524 2012;** MTR: Central), serving dim sum Saturday from 11am to 5pm and Sunday and holidays from 10am to 5pm.

Miramar Plaza, 1 Kimberley Rd., Tsim Sha Tsui. © **852/2368 6363.** www.Miramar-group.com. Dim sum HK$18–HK$38 (US$2.35–US$4.95). AE, MC, V. Mon–Sat 11:30am–5pm, Sun and holidays 10am–5pm, for dim sum. MTR: Tsim Sha Tsui.

Yan Toh Heen ★★★ CANTONESE   One of Hong Kong's top Cantonese eateries, this elegant restaurant with large windows treats diners to views of the harbor. A daily changing menu offers about two dozen varieties of dim sum.

In the InterContinental Hong Kong, 18 Salisbury Rd., Tsim Sha Tsui. © 852/2721 1211. www.hongkong-ic. intercontinental.com. Dim sum HK$38–HK$60 (US$4.95–US$7.80). AE, DC, MC, V. Mon–Sat noon–2:30pm, Sun and holidays 11:30am–3:30pm, for dim sum. MTR: Tsim Sha Tsui.

CENTRAL

Luk Yu Tea House ★★ *Finds* CANTONESE   The most authentic dim sum teahouse in Hong Kong is often so packed with regulars that mere tourists can't get a seat. Furthermore, trolleys with dim sum are pushed through the place only until 11am, after which there's only a Chinese menu. Yet it's worth the effort to come here; try to bring along a Chinese friend to help you with your selections.

24–26 Stanley St., Central. © 852/2523 5464. Dim sum HK$25–HK$55 (US$3.25–US$7.15). MC, V. Daily 7am–5:30pm for dim sum. MTR: Central.

Maxim's Palace *Value* CANTONESE   There's no better place for cheap dim sum than this enormously popular restaurant, located on the second floor of City Hall just a stone's throw from the Star Ferry. A recent refurbishment has put some unfortunate glaze on the windows, blocking the once-fabled views of the harbor (we can only hope it's temporary), but it's still a lively place to choose dim sum from trolleys, plus there's an English menu with photos and prices. It doesn't get much easier than this.

Low Block, City Hall, Connaught Road Central and Edinburgh Place. © 852/2526 9931. Dim sum HK$17–HK$29 (US$2.20–US$3.75). AE, DC, MC, V. Daily Mon–Sat 11am–3pm, Sun and holidays 9am–3pm, for dim sum. MTR: Central.

The Square CANTONESE   This smartly decorated restaurant, next to Hong Kong Station and ifc mall, offers only a dozen or so dim sum choices on weekdays but a greatly expanded dim sum menu on weekends and holidays. The restaurant is renowned for its steamed lobster dumplings and egg tarts with bird's nest, but even the humble steamed barbecued pork buns here are among the best I've had. Try to reserve a window seat from which you can watch the Star Ferry as it comes and goes from the Central pier (but note that it's in the smoking section).

Exchange Square II, Central. © 852/2525 1163. Dim sum HK$16–HK$58 (US$2.10–US$7.55). AE, DC, MC, V. Daily 11am–3pm, for dim sum. MTR: Central.

Zen Chinese CANTONESE   Starkly modern and hip, this Cantonese restaurant offers dim sum daily from an English menu, with more varieties available on the weekend.

The Mall, Pacific Place, 88 Queensway, Central. © **852/2845 4555.** Dim sum HK$30–HK$55 (US$3.85–US$7.05). AE, DC, MC, V. Mon–Fri 11:30am–3pm, Sat 11:30am–5pm, Sun 10:30am–5pm, for dim sum. MTR: Admiralty.

WAN CHAI

Fook Lam Moon ★★★ CANTONESE   This branch of the well-known expensive Cantonese restaurant (see above) offers dim sum from a Chinese menu only (no trolleys). Ask an English-speaking waiter for translations.

35–45 Johnston Rd., Wan Chai. © **852/2866 0663.** Dim sum HK$30–HK$60 (US$3.90–US$7.80). AE, DC, MC, V. Daily 11:30am–2:30pm for dim sum. MTR: Wan Chai.

8 Afternoon Tea

Colonial days are over, but the tradition of afternoon tea lives on in many of Hong Kong's best hotels. These are some of my favorites for a civilized midafternoon snack.

Clipper Lounge TEAS/CAKES   If you're in Central in the afternoon, stop by the brass-and-teak–decorated Clipper Lounge for one of England's finest traditions—afternoon tea. Besides 11 varieties of tea (or, if you must, coffee), you'll have a choice of English tea sandwiches, "savoury puffs," homemade scones with Devonshire clotted cream and jam, brownies, fruit tartlets, Windsor cakes, and other goodies to sample. A la carte items are also available, but if there are two of you, you're better off getting the tea-for-two special. At any rate, you'll probably want to skip lunch or dinner if you indulge here.

In the Mandarin Oriental Hotel, 5 Connaught Rd., Central. © **852/2522 0111.** www.mandarinoriental.com. Fixed-price afternoon tea HK$145 (US$19) for 1 person, HK$280 (US$36) for 2. AE, DC, MC, V. Daily 3–6pm. MTR: Central.

Lobby Lounge ★★ TEAS/CAKES   The InterContinental takes the honors of having the most gorgeous lobby view—soaring windows provide an almost surreal panorama of Victoria Harbour and Hong Kong Island. Feast your eyes on the view as you sip tea and indulge in finger sandwiches and pastries.

In the Hotel InterContinental Hong Kong, 18 Salisbury Rd., Tsim Sha Tsui. © **852/2721 1211.** www. hongkong-ic.intercontinental.com. Fixed-price afternoon tea for 2 HK$250 (US$32). AE, DC, MC, V. Daily 2:30–6pm. MTR: Tsim Sha Tsui.

Peninsula Hotel Lobby ★★★ TEAS/CAKES   The ornate lobby of The Peninsula hotel, built in 1928, is the most famous lobby in Hong Kong. A popular place to see and be seen, the lobby features soaring columns topped with elaborate gilded ceilings and sculpted figures of gods and angels, palm trees, a Tai Ping carpet, and classically styled furniture. As late as the 1950s, the lobby was divided into east and west wings—one for the British and one for everyone else, including, as one pamphlet put it, women "seeking dalliance." The fixed-price tea includes finger sandwiches, French pastries, and scones with clotted cream. No reservations are accepted, so you may have to wait for a table. A classical string quartet serenades you from an upstairs balcony.

In The Peninsula hotel, Salisbury Rd., Tsim Sha Tsui. © **852/2920 2888.** www.peninsula.com. Fixed-price afternoon tea HK$180–HK$220 (US$23–US$29). AE, DC, MC, V. Daily 2–7pm. MTR: Tsim Sha Tsui.

Exploring Hong Kong

Most people think of Hong Kong as, primarily, an exotic shopping destination. In the past decade, however, Hong Kong has revved up its sightseeing potential, opening new city parks and revamping older ones, constructing community art centers, expanding museums or developing new ones, and redesigning organized sightseeing tours to reflect the territory's changing demographics. Although some attractions closed after the handover, new ones have opened or are in the works, including Hong Kong's own Disneyland by 2006. On the other hand, if all you want to do is hike or lie on the beach, you can do that, too.

If you really want to do Hong Kong justice, plan on staying at least a week. However, since the city is so compact and its transportation is so efficient, you can see quite a bit of the city and its outlying islands in 3 to 5 days,

especially if you're on the go from dawn until past dusk.

To help you get the most out of your stay in Hong Kong, I've recommended itineraries below. However, the rest of the chapter gives you further information on the many attractions, parks, museums, organized tours, sports, and places of interest to children which will help you supplement and alter the below itineraries to your needs and likes.

Although the SAR is compact and easy to navigate, it makes sense to divide the city into sections when planning your sightseeing. The information on museums, parks, markets, and other attractions, therefore, is subdivided in this chapter according to area, making it easier to coordinate sightseeing and dining plans. Don't forget to also read over the suggested walking tours in chapter 7, since they include stops at several of Hong Kong's top attractions.

SUGGESTED ITINERARIES

If You Have 1 Day

If you only have 1 day to spend in Hong Kong, I feel sorry for you. Nevertheless, start the morning with a breakfast of dim sum in a lively Chinese restaurant (see the "Dim Sum" section of chapter 5, beginning on p. 153). For one-stop shopping, try one of the large stores specializing in Chinese products, such as Chinese Arts and Crafts Ltd.—you'll find one in Star House, right next to the Star Ferry in Tsim Sha Tsui (p. 212). Also in Tsim Sha Tsui, just a couple of minutes'

walk from the ferry, is the Hong Kong Museum of Art (p. 162), with its vast collection of Chinese antiquities and art.

Afterward, take the famous Star Ferry across Victoria Harbour to the Central District. There, near the ferry pier, board the shuttle bus that will take you to the tram bound for Victoria Peak (p. 160). Plan on spending at least an hour or more on The Peak, where you'll have fantastic views of Hong Kong if the weather is clear; if you have time, walk the 1-hour circular stroll around The Peak. If you still have time afterward or The Peak is shrouded in clouds, board the double-decker tram in Central for a unique view of north Hong Kong Island or follow one of my walking tours for Central or the Western District (see chapter 7).

In the evening, visit the Temple Street Night Market with its festive atmosphere and outdoor stalls selling clothing and accessories, as well as its palm readers, fortune-tellers, and street opera singers (p. 219).

If You Have 2 Days

After a dim sum breakfast (p. 153) and a quick stop at the Hong Kong Museum of Art (p. 162) with its collection of Chinese antiquities and art, ride the famous Star Ferry across the harbor and head straight to Victoria Peak (p. 160) for Hong Kong's best views and perhaps an hour's stroll around The Peak. Next, head to Stanley Market (p. 218), on the south end of the island, with its many shops and stalls selling clothing and souvenirs. For dinner, consider going to Aberdeen with its famous floating restaurant (p. 152). If you prefer to join an organized tour, take a sunset cruise that includes a meal at the Aberdeen floating restaurant. Tours can be booked through most hotels in Hong Kong (for more information on evening tours, see the "Night Tours" section of chapter 9, "Hong Kong After Dark," beginning on p. 235).

On your second day, board a ferry for one of the outlying islands. Cheung Chau (p. 248) is charming with its unhurried, small-village atmosphere; Lantau (p. 246) is famous for its giant outdoor Buddha and monastery. By midafternoon, try to be at the Hong Kong Museum of History (p. 164) in Tsim Sha Tsui East, Hong Kong's most important museum. Begin the evening with a cocktail at one of Hong Kong's many lounges that offer a view of the harbor, followed by dinner at a Chinese

or Western restaurant. Afterward, visit Temple Street Night Market (p. 219).

If You Have 3 Days

Start your first day with a dim sum breakfast at a Chinese restaurant (p. 153), followed by a quick visit to the Hong Kong Museum of Art (p. 162). Then, for your first breathtaking view of Hong Kong, ride the famous Star Ferry across Victoria Harbour. Afterward, for an even better perspective, take the tram to the top of Victoria Peak (p. 160), where you'll be rewarded with a spectacular view of the city—that is, if the weather is clear. Take an hour's walk along the circular path around Victoria Peak.

Have lunch on The Peak or at one of Central's many restaurants. In the afternoon, follow my do-it-yourself walking tour of the Western District (p. 187), where you can observe traditional Chinese life firsthand, shop for antiques, and visit the Man Mo Temple. For your first evening, try one of Hong Kong's organized evening tours, such as a sunset cruise to Aberdeen (p. 152).

On your second day, head to Stanley Market (p. 218) on south Hong Kong Island, where you can spend several hours shopping for clothing and souvenirs. After a late lunch in Stanley or afternoon tea in the historic lobby of The Peninsula hotel, head to Tsim Sha Tsui East for the Hong Kong Museum of History (p. 164) with its vivid representations of daily Chinese life through the ages. If time permits, explore the many shops along and around Nathan Road. In early evening, head for a cocktail lounge with a view of the harbor, followed by dinner and then a stroll through the Lan Kwai Fong nightlife district.

For your last morning in Hong Kong, get up early and head for one of the outlying islands. Cheung Chau (p. 248), with its small village, beach, and boat population, is good for a short excursion. Lamma (p. 252) is recommended if you want to do some hiking, swimming at a beach, or dining on seafood at a waterfront open-air restaurant. Lantau (p. 246) is a popular destination for its giant outdoor Buddha and adjoining monastery offering vegetarian lunches. Spend the afternoon following your own inclinations: another museum; a walking tour of Central (p. 182); Ocean Park with its aquarium and amusement rides (p. 174); or an organized tour of the New Territories (p. 176). After dinner at a traditional Chinese restaurant, take a stroll through Temple Street Night Market (p. 219) in Kowloon.

If You Have 5 Days or More

Consider yourself lucky! Spend the first 3 days as outlined above. Note, however, that if you're having an article of clothing custom-made, you should visit the tailor on your first day to discuss needs and fittings. Also, check the *Hong Kong Cultural Kaleidoscope* brochure, available at the tourist office, to see whether any of the free, 1-hour tours or cultural lectures offered through the "Meet the People" program pique your interest (p. 177).

On the fourth day, take a trip to the New Territories (see chapter 10 for more information). Alternatively, consider taking one of the excellent tours offered by the Hong Kong Tourism Board or a private tour company (p. 175). If you're not too tired by evening, take the tram to Victoria Peak (p. 160) for a romantic, spectacular nighttime view of Hong Kong, ablaze with glittering lights (the night view is

a must-see, even if you've already been to The Peak during the day). Alternatively, stroll the promenade along the Tsim Sha Tsui waterfront.

Devote the fifth day to all those things you haven't had time for—whether it's more shopping, sightseeing, or unstructured exploration. Visit another island, or, if you have children, make sure you visit Ocean Park (p. 174) with its performances by whales and dolphins, a shark aquarium, playground, and much more. If it's horse-racing season, try to get in on the action. For blitz shopping for fake designer handbags and watches, take the train into mainland China's Shenzhen district (p. 256), just across the Hong Kong border. If you've had something custom-made, don't forget to pick it up. For a memorable last evening in Hong Kong, splurge at one of Hong Kong's fine Chinese or Western restaurants with a view.

If you still have time to spare, I strongly urge you to cross the Pearl River Estuary by jetfoil to spend a day or two in the old Portuguese city of Macau, the first European settlement in the Far East (see chapter 11). On December 20, 1999, Macau reverted back to Chinese rule, becoming a special administrative region similar to Hong Kong. Not only is Macau cheaper than Hong Kong, but it is also very different, with its Mediterranean-influenced architecture in the old town, several great special-interest museums, fantastic Macanese cuisine, and more shopping opportunities.

1 Hong Kong's Top Attractions

The four activities I would recommend to every visitor to the SAR are: Ride the Star Ferry across the harbor; take the Peak tram to the top of Victoria Peak; ride one of the rickety old trams on Hong Kong Island; and take a ferry to one of the outlying islands (see chapter 10, "Side Trips from Hong Kong," for information on the islands). Nothing can beat the thrill of these four experiences, or give you a better insight into the essence of Hong Kong and its people. What's more, they're all incredibly inexpensive.

HONG KONG FERRIES

The stars of the Hong Kong show, of course, are the Star Ferries, green-and-white vessels that have been carrying passengers back and forth between Kowloon and Hong Kong Island since 1898. At only HK$1.70 (US20¢) for the regular, lower-deck fare, it's one of the cheapest—and yet most dramatic—5-minute rides in the world. The entire trip from loading pier to unloading pier takes about 7 minutes in all; there are approximately 400 crossings a day. (For tips on using the Star Ferry, see "Getting Around" in chapter 3, beginning on p. 50.)

Since a 5-minute ride isn't nearly enough time to soak up the ambience of Victoria Harbour, another great way to relax and view the skyline is on a ferry to an outlying island. While most of Hong Kong's 260 outlying islands are uninhabited, ferry trips to the most interesting ones are described in chapter 10. These ferries, which depart from the Central District, are by far the cheapest way to see Hong Kong harbor, with most trips lasting less than an hour. Some even offer an outside deck, where you can watch Hong Kong float past. In fact, part of the fun in visiting an outlying island is the ferry ride there and back.

VICTORIA PEAK

At 392m (1,308 ft.), Victoria Peak is Hong Kong Island's tallest hill, which naturally makes it the best place for spectacular views of the city and surrounding areas (if possible, go on a crystal-clear day). It's always been one of Hong Kong's most exclusive places to live, since, in addition to the views, the peak is typically cooler than the sweltering city below. More than a century ago, the rich reached the peak after a 3-hour trip in sedan chairs, transported to the top by coolies. Then, in 1888, the **Peak tram** began operations, cutting the journey from a grueling 3 hours to a mere 8 minutes. In 1989, the older, cast-iron green funicular cars with mahogany seats were replaced by new, modern cars imported from Switzerland, which increased the passenger load from 72 to 120 people.

The easiest way to reach the Peak Tram Station, located on Garden Road, is to take the no. 15C open-top shuttle bus that operates between the tram terminal and the Star Ferry in Central. (After exiting from the Star Ferry, turn left; shuttle buses depart from a traffic island located between the parking garage and City Hall.) Shuttle buses cost HK$3.20 (US40¢) and run every 10 to 20 minutes between 10am and 11:45pm. Otherwise, it's about a 10-minute walk to Garden Road and the tram station. Alternatively, you can take Minibus no. 15 from in front of the Star Ferry in Central directly to the top of Victoria Peak, but then you'd miss the tram unless you opt to take it down.

As for the trams, they depart every 15 minutes between 7am and midnight. The tram climbs almost vertically for 8 minutes before reaching the top of the peak—don't worry, there's never been an accident in its entire 100-odd years of operation. One-way tickets for the Peak tram cost HK$20 (US$2.60) for adults, HK$7 (US90¢) for seniors, and HK$6 (US80¢) for children. Round-trip tickets cost HK$30 (US$3.90), HK$14 (US$1.80), and HK$9 (US$1.15), respectively. Or, you can use an Octopus card. Upon reaching The Peak, you'll find

---

Tips **The Best Peek of the Peak**

For the best view when riding the Peak tram up to Victoria Peak, try to get a seat at the front, on the right side of the tram.

---

yourself at the very modern **Peak Tower** (www.thepeak.com.hk), designed by British architect Terry Farrell, which looks like a Chinese cooking wok. Head straight for the viewing terrace on Level 5, where you'll be privileged to one of the world's most breathtaking views, with the skyscrapers of Central, the boats plying Victoria Harbour, Kowloon, and the many hills of the New Territories undulating in the background.

Of the three attractions located in Peak Tower, the most well known around the world is probably **Madame Tussaud's,** Level 2, Peak Tower, 128 Peak Rd., Victoria Peak (© **852/3128 8288;** www.madame-tussauds.com.hk), with more than 100 life-size wax figures of celebrities, politicians, and historical figures. In addition to the usual figures—Marilyn Monroe, the Beatles, Winston Churchill, victims in a medieval torture chamber—there are also local heroes like Jackie Chan, Michelle Yeoh, and Bruce Lee. Be sure to bring your camera. It's open daily from 10am to 10pm and costs HK$95 (US$12) for adults and HK$55 (US$7.15) for seniors and children. You'll probably spend about 30 minutes here.

Another well-known attraction is **Ripley's Believe It or Not! Odditorium,** located on Level 3 of the Peak Tower (© **852/2849 0698;** www.ripleys.com). The 26th Ripley's museum to open worldwide, it contains oddities (and replicas of oddities) collected by Robert L. Ripley on visits to 198 countries over 55 years, including a shrunken head from Ecuador, torture items from around the world, a two-headed calf, and models of the world's tallest and fattest men. Be forewarned that some of the items are purely grotesque, or, at best, out of date in a more socially correct world. Still, human nature being what it is, probably everyone wants to visit one of these museums at least once, and children, of course, are fascinated. You probably won't be able to tear them away in less than an hour. It's open daily from 10am to 10pm and costs HK$90 (US$12) for adults and HK$50 (US$6.50) for seniors and children.

Peak Explorer, Level 4 of the Peak Tower (© **852/2849 0866;** www.the peak.com.hk/tower/explorer.html), is a 36-seat motion-simulator theater that features changing, 8-minute fast-paced films and seats that move, jerk, roll, and rock in accordance to the action on the screen. It's almost like being onboard the roller coaster, racecar, motorbike, or whatever is being shown, and is definitely not for those with motion sickness. Admission here is HK$62 (US$8.05) for adults and HK$35 (US$4.55) for seniors and children. It's open daily from 10am to 10pm.

If you wish, you can buy various combination tickets for the peak tram and attractions. A combination for everything—all three attractions and round-trip on the tram—costs HK$190 ($25) for adults and HK$115 ($15) for seniors and children. Frankly, I consider your time in Hong Kong better spent elsewhere (since you can find these attractions in many other places throughout the world), though if you have older children in tow, you may not have a choice.

When you're finished in Peak Tower, exit it via Level 4. Across the street is the **Peak Galleria,** a three-story complex with shops, restaurants, an outdoor children's playground, and a viewing terrace.

But the best thing to do atop Victoria Peak is to take a walk. One of my favorite walks in all of Hong Kong is the hour-long circular hike on Lugard Road and Harlech Road, both located just a stone's throw from the Peak tram terminus. Mainly a footpath overhung with banyan trees and passing lush vegetation, it snakes along the side of the cliff, offering great views of the Central District below, the harbor, Kowloon, and then Aberdeen and the outlying islands on the other side. Along the path are signboards identifying flora and fauna. You will also pass Victoria Peak mansions. At night, the lighted path offers one of the world's most romantic views. Don't miss it.

RIDING A TRAM

Just as the Star Ferry is the best way to see the harbor, the tram is the most colorful and cheapest way to see the northern end of Hong Kong Island, including the Central District, Western District, Wan Chai, and Causeway Bay. In fact, the tram is so much a part of Hong Kong life that it was chosen for Hong Kong's exhibit at the Vancouver '86 Expo. Dating from 1904, the tramline follows what used to be the waterfront (before the days of land reclamation). Old, narrow, double-decker affairs, the trams cut through the heart of the city, from Kennedy Town in the west to Shau Kei Wan in the east. There's only one detour—off to Happy Valley—so it's impossible to get lost.

In any case, if you're in Central, you can board the tram on Des Voeux Road Central. Climb to the upper deck and try to get a seat in the front row. (For more information on the fare and how to ride the tram, see "Getting Around" in chapter 3, beginning on p. 50.) I especially like to ride the tram at night, when neon signs are ablaze and the streets buzz with activity.

2 Museums & Galleries

If you plan to visit all six of Hong Kong's main museums—the Hong Kong Museum of Art, Hong Kong Museum of History, Hong Kong Space Museum, Hong Kong Science Museum, Hong Kong Museum of Coastal Defence, and Hong Kong Heritage Museum (located in Sha Tin in the New Territories; see p. 240)—you can save money by purchasing the Museum Pass for HK$30 (US$3.90) at any of the participating museums or Hong Kong Tourism Board Visitor Information and Services Centres. The total price of purchasing single tickets to all five museums is HK$75 (US$9.75). Note that museum admissions are free on Wednesdays.

Keep in mind, too, that municipal museums are closed December 25 and 26, January 1, and the first 3 days of the Chinese New Year. Private museums are usually also closed on bank holidays.

IN KOWLOON

Hong Kong Museum of Art ★★★ *(Finds*   Because of its convenient location on the Tsim Sha Tsui waterfront, just a 2-minute walk from the Star Ferry terminus, and its manageable size, this museum is the most worthwhile if your time is limited. I love popping in to see the special exhibits and the museum's vast collection of Chinese antiquities and fine art—shown on a rotating basis—that make this one of my top picks in Hong Kong. Feast your eyes on ceramics, bronzes, jade, cloisonné, lacquerware, bamboo carvings, and textiles, as well as paintings, wall hangings, scrolls, and calligraphy dating from the 16th century to the present. The works are arranged in five permanent galleries on three floors of exhibit space, plus two galleries devoted to changing exhibits. The Historical Pictures Gallery is especially insightful, with 1,000 works in oils, watercolors, pencil drawings, and prints that provide a visual account of life in Hong Kong, Macau, and Guangzhou (Canton) in the late 18th and 19th centuries. Another gallery displays contemporary Hong Kong works by local artists. You'll want to

Kowloon Attractions

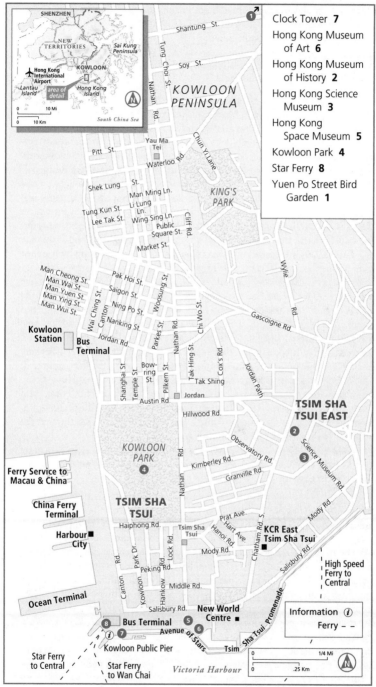

Clock Tower **7**

Hong Kong Museum
of Art **6**

Hong Kong Museum
of History **2**

Hong Kong Science
Museum **3**

Hong Kong
Space Museum **5**

Kowloon Park **4**

Star Ferry **8**

Yuen Po Street Bird
Garden **1**

SHENZHEN

NEW
TERRITORIES

Sai Kung
Peninsula

Hong Kong
International
Airport

KOWLOON

Lantau
Island

Hong Kong
Island

area of
detail

South China Sea

0   10 Mi
0   10 Km

Shantung St.

Tung Choi St.

Soy St.

Nathan Rd.

KOWLOON
PENINSULA

Chun Yi Lane

Pitt St.

Yau Ma
Tei

Waterloo Rd.

KING'S
PARK

Shek Lung St.

Man Ming Ln.

Li Lung Ln.

Tung Kun St.

Lee Tak St.

Wing Sing Ln.

Public
Square St.

Cliff Rd.

Market St.

Wylie

Man Cheong St.

Man Wai St.

Man Yuen St.

Man Ying St.

Man Wui St.

Pak Hoi St.

Saigon St.

Ning Po St.

Nanking St.

Wai Ching St.

Canton

Woosung St.

Chi Wo St.

Gascoigne Rd.

Kowloon
Station

Bus
Terminal

Jordan Rd.

Parkes St.

Nathan Rd.

Tak Hing St.

Cox's Rd.

Jordan Path

Shanghai St.

Temple St.

Bow-
ring
St.

Pilkem St.

Tak Shing

Jordan

Austin Rd.

Hillwood Rd.

TSIM SHA
TSUI EAST

Ferry Service to
Macau & China

KOWLOON
PARK

Nathan Rd.

Observatory Rd.

Science Museum Rd.

China Ferry
Terminal

Kimberley Rd.

Granville Rd.

TSIM SHA
TSUI

Harbour
City

Haiphong Rd.

Tsim Sha
Tsui

Prat Ave.

Hart Ave.

Hanoi Rd.

Chatham Rd. S.

KCR East
Tsim Sha Tsui

Mody Rd.

Canton Rd.

Park Dr.

Peking Rd.

Kowloon Rd.

Lock Rd.

Hankow Rd.

Mody Rd.

Middle Rd.

Salisbury Rd.

High Speed
Ferry to
Central

Ocean Terminal

Bus Terminal

Salisbury Rd.

New World
Centre

Avenue of Stars

Sha Tsui Promenade

Information ⓘ

Ferry - - -

Kowloon Public Pier

Tsim

Star Ferry
to Central

Star Ferry
to Wan Chai

Victoria Harbour

0   1/4 Mi
0   .25 Km

8 **7** ⓘ **4** **2** **3** **5** **6**

spend at least an hour here, though art aficionados may want to devote more time by renting audio guides for HK$10 (US$1.30). A bonus is the beautiful backdrop of Victoria Harbour.

Hong Kong Cultural Centre Complex, 10 Salisbury Rd., Tsim Sha Tsui. ℭ 852/2721 0116. www.lcsd.gov.hk/hkma. Admission HK$10 (US$1.30) adults; HK$5 (US65¢) children, students, and seniors. Free admission Wed. Fri–Wed 10am–6pm. MTR: Tsim Sha Tsui (exit E).

Hong Kong Museum of History ★★★ Kids   If you visit only one museum in Hong Kong, this should be it. Make it one of your first priorities, so you'll have a better understanding of what you see during the rest of your trip. Opened in 2001, this is Hong Kong's ambitious attempt to chronicle its long and fascinating history, starting with the formation of its natural history and its beginnings as a Neolithic settlement and continuing through its development as a fishing village and subsequent transformation into a modern metropolis. Through displays that include dioramas, replicas of fishing boats, models, reconstructed traditional housing, furniture, clothing, and items from daily life, the museum introduces Hong Kong's ethnic groups and their traditional means of livelihood, customs, and beliefs. These include the Tanka, who lived their entire lives on boats, the Five Great Clans who settled in what is now the New Territories and built walled communities, and the Hakka, primarily rice farmers.

You can peer inside a fishing junk, see what Kowloon Walled City looked like before it became a park, see the backstage of a Chinese opera, read about the arrival of European traders and the Opium Wars, study a map showing land reclamation since the 1840s, and see how Hong Kong changed under Japanese occupation (surprisingly, the section on Japanese occupation is quite extensive, considering that it takes up less than 4 years of Hong Kong's history). There are small movie theaters spread throughout, though showings in English are limited. One of my favorite parts of the museum is a re-created street of old Hong Kong, complete with a Chinese herbal-medicine shop actually located in Central until 1980, and reconstructed here. There are also 19th- and early-20th-century photographs, poignantly showing how much Hong Kong has changed through the decades. You can easily spend 2 hours here.

100 Chatham Rd. S., Tsim Sha Tsui East. ℭ 852/2724 9042. http://hk.history.museum. Admission HK$10 (US$1.30) adults, HK$5 (US65¢) children and seniors. Free admission Wed. Mon and Wed–Sat 10am–6pm; Sun and holidays 10am–7pm. MTR: Tsim Sha Tsui (a 20-min. walk from exit B2). Bus: 5 or 5C from the Star Ferry bus terminus.

Hong Kong Science Museum ★★ Kids   The mysteries of science and technology come to life here, with plenty of hands-on exhibits sure to appeal to children and adults alike. More than 500 exhibits cover four floors, with sections devoted to the life sciences; light, sound, and motion; meteorology and geography; electricity and magnetism; computers and robotics; construction; transportation and communication; occupational safety and health; energy efficiency; and food science and home technology. There is also an area specially designed for children 3 to 7. Visitors can play with different optical illusions, enter a rotating room to learn physics in a noninertial frame, "freeze" their shadows on a wall, pick up remote voices with a large parabolic disc, play with bubbles, navigate a flight over Hong Kong Island or Kowloon at night, watch the mechanisms of an eight-cylinder gasoline engine, and learn about herbs used in traditional Chinese medicine. There are exhibits designed to test a visitor's fitness, such as lung capacity, endurance, and blood pressure. There are more than 30 personal computers in the computer section, where guests can learn about computer software, including word processing for children and graphics production, and surf the Internet

for free (unfortunately, only two computers are for the Internet). This is a great place to bring kids on a rainy or humid day, when you'll want spend about 3 hours here. However, since this museum isn't unique to Hong Kong, I think childless adults can better spend their time elsewhere.

2 Science Museum Rd., Tsim Sha Tsui East. ℂ 852/2732 3232. http://hk.science.museum. Admission HK$25 (US$3.25) adults, HK$12.50 (US$1.60) children, students, and seniors. Free admission Wed. Mon–Wed and Fri 1–9pm; Sat–Sun and holidays 10am–9pm. MTR: Tsim Sha Tsui (a 20-min. walk from exit B2). Bus: 5 or 5C from the Star Ferry bus terminus.

Hong Kong Space Museum *Kids*   Located in front of The Peninsula hotel on the Tsim Sha Tsui waterfront, the Space Museum is easy to spot with its white-domed planetarium. It's divided into two parts: the Exhibition Halls with its Hall of Space Science and the Hall of Astronomy; and the Space Theatre. The Hall of Space Science explores the human journey into space, with exhibits on ancient astronomical history, science fiction, early rockets, manned space flights, and future space programs. There are also several interactive rides and exhibits (most with weight and height restrictions), including a ride on a virtual paraglider, a harness that holds occupants aloft with the same approximate gravity they'd experience walking on the moon, and a multi-axis chair developed for astronaut training that gives the sensation of tumbling through space. The Hall of Astronomy presents information on the solar system, solar science, the stars, and the universe. I find the museum, which opened in 1980, rather dated. Come only if you have kids and extra time on your hands, in which case you'll spend about an hour here.

The Space Theatre presents mostly OMNIMAX screenings with a projection system that produces an almost 360-degree panorama, as well as sky shows with a Zeiss star projector that can project up to about 9,000 stars. Forty-minute to hour-long shows are presented several times daily. Only a few are narrated in English, but for the others, free headsets are available with simultaneous English translations. You can buy Space Theatre tickets in advance at the museum, any URBTIX outlet, or by credit card by calling ℂ **852/2111 5999.** Call ℂ **852/ 2734 2722** for show schedules in English.

Hong Kong Cultural Centre Complex, 10 Salisbury Rd., Tsim Sha Tsui. ℂ 852/2721 0226. http://hk.space. museum. Admission to Exhibition Halls HK$10 (US$1.30) adults, HK$5 (US65¢) children, students, and sen-iors. Free admission on Wed. Space Theatre HK$24–HK$32 (US$3.10–US$4.15) adults, HK$12–HK$16 (US$1.55–US$2.10) children, students, and seniors. Mon and Wed–Fri 1–9pm; Sat–Sun and holidays 10am–9pm. MTR: Tsim Sha Tsui (exit E).

ON HONG KONG ISLAND

Flagstaff House Museum of Tea Ware ★★ *Finds*   Flagstaff House, located in Hong Kong Park, is the oldest colonial building in Hong Kong—the best place to go if you want to see typical Hong Kong architecture of 150 years ago. The house was completed in 1846 in Greek Revival style for the commander of the British forces. Now a museum devoted to the subject of tea culture in China, its collec-tion includes about 600 pieces of tea ware ranging from earthenware to porcelain, primarily of Chinese origin, dating from the 7th century to the present day. How-ever, only 150 or so pieces are on display at any one time, with exhibitions changed two or three times a year. I always find them fascinating, especially the exhibits describing the various kinds of tea and tea-making methods favored by the major dynasties. Don't miss the museum shop, which sells beautifully crafted teapots as well as teas. You can see everything here in about 30 minutes.

Hong Kong Park, 10 Cotton Tree Dr., Central. ℂ 852/2869 0690. www.lcsd.gov.hk/hkma. Free admission. Wed–Mon 10am–5pm. MTR: Admiralty (exit C1); then follow the signs through Pacific Place to Island Shangri-La Hotel/Hong Kong Park via 2 escalators.

The Hong Kong Planning and Infrastructure Exhibition Gallery ⭐ *(Finds)*
Its name is dry and unpromising, but anyone who has witnessed the SAR's changes over the past few decades will find this museum fascinating—Hong Kong is a never-ending work in progress. Over the next few decades, the city will continue to develop its tourism, transportation, and urban infrastructure at what seems like breakneck speed. The purpose of this museum is to help visitors visualize those changes through sophisticated computer simulation and high-tech models that project Hong Kong's new look two, ten, and 20 years from now. West Kowloon, embraced by a huge canopy to be designed by Norman Foster, will become one of the city's foremost cultural and entertainment centers when completed around 2012. Future works include a pedestrian promenade on Hong Kong Island stretching along the waterfront from Central to Causeway Bay; enlarged cargo capacity at the airport; a new town where Kai Tak Airport once stood, a fourth tunnel under the harbor, and 100km (62 miles) of new highway over the next decade. There are some fun exhibits, too, including a 3D flight over Sha Tin in the New Territories and a photo booth that takes your picture with a selected Hong Kong backdrop (like the giant Buddha on Lantau island) and then lets you e-mail it to friends for free. But the highlight of the museum is the "stroll" along Hong Kong's future waterfront via a three-dimensional panorama that surrounds you on all sides. The museum's location near Central's Star Ferry, on the north side of City Hall, makes it a convenient place to pop in. It can be toured in about 45 minutes.

3 Edinburgh Place, Central. ℂ 852/3101 6516. www.info.gov.hk/infrastructuregallery. Free admission. Wed–Mon 10am–6pm. MTR: Central.

Hong Kong Museum of Coastal Defence   Located in Lei Yue Mun Fort, one of Hong Kong's oldest and best-preserved British coastal fortresses dating from the Victorian period, this museum explores 600 years of the territory's coastal defense. Exhibits begin with the Ming and Qing dynasties, when coastal defenses guarded southern China against the invasion of Japanese pirates and Western imperialists, and continue through the Opium Wars, Hong Kong's role as a major base for the British navy, the Japanese 1941 invasion, and the recent

---

(Fun Fact **Did You Know?**

- The 1,355m (4,517-ft.) Tsing Ma Bridge, the world's second-longest road/rail suspension bridge, which connects the new international airport with Kowloon, is 95m (318 ft.) longer than San Francisco's Golden Gate Bridge and can withstand typhoon wind speeds up to 300km (186 miles) per hour.
- Hong Kong boasts several of the world's longest escalators. The world's two longest covered outdoor escalator systems are the four-section, 221m (738-ft.) system at Ocean Park and the 780m (2,600-ft.) Central/Mid-Levels escalator connecting Central to the Mid-Levels with a capacity of handling 210,600 passengers a day. The Hongkong Bank headquarters in Central boasts the two longest freely supported (no supporting walls along their lengths) escalators in the world.

City Hall **2**

Flagstaff House Museum of Teaware **8**

Hong Kong Museum of Coastal Defence **5**

Hong Kong Museum of Medical Science **4**

Hong Kong Park **8**

The Hong Kong Planning and Infrastructure Exhibition Gallery **3**

Man Mo Temple **4**

Peak Tram Terminal **7**

Star Ferry **1**

Zoological & Botanical Gardens **6**

Tramway

Post Office

0   100 Meters

0   1/10 Mi

Pacific Place

ADMIRALTY

Admiralty

Tamar St.

Queensway

Cotton Tree Drive

Harcourt Rd.

Lambeth Walk

Murray Rd.

HONG KONG PARK

Cotton Tree Dr.

Garden Rd.

CHATER GARDEN

Queen's Pier

City Hall

STATUE SQUARE

Chater Rd.

STATUE SQUARE

Club St.

Jackson Rd.

Edinburgh Place

Connaught Rd. Central

Bank St.

Des Voeux Rd. Central

Ice House St.

Queen's Rd. Central

Battery Path

Peak Tram

Star Ferry Pier

Hong Kong

General Post Office

Exchange Square

CENTRAL DISTRICT

Central

Douglas Lane

Connaught Rd. Central

Pedder St.

Queen's Rd. Central

Wyndham St.

Duddell St.

LAN KWAI FONG

Wellington St.

Wo On Lane

D'Aguilar St.

D'Aguilar St.

Wyndham St.

SOHO →

MID-LEVELS →

Upper Albert Road

Upper Albert Road

ZOOLOGICAL & BOTANICAL GARDENS

SHENZHEN

NEW TERRITORIES

Sai Kung Peninsula

KOWLOON

Hong Kong International Airport

Lantau Island

Hong Kong Island

Area of detail

South China Sea

0   10 Km

0   10 Mi

Life on the Water in Aberdeen

Situated on the south side of Hong Kong Island, Aberdeen is nestled around a naturally protected harbor. Famous for its colorful floating seafood restaurant and boat people who live on junks in Aberdeen Harbour, the town has undergone massive changes in recent years. Originally a typhoon shelter and land base for seafarers, it used to be a charming fishing village and boat-building port, supported primarily by several thousand junks and boat people. Many of the boat people, however, have since been moved to massive housing projects, and the waterfront surrounding Aberdeen is now crowded with high-rises. At anchor are almost as many yachts as fishing boats and junks.

Still, Aberdeen continues to be popular with the tourist crowd because of its remaining boat population and floating restaurant. Women operating sampans will vie for your dollars to tour you around the harbor, which is definitely worth the price since it's about the only thing to do here and is the best way to see the junks. Although the boat population is shrinking, you'll pass huge boats that house extended families; you'll see men repairing fishing nets, women hanging out their laundry, dogs barking, children playing, and families eating. I find the ride rather voyeuristic but fascinating just the same. There was a time when a boat person could be born, live, marry, and die onboard, hardly ever setting foot on shore. Nowadays, many young people move ashore to seek more stable employment.

A 20-minute tour from a licensed operator will cost approximately HK$60 (US$7.80) per person and is offered daily between 9am and 5:30pm from the Aberdeen Centre promenade. There are also old women with wide-brimmed straw hats who will try to persuade you to board their sampan, with the price open to bargaining and depending on the numbers of tourists around at the time. On one particularly slow day, for example, I was offered, and took, a sampan tour for HK$50 (US$6.50), and I was the only one in the boat.

Other Aberdeen attractions include the largest floating restaurant in the world—Jumbo Kingdom (p. 152), which offers free shuttle service from the Aberdeen Centre promenade—and a temple built in 1851. The temple is dedicated to Tin Hau, protectress of fishing folk, and is located at the junction of Aberdeen Main Road and Aberdeen Reservoir Road. A short taxi ride away is the huge Ocean Park amusement park with its thrill rides and aquarium.

To get to Aberdeen, take bus no. 7 from the Central outlying ferries pier; bus no. 70 from the Exchange Square Bus Terminal in the Central District; or bus no. 72 from Causeway Bay.

handover to the People's Liberation Army. On display are naval costumes, models of war junks, weaponry, photographs, and memorabilia. The fort itself, built by the British in 1887 to defend the eastern approaches to the harbor against possible attacks by Russia or France, retains its batteries, underground magazines, protective ditch, caponiers, and torpedo station. With its strategic location on the coast, it provides a panoramic view of the eastern approach to Victoria Harbour. You'll probably spend at least 1½ hours here.

175 Tung Hei Rd., Shau Kei Wan. ℂ 852/2569 1500. http://hk.coastaldefence.museum. Admission HK$10 (US$1.30) adults; HK$5 (US65¢) students, seniors, and children. Free admission Wed. Fri–Wed 10am–5pm. MTR: Shau Kei Wan (exit B2, then a 15-min. walk).

Hong Kong Museum of Medical Sciences ★ *Finds*   This museum charts the historical development of medical science in Hong Kong. It's located in the century-old, Edwardian-style former Pathological Institute, which was founded to combat the colony's most horrific outbreak of bubonic plague. Back then, British patients were treated upstairs, while the Chinese were relegated to the basement rooms. Several rooms remain almost exactly as they were, including an autopsy room and a laboratory filled with old equipment, while others serve as exhibition rooms devoted to such areas as the development of dentistry and radiology (note the X-ray of the bound foot). But what makes the museum particularly fascinating is its unique comparison of traditional Chinese and Western medicine, and its funding of research into Chinese medicine. Included are displays on acupuncture and traditional Chinese herbs. You can spend up to an hour here.

2 Caine Lane, Mid-Levels. ℂ 852/2549 5123. www.hkmms.org.hk. Admission HK$10 (US$1.30) adults, HK$5 (US65¢) children, students, and seniors. Tues and Thurs–Sat 10am–5pm; Wed 10am–7pm; Sun and holidays 1–5pm. MTR: Central; then bus no. 26 from Des Voeux Rd. in front of Hongkong Bank headquarters to Man Mo Temple; walk up Ladder St. (a particularly grueling set of stairs) to Caine Lane. Or, take Minibus 8 or 22 from in front of Central's Star Ferry to Ladder St. (pronounced Lau Tai Kai in Chinese).

3 Temples

For information on Po Lin Monastery and its adjacent Giant Tian Tan Buddha, see the section on Lantau island in "Side Trips from Hong Kong" in chapter 10, beginning on p. 246.

Chi Lin Buddhist Nunnery   Just one subway stop away from Wong Tai Sin (see below) is the Chi Lin Buddhist Nunnery, founded in the 1930s to provide religious, cultural, educational, and elderly care services to the Hong Kong community. Reconstructed in the 1990s in the style of Tang dynasty monastic architecture (A.D. 618–907), the nunnery is a successful union of ancient building techniques and modern technology. Imported yellow cedar from Canada was carved in China by skilled artisans and craftsmen and then reconstructed here like pieces in a jigsaw puzzle; no nails were used, but rather a system of wooden doweling and brackets. The main hall was modeled after the Foguang Monastery in Shanxi Province, while the double-eaved Hall of Celestial Kings is designed after the 11th-century Phoenix Hall outside Kyoto, Japan. On nunnery grounds are a lotus pond, sculpted bushes and bonsai, and statues of the Goddess of Mercy, God of Medicine, and others. Otherwise, there isn't much to see; this will appeal mostly to architects and East Asian scholars.

Chi Lin Rd., Diamond Hill. ℂ 852/2354 1712. Free admission. Daily 9am–4:30pm. MTR: Diamond Hill (exit C2) and then a 15-min. walk.

Man Mo Temple ★   Hong Kong Island's oldest and most important temple (Taoist) was built in the 1840s and is named after its two principal deities: Man, the god of literature, who is dressed in red and holds a calligraphy brush; and Mo, the god of war, wearing a green robe and holding a sword. Ironically, Mo finds patronage in both the police force (shrines in his honor can be found in all

Hong Kong police stations today) and the infamous triad secret societies. Two ornately carved sedan chairs in the temple were once used during festivals to carry the statues of the gods around the neighborhood. But what makes this evocative temple particularly memorable are the giant incense coils hanging from the ceiling, imparting a fragrant, smoky haze—these are purchased by patrons seeking fulfillment of their wishes, such as good health or a successful business deal, and may burn as long as 3 weeks. No flash photography is allowed inside the temple.

Hollywood Rd. and Ladder St., Western District. ☏ 852/2803 2916. Free admission. Daily 8am–6pm. Bus: no. 26 from Des Voeux Rd. Central (in front of the Hongkong Bank headquarters) to the 2nd stop on Hollywood Rd., across from the temple. Or, take the Mid-Levels Escalator to Hollywood Road.

Wong Tai Sin 🚻🚻　Located six subway stops northeast of Yau Ma Tei in the far north end of Kowloon Peninsula, Wong Tai Sin is Hong Kong's most popular Taoist temple and attracts worshippers of all three traditional Chinese religions: Taoism, Buddhism, and Confucianism. Although the temple itself dates only from 1973, it adheres to traditional Chinese architectural principles with its red pillars, two-tiered golden roof, blue friezes, yellow latticework, and multicolored carvings. The temple is very popular; everyone who comes here is seeking information about their fortunes—from advice about business or horse racing to determining which day is most auspicious for a wedding. Most worshippers make use of a bamboo container holding numbered sticks. After lighting a joss stick and kneeling before the main altar, the worshipper gently shakes the container until one of the sticks falls out. The number corresponds to a certain fortune, which is then interpreted by a soothsayer at the temple.

You can wander around the temple grounds, where there are halls dedicated to the Buddhist Goddess of Mercy and to Confucius; the Nine Dragon Garden, a Chinese garden with a pond, waterfall, and a replica of the famous Nine Dragons mural (the original is in Beijing's Imperial Palace); the Good Wish Garden, a replica of the Yi He Garden in Beijing with circular, square, octagonal, and fan-shaped pavilions, ponds, an artificial waterfall, and rocks and concrete fashioned to resemble animals; and a clinic with both Western medical services and traditional Chinese herbal treatments. Wong Tai Sin takes its name, in fact, from a legendary shepherd who learned the art of healing. A visit to this temple, surrounded by vast, government housing estates, provides insight into Chinese religious practices and is well worth a stop despite its out-of-the-way location.

2 Wong Tai Sin Estate. ☏ 852/2327 8141. www.siksikyuen.org.hk. Free admission to temple, though donations of about HK$1 (US15¢) are expected at the temple's entrance and for Nine Dragon Wall Garden; admission to Good Wish Garden HK$2 (US25¢) extra. Temple open daily 7am–5:30pm; gardens open Tues–Sun 9am–4pm. MTR: Wong Tai Sin (exit B2) and then a 3-min. walk (follow the signs).

4 Parks & Gardens

IN KOWLOON

KOWLOON PARK *(Kids)*　Occupying the site of an old military encampment first established in the 1860s, Kowloon Park (☏ 852/2724 3344) is Tsim Sha Tsui's largest recreational and sports facility, boasting an indoor heated Olympic-size swimming pool, three outdoor leisure pools linked by a series of waterfalls, an open-air sculpture garden featuring works by local and overseas sculptors, a Chinese garden, a fitness trail, an aviary, a maze formed by hedges, a children's playground, and a bird lake with flamingos and other waterfowl. On Sundays from 2:30 to 4:30pm there are free Kung Fu demonstrations at the Kung Fu

Corner. Not far from the Tsim Sha Tsui MTR station (take the A1 exit for Kowloon Park), it's easily accessible from Nathan, Haiphong, and Austin roads and is open daily from 6am to midnight, with free admission. The swimming pools (© **852/2724 4522**) are open daily from 6:30am to 9pm and charge HK$19 (US$2.45) for adults and HK$9 (US$1.15) for children.

KOWLOON WALLED CITY PARK ★★ *Finds*   Hong Kong's newest park is perhaps its finest. Although it doesn't boast the attractions of the city's other parks, the Kowloon Walled City Park, on Tung Tau Tsuen Road (© **852/2716 9962**), was designed to re-create the style of a classical Southern Chinese garden and is the largest such garden outside China. Beautifully landscaped with man-made hills, ponds, streams, pines, boulders, bonsai, bamboo, and shrubs, it features winding paths through a sculpture garden, flower gardens, pavilions, and a playground.

Even more fascinating is the site's history, described through photographs in a former administration office. More than 150 years ago, the site was on the seashore, making it perfect in 1847 for the construction of a Chinese fort to defend Kowloon after the British takeover of Hong Kong Island. After 1898, when the British took over the New Territories, the 500 soldiers occupying the fort were expelled. But China did not consider the site part of the leased territories, and for most of the next century, the Kowloon Walled City remained in sovereign limbo, ignored by British authorities. It developed a lifestyle of its own, with its own set of laws. An enclave of tenements and secret societies that flouted Hong Kong's building regulations and health standards, it served as a haven for squatters, refugees, criminals, prostitutes, and drug addicts. Densely packed and infested with rats, many parts of the warrenlike slum never saw the light of day. Hong Kong police ventured inside only in pairs. Following a special Sino-British agreement and years of lengthy negotiations over new housing for Walled City residents, the enclave was demolished in 1994. A few historic structures remain, however, including the Old South Gate entrance, wall foundations, and flagstone paths. To reach the park, take the MTR to Lok Fu station (exit B) and then walk 15 minutes on Junction Road to Tung Tau Tsuen Road; or take bus no. 1 from the Star Ferry in Tsim Sha Tsui to the stop opposite the park. It's open daily from 6:30am to 11pm, and admission is free.

YUEN PO STREET BIRD GARDEN ★★★ *Kids*   While in Hong Kong, you may notice wooden birdcages hanging outside shops or from apartment balconies, or perhaps even see someone walking down the street with a cage. Birds are favorite pets in Chinese households, and the price of a bird is determined not by its plumage but by its singing talents. To see more of these prized songbirds, visit the fascinating Yuen Po Street Bird Garden, Prince Edward Road West, which consists of a series of Chinese-style moon gates and courtyards lined with stalls selling songbirds, beautifully crafted wood and bamboo cages, live crickets and mealy worms, and tiny porcelain food bowls. Nothing, it seems, is too expensive for these tiny creatures. The lane is also crowded with scores of people buying and selling birds, or perhaps just taking their birds for an outing. This garden is very Chinese and a lot of fun to see; young children love it. Incidentally, next door is Flower Market Road, lined with flower shops, while on nearby Tung Choi Street is the Goldfish Market with exotic fish. To reach the Bird Garden, open daily from 7am to 8pm, take the MTR to Prince Edward Road station (exit B1 or B2) and walk 10 minutes east on Prince Edward Road West, turning left at the railway onto Yuen Po Street. Admission is free.

ON HONG KONG ISLAND

HONG KONG PARK ★★ *Kids*   Opened in 1991, Hong Kong Park, stretching 8 hectares (19 acres) along Supreme Court Road and Cotton Tree Drive, Central, features a dancing fountain at its entrance; Southeast Asia's largest greenhouse with more than 2,000 rare plant species, including desert and tropical jungle varieties; an aviary housing 800 exotic birds in a tropical rain-forest setting with an elevated walkway; various gardens; a children's playground; and a viewing platform reached by climbing 105 stairs. The most famous building on the park grounds is the Flagstaff House Museum of Tea Ware (p. 165). Since the marriage registry is located at the edge of the park, the gardens are a favorite venue for wedding photographs, especially on weekends and auspicious days of the Chinese calendar. The park is open daily from 6am to 11pm, the greenhouse and aviary are open daily 9am to 5pm, and the Museum of Tea Ware is open Wednesday through Monday from 10am to 5pm. Admission to all is free. To reach the park, take the MTR to Admiralty Station (exit C1), then follow the signs through Pacific Place and up the set of escalators.

VICTORIA PARK   The 17-hectare (42-acre) Victoria Park (© **852/2882 4151**) is one of Hong Kong's largest, located on Causeway and Gloucester roads in Causeway Bay and serving as the green lungs of the city. Constructed on reclaimed land formerly used for a typhoon shelter, it has tennis and squash courts, a 50m (164-ft.) swimming pool, soccer fields, basketball courts, playgrounds, a skating rink, a jogging track, and—my favorite—a pebble path for massaging the bottom of your feet. It is also popular in early morning for those practicing tai chi (shadow boxing). The Mid-Autumn Festival is held here, as well as a flower market a few days before Chinese New Year. The park is open 24 hours and is free. To reach it, take the MTR or tram to Causeway Bay.

ZOOLOGICAL & BOTANICAL GARDENS ★ *Kids*   Established in 1864, the Zoological and Botanical Gardens, Upper Albert Road, Central (© **852/ 2530 0154**), are spread on the slope of Victoria Peak, making it a popular respite for Hong Kong residents. Come here early, around 7am, and you'll see Chinese residents going through the slow motions of tai chi, a disciplined physical routine of more than 200 individual movements, designed to exercise every muscle of the body and bring a sense of peace and balance to its practitioners. In the gardens themselves, which retain some of their Victorian charm, flowers are almost always in bloom, from azaleas in the spring to wisteria and bauhinia in the summer and fall. More than 1,000 species of plants, most of them indigenous to tropical and subtropical regions and planted throughout the grounds, include Burmese rosewood trees, varieties of bamboo, Indian rubber trees, camphor trees, a variety of camellia, herbs, and the Hong Kong orchid. The small zoo houses 600 birds, 90 mammals, and 20 reptiles, including jaguars, orang-utans, tamarins, kangaroos, flamingos, a Burmese python, Palawan peacocks, birds of paradise from Papua New Guinea, cranes, and Mandarin ducks. The zoo is well known for its success in breeding birds on the verge of extinction and for supplying zoos around the world with new stock.

If you're tired of Central and its traffic, this is a pleasant place to regain your perspective. There's also a children's playground. Admission is free. The eastern part of the park, containing most of the botanical gardens and the aviaries, is open daily from 6am to 10pm, while the western half, with its reptiles and mammals, is open daily from 6am to 7pm. To reach it, take the MTR to Central and then walk 15 minutes up Garden Road to the corner of Upper Albert Road. Or take bus no. 3B or 12 from the Jardine House on Connaught Road Central.

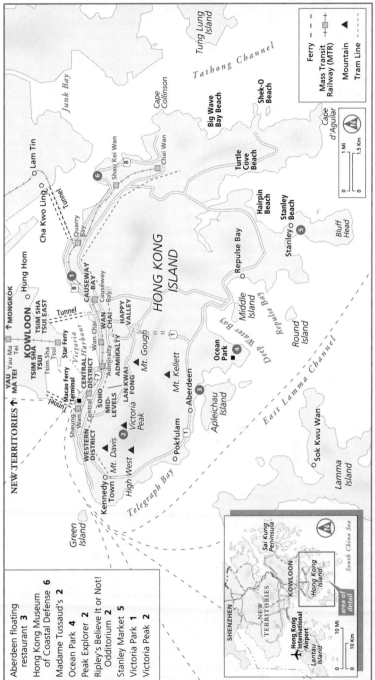

Ferry ----
Mass Transit Railway (MTR) ⊞
Mountain ▲
Tram Line ----

Tung Lung Island

Tathong Channel

Junk Bay

Cape Collinson

Big Wave Bay Beach

Shek-O Beach

Cape d'Aguilar

Lam Tin

Shau Kei Wan

Chai Wan

Turtle Cove Beach

Hairpin Beach

Stanley Beach

Cha Kwo Ling

Quarry Bay

Tunnel

6

8

Stanley

5

Bluff Head

Hung Hom

CAUSEWAY BAY

Causeway Bay

Repulse Bay

1

8

MONGKOK

KOWLOON

TSIM SHA TSUI

TSIM SHA TSUI EAST

Yau Ma Tei

YAU MA TEI

Tsim Sha Tsui

Star Ferry

Tunnel

WAN CHAI

Wan Chai

HAPPY VALLEY

Middle Island

Deep Water Bay

Repulse Bay

NEW TERRITORIES

Macau Ferry Terminal

CENTRAL DISTRICT

Central

SOHO

MID-LEVELS

ADMIRALTY

Admiralty

LAN KWAI FONG

HONG KONG ISLAND

Mt. Gough

1

Round Island

Sheung Wan

WESTERN DISTRICT

Victoria Peak

2

Mt. Kellett

Ocean Park

4

East Lamma Channel

Kennedy Town

Mt. Davis

High West

Victoria

Central Harbour

7

Mt. Gough

Aberdeen

3

Apleichau Island

Sok Kwu Wan

Poktulam

Telegraph Bay

Green Island

Lamma Island

Aberdeen floating
restaurant **3**
Hong Kong Museum
of Coastal Defense **6**
Madame Tussaud's **2**
Ocean Park **4**
Peak Explorer **2**
Ripley's Believe It or Not!
Odditorium **2**
Stanley Market **5**
Victoria Park **1**
Victoria Peak **2**

SHENZHEN

NEW TERRITORIES

Sai Kung Peninsula

KOWLOON

Hong Kong Island

South China Sea

area of detail

Hong Kong International Airport

Lantau Island

10 Km

5 Amusement Parks

Hong Kong Disneyland is scheduled to open some time at the end of 2005 or the beginning of 2006. The 126-hectare (310-acre) theme park, located on Lantau island, just 10 minutes from the airport, is the 11th Disney park and the second in Asia (the first was Tokyo Disneyland). Re-creating many of the exact designs of the original Disneyland in California, it will be familiar to anyone who has ever visited one of the other Disney theme parks, with classic Disney attractions and rides divided into Fantasyland, Adventureland, Tomorrowland, and Main Street, U.S.A. For more information, contact the Hong Kong Tourism Board at © **852/2508 1234** or check Hong Kong Disneyland's website at www.hongkongdisneyland.com.

Ocean Park ✦✦✦ *Kids* If you're a kid or a kid at heart, you'll love Ocean Park, a combination marine park and amusement center. Situated along a dramatic rocky coastline on the island's southern shore, the park is divided into two areas: a "lowland" and a "headland," connected by cable car and escalator. Because of the wide range of attractions, Ocean Park is interesting for children and adults alike. Facilities are first class, and Ocean Park is Asia's first accredited member of the American Zoo and Aquarium Association.

The lowland is subdivided into several areas and attractions. The most popular residents of Ocean Park are An An and Jia Jia, a pair of pandas presented as gifts from China. Aimed at youngsters are the Dinosaur Discovery Trail, with 17 life-like models of dinosaurs (the tyrannosaurus may be too scary for toddlers), and Kids' World, with its kiddie rides, playgrounds, remote-control cars and boats, shows geared toward children, and shooting-games arcade. Educational tours are given at Dolphin University (only one tour a day in English, however), where the audience can watch the training of dolphins at close range. Film Fantasia is a 100-seat theater with hydraulically actuated seats that move in time to the fast-paced action on the screen, kind of like riding a roller coaster without actually going anywhere but visually much more stimulating (participants must be at least 1.2m/4 ft. tall). Much gentler are walks through the magical Butterfly House (shaped, interestingly enough, like a caterpillar) with hundreds of free-flying butterflies, and, my favorite, the Golden Pagoda set in a lush garden, with more varieties of goldfish than you ever imagined possible, most of them from China. The pompommed fish, for example, have large pompomlike growths on their heads, while the bubble eyes, with huge bubbles under their eyes, are too bizarre for words.

From the lowland, visitors board cable cars for a spectacular 8-minute ride over a hill to the headland, while being treated to great views of the coastline and the South China Sea along the way. The headland area, situated on a peninsula that juts into the sea, is also subdivided into several areas and attractions. Pacific Pier features an artificial wave cove that is home to sea lions, penguins, and a shark aquarium, with more than 200 sharks and rays representing more than 30 species, viewed from an underwater tunnel. Ocean Theatre features shows by talented dolphins, sea lions, and a killer whale. But my favorite is the Atoll Reef, one of the world's largest aquariums, with 2,600 fish of 200 different species. The observation passageway circles the aquarium on four levels, enabling you to view the sea life—everything from giant octopi to schools of tropical fish—from various depths and from different angles. There are also thrill rides, including a Ferris wheel, a roller coaster that turns upside down three times, another roller coaster that follows a Wild West theme, and a rather wet ride on a "raging river." Other exhibits include a Japanese Garden; a 69m-high (230 ft.) Ocean Park

Tower offering revolving, panoramic views of Aberdeen and outlying islands; and an aviary with more than 2,000 birds.

After touring the headland, you can take the long escalator down to the Tai Shue Wan Entrance, from which it's a short taxi ride to Aberdeen with its sampan rides and floating restaurant. At any rate, to do Ocean Park justice, plan on spending a minimum of 4 hours here.

Aberdeen, Hong Kong Island. ℰ 852/2552 0291. www.oceanpark.com.hk. Admission HK$185 (US$24) adults, HK$93 (US$12) children. Daily 10am–6pm. Bus: Ocean Park Citybus 629 from the Admiralty MTR station or from the Central Star Ferry pier every 20 min.; you can buy round-trip tickets that include park admission. Or take no. 70 from Exchange Square in Central or no. 72 from Causeway Bay (get off at the 1st stop after the tunnel and then walk 20 min.).

6 Especially for Kids

Many of the above-listed attractions will appeal to children. On the Kowloon side, the **Space Museum** (p. 165) is very much oriented to children, with buttons to push, telescopes to look through, and computer quizzes to test what they've learned, not to mention the films featured in the Space Theatre. In the **Science Museum** (p. 164), more than 60% of its 500-some displays are hands-on, and there's also a special play area for children between the ages of 3 and 7. Across the Plaza is the **Museum of History** (p. 164), with life-size replicas and models that bring the history of Hong Kong to life. And don't forget **Kowloon Park** (p. 170), right on Nathan Road, which has a playground for children, a pond with flamingos and other waterfowl, an aviary, swimming pools, and lots of space to run. Another good destination for children is the **Yuen Po Street Bird Garden** (p. 171) with its thousands of birds.

On Hong Kong Island, the biggest draw for kids of all ages is **Ocean Park** (see above), which boasts a wide mix of things to do and see, including thrill rides; a shark aquarium; animal performances; life-size dinosaurs; and a children's section with kiddie rides, a playground, shows geared to children, and lots more. Of all the things to do in Hong Kong, this is probably the one kids enjoy most, though the 2005/2006 opening of **Hong Kong Disneyland** will provide stiff competition. For free entertainment, visit the **Zoological and Botanical Gardens** (p. 172) with its jaguars, monkeys, birds, and other animals, and **Hong Kong Park** (p. 172) with its greenhouse, aviary, children's playground, and climbing tower. Older kids will like **Victoria Peak** (p. 160), where there are not only fantastic views but also the attractions of Ripley's Believe It or Not! Odditorium, Madame Tussaud's, and the Peak Explorer, a motion-simulator theater with seats that move with the action on the screen.

7 Organized Tours & Cultural Activities

Hong Kong offers lots of organized tours, so if you're pressed for time, this may be the best way to go. Most major hotels have a tour desk where you can make bookings for city tours. In addition, I heartily recommend participating in one or more of the Hong Kong Tourism Board's Meet the People cultural activities, which are free, 1-hour tours, classes, or lectures given by local specialists covering everything from Chinese antiques to tai chi (shadow boxing).

LAND TOURS

For general sightseeing, **Gray Line** offers a variety of tours, with bookings available through most Hong Kong hotels or by calling ℰ **852/2368 7111** or searching www.grayline.com.hk. The Deluxe Hong Kong Island Tour is a

5-hour trip offered both morning and afternoon and includes stops at Man Mo Temple, Victoria Peak, Aberdeen, and Stanley. It costs HK$295 (US$38) for adults and HK$190 (US$25) for children.

Other tours take in the Po Lin Monastery and Giant Buddha on Lantau island or the New Territories; there are also sunset cruises (for information about organized evening tours, see the "Night Tours" section of chapter 9, "Hong Kong After Dark," beginning on p. 235). Most useful, in my opinion, are Gray Line's tours to the New Territories, since they cover large areas that would be very difficult, if not impossible, to reach in one day on your own. The "Land Between Tour" is a 6½-hour excursion that enables visitors to see how much this once-rural region has changed in the past couple decades, with traditional villages now overshadowed by huge government housing estates that house half of Hong Kong's population. Passing satellite towns with high-rise apartment buildings, farms, and villages, the bus stops at a temple, a lookout point on Hong Kong's tallest mountain, a traditional market at Tai Po, a fishing village to see how fisher folk breed fish in submerged cages, and a Cantonese restaurant for lunch. The price of this tour, with departures daily, is HK$395 (US$51) for adults and HK$345 (US$45) for children and seniors.

Gray Line's "Heritage Tour" also takes in the New Territories but emphasizes Hong Kong's past rather than the present and makes stops at historic Chinese sites that even Hong Kong residents seldom see. It's a must for those who are interested in local historical architecture; it also gives insight into clan life in the New Territories long before the region became part of colonial Hong Kong. Lasting approximately 5 hours, tours make stops at Tai Fu Tai, a Chinese-style ornate mansion built in 1865 by a high-ranking official, which is fascinating for its insight into how the rich lived; Tang Chung Ling, an ancestral hall belonging to one of the Five Great Clans; Lo Wai, a walled village built by the Tang clan; and the Man Mo Temple in Tai Po. Tours depart every Monday, Wednesday, Friday, and Saturday (except public holidays), and cost HK$295 (US$38) for adults and HK$245 (US$31) for children and seniors.

Splendid Tours & Travel (© 852/2316 2151; www.splendidtours.com) also offers a general city tour, excursions to Lantau and the New Territories, night tours, and cruises, which can also be booked through Hong Kong hotels.

BOAT TOURS

Since so many of Hong Kong's attractions are on or near the water, a variety of boat tours are available, including those given by Gray Line and Splendid Tours & Travel (see above). One of the most popular is the one-hour **Star Ferry's Harbour Tour** (© 852/2118 6201; www.starferry.com.hk/harbourtour), with boarding available at Tsim Sha Tsui, Central, Wan Chai, and Hung Hom ferry piers. Cost of the daily cruise, which has an on-board commentary, is HK$35 (US$4.55) for adults and HK$32 (US$4.15) for children and seniors.

Watertours (© 852/2926 3868; www.watertourshk.com), Hong Kong's largest tour operator of boat and junk cruises, offers a 2-hour cruise that includes a trip to a typhoon shelter and its junks and the firing of the Noon Day Gun in Causeway Bay (a holdover from colonial days that you can see if you're there, but don't go out of your way to see it) by Jardine Matheson & Co., Hong Kong's oldest trading company. The cost of this tour, which departs at 10:15am from the Kowloon public pier and 10:30am from Queen's Pier in Central and includes a dim sum buffet and drinks, is HK$220 (US$29) for adults and HK$130 (US$17) for children. Watertours also schedules more than a half dozen other longer boat trips, including a combination water-and-land tour and

> ## *Tips* A Junk Cruise for Free
>
> The best cruise deal in town is aboard the *Duk Ling,* an authentic Chinese junk. Free, 1-hour cruises, organized by the Hong Kong Tourism Board, are offered once a week. Contact the HKTB at © **852/2508 1234** or go to www.discoverhongkong.com for the latest schedule.

sunset and evening cruises aboard Chinese junks (for evening cruises, see the "Night Tours" section of chapter 9, "Hong Kong After Dark," beginning on p. 235). You can pick up a Watertours pamphlet at HKTB Visitor Information and Services Centres and in many hotels.

Hong Kong Dolphinwatch (© 852/2984 1414; www.hkdolphinwatch.com) offers 4-hour trips several mornings a week that include a bus ride to the new satellite town of Tung Chung followed by a luxury cruise to the natural habitat of the endangered Chinese pink dolphins (Indo-Pacific Humpback dolphins), which live off Lantau island within sight of power plants, factories, Tung Chung, and the new airport. Advance booking is necessary, and the cost is HK$280 (US$36) for adults and HK$140 (US$18) for children.

SPECIAL-INTEREST TOURS

"MEET THE PEOPLE" *Moments*   Through this unique program of free 1-hour tours, lectures, classes, and seminars, visitors can meet local specialists and gain in-depth knowledge of Hong Kong's traditions. Programs are updated and revised annually; past offerings have included such subjects as Chinese antiques, Cantonese opera, pearls, jade, *feng shui* (geomancy), and tai chi (shadow boxing), with something going on virtually every day of the week. Reservations are not necessary. For details on what, when, and where, pick up a *Cultural Kaleidoscope* brochure at a HKTB Visitor Information and Services Centre.

"COME HORSE RACING" TOUR   This tour, offered by both Gray Line and Splendid Tours (see "City Tours," above), allows visitors to experience the excitement of the races, at either Happy Valley or Sha Tin, an excitement that grows proportionally according to how much you bet. Tours are only scheduled during the horse-racing season—September to mid-June—usually on Wednesday evenings and on Saturday and/or Sunday afternoons. Two types of tours are available: The Classic Tour, costing HK$460 (US$60), includes a pre-race international buffet, personal entry badge to the luxurious Visitors' Box in the Hong Kong Jockey Club's Members' Enclosure, a HK$30 (US$3.90) betting voucher, transportation, guide services, and even hints to help you place your bets. The Race Tour, costing HK$190 (US$25), includes transportation and admission to the Betting Lounge within the Members' Enclosure. Tours are limited to tourists 18 years of age and older (be sure to bring your passport with you when booking and participating in this tour). Bookings can be made through the tour operators, hotel tour desks, or any HKTB Visitor and Information & Services Centres.

8 Outdoor Activities

Despite the fact that the SAR is densely populated, there's enough open space to pursue everything from golf to hiking to windsurfing. For the hardworking Chinese and expatriates, recreation and leisure are essential for relaxing and winding down. With that in mind, try to schedule your golfing, swimming, or hiking trips on weekdays unless you enjoy jostling elbows with the crowds.

GOLF

Golf courses can be crowded, so it's recommended you call the clubs beforehand to check whether they're are open and what tee-off times are available. It's best to book a tee-time in advance. For more information on courses in Hong Kong, contact the Hong Kong Golf Association (© 852/2504 8659; www.hkga.com).

The **Jockey Club Kau Sai Chau Public Golf Course** (© 852/2791 3344; www.kscgolf.com), carved out of an island formerly used by the British Army for shelling practice, offers great panoramic vistas and one of the world's finest public golfing facilities. There is one 18-hole course that charges HK$600 (US$78) on weekdays and HK$900 (US$117) on weekends. There's also a 9-hole course that costs HK$360 (US$47) and HK$530 (US$69), respectively. To reach it, take the MTR to Choi Hung and then board bus 92 or green minibus 1A to Sai Kung Bus Terminus, followed by the special "golfer's ferry" to Kau Sai Chau.

There are also private golf clubs that admit nonmembers on weekdays only. Most charge HK$1,400 (US$182) for greens fees on 18-hole courses. The **Hong Kong Golf Club** (www.hkgolfclub.org) maintains three 18-hole courses in **Fanling** (© 852/2670 1211) and a 9-hole course in **Deep Water Bay** (© 852/2812 7070). No advance reservations are taken, so visitors should first check availability by phone and then arrive early. To reach Fanling, take the KCR railway to Sheung Shui, followed by a 3-minute taxi ride. To reach Deep Water Bay, take bus no. 260 or 262 from Exchange Square in Central.

The **Discovery Bay Golf Club,** on Lantau island (© 852/2987 2112), has a beautiful 18-hole course developed by Robert Trent Jones Jr., offering great views of Hong Kong and the harbor. To reach it, take the 20-minute ferry ride from Central (next to the Star Ferry) to Discovery Bay, followed by a ride in a special shuttle bus. Another scenic 18-hole course and a 9-hole course, operated by the **Clearwater Bay Golf and Country Club** (© 852/2335 3888; www.cwbgolf.org), is located in Sai Kung in the New Territories, on a picturesque headland overlooking the South China Sea. To reach it, take the KCR railway to Sheung Shui, and then take a taxi.

HIKING

With 23 country parks—amounting to more than 40% of Hong Kong's space—there are many trails of varying levels of difficulty throughout Hong Kong, including hiking trails, nature trails, and family trails. Serious hikers, for example, may want to consider the famous **MacLehose Trail** in the New Territories, which stretches about 100km (62 miles) through eight country parks, from the Sai Kung Peninsula in the east to Tuen Mun in the west. The strenuous **Lantau Trail** is a 70km (43-mile) circular trail on **Lantau island** that begins and ends at Mui Wo (also called Silvermine Bay), passing several popular scenic spots and campsites along the way and including a 2½-hour trek to the top of Lantau Peak. Both the MacLehose and Lantau Trails are divided into smaller sections of varying difficulty, which means that you can tailor your hike to suit your own abilities and time constraints. Easier to reach is the 50km (31-mile) **Hong Kong Trail,** which spans Hong Kong Island's five country parks.

Hikers are advised not to hike alone and to check weather reports before departing; from May to October, irregular thunderstorms, typhoons, and heavy showers can cause flooding and landslides. The best hiking season is considered November to February. The Hong Kong Tourism Board has some trail maps and a hiking and wildlife guide book called *Exploring Hong Kong's Countryside: A Visitor's Companion.* HKTB also lists recommended hikes on its website, www.discoverhongkong.com.

JOGGING

The best places to jog on Hong Kong Island without dodging traffic are **Victoria Park's jogging track** in Causeway Bay, **Harlech Road** on Victoria Peak, and **Bowen Road,** which stretches 2.5 km (1½ miles) from Stubbs Road to Magazine Gap Road in the Mid-Levels and offers great views over the harbor. In addition, an inside track at the Happy Valley racecourse is open for runners when the horses aren't using the field. On the other side of the harbor, there's **Kowloon Park,** as well as the waterfront promenade along Tsim Sha Tsui and Tsim Sha Tsui East.

Remember that it can be quite hot and humid during the summer months, so try to jog in the early morning or in the evening.

SWIMMING

In addition to the many outdoor and indoor swimming pools at Hong Kong's hotels that are available for hotel guests, there are numerous public swimming pools, including those at **Kowloon Park** and **Victoria Park.** Prices are HK$19 (US$2.45) for adults and HK$9 (US$1.15) for children and seniors. Avoid hot weekends, when the pools can become quite crowded.

There are also about 40 **beaches** in the SAR that are free for public use; most of them have lifeguards on duty April to October, changing rooms, and snack stands or restaurants. Even on Hong Kong Island itself you can find a number of beaches, including Big Wave Bay and Shek O on the east coast, and Stanley, Deep Water Bay, South Beach (popular with the gay crowd), and Repulse Bay on the southern coast. Repulse Bay, by far the most popular beach in Hong Kong, becomes unbelievably crowded on summer weekends.

There are prettier beaches on the outlying islands, including Hung Shing Ye and Lo So Shing on Lamma, Tung Wan on Cheung Chau, and Cheung Sha on Lantau. It is, however, advisable to check on water pollution before plunging in, especially on the islands. Furthermore, I wouldn't recommend the waters around Sai Kung Peninsula. There seem to be fatal shark attacks here every couple of years, due to fish migration, though most of the public beaches have shark nets and guards patrolling the water.

TAI CHI

Tai chi (shadow boxing) is an ancient Chinese regimen designed to balance body and soul and thereby release energy from within. By strengthening both the mind and the body through seemingly fluid, slow movements that mask the strength and control required to perform the balletlike exercise, tai chi fosters a sense of well-being and nurtures self-discipline. It also helps develop balance, improves muscle tone and breathing, and aids in digestion. In Hong Kong, both young and old practitioners gather every morning in downtown parks and open public spaces to perform tai chi. Visitors, too, can join complimentary 1-hour **lessons** in English, offered by the Hong Kong Tourism Board's Meet the People cultural program, every Monday, Wednesday, and Thursday at 8am. Simply show up at the waterfront promenade outside the Hong Kong Cultural Centre on Tsim Sha Tsui near the Star Ferry, where you'll be led through the exercises

---

Fun Fact **Did You Know?**

Hong Kong won its first gold medal ever at the Centennial Olympic Games in Atlanta in 1996—in women's windsurfing.

by a tai chi master. Participants are advised to wear casual clothing and comfortable sport shoes with rubber soles. For information, contact the **Hong Kong Tourism Board** (© **852/2508 1234**).

9 Spectator Sports

A popular sporting event is the **Seven-A-Side Rugby Tournament** (called the Sevens), held in March or April. During the cooler winter months, a number of marathons are held, of which the best known are the **Hongkong-Shenzhen Marathon** in February and the **China Coast Marathon** in March. There are also tennis tournaments, including the **Super Tennis Classic** and the **Marlboro Championship.** If you enjoy watching golf, the highlight of the year is the **Hong Kong Open Golf Championships,** held in December at the Hong Kong Golf Club in Fanling (the New Territories).

If you're here anytime from September to mid-June, join the rest of Hong Kong at the **horse races.** Horse racing got its start in the colony in Happy Valley more than 150 years ago, when British settlers introduced the sport, making the Happy Valley track the oldest racecourse in Asia outside China. There is also a newer, modern track in Sha Tin (the New Territories), which can accommodate 90,000 spectators.

Without a doubt, horse racing is by far the most popular sporting event in Hong Kong. It's not, perhaps, the sport itself that draws so much enthusiasm, but rather the fact that, aside from the local lottery, racing is the only legal form of gambling in Hong Kong. The Chinese love to gamble, and there are more than 100 off-course betting centers throughout Hong Kong. Winnings are tax-free.

Races are held Wednesday evenings and some Saturday and Sunday afternoons. Both tracks feature giant color screens that show close-ups of the race in progress, photographs of jockeys and trainers, and videos of previous races. It's fun and easy to get in on the betting action, and you don't have to bet much—the minimum wager of HK$10 (US$1.30) per race is enough.

The lowest admission price is HK$10 (US$1.30), which is for the general public and is standing-room only. If you want to watch from the more exclusive Hong Kong Jockey Club members' enclosure (there are stands here so you can sit down), are at least 18 years old, and are a bona-fide tourist, you can purchase a temporary member's badge for HK$50 (US$6.50). It's available upon showing your passport at either the Badge Enquiry Office at the main entrance to the members' private enclosure (at either track) or at the off-course betting center near the Star Ferry concourse in Central. Tickets are sold on a first-come, first-served basis.

To reach Happy Valley Racecourse, take the tram to Happy Valley or the MTR to Causeway Bay (take the Times Square exit and walk towards the Wong Nai Chung Rd.). To reach Sha Tin Racecourse, take the KCR railway to Racecourse Station.

If you don't want to go to the races but would still like to bet on the winning horses, you can place your bets at one of the off-course betting centers. There's a convenient one near the Star Ferry concourse in the Central District and another one at 2–4 Prat Ave. in Tsim Sha Tsui.

On the other hand, an easy way to see the races is to take a guided tour to the tracks, described in "Organized Tours & Cultural Activities," earlier in this chapter. For information on current sporting events and future dates, contact the Hong Kong Tourism Board (© **852/2508 1234**).

Hong Kong Strolls

Surprisingly compact, Hong Kong is an easy city to explore on foot. If it weren't for the harbor, you could walk everywhere—Tsim Sha Tsui, Yau Ma Tei, the Central District, Wan Chai, and Causeway Bay. Walking affords a more intimate relationship with your surroundings, permits chance encounters with the unexpected, and lets you discover that vegetable market, temple, or shop you would have otherwise missed.

If, for example, you're in the Central District and want to have dinner in Causeway Bay, you can walk there in less than an hour, passing through colorful Wan Chai on the way. Causeway Bay is good for exploring, since it's full of little sidewalk markets, Japanese department stores, restaurants, and shops patronized by the locals. Another great place for walking is the Western District just west of Central, fascinating because it encompasses a wide spectrum of traditional Chinese shops, from chop makers to ginseng wholesalers. If you like panoramic views, nothing can beat the hour-long circular walk on Victoria Peak.

On the other side of the harbor, a walk up Nathan Road from the harbor to the Yau Ma Tei subway station takes less than 30 minutes, although you might want to browse in some of the shops and department stores along the

way. And Yau Ma Tei itself is another good place for wandering about since it, too, offers insight into the Chinese way of life with its markets and traditional shops. For easy strolling with great views of the harbor, walk along the waterfront promenade that stretches from the Star Ferry all the way through Tsim Sha Tsui East.

What follows are three recommended strolls: one through the Central financial district, where a few colonial-era buildings are sprinkled in among the modern skyscrapers; another through the Western District, with its Chinese shops and antiques stores; the third along Nathan Road in Kowloon, from Tsim Sha Tsui to Mong Kok.

If you're interested in additional self-guided walks throughout Hong Kong, be sure to pick up the free HKTB pamphlet called *Hong Kong Walks,* which covers points of interest in Central, the Western District, Yau Ma Tei, Mong Kok, Sha Tin in the New Territories, and Cheung Chau, Lantau, and Lamma islands. For more information, contact the Hong Kong Tourism Board (© **852/2508 1234**).

In addition to the three walks here, I also cover a couple of walks in the New Territories: The Ping Shan and Lung Yeuk Tau heritage trails, which highlight village life and architecture. See chapter 10 for more information.

WALKING TOUR 1 THE CENTRAL DISTRICT

Start:	Star Ferry terminus, Central District.
Finish:	Pacific Place, 88 Queensway, Central.
Time:	About 3 hours; add 1 to 2 hours if you include Victoria Peak.
Best Times:	Weekdays, when shops and restaurants are in full swing.
Worst Times:	Tuesday, when the Flagstaff House Museum of Tea Ware is closed; Saturday afternoon, Sunday, and public holidays, when some stores and restaurants in the Central District are closed.

The birthplace of modern Hong Kong, the Central District used to be called "Victoria," after Queen Victoria; it boasted elegant colonial-style buildings with sweeping verandas and narrow streets filled with pigtailed men pulling rickshaws. That's hard to imagine nowadays. With Central's gleaming glass-and-steel skyscrapers, there's little left of its colonial beginnings. Still, this is the logical starting place for a tour of Hong Kong. The handful of historic buildings scattered among towering monoliths symbolize both the past and the future of this ever-changing city. Yet, surprisingly, Central has several city parks, good for relaxation and sightseeing. If you have time, you can also take a trip to Victoria Peak from the tram terminus in Central.

If you're starting this tour from Tsim Sha Tsui, board the Star Ferry for an exhilarating ride across the world-famous harbor. You'll disembark in the heart of Central. Ahead of you—just outside the terminus—are all that remain of Hong Kong's once mighty fleet of:

❶ Rickshaw Drivers

First appearing in Japan (the name is derived from the Japanese *jinriksha,* which translates as "people-powered vehicle") and brought to Hong Kong in the 1870s, rickshaws are now tourist attractions rather than providers of transportation. In all my days in Hong Kong, I've never once seen a driver plying the streets of Central, and since no new licenses have been issued for years, the tradition will soon end when the last of the remaining ancient-looking men give up their trade. Most tourists prefer to have their photos taken sitting in a rickshaw rather than riding in one, but even that is likely to cost HK$50 (US$6.50). The drivers will also demand money if you take a picture of them. Negotiate the price beforehand.

To your right, just outside the ferry wickets, is the General Post Office. Continue walking inland from the Star Ferry terminus (with the post office to your right) to the underground pedestrian passage leading straight to:

❷ Statue Square

To your left after emerging from the underground passage is a cenotaph commemorating "The Glorious Dead" of both world wars. Across Chater Road is the larger part of the square. On the weekend, Statue Square and surrounding Central become the domain of Filipino housemaids, nannies, and waitresses, thousands of whom work in the SAR and send most of what they earn back home to their families. On their day off, they meet friends here, sitting on blankets spread on the concrete and sharing food, photographs, letters from home, and laughter, infusing the staid business district with a certain vitality and festivity. At any rate, a statue of Queen Victoria used to stand here, but it has been moved to Victoria Park. Perhaps appropriately for a town that was established to make money, the only statue remaining in the square is of a banker, Sir Thomas Jackson, former manager of the Hongkong and Shanghai Bank. It's interesting to note that he stands facing the:

Walking Tour 1: The Central District

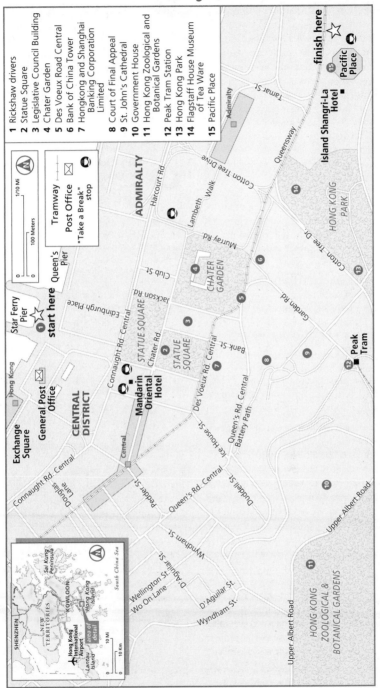

1 Rickshaw drivers
2 Statue Square
3 Legislative Council Building
4 Chater Garden
5 Des Voeux Road Central
6 Bank of China Tower
7 Hongkong and Shanghai Banking Corporation Limited
8 Court of Final Appeal
9 St. John's Cathedral
10 Government House
11 Hong Kong Zoological and Botanical Gardens
12 Peak Tram Station
13 Hong Kong Park
14 Flagstaff House Museum of Tea Ware
15 Pacific Place

Tramway
Post Office
"Take a Break" stop

❸ Legislative Council Building

Formerly the Supreme Court and looking curiously out of place in modern Central, the Legislative Council Building was built in the early 1900s by architect Aston Webb, who later redesigned Buckingham Palace, and now houses Hong Kong's lawmaking body, popularly known as "Legco." With its local pink-and-gray granite, Ionic columns, and Chinese roof, this neoclassical structure is typical of late-Victorian colonial architecture and boasts a carved-stone figure above the main portico of the Goddess of Justice holding scales. The building has two flags, one with the red star emblem of China and the other with the bauhinia flower of Hong Kong.

On the other side of the Legco building, to the east, is:

❹ Chater Garden

This was the site of the Hong Kong Cricket Club until the 1960s. Today, this is the only spot of green in the very heart of Central and is popular with those who practice tai chi (shadow boxing) in the early morning and among office workers on lunch break.

Running alongside the south edge of the garden is:

❺ Des Voeux Road Central

This road is easily recognizable by the tramlines snaking along it. What a contrast these quaint double-decker trams make when viewed against the high-rise banks on the other side of the street. Established in 1904 and now the city's oldest form of transportation, trams are the most colorful way to travel from the Western and Central districts to Causeway Bay, especially at night when Hong Kong is ablaze in neon. Des Voeux Road itself was constructed as part of an early-1800s land reclamation project; before that the waterfront was situated farther inland—at Queen's Road. Land reclamation has proceeded continuously throughout Hong Kong's history,

slowly encroaching on the harbor itself. One Hong Kong resident I met joked that so much land was being reclaimed it wouldn't be long before you could walk across the harbor. With Central's most recent reclamation project—which extended the ferry piers for outlying islands far into the water—the joke no longer seems quite so funny.

> **TAKE A BREAK**
> The most convenient place for a meal in this area is **Dot Cod Seafood Restaurant & Oyster Bar** (p. 136), in the Prince's Building with an entrance right on Statue Square (☎ **852/2810 6988**). It's owned by the Hong Kong Cricket Club but is open to anyone.
> Across the street, The Mandarin Oriental Hotel, just west of Statue Square at 5 Connaught Rd., Central, offers several convenient meal possibilities. Foremost is **Vong** (p. 133) on the 30th floor (☎ **852/2522 0111**, ext. 4028), a chic restaurant with stunning views and great Franco-Asian creations. After lunch, the Mandarin's **Clipper Lounge** (☎ **852/2522 0111**; see p. 156) is a cozy place for afternoon tea, finger sandwiches, scones, and other goodies.

Across from Chater Garden, on the other side of Des Voeux Road Central, is the:

❻ Bank of China Tower

This tower rises like a glass finger pointing into the sky. Designed by I. M. Pei, this 70-story futuristic building has a crisscross pattern reminiscent of bamboo. Locals have criticized the building, however, due to its insensitivity to *feng shui* (Chinese geomancy) principles and for its conspicuous ties to Communist mainland China.

The most conspicuous building on Des Voeux Road Central, however, is farther west. It's the headquarters for the:

❼ Hongkong and Shanghai Banking Corporation Limited

This company, at 1 Queen's Rd. Central, which generally shortens its name to HSBC, maintains offices in more than 20 countries around the world and employs more than 21,000 people. Hong Kong's first city hall once stood on this site. The Hongkong Bank, located here since 1865, issued the colony's first bank notes in 1881. The present building, designed in the mid-1980s by renowned British architect Sir Norman Foster and reputedly one of the most expensive buildings in the world (almost US$1 billion), attracts visiting architects the world over for its innovative external structure, rather than a central core. It was constructed from prefabricated components manufactured all over the world; the glass, aluminum cladding, and flooring came from the United States. Internal walls are removable, allowing for office reconfiguration. Walk underneath the bank's open ground plaza for a look up into this unique structure, or, if you choose, take the world's longest freely supported escalator up to the first floor. Much care was given to the angle of these escalators, as well as to many other aspects of construction, in order not to disturb the spirits (see the "*Feng Shui*—Restoring a Balance with Nature*"* box on p. 299 of the Appendix for more information about this) who reside here (altogether there are 62 escalators in the building, more than in any other office building in the world). Note, too, the two bronze lions you see at the entrance, which have been "guarding" the bank since 1935. You can rub their paws for good luck.

If you walk through the Hongkong Bank's open, ground-floor plaza to the other side, you'll find yourself on Queen's Road Central, where on the opposite side of the street you should take the stone steps leading up to a pathway overhung with branches, known as Battery Path, where you should turn left. Straight ahead is a handsome brick building, the 150-year-old:

❽ Court of Final Appeal

This building, which houses Hong Kong's highest court, was formerly the French Mission Building. Just beyond it is the cream-and-white–colored, Gothic-style:

❾ St. John's Cathedral

Inaugurated in 1849 and thought to be the oldest Anglican church in the Far East, this church was used for Japanese social functions during the Japanese occupation. You can enter the small church and take a look inside. It underwent extensive renovations following World War II but still retains quaint tropical characteristics like the ceiling fans.

Take a left out of the church and walk around it to busy Garden Road, where you should turn right and walk uphill. After passing the U.S. Consulate, you'll come to Upper Albert Road, where you should turn right. You'll soon see, on your right, the:

❿ Government House

Completed in 1855, this building served as the official residence of 25 British governors until 1997. During the World War II Japanese occupation, it also served as the headquarters of Lieutenant General Isogai, who ordered some extensive building renovations, a curious mix of Asian and Western architecture, including ceramic tile roofs and a tower reminiscent of Shinto shrines. Since the 1997 handover, the grand, whitewashed edifice has been used for official functions.

Across the street, on the corner of Upper Albert Road and Garden Road, is a staircase leading up to the main entrance of the:

⓫ Hong Kong Zoological and Botanical Gardens

This is a wonderful oasis of plants and animals (p. 172) that was established in 1864. It still imparts a Victorian atmosphere with its wrought-iron bandstand and greenhouse. Entrance is free, and the grounds are not too extensive, so it's worth taking the time to wander through to see its tropical botanical gardens, trees and plants, aviaries and birds, reptiles, and mammals such as apes. It opens daily at 6am, with the eastern half closing at 7pm and the western part at 10pm.

Exiting the same way you came in, cross to the other side of Garden Road and walk downhill, taking a right after passing the modern St. John's Building. Here, to your right, is the:

⑫ Peak Tram Station

When this station opened in 1888, the travel time to the top of Victoria Peak was reduced from 3 hours (by sedan chair) to 8 minutes. Today the tram is the steepest funicular railway in the world, and the view from the peak is the best in Hong Kong. I suggest you visit the peak twice during your stay: during the day for the great panoramic view of the city, and again at night for its romantic atmosphere. There's also a great, 1-hour circular walk around the peak, as well as attractions for children. In all, you'll probably want to spend at least an hour or two on the Peak, so if time is limited or it's foggy, save it for another day.

On the other side of the tram station, on Cotton Tree Drive, is:

⑬ Hong Kong Park

Before opening as a park in 1991, this was once the grounds of Victoria Barracks, a housing area for soldiers. In the park is the pink Rawlinson House, formerly the private residence of the Deputy General and now serving as a marriage registry. If it's a weekend or an auspicious day in the Chinese calendar, you'll find many newlyweds posing for pictures in the park. You'll also find a greenhouse, a great aviary with 800 birds, and a playground. Signs will direct you to the park's most important

building and Hong Kong's oldest surviving colonial-style structure, the:

⑭ Flagstaff House Museum of Tea Ware

Built in 1846, this museum (© **852/ 2869 0690;** see p. 165) houses a small collection of tea utensils, with descriptions of tea making through the various Chinese dynasties. It's open Wednesday through Monday from 10am to 5pm. Like everything else in the park, it's free. From here, walk past the fountain (a favorite backdrop for picture taking) to the escalators that will take you downhill to:

⑮ Pacific Place

This is a large complex filled with department stores, clothing boutiques, restaurants, and hotels. The nearest subway station from here is Admiralty Station, just a couple minutes' walk north, though you don't need to go outside to reach it; follow the signs via the air-conditioned walkway.

WINDING DOWN
There are many eating and drinking establishments in Pacific Place. **Dan Ryan's Chicago Grill** (© 852/2845 4600; see p. 120) is a casual bar and grill that remains open throughout the day for drinks, burgers, and other American favorites. **Zen Chinese** (© 852/2845 4555;** see p. 141) is the ultimate in Chinese hip dining, with a Zen-like decor and specialties that border on Cantonese nouvelle. **Grappa's** (© 852/2868 0086; see p. 137) is a moderately priced trattoria with an open kitchen and good food. But for all-you-can eat dining, **café TOO** (p. 136), in the Island Shangri-La Hotel at Pacific Place (© 852/2820-8571, ext. 8571), is an upscale buffet restaurant offering views of Hong Kong Park's greenery and beautifully presented international lunches and dinners.

WALKING TOUR 2 ▪ THE WESTERN DISTRICT

Start:	Pedder Street, Central District.
Finish:	Lan Kwai Fong, Central.
Time:	About 4 to 5 hours.
Best Times:	Tuesday to Friday mornings, when markets are in full swing.
Worst Times:	Sunday, when some shops are closed; Monday, when the Museum of Medical Sciences is closed.

While the Central District seems to be Western in style with its banks, high-rises, and smart department stores, the Western District is very Chinese—a fascinating neighborhood of family-owned shops and businesses, with nary a tourist in sight. Traditional herbs, ginseng, antiques, preserved fish, name chops, coffins, funeral items, Hong Kong's oldest temple, and an interesting museum comparing traditional Chinese and Western medicine are just some of the things you'll see in my favorite area on Hong Kong Island.

Named after Lieutenant William Pedder, Hong Kong's first harbor master, Pedder Street connects two of Central's major thoroughfares: Des Voeux Road Central (with its tram tracks) and Queen's Road Central. It is most well known to visitors, however, for its shopping, including the not-to-be missed (yet easily overlooked due to its modest size):

① Shanghai Tang

In the Pedder Building (© **852/2525 7333**), this small, chic shop (p. 217) is a reproduction of a Shanghai clothing department store as it might have looked in the 1930s, with gleaming wooden and tiled floors, raised cashier cubicles, ceiling fans, and clerks wearing traditional Chinese clothing. This is a great place to shop for typical Chinese goods in mod colors, from cheongsams to Chinese jackets, as well as funky accessories like Mao watches, home accessories, and gifts.

Just beside Shanghai Tang is the main entrance to the:

② Pedder Building

At 12 Pedder St., this has been a shopping center since 1926. It is now famous for its dozens of small factory outlets and clothing boutiques; look for the elevator that services the first to seventh floors. Be aware, however, that just a handful of shops here are true factory outlets. The rest are simply

taking advantage of the location to set up boutiques to sell their usual goods at regular prices; there are also some secondhand shops selling used designerwear. If you have the time, you might want to hunt for some bargains here. I usually take the elevator up to the sixth floor (there are no shops on the seventh floor) and then work my way down.

Across the street from the Pedder Building is the:

③ Landmark

This high-end shopping complex has brand-name boutiques, including Gucci, Tiffany & Co., Louis Vuitton, and Gianni Versace.

Head west on Des Voeux Road Central (the one with the tram tracks); in about 2 minutes you will come to:

④ Li Yuen Street East and Li Yuen Street West

These two parallel pedestrian lanes, which rise steeply to your left, are packed with stalls that sell clothing and accessories, including costume jewelry, Chinese jackets, handbags, belts, and even bras. If you see something you like, be sure to bargain for it. Walk up Li Yuen Street East, take a right, and then head back down Li Yuen Street West.

If you wish to visit a couple of local department stores, however, at the top of Li Yuen Street East, to the left on Queens Road Central, is the:

⑤ Yue Hwa Chinese Products Emporium

This is a great place to shop for Chinese souvenirs, furniture, arts and crafts, beaded purses, wooden vase stands, jewelry boxes, jade, traditional Chinese jackets, embroidery, Chinese medicines, and other products from the mainland. Located at 39 Queen's Rd., Central (⟨℗⟩ **852/2522 2333**), it's the next best thing to being in Beijing itself and is my favorite outlet for this popular chain.

After walking down Li Yuen Street West, turn left onto Des Voeux Road Central and continue walking west a couple of blocks, until (on your left) you see the entrance to the:

⑥ Central/Mid-Levels Escalator

Opened in 1994 as the world's longest covered escalator, it stretches 780m (2,600 ft.) from Central to the Mid-Levels on Victoria Peak. Contrary to its name, however, it is not one long continuous escalator but rather a series of escalators and moving sidewalks, with 29 entrances and exits. Designed to accommodate commuters who live in the Mid-Levels but work in Central and beyond, the escalators operate downhill from 6 to 10am and then reverse their direction and go uphill from 10:30am to midnight (after this time, you have to walk down the hill—there are stairs beside the escalators). If you travel its entire length, it takes about 20 minutes to go from one end to the other. Because of the foot traffic, the escalator has spawned a number of easily accessible new restaurants and bars, most in an area dubbed SoHo (more on this later).

Continue walking west on Des Voeux Road Central, past Jubilee Street with its Cyber Café at 12–13 Jubilee and ignoring the first sign directing you to the tourist office, turning left instead into a small, brick lane called Gilman's Bazaar. About halfway down on your left is a sign for the Hong Kong Tourism Board's:

⑦ Visitor Information & Services Centre

Located in **The Center,** 99 Queen's Rd. Central (⟨℗⟩ **852/2508 1234**), a bit off the beaten track, this new facility is nevertheless well equipped to help visitors with brochures, computers, and a knowledgeable staff, and is larger than the small office in the Star Ferry terminus in Kowloon. The Center, by the way, was supposed to end up as the tallest building in Hong Kong but fell short of its goal, probably due to a lack of funds. It is, however, the city's first building with a computer-controlled exterior lighting system capable of creating a million different colors and patterns, making it very visible indeed.

Back on Des Voeux Road Central, continue west 1 more block and turn left onto:

⑧ Wing Kut Street

This is another small lane lined with stalls that sell clothing, handbags, and other accessories for women. More interesting, however, are the small shops behind the stalls, which specialize in costume jewelry in a wide range of styles and prices. Some shops sell only wholesale, but others will sell to individual shoppers as well.

After walking through Wing Kut Street, take a right onto Queen's Road Central.

> **TAKE A BREAK**
> Located in the palatial-looking Grand Millennium Plaza, the upscale **Gaia Ristorante** (p. 134), 181 Queen's Road Central (⟨℗⟩ **852/2167 8200**), has a wonderful garden terrace, a contemporary interior, and very good Italian fare for both lunch and dinner.

Queen's Road Central will soon curve off to the left, but you'll want to keep walking straight westward onto Bonham Strand. Soon, to your right, just after the Hongkong Bank and Treasure Lake Seafood Restaurant, you'll see an interesting street:

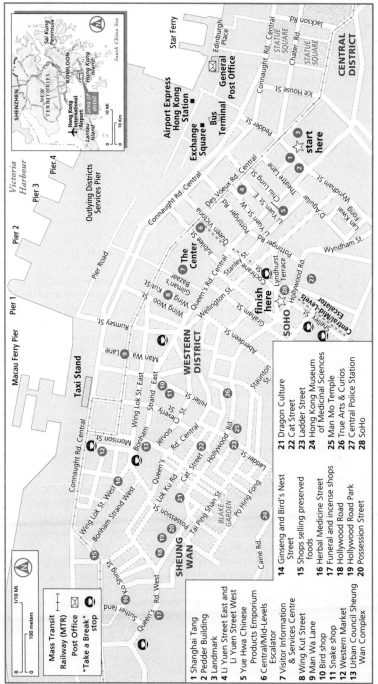

Legend / Key:

Mass Transit Railway (MTR)

Post Office ⊠

"Take a Break" stop ●

1 Shanghai Tang
2 Pedder Building
3 Landmark
4 Li Yuen Street East and Li Yuen Street West
5 Yue Hwa Chinese Products Emporium
6 Central/Mid-Levels Escalator
7 Visitor Information & Services Centre
8 Wing Kut Street
9 Man Wa Lane
10 Bird shop
11 Snake shop
12 Western Market
13 Urban Council Sheung Wan Complex

14 Ginseng and Bird's Nest Street
15 Shops selling preserved foods
16 Herbal Medicine Street
17 Funeral and incense shops
18 Hollywood Road
19 Hollywood Road Park
20 Possession Street

21 Dragon Culture
22 Cat Street
23 Ladder Street
24 Hong Kong Museum of Medicinal Sciences
25 Man Mo Temple
26 True Arts & Curios
27 Central Police Station
28 SoHo

⑨ Man Wa Lane

Since the 1920s this street has been the home of one of China's oldest trades—"chop" or carved-seal making. Sadly, the recent construction of many high-rises makes the stalls look out of place. Made from stone, ivory, jade, clay, marble, bronze, porcelain, bamboo, wood, soapstone, and even plastic, these seals or stamps can be carved with a name and are used by the Chinese much like a written signature.

You can have your own chop made at one of the several booths here, with your name translated into Chinese characters. It takes about an hour for a chop to be completed, so you may want to stop by again later after you've finished your walk. Calligraphy brushes are also for sale, and you can even have business cards made here with both English and Chinese characters; orders for that take about a day. Most stalls are

Chinese Gods

There are many gods in the Chinese world, each with different functions and abilities. There are household gods such as the kitchen god, as well as patron gods of various occupations, and gods who protect worshippers through certain stages of their lives. There is an earth god, a goddess of pregnant women, 60 gods representing each year of the 60-year Chinese calendar, a god of riches popular with shopkeepers, and a scholar god whose favor is curried by students.

Most popular in Hong Kong is **Tin Hau,** goddess of the sea and protector of seafarers (in Macau she is known as **A-Ma**). As the patron goddess of fisher folk, Tin Hau is honored by fishing communities throughout Hong Kong; there are more than two dozen Tin Hau temples, including those at Yau Ma Tei, Causeway Bay, Stanley, and Cheung Chau. According to popular lore, Tin Hau is the deification of a real girl who lived in Fujian Province around A.D. 900 or 1000 and who saved some fishermen during a storm. Her birthday is celebrated annually with gaily decorated junks and lion dances. Another popular goddess is **Kuan Yin** (called Kun Iam in Macau), the goddess of mercy, capable of delivering people from suffering or misery.

There are also several temples in Hong Kong devoted to **Man** (the god of literature and the patron of civil servants) and **Mo** (the god of war). Mo was a great warrior of the Han dynasty, deified not only for his integrity but his ability to protect from the misfortunes of war. Ironically, for this reason Mo is worshipped not only by soldiers and the Hong Kong police force but also by gang members of the underworld. Hong Kong's most famous Man Mo Temple is in the Western District on Hollywood Road.

One of the most popular gods in Hong Kong is **Wong Tai Sin,** believed to generously grant the wishes of his followers, cure sickness, and—best of all—dispense horse-racing tips. The Wong Tai Sin Temple, located in a district by the same name, is always crowded with worshippers, as well as fortune-tellers, making this one of the most interesting temple destinations in Hong Kong.

open Monday to Saturday from 10am to 6pm.

Back on Bonham Strand, continue west for 2 blocks. Just a few years ago, this area was known for its many snake shops, which did a roaring business from October to February. Now only a few remain, easily identifiable by cages of pythons, cobras, and banded kraits piled on the sidewalk, or by the wooden drawers lining the walls of the shop. Just past Mercer Street is Hillier Street (which is unmarked; it's the second street after Man Wa Lane, just past the corner fruit shop), where you should turn left for the:

⑩ Bird shop

At 3 Hillier St., this bird shop has hundreds of songbirds, exquisitely crafted wooden and bamboo cages, and tiny porcelain water bowls for sale.

A bit farther down, at 13 Hillier St., is a:

⑪ Snake shop

You can recognize this open-fronted shop by the many drawers lining its wall. Eaten as protection against the winter cold, snakes are often served in soup. They are also favored for their gallbladders, which are mixed with Chinese wine as cures for rheumatism. Who knows, you might see a shopkeeper fill a customer's order by deftly grabbing a snake out of one of the drawers, extracting the gallbladder, and mixing it in yellow wine. The snake survives the operation, but who knows what other fate it awaits. The more poisonous the snake, so they say, the better the cure. The mixture is also believed to be an aphrodisiac.

Backtrack to Bonham Strand and turn left, where you'll pass medicinal shops selling dried organic products such as mushrooms and roots; a tea merchant's shop; and, on the corner of Morrison Street, a rattan shop with handmade wares spilling out onto the sidewalks and hanging from hooks outside the shop. It takes an apprentice 3 years to learn the skills necessary to become a master rattan maker; the rattan itself comes from a climbing vine found throughout Asia. As a sign of the times, the shop has recently branched into plastic housewares. Take a

right here onto Morrison Street and walk to the end where, on the left, you'll find the handsome, redbrick:

⑫ Western Market

At 323 Des Voeux Rd., this market was built in 1906 and was used as a public market until 1988; it escaped demolition when the decision was made to renovate the imposing Edwardian/Victorian landmark into a bazaar for shops and artisans. On the ground floor are souvenir and gift shops that sell everything from Chinese seals to jade jewelry, with most shops open daily from 10am to 7pm. Up on the first floor, retailers sell bolts of colorful cloth, buttons, clasps, and other sewing accessories. On the top floor is The Grand Stage, noted for its afternoon tea dances daily from 2:30 to 6pm. Stop for a peek at Chinese couples as they glide dreamily across the ballroom floor.

TAKE A BREAK
There are several places in Western Market for casual dining, including eateries offering sandwiches, and desserts. The top floor **The Grand Stage** (☎ 852/ 2815 2311) offers dim sum for lunch until 2pm daily and Cantonese fare from 7pm to midnight. But if you're on a budget or like adventuresome dining, head to the **Cooked Food Centre** on the second floor of the Urban Council Sheung Wan Complex (described below), Bonham Strand, where the second floor has food stalls selling various noodle, vegetable, and other Chinese dishes. There are no English menus, since most of the patrons are neighborhood residents, vendors working inside the complex's market, or nearby blue-collar workers. It's open Monday to Saturday from 6am to an astonishing 2am.

From Western Market, backtrack on Morrison Street to Bonham Strand, where across the street you'll see the large:

⑬ Urban Council Sheung Wan Complex

One of Hong Kong's largest neighborhood markets, this complex, also called the Sheung Wan Civic Centre, open from 6am to 8pm, features fish and poultry on the ground floor, meats and vegetables on the first floor, and a large dining hall with stalls selling cheap, cooked meals on the second floor. Early morning is the best time to come, when women buy the day's food for their families and chefs purchase ingredients for their daily specials. Following the Chinese penchant for freshness, chickens are killed on the spot, boiled, and then thrown into machines that pluck them. Almost every part of every animal is for sale, including the liver, heart, and intestines. Wicker baskets may contain the discarded horns and skulls of bulls, with even the brains carved out—this is not a stop for the fainthearted.

Exit the market building back onto Bonham Strand, turn left, and continue straight ahead on Wing Lok Street. This street is nicknamed:

⑭ Gingseng and Bird's Nest Street

Obviously, shops here specialize in gingseng and bird's nest, both valued for their aid in longevity, energy, and a fair complexion. The kings of trade in this wholesale trading area are clearly ginseng, with more than 30 varieties on offer. The most prized are the red ginseng from North Korea, white ginseng from North America, and a very rare ginseng that grows wild in the mountains of northeastern China. Red ginseng is supposed to aid male virility, while the white variety helps cure hangovers.

By the way, this area has long had an exotic atmosphere—150 years ago it buzzed with activity as merchants from Shanghai, Canton (Guangzhou), Fujian, and other Chinese provinces and cities set up shop here, selling products from their native regions.

At the end of Wing Lok Street, turn left on Des Voeux Road West. Along this road you'll see:

⑮ Shops selling preserved foods

Dried and salted fish, flattened squid, oysters, scallops, abalone, sea slugs, fish bladders, starfish, shrimp, and many other kinds of seafood have been dried and preserved for sale here. You can buy bird's nest here, as well as shark's fin, and in winter there's also pressed duck and Chinese sausages made from pork and liver.

Continue west on Des Voeux Road, keeping your eyes peeled for a Park'n'Shop convenience store and Princeton Tower apartments on your left, at Des Voeux Road 92. Just past it is Sutherland Street, where you should turn left (Sutherland St. is unmarked; if you reach shop no. 98, you'll have gone too far). Almost immediately you will come to a somewhat larger street, Ko Shing Street. This street is nicknamed:

⑯ Herbal Medicine Street

for its many shops dealing in the herbal medicine trade. Based on the Asian concept of maintaining a healthy balance between the yin and yang forces in the body, the range of medicinal herbs is startling, including roots, twigs, bark, dried leaves, seeds, pods, flowers, grasses, insects (such as discarded cicada shells), deer antlers, dried sea horses, dried fish bladders, snake gall bladders, and rhinoceros horns. The herbalist, after learning about the customer's symptoms (most will not likely speak English) and checking the pulses in both wrists, will prescribe an appropriate remedy, using perhaps a bit of bark here and a seed there, based on wisdom passed down over thousands of years. A typical prescription might include up to 20 ingredients, which are often boiled to produce a medicinal tea.

Return to Sutherland and continue heading south (toward the playground). A few years back, this neighborhood was renovated and the Li Sing

Street Playground was built in its midst, displacing some of the narrow alleys favored by one of Hong Kong's oldest professions—street-side barbers. Once plentiful, street-side barbers are now going the way of the rickshaw, but just past the playground and basketball court, to the left, is the only makeshift barbershop remaining in this area. At the top of Sutherland Street, on busy Queen's Road West, I used to see an elderly woman who set up shop on the sidewalk, using only a couple of stools and a string. She used the string to pull out the facial hairs of her customers, an ancient method that few barbers can still perform. Like much of old Hong Kong, she and her trade have vanished.

TAKE A BREAK
There's no better place for Western food in this immediate vicinity than **Sammy's Kitchen** (p. 152), 204–206 Queen's Rd. W. (reached from Sutherland St. by turning right and walking about 2 minutes; ☎ 852/2548 8400). A landmark for more than 3 decades, it's owned by the gregarious and friendly Sammy Yip, who treats foreign guests like royalty. It's a good place for inexpensive lunchtime fare, an afternoon snack, for a soda or ice-cream sundae, or, in the evenings, fresh seafood, steaks, chicken, and house-invented specialties.

At the top of Sutherland Street, cross Queen's Road West and turn left, heading east. Here you'll pass several open-fronted:

⑰ Funeral and incense shops
Note the paper replicas of household goods and other items (such as houses, cars, running shoes, handbags, and even computers) hanging from the shops' eaves and ceilings. These are sold to accompany the deceased into the afterlife.

After the funeral shops, follow the sidewalk up and down a small hill. Shortly thereafter

you will see a road leading uphill to the right. It's the famous:

⑱ Hollywood Road
This road is a strange mixture of shops selling coffins, funeral items, furniture, and antiques. In fact, there are more antiques shops concentrated here along this rather long road than anywhere else in Hong Kong, and you'll find everything from woodblock prints and rosewood tables to Neolithic pots, Ming dynasty ceramic figures, silk carpets, snuff bottles, porcelain, and round-bellied smiling Buddhas. Built in 1844 to accommodate British troops stationed here, the road takes its name from the woods of holly that used to adorn the area.

First, however, before hitting all the stores just mentioned, to your left will be:

⑲ Hollywood Road Park
A pleasant garden oasis with a children's playground, a pond with goldfish, and Chinese pagodas, this park makes a nice stop for a few moments of relaxation before continuing.

Just past the playground, to your left, you'll soon pass a historic landmark:

⑳ Possession Street
There's no need to enter it, but you might be interested to know that it was here that the British first landed in 1841 and planted the Union Jack to claim the island for Britain. At the time, of course, this was part of the waterfront. One of the first antiques shops you'll come to is:

㉑ Dragon Culture
One of Hong Kong's largest and most respected shops, it's owned by Victor Choi, who has given lectures on Chinese antiques for the HKTB's Meet the People program. Browse his shop, at 231 Hollywood Rd. (☎ **852/2545 8098**), for everything from Tang pottery to Ming porcelain. If you want to learn more about antiques, pick up Choi's book *Collecting Chinese Antiques in Hong Kong*, which answers

frequently asked questions about antiques, including how to ship them home.

After Dragon Culture, turn left at Lok Ku Road and then right onto Upper Lascar Row, better known as:

㉒ Cat Street

For almost a century, Cat Street was famous for its antiques, which could be bought for a pittance; now, however, with the new antiques shops on Hollywood Road and the nearby Cat Street Galleries, Cat Street vendors offer a fantastic mix of curios and junk. Pleasantly dotted with potted palms, this pedestrian lane is worth a browse for jade, snuff bottles, watches, pictures, copper and brass kettles, old eyeglasses, birdcages, and odds and ends. You should bargain with the vendors who have laid their wares on the sidewalk; most of them do business Monday to Saturday from 11am to about 5pm. You can also bargain at the surrounding antiques shops, where prices are rather high to begin with. If you're not an expert, be wary of purchasing anything of value. During one of my visits, it seemed that every shop was offering fossilized "dinosaur eggs" for sale. How many can there be?

At the end of Cat Street, turn right and go up the stairs. Across the street you'll see unmistakable:

㉓ Ladder Street

This extremely steep flight of stairs was once a common sight on steep Hong Kong Island. Now, of course, Hong Kong Island has escalators and the Peak Tram, but you're going to find out exactly how steep and tiring these stairs are by taking them almost to the top before turning right and following the sign down the short flight of steps to the:

㉔ Hong Kong Museum of Medical Sciences

This museum (p. 169) is housed in a stately, 1905 Edwardian-style brick building, at 2 Caine Lane (© **852/ 549 5123**), that once served as the Pathological Institute, founded to combat Hong Kong's worst outbreak of bubonic plague, which eventually claimed 20,000 lives. With most rooms left intact and devoted to various aspects of early medicine practiced in colonial Hong Kong, it is the only museum in the world to compare traditional Chinese and Western medicine. You'll see acupuncture needles, an autopsy room, an X-ray of a bound foot (once considered a sign of beauty for Chinese women), Chinese medicinal herbs, and the Halvo Pelvic Distraction Apparatus, a Hong Kong invention for treating humped backs. Very fascinating. It's open Tuesday to Saturday from 10am to 5pm and Sunday from 1 to 5pm.

Head back down Ladder Street and turn right onto Hollywood Road, where you'll immediately see the:

㉕ Man Mo Temple

This is Hong Kong Island's oldest and most well known temple. It was in this area that the movie *The World of Suzie Wong* was filmed. The temple, which dates back to the 1840s and is open daily from 8am to 6pm, is dedicated to two deities: the god of literature (Man) and the god of war (Mo). Mo finds patronage both with the police force (shrines in his honor can be found in all Hong Kong police stations) and members of the underworld. Two ornately carved sedan chairs, dating from the 1800s and kept in the temple, were once used to carry the statues of the gods around the neighborhood during festivals. From the ceiling hang huge incense coils, which burn as long as 3 weeks, purchased by patrons seeking the fulfillment of their wishes. In a room to the right of the main hall is a small souvenir shop and an English-speaking fortune teller.

Return to Hollywood Road and turn right to continue walking toward its eastern end. Here you'll find more chic and upscale antiques shops, selling furniture, blue-and-white porcelain, and goods from other countries, including Korean chests and Japanese hibachi. One of my favorites is:

26 True Arts & Curios

Located at 89–91 Hollywood Rd. (© 852/2559 1485), this is a tiny shop packed with all kinds of surprises, from antique children's pointed shoes to porcelain, jewelry, and snuff bottles. It also carries about 2,000 temple woodcarvings, most of which are about 100 years old and small enough to carry with you on the plane.

Farther down, at 47 Hollywood Rd., just before the Central/Mid-Levels Escalator, are a couple of ancient-looking hole-in-the-wall shops selling bric-a-brac, old photographs and postcards of Hong Kong (including portraits of women engaged in that ageless profession), snuff bottles, and other interesting stuff.

Walk under the elevated people-mover, and just a bit beyond, to the right, on Old Bailey and Hollywood Road, is the former:

27 Central Police Station

Originally built in 1864 and expanded in 1919 and 1925, this is one of Hong Kong's largest clusters of Victorian-era buildings, built in the classical style. Plans call for the building's renovation into a new heritage center by 2009.

Return to the Central/Mid-Levels Escalator. Here, on the steep lanes flanking the escalator and on narrow side alleys, is Hong Kong's newest nightlife-and-dining district:

28 SoHo

Though SoHo stands for "south of Hollywood," the popularity of this area has made it blossom into side streets on both sides of Hollywood Road. Most establishments are tiny affairs, serving a great variety of ethnic cuisines at reasonable prices.

If you wish to return to Central, walk downhill on Cochrane Street (which runs underneath the escalator) to Queen's Road Central, where you should turn right.

WINDING DOWN

Since establishments are opening up in SoHo literally overnight, I suggest you simply walk along Shelley and Cochrane streets and their side streets until something catches your fancy. Otherwise, for a place you can't miss, head downhill to the bright-red exterior of **Dublin Jack,** 37 Cochrane St. (© 852/2543 0081). It's elbow-to-elbow with working expats after offices close, especially during the 11am-to-9pm happy hour.

Uphill, on the corner of Shelley and Staunton streets, is **Staunton Bar & Cafe** (© 852/2973 6611), one of the first venues to open in SoHo. For Mexican food, head up Shelley street to ¡Caramba! (p. 142), 26–30 Elgin St. (© 852/2530 9963), in SoHo, reached by going uphill on Shelley St. and turning right on Elgin St.

WALKING TOUR 3   KOWLOON

Start:	Star Ferry Terminus, Tsim Sha Tsui.
Finish:	Temple Street Night Market.
Time:	About 4 or 5 hours.
Best Times:	Sunday afternoon, when there are free Kung Fu performances in Kowloon Park and the Jade Market is likely to stay open as late as 6pm, allowing you to see nearby Temple Street Night Market as well.
Worst Time:	Thursday, when the Hong Kong Museum of Art is closed.

A stroll up Nathan Road through Tsim Sha Tsui and Yau Ma Tei will take you through the heart of Kowloon, past its famous hotels, restaurants, and shops, and on to the fascinating Chinese shops and markets in Yau Ma Tei and Mong

Kok. Because the Jade Market generally closes around 4pm and the nearby Temple Street Night Market isn't in full swing until 7pm, you'll have to decide which is most important to you and plan your time accordingly. If you only choose one, I'd opt for the Temple Street Night Market, though the nearby Ladies' Market, which is open all day, is very similar to the Temple Street market. Or, if you'd rather not visit Temple Street at night, a few vendors set up shop from about 4pm. Another possibility is to walk this tour on Sunday, when the Jade Market stays open later because of increased crowds. Finally, because this walk is such a long one, you might wish to either break it up into a 2-day stroll or cover only part of it, concentrating on those sights that interest you the most. And because the MTR is so efficient, it's no problem to return to the night market in the evening. Whatever you choose, a logical tour of Tsim Sha Tsui begins with the Star Ferry since, for more than a century, it served as the only link with Hong Kong Island.

Within the Star Ferry terminus itself is a Hong Kong Tourism Board's Visitor Information & Services Centre, where you can pick up free pamphlets, brochures, and maps of Hong Kong. In front of the Star Ferry concourse is Kowloon's main bus terminal; straight ahead, on the other side of the bus terminal, is a large, nondescript building, Star House, which contains mostly offices but also restaurants and shops. Of most interest to visitors is:

❶ Chinese Arts & Crafts

Located on the ground floor of Star House, 3 Salisbury Rd. (© **852/2735 4061**), this store is open daily from 10am to 9:30pm and is the most upscale store specializing in Chinese products, including embroidered tablecloths, jewelry, ceramics, arts and crafts, and clothing. It's also one of the safest places to buy jade.

Behind Star House to the left is Ocean Terminal, the port of call for cruise liners docking in Hong Kong. It's probably no accident that it is immediately adjacent to:

❷ Harbour City

This is Hong Kong's largest interconnected shopping mall and one of the largest shopping complexes in the world. Stretching more than .8km (½ mile) along Canton Road, it contains more than 700 shops. Enter it and you might not escape during this lifetime; better save shopping for another day. Instead, look just east of

the Star Ferry and bus terminals for the colonial-looking:

❸ Clock tower

Built in 1915, and now dwarfed by the buildings around it, this is the only structure remaining from Hong Kong's old train station, once the final stop for those traveling overland from London on the Orient Express. In 1975, the Kowloon-Canton Railway terminus moved to Hung Hom. Occupying the train station's former site is the modern:

❹ Hong Kong Cultural Centre

Opened in 1989 as the city's largest arena for the performing arts, this structure, in my opinion, is terribly misplaced. After all, why situate concert and theater halls that have no windows on waterfront property with one of the world's most stunning views? Still, the Cultural Centre does offer first-rate concerts of both Western and Chinese music, as well as free shows and events on Thursdays from 6 to 7pm and Saturdays from 2:30 to 4:30pm.

Walk through the Cultural Centre's ground floor to pick up a brochure detailing concerts and free events and exit the other side, or walk east between the clock tower and Victoria Harbour, where you'll find yourself on the:

Walking Tour 3: Kowloon

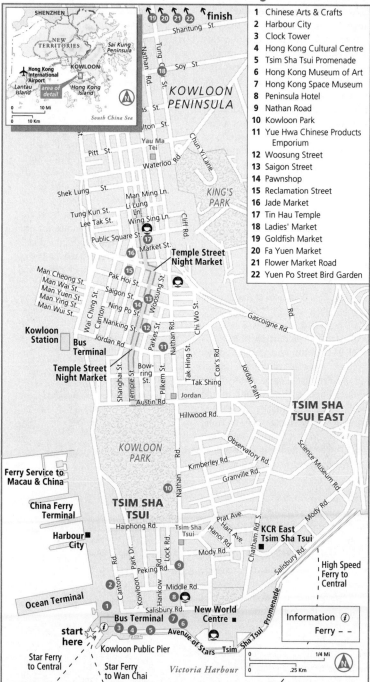

1 Chinese Arts & Crafts
2 Harbour City
3 Clock Tower
4 Hong Kong Cultural Centre
5 Tsim Sha Tsui Promenade
6 Hong Kong Museum of Art
7 Hong Kong Space Museum
8 Peninsula Hotel
9 Nathan Road
10 Kowloon Park
11 Yue Hwa Chinese Products Emporium
12 Woosung Street
13 Saigon Street
14 Pawnshop
15 Reclamation Street
16 Jade Market
17 Tin Hau Temple
18 Ladies' Market
19 Goldfish Market
20 Fa Yuen Market
21 Flower Market Road
22 Yuen Po Street Bird Garden

SHENZHEN

NEW TERRITORIES

Sai Kung Peninsula

KOWLOON

Hong Kong International Airport

Lantau Island

area of detail

Hong Kong Island

South China Sea

0   10 Mi
0   10 Km

finish

Shantung St.

Soy St.

KOWLOON PENINSULA

Tung St.

Nathan Rd.

Chun Yi Lane

KING'S PARK

Pitt St.

Waterloo Rd.

Yau Ma Tei

Chun Yi Lane

Cliff Rd.

Shek Lung St.

Man Ming Ln.

Li Lung Ln.

Wing Sing Ln.

Tung Kun St.

Lee Tak St.

Public Square St.

Market St.

Temple Street Night Market

Man Cheong St.
Man Wai St.
Man Yuen St.
Man Ying St.
Man Wui St.

Pak Hoi St.

Saigon St.

Ning Po St.

Nanking St.

Jordan Rd.

Wai Ching St.

Canton

Woosung St.

Parkes St.

Nathan Rd.

Chi Wo St.

Gascoigne Rd.

Rd.

Kowloon Station

Bus Terminal

Temple Street Night Market

Shanghai St.

Temple St.

Bow-ring St.

Pilkem St.

Tak Hing St.

Cox's Rd.

Jordan Path

Tak Shing

Austin Rd.

Jordan

Hillwood Rd.

TSIM SHA TSUI EAST

KOWLOON PARK

Observatory Rd.

Kimberley Rd.

Granville Rd.

Science Museum Rd.

Ferry Service to Macau & China

China Ferry Terminal

Harbour City

Nathan Rd.

Prat Ave.

Hart Ave.

Hanoi Rd.

Mody Rd.

KCR East Tsim Sha Tsui

Chatham Rd. S.

Mody Rd.

TSIM SHA TSUI

Haiphong Rd.

Tsim Sha Tsui

Park Dr.

Lock Rd.

Salisbury Rd.

High Speed Ferry to Central

Ocean Terminal

Canton Rd.

Kowloon Rd.

Peking Rd.

Hankow Rd.

Middle Rd.

Bus Terminal

Salisbury Rd.

New World Centre

Avenue of Stars

Tsim Sha Tsui Promenade

Information ℹ
Ferry – –

start here

Kowloon Public Pier

Star Ferry to Central

Star Ferry to Wan Chai

Victoria Harbour

Tsim Sha Tsui Promenade

0   1/4 Mi
0   .25 Km

⑤ Tsim Sha Tsui Promenade

Hugging the shoreline all the way from the Star Ferry to Hung Hom, the promenade offers a great vantage point of the harbor with its boat traffic, Hong Kong Island, and the Peak. It's also a good place for a romantic stroll at night, when the dazzling lights of Hong Kong Island are ablaze across the harbor. Nightly from 8 to 8:18pm, Hong Kong stages its "Symphony of Lights," an impressive laser and light show projected from 18 buildings on Hong Kong Island. Just a couple of minutes' stroll along the waterfront will bring you to the promenade's Avenue of Stars, where embedded plaques honor Hong Kong's most famous movie personalities, including Jackie Chan and Bruce Lee.

Just inland from the Avenue of Stars is one of my favorite museums in Hong Kong, the:

⑥ Hong Kong Museum of Art

Located at 10 Salisbury Rd. (✆ **852/ 2721 0116**), this museum contains an excellent collection of Chinese porcelain, bronzes, jade, lacquerware, bamboo carvings, and paintings of old Hong Kong and Macau, as well as works by contemporary Hong Kong artists. It even has windows. Don't miss it. The museum is open Friday to Wednesday from 10am to 6pm. See p. 162.

Beside the art museum, to the north is the:

⑦ Hong Kong Space Museum

Easy to spot because of its white-domed planetarium, the museum (10 Salisbury Rd.; ✆ **852/2721 0226**; see p. 165) is divided into two parts—the Space Theatre's planetarium, where films are projected onto the 75-foot domed roof, and exhibition halls devoted to space and space exploration. While there are many hands-on exhibitions and some simulator rides that make it a good bet for children, adults will probably find the museum outdated in today's high-tech

world. The Space Museum (also without windows) has stolen the view from Tsim Sha Tsui's most famous landmark, the venerable:

⑧ Peninsula Hotel

Right across the street from the Space Museum (and reached via the underground pedestrian passage), this hotel was built in 1928 to serve guests disembarking at the old train station. Guarded by the largest all-Rolls-Royce fleet in the world (13 at last count), The Peninsula is Hong Kong's grandest old hotel, with a new tower that restored harbor views to its front-facing rooms. Its lobby, reminiscent of a Parisian palace, with high gilded ceilings, pillars, and ferns, has long been a favorite spot for a cup of coffee and people-watching.

> **TAKE A BREAK**
> Many visitors feel that their Hong Kong stay would not be complete without dropping by the lobby of **The Peninsula hotel** (✆ 852/2920 2888). Classical music serenades guests throughout the afternoon and evening, but the best time to stop by is between 2 and 7:30pm daily, when an English-style afternoon tea is served for HK$165 to HK$220 (US$21–US$29).
>
> Another great place for afternoon tea is the **Lobby Lounge** of the Hotel Inter-Continental, 18 Salisbury Rd. (✆ 852/ 2721 1211), which offers fantastic views of the harbor and Hong Kong Island, along with its delicate finger sandwiches and tea daily from 2:30 to 6pm. See the "Afternoon Tea" section of chapter 5, on p. 156, for more information.

Walk to the busy road running alongside the east side of The Peninsula hotel:

⑨ Nathan Road

This is Kowloon's most famous street. It is also one of Hong Kong's widest and runs almost 4km (2½ miles) straight up the spine of Kowloon all the way to Boundary Road, the official border of the New Territories. Nathan Road is named after Sir Matthew Nathan, who served as governor at the time the road was constructed. After it was completed, it was nicknamed "Nathan's Folly." After all, why build such a wide road, seemingly leading to nowhere? Kowloon had very few people back then and even less traffic. Now, of course, Nathan Road is known as the "golden mile of shopping" because of all the boutiques and shops that line both sides.

You'll pass jewelry stores, electronics shops, optical shops, clothing boutiques, and many other establishments as you head north on Nathan Road. The side streets are also good hunting grounds for inexpensive casual wear, at prices comparable to those of Stanley Market. You'll want to return here to explore this area at leisure; shops are open until 9pm or later. After about 10 minutes (assuming you don't stop to shop along the way), you'll see a mosque on your left, built in 1984 to replace an older mosque built in the late 19th century for Muslim Indian troops belonging to the British army. Today, there are about 70,000 Muslims in Hong Kong; the mosque is not open to the public.

Just past the mosque, take the first steps you see leading up to:

❿ Kowloon Park

A good place to bring children for a romp through playgrounds and open spaces, Kowloon park also boasts a water garden, Chinese garden, sculpture garden (with Scotland's Sir Eduardo Paolozzi's bronze version of William Blake's *Concept of Newton*), aviary, woodland trail, maze made of foliage, and swimming pools. Best for visitors, however, are the free Kung Fu Chinese martial arts performances held every Sunday from 2:30 to 4:30pm featuring children and adult practitioners. Follow the signs to "Kung Fu Corner."

Walk through the park northward, past the indoor/outdoor public swimming pools, to Austin Road, where you should turn right until you hit Nathan Road again, where you should turn left. Be on the lookout to the left for:

⓫ Yue Hwa Chinese Products Emporium

On the corner of Jordan Road at 301–309 Nathan Rd. (**℃ 852/2384 0084**), this emporium caters primarily to the local Chinese with traditional Chinese products. Its goods from China include silk, porcelain, jade, clothing, furniture, medicinal herbs, and everyday household goods. Hours here are 10am to 10pm daily.

Yue Hwa marks the beginning of the Yau Ma Tei District. Its name translates roughly as "the place for growing sesame plants," but you won't see any such cultivation today. Rather, like the Western District on Hong Kong Island, Yau Ma Tei offers a look at traditional Chinese life, with shops that sell tea, chopping blocks, joss, bamboo steamers, baked goods, embroidery, herbs, and dried seafood.

Just past the Yue Hwa store, take the first left onto Nanking Street and the second right onto:

⓬ Woosung Street

Here you'll pass restaurants with live seafood in tanks and glazed ducks hanging from windows, an herbalist shop, a mahjong parlor, and other family-owned businesses. After 2 blocks (there's a 7-Eleven on the corner), take a left on:

⓭ Saigon Street

Here, on the left side of the street on the corner of Saigon and Temple streets, is a shop for herbal teas. Temple Street is the site of the famous Night Market, but if it's past 4pm, some vendors may have already set up shop (but more on that later).

A block farther along Saigon, on the corner of Saigon and Shanghai streets to the left, is a:

⑭ Pawnshop

Unlike U.S. pawnshops which double as stores selling unclaimed personal belongings after a prescribed length of time, in Hong Kong pawnshops simply hold items in storage, selling them to another store if the owner is unable to pay. Hong Kong pawnshops, therefore, look like secretive affairs, with walls shielding customers from casual street observers.

After walking 1 block farther east on Saigon, turn right onto:

⑮ Reclamation Street

This street, along with the nearby Yau Ma Tei Market, is an interesting stroll if you haven't yet visited a city market. You'll pass butcher shops and stores selling fish, fruits, and vegetables.

At the end of Reclamation Street, straight ahead past the elevated highway, is a small red building with "Welcome" written in many languages. It's the:

⑯ Jade Market

This fascinating covered market, in two separate structures, consists of some 400 stalls selling jade, pearls, and collectibles and is open from about 10am to approximately 4pm daily, though vendors stay open until 6pm or so if business warrants it (especially Sunday). The jade on sale here comes in a bewildering range of quality. The highest quality should be cold to the touch and translucent, but unless you know your jade, you're better off just coming here for a look. It's possible to infuse jade with color so that inferior stones acquire the brightness and translucence associated with more expensive stones. If you want a souvenir, get a pendant or bangle, but don't spend more than a few dollars on it. The freshwater pearls are also good buys. Although the Chinese here used to bargain secretly by using hand signals concealed underneath a newspaper so that none of the onlookers would know the final price, it appears that calculators have gained more popularity these days.

From the Jade Market, go east 1 block to Shanghai Street, where you will soon see the:

⑰ Tin Hau Temple

Shaded by banyan trees, this is one of many temples in Hong Kong dedicated to Tin Hau, the Goddess of the Sea. This popular community temple has a park, usually filled with people playing mahjong, and inner recesses filled with people asking favors or giving thanks. The temple has sections dating back more than a century. It also reveres deities of the city, the earth, and mercy. It's open daily from 8am to 6pm.

Depending on when you started this tour, at this point you may want to go back to your hotel room to rest and then take a taxi back to visit Yau Ma Tei's most famous attraction, the **Temple Street Night Market** (see the "Temple Street Night Market" box below). The market is in full swing after 7pm, though some vendors start setting up stalls at around 4pm.

TAKE A BREAK
The Dorsett Seaview Hotel, located across from the Tin Hau Temple in the heart of Yau Ma Tei at 262 Shanghai St. (© 852/ 2782 0882), has a lounge on its 19th floor offering views of surrounding Kowloon. It's open daily from 5pm to midnight; you can get two drinks for the price of one until 8pm.

The Eaton Hotel, 380 Nathan Rd. (just south of Kansu St.; © 852/2782 1818), is another good place to stop by for lunch or a drink. Planter's, just off the hotel's lobby on the fourth floor (enter the hotel on Pak Hoi St.), offers a buffet lunch Monday to Saturday until 2:30pm, as well as a happy hour daily from 5 to 9pm, with two drinks for the price of one and live music beginning at 7pm. Also off the lobby is an outdoor terrace, open noon to midnight for drinks and snacks; there's also a sophisticated lobby lounge. For a meal, in the basement of the Eaton Hotel is a Cantonese restaurant, **Yat Tung Heen Chinese Restaurant**, good for seafood and regional dishes.

Temple Street Night Market

The Temple Street Night Market is named after the street on which it's located. This market, with some stalls open from 4pm but busiest from 7 to 10pm, is a wonderful place to spend an evening, with its countless stalls that sell clothing, watches, lighters, imitation designer handbags, sunglasses, sweaters, cassettes, and more. The name of the game is bargaining. There are also seafood stalls, where you can eat inexpensive meals of clams, shrimp, mussels, and crab. Be sure to follow Temple Street to its northern end past the overpass and around the carpark; in the vicinity of the Tin Hau Temple, you'll find palm readers, musicians, and street singers (who favor Cantonese operas and pop songs). Several of the palm readers speak English.

The market is famous for its *dai pai dong* (Cantonese for "big rows of food stalls") that specialize in seafood. Fifty years ago, *dai pai dong* is where most Hong Kong families dined on an evening out, and they were found almost everywhere. Now the government has moved most food stalls into covered markets. The *dai pai dong* at this market are among the few remaining that retain their original ambience. You'll find several under one roof at the Temple Street Food Store at the intersection of Temple Street and Public Square Street, where you can dine inexpensively on clams, shrimp, mussels, and crab, sitting at simple tables in the middle of the action.

Otherwise, if it's early, you like markets, and you're still feeling energetic, walk north on Nathan Road about 10 minutes, taking a right on Dundas Street and then a left onto Tung Choi, home of the so-called:

⑱ Ladies' Market

This is where street vendors sell women's clothing and accessories, including handbags, Chinese jackets, sunglasses, watches, and shoes, as well as men's and children's clothing and toys at low prices, from about 12:30 to 10:30pm daily. Although this market used to be geared to local tastes (and their smaller sizes), an increasing number of tourists has turned it into a thriving market rivaling Temple Street Night Market. The Ladies' Market, in the heart of Mong Kok, extends from Dundas Street north to Argyle Street.

Continuing farther north on Tung Choi (past Mong Kok Rd., which you'll have to cross at the crosswalk to the left) soon brings you to the:

⑲ Goldfish Market

You'll recognize the Goldfish Market from the shop after shop selling exotic fish as well as other pets; most are open daily from 10am to 9pm. Aquariums are considered to bring good luck and are excellent for *feng shui* (geomancy).

Head 1 block east (right), and you'll find yourself on:

⑳ Fa Yuen Street

This is a local market with stalls selling more clothing, handbags, socks, belts, cheap toys, and fruit, at very inexpensive prices. There probably won't be another tourist in sight here and you may pick up some bargains to boot.

At the end of Fa Yuen Street, turn right to cross Prince Edward Road West at the pedestrian light, turn left onto Sai Yee Street, and then take the first right for:

㉑ Flower Market Road

Shop after open-fronted shop here sells orchids, roses, and other wonderfully aromatic flowers, at prices so inexpensive you'll wish you could take some home. More transportable but not nearly as appealing are the plastic flowers also sold on this street. Shops are open daily from around 7am to 7pm.

At the end of the road is the:

㉒ Yuen Po Street Bird Garden

This is an attractive series of Chinese-style open courtyards lined with shops selling songbirds, intricately fashioned birdcages, live crickets, and tiny porcelain water bowls. Note, too, the men who bring their pet birds here for an outing. This place is very Chinese and makes for some great photographs. It's open daily from 7am until 8pm.

After exploring this area of Mong Kok, walk back to Nathan Road for the Prince Edward MTR station.

Shopping

No doubt about it—one of the main reasons people come to Hong Kong is to shop. According to the Hong Kong Tourism Board (HKTB), visitors here spend more than 50% of their money on shopping. In fact, the Hong Kong Special Administrative Region (SAR) is such a popular shopping destination that many luxury cruise ships dock longer here than they do anywhere else on their tours. I doubt that there's ever been a visitor to Hong Kong who left empty-handed. In addition to my below suggestions, you might also want to get a copy of *Suzy Gershman's Born to Shop Hong Kong, Shanghai & Beijing* to help you find what you're looking for.

1 The Shopping Scene

BEST BUYS

Hong Kong is a duty-free port, which means that imported goods are not taxed in the SAR with the exception of only a few luxury goods like tobacco and alcohol. What's more, there is no sales tax in Hong Kong. Thus, you can buy some goods in the SAR at a cheaper price than in the country where they were made. It's less expensive, for example, to buy Japanese products such as designer clothing, cameras, electronic goods, and pearls in Hong Kong than in Japan itself. In fact, all my friends who live in Japan try to visit the SAR at least once or twice a year to buy their business clothes, cosmetics, and other accessories.

Although not as cheap as it once was, clothing is probably one of the best buys in Hong Kong, simply because of the sheer quantity and variety. If you've looked at the labels of clothes sold in your own hometown, you've probably noticed that many say MADE IN HONG KONG or MADE IN CHINA. Both custom-made and designer garments remain affordable in Hong Kong, including three-piece business suits, leather outfits, furs, sportswear, and jeans. Even cheaper are factory outlets and small stores where you can pick up inexpensive fashions for a song. But even when I end up paying about as much for an outfit as I would back home, I know I've purchased unique clothing in Hong Kong that's impossible to find in homogenized shopping malls.

Hong Kong is also a great place to shop for other Chinese products, including porcelain, tableware, jade, cloisonné, silk, handicrafts, hand-embroidery, Chinese herbs, exotic teas from China's many provinces, and artwork. You'll also find crafts and goods from other parts of Asia, including Thailand, India, the Philippines, and Indonesia.

Other good buys include Chinese antiques, shoes, gold jewelry, furniture, carpets, leather goods, luggage (you'll probably need a new bag just to lug your purchases home), handbags, briefcases, cosmetics, and eyeglasses. Hong Kong is also one of the world's largest exporters of watches and toys. As for electronic goods and cameras, they are not the bargains they once were. Make sure, therefore, to check prices on goods at home before you come to the SAR so that you can accurately assess a bargain. The best deals are on recently discontinued models, such as last year's Sony Discman.

If you're interested in fake name-brand watches, handbags, or clothing to impress the folks back home, you've come to the right place. Although illegal, fake name-brand goods were still being sold at Hong Kong's night markets during my last visit by vendors who were ready to flee at the first sight of an official (even cheaper prices are offered for fake designer handbags and watches just across the border in mainland China; see chapter 10, "Side Trips from Hong Kong"). Of course, if customs officials spot these fake goods in your bags when you return home, they'll be confiscated. Approximately half the fake goods seized by US customs agents come from mainland China.

WHEN TO SHOP

Because shopping is such big business in Hong Kong, most stores are open 7 days a week, closing only for 2 or 3 days during the Chinese New Year. Most stores open at 10am and remain open until 7pm in Central, 9pm or 10pm in Tsim Sha Tsui and Yau Ma Tei, and 9:30pm in Causeway Bay. Street markets are open every day.

The biggest and best seasonal sale takes place around the Chinese lunar new year, generally in February. All the major department stores as well as shops in many of the huge shopping complexes hold sales at this time, with prices discounted about 40%. There is also a summer sale, usually in June or July, as well as end-of-season sales in the early spring and early autumn.

GUARANTEES & RECEIPTS

It's always a good idea to obtain a receipt from the shopkeeper for your purchases, if for no other reason than as proof of value when going through customs upon returning home. You'll also need a receipt if the product you've purchased is defective. A receipt should give a description of your purchase, including the brand name, model number, serial number, and price for electronic and photographic equipment; for jewelry and gold watches, there should be a description of the precious stones and the metal content. If you're making a purchase using a credit card, you should also ask for the customer's copy of the credit card slip, and make sure "HK$" appears before the monetary total.

If you're interested in a camera, electronic goods, watch, or any other expensive product, be sure to inspect the product carefully and make sure its voltage is compatible with that of your home country. Before purchasing, make sure that all parts, pieces, and the warranty card of your purchase are included in the box. Ask the shopkeeper for a manufacturer's guarantee, which should include the name and/or symbol of the sole agent in the SAR, a description of the model and serial number, date of purchase, name and address of the shop where you bought it, and the shop's official chop or stamp. Different products and models of the same brand may carry different warranties—some valid worldwide, others only in Hong Kong. Worldwide guarantees (which is what you'll want) must carry the name and/or symbol of the sole agent in Hong Kong for the given product. If you're in doubt, check with the relevant Hong Kong sole agent (information on sole agents for Sony, Rolex, and others can be obtained by calling the **Consumer Council Hotline** at ⓒ **852/2929 2222**).

COMPARISON SHOPPING & BARGAINING

The cardinal rule of shopping in Hong Kong is to shop around. Unless you're planning to buy antiques or art, you'll probably see the same items in many

Tips **A Shopping Warning**

Hong Kong is a buyer-beware market. Name brands are sometimes fakes; that cheap jade you bought may actually be glass; and electronic goods may not work. To make things worse, the general practice is that goods are usually not returnable, and deposits paid are not refundable.

On a personal aside, I decided to buy a digital Sony camcorder and checked approximately 10 electronic stores, where I received price quotes ranging from HK$3,500 to HK$12,000 (US$455–US$1,560) for the exact same model. When I returned to the cheapest stores and asked to see the camcorder, however, I was told it was suddenly "out of stock," but the salesmen said they would be happy to show me a similar model for a slightly higher price. The problem is that there are so *many* models—including many that never make it to Western markets—that it's difficult to know exactly what you're getting and what constitutes a fair price. In the end, I fell for the old bait-and-switch and bought a discontinued Sony camcorder at a higher price than what I would have paid for a newer model in the United States. I didn't do my homework *before* departing home (even checking the Sony website while in Hong Kong would have been a smart move), and I ended up paying for my mistake.

To be on the safe side, try to make your major purchases at HKTB member stores, which display the HKTB logo (a gold circle with black Chinese calligraphy in the middle and the words "Quality Tourism Services") on their storefronts. There are hundreds of member stores, all listed in a directory called *A Guide to Quality Shops and Restaurants* that you can get free from the HKTB and at www.discoverhongkong. com/qts. Both give the names, addresses, and phone numbers of shops that sell everything from audio-video equipment to jewelry, clothing, optical goods, antiques, and custom-made clothing. HKTB member stores are required to give accurate information on the products they sell and to respond promptly to justified complaints. Even more important, the Hong Kong Tourism Board will provide after-sales assistance for purchases from its member stores. Of course, prices are often higher than at nonmember stores, but the payoff should be peace of mind and reassurance that you are paying a fair price. In addition, if you patronize a shop as part of a group tour arranged by travel agents who are members of the **Travel Industry Council of Hong Kong** (© 852/2807 0707), you are guaranteed a full refund within 14 days of purchase provided goods are unused and intact and you have the original sales receipt.

If you have any complaints against a member store, call the **HKTB** (© 852/2508 1234) multilingual Visitor Hotline daily between 8am and 6pm, or the **Consumer Council Hotline** (© 852/2929 2222) Monday to Friday from 9am to 5pm and Saturday from 9am to noon. In case of a serious dispute you can also call the **Hong Kong Police** (© 999) 24 hours a day.

different shops on both sides of the harbor. If you've decided to buy a washable silk blouse for that favorite niece, for example, check a few stores to get an idea of quality, color, and style. With the exception of department stores and designer boutiques, you may be able to bargain for your purchase, though I've noticed that some shopkeepers are less willing to bargain than they once were. Still, at some of the smaller, family-owned stores, a good strategy is to ask what the "best" price might be. You should also ask for a discount if you're buying several items from the same store, and generally speaking, you can get a better price if you pay with cash rather than by credit card. How much you pay will depend on your bargaining skills and how many items you intend to purchase. Begin your comparison shopping as soon as you arrive in Hong Kong, so that you can get an idea of the differences in prices. As for street markets, you most certainly must bargain, though nowadays some vendors will just shake their heads and say their prices are fixed. If vendors are willing to bargain, sometimes just saying the item is too expensive and walking away will suddenly get you that "special price."

SHIPPING

Many stores, especially the larger ones, will pack and ship your purchases home for you. Since basic insurance usually insures only against loss, it's a good idea to buy an all-risk insurance for valuable or fragile goods, available at the store. However, since these policies can be expensive, find out whether using your credit card to make your purchase will provide automatic free insurance.

In addition, all upper-bracket and most medium-range hotels offer a parcel-wrapping and mailing service. If you decide to ship your purchases home yourself, the easiest thing to do is to stop by the post office and buy ready-made boxes, which come with everything you need to ship goods home. Packages sent to the United States or Europe generally take 6 to 8 weeks by surface mail and 1 week by airmail. For major purchases, you can also buy postal insurance covering damage or loss in transit.

2 Great Shopping Areas

Hong Kong is so filled with shops, boutiques, street markets, department stores, and malls, it's hard to think of places where you *can't* shop. Still, there are specific hunting grounds for various products, as well as areas that have greater concentrations of shops than elsewhere.

Tsim Sha Tsui has the greatest concentration of shops in Hong Kong. Nathan Road, which runs through Kowloon for 4km (2½ miles) from the harbor to the border of the New Territories, is lined with stores selling clothing, jewelry, eyeglasses, cameras, electronic goods, crafts from China, shoes, handbags, luggage, watches, and more. There are also tailors, tattoo artists, and even shops that will carve your name into a wooden chop (a stamp used in place of a signature for official documents). Be sure to explore the side streets radiating off Nathan Road for shops specializing in washable silk and casual clothing and for export overruns of fun, youth-oriented fashions at modest prices. There are also department stores, Chinese emporiums, and shopping arcades, as well as several huge shopping malls. Harbour City, on Canton Road, for example, is gigantic; it is comprised of Ocean Centre, Ocean Galleries, Ocean Terminal, the Hongkong Hotel Arcade, and the Gateway Shopping Arcade. Farther north, in Yau Ma Tei, is Hong Kong's most famous outdoor market, the Temple Street Night Market, with vendors selling clothing, CDs, watches, toys, mobile phones, and

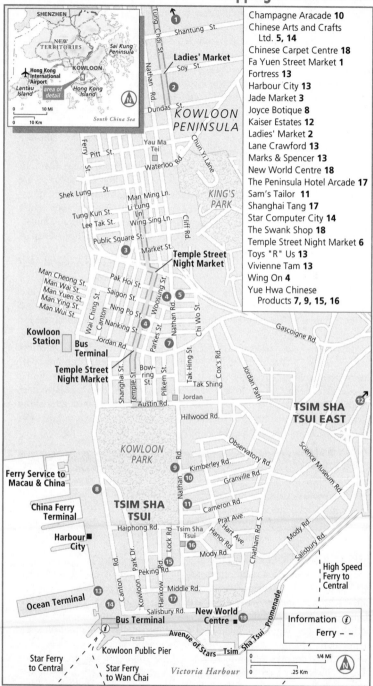

Shopping in Tsim Sha Tsui

Champagne Aracade **10**
Chinese Arts and Crafts
  Ltd. **5, 14**
Chinese Carpet Centre **18**
Fa Yuen Street Market **1**
Fortress **13**
Harbour City **13**
Jade Market **3**
Joyce Botique **8**
Kaiser Estates **12**
Ladies' Market **2**
Lane Crawford **13**
Marks & Spencer **13**
New World Centre **18**
The Peninsula Hotel Arcade **17**
Sam's Tailor **11**
Shanghai Tang **17**
Star Computer City **14**
The Swank Shop **18**
Temple Street Night Market **6**
Toys "R" Us **13**
Vivienne Tam **13**
Wing On **4**
Yue Hwa Chinese
  Products **7, 9, 15, 16**

accessories. The nearby Ladies' Market is also great for inexpensive clothing and accessories. There are also specialist markets in Yau Ma Tei and Mong Kok selling everything from clothing and flowers to goldfish, songbirds, and jade.

For upscale shopping, **Central** is the place where you'll find international designer labels. The Landmark, Prince's Building, Alexandra House, and Chater House boast boutiques selling jewelry, clothing, leather goods and more, with names ranging from Armani, Cartier, and Chanel to Gucci, Louis Vuitton, and Tiffany & Co. Pacific Place is an upscale shopping mall selling everything from clothing to electronics; ifc mall sells clothing and accessories. Central is also a good place to shop for Chinese imports and souvenirs, especially at the hip Shanghai Tang and the Yue Hwa Chinese Products Emporium.

Another happy hunting ground is **Causeway Bay** on Hong Kong Island. In contrast to Tsim Sha Tsui, it caters more to locals than to tourists, and prices are often lower. In addition to small shops selling everything from shoes and clothing to Chinese herbs, there are a couple of Japanese department stores and a large shopping complex called Times Square specializing in clothing and housewares. Also check the area around Jardine's Crescent (p. 218), an open-air market with cheap clothing, food, and produce.

One of my favorite places to shop for inexpensive fashions is **Stanley Market** on the southern end of Hong Kong Island, where vendors sell silk clothing and business and casual wear. In recent years, shops specializing in Chinese crafts and products have also opened in Stanley Market. For shoes, get on the tram and head for Happy Valley; on Leighton Road and Wong Nai Chung Road (near the racecourse) there are rows of shoe and handbag shops.

Antiques and curio lovers usually head for **Hollywood Road** and **Cat Street** in the Western District on Hong Kong Island, where everything from snuff bottles to jade carvings and Ming vases is for sale. Chinese handcrafts, including porcelain, furniture, silk clothing, and embroidery, are sold in Chinese-product department stores and Chinese arts-and-crafts shops located on both sides of the harbor. Several deluxe hotels boast arcades housing designer boutiques, most notably The Peninsula and Regent.

3 Shopping A to Z

The stores listed below are just a few of the thousands upon thousands in the SAR. For more detailed coverage, see the booklet *A Guide to Quality Shops and Restaurants,* which lists shops that are members of the HKTB, or check the website www.discoverhongkong.com/qts. You might also want to look at *Suzy Gershman's Born to Shop Hong Kong, Shanghai & Beijing.*

ANTIQUES & COLLECTIBLES

Several of the Chinese-product stores, listed under "Chinese Craft Emporiums" later in this chapter, also stock antiques, especially porcelain. Additionally, some hotel shopping arcades have shops specializing in antiques. Antiques buffs should also inquire at HKTB whether international auctioneers Christie's or Sotheby's are holding one of their regular sales for antiques in Hong Kong.

The most famous area for antiques and chinoiserie, however, is around **Hollywood Road** and **Cat Street,** both above the Central District on Hong Kong Island. This area gained fame in the 1950s following the 1949 revolution in China (which flooded the market with family possessions). Hollywood Road twists along for a little more than .8km (½ mile), with shops selling original and reproduction Qing and Ming dynasty Chinese furniture, original prints, scrolls, porcelain, clay figurines, silver, and rosewood and black-wood furniture, as well as fakes and curios. Near the western end is Upper Lascar Row, popularly known as Cat Street, where sidewalk vendors sell snuff bottles, curios, and odds and ends, as well as reproductions. At the eastern end of Hollywood Road, near Pottinger Street, is a cluster of chic antiques shops displaying furniture and blue-and-white porcelain, including goods from neighboring Asian countries such as Korean chests and Japanese hibachi. If you're a real antiques collector, I suggest you simply walk through the dozens of shops on and around Hollywood Road. Most are open daily from 10am to 6pm.

If you cannot tell the difference between originals and reproductions, you're better off shopping at one of the HKTB member stores, which display HKTB's gold circle and calligraphy logo. Be sure to ask whether an antique has been repaired or restored, as this can affect its value. If the piece is quite expensive, ask that it be tested. (The most important rule is to shop with reputable dealers when buying expensive pieces. And make sure that if the test turns out negative, the shop will pay for the test. As you can see, this process takes time, money, and effort.) Wood, for example, can be tested using carbon-14 dating, while ceramics can be tested with the Oxford Test. The authenticity of bronze, jade, glass, and stone can also be determined through testing. If you're purchasing anything more than 100 years old, request a Certificate of Antiquity detailing its age and origin, along with a receipt detailing your purchase. Although it's illegal to smuggle antiques out of mainland China, many smuggled items do in fact end up in Hong Kong, where it is legal to then sell, buy, and own them. Needless to say, this has caused friction between China and Hong Kong, especially when international auction houses have sold well-documented smuggled Chinese antiques.

Arch Angel Antiques   Established in 1988, this is one of Hollywood Road's largest shops for Asian antiques and art, including museum-quality ceramics, furniture, Ming dynasty figurines, terracotta animals, boxes, and collectibles. In addition to this three-story main shop, nearby galleries showcase ancient ceramics, bronze Buddhas, terracotta figures, stone sculptures, and contemporary Vietnamese art. Every antique item for sale is accompanied by a detailed certificate of authenticity. The main shop is open daily from 9:30am to 6:30pm. 53–55 Hollywood Rd., Central. ℭ **852/2851 6848.** MTR: Central.

Cat Street Galleries   Cat Street Galleries, on a street parallel to Cat Street, houses several individually owned booths of arts and crafts and expensive antiques from the various dynasties, making it a good place to begin an antiques shopping odyssey. It's open Monday to Friday from 11am to 6pm and Saturday from 10am to 6pm. 38 Lok Ku Rd., Central. ℭ **852/2543 1609.** MTR: Sheung Wan. Bus: 26 (from Des Voeux Rd. Central in front of the Hongkong Bank) to the 2nd stop on Hollywood Rd., at Man Mo Temple.

China Art   This family-owned shop, which has the elegance of an art gallery with its mixed displays of furniture and art, is one of Hong Kong's best for restored antique Chinese furniture, including chairs, tables, folding screens, chests, and wardrobes, mostly from the Ming dynasty (1368–1644). Located across from the Central Police Station, it's open Monday to Saturday from 10:30am to 6pm and Sunday and holidays from 1 to 6pm. (An additional showroom warehouse, open only by appointment, is located in Cat Street Galleries; see above). 15 Hollywood Rd., Central. ℭ **852/2542 0982.** www.chinaart.com.hk. MTR: Central. Bus: 26 (from Des Voeux Rd. Central in front of the Hongkong Bank) to Hollywood Rd.

Dragon Culture *(finds)* All serious fans of Chinese antiques eventually end up here. One of the largest and most knowledgeable purveyors of antiques in Hong Kong, Victor Choi began collecting Chinese antiques in the 1970s, traveling throughout China from province to province and to all the major cities. He shares his expertise in three books: *Collecting Chinese Antiquities in Hong Kong* (a must for both the novice and experienced buyer), *Horses for Eternity,* and *Antiquities through the Ages,* which you can purchase in his shop. Choi has also given lectures on Chinese antiques in the HKTB's Meet the People program. With another gallery nearby at 184 Hollywood Rd. (© **852/2815 5227**) and another one in New York, he carries Neolithic pottery, three-color glazed pottery horses from the Tang dynasty, Ming porcelains, bronzes, jade, wood carvings, snuff bottles, calligraphy, paintings, brush pots, stone carvings, and more, and also provides authenticity for all items he sells. According to Choi, prices for antiques are a fourth of what they'd fetch in New York. Both his Hong Kong shops are open Monday to Saturday from 10am to 6pm. 231 Hollywood Rd., Sheung Wan. © **852/2545 8098**. www.dragonculture.com.hk. MTR: Sheung Wan. Bus: 26 (from Des Voeux Rd. Central in front of the Hongkong Bank) to the 2nd stop on Hollywood Rd., at Man Mo Temple.

Teresa Coleman Fine Arts Established in 1982, this gallery is best known for its collection of antique embroidered costumes from the Chinese imperial court, with approximately 2,000 pieces dating from the Ching Dynasty (1644–1911). Complimenting the collection are costume accessories and ornaments, including fans, lacquered boxes, and jewelry. The shop also has a good collection of antique oriental rugs from Tibet and China. It's open Monday to Saturday from 9:30am to 6pm. 79 Wyndham St., Central. © **852/2526 2450**. www.teresa coleman.com. MTR: Central.

True Arts & Curios *(finds)* This tiny shop is so packed with antiques and curios that there's barely room for customers. Although everything from snuff bottles, porcelain, antique silver, earrings, hair pins, and children's shoes (impractical but darling, with curled toes) are stocked, the true finds here are some 2,000 intricate wood carvings, pried from the doors and windows of dismantled temples and homes. You'll find them hanging from the ceiling and in bins, many of them dusty and grimy from years of neglect. The best ones are carved from a single piece of wood, masterpieces in workmanship and available at modest prices. It's open Monday to Saturday from 10:30am to 6:30pm and Sunday from 2:30 to 6:30pm. 89–91 Hollywood Rd., Central. © **852/2559 1485**. MTR: Sheung Wan.

ART GALLERIES

Several Hong Kong art galleries specialize in contemporary art from mainland China and Hong Kong. These are two of the most well known.

Hanart TZ Gallery This very tiny gallery (in the same building as American Express) has been exhibiting, promoting, and selling experimental art from mainland China, Hong Kong, and Taiwan since 1983. Its owner/curator, Chang Tsong-zung, has given lectures on the contemporary local art scene for HKTB's Meet the People program. Exhibition space is small, so be sure to ask for recent catalogues. It's open Monday to Saturday from 10am to 6:30pm. 202 Henley Bldg., 2nd floor, 5 Queen's Rd., Central. © **852/2526 9019**. www.hanart.com. MTR: Central.

Schoeni Art Gallery This 5,000-square-foot gallery shows contemporary Chinese oil paintings by both up-and-coming and established artists. A smaller gallery at nearby 27 Hollywood Rd. (© **852/2542 3143**) specializes in contemporary works by European and Asian artists. Both are open Monday to Saturday from 10:30am to 6:30pm. 21–31 Old Bailey St., Central. (©) **852/2869 8802.** www.schoeni. com.hk. MTR: Central.

CARPETS

Hong Kong is a good place to shop for Chinese, Indian, Persian, and other types of carpets and rugs. Additionally, the locally-made Tai Ping carpets are famous the world over, produced in Hong Kong with virgin wool imported from New Zealand.

For imported carpets from India and the Middle East, there are several shops along the **Hollywood Road** and **Wyndham Street** areas in Central. For hand-knotted wool or silk Chinese carpets, be sure to check out the Chinese Craft Emporiums (listed below).

The **Chinese Carpet Centre,** in Shop 5 on the ground floor of the New World Centre at 18–24 Salisbury Rd., Sim Sha Tsui ((©) **852/2730 7230;** MTR: Tsim Sha Tsui), stocks more than 100,000 Chinese carpets, mostly handmade of silk, wool, or cotton but also machine-made acrylic.

For Tai Ping carpets, there's a conveniently located showroom in Shop 213 of the Prince's Building, 10 Chater Road, Central ((©) **852/2522 7138;** www.taiping carpets.com; MTR: Central). If you don't see what you like, you can have one custom-designed, specifying the color, thickness, and direction of the weave. It takes about 3 months to make a carpet; the company will ship it to you.

CHINA (PORCELAIN)

Chinaware, a fine, translucent earthenware, was first brought from China to Europe by the Portuguese in the 16th century. Its name was subsequently shortened to "china," and Hong Kong remains one of the best places in the world to shop for both antique (mainly from the Manchu, or Ching, dynasty, 1644–1911) and contemporary Chinese porcelain. Traditional motifs include bamboo, flowers, dragons, carp, and cranes, which adorn everything from dinner plates to vases, lamps, and jars. Also popular is translucent porcelain with a rice grain design. And, of course, European and Japanese china is also available in Hong Kong, including Meissen, Wedgwood, and Noritake.

Probably the best place to begin looking for Chinese porcelain is at one of the Chinese-product stores, listed below under "Chinese Craft Emporiums." In addition, malls and shopping centers (see "Megamalls & Shopping Centers," later in this chapter) like Pacific Place in Admiralty, Times Square in Causeway Bay, and Harbour City in Tsim Sha Tsui also have porcelain shops. Nowadays, contemporary china is generally both dishwasher- and microwave-safe.

Overjoy Porcelain Factory   With more than 400 stock designs, dinner services are the specialty here. You may also mix and match, or even create your very own design. Sets are usually commissioned for either 6, 8, or 12 diners and take 4 to 6 weeks to complete. It's open Monday to Saturday from 10am to 6pm, but because it's in the New Territories, you'd be wise to call first. Or, visit its smaller shop on the first floor of Fleet Arcade, Fenwick Pier Lung King St., Wan Chai ((©) **852/2511 2763;** MTR: Wan Chai), open the same hours. 1st floor, Block B of Kwai Hing Industrial Building, 10–18 Chun Pin St., Kwai Chung, New Territories. (©) **852/2487 0615.** MTR: Kwai Hing station; then take a taxi.

Wah Tung China Company   This is reputedly the largest company specializing in hand-painted antique porcelain reproductions, especially huge pieces like vases and garden stools. Its vast collection covers all Chinese artistic periods, including Song dynasty celadons, Canton Rose, Chinoiserie, Chinese Imari, and 17th- and 18th-century Chinese export porcelain. It's open Monday to Saturday from 10am to 8pm and Sunday from 11am to 7pm. A second shop is located at 59 Hollywood Rd., Central (© **852/2543 2823;** MTR: Central), open Monday to Saturday from 10am to 7pm and Sunday from 11am to 6pm. 8 Queen's Road East, Central. © **852/2520 5933.** www.wahtungchina.com. MTR: Admiralty.

CHINESE CRAFT EMPORIUMS

In addition to the shops listed here, which specialize in traditional and contemporary arts, crafts, clothing, souvenirs, and gift items from China, there are several souvenir shops at Stanley Market (located in Stanley on the southern end of Hong Kong Island) that carry lacquered boxes, china, embroidered tablecloths, figurines, and other Chinese imports.

Chinese Arts and Crafts Ltd   In business for more than 30 years, this is the best upscale chain for Chinese arts and crafts and is one of the safest places to purchase jade. Prices are high, but so is the quality. You can also buy silk dresses and blouses, beautiful Chinese jackets, arts and crafts, antiques, jewelry, watches, carpets, cloisonné, furs, Chinese herbs and medicine, rosewood furniture, chinaware, Chinese teas, and embroidered tablecloths or pillowcases here—in short, virtually all the upmarket items that China produces. It's a great place for gifts in all price ranges. The main shop, spread on two floors and located in Star House near the Star Ferry, is open daily from 10am to 9:30pm. Branches are conveniently located in the Nathan Hotel, 378 Nathan Rd., Yau Ma Tei (© **852/ 2730 0061;** MTR: Jordan); 59–65 Queen's Road Central (© **852/2901 0338;** MTR: Central); Shop 230 in Pacific Place, 88 Queensway, Central (© **852/2523 3933;** MTR: Admiralty); and in the China Resources Building, 26 Harbour Rd., Wan Chai (© **852/2827 6667;** MTR: Wan Chai). 3 Salisbury Rd., Tsim Sha Tsui. © **852/2735 4061.** www.crcretail.com. MTR: Tsim Sha Tsui.

Chinese Products   Yue Hwa caters to a local clientele with both traditional Chinese and everyday products. The main shop in Yau Ma Tei stocks everything from household goods to clothing, shoes, jade jewelry, arts and crafts, china, linens, furniture, tea, foodstuff, medicinal herbs like dried sea horses, and even antlers. It was here that I bought some friends a gag wedding gift years ago— Chinese whiskey with preserved lizards in it, all for only HK$25 (US$3.25)— definitely a bargain.

The branch stores specialize primarily in Chinese handcrafts and jewels. My favorite is the one at 39 Queen's Rd. Central, in Central (© **852/2522 2333;** MTR: Central), with a wealth of silk clothing and other traditional items. Other branches include: Park Lane Shopper's Boulevard at 143–161 Nathan Rd., Tsim Sha Tsui (© **852/2739 3888;** MTR: Tsim Sha Tsui); basement of Mirador Mansion, 54–64 Nathan Rd., Tsim Sha Tsui (© **852/2368 9165;** MTR: Tsim Sha Tsui); 1 Kowloon Park Dr. and Peking Rd., Tsim Sha Tsui (© **852/2317 5333;** MTR: Tsim Sha Tsui); and 375–379 Hennessy Rd., Wan Chai (© **852/ 3162 8998;** MTR: Wan Chai). 301–309 Nathan Rd., Yau Ma Tei, Kowloon. © **852/2384 0084.** www.yuehwa.com.sg. Daily 10am–10pm. MTR: Jordan.

Shanghai Tang *Finds*   You are stepping back into the Shanghai of the 1930s when you enter this small but upscale two-level store with its gleaming wooden and tiled floors, raised cashier cubicles, ceiling fans, and helpful clerks wearing classical Chinese jackets. This is Chinese chic at its best, with neatly stacked rows of updated versions of traditional Chinese clothing, ranging from cheongsams and silk pajamas to padded jackets, caps, and shoes—all in bright, contemporary colors and styles. If you're looking for a lime-green or shocking pink padded jacket, this is the place for you. There are even Shanghai tailors on hand to custom-make something for you. You will also find children's clothing and funky accessories and home furnishings, from Mao-emblazoned watches to silk-covered photo albums, beaded picture frames, and silver chopsticks. It's open Monday to Saturday from 10am to 8pm and Sunday from 11am to 7pm. There are tiny branches in The Peninsula hotel, Salisbury Road, Tsim Sha Tsui (✆ **852/2537 2888;** MTR: Tsim Sha Tsui) and in Shop 6E140 of Hong Kong International Airport (✆ **852/2261 0606**), but the main shop has the best selection. Its sign is hidden under the eaves of the Pedder Building, so you may have to search for it. Pedder Building, 12 Pedder St., Central. ✆ 852/2525 7333. www.shanghaitang.com. MTR: Central.

DEPARTMENT STORES

It will probably come as no surprise to learn that the SAR has a great many department stores. Wing On and Lane Crawford, two upmarket local chain department stores, offer a nice selection of clothing, accessories, and local and imported designer fashions, gift items, and cosmetics. Japanese department stores are also quite popular with the locals, with a couple located in Causeway Bay.

LOCAL DEPARTMENT STORES

Lane Crawford Ltd   This chic and upscale department store is a hometown favorite for its large clothing and accessory departments for the whole family and its home furnishings, including shoes, handbags, silver, crystal, and cosmetics. It has branches on both sides of the harbor (the branch at Pacific Place is probably the best) and is similar to established chain stores in England and the United States. This main store is open daily from 10am to 9pm. Other branches can be found at: Pacific Place, 88 Queensway, Central (✆ **852/2118 3668;** MTR: Admiralty); Times Square, 1 Matheson St., Causeway Bay (✆ **852/2118 3638;** MTR: Causeway Bay); and Shop 100, Ocean Terminal, Harbour City, 3 Canton Rd., Tsim Sha Tsui (✆ **852/2118 3428;** MTR: Tsim Sha Tsui). Podium 3, ifc mall, Central. ✆ 852/2118 3388. www.lanecrawford.com. MTR: Central.

Wing On   Founded in Shanghai almost a century ago and one of Hong Kong's oldest department stores, this main shop offers a wide selection of clothing, jewelry, accessories, and household items, with branches mostly in outlying areas (though a convenient branch can be found at Wing On Kowloon Center across from the Nathan Hotel, 345 Nathan Rd., Yau Ma Tei ✆ **852/2710 6288;** MTR: Jordan). The main branch is open daily from 10am to 7:30pm. 211 Des Voeux Rd., Sheung Wan. ✆ 852/2852 1888. www.wingonet.com. MTR: Sheung Wan.

JAPANESE DEPARTMENT STORES

Mitsukoshi   Mitsukoshi is a long-established department store; it first opened as a kimono shop in Japan in the 1600s and is still one of Japan's most exclusive stores. Today it houses the boutiques of well-known designers of shoes, accessories, and clothing, with high prices to match; it also carries lingerie, cosmetics, household goods, and toys. It's open daily from 10:30am to 10pm. 500 Hennessy Rd., Causeway Bay. ✆ 852/2576 5222. www.mitsukoshi.com.hk. MTR: Causeway Bay.

Seibu   One of the largest department-store chains in Japan (its Tokyo store is the third-largest department store in the world), this was Seibu's first store to open outside Japan. An upscale, sophisticated department store targeting Hong Kong's affluent yuppie population, it is the epitome of chic, from its Art Deco Italian furnishings to fashions from the world's top design houses. More than 65% of its merchandise is European, and 25% is from Japan. The Loft department carries well-designed housewares and gifts, while Seed is the place to go for the latest fashions. The food department in the basement is especially good, stocking many imported items that are not available elsewhere in Hong Kong; it's also a good choice in inexpensive dining, with various counters specializing in international fare. It's open Sunday to Wednesday from 10:30am to 8pm and Thursday to Saturday from 10:30am to 9pm. There's a small branch in the Windsor House, 311 Gloucester Rd., Causeway Bay (© **852/2890 0333;** MTR: Causeway Bay). Pacific Place, 88 Queensway, Central. © **852/2868 0111.** MTR: Admiralty.

Sogo   Sogo is much larger and more egalitarian than the other Japanese department stores listed above; its goods are cheaper and its prices lower. Consequently, the 12-story store is often packed (particularly on Sun), filled with families shopping for clothing, toys, furniture, household goods, and electrical appliances. In the second basement is a large supermarket. Sogo is open daily from 10am to 10pm. East Point Centre, 555 Hennessy Rd., Causeway Bay. © **852/2833 8338.** www.sogo.com.hk. MTR: Causeway Bay.

OTHER DEPARTMENT STORES
Marks & Spencer   Known in Britain for its great prices on clothing and affectionately nicknamed "Marks & Sparks," this import from the United Kingdom (but with smaller sizes) is open daily from 10am to 8pm. It also has several branches on the Hong Kong side, including in Central Tower, 28 Queen's Rd. Central (© **852/2921 8059;** MTR: Central); Pacific Place, 88 Queensway, Central (© **852/2921 8891;** MTR: Admiralty); and Times Square, 1 Matheson St., Causeway Bay (© **852/2923 7970;** MTR: Causeway Bay). Ocean Centre, Harbour City, Canton Rd., Tsim Sha Tsui. © **852/2926 3346.** www.marksandspencer.com. MTR: Tsim Sha Tsui.

ELECTRONICS
Because there is no import-duty or sales tax and because Hong Kong may offer the latest models months before they're available in other countries, shopping for electronic goods has long been a popular tourist pastime. However, prices have increased for electronic products in recent years, so if you're interested in buying a digital camera, camcorder, DVD or MP3 player, computer, mobile phone, or other electronic product, be sure to check prices at home before coming to Hong Kong to make sure that what you want to buy here is really a bargain. Then, head to Tsim Sha Tsui for the many shops along Nathan Road and surrounding streets specializing in electronics galore. Compare prices first, and to be on the safe side, only shop in stores that are members of HKTB and skip those that do not have price tags. Otherwise, you may end up buying a discontinued model at inflated prices (see "A Shopping Warning," earlier in this chapter). **Fortress** (www.fortress.com.hk) is a big-name chain with locations throughout Hong Kong, including major shopping malls and tourist areas (there are two in Harbour City alone). In Central there's a convenient Fortress in the Melbourne Plaza, 33 Queen's Rd. Central (© **852/2121 1077;** MTR: Central).

Camera buffs may wish to check out the used-camera stores at the Champagne Arcade, located beside the Miramar Hotel on Kimberley Road, or Stanley Street in Central for photographic equipment. For computers and software, try dedicated malls such as **Star Computer City,** located on the second floor of the Star House across from the Tsim Sha Tsui Star Ferry terminal at 3 Salisbury Rd., or the **In Square Computer Plaza,** located on the 10th through 12th floors of the Windsor House, 311 Gloucester Rd. in Causeway Bay. In any case, whatever you buy, be sure to inspect every piece of equipment before leaving the store (do not assume what's inside a box matches the picture on the outside and check to make sure instructions are in English), make sure equipment works and that its voltage is compatible with yours at home, and obtain warranties and receipts. For computers, look for complete packages that offer computer, printer, scanner, and software at competitive prices, and be sure that the loaded software is in English.

A fun place for adventuresome shoppers is **Apliu Street** (beside Cheung Sha Wan Station), which functions as a street market for second-hand electronic goods and a hodgepodge of junk, including fishing poles, pots and pans, and more. The market is open weekdays from about 11am to 8pm and weekends from 11am to 11pm. You need to know your goods here, and be sure to bargain fiercely. Don't neglect the many stores behind the vendors, either, selling new and used mobile phones, watches, batteries, and more.

FABRICS

Many tailors stock their own bolts of fabric, but for one-stop fabric shopping with larger selections, the place to go is the **Western Market,** 323 Des Voeux Rd. Central, in the Western District. The first floor of this 1906 renovated brick building is lined with shop after shop selling every imaginable type of cloth, from upholstery fabric and silk to linens and Indian cottons, with approximately 16 vendors in all. The salespeople can advise almost to the inch how much fabric you'll need for any outfit, even if all you have to show them is a drawing. The Western Market shops are open daily from 10am to 7pm. The nearest MTR station is Sheung Wan, or take the tram to Sheung Wan.

Other good places to look for silk are the emporiums listed under "Chinese Craft Emporiums," above.

FASHION

Ever since Hong Kong received a large influx of Shanghainese tailors following the revolution in China in 1949, Hong Kong has been a center for the fashion industry. Today, clothing remains one of Hong Kong's best buys, and many major international design houses have boutiques here; several have factories as well, either here or just across the border in Guangzhou (p. 257). There are also a number of Hong Kong designers to watch out for, including Vivienne Tam, Walter Ma, Lulu Cheung, and Barney Cheng.

For a wide range in prices, the department stores listed above are best for one-stop shopping for the entire family, as are Hong Kong's many malls and shopping centers. Otherwise, small, family-owned shops abound in both Tsim Sha Tsui and Stanley Market, offering casual wear, washable silk outfits, and other clothing at very affordable prices. Cheaper still are factory outlets and street markets (see below).

If you're looking for international designer brands and don't care about price, there are several arcades and shopping centers known for their brand names. The **Landmark,** located on Des Voeux Road Central in Central, is an ultrachic shopping complex boasting the highest concentration of international brand names in Hong Kong, including Gucci, Tiffany & Co., Polo/Ralph Lauren, Manolo Blahnik, Marc Jacobs, Versace, Missoni, Kenzo, Sonia Rykiel, Louis Vuitton, Lanvin, and Christian Dior, as well as restaurants and other shops. The shops here are generally open daily from 10:30am to 7:30pm. Other nearby fashion centers known for their international designer boutiques (and linked to the

Landmark via elevated walkways) include the **Prince's Building,** next to the Mandarin Hotel, with boutiques for a. testoni, Cartier, Chanel, Hugo Boss, and others; **Alexandra House** with outlets for Prada and Yves Saint Laurent among others; and Chater House, with several Armani shops that sell everything from household items to clothing and cosmetics. Across the harbor, **The Peninsula hotel,** on Salisbury Road in Tsim Sha Tsui, has concessions for Hermès, Louis Vuitton, Loewe, Chanel, Gucci, Dior, Shanghai Tang, Prada, and Manolo Blahnik, to name only a few of the 80-some shops.

For trendier designs catering to an upwardly mobile younger crowd, check out the **Joyce Boutique** chain, the first fashion house in Hong Kong, established in the 1970s by Joyce Ma to satisfy Hong Kong women's cravings for European designs. Today her stores carry clothing by Issey Miyake, John Galliano, Stella McCartney, Yohji Yamamoto, Rei Kawakubo (Comme des Garçons), and others on the cutting edge of fashion. You'll find Joyce shops at 18 Queen's Rd. Central, Central District (© **852/2810 1120;** MTR: Central); 334 Pacific Place, 88 Queensway, Central (© **852/2523 5944;** MTR: Admiralty); and Shop G106 in The Gateway, Canton Rd., Tsim Sha Tsui (© **852/ 2367 8128;** MTR: Tsim Sha Tsui). Bargain hunters in the know head to the Joyce Warehouse, located on the south end of Hong Kong Island near Aberdeen, on the 21st floor of Horizon Plaza, 2 Lee Wing St., Ap Lei Chau (© **852/2814 8313;** bus: M590 from Exchange Square in Central to Ap Lei Chau). You never know what you may find among the discounted, off-season designer wear, but discounts run 30% to 70% off the original prices (closed on Mon).

For clothing by local designers, shop for Barney Cheng's classy evening wear at The Swank Shop in the New World Centre, 18–24 Salisbury Rd., Tsim Sha Tsui (© **852/2736 8757;** MTR: Tsim Sha Tsui); and the Chinese chic designs with a Western twist by Vivienne Tam at Shop 209, Pacific Place, 88 Queensway, Central (© **852/2918 0238;** MTR: Admiralty); Shop 2095, ifc mall, 8 Finance St., Central (© **852/2868 9268;** MTR: Central); Shop 215, Times Square, Causeway Bay (© **852/2506 0098;** MTR: Causeway Bay); and Shop G310, Harbour City, Tsim Sha Tsui (© **852/2117 0028;** MTR: Tsim Sha Tsui).

FACTORY OUTLETS   Savvy shoppers head for Hong Kong's factory outlets to buy at least some of their clothes. These outlets sell excess stock, overruns, and quality-control rejects; because these items have been made for the export market, the sizes are Western. Bargains include clothes made of silk, cashmere, cotton, linen, knitwear, and wool, and some outlets have men's and children's clothing as well. Some manufacturers even produce clothing for famous designer labels, though it's not unusual to find labels cut out. Unfortunately, outlets are scattered throughout the territory, though there are clusters in the Central District on Hong Kong Island and Hung Hom in Kowloon.

There are, however, a few caveats about shopping in factory outlets. For one thing, you never know in advance what will be on sale, and sometimes the selection is disappointing. Some outlets do not have fitting rooms, and it's important to carefully examine garments inside and out for tears and stains. What's more, some outlets are indistinguishable from upmarket boutiques, with prices to match. Unfortunately, it seems that some shops simply call themselves "factory outlets" because that's what tourists are looking for. Thus, unless you have lots of time, it may not be worth your while to go to the outlets in Hung Hom in search of a good deal. Several street markets—notably Ladies' Market in Mong Kok (see "Markets" below)—also serve as outlets for mainland factories.

On Hong Kong Island, the best-known building that houses factory-outlet showrooms is the **Pedder Building,** 12 Pedder St., Central. During my last visit, I counted 30-some shops here located on six floors, but many of these shops are not factory outlets—they're simply regular boutiques with the same merchandise at the same prices found at their other branches. In addition, a new trend seems to be shops selling used designerwear, shoes, and handbags, making it good for bargains in last season's fashions. In any case, it's convenient to have so many shops in one building and it's fun to just poke around here.

On the Kowloon side, the largest concentration of factory outlets is in Hung Hom, clustered in a group of warehouse buildings called **Kaiser Estates** on Man Yue Street. Although the Kaiser Estates comprise huge concrete factory buildings, the outlet shops inside look just like ordinary shops. To reach the Kaiser Estates, take bus no. 5C from the Tsim Sha Tsui Star Ferry bus terminal to Ma Tau Wai Road (the third stop after the KCR Kowloon Railway Station).

For a list of factory outlets along with their addresses, telephone numbers, and types of clothing, pick up the typed sheet called *Clothing & Accessories* at HKTB offices. Most outlets are open from 10 or 11am to 7pm Monday to Friday, with shorter hours on Saturdays. Some are open Sunday as well.

JEWELRY

According to the HKTB, Hong Kong has more jewelry stores per square mile than any other city in the world. Gems are imported duty-free from all over the world, and Hong Kong is reputedly the world's fourth-largest trading center for diamonds. Gold jewelry, both imported and locally made, is required by law to carry a stamp stating the accurate gold content.

Jade, of course, remains the most popular item of jewelry for both visitors and Chinese. It's believed to protect wearers against illness and ward off bad luck. The two categories of jade are jadeite and nephrite. Jadeite (also called Burmese jade) is generally white to apple green in color, although it also comes in hues of brown, red, orange, yellow, and even lavender. It may be mottled, but the most expensive variety is a translucent emerald green. Nephrite, which is less expensive, is usually a dark green or off-white. In any case, true jade is so hard that supposedly even a knife leaves no scratch. Unless you know your jade, your best bet is to shop in one of the Chinese-product stores, listed earlier in this chapter under "Chinese Craft Emporiums." For less expensive pieces and souvenirs, visit the Jade Market, described below under "Markets."

Pearls, almost all of which are cultured, are also popular among shoppers in Hong Kong. There are both sea- and freshwater pearls, available in all shapes, sizes, colors, and lusters. For inexpensive strands, check the vendors at the Jade Market. There are also many shops along Nathan Road in Tsim Sha Tsui that retail pearls.

If you're a real jewelry fan, you'll want to visit some of the jewelry factory outlets scattered throughout Hong Kong. For a list of jewelry factory outlets, contact the Hong Kong Tourism Board.

MARKETS

Markets offer the best deals in Hong Kong, though a lot depends on how well you can bargain. Be sure to scrutinize the items that interest you carefully, since you won't be able to return them. Check clothing for faults, tears, cuts, marks, and uneven seams and hemlines. Make sure electronic gadgets work; the cheap Pikachu alarm clock I bought my son lasted only a week: It's a buyer-beware market in the SAR.

HONG KONG ISLAND

STANLEY   Stanley Market is probably the most popular and best-known market in Hong Kong. Located on the southern coast of Hong Kong Island on a small peninsula, it's a great place to buy inexpensive clothing, especially sportswear, cashmere sweaters, silk blouses and dresses, and even linen blazers and outfits suitable for work. Men's, women's, and children's clothing are available. During my last visit, shopkeepers were not keen about bargaining unless you're buying several pieces, no doubt because tourists come here by the busload. In fact, Stanley is not as cheap as it once was, and many shops have remodeled into chic boutiques. Still, you're bound to find at least something you're wild about, especially if you like cheap, fun fashions. The inventory changes continuously— one year it seems everyone is selling tie-dyed shirts, the next year it's linen suits, washable silk, Chinese traditional jackets, or Gore-Tex coats. I usually walk through the market first, taking note of things I like and which stores they're in, and then I compare prices as I walk through. Most stores carry the same products, so it pays to comparison-shop. In addition to clothing, there are also many souvenir shops selling Chinese paintings, embroidered linen, beaded purses, handicrafts, curios, and jewelry.

To reach Stanley, take bus no. 6, 6A, 6X, or 260 from Central's Exchange Square bus terminal near the Star Ferry (bus no. 260 also makes stops in front of the Star Ferry terminal and Pacific Place) or Minibus 40 from Causeway Bay. The bus ride to Stanley takes approximately 30 minutes. From Kowloon, take bus no. 973 from Mody Road in Tsim Sha Tsui East or from Canton Road in Tsim Sha Tsui. The shops are open daily from 9:30 or 10am to about 6:30pm.

LI YUEN STREET EAST & WEST   These two streets are parallel pedestrian lanes in the heart of the Central District, very narrow, and often congested with human traffic. Stalls are packed with Chinese jackets, handbags, clothes, scarves, sweaters, toys, baby clothes, watches, makeup, umbrellas, needles and thread, knickknacks, and even brassieres. Don't neglect the open-fronted shops behind the stalls. Some of these are boutiques selling fashionable but cheap clothing as well as shoes, purses, and accessories. These two streets are located just a couple of minutes' walk from the Central MTR station or the Star Ferry, between Des Voeux Road Central and Queen's Road Central. Vendors are open daily from 10am to 7pm.

JARDINE'S CRESCENT   The open-air market that spreads along this narrow street in Causeway Bay is a traditional Chinese market for produce, household goods, cheap clothing, and accessories, including shoes, costume jewelry, handbags, hair accessories, children's clothing, and cosmetics. Though you may not find something worth taking home at this very local market, it's fun just to walk around. The nearest MTR station is Causeway Bay (take exit F), but you can also reach this area easily by tram. It's open daily from 11am to 8pm.

WANCHAI MARKET   This local market, centered on Spring Garden Lane and Wan Chai Road (between Johnston Rd. and Queen's Rd. East), is very much a local market, attracting housewives with its wet markets and household goods, but also young office workers with its stalls selling clothing originally meant for export at very competitive prices. It's located near the Wanchai MTR Station and is open daily from 7am to 7pm.

KOWLOON

JADE MARKET   Jade, believed by the Chinese to hold mystical powers and to protect its wearer, is available in all sizes, colors, and prices at the Jade Market, located at the junction of Kansu Street and Battery Street in two temporary structures in the Yau Ma Tei District. The jade comes from Burma, China, Australia, and Taiwan. Unless you know your jade, you won't want to make any expensive purchases here, but the quality of jade sold here is great for bangles, pendants, earrings, and inexpensive gifts. This market is also recommended for pearls, especially inexpensive freshwater pearls from China. Otherwise, this market is fun just for its unique atmosphere.

The Jade Market is open daily from 10am to about 4pm (mornings are best), though vendors stay until 6pm on busy days like Sunday. It's located halfway between the Yau Ma Tei and Jordan MTR stations or is less than a 30-minute walk from the Star Ferry.

LADIES' MARKET   If you want to shop at a market on the Kowloon side in the daytime, this very large market is your best bet. Stretching along Tung Choi Street (between Argyle and Dundas sts.) in Mong Kok, it serves as a lively market for inexpensive women's and children's fashions, shoes, socks, hosiery, jewelry, sunglasses, watches, handbags (including fake designer handbags), and other accessories. Some men's clothing is also sold. Although many of the products are geared more to local tastes and sizes, an increasing number of tourists has brought more fashionable clothing and T-shirts in larger sizes, and you may find some great bargains here. The atmosphere is fun and festive, especially at night. The nearest MTR station is Mong Kok. Vendors are open daily from about 12:30 to 10:30pm.

FA YUEN STREET MARKET   Located just a few minutes' walk north of Ladies' Market, north of Mong Kok Road, this street market is geared to local residents rather than tourists and offers clothing for women and children, as well as toys and produce. With laundry fluttering from the apartments above, this is a typical Mong Kok Street, full of character. The nearest MTR station is Prince Edward, and stalls are open from 9:30am to 8pm daily.

TEMPLE STREET NIGHT MARKET   Temple Street, in the Yau Ma Tei District of Kowloon, is a night market that comes to life when the sun goes down. It offers the usual products sold by street vendors, including T-shirts, jeans, menswear, watches, lighters, pens, sunglasses, jewelry, CDs, mobile phones, electronic gadgets, alarm clocks, luggage, and imitation designer watches and handbags. Bargain fiercely, and check the products carefully to make sure they're not faulty or poorly made. The night market is great entertainment, a must during your visit to Hong Kong, though the surge of shoppers can be overwhelming. If you follow the market north around the left side of the car park (the wares here get decidedly more racy—sex toys, and so on), you'll come to the Tin Hau Temple where there are fortune-tellers and sometimes even street-side performers singing Chinese opera. Although some vendors begin setting up shop at 4pm, the Night Market is busiest from about 7pm until it closes at 10pm, and is located near the Jordan MTR station.

MEGAMALLS & SHOPPING CENTERS

Hong Kong boasts shopping complexes that are so huge I call them "megamalls." Aside from the more convenient ones listed below, other Hong Kong megamalls include **Festival Walk** (located above Kowloon Tong MTR Station), the **New Town Plaza** in Sha Tin in the New Territories, and the **Taikoo Shing City Plaza,** located at the Taikoo MTR station on Hong Kong Island.

Harbour City   This is the largest of the megamalls and certainly one of the largest in Asia. Conveniently located right next to the dock that disgorges passengers from cruise liners and just east of the Star Ferry, it encompasses several zones to make navigation easier (The zones are designated different colors on the map of Harbour City. To most people, Harbour City will seem like one huge mall and the zones won't mean anything to them. But stores and restaurants often give their zone, like Ocean Terminal, as their address.): Ocean Terminal with its many shops relating to kids and sportswear; Ocean Centre, anchored by Marks and Spencer department store; the Hongkong Hotel Arcade, consisting mostly of the Lane Crawford department store and restaurants; and the Gateway Arcade at its northernmost end. All zones are interconnected by air-conditioned walkways. The complex stretches more than .8km (½ mile) along Canton Road. There are more than 700 outlets, with shops selling clothing, accessories, jewelry, cosmetics, antiques, electronic goods, furniture, housewares, toys, Asian arts and crafts, and much more. Some shops are closed on Sunday but otherwise the hours are about 10 or 11am to 8 or 9pm. Canton Rd., Tsim Sha Tsui. (🕾 852/2118 8601. www.harbourcity.com.hk. MTR: Tsim Sha Tsui.

ifc mall   ifc mall is part of a massive redevelopment taking place beside Hong Kong Station, terminus of the Airport Express, and includes two office buildings and the world's largest Four Seasons Hotel (open by summer 2005). The ifc mall is a smart-looking, three-level complex housing more than 200 high-end shops and restaurants, as well as open-air terraces with views of the harbor. While not nearly as large as the other malls mentioned here, its location, just minutes from the Star Ferry and practically on top of Hong Kong Station, is convenient and its restaurants boast great views. Most shops are open daily from 10am to 8pm. 8 Finance St., Central. (🕾 852/2295 3308. www.ifc.com.hk. MTR: Central.

Pacific Place   Pacific Place was the largest and most ambitious commercial project to hit Central when it opened more than 15 years ago; in fact, it shifted the city center toward the east. With the opening of Hong Kong Station and the new ifc mall to the west, Pacific Place is no longer the center of attention, but it still ranks as one of Hong Kong's swankiest malls. Besides three hotels, Pacific Place boasts approximately 200 retail stores and restaurants and three major department stores (Marks & Spencer, Lane Crawford, and Seibu). Most shops are open daily from about 10:30am to 8pm. 88 Queensway, Central. (🕾 852/2844 8988. www.pacificplace.com.hk. MTR: Admiralty.

Times Square   This stylish center offers 16 floors of shopping and dining. In the basement are fast-food outlets and stores selling health and beauty products, while the next six floors offer clothing, shoes, handbags, jewelry, watches, and other accessories. Shops dealing in computers, electronics, and home appliances dominate the seventh and eight floors, while the ninth floor is the place to go for children's clothing and toys. Marks & Spencer and Lane Crawford department stores are also here, but one of Times Square's major draws is its Food Forum on the top four floors, home to more than a dozen top-grade restaurants. Most shops are open daily from 10am to 10pm. 1 Matheson St., Causeway Bay. (🕾 852/ 2118 8900. www.timessquare.com.hk. MTR: Causeway Bay.

TAILORS

The 24-hour suit is a thing of the past, but you can still have clothes custom-made here in a few days. Tailoring in Hong Kong really began in the 1950s, when tailor families from Shanghai fled China and set up shop in Hong Kong. Today, prices are no longer as low as they once were, but they're often about what you'd pay for a ready-made, top-quality garment back home; the difference, of course, is that a tailor-made garment should fit you perfectly. The standards of the better, established shops rival even those of London's Savile Row—at less than half the price. A top-quality man's suit can run about HK$8,000 (US$1,039) or more, including fabric, while a silk shirt can cost HK$800 (US$104).

Tailors in Hong Kong will make anything you want, from business suits and evening gowns to wedding dresses, leather jackets, and monogrammed shirts. Some stores will allow you to provide your own fabric, while others require that you buy theirs. Many tailors offer a wide range of cloth from which to choose, from cotton and linen to very fine wools, cashmere, and silk. Hong Kong tailors are excellent at copying fashions, even if all you have is a picture or drawing of what you want.

On average, you should allow 3 to 5 days to have a garment custom-made, with at least two or three fittings. Be specific about what you want, such as lining, tightness of fit, buttons, and length. If you aren't satisfied during the fittings, speak up. Alterations should be included in the original price (ask about this during your first negotiations). If, in the end, you still don't like the finished product, you don't have to accept it. However, you will forfeit the deposit you are required to pay before the tailor begins working, about 50% of the total cost.

With more than 2,500 tailoring establishments in Hong Kong, it shouldn't be any problem finding one. Some of the most famous are located in hotel shopping arcades and shopping complexes, but the more upscale the location, the higher the prices. Tsim Sha Tsui abounds in tailor shops; one of the most well known is Sam's Tailor, 94 Nathan Rd., Tsim Sha Tsui (© 852/2367 9432; www.samstailor.com; MTR: Tsim Sha Tsui), whose clients have included former U.S. president Bill Clinton and designer Armani. In any case, your best bet is to deal only with shops that are members of the HKTB or those you have used before. Member shops are listed in the booklet *A Guide to Quality Merchants*, talked about earlier in this chapter.

Once you've had something custom-made and your tailor has your measurements, you will more than likely be able to order additional clothing later, even after you've returned home.

TOYS

Even though Hong Kong is one of the world's leading exporters of toys, they seem to be in short supply in Hong Kong itself. There is, however, an abundance of cheap plastic toys from mainland China; I've done some of my best (cheapest) shopping at Hong Kong's many outdoor markets. In addition to the shop below, the ninth floor of Times Square (p. 220) in Causeway Bay has several clothing and toy stores geared toward children.

Toys 'R' Us   This is one of the largest, if not *the* largest, toy store in Hong Kong. A huge department store, it offers games, sporting goods, hobby goods, baby furniture, books, clothing, and, of course, toys galore, including toys from mainland China, Japan, and other Asian countries that never reach U.S. markets (where else could you find a children's play dim sum set?). It's open daily from 11am to 9pm. Shop 032, in Ocean Terminal, Harbour City, 5 Canton Rd., Tsim Sha Tsui. © 852/2730 9462. www.toysrus.com.hk. MTR: Tsim Sha Tsui.

9

Hong Kong After Dark

Nightlife in Hong Kong seems pretty tame when compared with that in Tokyo or Bangkok. With the world of Suzie Wong in Wan Chai now a shadow of its former wicked self, Hong Kong today seems somewhat reserved and, perhaps to some minds, yawningly dull. For the upper crust who live here, exclusive clubs are popular for socializing and entertaining guests, while the vast majority of Chinese are likely to spend their free evenings at one of those huge lively restaurants.

Yet it would be wrong to assume that the SAR has nothing to offer in the way of nightlife—it's just that you probably won't get into any trouble enjoying yourself. To liven things up, Hong Kong stages several annual events, including the Hong Kong Arts Festival held in February/March, and the Hong Kong International Film Festival held in April. There are cultural activities and entertainment throughout the year, including theater productions, pop concerts, and Chinese opera and dance performances. In addition, there are plenty of that finest of British institutions—the pub—not to mention sophisticated cocktail lounges, discos, hostess clubs, and topless bars. There are even a couple of nightlife districts in the Central District: in the vicinity of Lan Kwai Fong Street and D'Aguilar Street, where a string of bars and restaurants have long added a spark to Hong Kong's financial district; and SoHo,

along the Central/Mid-Levels Escalator, with its ever-growing number of ethnic restaurants and bars. Business is so good, some predict a future merging of the two as more and more establishments set up shop. Wan Chai has also witnessed a revival with a spate of new bars and restaurants, while Knutsford Terrace, a small alley on the north end of Tsim Sha Tsui, is popular for its open-fronted bars and restaurants. You can party until dawn; indeed, some bars and discos don't take off until after midnight.

Remember that a 10% service charge will be added to your food/drinks bill. If you're watching your Hong Kong dollars, keep in mind that one of the best traditions in the city is its "happy hour," when many bars offer two drinks for the price of one or drinks at lower prices. Actually, "happy hours" would be more appropriate, since the period is generally from 5 to 7pm and often even longer than that. Furthermore, many pubs, bars, and lounges offer live entertainment, from jazz to Filipino combos (musicians and singers together performing all kinds of music genres), which you can enjoy simply for the price of a beer. There are also a variety of ways to enjoy yourself at night without spending money—for example, strolling along the Tsim Sha Tsui harbor waterfront or around Victoria Peak, or browsing at the Temple Street Night Market.

> **Tips** **Information, Please**
>
> To find out what's going on during your stay in the SAR, be sure to pick up *What's On—Hong Kong,* an HKTB leaflet published weekly that tells what's happening in theater, music, and the arts, including concerts and Chinese opera. *HK Magazine,* distributed free at restaurants, bars, and other outlets around town and aimed at a young readership, is a weekly that lists what's going on at the city's theaters and other venues, including plays, concerts, the cinema, and events in Hong Kong's alternative scene. *Where Hong Kong, CityLife,* and *bc* are three other free magazines published monthly with nightlife information and special events. Finally, you can also find out what's going on for the upcoming week by visiting the Hong Kong Tourist Board online at **www.discoverhongkong.com**.

1 The Performing Arts

The busiest time of the year for the performing arts is the month-long **Hong Kong Arts Festival,** held every year in February and March. This international 3-week affair features artists from around the world performing with orchestras, dance troupes, opera companies, and chamber ensembles. Appearing at past festivals, for example, were the Hong Kong Philharmonic Orchestra, the London Philharmonic, the Empire Brass from Boston, the Hong Kong Chinese Orchestra, the Stuttgart Ballet, the Paul Taylor Dance Company, and the Georgian State Dance Company from Russia. City Hall, located in Central just east of the Star Ferry concourse, sells tickets to performances, which are priced from HK$60 to HK$650 (US$7.80–US$85). For information about the Hong Kong Arts Festival programs and future dates, call ✆ **852/2824 2430** or visit www.hk. artsfestival.org.

To obtain tickets for the Hong Kong Arts Festival, as well as tickets throughout the year for classical-music performances (including the Hong Kong Philharmonic Orchestra and the Hong Kong Chinese Orchestra), Chinese opera, rock and pop concerts, theatrical productions, dance, and other major events, contact the **Urban Council Ticketing Office (URBTIX),** the ticketing system run by the government's Leisure and Cultural Service Department. There are convenient URBTIX outlets in City Hall, Low Block, 7 Edinburgh Place in Central, open daily from 10am to 9:30pm, and the Hong Kong Cultural Centre, 10 Salisbury Rd. in Tsim Sha Tsui, open daily from 10am to 9:30pm. Drop by one of the outlets, or reserve a ticket in advance by calling URBTIX at ✆ **852/2734 9009.** Tickets reserved by phone must be picked up within 3 days of the order. You can even book tickets before arriving in Hong Kong, either by calling the Credit Card Hotline at ✆ **852/2111 5999,** from 10am to 8pm daily Hong Kong time, or through the URBTIX website at www.urbtix.gov.hk. The Hong Kong Tourism Board's website, www.discoverhongkong.com, also offers e-ticketing.

Full-time students and senior citizens are often eligible for half-price tickets, so be sure to ask when making reservations.

PERFORMING-ARTS COMPANIES
CHINESE OPERA

Chinese opera predates the first Western opera by about 600 years, although it wasn't until the 13th and 14th centuries that performances began to develop a structured operatic form, with rules of composition and fixed role characterization. Distinct regional styles also developed, and even today there are marked differences among the operas performed in, say, Peking, Canton, Shanghai, Fukien, Chiu Chow, and Sichuan.

Most popular in Hong Kong, however, is Peking-style opera, with its spectacular costumes, elaborate makeup, and feats of acrobatics and swordsmanship, and the less flamboyant but more readily understood Cantonese-style opera. Plots usually dramatize legends and historical events and extol such virtues as loyalty, filial piety, and righteousness. Accompanied by seven or eight musicians, the performers sing in shrill, high-pitched falsetto, a sound Westerners sometimes do not initially appreciate. Although lyrics are in Chinese, body language helps translate the stories.

Another aspect of Chinese opera that surprises Westerners is its informality. No one minds if spectators arrive late or leave early; in fact, no one even minds if a spectator, upon spotting friends or relatives, makes his or her way through the auditorium for a chat.

For visitors, the easiest way to see a Chinese opera is during the **Hong Kong Arts Festival** (see above), held from about mid-February to early March each year. Alternatively, Cantonese opera is a common feature of important Chinese festivals, such as the birthday of Tin Hau or the annual Bun Festival on Cheung Chau island, when temporary bamboo theaters are erected.

Otherwise, Cantonese opera is performed fairly regularly at Town Halls in the New Territories, as well as in City Hall in Central and the Hong Kong Cultural Centre in Tsim Sha Tsui. However, Chinese opera is immensely popular in Hong Kong, so much so that tickets for these shows sell out well in advance, making it almost impossible for tourists to attend performances. If you're still determined to try, call URBTIX in advance of your arrival in Hong Kong, book online (see above), or, once in the SAR, contact the HKTB or check with one of the tourist publications for information on what's playing and then call or drop by URBTIX. Alternatively, the concierge of your hotel may be able to secure seats. Prices generally range from about HK$100 to HK$300 (US$13–US$39).

CLASSICAL MUSIC

Hong Kong Chinese Orchestra   Established in 1977, the Hong Kong Chinese Orchestra is the world's largest professional Chinese-instrument orchestra. It features more than 80 full-time musicians who perform both traditional folk music and full-scale contemporary works, including commissioned pieces, in approximately 30 concerts annually. Musicians play a wide range of traditional and modern Chinese instruments (mainly stringed Chinese instruments, which are

---

(**Fun Fact**   **Did You Know?**

- The world's largest professional Chinese instrument orchestra is the more-than-80-member Hong Kong Chinese Orchestra (see above), which uses traditional and modern Chinese musical instruments.
- Club BBOSS (p. 234), in Tsim Sha Tsui East, is the world's largest Japanese-style hostess club, occupying 70,000 square feet.

Impressions

Hong Kong illuminated . . . is wonderful. Imagine a giant Monte Carlo with a hundred times as many lights!
        —Alfred Viscount Northcliffe, *My Journey Round the World*, 1923

---

completely different from Western violins, cellos, and so on), as well as suitable Western instruments, combining them with Western orchestrations or Chinese music. Performing at the Hong Kong Cultural Centre, 10 Salisbury Rd., Tsim Sha Tsui (© 852/2734 2009), and City Hall, Edinburgh Place, Central District (© 852/2921 2840). www.hkco.org. Tickets HK$90—HK$150 (US$12–US$19). MTR: Tsim Sha Tsui for Cultural Centre or Central for City Hall.

Hong Kong Philharmonic Orchestra   The Hong Kong Cultural Centre is the home of the city's largest (Western-style) orchestra: the Hong Kong Philharmonic, founded in 1975. It performs regularly from September to July and at other scheduled events throughout the year, such as providing live accompaniment to the Hong Kong Ballet. Its conductor is Edo de Waart; guest conductors and soloists appear during the concert season. In addition to Western classical pieces, its repertoire is enriched by works commissioned from Chinese composers. Performing at the Hong Kong Cultural Centre, 10 Salisbury Rd., Tsim Sha Tsui (© 852/ 2734 2009), and City Hall, Edinburgh Place, Central District (© 852/2921 2840). www.hkpo. com. Tickets HK$60–HK$250 (US$7.80–US$32). MTR: Tsim Sha Tsui for Cultural Centre or Central for City Hall.

DANCE

Both the **Hong Kong Ballet Company** and the **Hong Kong Dance Company** have extensive repertoires. The Hong Kong Ballet Company (© 852/2573 7398; www.hkballet.com), founded in 1979, performs both classical works and modern pieces, usually at the Cultural Centre or the Hong Kong Academy for Performing Arts. The Hong Kong Dance Company (© 852/3103 1888; www. hkdance.com) specializes in traditional Chinese dance and the development of Chinese dance in modern forms, with about five major productions each year.

THEATER

Most plays presented in the SAR are performed in Cantonese. Hong Kong's leading local troupes are the **Chung Ying Theatre Company,** a community ensemble that plays in a wide range of venues, from schools and seniors' homes to Hong Kong's main theaters, often performing works by local writers, and the **Hong Kong Repertory Theatre,** which performs original Chinese works. Both perform in Cantonese at various venues, including City Hall in Central and the Hong Kong Cultural Centre in Tsim Sha Tsui. Prices range from about HK$100 to HK$160 (US$13–US$21).

Otherwise, your best bet for English-language performances is at the **Fringe Club,** 2 Lower Albert Rd., Central (© 852/2521 7251; www.hkfringe.com.hk; MTR: Central), a venue for experimental drama (in English and Cantonese), live music, comedy, art exhibitions, and other happenings, from mime to magic shows. The Fringe Club occupies a former dairy-farm depot built in 1813 and consists of two theaters, exhibition space, a restaurant, and a bar.

MAJOR CONCERT HALLS

City Hall   Located right beside the Star Ferry concourse, City Hall's Low Block has a 1,500-seat balconied concert hall, as well as a 470-seat theater used for plays and chamber music. Exhibitions are frequently held in the foyer, while the lobby has pamphlets of upcoming events. Connaught Rd. and Edinburgh Place, Central District. © 852/2921 2840. www.cityhall.gov.hk. Box office open daily 10am–9:30pm. MTR: Central.

Hong Kong Academy for Performing Arts   Located across the street from the Arts Centre, the academy is Hong Kong's institution for vocational training in the performing arts. It also features regular performances in theater and dance, by both local and international playwrights and choreographers. Its Theatre Block is composed of six venues, including the Lyric Theatre, Drama Theatre, Orchestral Hall, and Recital Hall; there's also an open-air theater. 1 Gloucester Rd., Wan Chai. © 852/2584 88633. www.hkapa.edu. MTR: Wan Chai.

Hong Kong Arts Centre   Built on Wan Chai's new waterfront of reclaimed land, the Arts Centre hosts the Hong Kong Arts Festival and other international presentations, as well as performances by Hong Kong's own amateur and professional companies. It offers a regular schedule of plays or dances, exhibition galleries, and showings of foreign films. There are three auditoriums: Shouson Theatre, McAulay Studio Theatre, and Lim Por Yen Film Theatre. 2 Harbour Rd., Wan Chai. © 852/2582 0200. www.hkac.org.hk. Box office open Mon–Fri 9am–6pm. MTR: Wan Chai.

Hong Kong Cultural Centre   Sandwiched in between the Space Museum and the Star Ferry concourse, the Hong Kong Cultural Centre is the territory's largest arena for the arts. Opened in 1989, this complex is a good bet for free music and events, including family shows on Saturday afternoon from 2:30 to 4:30pm that may include Chinese dance, a magic show, or music. Thursday Happy Hour, from 6 to 7pm, features Chinese classical music, Western music, puppetry, and other performances by local performance groups. Pick up a monthly leaflet of events at the Centre or call © 852/2734 32820 for program enquiries.

Otherwise, the pride of the Cultural Centre is its 2,100-seat Concert Hall, home of the Hong Kong Philharmonic Orchestra. It features a 93-stop, 8,000-pipe Austrian Rieger organ—one of the world's largest. Two levels of seating surround the stage, which is set near the center of the oval hall. There are also two theaters, the Grand Theatre, used for musicals, large-scale drama, dance, film shows, and Chinese opera, and the smaller Studio Theatre, designed for experimental theater and dance. 10 Salisbury Rd., Tsim Sha Tsui. © 852/2734 2009. www.hk culturalcentre.gov.hk. Box office open daily 10am–9:30pm. MTR: Tsim Sha Tsui.

2 The Club & Music Scene

LIVE MUSIC

Hong Kong does not have the kind of jazz-, rock-, or blues-club scene that many other cities do. On the other hand, live music is such a standard feature of many restaurants, hotel cocktail lounges, and bars, that it would be hard *not* to hear live music in the SAR. Although a few establishments levy a cover charge, most charge absolutely nothing.

Bars, lounges, and clubs offering live music include **Chasers, Hard Rock Cafe, Lobby Lounge** (in the Hotel InterContinental Hong Kong), and **Ned Kelly's Last Stand,** all in Kowloon; the **Captain's Bar** and **Insomnia** in Central; **Dusk til Dawn, Joe Bananas,** and **The Wanch** in Wan Chai; and **ToTT's Asian Grill & Bar** in Causeway Bay.

Among the many restaurants with free live music are **Avenue Restaurant & Bar, Gaddi's, Hugo's,** and **Sabatini,** all in Kowloon; **Mandarin Grill** and **Petrus** in Central; and **Cafe Deco** and **The Peak Lookout** on the Peak. For more information on all these establishments, refer to their individual listings throughout this chapter and in chapter 5, "Where to Dine in Hong Kong."

Because live music is regarded more as a sidelight than the raison d'être of most Hong Kong establishments, if you're serious about music, you will want to head straight to one of these two venues described below.

48th Street Chicago Blues *(Value)* Music is clearly king at this tiny joint, owned by local blues musician Tommy Chung, who performs Saturday nights with his All Blues band. The rest of the week, local Chinese, Japanese, and Southeast Asian musicians play blues, jazz, fusion, and rock. Mondays are jam nights, while Sundays showcase new and emerging talent. It's open 5pm to 3am nightly, with live music beginning around 9:30 or 10:30pm. 2A Hart Ave., Tsim Sha Tsui. ℂ 852/2723 7633. www.48chicagoblues.com. No cover Sun–Thurs; cover HK$128 (US$17) Fri–Sat, including 2 drinks. MTR: Tsim Sha Tsui.

Fringe Club *(Finds)* Hong Kong's best-known venue for alternative events offers live music most Fridays and Saturdays from 10:30pm at its Fringe Gallery, including jazz, funk, folk, and blues, as well as other musical programs other days of the week. Call for an updated listing, visit its website, or pick up the Fringe Club's monthly calendar. 2 Lower Albert Rd., Central. ℂ 852/2521 7251. www.hk fringeclub.com. Cover HK$80 ($10) for most events. MTR: Central.

DANCE CLUBS

Disco fever has cooled considerably since the heady days of the early 1980s, with only a couple of discos weathering the years. More prevalent are small, simple bars that metamorphose into miniature discos late at night or on weekends, as well as trendy clubs that cater mostly to their in-crowd members but may occasionally allow nonmembers on slow nights (the best plan of action to get into a membership club is to dress smartly, come on a weeknight or early in the evening, and be nice to the doorman). Discos and dance clubs in Hong Kong generally charge more on weekend nights, but the admission price usually includes one or two free drinks. After that, beer and mixed drinks are often priced the same. Bars, whether with DJs or live music, rarely charge cover.

In addition to the discos below, check "The Bar, Pub & Lounge Scene" section below for establishments that offer dancing. These include **Bahama Mama's** and **Delaney's** in Kowloon; **Al's Diner, Alibi, California, Captain's Bar, Club 97, Curve, D'Apartment, Dragon-I, Insomnia,** and **Lux** in Central; and **Carnegies, Joe Banana's,** and **Klong** in Wan Chai; and **ToTT's Asian Grill & Bar** in Causeway Bay.

CENTRAL DISTRICT

C Club With a seductive interior of velvet sofas and a curved bar, all bathed in red lighting, this basement club packs 'em in with what management calls "sexy house" music, including funk, R&B, soul, and Latino. If you come on a weekend, be prepared to join the queue of beautiful people lined up outside waiting to be let in, but at least you don't have to be a member. It's open Monday to Thursday from 6pm to 2am, Friday from 6pm to 5am, and Saturday from 9pm to 5am, with happy hour weekdays until 9pm. California Tower, 30–32 D'Aguilar, Lan Kwai Fong, Central. ℂ 852/2526 1139. www.lankwaifong.com. No cover Mon–Thurs; cover HK$200 (US$26) Fri–Sat, including 2 drinks. MTR: Central.

Propaganda Hong Kong's longest-standing and most popular gay disco, Propaganda moved into upgraded quarters a few years back in the new SoHo nightlife district, with a discreet entrance in a back alley (it's a bit hard to find; look for the alley off Pottinger St.). Only about 5% of the people who come through the doors are straight, but everyone is welcome. Come late on a weekend if you want to see

Mad About Mahjong

You don't have to be in Hong Kong long before you hear it—the clack-ity-clack of mahjong, almost deafening if it's emanating from a large mahjong parlor. You can hear it at large restaurants (there are usually mahjong parlors in side rooms), at wedding celebrations, in the middle of the day, and long into the night. In a land where gambling is illegal except at the horse races, mahjong provides the opportunity for skillful gambling.

Although mahjong originated during the Sung dynasty almost 1,000 years ago, today's game is very different and more difficult and is played with amazing speed. Essentially, mahjong is played by four people, using tiles that resemble dominoes and bear Chinese characters and designs. Tiles are drawn and discarded (by slamming them on the table), until one player wins with a hand of four combinations of three tiles and a pair of matching tiles. But the real excitement comes with betting chips that each player receives and which are awarded to the winner based on his or her combination of winning tiles. Excitement is also heightened by the speed of the game—the faster tiles are slammed against the table and swooped up, the better. Technically, the mahjong game is over when a player runs out of chips, though it's not unusual to borrow chips to continue playing. There are lots of stories in Hong Kong of fortunes made and lost in a game of mahjong. Many hard-core players confess to an addiction.

this alternative hotspot at its most crowded. It's open Tuesday to Thursday from 9pm to 3:30am, Friday and Saturday from 9pm to 5am. 1 Hollywood Rd., Central. © 852/2868 1316. No cover Tues–Thurs; cover HK$100 (US$13) Fri; HK$120 (US$16) Sat before 10:30pm, HK$160 (US$21) Sat 10:30pm–3:30am, HK$100 (US$13) Sat after 3:30am. MTR: Central.

CAUSEWAY BAY & WAN CHAI

Club ING   This hotel club is more egalitarian than most, since it's located in a hotel near the convention center and is a bit off the beaten track for bar hoppers. Attracting a mixed local crowd in addition to conventioneers and out-of-towners, this club offers three different sections, including a small dance floor, bar areas, and karaoke rooms. Happy hour is Monday and Tuesday from 5pm to 2am, Wednesday from 5 to 8pm, and Thursday and Friday from 5 to 9pm. On Thursdays, ladies drink for free. It opens Monday to Saturday at 4:30pm, closing at 2am Monday to Thursday and at 4am Friday and Saturday. Renaissance Harbour View Hotel Hong Kong, 4th fl., 1 Harbour View, Wan Chai. © 852/2824 0523. No cover Mon–Thurs; cover HK$110 (US$15) Fri–Sat, including all-you-can-drink Fri until 1:30am. MTR: Wan Chai.

3 The Bar, Pub & Lounge Scene

KOWLOON

For concentrated nightlife in Tsim Sha Tsui, head to Knutsford Terrace, a narrow, alley-like pedestrian lane just north of Kimberley Road, where you'll find a row of open-fronted bars and restaurants, many with outdoor seating.

Aqua Spirit   This glam newcomer is one of Hong Kong's hottest bars, due in no small part to its unbeatable location on the 30th floor of a Tsim Sha Tsui highrise, where slanted, soaring windows give an incredible bird's-eye-view of the city. Circular booths shrouded behind strung beads, designer drinks, and a voyeur's dream location on an open mezzanine overlooking diners at the 29th-floor Aqua, which serves passable Italian and Japanese fare, make this one of Kowloon's trendiest venues. Note that there's a minimum drink charge of HK$120 (US$16). Entrance to both Aqua and Aqua Spirit is on the 29th floor. The bar is open Sunday to Thursday from 6pm to 1am and Friday and Saturday from 6pm to 3am. 1 Peking Rd., Tsim Sha Tsui. (C) 852/3427 2288. MTR: Tsim Sha Tsui.

Bahama Mama's   One of many bars lining Knutsford Terrace, this one is decorated in a kitschy Caribbean theme and offers a few tables outside, Foosball, and a small dance floor and in-house DJ. Happy hour is daily from 5 to 9pm, as well as Monday to Thursday from midnight to 3am. Drink specialties include fruit cocktails, frozen margaritas, and tequila shots. Maybe that's what leads to late-night dancing on the bar. It's open Monday to Thursday from 5pm to 3am, Friday and Saturday from 5pm to 4am, and Sunday from 6pm to 2am. 4–5 Knutsford Terrace, Tsim Sha Tsui. (C) 852/2368 2121. MTR: Tsim Sha Tsui.

Chasers   Next to Bahama Mama's, this is among the most popular and longest-standing bars on Knutsford Terrace, filled with a mixed clientele that includes both the young and the middle-aged, foreign and Chinese. One of Hong Kong's first late-night haunts to actively promote the live-music scene and famous for its shooters, it features a house Filipino band nightly from 10:30pm, playing rock, jazz, rhythm and blues, and everything in between. There is no cover charge. Happy hour is from 3 to 10pm Monday to Friday and from noon to 9pm Saturday and Sunday. It's open Monday to Friday from 3pm to 6am and Saturday and Sunday from noon to 6am. 2–3 Knutsford Terrace, Tsim Sha Tsui. (C) 852/ 2367 9487. MTR: Tsim Sha Tsui.

Delaney's   This very successful, upmarket Irish pub is decorated in old-world style with its old posters and photographs. Its convivial atmosphere gets an extra boost from a Tuesday quiz night with prizes for winners and from a DJ on Friday nights, both free of charge. The great selection of draft beers and whiskeys also doesn't hurt. Big soccer and rugby events are shown on a big screen. In addition to a set carvery lunch offered Sundays, it also has an a la carte menu listing Irish stew, beef and Guinness pie, corned beef and cabbage, and other Irish favorites. Happy hour is from 5 to 9pm daily; open hours are daily from 9am to 2:30am. There's another Delaney's in Wan Chai at 18 Luard Rd. ((C) **852/2804 2880**). 71–77 Peking Rd., Tsim Sha Tsui. (C) **852/2301 3980**. MTR: Tsim Sha Tsui.

Hard Rock Cafe   You can come to this international chain for a burger, fish and chips, fajitas, or a steak, but you can also come for its nighttime ambience, when a DJ enlivens the scene daily from 7pm and a live band takes over every night except Mondays from 9:30pm. Best of all, there's no cover charge. It's open Sunday to Thursday from 11am to 1am and Friday and Saturday from 11am to 3am. On the ground floor of the Silvercord Building, 30 Canton Rd., Tsim Sha Tsui. (C) **852/2375 1323**. MTR: Tsim Sha Tsui.

Lobby Lounge *Value*   This comfortable cocktail lounge boasts gorgeous water-level views of Victoria Harbour and Hong Kong Island. You'll fall in love all over again (with Hong Kong, your companion, or both) as you take in one of the world's most famous views (this is a very civilized place for watching the nightly Symphony of Lights laser show), listen to a live jazz band (from 6–11pm), and imbibe one of the bar's famous martinis or one of its signature Nine Dragons cocktails. Unlike other hotel cocktail lounges with live music, the Lobby Lounge doesn't impose a minimum drink charge. It's open daily from 8am to 2am. In Hotel InterContinental Hong Kong, 18 Salisbury Rd., Tsim Sha Tsui. © 852/2721 1211. MTR: Tsim Sha Tsui.

Murphy's   Seven TV screens beaming in sports also beams in the guys, making this Irish pub a lively place indeed during testosterone-high sporting events. Otherwise, it's a decent place for pub grub (potato skins, Irish oysters, steak and porter pie, corned beef and cabbage) or the weekend roast. It also has a few computers where you can check e-mail simply for the price of a drink. Happy hour is from 5 to 8pm daily. It's open Monday to Friday 11am to 2am and Saturday and Sunday from 10am to 2am. 32 Nathan Rd., Tsim Sha Tsui. © 852/2782 3344. MTR: Tsim Sha Tsui.

Ned Kelly's Last Stand   Named after one of Down Under's most famous outlaws, this is a lively Aussie saloon, with free live Dixieland jazz daily from 9:30pm to 1am and attracting a largely middle-aged crowd. It serves Australian chow, including juicy pork sausages with mashed potatoes and onion gravy; beef stew; fish and chips; Australian sirloin steak; Irish stew; hamburgers; and cottage pie (baked bowl of minced beef, onions, vegetables, and mashed potatoes). Happy hour is from 11:30am to 9pm, with reduced prices. It's open daily from 11:30am to 2am. 11A Ashley Rd., Tsim Sha Tsui. © 852/2376 0562. MTR: Tsim Sha Tsui.

Sky Lounge   This plush and comfortable lounge is on the top floor of the Sheraton, affording one of the best and most romantic views of the harbor and glittering Hong Kong Island. Unless you're a hotel guest, from 8pm onward there's a minimum drink charge of HK$118 (US$15) per person. Or, come earlier for the afternoon tea buffet, available Saturday and Sunday from 2 to 6pm for HK$128 (US$17) and weekdays from 4 to 6pm for HK$85 (US$11). It's open Monday to Thursday from 4pm to 1am, Friday from 4pm to 2am, Saturday from 2pm to 2am, and Sunday from 2pm to 1am. In the Sheraton Hotel and Towers, 20 Nathan Rd., Tsim Sha Tsui. © 852/2369 1111. MTR: Tsim Sha Tsui.

CENTRAL DISTRICT

Agave   Fans of Mexico's most famous spirit should make a point of visiting this showcase for tequila in Hong Kong, with approximately 150 brands of 100% agave tequila on offer, as well as 30 different kinds of margaritas. An open-fronted, noisy bar in Lan Kwai Fong, it has a daily happy hour from 5 to 8:30pm. Open Sunday through Thursday from 5pm to 1:30am and Friday and Saturday from 5pm to 3:30am. 33 D'Aguilar St., Central. © 852/2521 2010. MTR: Central.

Al's Diner   Rather innocent-looking during the day, this hamburger joint transforms into one of Lan Kwai Fong's most extroverted party scenes on weekend nights, no doubt fueled by the house specialty, jello shots (jello laced with vodka), and music supplied by a DJ. A few shots, and you may find yourself joining the others dancing on the tables. Two drinks for the price of one are offered during happy hour Monday to Friday from 4 to 8pm. It opens daily at 11:30am, closing at 1am Sunday to Wednesday, 2am on Thursday, and 4am Friday and Saturday. 39 D'Aguilar St., Central. © 852/2869 1869. MTR: Central.

California   Located in Central's nightlife district, this chic bar was once the place to see and be seen—the haunt of young nouveaux riches in search of a definition. Newer establishments have since encroached upon California's exalted position, but it remains a respected and sophisticated restaurant/bar, with silent TV screens showing music videos or sporting events almost everywhere you look. You might consider starting your night on the town here with dinner and drinks—the menu exalts Californian cuisine with a wide range of pastas, pizzas, sandwiches, and main courses like Norwegian salmon with mussels, chorizo, new potatoes and fennel broth, though hamburgers (the house specialty) remain hugely popular. A plus to coming early is happy hour from 5 to 10pm, with two drinks for the price of one. On Friday and Saturday nights from 11pm to 4am, it becomes a happening disco, with hot DJs playing the latest hits. This place is usually packed, so be prepared for crowds. It's open Monday to Thursday from noon to midnight, Friday and Saturday from noon to 4am, and Sunday from 6pm to midnight. 24–26 Lan Kwai Fong St., Central. ℂ **852/2521 1345.** MTR: Central.

Captain's Bar   That this refined bar is popular with Hong Kong's professional crowd, especially at the end of the working day, comes as no surprise considering that it's in the Mandarin Oriental hotel, a longtime favorite with business travelers. Well known for its expertly made martinis, its pints of beer served in aluminum and silver tankards, and its weekday roast beef lunches, it's a small, intimate place, with seating at the bar or on couches. Live music begins nightly at 9pm; there's even a small dance floor for those inclined to shuffle around. It's open Monday to Saturday from 11am to 2am and Sunday 11am to 1am. In the Mandarin Hotel, 5 Connaught Rd., Central. ℂ **852/2522 0111.** MTR: Central.

Club 97   Opened more than 20 years ago and still one of Lan Kwai Fong's most revered nightlife establishments, this club underwent a transformation a few years back that changed it from a disco to a sophisticated lounge, in recognition that its customers had grown up and were more prone to predinner cocktails or late-night drinks rather than disco dancing. There's still a small dance floor, but gone is the foreboding entrance that once turned away any but the in crowd. Rather, an open-fronted facade invites a mixed clientele of gays and straights. Weekly events to watch out for are the Friday gay happy hour complete with drag shows, and Sunday reggae night, which draws a huge crowd wishing to chill out before the workweek begins. In any event, this place is a must for any decent pub crawl through Lan Kwai Fong. It's open Monday to Thursday from 6pm to 2am (happy hour 6–9pm), Friday 6pm to 4am (happy hour 7–9pm), Saturday 7pm to 4am (happy hour 6–9pm), and Sunday 8pm to 3am (happy hour 8–10pm). 9 Lan Kwai Fong, Central. ℂ **852/2810 9333.** MTR: Central.

Curve   This is one of Hong Kong's friendliest and most crowded gay bars, though it caters to partyers of all persuasions with two levels for drinking and dancing. It's located on a hill above Lan Kwai Fong (on the long staircase beside The Centurium) and is open daily from 8pm to 3am (happy hour daily to 10pm). 2 Arbuthnot Rd., Central. ℂ **852/2523 0998.** No cover (except for special events once or twice a month, when it's HK$100–HK$200/US$13–US$26, including 1 or 2 drinks). MTR: Central.

D'Apartment   This basement bar has a cute premise: Each room is decorated like a room in an apartment. You can lie on a bed in the bedroom and watch a TV screen, chat in the living room on sofas and armchairs, lounge on beanbag chairs in the playroom, or peruse the books in the library. All it lacks is the kitchen. Of course, once the resident DJ starts spinning tunes for the tiny dance floor and the crowds surge, some visitors may feel like they've time traveled to their first college apartment. It's open Monday to Thursday 6:30pm to 3am, Friday from 5:30pm to 5am, and Saturday from 7pm to 5am. Happy hour is from 6:30 to 9pm. California Entertainment Building, 34–36 D'Aguilar, Central. ℂ **852/2523 2002.** MTR: Central.

Dragon-i   This is one of Hong Kong's most talked-about bars; the fact that it lures models with promises of free drinks is obviously good for business, since it also brings in those who like to ogle models. Its interior is bathed in red from the glow of lanterns, while the outdoor patio, decorated with huge birdcages, provides some relief from the crowds, especially when things start hopping from 11:30pm when a DJ stirs action on the dance floor. The bar's other incarnation is as a venue for lunch or dinner (its all-you-can-eat lunch for HK$108/US$14 includes dim sum and sushi); happy hour is from 6 to 9pm. Located on a hill above Lan Kwai Fong, it's open Monday, Tuesday, and Thursday from noon to 3am and Wednesday, Friday, and Saturday from noon to 5am, but you'll never get in on Wednesday, Friday, or Saturday unless you're a dead ringer for Uma Thurman. The Centurium, 60 Wyndham St., Central. (☎ 852/3110 1222. MTR: Central.

Dublin Jack   It's easy to spot this cozy Irish pub with its bright-red exterior, located right next to the Central/Mid-Levels Escalator Link in Central's SoHo entertainment district. It's so packed with expats on their way home to the Mid-Levels after a day's work in Central, it's hard to elbow your way in through the door. Maybe it's because of its whisky—more than 50 brands of Irish and 100 kinds of Scottish whiskies—or the ubiquitous screens broadcasting rugby and other British sports. Happy hour, with reduced drink prices, is from 11am to 9pm daily. The multilevel bar is open daily from 11am to 2am. 37 Cochrane St. (at Lyndhurst Terrace), Central. (☎ 852/2543 0081. MTR: Central.

Insomnia   One of Lan Kwai Fong's most popular bars, it's aptly named, since live music by a Filipino band doesn't get underway until 10:30pm and it's at its most packed in the wee hours of the morning, when there's no room to spare on the crowded dance floor. Happy hour is from 5 to 9pm. It's open daily from 8am to 6am, leaving insomniacs 2 hours with nowhere to go. 38–44 D'Aguilar St., Central. (☎ 852/2525 0957. MTR: Central.

Lux   Although this classy venue in the heart of Lan Kwai Fong serves as both a restaurant and a bar, it seems most successful as a bar, especially on Friday and Saturday nights when it morphs into a dance club after midnight. Its contemporary Mediterranean-influenced food, however, is not to be overlooked, particularly if you're in the mood for lobster and prawn raviolini or tuna with a black-olive pesto. In fact, if you want an intimate dinner followed by drinks or dancing, this sophisticated establishment might be just right for you. Happy hour is Monday to Saturday from 6 to 9pm and Sunday from 11am to 9pm. It's open Monday to Saturday from noon to 3pm for lunch and from 6 to 11pm for dinner, closing at 1am Monday to Thursday and at 3am Friday and Saturday. On Sunday it's open from 11am to 1am. California Tower, 30–32 D'Aguilar St., Central. (☎ 852/2868 9538. MTR: Central.

Staunton's Bar & Café   Located on the corner of Staunton and Shelley streets, beside the Central/Mid-Levels Escalator, this was one of the first of many bars and restaurants that now give the SoHo district its unique, homey atmosphere. Above the open-fronted ground-floor bar (which boasts views of commuters going up the escalator) is a restaurant serving contemporary Mediterranean Italian fare. Happy hour is from 5 to 9pm daily, with 25 wines on offer by the glass, and open hours here are daily from 9am to 2am. 10–12 Staunton St., Central. (☎ 852/2973 6611. MTR: Central.

CAUSEWAY BAY & WAN CHAI

Wan Chai, once Hong Kong's most notorious nightlife scene for raunchy bars and prostitution, is back on the scene with a growing number of bars and erotic shows with female dancers, concentrated mostly on Lockhart and Luard roads.

Carnegie's   Imported from Singapore and dedicated to classic rock music, this bar attracts crowds with daily promotions, DJs that play the Eagles and Springsteen, and a happy hour daily from 6 to 7pm. Tuesday is vodka night, with cheap drinks from 9pm. Wednesday is ladies' night, with free champagne from 9pm. Sunday is Corona night, with cheap prices and a live band. It's open Monday, Tuesday, and Thursday from 11am to 2am, Wednesday and Friday from 11am to 4am, Saturday from noon to 4am, and Sunday from noon to 1am. 53–55 Lockhart Rd., Wan Chai. ✆ 852/2866 6289. MTR: Wan Chai.

Dusk til Dawn   This is one of my top picks for an evening out in Wan Chai. It attracts a mostly expat and Southeast Asian clientele, who come to take advantage of its 5-to-11pm daily happy hour, food and snack menu served until 5am, and nightly free live music starting at 10pm. Open Monday through Friday from noon to 6am and Saturday and Sunday from 3pm to 6am. 76–84 Jaffe Rd., Wan Chai. ✆ 852/2528 4689. MTR: Wan Chai.

Joe Bananas   This has long been one of the most popular hangouts in Wan Chai, maybe because it's reportedly also one of Hong Kong's best pickup bars. It's also a very popular place for lunch. Called "JB's" by the locals, it sports a casual, beach-house decor. A live band entertains Monday to Saturday from 8pm to midnight, followed by a DJ, but a HK$100 (US$13) cover, which includes one drink, is charged only Friday and Saturday (though women get in free until 1am). Wednesday is Ladies' Night, with free drinks for women from 6pm to midnight. Happy hour is from 8 to 10pm daily. It's open Monday to Thursday from 11:30am to 5am, Friday from 11:30am to 6am, Saturday from 3pm to 6am, and Sunday from 5pm to 5am. 23 Luard Rd., Wan Chai. ✆ 852/2529 1811. MTR: Wan Chai.

Klong Bar & Grill   Wishing to evoke steamy, sensual Bangkok, this new establishment takes its name from the many canals that lace Thailand's capital. Its open-fronted ground-floor bar and grill, with an open kitchen turning out delectable Thai barbecue, looks like any Asian bar, dark and slightly rough around the edges. Go upstairs, however, and it's a whole different place, very posh and upmarket, with well-dressed urbanites crowded around a huge U-shaped bar and lounging in the corner "opium den." Things do get crazy, however, especially when both professionals and amateurs are encouraged to hop on the bar and perform an exotic pole dance, which probably happens most on Wednesday nights when ladies are served free vodka. Still, it's a long cry from Bangkok's truly wild and steamy (and raunchy to some) nightlife scene. A DJ hits the scene on Friday and Saturday nights. With happy hour daily from 6 to 10pm, it's open daily from 6pm until 3am or later. The Broadway, 54–62 Lockhart Rd., Wan Chai. ✆ 852/2217 8330. MTR: Wan Chai.

Old China Hand   This is one of the old-timers in Wan Chai (since 1977), an informal English pub popular with older expats but welcoming to tourists as well with its open facade good for people-watching. In the tradition of the pub lunch, meals include steak-and-kidney pie, fish and chips, sandwiches, salads, chili con carne, and a fixed-price lunch priced at HK$49 (US$6.35). Happy hour is daily from noon to 10pm and midnight to 2am. There's live music Sundays from 5 to 11pm. It's open 24 hours on Friday and Saturday; the rest of the week it's open from 8am to 5am. 104 Lockhart Rd., Wan Chai. ✆ 852/2527 9174. MTR: Wan Chai.

ToTT's Asian Grill & Bar   This flashy bar and grill, with a blood-red interior and zebra-striped chairs, offers fabulous views of Victoria Harbour and Kowloon from its 34th-floor perch. There's live music and dancing Monday through Saturday nights from 10pm, with a minimum drink/snack charge of HK$168 (US$22) on weekends only (there's no minimum charge for hotel guests or diners who eat here; see p. 144 for the restaurant's review). Happy hour is from 5 to 8pm. The bar is open Sunday to Thursday from 5pm to 1am and Friday and Saturday from 5pm to 2am. In the Excelsior Hotel, 281 Gloucester Rd., Causeway Bay. ✆ 852/ 2837 6786. MTR: Causeway Bay.

The Wanch   Offering free live music nightly, this unpretentious bar is a good bet for Wan Chai bar hopping. Tuesdays feature an all-female Filipino band, Wednesday is jam night, and Sundays it's sing-along music. Live music begins at 9pm Monday to Thursday, 10pm Friday and Saturday, and 3pm Sunday. Happy hour is generous: all day Monday, Tuesday to Thursday all day except 10pm to midnight, and Friday to Sunday all day except 9pm to 1am. Hours here are Monday to Saturday 11am to 2am and Sunday noon to 2am. 54 Jaffe Rd., Wan Chai. ✆ 852/2861 1621. MTR: Wan Chai.

TOPLESS BARS & HOSTESS CLUBS

Hong Kong's world of hostess clubs and topless bars has changed in the past 40 years. Back in the 1950s and 1960s, Wan Chai was where the action was, buzzing with sailors fresh off their ships and soldiers on leave from Vietnam. Then, it was a world of two-bit hotels, raunchy bars, narrow streets, and dark alleyways where men came to drink and brawl and spend money on women.

Today, most of Wan Chai has become respectable (and a bit boring)—an area full of new buildings, mushrooming high-rises, and Hong Kong's expansive convention center. There is a small pocket of depravity, however, concentrated mostly on Lockhart and Luard roads and consisting of bars catering to young revelers and shows of erotic dancers. To be on the safe side, stick to the two longtime recommendations described below. If you decide to explore on your own, be sure you know all the charges, including admission charges, the prices of drinks, and extra charges for shows or hostesses.

BBOSS   This dazzling, 70,000-square-foot hostess club can seat 3,000 people and was the largest Japanese-style nightclub in the world when it opened in 1984. Even larger ones have since opened in China, but this place is still so big that a full-size electric replica of an antique Rolls-Royce delivers customers along a "highway" to their seats. There are three nightly stage shows, at 9:20, 10:15, and 11:10pm, complete with a rotating stage so that everyone gets a chance to ogle the scantily clad performers. There's also a 20-member band, a smaller combo band, and a dance floor. Couples are welcome, though single women are not allowed, as they would compete with the scores of hostesses who flatter and chat with male customers. Big spenders can even take hostesses away from the club for the evening (escort services are big business in Hong Kong, as a perusal of any local newspaper will show). In any case, how much you end up spending will be determined by how many drinks you consume, how long you entertain a hostess at your table (it costs HK$1,000/US$130 for 2 hr. during the day and HK$1,200/US$156 for 2 hr. at night, not including her drinks), and what time of the day or night you visit. If you're not careful, you could spend a fortune here. On the other hand, the place is so overdecorated in bows and the color pink, 1 hour may be all you can stand; in that case, come for one of the 30-minute shows (see times above), which costs HK$200 (US$26) per person, including a soft drink. However, since these shows all happen after 9pm, you'll sill need to spend the HK$520 (US$68) drink minimum charge on top of the show charge. It's open daily from 1pm to 4am. New Mandarin Plaza, 14 Science Museum Rd., Tsim Sha Tsui East. ℰ 852/2369 2883. Minimum drink/snack charge HK$460 (US$60) until 9pm, HK$520 (US$68) after 9pm. MTR: Tsim Sha Tsui, then take a taxi.

Bottoms Up   For more than 30 years, this basement establishment was located in Tsim Sha Tsui and had explicit pictures of its namesake at the entranceway. In 2004, however, it moved across the harbor to Wan Chai, no doubt to be closer to like-minded businesses. In any case, this is probably the best place to go if you want a topless joint. Welcoming tourists, couples, and unaccompanied men (but not unaccompanied women), the old Bottoms Up was used as a location shot in the James Bond movie *Man with the Golden Gun.* It's open daily from 6:30pm to 3:30am. 37–39 Lockhart Rd., Wan Chai. ℰ 852/2721 4509. MTR: Wan Chai.

4 Only in Hong Kong
NIGHT TOURS
If you have only 1 or 2 nights in Hong Kong and you're uncomfortable roaming around on your own, I recommend an organized night tour. **Watertours,** an old Hong Kong company that specializes in boat tours, offers two evening tours that combine harbor cruises with various land activities. The Aberdeen & Harbour Night Cruise, for example, includes a sunset cruise with unlimited drinks, dinner aboard the Jumbo Kingdom floating restaurant in Aberdeen, and a stop at a scenic overlook midway up Victoria Peak. This 4½-hour tour is offered nightly and costs HK$660 (US$86), including dinner. There are also shorter evening cruises (without dinner); Watertours offers nightly cocktail cruises at 6:15pm and night cruises at 9:30pm. Both tours last approximately 90 minutes and cost HK$290 (US$38), including unlimited free drinks. Watertours can be booked through most hotels or by calling ℰ 852/2926 3868 (www.watertours hk.com). Other tour companies offering night tours (these two concentrate on land tours but also offer evening cruises) include **Gray Line** (ℰ 852/2368 7111;** www.grayline.com.hk) and **Splendid Tours & Travel** (ℰ 852/2316 2151;** www.splendidtours.com).

If you're in Hong Kong anytime from September to May on a Wednesday evening, you can go to the **horse races** in **Happy Valley** or **Sha Tin.** Although you can go on your own for as little as HK$10 (US$1.30), you can also take an organized trip to the races offered by both Gray Line and Splendid Tours, which includes a meal, a seat in the Royal Jockey Club members' stand, and racing tips. (For more information, see p. 177.)

NIGHT STROLLS
One of the most beautiful and romantic sights in the world must be from **Victoria Peak** at night. The peak tram, which costs only HK$30 (US$3.90) round-trip and runs daily until midnight, deposits passengers at the Peak Tower terminal. From the terminal, turn right, and then turn right again onto a pedestrian footpath. This path, which follows Lugard Road and Harlech Road, circles the peak, offering great views of glittering Hong Kong. Popular with both lovers and joggers, the path is lit at night and leads past expensive villas and primeval-looking jungles. Definitely the best stroll in Hong Kong, it takes about an hour.

On the other side of the harbor, there's a promenade along the **Tsim Sha Tsui waterfront,** which is popular among young Chinese couples. It stretches from the Star Ferry terminus all the way through Tsim Sha Tsui East, with very romantic views of a lit-up Hong Kong Island across the choppy waters. Best of all is the nightly "Symphony of Lights" from 8 to 8:18pm, when an impressive laser and light show is projected from 18 buildings on Hong Kong Island.

The Tsim Sha Tsui waterfront is very safe at night, as it has lots of people. As for Victoria Peak, I have walked it alone several times at night, but to be honest, it's probably best with someone else.

NIGHT MARKETS

If you're looking for colorful atmosphere, head for the **Temple Street Night Market** (p. 219), near the Jordan MTR station in Kowloon. Extending for several blocks, it has stalls where clothing, accessories, toys, pens, watches, sunglasses, cassettes, household items, and much more is sold. Be sure to bargain fiercely if you decide to buy anything, and be sure to check the merchandise to make sure it isn't going to fall apart in 2 weeks. This is also a good place for an inexpensive meal at one of the *dai pai dong* (roadside food stalls), which specialize in seafood, including clams, shrimp, mussels, and crab.

But the most wonderful part of the market is its northern end, to the right, around the white parking area. There, near the Tin Hau temple, you'll find palm readers and fortune-tellers, some of whom speak English, as well as street musicians and singers. You'll have to hunt for the tiny alleyway of musicians, where group after group has set up their own stages and are surrounded by an appreciative audience. Cantonese pop songs and operas are among the favorites, and when the musicians do an especially good job, they are rewarded with tips. Get there before 9pm to see the musicians. Otherwise, although some vendors set up shop as early as 4pm, the market is in full swing from about 7 to 10pm daily.

Farther north, near the Mong Kok MTR station, is the **Ladies' Market** (p. 219), which stretches along Tung Choi Street between Argyle and Dundas streets. It's a great place to shop for inexpensive women's, men's, and children's fashions and accessories, including watches, handbags, T-shirts, and other goods. It's not quite as touristy as the Temple Street Night Market, and the atmosphere is fun and festive. It's open daily from about 12:30 to 10:30pm.

10

Side Trips from Hong Kong

Mention Hong Kong and most people think of Hong Kong Island, Victoria Peak, the shops and neon of Tsim Sha Tsui, the Star Ferry crossing Victoria Harbour, and the high-rises of the Central District. What they don't realize is that Hong Kong Island and Kowloon comprise only 10% of the entire territory—the New Territories and the outlying islands make up the other whopping 90%.

If you have a day or two to spare, or even just an afternoon, I suggest that you spend it on a trip outside the city in one of the SAR's rural areas. Escape the bustle and chaos of the city to one of the region's small villages in the countryside, especially on the islands, and you'll have the chance to glimpse an older and slower way of life, where traditions still reign supreme and where lifestyles have a rhythm all their own.

1 The New Territories

Before the 1980s, the New Territories were made up of peaceful countryside, with duck farms, fields, and old villages. No longer. A vast 1,008-sq.-km (389-sq.-mile) region that stretches from Kowloon to the border of mainland China, the New Territories are Hong Kong's answer to its growing population. Huge government housing projects have mushroomed throughout the New Territories, especially in towns along the railway and subway lines. Once-sleepy villages have become concrete jungles virtually overnight.

Close to one-half of Hong Kong's population—about 3.3 million people—lives in the New Territories, mostly in subsidized housing. The New Territories, therefore, are vitally important to the SAR, its well-being, and its future. For visitors to ignore the area completely would be shortsighted; many find the housing projects, in some suburbs stretching as far as the eye can see, nothing short of astounding. If, on the other hand, it's peace and quiet you're searching for, don't despair. The New Territories are so large and so mountainous that not all the land has been turned into housing, and the area still makes an interesting side trip—it's so different from the city itself that it's almost like visiting an entirely different country.

Traveling in the New Territories, you may notice women wearing wide-brimmed hats with a black fringe and pajama-like clothing; many of them have gold-capped teeth as well. These women are Hakka, as are most of the farmers of the New Territories. They keep to themselves, preserving their customs and dialect. During the Ming dynasty (1368–1644), some of the Hakka clans in the area built walls around their homes to protect themselves against roving bandits and invaders. A handful of these walled villages still exist today, along with ancestral halls and other ancient, traditional buildings. One of my favorite things to do in the New Territories is to walk one of two Heritage Trails, both of which highlight village life in the New Territories and take you past significant historic buildings and walled villages. Both trails are described in more detail later, but be sure to pick up HKTB's two pamphlets, the *Lung Yeuk Tau Heritage Trail* and the *Ping Shan Heritage Trail.* I also suggest that before visiting any walled village, try to see the Sam Tung Uk Museum in Tsuen Wan (also described later), since it will greatly enrich your visit to a lived-in walled village.

As for getting around the New Territories, the Kowloon-Canton Railway (KCR) is the fastest and most convenient way to reach major destinations. All KCR train stations have free maps in English of their immediate surroundings, complete with descriptions of buses that serve the area. Simply stop by the ticket or customer service counter at your destination and ask for the station's map. Another useful pamphlet is the free HKTB leaflet, "Major Bus Routes in the New Territories," which tells you which bus to take, the fare, and the frequency of buses along the route.

If your time is limited, a good tactic for seeing the New Territories is to leave the driving to someone else and opt for an organized tour. The "Land Between" Tour emphasizes both the rural side of Hong Kong and its urban development, enabling visitors to learn about the lifestyle, customs, and beliefs of the local people. It visits a temple, a traditional market in Tai Po, and a fishing village, passing through sprawling satellite towns on the way. The Heritage Tour, a must for architectural buffs, covers historic Chinese architectural sites spread throughout Kowloon and the New Territories, including a restored 18th-century walled village, a Man Mo temple, an ancestral hall, and Tai Fu Tai, a stately country mansion. It's impossible for the individual traveler to cover as much ground in a single day as is covered on one of these tours. For more information on these tours and other tours, see "Organized Tours & Cultural Activities" in chapter 6, beginning on p. 175.

SEEING THE NEW TERRITORIES BY KOWLOON-CANTON RAILWAY (KCR)

For years, every visitor to the New Territories took the train to the border for a look into forbidden and mysterious China. Now, of course, it's easy to get permission to enter China, and the border lookout has lost its appeal—the view was never very exciting anyway. Still, you might want to take the train up into the New Territories just for the experience, as well as for the interesting stops you can make on the way. From the KCR East Tsim Sha Tsui Station at the southern tip of Kowloon, the trip by KCR East Rail costs only HK$9 (US$1.15) one-way for ordinary class and HK$18 (US$2.35) for first class and takes just 30 minutes to go to the end of the line: Sheung Shui. Trains depart every 3 to 8 minutes.

After departing East Tsim Sha Tsui Station, the Kowloon-Canton Railway (KCR) East Rail will take you along 32km (20 miles) of track, passing through such budding satellite towns as Sha Tin, University Station, Tai Po Market, and Fanling before reaching Sheung Shui—your last stop unless you have a visa to enter China. The train makes a total of 11 stops along the way, enabling you to get out and do some exploring on your own. I have arranged the towns below in the order in which you'll reach them when traveling north from Kowloon. The names of the towns are also the names of the KCR stations.

TAI WAI

Tai Wai, the first stop on the KCR after passing into the New Territories, was once a small village but has now been engulfed by Sha Tin, described below. Near the station are a couple of sights worth seeing if you're restricting your sightseeing to Sha Tin or have lots of time (ask for the "Tai Wai Station Street Map and Information" at Tai Wai Station; in addition, *Hong Kong Walks,* a free brochure at HKTB, gives instructions on how to reach attractions in Sha Tin on foot). **Che Kung Temple,** 7 Che Kung Miu Road (© **852/2603 4049**), is a modern Taoist temple honoring Che Kung, a general from the Sung dynasty (A.D. 960–1279) credited with suppressing a revolt in southern China and safe-guarding villagers from a plague. You'll find a giant statue of Che Kung inside, holding his sword, but the temple is popular with nearby residents mainly for the fortune-tellers on hand. Many also bring food offerings and burn incense to ask for blessings. To reach the temple, follow the exit with the sign "Che Kung Temple" (or turn left from Tai Wai Station onto Hung Mui Kuk Rd.), and walk to Che Kung Miu Road, which you should cross via the pedestrian pass and then turn left. The temple will be on your right, past Chui Tin Street. Admission is free, and it's open daily from 7am to 6pm.

Just a 15-minute walk east of the temple, on the other side of Lion Rock Tunnel Road on Sha Kok Road, is **Tsang Tai Uk** (also called Shan Ha Wai, which means Walled Village at the Mountain Foot), a tiny, walled village built in the 1840s for members of the Tsang clan (Tsang Tai Uk translates as "Mr. Tsang's Big House"). With its high, thick walls, four parallel rows, two side columns of houses, and central courtyard with the ancestral halls (and a painting of the clan founder) in the middle, it's typical of Hakka settlements in Guangdong Province (formerly Canton Province). Although not as old nor as famous as other walled villages, Tsang Tai Uk is, in my opinion, more intriguing and interesting because it has been spared the intrusion of the modern apartments that now plague most villages. Still occupied by about 300 members of the Tsang clan, it looks like a vision of communal life from Hong Kong's not-so-distant past, with children playing in the grassy field out front, seniors sitting in doorways, and women drawing water from courtyard wells.

The recent addition of public toilets has made life easier, as most of the 99 apartments are without private facilities and residents formerly relied on chamber pots. Since Tsang Tai Uk is off the tourist pathway and serves as home to a number of families, visitors should be respectful of the inhabitants' privacy when visiting the compound. Tsang Tai Uk is about a 15-minute walk from Che Kung Temple (above), but getting there is confusing despite a few small signs. Best is to have the concierge of your hotel write out the name in Chinese so you can show people for directions; there's also a map and directions in the HKTB booklet *Hong Kong Walks.*

North, across the river from Che Kung Temple and Tsang Tai Uk, is the **Hong Kong Heritage Museum** ★★, 1 Man Lam Road (📞 **852/2180 8188;** http://hk.heritage.museum), in my opinion the main reason for a visit to the area. Opened in 2001, it presents both the history and culture of the New Territories in a series of themed exhibitions. Foremost is the New Territories Heritage Hall, with displays relating to the customs, religions, and lifestyle of the early fishermen and settlers and how they have changed over the centuries. A barge loaded for market, an ancestral hall, traditional clothing, and other items are also on display. Particularly stunning are the models showing the growth of Sha Tin since the 1930s. I also like the Cantonese Opera Heritage Hall, a must for anyone wishing to gain insight into the history and characteristics of this unique form of entertainment, with musical instruments, elaborate costumes and headgear, and a typical backstage scene. The Chao Shao-an Gallery shows the works of Chao Shao-an (1905–98), a Hong Kong artist famous for his bird-and-flower paintings, while the T. T. Tsui Gallery of Chinese Art contains porcelains, bronzes, furniture, jade, and other works of Chinese art dating from the Neolithic period to the 20th century. For the kids, there's also a toy museum and the hands-on Children's Discovery Gallery, where they can practice being an archaeologist, wear traditional costumes, and learn about marshes. Allow at least 2 hours here. It's open Monday and Wednesday through Saturday from 10am to 6pm and Sunday and holidays from 10am to 7pm. Admission is HK$10 (US$1.30) for adults and HK$5 (US65¢) for children, students, and seniors. Admission is free on Wednesdays. It's located about halfway between Tai Wai and Sha Tin stations, about a 15-minute walk from each. On weekends and holidays from 1pm, there's a free shuttle bus from Sha Tin Station (take Exit B1 and turn left) departing every 10 minutes.

SHA TIN

This is Hong Kong's prime example of a budding satellite town, with a population approaching 640,000. Fewer than 13km (8 miles) north of Tsim Sha Tsui, it's also home to a modern **horse racetrack,** as well as a huge shopping mall called the **New Town Plaza,** located next to the Sha Tin KCR Station and featuring a frequent 10-minute performance by an illuminated, computer-controlled musical indoor fountain. Shops here are open from 10am to 10pm daily.

Most interesting for the visitor here, however, is the **Monastery of 10,000 Buddhas,** located on a hill west of the Sha Tin railway station (take the left-hand exit from the station and follow the signs a couple minutes to the foot of the hill). It takes about a half hour's energetic walk to reach the actual monastery; first you have to climb more than 400 twisting steps, flanked by gold-colored statues. The temple was established in the 1950s by a monk named Yuet Kai, who wrote 98 books on Buddhism. He's still at the temple—well, actually, his body is still there. He's been embalmed and covered in gold leaf and sits behind a glass case. In attendance are more Buddha images than you've probably ever seen gathered in one place. In fact, despite the monastery's name, there are almost 13,000 of the tiny statues lining the walls, and no two are exactly alike. Also on the grounds are a nine-story pink pagoda and a very simple vegetarian dining hall. The temple affords a good view of Sha Tin's high-rise housing estates and the surrounding mountains. Admission is free, and it's open daily from 9am to 5pm.

Where to Dine

My first choice for lunch or dinner is overwhelmingly **Yucca de Lac,** Ma Liu Shui, Sha Tin (📞 **852/2691 1630**). Opened in 1964 when Sha Tin was still a sleepy village, it has an enviable location on a hill with a shaded, outdoor terrace affording a dreamy view of Tolo Harbour and high-rises. Umbrellas, strung lights, streams, and flowering bushes give it a festive atmosphere. The English menu lists more than 200 Cantonese dishes (pigeon is a specialty), with most priced between HK$75 and HK$130 (US$9.75–US$17). MasterCard and Visa are accepted, and it's open from 11am to 11pm daily. You can best reach it by taxi. Note, however, that this is prime real estate and the restaurant's days may be numbered. Be sure to telephone first.

The **Monastery of 10,000 Buddhas** has a very simple dining hall (© **852/ 2699 4144**) serving vegetarian dishes from an English menu, sweet-and-sour garoupa (not real fish, of course), deep-fried taro "fish," fried bean curd, and other choices, with dishes costing HK$35 to HK$40 (US$4.55–US$5.20). No credit cards are accepted and it's open daily from 10am to 5pm.

Otherwise, the **New Town Plaza,** Sha Tin's massive shopping mall, located beside the Sha Tin KCR station, is a good place for a snack or quick meal, with cafeterias, fast-food outlets, and restaurants serving both Western and Chinese fare. The largest restaurant here is **Maxim's Palace Chinese Restaurant** on the sixth floor (© **852/2693 6918**), open daily from 7:30am to 11:45pm and serving dim sum and Cantonese food, including barbecued Peking duck, roasted goose, deep-fried crispy chicken, and seafood. Other Maxim's group restaurants here are **Peking Garden Restaurant** (© **852/2681 4888**) on the third floor and **Chiuchow Garden Restaurant** (© **852/2694 1688**) on the fifth floor. For inexpensive Western fare, head for the **Spaghetti House** in Shop 153 (© **852/ 2697 9009**), one in a chain of successful American-style spaghetti-and-pizza parlors, open daily from 11am to 11pm; or **Oliver's Super Sandwiches** in Shop 404 (© **852/2892 7226**), specializing in sandwiches, baked potatoes with various toppings, and bagels. It's open daily from 7:30am to 10:30pm.

UNIVERSITY

This stop, which is actually still within the boundaries of budding Sha Tin, serves students going to Chinese University. But your main interest will be its art museum and a ferry ride through Tolo Harbour.

The permanent collection of the **Chinese University Art Museum** at Chinese University (© **852/2609 7416;** www.cuhk.edu.hk/ics/amm) is made up of more than 1,000 paintings and examples of calligraphy by Guangdong artists dating from the Ming period to the present, as well as bronze seals, rubbings of stone inscriptions, jade flower carvings, Chinese ceramics, and other decorative arts, displayed on a rotating basis. There are also special exhibitions of art. The museum occupies four levels of a modern building with a Chinese garden in a central courtyard but is actually quite small; you can see everything in about 30 minutes, so only aficionados of Chinese art will want to make the extra effort to come here. It's open Monday to Saturday from 10am to 4:45pm and on Sunday from 12:30 to 5:30pm (closed on public holidays); admission is free. To reach it from the KCR University Station, take one of the free Chinese University Hong Kong shuttle buses departing every 20 or 30 minutes, getting off 5 minutes later near the administration building.

University is also where you get off if you want to take a ferry around **Tolo Harbour.** Located in the northeastern edge of the New Territories and surrounded by grassy low hills and lush woodlands, Tolo Harbour is home to several fishing villages, including Tap Mun. From University Station, it's a 20-minute walk to Ma Liu Shui, where you board the ferry for a leisurely trip to three villages around the harbor. The ferry departs Ma Liu Shui only twice a day, at 8:30am and 3pm, with additional sailings weekends and holidays at 12:30pm. Since the first ferry may be a little too early, I would suggest taking an afternoon cruise. The 3pm ferry makes stops at Sham Chung and Lai Chi Chong before arriving at Tap Mun at 4:20pm. The return ferry departs Tap Mun at 5:30pm for the trip back to Ma Liu Shui. This gives you a little time to do some sightseeing, but make sure you return to the Tap Mun ferry dock by 5:30pm because there are no hotels here. The ferry gets back to Ma Liu Shui at 6:45pm. The entire round-trip ride costs HK$32 (US$4.15) on weekdays and HK$50 (US$6.50) on weekends and holidays. HKTB has a leaflet on Tolo Harbour with a timetable, but it would be wise to double-check with the Tsui Wah Ferry company itself by calling 🕻 **852/2272 2000** (www.traway.com.hk).

TAI WO

One of the new satellite towns of the New Territories, Tai Po was first settled by Tanka boat people more than 1,000 years ago because of its strategic location on a river that flows into Tolo Harbour. Today many Hakka farmers and residents call it home. Just a short taxi ride or a 15-minute walk from the Tai Wo KCR station (ask for the *Tai Wo Station Street Map and Information* pamphlet at the station) is the small **Hong Kong Railway Museum,** 13 Shung Tak St. (🕻 **852/2653 3455;** http://hk.heritage.museum). It occupies what was formerly the very tiny Tai Po Market railway station, built in 1913 in traditional Chinese style with ceramic figurines cresting its gabled roof. Besides the station's original waiting hall and ticket office, the museum displays a few model trains, historic photographs of Tai Po, a narrow-gauge steam locomotive, and some vintage railway coaches dating from the early 1900s; its main appeal is to railway buffs, who will probably want to spend about 15 minutes here. It is open (and free) Wednesday to Monday from 9am to 5pm.

From the museum, you should visit the nearby **Man Mo Temple** by exiting from the museum's main entrance, walking downhill 1 block, and then turning left onto Fu Shin Street, a pedestrian lane that has been serving as Tai Po's market for more than a century. It bustles with activity from 7am to 6pm as housewives shop here twice daily to secure the freshest produce, fish, dried herbs, and other ingredients for the day's meals. Booths also sell Hakka-style clothing, including the distinctive broad-brimmed hats with black fringe. At the end of Fu Shin Street is the small Man Mo Temple, founded in 1893 to commemorate the founding of Tai Po Market. Dedicated to the Taoist gods of war and literature, the temple is a popular spot for older residents to gather and play mahjong or simply pass the time. Note the two-storied compounds on both sides of the main entrance—they were once used by market administrators and for housing overnight guests. As at the Man Mo Temple on Hong Kong Island (p. 169), huge incense coils suspended from the temple's ceiling are purchased by worshippers and burn for more than 2 weeks.

FANLING

A small farming settlement for several centuries, Fanling is now a huge satellite town. There is, however, a traditional part of Fanling that preserves its rural atmosphere and is the raison d'etre of the **Lung Yeuk Tau Heritage Trail.** Many of the historic buildings along the trail are legacies of the Tang clan, the first and largest of the Five Great Clans to settle in the New Territories. Royal descendants of the eldest son of the princess of the Southern Song dynasty (1127–1279), they established five *wais* (walled villages) and six *tsuen* (villages) in the area around Luk Yeuk Tau, which takes its name from the nearby Mountain of the Leaping

Dragon. The trail, which stretches about 2.25km (1.4 miles) and takes approximately one hour to complete, passes more than a dozen historic structures along the way, including four walled villages, a study hall, a Tin Hau temple, and one of Hong Kong's largest ancestral halls, built in 1525 to honor the founding Tang ancestor. It also passes vegetable plots, tended by Hakka women wearing traditional fringed hats.

To reach the Lung Yeuk Tau Heritage Trail, take minibus no. 54K from the east exit of Fanling Station to Lo Wai walled village. Near the end of the trail, at the San Wai walled village, take bus no. 56K back to Fanling Station. Be sure to pick up the free brochure *Lung Yeuk Tau Heritage Trail,* which contains a map and information on historic buildings, at one of the HKTB Visitor Information and Services Centres.

Where to Dine

The most memorable place to dine in Fanling is at **Fung Ying Seen Koon,** 66 Pak Wo Rd. (*©* **852/2669 9186**), a Taoist temple established in 1929. It offers vegetarian food daily from 11am to 5:30pm in a simple dining room to the left of the main hall. Main dishes on the English menu, ranging in price from HK$37 to HK$65 (US$4.80–US$8.45), include hot and spicy bean curd and fried elm fungus with three kinds of mushroom. There are also set meals for two or more people, costing HK$105 (US$14) for two and HK$150 (US$19) for three. No credit cards are accepted. To reach Fung Ying Seen Koon, visible from Fanling Station, take the west exit and go through the pedestrian underpass.

SHEUNG SHUI

Once its own market town, Sheung Shui, the last stop before the China border, has been swallowed up in the budding satellite town that now spreads out from Fanling. Although much of Sheung Shui's charm has been lost due to the construction of modern buildings all around, it's still more peaceful than other old villages that are closer to the beaten path. Of all the historic, traditional Chinese buildings in the New Territories, few impress me as much as **Tai Fu Tai** ✦✦, built in 1865 and the only Mandarin mansion restored and remaining in Hong Kong. It belonged to Man Chung-luen, the 21st generation of the Man clan, a merchant and scholar who attained the highest grade in the Imperial Chinese Civil Service Examinations. Constructed of granite and bricks and adorned with colorful ceramic figurines, fine plaster moldings, woodcarvings, and murals, it is striking for its simplicity, a stark contrast to mansions built by Westerners of the gentry class of the same period. Constructed like a miniature fort, without windows but with an inner courtyard to let in light, it contains a main hall, side chambers, bedrooms, study, kitchen, servants' quarters, and lavatory. In the back of the main hall is a portrait of Man Chung-luen, flanked by pictures of his two wives and two sons. Not shown are his eight daughters. Remarkably, the mansion was occupied by members of the Man clan until the 1980s. Nearby is the **Man Lun Fung Ancestral Hall,** built to honor the 8th member of the Man clan. Both Tai Fu Tai and the ancestral hall are open free to the public Wednesday to Monday from 9am to 1pm and 2 to 5pm. To reach them, take bus no. 76K from Sheung Shui KCR station traveling in the direction of Yuen Long (West) about 30 minutes to San Tin (near the post office), followed by a 5-minute walk back along Castle Peak Road to the signposted entrance. Since it's a bit difficult and time-consuming to visit on your own, you might want to take the Hong Kong Tourist Board's guided Heritage Tour to visit this site.

ELSEWHERE IN THE NEW TERRITORIES
TSUEN WAN AND TIN SHUI WAI

If I were to choose only one quick destination in the New Territories, it would be Tsuen Wan with its excellent walled-village museum. It's easily reached by taking the MTR Tsuen Wan Line, which runs from Central through Tsim Sha Tsui and Kowloon, to the last stop. Tsuen Wan was a small market town just 100 years ago, with a population of about 3,000 Hakkas and a thriving incense pow-der–producing industry. Then, as the first designated satellite town of the New Territories, it grew to a population of more than 275,000 residents, living mostly in high-rise housing estates.

The main reason for visiting Tsuen Wan is its excellent **Sam Tung Uk Museum** ★★★, 2 Kwu Uk Lane, Tsuen Wan (© 852/2411 2001; http://hk.heritage.museum), located just a few minutes' walk from Tsuen Wan MTR sta-tion by taking exit E and then turning left. The museum is actually a restored Hakka walled village, built in the 18th century by members of the farming Chan clan. It consists of tiny lanes lined with tiny tile-roofed homes, four houses that have been restored to their original condition, an ancestral hall, two rows of side houses, an exhibition hall depicting Tsuen Wan's history, and an adjacent land-scaped garden. The four windowless restored houses are furnished much as they would have been when occupied, with traditional Chinese furniture (including elegant black-wood furniture), and contain farm implements, kitchens, and lavatories. Although as many as 300 clan members once lived here, the village was abandoned in 1980. Today the museum is a tiny oasis in the midst of mod-ern high-rise housing projects. The museum is open Wednesday to Monday from 9am to 5pm, and admission is free.

From the MTR Tsuen Wan Station, it's a 15-minute walk on Tai Ho Road to Tsuen Wan West Station, a stop on the new KCR West Rail line (stop by the customer service counter at MTR Tsuen Wan Station to pick up the "Location Map," which shows the location of both stations). From Tsuen Wan West Sta-tion, take the West Rail four stops to Tin Shui Wai Station.

At Tin Shui Wai Station, take exit E for the **Ping Shan Heritage Trail,** the start of which is easy to spot by its ancient pagoda (be sure to pick up the free *Ping Shan Heritage Trail* brochure at HKTB). This wonderful walking trail is only 1km (.62 miles) long and takes less than 30 minutes to complete, yet it passes a wealth of traditional Chinese structures along the way, most relating to the pow-erful Tang clan, who settled the Ping Shan area in the 12th century. The Tsui Sing Lau Pagoda (open 9am–1pm and 2–5pm; closed on Tues) is the only ancient pagoda in Hong Kong, constructed more than 600 years ago to improve the area's *feng shui* (geomancy) and ward off evil spirits. A small flea market, held near the pagoda on weekends and holidays, sells toys, clothing, jewelry, and accessories.

Other highlights of the trail are a walled village, two temples, and a study hall built for members of the Tang clan studying for the Imperial Civil Service Exam-ination. But the main attraction is the 700-year-old Tang Ancestral Hall (open daily 9am–1pm and 2–5pm), still used by the Tang clan for ancestral worship, ceremonies, and festivals. Admission to this and other structures along the trail is free.

Where to Dine

Next to the Tsui Sing Lau Pagoda is the **Gallo Café,** 250 Sheung Cheung Wai (© 852/2495 5555), called Dai Gong Guy in Chinese, which translates as Big

Rooster (look for the rooster on top of the restaurant and the replica water buffalo at its entrance). With outdoor seating, a covered pavilion, and an air-conditioned dining room, it specializes in free-range chicken, which is steamed and delivered whole to the table for HK$108 (US$14). Another good choice is the deep-fried eel, basted with honey and mandarin (Kam Gut Mud Heung Sin). Sandwiches are also available. It's open daily from 7am to midnight, and no credit cards are accepted.

SAI KUNG

Located on the eastern coast of the New Territories, Sai Kung is the second largest and least populated of Hong Kong's 18 districts and encompasses three country parks. It's popular for its scenery, nature trails, and Sai Kung Town with its harbor-front seafood restaurants.

To reach Sai Kung Town, take the MTR to Choi Hung Station, and then board minibus no. 1A for a 20-minute ride to Sai Kung Town. The bus will deposit you at the bus terminal near the waterfront, where you should turn right and walk along the harbor to the local fish market. Around 5pm each evening, sampans docked at the public pier sell live fish to tourists and residents alike. Here, too, are many seafood restaurants with outside tanks holding live prawns, crabs, lobster, abalone, moray eels, stonefish, garoupa, and other creatures of the sea. Behind the waterfront restaurants, on Sai Kung Tai Kai Street, is Sai Kung Old Town with its narrow, twisting lanes lined with shops selling incense, dried seafood, herbs, and provisions.

Hiking

For some hiking, board bus no. 94 (going in the direction of Wong Shek Pier) from Sai Kung's bus terminal and ride 20 minutes to Pak Tam Chung. Here you'll find the **Sai Kung Country Park Visitor Center** (© **852/2792 7365**), open Wednesday to Monday from 9:30am to 4:30pm. In addition to displays on agriculture, fishing, rural culture, and village life, it has a model of Sai Kung Country Park, as well as a hiking map.

Beside the visitor center is a barrier gate, restricting vehicular access to Tai Mong Tsai Road. If you follow this road to its junction with Pak Tam Road, you'll find the starting point of the 100km-long (62-mile) **MacLehose Trail,** which winds through eight country parks and ends at Tuen Mun in the western part of the New Territories. It's divided into 10 stages of various difficulty; the beginning stage, which runs along the High Island Reservoir, is one of the easiest.

Where to Dine

No trip to Sai Kung Town would be complete without dining on fresh seafood at one of the town's waterfront seafood restaurants. I suggest simply wandering from tank to tank of live fish, shellfish, and other delectables until something catches your fancy, but for a specific recommendation, try the Cantonese **Chuen Kee Seafood Restaurant,** 51 Hoi Pong St., Sai Kung Town (© **852/2791 1195**). After selecting your lobster, prawns, or fish from its live tanks, after which it will be weighed by the catty (one catty is about 1½ lb.), you'll be given a number and your selections will be sent directly to the kitchen, along with your directions for cooking. My favorite: crab sautéed with ginger and shallots. As with most Cantonese restaurants, however, the seafood is mainly steamed. Prices depend on market price, with most meals costing about HK$300 to HK$350 (US$39–US$45) per person (MasterCard and Visa accepted). It's open daily from 11:30am to 10:30pm.

2 The Outlying Islands

There are some 260 outlying islands around Hong Kong, most of them barren and uninhabited. Because construction in the New Territories is booming and transportation to underpopulated areas there can be slow, the islands offer the best opportunity to see something of rural Chinese life. What's more, they're easy to reach—hop on a ferry in Central and then sit back and enjoy the view. Taking a ferry to an outlying island is the cheapest harbor cruise there is, making getting there part of the fun.

Three of the most accessible and popular islands are **Lantau, Cheung Chau,** and **Lamma.** Each offers something different: Lantau is famous for its giant outdoor Buddha—one of Hong Kong's major attractions—and Po Lin Monastery with its vegetarian meals; Cheung Chau, with its beach, boat population, and thriving fishing community, is a popular destination for families and is the best choice for immersion into village life; and Lamma, known for its open-air seafood restaurants, hiking trail, and beaches, is best for getting away from it all.

Ferries depart approximately every hour or so from Hong Kong Island's Central Ferry Piers (also called Outlying Islands Ferry Piers), piers built out into the harbor on reclaimed land less than a 5-minute walk west of the Star Ferry. You can purchase your ticket at the piers just prior to departure or use the magnetic Octopus transportation card, but avoid going on Sunday when the ferries are packed with city folks on family outings. The fares are also slightly higher on Saturday afternoon and Sunday, though they're never very expensive—HK$14 to HK$16 (US$1.80–US$2.05) for ordinary class depending on the destination, HK$25 to HK$31 (US$3.25–US$4) for a deluxe ticket. On weekdays and before noon on Saturday, tickets cost just HK$10 to HK$11 (US$1.30–US$1.35) for ordinary class and HK$17 (US$2.20) for deluxe. If you're headed for Lantau or Cheung Chau, go deluxe class, since this upper-deck ticket entitles you to sit on an open deck out back—a great place to watch the harbor float past when the weather is nice. In addition, deluxe cabins are the only ones that are air-conditioned, a plus when humidity is at its peak. Note that ferries to Lamma have no deluxe class or outside deck.

On Saturday afternoon and Sunday, there is additional infrequent ferry service from Tsim Sha Tsui's Star Ferry concourse to Lantau and Cheung Chau, but it may not offer deluxe class. There is also a quicker hover-ferry service (called "Fast Ferries") to Lantau, Cheung Chau, and Lamma used mostly by commuters, but I personally prefer the slower ferries because the view is better and they have outdoor decks. In any case, by ferry it takes only 20 to 35 minutes to reach Lamma, 55 minutes to reach Cheung Chau, and 40 to 50 minutes to reach Lantau.

For information on ferry schedules and prices, drop by the Hong Kong Tourist Board for a free copy of timetables and prices.

LANTAU

Inhabited since Neolithic times and twice the size of Hong Kong Island, Lantau is Hong Kong's largest island. But while Hong Kong Island has a population of

---

Tips **The Best Seat on Ship**

The best view aboard ferries to the outlying islands is on the left side of the boat, as Central, the Western District, and Hong Kong Island glide past in all their glory.

more than a million, **Lantau** ✦✦✦ has only about 84,000. Much of its population growth has occurred only recently, first with the founding of Discovery Bay, a large, modern, and expensive settlement of condominiums popular with expats, and then with Hong Kong's new airport, which brought with it the creation of a new satellite town at Tung Chung, with a population of more than 25,000. Hong Kong Disneyland, opening at the end of 2005 or beginning of 2006 on reclaimed land just 2km (1½ miles) from Discovery Bay, will also add to the island's population and popularity.

Yet much of Lantau remains mountainous and lush. Country parks make up more than half of the island, with 69km (43 miles) of marked hiking trails. Lantau is an island of high peaks, remote and isolated beaches, small villages, temples, and monasteries. But one of the main draws is its Giant Tian Tan Buddha, the largest seated outdoor Buddha in the world, and to eat a vegetarian meal at the nearby Po Lin Monastery. Because of the ferry and bus rides required to get there and back, allow at least 5 hours for a visit to Lantau.

Ferries, with both ordinary and deluxe class, depart from Central Ferry Pier no. 7 in Central approximately every 2 hours or less between 6:10am and 10:30pm and arrive about 50 minutes later at Silvermine Bay, known as *Mui Wo* in Chinese. There is also more frequent hover-ferry service from the same pier, which gets you there in about 40 minutes. In Mui Wo there is a hotel fronting the bay as well as some restaurants, but otherwise, there isn't much of interest. As soon as you exit the ferry pier, you'll see a bus terminal with buses going to other parts of the island, with departures coinciding with the arrival of the ferries. For the Giant Buddha and Po Lin Monastery, take bus no. 2 bound for Ngong Ping (Po Lin Monastery). The exact bus fare of HK$16 (US$2.05) Monday to Saturday and HK$25 (US$3.25) on Sunday and public holidays is required, so come with lots of change or use the handy Octopus transportation card. The bus hurtles around hair-raising curves and up and down through lush countryside—not for the faint of heart. The duration of the ride from Silvermine Bay to Po Lin Monastery takes about 45 minutes.

If you don't wish to ride the ferry, you can also reach Lantau by taking the Tung Chung MTR Line, which was extended to Lantau to serve staff working and living near the new airport. It takes about 35 minutes to ride from Hong Kong Station in Central to Tung Chung, the end terminus. In Tung Chung, bus no. 23 reaches Ngong Ping in about 50 minutes (the fare is the same as from Mui Wo) and the ride is no less hair-raising. In 2006, a cable car from Tung Chung will deliver visitors directly to Ngong Ping in just 17 minutes, eliminating the roller-coaster bus ride.

EXPLORING LANTAU

The most famous attractions on Lantau are the **Giant Tian Tan Buddha** and **Po Lin Monastery,** both situated on the plateau of Ngong Ping at an elevation of 738m (2,460 ft.). The Buddha is so huge that you'll have your first glimpses of it en route on the bus. More than 30m (100 ft.) tall and weighing 250 tons, it's the world's largest seated outdoor bronze Buddha and can be seen as far away as Macau (or so it is claimed) on clear days. There are 260-some steps leading up to the Buddha itself, but first you should stop at the ticket office at the bottom of the steps to purchase a meal ticket, since the other reason people come to Po Lin is to eat. The monastery is famous for its vegetarian lunches, served in a big dining hall (see "Where to Dine," below). Your meal ticket, which specifies the time for your communal meal, doubles as your admission ticket to a small museum inside the base of the statue, but there isn't much to see here.

Rather, the best part is the view of the surrounding countryside from the statue's platform, which is free. The Giant Buddha is open daily from 10am to 6pm.

From the statue, walk a couple minutes to the colorful Po Lin Monastery, largest and best known of the dozens of Buddhist monasteries on Lantau. Po Lin (which means "precious lotus") was first established more than 100 years ago by reclusive monks; the present buildings date from 1921 and 1970. The ornate main temple houses three magnificent bronze statues of Buddha, representing the past, present, and future; it also has a brightly painted vermilion interior with dragons and other Chinese mythical figures on the ceiling. You'll probably want to spend about a half hour wandering through the grounds here. If you're truly adventurous or energetic, you can climb to the top of nearby Lantau Peak, the second-tallest peak in Hong Kong (1,000m/3,000 ft.); plan on 3 hours for the hike up and back.

From Po Lin, you can reboard the bus that will take you back to Mui Wo (Silvermine Bay), with departures once or twice an hour, or Tung Chung, with departures twice or thrice an hour (I always check departure times upon arrival at Po Lin, so I don't have to sit around after a just-missed bus). Energetic travelers may even opt to hike down to Tung Chung in about 3 hours, along a route covered in the free HKTB brochure *Hong Kong Walks.*

Where to Dine

Po Lin Monastery ★★ VEGETARIAN   Po Lin Monastery, offering fixed-price vegetarian meals, is the most famous place to eat on the island. Buy your lunch ticket from the counter at the base of the Giant Buddha or at the monastery itself; your ticket is for a specific time, at an assigned table. Two different meals of soup, vegetarian dishes, and rice are available: the ordinary, HK$55 (US$7.15) meal is served in an unadorned dining hall and the procedure is rather unceremonious, with huge dishes of vegetables, rice, and soup brought to communal tables. Grab a plastic bowl and chopsticks and help yourself. Packed with Chinese families, the dining hall here is certainly colorful. The HK$98 (US$13) "Deluxe" meal is served in a smaller adjacent "VIP Room" and is popular mostly with foreign visitors. Meals here are served on china plates, and the food is a notch above the cheaper meal. Both, however, are good and plentiful. There's also a snack menu available at an open-air counter at the monastery; it consists of fried noodles and bean curd; skip it.

Ngong Ping. ✆ 852/2985 5248. Fixed-price lunch HK$55 or HK$98 (US$7.15 or US$13). No credit cards. Daily 11:30am–4:30pm.

CHEUNG CHAU

If you have only 3 or 4 hours to spare and don't want to worry about catching buses and finding your way around, Cheung Chau is your best bet. In fact, if I were forced to select only one island to show visiting friends on a limited time schedule, Cheung Chau would be it. Only 12km (7½ miles) from Hong Kong Island, it's a 55-minute ride by ordinary ferry ride from outlying-ferry pier no. 6 in Central, with ferries leaving approximately every hour and offering scenic harbor views from the outdoor deluxe-class deck. Even quicker are the fast ferries, also departing every hour and making the trip in 30 minutes. Despite its name (Cheung Chau means "Long Island"), Cheung Chau is a tiny, dumbbell-shaped island (only 2.5 sq. km/1 sq. mile), with more than 25,000 residents concentrated in a thriving fishing village. There are no cars on the island, making it a delightful place for walking around and exploring rural village life. The

Cheung Chau

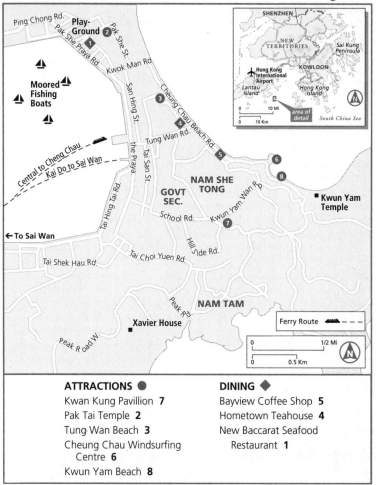

ATTRACTIONS ●
Kwan Kung Pavillion **7**
Pak Tai Temple **2**
Tung Wan Beach **3**
Cheung Chau Windsurfing
    Centre **6**
Kwun Yam Beach **8**

DINING ◆
Bayview Coffee Shop **5**
Hometown Teahouse **4**
New Baccarat Seafood
    Restaurant **1**

island is especially popular with Chinese families for its rental bicycles and beach, but my favorite thing to do here is to walk the tiny, narrow lanes of Cheung Chau village. Be sure to pick up the free HKTB brochure *Hong Kong Walks,* which includes a stroll on Cheung Chau and a map.

Inhabited for at least 2,500 years by fisher folk and serving as a haven for smugglers and pirates until the 1920s, Cheung Chau still supports a small population of fishing families, with fishing and tourism the island's main industry. Junks are built on Cheung Chau after a design hardly changed through the centuries, entirely from memory and without the aid of blueprints. The waterfront where the ferry lands, known as the Praya, buzzes with activity as vendors sell fish, lobster, and vegetables. The village itself is a fascinating warren of narrow alleyways, food stalls, open markets, and shops selling everything from medicinal herbs and incense to dried fish, rice, haircuts, and—a reflection of the island's tourist trade—sun hats, sunglasses, and beach toys.

EXPLORING CHEUNG CHAU

Although there seem to be fewer and fewer junks in Cheung Chau's harbor each time I visit, a small group of fishermen and their families still live on their junks here. I like this harbor more than Aberdeen because boats are moored right next to the waterfront, and I find it amazing how many families keep dogs aboard their boats (not to mention radar systems and computers). If you wish, you might consider taking a *kai do,* a water taxi, past the junks and fishing boats to Sai Wan—it shouldn't cost more than HK$5 (US65¢) for the 5-minute ride and may even be cheaper than that; board it at the public pier next to the ferry pier. At Sai Wan, a tiny settlement with nary a tourist shop in sight, there's a temple dedicated to **Tin Hau,** goddess of the sea and protectress of fisher folk. There's also Cheung Po Tsai Cave, reportedly a hideout of a 19th-century pirate. Steep, narrow, low, and dark, it should be skipped unless you're prepared to bring a flashlight or buy one from a vendor, and you're willing to inch your way through the tunnel with a queue of other tourists, exiting by climbing up a smooth-surfaced cliff. The cave is definitely not for the fainthearted, claustrophobic, or generously proportioned, and in my opinion it's just not worth it.

At any rate, from San Wai, you can walk back to Cheung Chau village in less than 15 minutes by taking the road that hugs the harbor. Alternatively, you can take a longer, 45-minute hike back to the village via Peak Road, one of the main roads on the island, which runs along the crest of a lushly wooded hill with good vistas of the sea. Along the way, you'll pass a huge Chinese cemetery on a hillside (blessed with excellent *feng shui*) and the Kwan Kung Pavilion, dedicated to the god of war and righteousness. As for seeing Cheung Chau village, begin with a stroll along the **Praya**—the waterfront promenade right in front of the ferry pier. It's a good place from which to observe the many junks and fishing boats in the harbor. To the right as you leave the ferry pier are several open-air restaurants (and, as a sign of the times, a new McDonald's), as well as the unimaginative-looking Regional Council Cheung Chau Complex, which houses a library, post office, and city market (open daily 6am–8pm) with more than 200 stalls that sell everything from fresh seafood to vegetables.

On the opposite end of the Praya (to the left as you leave the ferry) are more waterfront restaurants, shops with bicycles to rent, and souvenir shops. After about a 3-minute walk, take a right at the playground onto Pak She Fourth, at the end of which is the **Pak Tai Temple,** guarded by two stone lions. Built in 1783, it's dedicated to the "Supreme Emperor of the Dark Heaven," long worshipped as a Taoist god of the sea. Inside is an iron sword measuring almost 1.5m (5 ft.) in length that was found by local fishermen and thought to be 1,000 years old, as well as a sedan that is used to carry the statue of Pak Tai around the village during festivals. Before the altar are also statues of two formidable generals, Thousand Miles Eye and Favourable Wind Ear, who together can hear and see anything. Beside the temple, on a shaded terrace, old villagers are almost always engaged in games of mahjong.

The most important festival here is the Bun Festival, held in late April or May. It originated a century ago following a terrible plague, and is famous throughout Hong Kong. It features 15m-tall (50-ft.) towers of buns (yes, they're edible!), but the biggest attraction is the parade of children who "float" through the streets suspended by hidden wires and rods.

Leaving the Pak Tai Temple, take a left onto Pak She Street, which later becomes San Hing Street. As you walk back to the center of the village, you'll pass open-fronted shops that sell incense, paper funeral objects such as cars (cremated with the deceased to accompany them to the next life), medicinal herbs, lotus-seed cakes, pungent shrimp paste, jade, rattan, cheap toys, and other local goods, vegetables, and meat. You'll also pass people's homes with the living rooms that hold the family altar opening onto the street. This is the traditional Chinese home, with the family business and communal rooms on the ground floor and the bedrooms up above. All day long you can hear people playing mahjong.

At the end of San Hing Street, at a square, take a left to Tung Wan Road, which cuts across the thinnest part of the island from the Praya with its ferry to Tung Wan Beach. Here, just past the square, is a gnarled old banyan tree, which is considered to be the dwelling place of the spirit of health and fertility. At the end of Tung Wan Road is **Tung Wan Beach,** the most popular beach on the island, with lifeguards, and shark nets. Nearby, past the playground and War-wick Hotel, is another, smaller public beach, **Kwun Yam Beach,** and the **Cheung Chau Windsurfing Centre** (✆ 852/2981 8316), with a pleasant outdoor cafe and rental windsurfing boards ranging from HK$110 to HK$220 (US$14–US$28), depending on the size, for 2 hours. Unfortunately, views from both beaches are marred by views of the Lamma power plant and Hong Kong Island's high-rises.

From Tung Wan Beach, it's only a few minutes' walk via Tung Wan Road back to the Praya and ferry pier.

WHERE TO DINE
Bayview Coffee Shop INTERNATIONAL   The Warwick Hotel, located on the beach, is a good choice for a simple lunch. Its casual coffee shop is an enclosed terrace with a good view of the beach and offers a limited menu of noo-dle and rice dishes, sandwiches, dim sum, and Chinese food like sweet and sour garoupa.

In the Warwick Hotel, Tung Wan Beach. ✆ 852/2981 0081. Sandwiches and main dishes HK$30–HK$120 (US$3.90–US$16). AE, DC, MC, V. Daily 11:30am–2:30pm. Take Tung Wan Rd. to Tung Wan Beach, about a 7-min. walk from the ferry pier.

Hometown Teahouse TEA/SUSHI   This is a quirky teahouse, a laid-back and pleasant island oasis on the village's main passageway between the Praya and Tung Wan Beach. It's owned and managed by a Japanese woman, Takahiko-san, and her artist husband. Only a few items—sushi rolls with crab or sausage and herbal teas like ganoderma tea (which is thought to boost energy levels)—are available at the "counter," which is nothing more than an open window of a small house. Most people order the sushi set, which comes with tea, sushi, and a cookie. The teahouse itself is an outdoor terrace with a few tables and chairs.

12 Tung Wan Rd. ✆ 852/2981 5038. Rolled sushi HK$9–HK$16 (US$1.15–US$2.10); sushi set HK$20 (US$2.60). No credit cards. Daily noon–midnight.

New Baccarat Seafood Restaurant ✿ CANTONESE   On the Praya, the last of many open-air restaurants now crowding the waterfront but also one of the oldest (located near the Pak Tai Temple on the corner of Pak She St. beside a playground), this simple spot offers outdoor seating under a canopy with a view of the harbor. Owned by a fishing family and sporting tanks of live sea crea-tures, it specializes in fresh seafood, including crab, lobster, squid, scallop, prawn, shrimp, and various other fish.

9A Pak She Praya St. ✆ 852/2981 0606. Main dishes HK$40–HK$100 (US$5.20–US$13). V. Daily 11am–10:30pm. Turn left from the ferry and walk along the Praya about 4 min.

LAMMA

Lamma is the island to visit if you want to escape city life, do some pleasant hiking, swim, or dine alfresco on fresh seafood with views of a peaceful waterfront. The closest of the outlying islands, only 20 to 35 minutes by ordinary and fast ferry from outlying-ferry pier no. 4 in Central, Lamma is Hong Kong's third-largest island, has a population of about 12,000, and is still largely undeveloped. There are no cars on the island, and a 1½-hour hiking trail connects Lamma's two main villages—Yung Shue Wan and Sok Kwu Wan—both served by ferries from Hong Kong Island. Yung Shue Wan, with a large and youthful foreign population, has a decidedly bohemian laid-back atmosphere, while much smaller Sok Kwu Wan is popular for its open-air seafood restaurants. If it's summer, don't forget to bring your bathing suit, since there are several beaches along the trails. You'd be smart, too, to buy bottled water from one of the many stores in either Sok Kwu Wan or Yung Shue Wan before setting out on the trail. In addition, try to avoid Sundays, when the trail is crowded with families, seniors walking dogs, and even bicycles. For a map of the island, pick up the free HKTB brochure *Hong Kong Walks*.

EXPLORING LAMMA

Although ferries from Central will deposit you at either Yung Shue Wan or Sok Kwu Wan, I personally prefer to land at Sok Kwu Wan for a light seafood meal, hike 20 minutes to a nearby beach, and then continue onward to Yung Shue Wan for drinks or dinner before heading back to Central. The advantage of this route is that ferry service is more frequent from Yung Shue Wan, which means you're not constricted to a time schedule. However, you might choose to hike the trail in reverse from my description below. If you do, remember that ferries to and from Sok Kwu Wan are less frequent, so you'll have to time your arrival and departure with precision. The hike between the two villages along a marked, concrete footpath takes about 1½ hours and is a true delight, with great views of the surrounding sea and, in the distance, even Ocean Park and Aberdeen on Hong Kong Island.

Tiny **Sok Kwu Wan** is famous for its open-air seafood restaurants and is a popular destination for those lucky enough to own pleasure boats. These restaurants are aligned along the small waterfront, extended over the water on stilts, and shaded by canopies; they offer views of the harbor (and, unfortunately, of denuded hills belonging to a defunct cement factory across the harbor; there is talk of eventual landscaping, but only time will tell). All restaurants here have tanks of fresh seafood from which you can choose your own meal. Fresh seafood is available by the *catty* (one catty is about 1⅓ lb.). Prices for a catty vary each day, depending on supply and demand. One catty of prawns will cost approximately HK$150 to HK$175 (US$20–US$23), with half a catty usually enough for two people. A catty of lobster will cost about HK$250 to HK$280 (US$33–US$36), though small lobsters for one person are available for about HK$100 (US$13). If you go all out, meals here will average about HK$250 (US$33) a person.

Incidentally, as you dine, you'll notice fish-breeding rafts in the harbor, some also supporting family homes. According to one restaurant manager, however, very little fishing is still done nowadays in local waters because of contamination. The manager assured me that only imported fish is served in Sok Kwu Wan's restaurants and that locally caught or bred fish is consumed only by local Chinese. Another restaurant owner, however, proudly told me that his fish came from the harbor fish farm. The restaurant I recommend in Sok Kwu Wan serves only imported fish.

Turning right out of the ferry pier and walking past the many seafood restaurants of Sok Kwu Wan, you will soon come to a small, 150-year-old Tin Hau temple on the edge of town. Continue on the concrete path that hugs the harbor about 10 minutes to Lo So Shing School, where, if you wish to swim, you can turn left and follow the dirt path another 10 minutes to **Lo So Shing Beach.** Prettily situated in a small bay, this is the island's nicest and least crowded beach, offering changing rooms and lifeguards on duty from April to October daily from 9am to 6pm.

Otherwise, continuing on the main pathway takes you through lush and verdant valleys, with butterflies flitting across the path and roosters crowing from the distance, before ascending to a hillside pavilion overlooking the scandalous cement factory. From this point, the path climbs higher onto barren and windswept hills. About halfway along the trail, on the top of a peak, is a pagoda where you can take a rest and enjoy the view of the South China Sea. After that, the barren hills give way to valleys and trees and then **Hung Shing Yeh Beach,** which also has changing facilities, showers, toilets, and lifeguards on duty in the summer. If it's hot, it may be hard to resist joining the throngs of families and taking another dip in the water. Regrettably, however, the beach is overshadowed by an unsightly power station.

The hiking path resumes on the other side of the beach. In less than 20 minutes, you'll reach **Yung Shue Wan,** but it takes a while to walk past a new development before reaching Yung Shue Wan Main Street and the center of town. Yung Shue Wan, which translates as "Banyan Tree Bay," is Lamma's main town. It used to be small and undeveloped, with old houses and small garden plots, but new apartment buildings and shops have sprung up on its hillsides in the past decade. A sizable population of expatriates has settled here, and the town is unfortunately blighted by that unsightly power station. What's more, small motorized wagons carrying building supplies zip around as if they can't get to construction sites soon enough. Compared to how the village looked in the early 1980s, I can barely recognize the place. Still, the village has a laid-back, slow-paced tropical-island atmosphere, making it a pleasant place to while away an hour or more at a local restaurant, bar, or a shop selling Southeast Asian artifacts.

WHERE TO DINE

Bookworm Café ★★ *(Finds)* VEGETARIAN   Lined with shelves of used books and serving as an informal resource and meeting center for Yung Shue Wan's expat residents, and with occasional jam sessions, video nights, and other happenings, this casual restaurant is a great alternative to seafood. The interesting menu includes sandwiches, veggie and tofu burgers, and salads like the "veg-out" salad plate with roasted eggplant, avocado, feta cheese, and black olives on a bed of mixed greens and herbs with Lebanese bread. There are also various teas and fresh juices. Dining is either in a small, air-conditioned room or across the street on an open terrace.

79 Yung Shue Wan Main St., Yung Shue Wan. © 852/2982 4838. Main dishes HK$35–HK$80 (US$4.55–US$10). MC, V. Mon–Fri 10am–9pm; Sat and holidays 9am–10pm; Sun 9am–9pm.

Concerto Inn *(Kids)* WESTERN/CHINESE/SNACKS   Located right on Hung Shing Yeh Beach, about a 30-minute walk from the ferry pier in Yung Shue Wan, this clean, low-key establishment offers both accommodations and a pleasant cafe, with outdoor, covered seating beside a running fountain and views of the beach. Its menu is limited, but the restaurant makes a comfortable stop along the hiking trail for a hamburger, sandwich, spaghetti, satays, rice and noo-dle dishes, ice cream, juice, or beer. A toddlers' play area in back makes for a good diversion for the little ones, especially on crowded days when service can be a bit slow.

Hung Shing Yeh Beach, Yung Shue Wan. © **852/2982 1668.** Main dishes HK$48–HK$57 (US$6.25–US$7.40). AE, DC, MC, V. Daily 8am–9:30pm.

Man Fung Restaurant ⚐ CANTONESE/SEAFOOD

If you start your hike at Sok Kwu Wan and end up hungry on this side of the island, this restaurant is my number-one choice for a hearty meal. Located just a minute's walk from the ferry pier, it offers pleasant outdoor seating right by the water with a view of the harbor and town. Specialties are its fresh seafood straight from the tank, includ-ing lobster served with a cheese sauce; fried prawns with garlic and butter; steamed crab with chili; and various other fish, scallop, and seafood dishes avail-able at market price (inquire first before ordering). Otherwise, the menu lists pork, beef, chicken, and pigeon dishes, as well as vegetarian dishes such as deep-fried bean curd with chili, fried broccoli and baby corn with garlic, sweet-and-sour bean curd, and braised eggplant in a hot pot. There are also pitchers of Carlsberg draft beer as well as wine from France and Portugal.

5 Yung Shue Wan Main St., Yung Shue Wan. © **852/2982 0719.** Main dishes HK$50–HK$70 (US$6.50–US$9.10). AE, MC, V. Daily 11am–10pm.

Rainbow Seafood Restaurant ⚐⚐ CANTONESE/SEAFOOD

This is the largest open-air restaurant on Sok Kwu Wan's waterfront, easily recogniza-ble by its whir of ceiling fans and red lanterns. Farther from the pier (and the cement factory across the harbor) than many other restaurants, it therefore offers a better view of the harbor and boat rafts (don't confuse it with its smaller branch just beside the ferry pier, which does nevertheless have the added con-venience of an air-conditioned bar). A nice touch is the water sprayed over its canopy to cool the restaurant on hot summer days. A member of the Hong Kong Tourist Board and serving only imported fish from the South China Sea, it offers an English menu with photographs of its main dishes, including a vari-ety of fresh seafood dishes, with prices for lobster, prawn, and fish clearly marked. Among its specialties are steamed garoupa, lobster available several ways (fried lobster with a cheese sauce is most popular), and fried crab with gin-ger and scallions. There are two fixed-priced feasts for two persons or more, costing HK$320 and HK$380 (US$42 and US$49) per person. Incidentally, this restaurant also offers free ferry service to and from Queen's Pier (in Cen-tral, near Star Ferry) and from Kowloon Public Pier in Tsim Sha Tsui; be sure to call first and make a reservation.

17 1st St., Sok Kwu Wan waterfront. © **852/2982 8100.** www.rainbowrest.com.hk (click the E in the lower left of the screen for English). Seafood dishes HK$60–HK$160 (US$7.80–US$21). AE, DC, MC, V. Daily 10am–10pm.

A LOCAL BAR

The Island Bar   Located next to Man Fung Restaurant on the waterfront, just a minute's walk from the ferry pier, this is a longtime bar and local *gwailo* (foreign) hangout, popular with a mostly middle-aged crowd. Owned by expats living in Yung Shue Wan, it's a comfortable place to wait for the next ferry, play darts, and meet the locals. Happy hour is from 6 to 8pm daily.

6 Yung Shue Wan Main St., Yung Shue Wan. © **852/2982 1376.** Mon–Fri 6pm–2am; Sat–Sun and holidays noon–2am.

3 China

Hong Kong is a major gateway to China. Many first-time visitors to the mainland join an organized tour for excursions to the mainland, though it's certainly easy enough to do so on your own. Avid shoppers with a sense of adventure will want to make a day trip across the border to Shenzhen a priority, where fake designer watches and handbags are sold for a song.

ORGANIZED TOURS

Virtually all hotels in Hong Kong work with tour agencies that offer a variety of excursions to China, ranging from 1-day trips to Guangzhou or Shenzhen to 11-day trips that include Guangzhou, Beijing, and other major destinations. Most of these trips follow identical itineraries at similar prices. For example, I joined a 1-day guided tour of Shenzhen (Shekou) and Guangzhou. In Shenzhen, we were shown a small, musty museum containing three terra-cotta figures taken from the tomb of China's first emperor near the city of Xi'an; and in Guangzhou, a local market; an unenlightened zoo with cramped, littered cages and a couple of panda bears; Six Banyan Temple; and the outside of a concert hall built in 1931 as a memorial to Sun Yat-sen (on weekdays, tours also take in a local kindergarten). What I most enjoyed about the trip, offered by Splendid Tours for HK$1,230 (US$160) per person, was the journey by hover ferry to Shenzhen, the bus trip to Guangzhou, and the trip back by KCR railway, as these allowed good vistas of the surrounding countryside. The so-called attractions, however, were not worth seeing. In my opinion, you (and your pocketbook) are better off making the journey on your own, since the attractions are dismal. What I really enjoyed was the ride through the countryside for the contrast it provides with Hong Kong, especially in rural Guangdong Province with its duck and fish farms, rice fields and banana groves, and simple living conditions.

Companies offering organized trips into China (none of them have 1-day trips just for shopping) include **Splendid Tours** (© **852/2316 2151;** www.splendidtours.com), **Gray Line Tours** (© **852/2368 7111;** www.grayline.com.hk), and **China Travel Service** (see "Visas," below), the official travel agency of the People's Republic of China. Unsurprisingly, CTS offers the most extensive list of tours, with trips that include Beijing, Guilin, Shanghai, Xi'an, and other major cities. CTS's 11-day trip, for example, includes train and plane travel from Hong Kong to Guangzhou, Guilin, Beijing, Xian, and Shanghai before returning to Hong Kong. The cost of this trip runs HK$13,660 to HK$14,230 (US$1,774–US$1,848), depending on the season.

VISAS

If you join an organized tour, your visa for China will be taken care of by the tour agency. Tour prices include the price of tour group visas (which cost less than individual visas). You can book tours up to the day before departure if there's room, but most charge more if you book later than 11:30am the day before departure, since the company will have to apply for an individual rush visa rather than submitting your passport along with the others for a group visa. But if you wish to visit China on your own, you'll need to obtain a visa yourself. Your hotel or a travel agency may be able to arrange this for you. Having your hotel's concierge or tour desk do the work certainly saves time, but prices can be high. Travel agencies are cheaper, but you'll have to first apply and then return to pick up the visa. You can also save money by planning ahead, as rush orders for visas add to the price.

One of the most popular places to apply for a visa is at a **China Travel Service (CTS),** the official travel agency of the People's Republic of China. There are several branches in Hong Kong, including 78 Connaught Rd. Central, Central District (℄ **852/2853 3533;** MTR: Central); 62 Sai Yee St., Mong Kok (℄ **852/ 2789 5970;** MTR: Mong Kok); and 27–33 Nathan Rd., Tsim Sha Tsui (℄ **852/ 2315 7188;** MTR: Tsim Sha Tsui), which is the most convenient with the most convenient hours: It's open Monday to Friday from 9am to 7pm, Saturday from 9am to 5pm, and Sunday and holidays from 9am to 12:30pm and 2 to 5pm.

To fill out an application for your visa, you will need your passport (with an expiration date of not less than 6 months) and one passport photograph (you can have your portrait taken here for HK$35/US$4.55; otherwise, there's a portrait machine at the nearby YMCA Salisbury on Salisbury Rd., as well as the Tsim Sha Tsui MTR station). It's best to make your visa application at least 3 business days prior to departure; cost of a single-entry visa (valid for 30 days) is HK$210 (US$27). However, if you're in a hurry, you can obtain a visa more quickly by paying more: For HK$360 (US$47), your visa will be processed and available for pickup by 2pm the next day; for HK$480 (US$62), visa applications made before noon will be available by 5:30pm the same day. The cost for a visa at CTS is better than most places (especially hotel tour desks). Note, however, that at the time of going to press, Americans applying for visas were required to pay an extra HK$250 (US$32) to the fees above. While all the visa officials I talked to agreed that it was a retaliatory measure, reasons for the retaliation differed, ranging from U.S. criticism of human rights in China to the fingerprinting of Chinese entering the U.S.

In addition to CTS, another convenient (and even cheaper!) travel agency is **Shoestring Travel,** on the fourth floor of Alpha House on the corner of Peking and Nathan roads, right next to CTS (℄ **852/2723 2306**). Open Monday to Friday from 8am to 7pm and Saturday, Sunday, and holidays from 8am to 6pm, it charges HK$180 (US$23) for a single-entry visa if you can wait 2 business days, HK$400 (US$52) if you need it the same day. Again, Americans pay extra.

SHENZHEN

If you're planning a 1-day trip to China, your destination will be either Shenzhen or Guangzhou (see below). **Shenzhen,** located across the Hong Kong–China border, was established in the 1980s as one of China's first Special Economic Zones. Today, this experiment with capitalism looks almost like Hong Kong with its million people, concrete high-rises, traffic, industries, and relative prosperity. In recent years, it has become a shopping mecca for day-trippers, who come for fake designer handbags, watches, and other goods at prices much cheaper than in Hong Kong. However, the HK$460 (US$60) minimum Americans now pay for a single-entry visa makes shopping Shenzhen less of a bargain.

You can travel to Shenzhen via the KCR Kowloon-Canton railway, with trains departing Kowloon KCR Railway Station in Tsim Sha Tsui East every 3 to 8 minutes between 5:30am and 11pm. The trip from Tsim Sha Tsui East to Lo Wu, the border crossing (open daily 6:30am–midnight), takes about 40 minutes. Cost of the KCR from Hung Hom to Lo Wu is HK$33 (US$4.30) for ordinary class and HK$66 (US$8.55) for first class. Prices are slightly cheaper if you have an Octopus card, but if you're traveling first class, you'll have to swipe your card once again on the train platform at the First Class Processor located in front of the first-class compartment. The Lo Wu Border Control is one of the busiest border crossings in the world. Avoid traveling through it on weekends and holidays, if possible, when crowds of day-trippers can make the wait to cross over very long.

After going through Customs, you can walk across the border into Shenzhen. Just across the border is a huge shopping mall called Luohu Commercial City, with five floors of tiny shops selling a bewildering amount of inexpensively priced handbags, shoes, watches; jewelry; clothing (including Chinese padded jackets); and bolts of cloth. As for imitation designer bags and pirated DVDs, Chinese officials have cracked down on counterfeit goods (half the fake goods seized by US Customs agents in 2002 came from China, which should give would-be purchasers pause as well). That is not to say that such goods are unavailable. When I agreed, at a shopkeeper's insistence, to look at imitation handbags, I was whisked to a concealed backroom closet with rows and rows of bags. In a tiny electronics shop, the owner closed all his doors and sent his assistant scurrying up a concealed hole in the drop ceiling to retrieve pirated DVDs (don't bother buying DVDs—most of the time they aren't fully copied or they don't work). I can't believe that police, who regularly patrol Luohu Commercial City, are clueless, but the game seems to satisfy everyone. There are also shops offering combination manicures and pedicures for as little as HK$30 (US$3.90), but lack of hygienic conditions may discourage most tourists from giving them a whirl. In any case, bargaining is the name of the game, and since there are no ATMs around, be sure to bring plenty of HK dollars. You should also guard your belongings against pickpockets. Shops are open daily from 10am to 10pm.

As for tourist attractions, they're limited to Splendid China, a theme park with more than 80 miniatures of China's most historic buildings, sites, and scenic wonders, including the Great Wall and the Forbidden City; Window of the World, which re-creates famous buildings, monuments, and scenic spots from around the world, including the Taj Mahal, Eiffel Tower, and Grand Canyon; and China Folk Cultures Villages, which presents the art and cultures of China's various ethnic groups with life-size villages and people dressed in native dress. All three are clustered together about 13km (8 miles) west of the border crossing and are included in several 1-day tours offered by tour companies listed above. Most visitors to Shenzhen, however, come for the shopping.

FARTHER AFIELD

Farther afield is **Guangzhou (Canton),** capital of Guangdong Province with a population of 7.5 million. Guangzhou has a famous open-air market, Qingping Market, which has a somewhat lurid reputation for the exotic animals sold there for food, but it also has antiques, herbs, flowers, and a bird market. Otherwise, the sights are confined to a Buddhist temple and the monuments and statues in the city's largest park, Yuexiu Yuan, that include a memorial to Sun Yat-sen. You can reach Guangzhou by KCR railway in about 2 hours; cost of this trip is HK$230 (US$30) for "premium" class, HK$190 (US$25) for first class, and HK$180 (US$23) for second class. At last check, through-train service to Guangzhou departed Kowloon KCR Railway Station in Hung Hom at 8:25, 9:25, and 11:05am and 12:10, 1:25, 2:30, 4:45, and 6:15pm.

Be forewarned, however, that since tourist attractions in Shenzhen and Guangzhou are extremely limited, if you're really interested in a trip to China, you should plan on traveling to Shanghai, Beijing, and beyond. For more information on China, see *Frommer's China.*

11

Macau

Hanging from China's gigantic underbelly on its southeastern coast, Macau covers all of 27 sq. km (almost 11 sq. miles). About 64km (40 miles) west of Hong Kong across the Pearl River Estuary, it served as Portugal's last holdout in Asia until 1999, when it was handed back to China. Portugal's other former Asian strongholds, Goa and Malacca, had long before been claimed by neighboring powers.

In 1993 the *Guinness Book of World Records* declared Macau the most densely populated territory in the world, with more than 69,000 people per square mile. Today, due to a vigorous policy of land reclamation that has more than doubled its size over the last few decades, figures hover around 47,130 residents per square mile, admittedly still one of the highest densities in the world. Yet because of its diminutive size, Macau is more easily navigated compared with Hong Kong. And with its mixture of Portuguese and Chinese elements, Macau feels different from Hong Kong, too, different from China—different from anywhere else. Maybe it's the jumble of Chinese signs and stores mixed in with freshly painted colonial-style buildings, or the Buddhist and Taoist temples alongside Catholic churches. Maybe it's because people smile here more readily than they do in Hong Kong, seem more relaxed, and friendlier. It's an attractive mix—Portuguese flair blended with Chinese practicality.

With its unique mixture of cultures, Macau makes an interesting day trip or overnight stay if you want to get away from the bustle of Hong Kong

after a business trip or strenuous traveling itinerary. Consisting of a small peninsula and two tiny islands connected to the mainland by bridges, it's the ideal place to relax, and although Macau's Las Vegas–style casinos are undoubtedly a major attraction (especially for Chinese), there are also beaches, fortresses, churches, temples, gardens, and excellent museums to explore. What's more, although prices have risen over the years, Macau's hotels are still cheaper than their counterparts in Hong Kong—you can bask in luxury in Macau for a fraction of what you'd pay in the former British colony; and as a duty-free port, Macau has also become something of a shopping mecca. And finally, Macanese cuisine, unique to Macau and combining ingredients from former Portuguese trading ports from around the world, is both inexpensive and delicious, especially when accompanied with Portuguese wine. If you're looking for a vacation from your vacation, I heartily recommend Macau.

Macau today is experiencing something of a revival with the lure of its resort hotels, spanking-new boutiques and restaurants, top-class casinos, and increased transportation service both local and international. In fact, Macau is changing so rapidly that old-timers are right when they complain that the place isn't what it used to be—it's *more* than it used to be, with land reclamation and new construction dramatically altering the city's skyline in just 10 short years, and there seems to be no end in sight. The small downtown, built in the era of pedicabs with its narrow lanes, is ill-equipped to deal with Macau's ever-increasing traffic. Indeed, city planners seem so intent on expansion, I fear that much of Macau's unique architectural legacy and charm will be lost in an ever-growing concrete jungle.

Even Macau's Portuguese legacy has been under threat since the handover. The number of Portuguese remaining in Macau has fallen from 4,000 in the mid-1990s to about 1,000 residents today. There are approximately 20,000 Macanese, of mixed Chinese and Portuguese heritage. Although Portuguese was the only official language until as late as 1991, 96% of Macau's 455,000 residents are Chinese (half of whom were born in China), which means that you hardly ever hear Portuguese spoken. Though it remains an official language, Portuguese is in danger of losing ground outside official circles, as English and Putonghua (Mandarin) become the languages of choice for business and tourism.

Still, there have been many positive developments. About 15 years ago, Macau's downtown was crumbling and neglected, and there were few attractions beyond its casinos and a couple of ruined forts and churches. In the 1990s, however, the small downtown underwent a major renovation, with the restoration of its main plaza and its Mediterranean-influenced, colonial-era buildings with their arched, shuttered windows. In addition, the opening of several excellent, special-interest museums and attractions greatly enhanced Macau's tourist circuit. Increased tourism—particularly from mainland China—has brought increased revenue, benefiting the local economy. Gambling in particular is a mainstay of Macau's economy, accounting for half the government's revenue. In other words, there's something for everyone here—beaches, churches, museums, attractions, and nightlife—all in a setting found nowhere else in the world.

1 Frommer's Favorite Macau Experiences

- **Following the Mosaic Pathway to St. Paul's Church:** From Largo do Senado, Macau's main, colonial-era square, follow the wavy-patterned mosaic tiles through the old city uphill to the ruins of St. Paul's Church (p. 278), Macau's most photographed facade.
- **Dining on Local Macanese and Portuguese Specialties:** African chicken, spicy prawns, sole, and codfish are just some of the culinary treats for the visitor to Macau, all available at very reasonable prices. Portuguese wine, the perfect accompaniment to both Macanese and Portuguese food, is also a bargain. See the "Where to Dine" section, later in this chapter, for more information.
- **Splurging for a Room at a Resort Hotel:** After the traffic and crowds of Hong Kong, there's nothing more relaxing than gazing at the sea from your hotel room, sunning at an outdoor pool surrounded by greenery, and feeling tension and aches melt away under the expert care of a masseuse. Macau has three resort hotels with extensive spa and fitness facilities. See the "Where to Stay" section, later in this chapter, for more information.
- **Learning About Macau's History at the Museum of Macau:** Macau's history museum (p. 279) is a delight, built into the ruins of a fortress and highlighting not only the history of Macau but also unique Macanese traditions, culture, architecture, and cuisine.
- **Visiting Lou Lim Iok Garden Early in the Morning:** Get to this Chinese garden (p. 282) early in the morning, when you're apt to see the locals going

A Blending of Cultures

Macau was born centuries before Hong Kong was even conceived. Portuguese ships first landed in southern China in 1513; in 1557, Portugal acquired Macau from China. Before long, Macau had achieved a virtual monopoly on trade between China, Japan, and Europe, making the city Portugal's most important trading center in Asia and the greatest port in the East in the early 1600s.

As the only Europeans engaged in trade in Asia, the Portuguese made a fortune acting as middlemen. Every spring, Portuguese ships laden with Indian goods and European crystal and wines sailed out of Goa, anchored in Malacca to trade for spices, stopped in Macau for silk brought down from China, and then traveled on to Nagasaki to trade the silk for silver, swords, and lacquerware. Using the monsoon winds, the ships returned to Macau to trade silver for more silk and porcelain, then sailed back to Goa where the exotic Asian goods were shipped to eager customers in Europe. The complete circuit from Goa and back took several years.

As Macau grew and prospered, it also served as an important base for the attempt to introduce Christianity to China and Japan, becoming a springboard for Jesuit missionaries to China and a refuge for Asian Christians, including Japanese Christians who faced persecution and death at home. Many Portuguese married local Chinese, creating a new community of Macanese (Eurasian) families with a blend of the two cultures. This blending is still evident today in Macanese cuisine and architecture, as well as in the population.

through the motions of tai chi, playing traditional Chinese music, and taking birds for walks in cages.

- **Stopping for Some Culture at the Leal Senado:** Macau's most outstanding example of Portuguese colonial architecture has a gallery where shows are mounted without much advance notice. Stop by (p. 265) and be surprised. Best of all, it's free.
- **Strolling through Macau's Fisherman's Wharf:** Macau's biggest project (p. 286) since the 1999 handover features restaurants, souvenir shops, an amusement park, disco, a playground, a man-made volcano and more, nestled in a village-like setting along the waterfront.
- **Swimming on Colôane Island:** Two public beaches, Cheoc Van and Hac Sa (p. 284), feature lifeguards on duty, dining facilities, and public swimming pools. Afterward, retire for a drink or a Portuguese meal at Fernando's (p. 284), a beach shack on Hac Sa.
- **Trying Your Luck at the Horse and Dog Races:** Admission to the races in Macau is so cheap, it's practically free. And who knows? You could strike gold. These are great places (p. 285) to observe local passions.
- **Observing the Chinese Gambling at the Ornate Floating Casino:** This moored boat (p. 285) is abuzz 24 hours a day with gambling fever. Drop by and observe the Chinese gambling, or try your luck with the slot machines on the upper deck.

Needless to say, because of Macau's obvious prosperity, it attracted jealous attention from other European nations. Dutch invasions were repelled several times in the first decades of the 1600s. In response to the threat of invasion, the Portuguese built a series of forts; some still exist.

In the 1630s, Japan closed its doors to foreign trade, granting a limited admittance only to the Dutch. This was a great blow for Macau, but the coup de grace came in 1841 when the British established their own colony on Hong Kong Island, only 64km (40 miles) away. As Hong Kong's deep natural harbor attracted trading ships, Macau lost its importance as a base for trade and slowly sank into obscurity.

However, Macau gained a new foothold in the world of trade in the 1970s by producing electronics, clothing, toys, and other items for export. At the same time, tourism began to grow, and with the establishment of casinos, Macau attracted a large number of Chinese gamblers from Hong Kong. In recent years, the construction of ever-larger resort hotels and casinos has lured even more leisure tourists, especially since the 1995 opening of Macau's international airport, which made Macau easily accessible for the first time in its history.

On December 20, 1999, Portugal's 442 years of rule came to an end, with Macau's transition from colony to Special Administrative Region of China. Like Hong Kong, Macau is permitted its own internal government and economic system for another 50 years. Tourism has blossomed since the handover, with visitors from Hong Kong and mainland China accounting for almost 90% of Macau's annual 11 million tourists.

- **Watching the Sun Set from Macau Tower:** This 220m-high (732 ft.) Space Needle wannabe (p. 280) looks out of place in tiny Macau, but you can't beat it for its views: 55km (34 miles) on clear days. Come for a drink in its lounge or dinner in its revolving restaurant.
- **People-Watching After Midnight:** After the sun goes down, Macau's nighttime revelers head to the Docks, a string of bars and discos with sidewalk seating. But the action doesn't really start hopping until after midnight.

2 Orientation
ENTRY REQUIREMENTS
Entry procedures into Macau are very simple. If you are American, Canadian, Australian, or New Zealander, you do not need a visa for Macau for stays of up to 30 days—all you need is your passport. Residents of the United Kingdom and Ireland can stay up to 90 days without a visa.

VISITOR INFORMATION
ON THE INTERNET   You can obtain information on Macau on the Internet by visiting the Macau Government Tourist Office's website at **www.macau tourism.gov.mo.**

OVERSEAS   There is no **Macau Government Tourist Office (MTGO)** in the United States. In England, contact MTGO at 1 Battersea Church Rd., London

SW11 3LY (℗ **207/771-7006;** fax 207/771-7181; macau@cibgroup.co.uk). Other worldwide offices include Level 17, Town Hall House, 456 Kent St., Sydney, Australia NSW 2000 (℗ **02-9264-1488;** fax 02-9267-7717; macau@ worldtradetravel.com); and Level 5, Ballantyne House, 101 Customs St. E., P.O. Box 3779, Auckland, New Zealand (℗ **09/308-5206;** fax 09/308-5207; macau@aviationandtourism.co.nz).

IN HONG KONG   Your first stop for information about Macau should be as soon as you arrive in Hong Kong, at the Hong Kong International Airport. In the arrivals lobby, at A06, you'll find the **Macau Government Tourist Office (MTGO)** information counter (℗ **852/2769 7970**), open daily from 9am to 10pm (closed for lunch 1–1:30pm and dinner 6–6:30pm). Stop here for a wealth of printed material about hotels and sightseeing in Macau. In addition, there's another MTGO information bureau at the Macau Ferry Terminal, the departure pier for most jetfoils and other craft bound for Macau. You'll find it on the third-floor Departure Floor, in room 336 of the Shun Tak Centre, 200 Connaught Rd., in Central (℗ **852/2857 2287**). It's open daily from 9am to 1pm and 2:15 to 5:30pm. Be sure to pick up a map of Macau, as well as the tourist tabloid *Macau Travel Talk; Where,* a quarterly with information on cultural activities, sightseeing, shopping, and entertainment; and *What's On,* a leaflet with information on festivals, exhibitions, and events.

IN MACAU   Once in Macau, you'll find a **MGTO** at the Macau Ferry Terminal, located just outside customs and open daily from 9am to 10pm; there is also a MGTO at Macau International Airport, open for all incoming flights. For complete information, however, your best bet is the **main Macau Government Tourist Office,** Largo do Senado, located in the center of town on the main plaza just across from the water fountain; it's open daily from 9am to 6pm. Other tourist information offices are located at St. Paul's Church, open daily from 9am to 1pm and 2:15 to 6pm; at Guia Fort and Lighthouse, open daily from 9am to 1pm and 2:15 to 5:30pm; and the Border Gate (also called Barrier Gate and serving visitors from mainland China), open daily from 9am to 1pm and 2:30 to 6pm. For information by telephone, call the Tourist Hotline at ℗ **853/333000.**

GETTING THERE
BY BOAT   Located only 64km (40 miles) from Hong Kong across the mouth of the Pearl River, Macau is most easily accessible from Hong Kong by high-speed jetfoil, with most departures from the **Macau Ferry Terminal,** located just west of the Central District in the Shun Tak Centre, 200 Connaught Rd., on Hong Kong Island. Situated above the Sheung Wan MTR station, the Shun Tak Centre houses booking offices for all forms of transportation to Macau, as well as the Macau Government Tourist Office (Room 336, on the same floor as boats departing for Macau). On the Kowloon side, limited service is available also from the China Ferry Terminal on Canton Road, Tsim Sha Tsui, where boats also depart for China. The nearest MTR station for this terminal is Tsim Sha Tsui.

The fastest, most convenient way to travel to Macau is via sleek **jetfoils** and **catamarans,** operated by **TurboJET** (℗ **852/2859 3333** in Hong Kong; **853/ 7907039** in Macau; www.turbojet.com.hk). The trip to Macau takes approximately 1 hour. Jetfoils depart from the Macau Ferry Terminal west of Central about every 15 to 30 minutes, 24 hours a day. One-way fares Monday to Friday are HK$243 (US$32) for super class and HK$141 (US$18) for economy class; fares on Saturday, Sunday, and holidays are HK$259 (US$34) in super class and

HK$153 (US$20) in economy. Fares for night service (5:45pm–6am) are HK$274 (US$36) in super class and HK$175 (US$23) in economy. Seniors older than 60 and children younger than 12 receive a HK$15 (US$1.95) discount. Fares from the China Ferry Terminal in Tsim Sha Tsui are slightly cheaper but departures are less frequent.

Note that the Hong Kong government levies a HK$19 (US$2.45) departure tax for those traveling to Macau. Likewise, passengers leaving Macau are charged a departure tax of $20 ptcs (US$2.60). However, there's no need to worry about this, since departure taxes are already included in the price of your ticket. For this reason, tickets for travel from Macau to Hong Kong are $1 ptc (US15¢) more than the ticket prices quoted above, reflecting the departure tax.

If you plan to travel on a weekend or holiday, it's wise to buy round-trip tickets well in advance. Tickets can be purchased at either the Macau Ferry Terminal on Hong Kong Island or the China Ferry Terminal in Kowloon, as well as at all China Travel Service branches in Hong Kong (p. 256) and at the TurboJET Service Counter at Sheung Wan MTR Station, Exit D. You can also book by credit card by calling © 852/2921 6688 in Hong Kong. All tickets are for a specific time and cannot be changed. If, however, you've purchased your ticket in advance and then decide you'd like to leave at an earlier time, head for the special queue for standby passengers available at both Shun Tak Centre and in Macau. There is often a good chance that you can get a seat, except during peak periods.

If you plan to spend only 1 or 2 nights in Macau, consider leaving most of your luggage at your Hong Kong hotel, at the Luggage Services Centre on the ground floor of Shun Tak Centre, or in computer-monitored lockers located at both the Hong Kong Island and Kowloon Macau ferry terminals. Then travel to Macau with only small, hand-carried bags. Otherwise, you could end up paying an extra charge. Passengers traveling on a TurboJET are allowed only one hand-carried bag, not to exceed 9.9kg (22 lb.). One additional piece of luggage may be checked in prior to departure, with charges ranging from HK$20 to HK$40 (US$2.60–US$5.20) depending upon its weight. Additional checked-in luggage will be subject to the carrying capacity of the jetfoil. Baggage must be at the check-in counter, located just before customs, 20 minutes before the jetfoil's departure. Obviously, your life will be easier if you leave heavy luggage in Hong Kong.

If you're arriving at Hong Kong International Airport and wish to travel directly to Macau, you can do so via TurboJET's new Sea Express service (www.turbojetseaexpress.com.hk) without passing through Hong Kong customs and immigration formalities (if you do pass through customs, you will not be allowed to take the Sea Express). After purchasing your Sea Express ticket and producing your baggage identification tag for baggage reclaim at the Air/Sea Transfer Desk (your luggage will be retrieved from baggage claim by a TurboJET employee), you will board a bus for a seven-minute shuttle to the SkyPier, take the TurboJET directly to Macau, and go through customs there. Baggage is limited to 20kg (44 lb.) in economy class and 30kg (66 lb.) in super class, except for passengers from North America, who are allowed two pieces of baggage, with each piece not to exceed 32kg (70 lb.). There are four sailings daily (at 11:50am and 3:30, 6:15, and 9:15pm), with fares costing HK$180 (US$14) for economy class and HK$280 (US$36) for super class.

BY PLANE   Macau's new **International Airport** (© 853/861111; www.macau-airport.gov.mo) opened in November 1995, heralding the birth of Air Macau, the territory's fledgling carrier. The airport is located on reclaimed land on Taipa Island and is conveniently connected to the peninsula by a bridge and bus service. The airport serves flights mainly from China, including Beijing and Shanghai, as well as from several other cities, including Taipei, Singapore, Seoul, Manila, and Bangkok. Departure tax from Macau International Airport is $80 ptcs (US$10) for adults and $50 ptcs (US$6.50) for children for destinations in China. For other destinations, the departure tax is $130 ptcs (US$17) and $80 ptcs (US$10), respectively. Contact your travel agent or the Macau Government Tourist Office for more information.

ARRIVING IN MACAU

Passengers traveling by boat arrive at the Macau Ferry Terminal, located on the main peninsula. After going through customs, stop by the Macau Government Tourist Office for a map and brochures, including the useful *Macau Guide Book*. In the arrivals hall there's also a counter for hotels operating shuttle buses. Most expensive and moderately priced hotels operate free shuttle services from the terminal, including the Holiday Inn, Hyatt Regency, Mandarin Oriental, Lisboa, Pousada de São Tiago, Westin Resort Macau, and Sintra. Otherwise, city buses 3, 3A, and 10 travel from the terminal to Avenida Almeida Ribeiro, the main downtown street. The fare is $2.50 ptcs (US30¢).

From the airport, there's an airport bus, AP1, which travels from the airport to the ferry terminal, Holiday Inn, Lisboa Hotel, and the Border Gate. The fare for this is $6 ptcs (US80¢). A taxi to the Lisboa costs approximately $40 ptcs (US$5.20).

MONEY

Even though the **pataca** (ptc) is Macau's official currency, you can use your Hong Kong dollars everywhere, even on buses and for taxis (though you are likely to receive change in patacas). The pataca is pegged to the Hong Kong dollar at the rate of $103.20 ptcs to HK$100; however, on the street and in hotels and shops, the Macau pataca and Hong Kong dollar are treated as having equal value. I suppose, therefore, that you could save a minuscule amount by exchanging your money for patacas (US$1 equals $8 ptcs), but I rarely have done so and don't consider it worth the hassle for short stays in Macau. You may wish to exchange a small amount—say, HK$20 (US$2.60), but keep in mind that the pataca is *not* accepted in Hong Kong. In addition, most Macau hotels and their restaurants, as well as restaurants catering largely to tourists, list room rates and menu items in Hong Kong dollars. For the sake of simplicity, the hotel rates given below are quoted in HK$, but this could just as well read "patacas." Outside of hotels, restaurants are more likely to give prices in patacas, but sometimes they use HK$, too. Attractions, however, always use patacas. To mirror the most common pricing practices in Macau, I use HK$ for hotels and restaurants but patacas for attractions listed below.

CITY LAYOUT

Macau comprises a small peninsula and Taipa and Colôane, two islands that have merged due to land reclamation and are linked to the mainland by bridges. The peninsula—referred to as Macau—is where you'll find the city of Macau, as well as the ferry terminal and most of its hotels, shops, and attractions. The ferry terminal is located on what is called the Outer Harbour, which faces Taipa and connects to the South China Sea. On the opposite side of the Peninsula is the Inner Harbour, which faces China. Although I used to love the Outer Harbour for its dreamy view of boats plying the Pearl River waterway and the tree-shaded Avenida da República, which ran along the waterfront, land reclamation, including new highways, high-rises, the Macau Tower, and Fisherman's Wharf, has rendered the Outer Harbour a horror zone. I'd advise fleeing this side of the peninsula as hastily as possible for downtown and the more colorful Inner Harbour. Walking along the Inner Harbour from Avenida Almeida Ribeiro to the Maritime Museum, you will see an unchanged Macau, with decaying buildings, small family businesses, street-side barbers, and, occasionally, fish laid out on sidewalks to dry. In the evening, however, you may want to return to the Outer Harbour, where Macau's nightlife district, called The Docks, spreads along the waterfront near the Statue of Kun Iam. Fisherman's Wharf, with its restaurants, shops, and other diversions, is also well worth a visit.

Near the middle of the peninsula is Guia Hill, the highest natural point of Macau. Because of its strategic location, a fort was constructed atop the hill in the 1630s, followed in 1865 by a lighthouse, the first of its kind on the China coast. Also on the grounds of Guia Fort are a small chapel and a tourist-information counter (open daily 9am–1pm and 2:15–5:30pm). A jogging path, complete with exercise stations, circles the top of the hill. Although there's not much to do on Guia Hill, it does provide a good overview of Macau. You can reach it by taking bus no. 9 to Flora Garden and then boarding what must be the world's shortest ropeway to the top of the hill.

Connecting the two harbors is Macau's main road, Avenida Almeida Ribeiro, remarkably without traffic lights despite nightmarish traffic. About halfway down its length is the attractive Largo do Senado, or Senate Square, Macau's main plaza. Lined with colonial-style buildings painted in hues of yellows and pinks, it is paved in a wave pattern of colored mosaic tiles, which lead from the square to the ruins of St. Paul's Church crowning the crest of a hill. On the other side of the square is **Leal Senado,** Macau's most outstanding example of Portuguese colonial architecture. Radiating from Avenida Almeida Ribeiro in all directions is old Macau, a fascinating warren of narrow streets, street markets, open-fronted family shops, and a cacophony of sounds, sights, and smells.

Taipa, closest to the mainland and connected by three bridges, has witnessed a construction boom over the past decades, with the addition of high-rise apartments and Macau's airport. In its midst is the picturesque Taipa Village with its many restaurants. Connected to Taipa by a causeway of reclaimed land (nicknamed Cotai) is Colôane, largely undeveloped and the site of Macau's best beaches. In fact, reclaimed land connecting the two islands is so extensive (4.7 sq. km/almost 2 sq. miles), in reality they are now just one fused island. Population on the two islands has exploded from only 10,000 residents in 1991 to now more than 48,000, concentrated mostly on Taipa.

GETTING AROUND

Because the peninsula is less than 4.75km (3 miles) in length and 1.5km (1 mile) at its greatest width, you can walk to most of the major sights. If you get tired, you can always jump into one of the licensed metered **taxis,** all painted black and beige and quite inexpensive. To overcome the language barrier, MGTO has supplied most taxis with a destination guide listing most destinations in both English and Chinese. The charge is $10 ptcs (US$1.30) at flag fall for the first 1.5km (1 mile), then $1 ptc (US15¢) for each subsequent 200m (660 ft.). A taxi from the peninsula all the way to Hac Sa Beach on Colôane Island costs about $85 ptcs (US$11). Luggage costs $3 ptcs (US40¢) per piece, and there's a surcharge of $5 ptcs (US65¢) if you go all the way to Colôane. There is no surcharge, however, for the return journey to Macau. To order a taxi by phone, call © 853/939939 or 853/519519.

Public buses run daily from 7am to midnight, with fares costing $2.50 ptcs (US30¢) for travel within the Macau peninsula, $3.30 ptcs (US45¢) for travel to Taipa, and $4 ptcs to $5 ptcs (US50¢–US65¢) for travel to Colôane. Bus nos. 3, 3A, and 10, for example, travel from the front of the ferry terminal past the Lisboa Hotel to the main street, Avenida Almeida Ribeiro, in the city center and then continue to the Inner Harbour. Buses going to Taipa and Colôane islands stop for passengers at the bus stop in front of the Hotel Lisboa, located on the mainland near the Macau-Taipa Bridge. Bus nos. 11, 22, 28A, 33, and 34, as well as the airport bus AP1, travel between Macau and Taipa; bus nos. 15, 21, 21A, 25, 26, and 26A connect Macau, Taipa, and Colôane. The MGTO has a free map with bus routes.

There are also **pedicabs,** tricycles with seating for two passengers. Even as late as the early 1980s, this used to be one of the most common forms of transportation in Macau for the locals. But increased traffic and rising affluence have rendered pedicabs almost obsolete, and I suppose they will eventually vanish from the city scene much like the Hong Kong rickshaw. Today, pedicab drivers vie mostly for the tourist dollar, charging about $150 ptcs (US$20) for an hour of sightseeing, but keep in mind that there are many hilly sights you can't see by pedicab. The most popular route is along the Praia Grande Bay around the tip of the peninsula, and back via Rue do Almirante Sérgio. Be sure to settle on the fare, the route, and the length of the journey before climbing in. You'll find them parked outside the ferry terminal and Lisboa Hotel.

FAST FACTS: Macau

American Express You'll find an American Express counter in the Hotel Lisboa, Avenida da Amizade (🕐 853/579898), open 24 hours for all those gamblers.

Area Code The international telephone country code for Macau is 853. From Hong Kong, dial **001/853** before the number. When dialing an international number from Macau, you must first dial **00,** followed by the country code. However, when calling Hong Kong from Macau, you need only dial the prefix **01.**

Currency Macau's currency is the *pataca.* Like the Hong Kong dollar, the pataca is identified by the "$" sign, sometimes also written "M$" or "MOP$." To avoid confusion, I have identified patacas by the shortened "ptcs." The pataca is composed of 100 *avos.* Coins come in 10, 20, and 50 avos and 1, 5, and 10 patacas. Banknotes are issued for 10, 20, 50, 100, 500, and 1,000 patacas. The Macau pataca is pegged to the Hong Kong dollar (which is in turn pegged to the U.S. dollar) at a rate of $103.20 ptcs to HK$100; if you're going to be in Macau for only a short time, there's no need to change your money into patacas since Hong Kong dollars are readily accepted everywhere in Macau. Hotel rates, in fact, are generally quoted only in Hong Kong dollars. If you do exchange U.S. dollars, you'll receive approximately $8 ptcs for each US$1.

Emergencies Dial 🕐 **999** for medical emergencies and 🕐 **112** for the police's special tourist hotline, both free calls. For the fire department, dial 🕐 **853/572222,** a toll call. However, if necessary you can call 🕐 **999** and the operator will transfer you to the police or fire departments.

Hospitals If you need to go to a hospital, contact the S. Januario Hospital, Estrada do Visconde de S. Januario (𝄪 **853/313731**), or Kiang Wu Hospital, Estrada Coelho do Amaral (𝄪 **853/371333**), both with 24-hour emergency service.

Language Both Portuguese and Chinese are official languages, with Cantonese the most widely spoken language. However, hotel and restaurant staffs usually understand English.

Mail Mailboxes are red in Macau. The main post office (𝄪 **853/323666**), located in the city center on Largo do Senado, is open Monday to Friday from 9am to 6pm and Saturday from 9am to 1pm. It costs $4.50 ptcs (US60¢) to send a postcard or letter weighing up to 10g via airmail to the United States.

Taxes Hong Kong levies a HK$19 (US$2.45) tax for boat departures for Macau, while the Macau government levies a $20 ptcs (US$2.60) departure tax, but note that the tax is already included in the price of the ticket. Hotels levy a 5% government tax and a 10% service charge on room rates. Restaurants also levy a 10% service charge, but government tax has been waived on the consumption of food and beverages.

Telephone For local calls made from public phone booths, it costs $1 ptc (US15¢) for every 3 minutes. Telephones in Macau also offer international direct dialing, though in your hotel room, you may have to go through the hotel operator. It costs $5.50 ptcs (US70¢) for a 1-minute phone call to the United States during peak hours (Mon–Sat 6am–noon and 8pm–midnight) and $4.50 ptcs (US60¢) on Sundays and off-peak hours. If you think you'll be making a lot of international telephone calls, purchase a prepaid phone card for $50, $100, or $150 ptcs (US$6.50, US$13, or US$19) at **Edificio CTM,** Rua Pedro Coutinho, 25 (𝄪 **853/1000**), which also has information regarding use of your own mobile phone in Macau. For international directory assistance, dial 𝄪 **101;** for local directory enquiries, dial 𝄪 **181.**

Water Macau's water is from China and is purified and chlorinated. However, distilled water is supplied in restaurants and hotel rooms.

3 Where to Stay

Most of Macau's hotels are located in the city of Macau on the peninsula, providing convenient access to most of Macau's sights. For a more relaxed getaway, however, there are a few hotels on the islands, mostly in a resort setting.

In addition to the room rates given below (which are the same whether you pay in Hong Kong dollars or in patacas), there is a 10% hotel service charge and a 5% government tax. Except for some of the moderate and inexpensive hotels, most charge the same price for single or double occupancy. However, as in Hong Kong, the prices given below are rack rates; you should be able to bargain for a better rate, especially in the off season. If you plan on visiting Macau during Chinese New Year, Easter, July, or August, or when the Grand Prix is held in November, you should book well in advance. Weekends can also be quite busy. Otherwise, you shouldn't have any difficulty securing a room even on short notice, though if you have a specific hotel in mind, it's always a good idea to reserve in advance. Since most of Macau's hotels have reservations facilities in Hong Kong, I've included the Hong Kong reservation telephone numbers when available. For more complete information about hotel restaurants, see "Where to Dine," later in this chapter.

EXPENSIVE

Hyatt Regency Macau ★★★ (Value) (Kids)   If you're looking for a resort getaway with a tropical, Mediterranean atmosphere, extensive recreational facilities for the entire family, restaurants that are among the best in Macau, and comfortable rooms, the Hyatt is a good choice. It's located on Taipa Island but offers free shuttle service to the mainland, just a 5-minute drive away. Adjoining the hotel is the Taipa Island Resort, a sprawling, 1.25-hectare (3-acre) complex set amidst lush greenery with an outdoor heated pool open year-round, tennis and squash courts, fitness center, and more. For families, there's the children's wading pool, playground, game room, child-care center, babysitting services, and, for children ages 5 to 12, Camp Hyatt, with fun activities offered weekends and during school and public holidays. If you feel like exploring or dining on local cuisine, the quaint Taipa Village is only a 15-minute walk away.

The guest rooms feature black rattan furnishings, Asian artwork, and shuttered windows. Since the least expensive rooms face inland toward new apartment construction, consider springing for a harbor view with Macau's rapidly changing skyline. In short, you could easily spend days here, unwinding and relaxing. Note that the swimming pool, aerobics class, and exercise room are free, but there is a charge to use the health spa with its steam rooms, sauna, and Jacuzzi. But what makes this place a real bargain are its floating rates, the range for which is given below. Check the hotel's website for current fares.

2 Estrada Almirante Marqués Esparteiro, Taipa Island, Macau. © **800/233-1234** in the U.S. and Canada, 853/831234, or 852/2546 3791 for reservations in Hong Kong. Fax 853/830195. www.macau.hyatt.com. 326 units. HK$800–HK$1,750 (US$104–US$227) single or double; HK$1,100–HK$2,050 (US$143–US$266) Regency Club; from HK$5,300 (US$688) suite. One child under 12 free in parent's room (maximum 3 persons per room). AE, DC, MC, V. Free shuttle bus from ferry terminal, or bus no. 28A from the ferry terminal. **Amenities:** 3 restaurants (Macanese, international buffet, Chinese); lounge; 24-hr. outdoor heated pool open year-round; outdoor children's pool; 4 floodlit outdoor tennis courts; 2 indoor squash courts; multipurpose court for volleyball, basketball, badminton, and soccer; playground; health club and spa; rental bicycles; wonderful child-care center for children 2–8; Camp Hyatt for children 5–12; game room with video games, table tennis and pool tables; concierge; free shuttle to ferry and Hotel Lisboa; business center; 24-hr. room service; massage; babysitting; same-day laundry/dry-cleaning service; executive-level rooms; in-house doctor. *In room:* A/C, satellite TV w/pay movies, minibar, coffeemaker, hair dryer, safe.

Mandarin Oriental Macau ★★★ (Kids)   A companion hotel of the Mandarin Oriental in Hong Kong and the Oriental in Bangkok, this has long been one of Macau's most exclusive hotels, with room rates much lower than you'd pay in Hong Kong. Located about a 7-minute walk from the ferry terminal in the direction of downtown, it used to enjoy a rather isolated spot right on the Outer Harbour, but huge land-reclamation projects (including Fisherman's Wharf) have robbed the hotel of waterfront views, not to mention peace and quiet. On the plus side, the hotel claimed a small portion of the new land for its state-of-the-art resort facility, which includes a free-form outdoor swimming pool (heated in winter and chilled in summer) landscaped against a waterfall; a water slide, pool, playground, and children's center for the kids; and a gorgeous spa offering various types of massage, body scrubs and wraps, facials and more. As for the hotel, although its exterior is rather nondescript, if not downright ugly, the interior is beautifully designed and elegantly decorated throughout with imports from Portugal, including blue-and-white tiles, chandeliers, tapestries, and artwork. Guest rooms are decorated in Portuguese fabrics and natural teak. For families, a huge plus are the baby-care amenities provided free of charge on

Macau

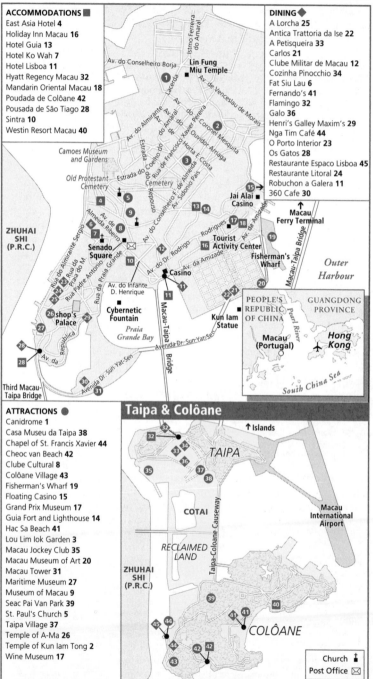

Taipa & Colôane

Church ✝
Post Office ✉

request, including diapers, wipes, and baby shampoo. The least expensive rooms face inland, while the best are those on the top four Mandarin executive floors with large balconies overlooking the resort.

956–1110 Avenida da Amizade, Macau. ℂ 800/526-6566 in the U.S. and Canada, 853/567888, or 852/2881 1288 for reservations in Hong Kong. Fax 853/594589. www.mandarinoriental.com. 435 units. HK$1,900–HK$2,300 (US$247–US$299) single or double; HK$2,600–HK$3,000 (US$338–US$390) Mandarin floors; from HK$5,100 (US$662) suite. AE, DC, MC, V. Free shuttle bus from ferry terminal or bus 3A from ferry terminal. **Amenities:** 4 restaurants (Italian, Cantonese, international, Thai); bar; 24-hr. casino; outdoor heated pool open year-round; kids' pool; 4 outdoor floodlit tennis courts; 2 indoor squash courts; playground; health club and spa; outdoor Jacuzzi; children's day-care center for ages 3–12; game room; concierge; business center; shopping arcade; salon; 24-hr. room service; massage; babysitting; same-day laundry/dry-cleaning service; executive-level rooms; doctor on call. In room: A/C, satellite TV w/pay movies, high-speed dataport, minibar, coffeemaker, hair dryer, safe.

Pousada de São Tiago 🌟🌟 (Finds)

Built around the ruins of the Portuguese Fortress da Barra, which dates from 1629, this charming inn on the tip of the peninsula is perfect for travelers who prefer romantic, atmospheric getaways over chain hotels. The entrance is dramatic—a flight of stone stairs leading through a cavelike tunnel that was once part of the fort, with water trickling in small rivulets on one side of the stairs. Once inside, guests are treated to the hospitality of a Portuguese inn, with ornately carved wooden bedroom furniture imported from Portugal and the use of stone, brick, and Portuguese blue tile throughout. Os Gatos, a terrace restaurant shaded by banyan trees, is a great place to while away an afternoon, as is the nearby outdoor swimming pool; and most of the rooms, all of which face the sea, have balconies. Although lacking the recreational resort facilities of other hotels in this category, this place is a true find. No wonder it's a popular spot for local weddings. The Maritime Museum and A-Ma Temple are within easy walking distance; you can also walk to the city center in about a half hour.

Avenida da República, Fortaleza de São Tiago da Barra, Macau. ℂ 853/378111, or 852/2739 1216 for reservations in Hong Kong. Fax 853/552170. www.saotiago.com.mo. 24 units. HK$1,620–HK$1,960 (US$210–US$254) single or double; from HK$2,300 (US$299) suite. AE, DC, MC, V. Free shuttle bus (on request) or bus no. 28B from ferry terminal. **Amenities:** Restaurant (Macanese/Portuguese/Mediterranean); lounge; outdoor pool; room service 8am–10:30pm; babysitting; same-day laundry/dry-cleaning service. In room: A/C, cable TV, minibar, hair dryer.

Westin Resort Macau 🌟🌟🌟 (Kids)

Opened in 1993, this is Macau's most stunning luxury resort hotel, complete with beautifully landscaped grounds, indoor and outdoor swimming pools, a health club with free yoga, aerobics, tai chi, and other exercise classes, excellent restaurants, and Macau's first golf course (accessed from the top floor of the resort). Located just a stone's throw from Hac Sa Beach on Colôane Island (with its popular Fernando's restaurant), it's a bit far from the center of town (about a 20-min. ride from the ferry pier on the hotel's complimentary shuttle bus, with departures every 30–60 min.), but the management is betting that most prospective guests are those who want to get away from it all. Families are catered to with a child-care center; Westin Kids' Club, which provides a multitude of activities for children under 12; a wading pool; and a playground. The hotel, Mediterranean in design and atmosphere, is spacious and airy, with a red terra-cotta tile roof and a comfortable lounge off the lobby that takes advantage of the idyllic setting by providing lots of windows that overlook the sea. Constructed in tiers to harmonize with the hillside overlooking Hac Sa Beach, each of the eight-storied hotel's very spacious, vibrantly colored rooms faces either the South China Sea or the beach (sea views are better) and features glass sliding doors opening onto—I love this—a huge 25-sq.-m (270-sq.-ft.) private terrace with plants and patio furniture (for real luxury, you can succumb to an outdoor Chinese-style massage here). Roomy bathrooms have everything from shaving/ makeup mirrors to separate tubs and shower stalls. Room rates are based on altitude, with the highest floors costing more.

1918 Estrada de Hac Sa, Colôane Island, Macau. © 800/228-3000 in the U.S. and Canada, 853/871111, or 852/2803 2333 for reservations in Hong Kong. Fax 853/871122. www.westin-macau.com. 208 units. HK$2,100–HK$2,450 (US$273–US$318) single or double; from HK$5,500 (US$714) suite. Children under 19 stay free in parent's room. Spa, dining, and golf packages available. AE, DC, MC, V. Free shuttle bus from ferry terminal, airport, and Hotel Lisboa. **Amenities:** 2 restaurants (Cantonese, international); bar; lounge; outdoor swimming pool open year-round; outdoor children's pool; indoor pool; 18-hole golf course; golf-driving range; minigolf course; 8 outdoor floodlit tennis courts; 2 indoor squash courts; basketball court; croquet; jogging lanes, health club and spa; indoor and outdoor Jacuzzis; solarium; rental bikes; children's day-care center; Westin's Kids Club (ages 4–12) and playground; game room; small 24-hr. business center with free access to the Internet; 24-hr. room service; massage; babysitting; same-day laundry/dry-cleaning service. *In room:* A/C, satellite TV w/pay movies, high-speed dataport, minibar, coffeemaker, hair dryer, iron/ironing board, safe.

MODERATE

Holiday Inn Macau   Opened in 1993, this well-known chain is familiar to North American guests; however, though the hotel is comfortable enough, it falls short of what you've come to expect if you've stayed at other Holiday Inns in Asia, where the level of service and facilities is higher than in North American properties. The hotel is situated in a rather drab area of high-rises between the ferry terminal and downtown, and, like most moderately priced Macau hotels, caters largely to gamblers and tour groups, mostly from Hong Kong, Taiwan, and China. Rooms, all with two double beds or queen- or king-size beds, are simple and unimaginative and are tiny compared to their U.S. counterparts. Steer clear of the standard rooms, which are on lower floors and face another building. Rather, splurge instead on a deluxe room, being sure to request a room on the 25th floor or higher facing the front, where you have a glimpse of the harbor far away. A plus is that the hotel is about a 10-minute walk from the main downtown area of Avenida de Almeida Ribeiro. And its bar, Oskar's Pub, is a popular hangout for the local after-work crowd.

Rua de Pequim, 82–86, Macau. © 800/465-4329 in the U.S. and Canada, 853/783333, or 852/8009 65646 in Hong Kong. Fax 853/782321. www.holiday-inn.com. 410 units. HK$1,000–HK$1,480 (US$130–US$192) single or double; HK$1,680 (US$218) executive floor; from HK$3,300 (US$429) suite. Children under 12 stay free in parent's room. AE, DC, MC, V. Free shuttle bus from ferry terminal. **Amenities:** 2 restaurants (International/Macanese, Cantonese); bar; small indoor pool; exercise room; Jacuzzi; sauna; steam room; game room; business center; 24-hr. room service; babysitting; coin-op laundry; same-day laundry/dry-cleaning service; executive-level rooms. *In room:* A/C, satellite TV w/pay movies, minibar, coffeemaker, hair dryer, safe.

Hotel Lisboa 😾 *(Finds*   The Lisboa is in a class by itself. Built in 1969, it's a Chinese version of Las Vegas on acid—huge, flashy (check out the peacocklike decoration on its roof), and with a bewildering array of facilities that make it almost a city within a city. I always get lost in this hotel. Located near the water and one of the bridges to Taipa Island, it also has great *feng shui,* which may explain why its 24-hour casino is one of the most popular in Macau, especially among Hong Kong and mainland Chinese. There are also countless restaurants (even the front-desk staff is unsure how many), shops, and nighttime diversions, including the Crazy Paris Show with a revue of scantily clad European women and countless more Chinese women roaming the shopping complex's halls hoping for some short-term business from a lucky gambler. Ah, the Lisboa. As for rooms, they're located in an older East wing and a tower that was completed in 1993. The tower, which added 14 floors, offers the best—and most expensive—harbor views, including rooms with traditional Chinese architecture and furniture that are a bit over the top. Otherwise, standard rooms have a few perks that make them recommendable, including Jacuzzi tubs, free local calls, and ornate decor. In short, this is the place to be if you want to be in the thick of it, though don't expect any personal time with the busy staff. I suspect some guests check in and never leave the premises. If they do, they'll find buses traveling to the outlying islands and other parts of Macau stopping right out the front door; downtown Macau is only a 5-minute walk away.

2–4 Avenida de Lisboa, Macau. ✆ 853/377666, or 852/2546 6944 for reservations in Hong Kong. Fax 853/567193. www.hotelisboa.com. 927 units. HK$1,480–HK$2,800 (US$192–US$364) single or double; from HK$3,800 (US$494) suite. Children under 13 stay free in parent's room. AE, DC, MC, V. Free shuttle bus or bus no. 3, 3A, 10A, 28A, or 28B from the ferry terminal. **Amenities:** 18 restaurants (some 24 hr.); 2 bars; lounge; nightclub; 24-hr. casino; outdoor heated pool; health club;; shopping arcade; salon; 24-hr. room service; same-day laundry/dry-cleaning service. *In room:* A/C, satellite TV w/free movies, minibar, coffeemaker (but no coffee), hair dryer, safe.

Pousada de Colôane ★ *(Finds* This small, family-owned property, perched on a hill above Cheoc Van Beach with views of the sea, is a good place for couples and families in search of a reasonably priced isolated retreat. Opened in 1977 as Macau's first beach property, it's a relaxing, rather rustic place, with modestly furnished rooms, nothing fancy but all with balconies facing the sea and popular public beach. For some visitors it awakens memories of beachside vacations from childhood. There's an outdoor terrace where you can relax over drinks with views of the sunset, and the inn's Portuguese restaurant is especially popular for its Sunday lunch buffet offered during peak season. The main drawback is one of access, but buses to Macau pass by frequently; when arriving at the Macau ferry terminal, you're best off traveling to the hotel by taxi (fares average HK$80/US$10).

Praia de Cheoc Van, Colôane Island, Macau. ✆ 853/882144. Fax 853/882251. www.hotelpcoloane.com.mo. 22 units. HK$680–HK$750 (US$88–US$98) single or double. Weekday discounts available. MC, V. Bus: 21A, 25, or 26A from Lisboa Hotel (tell the bus driver you want to get off at the hotel). **Amenities:** Restaurant (Portuguese); bar; outdoor pool; children's pool; playground. *In room:* A/C, TV, minibar.

Sintra   With the best central location of any of the moderately priced hotels, the Sintra, under the same management as Hotel Lisboa, enjoys a prime spot in the heart of Macau, within easy walking distance of Avenida de Almeida Ribeiro (Macau's main street), Largo do Senado, and the Hotel Lisboa with its 24-hour casino. Originally built in 1975 but completely overhauled in the mid-1990s, it looks good for its age and the staff is friendly. Standard rooms face another building but are large. Even roomier are the higher-priced rooms occupying higher floors; individual bookings (not through a travel agency) are often upgraded to one of these rooms if space is available. Of note for night owls is the hotel's one restaurant, open 24 hours.

Avenida de D. João IV, Macau. ✆ 853/710111, or 852/2546 6944 for reservations in Hong Kong. Fax 853/567769. www.hotelsintra.com. 240 units. HK$860–HK$1,260 (US$112–US$164) single or double; HK$1,280–HK$1,580 (US$166–US$205) executive floor; from HK$1,860 (US$242) suite. Children under 13 stay free in parent's room. AE, DC, MC, V. Free shuttle bus or bus no. 3A or 10 from the ferry terminal. **Amenities:** Restaurant (International/Cantonese); sauna (men only); business center; shopping arcade; 24-hr. room service; same-day laundry/dry-cleaning service; executive-level rooms. *In room:* A/C, satellite TV w/pay movies, minibar, hair dryer.

INEXPENSIVE

East Asia Hotel   This is one of Macau's better choices for inexpensive accommodation in the heart of the city (I've seen some pretty grim hotels and guesthouses in this category), located near the Inner Harbour just off Avenida de

Almeida Ribeiro in an area filled with local color and atmosphere. Some of that local color extends to a room just off the lobby where a bevy of beauties await phone calls or customers, which may admittedly be a bit too atmospheric for some (prostitution is not legal here, even though prostitutes are blatant—the law is obviously not enforced). Still, the renovated, 60-year-old hotel features a polite staff and large, perfectly fine rooms with clean, tiled bathrooms and complimentary Chinese tea. The least expensive rooms are windowless and a bit depressing. Best are rooms on higher floors offering good views, including some of the Inner Harbour.

Rua da Madeira 1–A, Macau. ☎ 853/922433, or 852/2540 6333 for reservations in Hong Kong. Fax 853/922430. 98 units. HK$260–HK$340 (US$39–US$44) single; HK$400–HK$500 (US$52–US$65) twin. Weekday discounts available. AE, MC, V. Bus: 3, 3A, or 10 from the ferry terminal. **Amenities:** Restaurant (Chinese). In room: A/C, TV.

Hotel Guia ⭐ Located on the slope of Guia Hill, below the Guia Fort and Lighthouse and surrounded by traditional colonial architecture, this is one of Macau's more secluded inexpensively priced hotels. It's also one of the most welcoming, small and personable with a friendly staff and spotless rooms that range from those facing inland to those with little balconies facing the sea. By far the best are those with a view of Guia Lighthouse and the harbor in the background—request a room with a balcony on the highest (fifth) floor. Some rooms even have high-speed Internet access and LCD TV screens. The only drawback to its quiet residential location is that it's a bit far from the action, but a free shuttle bus makes runs every half hour or so to and from the ferry pier and the Hotel Lisboa. A nearby jogging path on Guia Hill makes this an ideal choice for joggers and walkers.

Estrada do Engenheiro Trigo 1–5, Macau. ☎ 853/513888. Fax 853/559822. guia@macau.ctm.net. 90 units. HK$520–HK$720 (US$68–US$94) single or double; from HK$850 (US$110) suite. AE, DC, MC, V. Free shuttle bus or bus no. 28C from ferry terminal. **Amenities:** Restaurant (Chinese seafood); nightclub/disco; room service 9am–11pm; same-day laundry/dry-cleaning service. In room: A/C, cable TV w/free movies, minibar, coffeemaker (but no coffee), hair dryer.

Hotel Ko Wah *Value* Despite its name, this is actually a guesthouse. There are many guesthouses around the Inner Harbour, Macau's oldest district, but most are of very low standards. This one, on picturesque Rua da Felicidade, is better than most, with a white-washed long corridor adorned with fake flowers and with rooms on either side. Some of the rooms have windows, others don't, but all have the basics including bathrooms. If all you're looking for is cheap accommodation in the heart of Macau's most colorful old town, this place fits the bill.

Rua da Felicidade, 3rd floor, Macau. ☎ 853/375599. 27 units. HK$130 (US$17) single; HK$180 (US$23) double. No credit cards. Bus: 3, 3A, or 10 from ferry terminal. In room: A/C, TV.

4 Where to Dine

As a former trading center for spices and a melting pot for Portuguese and Chinese cultures, it's little wonder that Macau developed its own very fine cuisine. The Portuguese settlers brought with them sweet potatoes, peanuts, and kidney beans from Brazil, piri-piri peppers from Africa, chilies from India, and codfish, coffee, and vegetables from Europe. In turn, the Chinese introduced rhubarb, celery, ginger, soy sauce, litchis, and other Asian foods. The result is Macanese cuisine. One of the most popular dishes is African chicken, grilled or baked with chiles and piri-piri peppers, but I also love *minchi,* a Macanese dish of minced beef prepared with fried potatoes, onion, and garlic. Other favorites include Portuguese chicken

(chicken baked with potatoes, tomatoes, olive oil, curry, coconut, saffron, and black olives), *bacalhau* (codfish), Macau sole, *caldeirada* (seafood stew), spicy giant shrimp, baked quail and pigeon, curried crab, Portuguese sausage, and *feijoada* (a Brazilian stew of pork, black beans, cabbage, and spicy sausage). There are also restaurants specializing in traditional Portuguese cuisine, and, of course, countless Chinese restaurants. And don't forget Portuguese wine, inexpensive and a great bargain. Most famous is the *vinho verde*, a young wine served very cold that is refreshing on hot summer days.

Restaurants will add a 10% service charge to your bill, but as you'll discover, even the "expensive" restaurants in Macau would be a bargain in Hong Kong.

VERY EXPENSIVE

Robuchon a Galera *Overrated* FRENCH   This is by far Macau's most exclusive—and expensive—restaurant, with an elegant decor and a polished staff. Still, it's hard not to wonder why renowned French chef Joel Robuchon chose Macau to showcase his talents (he passed over Maxim's on New York's Times Square in favor of Macau) and whether there are enough patrons willing to pay top dollar when so many other tantalizing, more reasonably priced restaurants abound. In any case, Robuchon flies in four times a year to supervise the change of the seasonal menu, which in the past has included such offerings as lobster cooked on rock salt and served with girolles mushroom, zucchini and fettuccine, and duck breast roasted in spices with turnip and foie gras. While beautifully presented, main courses sometimes fall short and seem too highly priced for what they are. Appetizers, however, are wonderful; the cheese, dessert, and after-dinner-drink trolleys are hard to pass up; and the wine list is probably the best in town. However, I recommend spending your money elsewhere, unless, of course, you strike it big at the casino.

In the Hotel Lisboa, 3rd floor of Lisboa Tower, Avenida da Amizade. © 853/377666. Reservations recommended. Main dishes HK$250–HK$460 (US$32–US$60); 11-course tasting menu HK$1,400 (US$182); fixed-price lunch HK$288 (US$37). AE, DC, MC, V. Daily noon–2:30pm and 6:30–11pm (last order). Bus: 3, 3A, 8, 8A, 9, 9A, 10, 10A, 10B, 11, 12, 21, 21A, 22, 23, 25, 26, 26A, 28A, 28B, 32, 33, or AP1.

EXPENSIVE

Clube Militar de Macau *Finds* MACANESE/PORTUGUESE   This is certainly one of Macau's most atmospheric dining halls, located in the Macau Military Club, built in 1870 as a private cultural and recreation center for military officers. Painted a bright pink, this striking colonial building behind the Hotel Lisboa opened its restaurant to the public in 1995, offering nonmembers the chance to dine in style in its old-fashioned dining hall with its tall ceilings, whirring ceiling fans, arched windows, wood floor, and displays of antique Chinese dishware. As for the food, it's best to stick to the classics, such as Portuguese green vegetable soup, roasted codfish with hot olive oil and garlic, seafood stew in a white-wine sauce, sirloin steak Portuguese-style, stewed lamb leg in red wine, or African chicken. The lunch buffet is a downtown favorite, and the list of Portuguese wines is among the best in town.

Avenida da Praia Grande, 795. © 853/714009. Reservations recommended for lunch. Main courses HK$90–HK$168 (US$12–US$22); fixed-price lunch or dinner HK$90 (US$12); lunch buffet HK$130 (US$17). MC, V. Daily noon–3pm and 7–11pm. Bus: 3, 3A, 8, 10, 10A, or 10.

Os Gatos *Finds* MACANESE/MEDITERRANEAN   Os Gatos occupies a wonderful tree-shaded brick terrace that faces the Pearl River. It's a great place to stop for a meal, snack, or drink if you're walking around the tip of the peninsula (something I try to do on every trip to Macau) or visiting the nearby Maritime Museum or A-Ma Temple. If you wish, you can also sit in air-conditioned comfort inside a glass-enclosed room. The menu offers a blend of Mediterranean and Macanese food, including poached bacalhau, seafood paella, baked salmon with garlic and basil, king crab in tomato sauce, and pastas. Or, come for the afternoon tea set served from 3 to 6pm for HK$95 (US$12). The restaurant itself is located in the delightful Pousada de São Tiago Hotel, a romantic and intimate getaway.

In the Pousada de São Tiago Hotel, Avenida da República. (C) 853/378111. www.saotiago.com.mo. Main courses HK$116–HK$164 (US$15–US$21). AE, DC, MC, V. Daily 11am–11:30pm. Bus: 6, 9, 28B.

Restaurante Espaco Lisboa *(★) (Finds* PORTUGUESE   This is a tiny two-story restaurant, popular with the locals for its traditional, country-style Portuguese food. Located in a Chinese village house just off the main square in Colôane Village (Vila Colôane), just a few minutes' walk from the St. Francis Xavier Chapel, it offers so many great choices it's hard to know where to start. Fried codfish cakes, an assortment of Portuguese sausages, or the sautéed clams with garlic and coriander are a good launch to a feast here, followed, perhaps, by the traditional Portuguese cabbage soup. For the main course, which comes with side dishes, you might opt for the roast codfish served with potatoes and hot olive oil and garlic or the tenderloin steak Portuguese style, fried with garlic and white wine and served with Portuguese honey ham, fried egg, and potatoes. And to top it all off? How about mango ice cream, served with cherry sauce *au flambé*. In nice weather, you may want to sit at one of the three tables outside on the tiny balcony, where you can look upon ancient tiled roofs and listen to the clicking of mahjong.

Rua das Gaivotas, 8, Colôane Village, Colôane Island. (C) 853/882226. Reservations recommended on weekends. Main courses HK$83–HK$198 (US$11–US$26). MC, V. Mon–Fri noon–3pm and 6:30–10pm; Sat–Sun noon–10:30pm. Bus: 15, 21, 21A, 25, 26, or 26A.

360 Cafe INTERNATIONAL   This is Macau's most conspicuous restaurant, more than 219m (730 ft.) above reclaimed ground in the soaring Macau Tower. Opened in 2001, the tower contains an observation deck and lounge, with an admission of HK$70 (US$9.10). Head instead to the tower's revolving restaurant, where for the price of a buffet meal you'll get an equally good view. It takes 1½ hours for a complete spin, giving you ample time to sample the various Southeast Asian, Chinese, Macanese, and Continental dishes available as you soak in the view. Safety precautions make this Macau's only nonsmoking restaurant.

In the Macau Tower, Lago Sai Van. (C) 853/9888660. www.macautower.com.mo. Reservations recommended weekends. Buffet lunch HK$148 (US$19); buffet dinner HK$238 (US$31). HK$10 (US$1.30) extra on weekends and public holidays. Daily 11:30am–3pm and 7–11pm. AE, DC, MC, V. Bus: 23 or 32.

MODERATE

A Lorcha PORTUGUESE   Just a stone's throw from the Maritime Museum and A-Ma Temple, this is the best place to eat if you find yourself hungering for Portuguese food in this area. Look for its whitewashed walls, an architectural feature repeated in the interior of the tiny restaurant with its arched, low ceiling. Casual yet often filled with businesspeople, it offers *feijoada* (a Brazilian stew of pork, black beans, cabbage, and spicy sausage), codfish in a cream sauce, char-grilled king prawns, clams prepared in garlic and olive oil, grilled lamb chops, baked minced beef potato pie, and other traditional dishes that are consistently good. Its name, by the way, refers to a type of Portuguese boat, which is appropriate for a colony founded by seafaring explorers.

Rua do Almirante Sérgio, 289. © 853/313193. Reservations recommended for lunch. Main courses HK$65–HK$128 (US$8.45–US$17). AE, DC, MC, V. Wed–Mon 12:30–3pm and 6:30–11pm. Bus: 1, 1A, 2, 5, 6, 7, 9, 10, 10A, 11, 18, 21, 21A, 28B, or 34.

A Petisqueira PORTUGUESE A small, unpretentious restaurant just off Taipa Village's main road, on the corner of Rua de S. João and Rua das Virtudes, it offers typical Portuguese fare, including codfish grilled, roasted, or boiled; grilled sole with lemon butter sauce; grilled quail; grilled king prawns; paella; fried tenderloin steak Portuguese-style; grilled sea bass; and curried crab. All grilled dishes are cooked over a charcoal grill. The fresh cheeses are especially recommended. Of course, everything tastes better with Portuguese wine.

Rua S. João, 15, Taipa Village, Taipa Island. © 853/825354. Main courses HK$65–HK$135 (US$8.45–US$18). MC, V. Mon–Fri noon–3pm and 6:30–11pm; Sat–Sun and holidays noon–11pm. Bus: 11, 22, 28A, 30, 33, 34, or 35.

Cozinha Pinocchio PORTUGUESE/MACANESE Opened in 1977, Taipa Island's first Portuguese restaurant is still going strong, though some who have known it since its early days claim that the atmosphere became more staid when a roof was added to the original roofless two-story brick warehouse. Nevertheless, things are still hopping—people crowd its doors for specialties like curried crab, king prawns, charcoal-grilled sardines, fried codfish cakes, grilled spareribs, roast veal, roast quail, and Portuguese-style cooked fish. The wine list is extensive.

Rua do Sol, Taipa Village, Taipa Island. © 853/827128. Main courses HK$48–HK$128 (US$6.25–US$17). DC, MC, V. Daily 11:45am–11:45pm. Bus: 11, 22, 28A, 30, 33, 34, or 35.

Fat Siu Lau MACANESE This is Macau's oldest restaurant (dating from 1903), but its three floors of dining have been renovated in upbeat modern Art Deco. Its exterior matches all the other storefronts on this renovated street—whitewashed walls and red shutters and doors—which used to serve as Macau's red-light district. Macanese cuisine is served here, including roast pigeon marinated according to a 90-year-old secret recipe; spicy African chicken; curried crab; garoupa stewed with tomatoes, bell pepper, onion, and potatoes; and grilled king prawns.

Rua da Felicidade, 64. © 853/573580. Main courses HK$45–HK$135 (US$5.85–US$18). DC, MC, V. Daily 11:30am–11:30pm. Bus: 3, 3A, 5, 6, 7, 8, 10, 11, 18, 19, 21, or 21A.

Fernando's *Finds* PORTUGUESE For years, Fernando's was just another shack on Hac Sa Beach. Although outwardly there is nothing to distinguish it from the others (it's the brick one closest to the beach, below the vines), a pavilion was added out back, complete with ceiling fans and an adjacent open-air bar with outdoor seating (open daily noon–midnight), making it *the* place to dine on the beach. Now everyone knows Fernando's, and even though there's no air-conditioning (that goes for the kitchen as well), it doesn't seem to deter the faithful who pilgrimage here, especially on weekends, when you'll probably have to wait for a table. Outspoken Fernando is usually on hand, holding court. The menu is strictly Portuguese (it's even written only in Portuguese) and includes prawns, crabs, mussels, codfish, feijoada, veal, chicken, pork ribs, suckling pig, beef, and salads. The bread all comes from the restaurant's own bakery, and the vegetables are grown on the restaurant's own garden plot across the border in China. Only Portuguese wine is served, stocked on a shelf for customer perusal (there is no wine list). It's all very informal, and not for those who demand pristine conditions.

Praia de Hac Sa, 9, Colôane. © 853/882264 or 853/882531. Reservations not accepted. Main courses HK$60–HK$148 (US$7.80–US$19). No credit cards. Daily noon–9:30pm. Bus: 15, 21A, 25, or 26A.

Flamingo ★★★ *Value* MACANESE   If I had time for only one memorable meal in Macau, this would be a serious contender. Decorated in hot pink, this restaurant has a great Mediterranean ambience, with ceiling fans, swaying palms, and a terrace overlooking lush landscaping and a duck pond. For lightweights unaccustomed to alfresco dining, an air-conditioned enclosure was recently added, but for me the real pleasure of dining here is the terrace. The bread is homemade, and the specialties are a unique blend of Portuguese, Chinese, African, Indian, and Malay spices, resulting in delicious, authentic Macanese fare. For an appetizer, try the stuffed crab, followed by a main course like pan-fried Macau sole; spicy king prawns with chile sauce; curried crab; or African chicken. Dining here is a great value considering the ambience and the food. A strolling three-man band sets the mood.

In the Hyatt Regency Hotel, Taipa Island. © **853/831234.** www.macau.hyatt.com. Reservations recommended Sat–Sun. Main courses HK$70–HK$100 (US$8.85–US$13); fixed-price lunch HK$88 (US$11). AE, DC, MC, V. Daily noon–3pm and 7–11pm. Bus: 11, 21, 21A, 22, 25, 26, 26A, 28A, 30, 33, 34, 35, or AP1.

Galo ★ PORTUGUESE/MACANESE   A delightful, two-story house in Taipa Village has been converted into this informal and festively decorated restaurant specializing in local cuisines and unique creations of the talented owner/chef. "Galo" means rooster in Portuguese; look for the picture of the rooster outside the restaurant, just off the main pedestrian street. Its menu, which includes photographs of each dish, offers such house specialties as Macau crabs, prepared with a mixture of Shanghainese and Macanese ingredients, rather than curry. You might also want to try giant prawns, mussels, African chicken, Portuguese broad beans, or the mixed grill. In any case, be sure to start out with the *sopa da casa* (house soup), made from potatoes, red beans, onions, and vegetables simmered in broth from boiled beef and sausages. Delicious!

Rua dos Clérigos, 45, Taipa Village, Taipa Island. © **853/827423** or 853/827318. Main courses HK$43–HK$130 (US$5.60–US$17). MC, V. Mon–Fri 11:30am–3pm and 6–10:30pm; Sat–Sun 11:30am–10:30pm. Bus: 11, 22, 28A, 30, 34, or 35.

Henri's Galley Maxim's MACANESE/PORTUGUESE   Located on the Outer Harbour below the venerable Bela Vista (now the Portuguese Embassy), this 30-year-old restaurant was once *the* place to dine on the tree-shaded waterfront. Now the Bela Vista has closed as a hotel, the waterfront has been compromised with reclaimed land (and the Macau Tower), and Macau's socially conscious have moved on to trendier restaurants. Still, this remains a good choice for Macanese and Portuguese cuisine. It's owned by Henri Wong, a jovial and friendly man who used to be chief steward in a galley at sea; he has decorated his restaurant as though he were still aboard ship. The waiters, dressed as stewards, are attentive and there are a few seats outdoors under umbrellas. Specialties of the house include fried Macau sole, Portuguese roast fish, African chicken, Portuguese baked chicken, *bacalhau* (codfish), feijoada, curry crab, spicy giant prawns, steaks, and stuffed crabmeat in its shell, but there are also sandwiches priced at less than HK$42 (US$5.45).

Avenida da República, 4. © **853/556251** or 853/562231. www.henrisgalley.com.mo. Main courses HK$60– HK$192 (US$7.80–US$25). AE, MC, V. Daily 11am–11pm. Bus: 28B.

O Porto Interior ★ *Value* MACANESE/PORTUGUESE   Located on the Inner Harbour not far from the Maritime Museum and A-Ma Temple, this comfortable, classy restaurant decorated in colonial style with woodwork carvings, a brick floor, and decorative birdcages offers surprisingly inexpensive fare, making it a good value. You might wish to start with grilled Portuguese sausage, spicy shrimp, or the seafood supreme soup, served inside a bread bowl. Main dishes range from Macau curry crab and Macanese garlic king prawns to African chicken, black pepper steak, and *minchi.*

Rua do Almirante Sérgio, 259B. ℰ **853/967770.** Main courses HK$55–HK$120 (US$7.15–US$16). AE, DC, MC, V. Daily noon–11:30pm. Bus 1, 1A, 2, 5, 6, 7, 8, 9, 10, 10A, 11, 18, 21, 21A, or 28B.

Restaurante Litoral ⋆⋆ MACANESE   Exactly which restaurant serves the most "authentic" Macanese food in town is a hotly contested subject, but this attractive restaurant with its dark-gleaming woods, white-washed walls, and stone floor can certainly lay claim to the title. All the traditional favorites are here, including curry crab, curry prawns, African chicken, feijoada, and *minchi,* but Portuguese specialties like codfish baked with potato and garlic, roast Portuguese sausage, and Portuguese green soup are not overlooked. Wash it all down with Portuguese wine or beer. It's located along the covered sidewalk not far from the Maritime Museum and A-Ma Temple.

Rua do Almirante Sérgio, 261A. ℰ **853/967878.** Main courses HK$78–HK$148 (US$10–US$19). AE, MC, V. Daily noon–3pm and 6–11pm. Bus: 1, 1A, 2, 5, 6, 7, 9, 10, 10A, 11, 18, 21, 21A, 28B, or 34.

INEXPENSIVE

Antica Trattoria da Ise ITALIAN   This casual, upstairs restaurant, located near the Docks nightlife district, is always crowded. Simply decorated with cast-iron chandeliers, plants, and palm trees, it offers 18 different kinds of pizza, as well as pastas and main courses like baked salmon with lemon thyme and T-bone steak with mint, basil, parmesan, garlic, and lemon dressing.

Avenida Sir Anders Ljungstedt, Edificio Vista Magnifica Court, no. 40–46. ℰ **853/755102.** Reservations recommended. Pizza HK$47–HK$95 (US$6.10–US$12); main dishes HK$60–HK$95 (US$7.80–US$12). AE, MC, V. Daily noon–11pm. Bus: 1A, 8, 12, or 23.

Carlos PORTUGUESE   Just a block inland from the Docks nightlife district, this bare room with a tall ceiling offers no-nonsense, home-cooked Portuguese food at very reasonable prices, assuring it a faithful clientele. The menu is extensive and includes all the classics, but standouts include the shrimp in garlic sauce and the clams and pork stewed in white wine and herbs.

Rua Cidade de Braga. ℰ **853/751838.** Main dishes HK$55–HK$100 (US$7.15–US$13). No credit cards. Tues–Sun 11am–3pm and 6–11pm. Bus: 1A, 8, 12, or 23.

Nga Tim Cafe *Finds* CHINESE/MACANESE   This lively, open-air, pavilion restaurant is on the tiny main square of Colôane Village, dominated by the charming Chapel of St. Francis Xavier. Its popularity with the locals on weekends and holidays lends it a festive, community-affair atmosphere; it's a great place for relaxing and people watching. The food, which combines Chinese and Macanese styles of cooking and ingredients, is in a category all its own, with many unique dishes not available anywhere else. Try the salt-and-pepper shrimp, chicken in an earthen pot, grilled duck with lemon sauce, steamed chicken with garlic, scallops with broccoli, or crab curry, accompanied by Portuguese wine or fresh fruit juice. This is a good place to rub elbows with the natives.

Rua Caetano, No. 8, Colôane Village, Colôane Island. ℰ **853/882086.** Main courses HK$32–HK$88 (US$4.15–US$11). MC, V. Daily 11:30am–1am. Bus: 15, 21, 21A, 25, 26, or 26A.

5 Exploring Macau

THE TOP ATTRACTIONS

St. Paul's Church ⋆⋆   The most famous structure in Macau is the ruin of St. Paul's Church. Crowning the top of a hill in the center of the city and

---

Tips Museum Mania

If museums are your passion, save money by purchasing the Museums Pass, valid for 5 days and allowing entry to six museums, including the Grand Prix Museum, Wine Museum, Museum of Macau, Maritime Museum, and Macau Museum of Art. Passes, which cost $25 ptcs (US$3.25) for adults and $12 ptcs (US$1.55) for children and seniors, can be purchased at any of the museums. (The sixth museum is Lin Zexu Museum of Art, which is not covered below, since most people come to Macau only on a day trip or, at the most, 2 or 3 days and probably don't have time to see even five museums. Nevertheless, the Lin Zexu Museum centers on Lin Zexu, who was commissioned by Beijing in the 1830s to abolish the opium trade. It is not as conveniently located as the other museums included on this pass.)

---

approached by a grand sweep of stairs, only its ornate facade and some excavated sites remain. It was designed by an Italian Jesuit and built in 1602 with the help of Japanese Christians who had fled persecution in Nagasaki. In 1835, during a typhoon, the church caught fire and burned to the ground, leaving only its now-famous facade. The facade is adorned with carvings and statues depicting Christianity in Asia, a rather intriguing mix of images: a Virgin Mary flanked by a peony (representing China) and a chrysanthemum (representing Japan), and a Chinese dragon, a Portuguese ship, and a demon. Beyond the facade is the excavated crypt, where in glass-fronted cases are the bones of 17th-century Christian martyrs from Japan and Vietnam. Here, too, is the tomb of Father Allesandro Valignano, founder of the Church of St. Paul and instrumental in establishing Christianity in Japan. Next to the crypt is the underground Museum of Sacred Art, which you can tour in about 20 minutes. It contains religious works of art produced in Macau from the 17th to 20th centuries. Included are very interesting 17th-century oil paintings by exiled Japanese Christian artists, crucifixes of filigree silver, carved wooden saints, and other sacred objects. Incidentally, also at St. Paul's Church is a counter of the Macau Government Tourist Office, open daily from 9am to 1pm and 2:15 to 6pm.

Rua de São Paulo. © 853/358444. Free admission. Grounds open daily 24 hr.; museum Wed–Mon 9am–6pm. Bus: 2, 3, 3A, 5, 9, 9A, 12, 16, 22, or 25 to Largo do Senado Square (off Avenida Almeida Ribeiro), then follow the wavy, tiled sidewalk leading uphill to the northeast about 10 min.

Museum of Macau ★★★   Located in the bowels of ancient Monte Fortress, this very ambitious project opened in 1998 and provides an excellent overview of Macau's history, local traditions, and arts and crafts. If you see only one museum in Macau, it should be this. Entrance is via an escalator located near St. Paul's Church. Arranged chronologically, the first floor depicts the beginnings of Macau and the arrival of Portuguese traders and Jesuit missionaries. Particularly interesting is the room comparing Chinese and European civilizations at the time of their encounter in the 16th century, including descriptions of their different writing systems, philosophies, and religions. The second floor deals with the daily life and traditions of old Macau, including festivals, wedding ceremonies, and industries ranging from fishing to fireworks factories. Displays include paintings and photographs depicting Macau through the centuries, traditional games and toys, an explanation of Macanese cuisine and architecture, and a re-created street in Macau lined with colonial and Chinese facades and containing tea, pastry, and traditional Chinese pharmacy shops. The top floor, the only one above ground, is of modern Macau and its plans for the future. From here you can exit to the wall ramparts of the fort, which was built by the Jesuits about the same time as St. Paul's, and largely destroyed by the same fire. You'll want to spend at least an hour here.

Citadel of São Paulo do Monte (St. Paul Monte Fortress). (📞 853/357911. www.macaumuseum.gov.mo. Admission $15 ptcs (US$1.95) adults, $8 ptcs (US$1.05) seniors and children. Tues–Sun 10am–6pm. Located next to St. Paul's Church.

Macau Tower *(Overrated)*   Does the world really need another tower? Local authorities apparently thought so, opening the Macau Tower Convention & Entertainment Centre in 2001. In addition to exhibition and convention space, it contains restaurants and shops, but the crowning glory is the 330m (1,100-ft.) tower, with an observatory about 219m (730 ft.) high. Since admission to the outdoor observation deck and indoor lounge is rather exorbitant by Macau standards, I personally think you are best off coming for a meal in the revolving **360 Cafe** (p. 275). However, thrill seekers take note: The indoor observation lounge has a glass-floored section that gives the illusion of standing on thin air. But real dare devils will want to tour the observation deck's *outside* ramparts with the safety of harnesses and ropes, which costs $220 ptcs (US$29) on weekdays and $250 ptcs (US$32) weekends and holidays; half price for children and seniors. Other ways to have fun with Macau Tower: climbing the mast (a 2-hr. ordeal); climbing 32m (106 ft.) up the tower's concrete shaft on what may be the world's highest artificial climbing wall; bungee jumping 233m (769 ft.); and more.

Lago Sai Van. (📞 853/933339. www.macautower.com.mo. Admission to observatory $70 ptcs (US$9) adults, $35 ptcs (US$4.55) children and seniors. Daily 10am–9pm. Bus: 23 or 32.

MORE MUSEUMS

Grand Prix Museum   One of two museums located in the Tourist Activity Center (see the Wine Museum, below), a 10-minute walk from the Macau Ferry Terminal, the Grand Prix Museum opened in 1993 to celebrate the 40th anniversary of the Macau Grand Prix. Its display hall is filled mainly with cars and motorcycles that have competed in the race through the years. Most interesting for visitors, perhaps, are the two simulators, each of which costs $20 ptcs (US$2.60) extra and gives visitors the thrill of "experiencing" the Grand Prix (participants must be 12 years or older). One lets you be the driver as you steer and race other drivers on the Guia Circuit (first-timers might want to request automatic transmission!); the other lets you be a passenger of a real car driven in the 1995 Grand Prix. Be warned—a closed-circuit TV outside the simulator allows spectators to watch your every facial expression. Together with the Wine Museum (see below), you'll spend less than an hour here.

Centro de Actividades Turisticas Macau, Rua de Luis Gonzaga Gomes. (📞 853/7984108. Admission $10 ptcs (US$1.30) adults, $5 ptcs (US65¢) children 11–18, free for seniors and children younger than 11. Combination ticket to Grand Prix Museum and Wine Museum $20 ptcs (US$2.60). Wed–Mon 10am–6pm. Bus: 1A, 3, 3A, 10, 10A, 10B, 12, 17, 23, 28A, 28B, 28C, 32, or AP1.

Clube Cultural   Located on Macau's main street not far from Senado Square, this historic building was once a traditional pawnshop. Today it serves as a museum outlining the pawnshop business in Macau. Unlike pawnshops in the West, this pawnshop held personal possessions for up to 3 years, safeguarded against fires, floods, and theft in a thick-walled tower. There isn't a lot to see here (you can tour the entire building in about 15 min.), so be sure to stop by the second-floor shop selling local souvenirs and stop for refreshment at the third-floor tea room.

Avenida Almeida Ribeiro 396. ℂ **853/921811.** www.culturalclub.net. Admission $5 ptcs (US65¢). Daily 10am–7pm. Closed 1st Mon of every month. Bus: 2, 5, 7, 8, 9, 9A, 12, 16, 22, or 25.

Macau Museum of Art 𝄞   Located in the new Macau Cultural Centre on reclaimed land in the Outer Harbour, this small but interesting museum displays historical paintings, Chinese calligraphy, pottery, and works by contemporary local artists. Particularly fascinating are paintings by Western artists such as British painter George Chinnery and others, who painted scenes, people, and customs of Macau and Guangdong, including depictions of the port town as it looked long ago. Their works were often copied and then sold to visiting foreigners as souvenirs. Also impressive is the collection of Shiwan ceramic figurines. There are also temporary exhibitions. Depending upon your interest, you'll spend anywhere from 30 to 60 minutes here.

Macau Cultural Centre (Novos Aterros do Porto Exterior/NAPE), Avenida Xian Xing Hai. ℂ **853/7919814.** www.artmuseum.gov.mo. Admission $5 ptcs (US65¢) adults, $3 ptcs (US40¢) students and children, free for seniors; free admission Sun. Tues–Sun 10am–6:30pm. Bus: 1A, 8, 12, 17, or 23.

Maritime Museum 𝄞 *Kids*   Macau's oldest museum, ideally situated on the waterfront of the Inner Harbour where visitors can observe barges and other boats passing by, does an excellent job of tracing the history of Macau's lifelong relationship with the sea. It's located at the tip of the peninsula, across from the Temple of A-Ma, in approximately the same spot where the Portuguese first landed. The museum begins with dioramas depicting the legend of A-Ma, protectress of seafarers and Macau's namesake, and continues with models of various boats, including trawlers, Chinese junks, Portuguese sailing boats, and even modern jetfoils. There are also life-size original boats on display, ranging from the sampan to an ornate festival boat. Various fishing methods are detailed, from trawling and gill netting to purse seining, as well as various voyages of discovery around the world. The museum also has nautical equipment, navigation instruments used by the Portuguese and Chinese, and—a hit with children—a small aquarium, with tanks of exotic fish and a collection of shells. You'll probably spend about an hour here.

Largo do Pagode da Barra, 1. ℂ **853/595481.** www.museumaritimo.gov.mo. Admission $10 ptcs (US$1.30) adults, $5 ptcs (US65¢) children, free for seniors and children under 10. Sun and holidays half price. Wed–Mon 10am–5:30pm. Bus: 1, 1A, 2, 5, 6, 7, 9, 10, 10A, 11, 18, 21, 21A, 28B, or 34.

Wine Museum   Located in the same building as the Grand Prix Museum (see above), this is Asia's first museum dedicated to wine. Modeled like a wine cellar, it begins with a brief history of wine making, starting with its discovery by Egyptians and Phoenicians in 6000 to 4000 B.C. and its spread from Greece through the rest of Europe, reaching Portugal around A.D. 1100. On display are wines (the oldest is an 1815 Madeira), wine presses, storage barrels, harvesting tools, and other wine-making equipment, as well as descriptions of every wine-growing region in Portugal. Wine production in China is also presented. A museum highlight is the free wine tasting of red, white, or verde wine. Bottles of Portuguese wine can also be purchased.

Centro de Actividades Turisticas Macau, Rua de Luis Gonzaga Gomes. ℂ **853/7984188.** Admission $15 ptcs (US$1.95) adults, $5 (US65¢) children 11–18, free for seniors and children younger than 11. Combination ticket to Wine Museum and Grand Prix Museum $20 ptcs (US$2.60) adults, $10 ptcs (US$1.30) children. Wed–Mon 10am–6pm. Bus: 1A, 3, 3A, 10, 10A, 12, 17, 23, 28A, 28B, 28C, 32, or AP1.

TEMPLES

Temple of Kun Iam Tong (Temple of the Goddess of Mercy) ★★   Of
the many temples in Macau, one of the most important is the Temple of Kun
Iam Tong, founded in the 13th century. Its present buildings, with ornate porcelain figurines adorning its roofs, date from 1627. The most significant historical
event that took place at this largest and wealthiest of Macau's Buddhist temples
was the 1844 signing of the first treaty of trade and friendship between the
United States and China; the round granite table where the treaty was signed is
still here. The temple houses images of Buddha, representing the past, present,
and future, as well as the goddess of mercy (Kun Iam) dressed in the costume of
a Chinese bride. She is attended by 18 gold-lacquered figures lining the walls
that represent the 18 wise men of China. Curiously enough, the figure on the
left with bulging eyes and mustache is identified here as Marco Polo, who, having embraced Buddhism, came to be viewed as one of China's 18 wise men.
Behind the temple is a landscaped Chinese garden; it has four banyan trees with
intertwined branches, popularly known as the Lovers' Tree and considered sym-
bols of marital fidelity. According to local legend, the trees grew from the burial
site of two lovers who committed suicide when they were forbidden to marry.
Although the original trees died, new ones have taken their place.

   As you wander through the various buildings on the temple grounds, you will
notice small funeral rooms with altars dedicated to the newly deceased, complete
with photographs, offerings of fruit and other food, and paper money to assist the
departed in the afterlife. You may even chance upon a funeral service, in which
participants are dressed in white. Please show respect by being quiet, and refrain
from taking photographs. It is also considered bad manners—not to mention bad
luck—to take a picture of a monk without his permission. In any case, a visit to
this temple is like going back in time; allow 20 minutes in this time capsule.

Avenida do Coronel Mesquita. Free admission. Daily 7am–6pm. Bus: 12, 17, 18, 19, 22, or 23.

Temple of A-Ma ★★   Another important temple is situated at the bottom of
Barra Hill at the entrance to the Inner Harbour, across from the Maritime
Museum. It is Macau's oldest Chinese temple, with parts of it dating back more
than 600 years. This temple is dedicated to A-Ma, goddess of seafarers. According to legend, a poor village girl sought free passage on a boat but was refused
until a small fishing boat came along and took her onboard. Once the boat was
at sea, a typhoon blew in, destroying all boats except hers. Upon landing at what
is now Barra Hill, the young girl revealed herself as A-Ma, and the fishermen
repaid their gratitude by building this temple on the spot where they came
ashore. The temple was already here when the Portuguese arrived; they named
their city A-Ma-Gao (Bay of A-Ma) after this temple. The name has been shortened to Macau now, of course. The temple has images of A-Ma and stone carvings of the Chinese fishing boat that carried A-Ma to Macau. The temple,
spreading along the steep slope of a hill with views of the water, has good *feng
shui*. There are several shrines set in the rocky hillside, linked by winding paths
through moon gates. The uppermost shrine honors Kun Iam, the Goddess of
Mercy, and affords good views of the Inner Harbour.

Rua de S. Tiago da Barra. Free admission. Daily 6am–6pm. Bus: 1, 1A, 2, 5, 6, 7, 9, 10, 10A, 11, 18, 21, 21A,
28B, or 34.

A GARDEN

Lou Lim Iok Garden *Finds*   Macau's most flamboyant Chinese garden was
built in the 19th century by a wealthy Chinese merchant and modeled after the

famous gardens in Suzhou, China. Tiny, with narrow winding paths, bamboo groves, rock grottoes, a nine-turn zigzag bridge (believed to deter evil spirits), and ponds filled with carp, it's a nice escape from the city. If possible, come in the morning, when the garden is filled with Chinese doing tai chi exercises, musicians practicing traditional Chinese music, and bird lovers strolling with their birds in ornate wooden cages.

Estrada de Adolfo Loureiro. © 853/356622. Free admission. Daily 6am–6pm. Bus: 2, 4, 5, 7, 8, 8A, 9, 9A, 12, 16, 18, 19, 22, 23, 25, or 28C.

TAIPA & COLÔANE ISLANDS

Macau's two islands—Taipa and Colôane—are the city's breathing space, Macau's playground, a good place to get away from it all.

TAIPA

Closest to the mainland, Taipa was accessible only by ferry until 1974, when the Macau-Taipa Bridge was finally completed. Two additional bridges have led to increased development on Taipa, including unsightly new apartment blocks and booming suburbs that have pushed the population on this small, 6.5-sq.-km (2½-sq.-mile) island to 42,000. Taipa is also the home of several luxury hotels, Taipa Village with its popular restaurants and colonial architecture, a former

---

Car Races & Fireworks—The Heat Is On!

Of Macau's several annual events, none is as popular or draws as many enthusiasts as the Macau Grand Prix, held in mid- to late November, and the Macau International Fireworks Display Contest, held on subsequent Saturdays through September.

The **Macau Grand Prix**, first staged in 1954, features races for motorcycles, production cars (international group A), and Formula Three racers, and attracts drivers from all over the world. Very similar to the famous circuit in Monaco, the 6km (3¾-mile) Guia Circuit, which winds through town near the ferry terminal and is lined with grandstands along the way, includes the winding roads of Guia Hill, hard corners around the waterfront, and the straightaway along the Outer Harbour. Champion drivers can complete a lap in as little as 2 minutes and 20 seconds. Tickets for stands during the 2 practice days cost HK$100 (US$13), while race-day tickets range from HK$350 to HK$600 (US$46–US$78). For ticket inquiries, contact the Macau Government Tourist Office. Note, however, that ferry tickets and hotel accommodations in Macau are tight during the races.

Macau's other major competition, the **Macau International Fireworks Display Contest,** has a more universal appeal with its dazzling displays of fireworks spread over 5 nights. Begun in 1988, it is now the world's biggest fireworks contest, with almost a dozen international teams competing. Displays last 20 minutes and are judged using criteria such as the height reached by the fireworks, the explosive bang and spread of each firework, color and variety, and the overall choreographic effect of each display. The best places to view the fireworks are along the Praia Grande, from Penha Hill, or from the Macau-Taipa Bridge.

firecracker factory, temples, the United Chinese Cemetery with its blend of Confucianist, Taoist, and Buddhist influences, a university, Macau Stadium, and the Macau Jockey Club for horse racing.

For history and architecture buffs, the first stop should be **Taipa Village** ⟨★⟩, a small traditional community of narrow lanes, alleys, squares, and two-story colonial buildings painted in hues of yellow, blue, and green. Although now almost completely engulfed by nearby housing projects, village life remains in full view here, with women sorting the day's vegetables on towels in the street, children playing, and workers carrying produce and goods in baskets balanced from poles on their shoulders. On or near Rua do Cunha, the picturesque pedestrian-only main street with its hanging baskets of flowers, are a number of fine, inexpensive restaurants, making dining reason enough to come (see "Where to Dine," earlier in this chapter).

But for sightseeing, the best place to visit is the **Casa Museu da Taipa (Taipa House Museum),** on Avenida da Praia (✆ **853/827088**). It is one of five colonial-style buildings lining the street—homes that belonged to Macanese families in the early 1900s. Combining both European and Chinese design as a reflection of the families' Eurasian heritage, the Casa Museu has a dining and living room, study, kitchen, upstairs bedrooms, and large verandas that face banyan trees and the sea, reflecting the fact that most entertaining in this small colonial outpost took place at home. The home is filled with period furniture, paintings, art, and personal artifacts reflective of a dual heritage. The museum is open Tuesday to Sunday from 10am to 6pm, and admission is $5 ptcs (US65¢). Other buildings on the banyan-shaded Praia open to the public contain displays relating to the history of Taipa and its inhabitants, and traditional regional costumes of Portugal. Next to the buildings, on a hill, is Our Lady of Carmel Church, built in the 19th century for the devout Macanese Catholics.

The easiest way to reach Taipa Village is via one of the buses that stops in front of the Hotel Lisboa near the bridge on the mainland. Bus nos. 11, 15, 22, 28A, 30, 33, 34, and 35 all go to Taipa Village.

COLÔANE

Farther away and connected to China via bridge and to Taipa via a huge added strip of reclaimed land that has essentially made the two islands one, Colôane once served as a haven for pirates who preyed upon the rich trading ships passing by. The last pirate raid was as late as 1910, when bandits kidnapped 18 children and demanded ransom. Government forces eventually overpowered the pirates, freeing all the children. At any rate, Colôane today, measuring 7.75 sq. km (3 sq. miles) but with a population of only 4,000, is less developed than Taipa and is known for its beaches, pine trees, eight marked hiking trails, golf course, and traditional village. Two of the most popular **beaches** are Cheoc Van and Hac Sa (which means "black sand"). Both beaches have lifeguards on duty in the summer, restaurants, and nearby public swimming pools that are open until 10pm. To reach them, take bus no. 21A or 26A from Avenida de Almeida Ribeiro in the city center or from the Lisboa Hotel; bus no. 25 also runs from the Lisboa Hotel to both beaches.

For a bit of greenery, visit **Seac Pai Van Park** (✆ **853/870277**), a 20-hectare (50-acre) expanse on the island's western end with a walk-in aviary; a small zoo containing monkeys, cows, goats, geese, rabbits, and other animals; hillside trails; a small botanical garden; a playground; and the Museum of Nature and Agriculture, dedicated to the geography, agriculture, flora, and fauna of Macau. The museum is open Tuesday to Sunday from 10:30am to 4:30pm, while the park is open Tuesday to Sunday from 9am to 6pm. Admission to both the park and the museum is free. To reach the park, take bus no. 21A or 26A from Avenida de Almeida Ribeiro in the city center or from the Lisboa Hotel; bus nos. 25 and 26 also stop at the park.

Farther along the coast is the laid-back, quaint community of **Colôane Village** ★★. Now that Taipa Village has suffered so much surrounding development, I find Colôane Village much more picturesque and a worthy destination if exploring the islands. Located on the southwestern tip of the island, it is so close to China that it almost seems like you can reach out and touch it. Boats headed to and from China pass through the narrow waterway. The social center of the village revolves around a small, tiled square, which is lined on two sides with cloistered cafes. In its center is a monument erected in 1928 to commemorate those who fought in the 1910 battle against the pirates. At its end is the small but sweet **Chapel of St. Francis Xavier,** built in 1928 and dedicated to Asia's most important and well known Catholic missionary. The church, built in classic Portuguese style, would seem rather plain if it weren't for its exuberant Asian artwork.

6 Gambling, Shopping & Nightlife

GAMBLING

The Chinese so love gambling that it's often said that if two flies are walking on the wall, the Chinese will bet on which one will walk faster. It's not surprising, therefore, that mainland and Hong Kong Chinese make up almost 90% of the 11 million annual visitors to Macau. Since the only legal gambling in Hong Kong is comprised of the horse races and mahjong, you can bet that most of the Chinese come to Macau to gamble, whether it's at the casinos or the tracks.

CASINOS   In 2002, a 40-year monopoly on gambling ended, paving the way to grander casinos and an upsurge in Las Vegas–style entertainment. As of now, there are more than a dozen casinos in Macau, all open 24 hours. Some are fancy, others aren't, but none allow photographs to be taken, and shorts may not be worn. Admission is free, but some require you show a passport to enter.

Several hotels have casinos, including the **Mandarin Oriental** and **Hotel Lisboa,** all of which offer blackjack, baccarat, roulette, and Chinese games. The Hotel Lisboa, which boasts one of the busiest casinos, also offers hundreds of slot machines (known, appropriately enough, as "hungry tigers" in Chinese). In the past couple years, several themed, Las Vegas–style casinos have opened their doors, including **Pharaoh's Palace,** in the Landmark on Avenida da Amizade (© 853/788111), designed with motifs from ancient Egypt, and the **Sands Macau,** near the ferry terminal and Fisherman's Wharf (© 853/883388; www.sands.com.mo). In 2006, Macau's reputation as a gambling destination will skyrocket with the opening of the **Venetian Macau,** a resort on Cotai (the strip of reclaimed land between Taipa and Coloane) complete with casino, hotel, canals, gondolas, shopping mall, and more.

For a glimpse of gambling Chinese style, be sure to take a stroll through the ornately decorated **Macau Palace Floating Casino,** moored in the Outer Harbour not far from the Mandarin Oriental Hotel.

RACETRACKS   The **Macau Jockey Club** has its racetrack on Taipa Island (© 853/820868; www.macauhorse.com); it features horse racing most Saturdays and/or Sundays at 2pm and Tuesdays at 7:30pm, September through August. The minimum bet is $10 ptcs (US$1.30). Transportation is available by both public buses and air-conditioned coaches, which depart from in front of the Hotel Lisboa; tickets for the coach and raceway are available in the hotel lobby. The grandstand, which is air-conditioned, charges an admission of $20 ptcs (US$2.60); outdoor public stands are free. Call for more information or stop by the Macau Government Tourist Office. Take bus no. 11, 15, 22, 28A, 30, 33, 34, 35, or AP1.

For racing of a different sort, check out the greyhound races, held year-round on Monday, Thursday, Friday, and Sunday at 7:30pm at the open-air **Canidrome,** Avenida General Castelo Branco, located near the border gate to China (© 853/333399). An admission charge of $10 ptcs (US$1.30) is applied to the first bet; minimum bet is $10 (US$1.30). Take bus no. 1, 1A, 3, 4, 5, 7, 9, 9A, 25, or 34.

SHOPPING

A duty-free port, Macau has long been famous for its jewelry stores, especially those offering gold jewelry along Avenida do Infante D. Henrique and Avenida de Almeida Ribeiro. Many Chinese consider buying gold as an investment. Market prices per tael (1.2 oz.) of gold are set daily. When buying gold or jewelry, always request a certificate of guarantee.

After gold, Portuguese wines are another good bargain, as are Chinese antiques and leather garments. In recent years, a number of fashionable clothing boutiques have also opened in the center of town. To my mind, they seem a bit out of place amid the crumbling colonial architecture; in any case, these boutiques can also be found in Hong Kong. More colorful are the clothing stalls near Largo do Senado square, many of which sell overruns and seconds from Macau's many garment factories. Another colorful local shopping experience is the **Red Market,** located on the corner of Avenida Almirante Lacerda and Avenida Horta e Costa. Built in 1936 in Art Deco style, it houses a lively food market open daily from 7:30am to 7:30pm. A street market extends from the Red Market to Rotunda de Carlos Maia, a district popularly dubbed the Three Lamps District and a fun place to browse for cheap clothing. To reach the Red Market, take bus no. 1, 1A, 3, 4, 5, 8, 16, 17, 23, 25, 26, 26A, 32, 33, or 34 to Mercado Vermelho.

A significant indication of change was the 1993 opening of Macau's first full-fledged department store, **New Yaohan**—conveniently situated next to the ferry terminal (© 853/725338). Modeled after Japanese department stores, this four-floored shopping extravaganza is open daily from 11am to 10:30pm. (While Hong Kong department stores tend to focus on clothing and accessories, this store distinguishes itself by having departments for toys, gifts, electronics, household goods, cosmetics, and other items in addition to clothing and accessories, as well as a top floor devoted to restaurants, all very similar to how department stores are laid out in Japan.) But the biggest and most conspicuous addition to Macau's shopping and entertainment scene is **Fisherman's Wharf,** which stretches on reclaimed land in the Outer Harbour from the Macau Palace Floating Casino to the Macau Museum of Art. Opened in 2004, it is divided into themed port "towns" including Amsterdam, Lisbon, Cape Town, and New Orleans, and features shops, restaurants, bars, a disco, a manmade "active" volcano, an amusement park, playground, hotels, and amphitheater.

On the islands, there's a **weekly outdoor market** held Sundays from 11am to 8pm in Taipa Village, with booths selling traditional crafts, souvenirs, clothing, toys, and food. In Colôane Village, check out **Asian Artefacts,** 9 Rua dos Negociantes (© 853/881022), which sells restored antique furniture from North

China, including trunks, chests, tables, chairs, and more, as well as handicrafts from Thailand, India, and other Asian countries. It's open from 10am to 7pm daily and can arrange shipping.

NIGHTLIFE

For many years, Macau's only nighttime entertainment outside gambling and the horse races centered on hotel bars and lounges. While these are still recommendable for a drink and live entertainment, one of the few benefits to have arisen from the otherwise hideously sterile reclaimed-land development on the Outer Harbour is **Fisherman's Wharf** with its many bars and restaurants (see above) and **the Docks,** an unofficial name given to a string of sidewalk cafes and bars lining Avenida Dr. Sun Yat-sen near the Kun Iam Statue. The Docks is a great place for a drink and watching the parade of people file past. True to Macau's Mediterranean roots, the action doesn't start until after 10pm and is at its most frenetic after 1am. For a suggestion, try **Moonwalker** (© 853/751326), open daily from 4pm to 4am and offering live music Wednesday through Monday nights from 10pm. A great place to watch the sun go down is **180 Lounge and Grill** in the Macau Tower (© 853/9888659), open daily from noon to 1am and with live music Monday to Saturday from 8:30pm to midnight.

Appendix:
Hong Kong in Depth

Although some people might erroneously believe that Hong Kong's history began after the British took control of the island in 1842, it actually began millennia before that. Stone, bronze, and iron artifacts indicate that Hong Kong Island has been inhabited for at least 6,000 years, and more than 100 Neolithic and Bronze Age sites have been identified throughout the territory, including a 5,000-year-old kiln unearthed on Lantau island, 4,000-year-old burial grounds, a 2,000-year-old brick tomb, and Neolithic rock carvings.

1 History 101

EARLY SETTLERS

Although the area now called Hong Kong became part of the Chinese empire some 2,200 years ago during the Han dynasty, it was not until after the 12th century that the area became widely settled. Foremost were settler families, known as the Five Great Clans, who built walled cities complete with moats and gatehouses to protect their homes against roving pirates; a few of these walled cities remain. First to arrive was the Tang clan, who built at least five walled villages and maintained imperial connections with Beijing for 800 years, until the end of the 19th century. The other four clans were the Hau, Pang, Liu, and Man. The clans were joined by the Tanka people, who lived their whole lives on boats anchored in sheltered bays throughout the territory, and by the Hoklos, another seafaring people who established coastal fishing villages. They were followed by the Hakka, primarily farmers who cultivated rice, pineapples, and tea. There were also garrison troops stationed at Tuen Mun and Tai Po (now major satellite towns in the New Territories) to guard pearls harvested from Tolo Harbour by Tanka divers, while forts to guard against invasion were constructed at Tung Chung and other coastal regions.

Dateline

- **4,000–1,500 B.C.** Early settlers of Asian Mongoloid stock spread throughout South China, including Hong Kong, leaving behind Neolithic artifacts ranging from pottery and stone tools to burial grounds.
- **221 B.C.** Hong Kong becomes part of the Chinese empire with unification of China by the first emperor of Qin.
- **960–1500s** Pirates roam the seas around Hong Kong.
- **1514** Portuguese traders establish a base on Hong Kong.
- **1839** The Chinese emperor attempts to abolish the opium trade and destroys the British opium stockpile; the Royal Navy retaliates by firing on Chinese war junks, starting the first Opium War.
- **1841** British naval Capt. Charles Elliot seizes Hong Kong Island and declares himself governor.
- **1842** The first Opium War ends in the Treaty of Nanking, ceding Hong Kong Island to Britain in perpetuity.
- **1846** Hong Kong's population is 24,000. First horse races held at Happy Valley.
- **1856** Chinese officials searching for pirates arrest the crew of a British ship, prompting the second Opium War, which ends in 1858.
- **1857** A popular Chinese baker, Cheong Ah Lum, is accused of putting arsenic into his bread and poisoning nearly 300 Europeans in retaliation for

TEA & OPIUM

Hong Kong's modern history, how-ever, begins a mere 160-some years ago, under conditions that were far less than honorable. During the 1800s, the British were extremely eager to obtain Chinese silk and tea. Tea had become the national drink, but the only place it was grown was China, from which it was being imported to England in huge quanti-ties. The British tried to engage the Chinese in trade, but the Chinese were not interested in anything offered—only silver bullion would do. The Chinese also forbade the British to enter their kingdom, with the exception of a small trading depot in Canton.

But then the British hit upon a commodity that proved irresistible—opium. Grown in India and exported by the British East India Company, this powerful drug enslaved everyone from poor peasants to the nobility, and before long, China was being drained of silver, traded to support a drug habit. The Chinese emperor, fearful of the damage being wreaked on Chinese society and alarmed by his country's loss of silver, declared a ban on opium imports in the 1830s. The British simply ignored the ban, smug-gling their illegal cargo up the Pearl River. In 1839, with opium now India's largest export, the Chinese con-fiscated the British opium stockpiles in Canton and destroyed them. The British responded by declaring war and then winning the struggle. As a result of this first Opium War, waged until 1842, China was forced to open new ports for trade, agree to an exor-bitant cash indemnity for the loss of the destroyed opium, and cede Hong Kong Island in perpetuity to the British in a treaty China never recog-nized. Not only was this Treaty of Nanking demoralizing to the Chinese, it also ensured that their country remain open to the curse of opium.

the Opium Wars. He is acquitted but deported to China.

- **1860** Victorious in the second Opium War and seeking a foothold on the mainland, Britain forces China to cede Kowloon Peninsula and Stonecutters Island to the British in perpetuity in the First Convention of Peking. Popu-lation reaches 94,000.
- **1865** Hongkong and Shanghai Bank founded.
- **1888** The Victoria Peak tram is com-pleted, reducing the journey to the peak from 3 hours to 8 minutes.
- **1898** With the signing of the Second Convention of Peking, the New Terri-tories are leased to Britain for 99 years, for which Britain pays nothing.
- **1900** Hong Kong's population is 263,000.
- **1904** The street tramway system is constructed along the waterfront on Hong Kong Island.
- **1910** The Kowloon Railway is com-pleted, linking Hong Kong with China.
- **1911** The Manchu dynasty is over-thrown by Sun Yat-sen's Nationalist revolution; refugees flood into Hong Kong.
- **1925** Hong Kong's first and only gen-eral strike; Nationalists and Commu-nists join in a United Front, organizing anti-foreign strikes and boycotts in China that spread to Hong Kong, paralyzing the economy.
- **1938** Japan seizes Canton; Hong Kong becomes an arms-smuggling route for the Nationalist forces, now under Chiang Kai-shek; 500,000 Chi-nese refugees flee into Hong Kong.
- **1941** Japanese forces occupy Hong Kong and begin deporting residents to the mainland to ease food and housing shortages.
- **1945** The British resume control of Hong Kong following World War II. Hong Kong's pre-war population of 1.6 million now stands at 600,000.
- **1949** Mao declares the founding of the People's Republic; a subsequent flood of refugees to Hong Kong causes the Communist government to seal the Chinese–Hong Kong border.

continues

And although opium was the cause of the war, it was never even mentioned in the Treaty of Nanking.

Following the second Opium War, waged from 1856 to 1858 as the British sought more trading ports and pushed for the legalization of the opium trade, the tip of Kowloon Peninsula and Stonecutters Island were added to the colony in 1860. In 1898, Britain decided it needed more land for defense and dictated a lease for the New Territories (where approximately 100,000 Chinese were living at the time), including more than 200 outlying islands, for 99 years, until 1997.

THE PROMISED LAND

When the British took control of Hong Kong Island in 1842, some 7,000 Chinese lived on the island in farming and fishing communities. Although Hong Kong had a deep and protected harbor, no one, including the Chinese, was much interested in the island itself, and many in the British government considered its acquisition an embarrassing mistake. No sooner had the island been settled than a typhoon tore through the settlement. Repairs were demolished only 5 days later by another tropical storm. Fever and fire followed, and the weather grew so oppressive and humid that the colony seemed to be enveloped in a giant steam bath.

Yet, while the number of headstones in the hillside cemetery multiplied, so did the number of the living, especially as word spread of the fortunes being made by traders who had established trading houses. By the turn of the century, the number had swelled to 300,000. British families lived along the waterfront and called it Victoria (now the Central District), slowly moving up toward the cooler temperatures of Victoria Peak. The Chinese, barred from occupying The Peak and other European-only neighborhoods, resided in a shantytown farther west,

- **1950** Mass influx of refugees continues following the fall of Shanghai to the Communists. Population of Hong Kong reaches 2 million.
- **1953** Following a huge fire in a squatter camp, Hong Kong begins an ambitious public housing program to house its still-growing population of refugees.
- **1966** A fare increase on the Star Ferry prompts clashes between Chinese and the police.
- **1967** The Cultural Revolution in China leads to pro-Communist riots in Hong Kong; 51 people are killed, and hundreds more are wounded or arrested in the fighting.
- **1972** First cross-harbor tunnel opens.
- **1979** Establishment of Hong Kong's Mass Transit Railway subway system. Hong Kong governor Sir Murray MacLehose goes to Beijing for the first Sino-British discussions on the return of Hong Kong to Chinese rule.
- **1981** British Parliament downgrades Hong Kong passports to prevent an exodus of Hong Kong Chinese to the United Kingdom.
- **1984** China and Britain sign the Joint Declaration for the handover of Hong Kong to China in 1997.
- **1989** Events at Tiananmen Square in Beijing send shock waves through Hong Kong. Some 80,000 demonstrators brave a typhoon in support of the pro-democracy uprising.
- **1992** Hong Kong governor Chris Patten announces new democratic reforms.
- **1995** Elections for the Legislative Council brings landslide victory for the Democrats; China announces it will dissolve the legislature after the handover.
- **1997** Britain transfers Hong Kong to Communist China, ending 156 years of British rule, in an agreement that allows Hong Kong—now a Special Administrative Region—to retain many of its freedoms for at least 50 years. Four thousand Chinese troops march in; Tung Chee-hwa becomes chief executive of the SAR. Hong Kong's first outbreak of avian flu at the end of the year, killing six people, prompts the new government to order the slaughter of 1.3 million chickens.

now called the Western District. Conditions were so appalling that when the bubonic plague struck in 1894, it raged for almost 30 years, claiming more than 20,000 lives.

Hong Kong's growth in the 20th century was no less astonishing in terms of both trade and population. In 1900, approximately 11,000 ships pulled into Hong Kong harbor; just a decade later, the number had doubled. In 1911, the overthrow of the Manchu dynasty in China sent a flood of refugees into Hong Kong, followed, in 1938, by an additional 500,000 immigrants. Another mass influx of Chinese refugees arrived after the fall of Shanghai to the Communists in 1950. From this last wave of immigrants, including many Shanghai industrialists, emerged the beginnings of Hong Kong's now-famous textile industry. Throughout the 1950s, Hong Kong grew as a manufacturing and industrial center for electronics, watches, and other low-priced goods. By 1956, Hong Kong's population stood at 2.5 million.

CHANGE, UNREST & THE LAST OF THE BRITISH

As a British colony, Hong Kong was administered by a governor appointed by the queen. There were no free elections, and the Legislative Council, Hong Kong's main governing body, was also appointed. As 1997 drew nearer, marking the end of the 99-year lease on the New Territories, it soon became clear that China had no intention of renewing the lease or renegotiating a treaty it had never recognized in the first place.

Finally, after more than 20 rounds of talks and meetings, Britain's Prime Minister Margaret Thatcher signed the Sino-British Joint Declaration of 1984, agreeing to transfer all of Hong Kong to Chinese Communist rule on June 30, 1997. China declared Hong Kong a "Special Administrative Region," granting it special privileges under a "one country, two systems" policy that guaranteed Hong Kong's capitalist lifestyle and social system for at least 50 years after 1997. Under provisions set forth in the Sino-British Joint Declaration and in Hong Kong's constitution, the Basic Law, Hong Kong would remain largely self-governing, and its people would retain rights to their property, to freedom of speech, and to travel freely in and out of Hong Kong. Throughout the negotiations, however, Hong Kong's residents were never consulted.

Then came the events of June 1989 in Tiananmen Square, in which hundreds of students and demonstrators were attacked by Chinese authorities in a brutal

- **1998** Hong Kong's first election under Chinese rule allows for one-third of the Legislative Council to be elected by popular vote; Democrats win the most seats. Hong Kong's new airport at Chep Lak Kok opens.
- **1999** Hong Kong's Court of Final Appeal rules that according to its constitution, Hong Kong residency can be extended to any mainland Chinese with one Hong Kong parent; Tung Chee-hwa invites Beijing to review the immigration ruling, which is subsequently overturned.
- **2000** Hong Kong's freedom of the press is threatened after a mainland official warns Hong Kong media against covering independence for Taiwan, followed by a crackdown on pornography.
- **2002** Hong Kong's highest court affirms the mainland's 1999 reversal of its earlier ruling on migrants and orders 7,300 "unlawful migrants" back to the mainland. Only 3,000 comply, with the rest of the "abode seekers" forcibly removed, causing great public outcry.
- **2003** An outbreak in Hong Kong of severe acute respiratory syndrome (SARS) spreads around the globe, infecting more than 8,000 people and delivering a shocking blow to Hong Kong's economy.

move to quash the pro-democracy movement. China's response to the uprising sent shock waves through Hong Kong and led to rounds of angry protest.

Those who could, emigrated, primarily to Australia, Canada, and the United States; at its height, more than 1,000 were emigrating each week. After all, nearly half of Hong Kong's Chinese are refugees from the mainland, and as one Hong Kong Chinese told me, his family fled to escape Communist rule, so why should he stay after 1997? Approximately 90% of Hong Kong's Chinese, however, remained, confident or at least hopeful that China realized it had more to gain by keeping Hong Kong as it was. In a move that angered Communist China, Hong Kong Chinese were granted more political autonomy during the last few years of the colony's existence than in all the preceding 150 years, including various democratic reforms such as elections for the Legislative Council. Some early emigrants began returning to Hong Kong, confident they could do better in their native country and willing to wait to see how life might change under the Chinese. In any case, now they had a safety net: foreign passports.

On June 30, 1997, the last British governor of Hong Kong, Chris Patten, sailed out of Hong Kong, and Tung Chee-hwa, appointed by Beijing, became the new chief executive of the Special Administrative Region (SAR). Mainland China celebrated the event as the end of more than 100 years of shame. On July 1, it dissolved Hong Kong's elected Legislative Council and replaced it with a hand-picked Provisional Legislature until a new Legislative Council, with both elected and appointed members, could be formed.

SINCE THE HANDOVER

Hong Kong's first elections under Chinese rule, held in May 1998, allowed for one-third of the 60-member legislature to be elected by direct popular vote, with the Democrats—Hong Kong's largest party, led by the SAR's main opposition figure Martin Lee—winning the most seats (although full suffrage, with a fully elected legislature and chief executive, is declared a goal in the Basic Law, there is no timetable). Meanwhile, like the rest of Asia, Hong Kong was hit hard by economic recession, made worse by manufacturers moving across the Chinese border into Shenzhen to take advantage of cheaper land prices and cheaper wages. Approval ratings for Tung and other government officials plunged, especially after unemployment hit 4.5%, a 15-year high.

After the handover, the SAR began allowing 150 mainland Chinese to migrate to Hong Kong every day—more than 54,000 a year. In January 1999, Hong Kong's Court of Final Appeal ruled that the Basic Law also granted automatic Hong Kong residency to any mainland Chinese with one Hong Kong parent, even if that parent gained residency after the child was born. However, fearing unplanned population growth, with an estimated 1.6 million additional qualified immigrants potentially pouring in from the mainland, coupled with increased unemployment, Tung Chee-hwa asked Beijing to review the immigration ruling, a move interpreted by critics as a threat to the judicial independence of the SAR. China responded by overturning the immigration judgment issued by Hong Kong's highest court and providing a narrower interpretation of the Basic Law, thereby cutting the number of potential new immigrants over the next decade from 1.6 million to about 200,000. Only mainland children who were born *after* a parent received legal resident status were given a "right of abode." In January 2002, Hong Kong's Court of Final Appeal affirmed the Chinese government's reversal of its earlier ruling and ordered 7,300 "unlawful migrants" to leave the SAR by March 31. Only 3,000 complied; the remaining 4,300 were forcibly removed to the mainland by police.

But the biggest rift in Hong Kong-Beijing relations came in 2003, when an anti-subversion bill was introduced by Tung Chee-hwa's Beijing-backed administration. The measure, meant to outlaw subversion, sedition, treason, the theft of state secrets, and other crimes against the state, brought more than 500,000 protesters to Hong Kong's streets on July 1, 2003, making it the SAR's largest protest since the Tiananmen Square massacre. Opponents of the measure said it would erode political freedoms and curb free speech. Although Tung withdrew the bill, some critics contend he did so only after a key ally quit his Cabinet, leaving him with insufficient support to enact the law.

Another blow to Hong Kong democracy came in 2004, when Beijing ruled against a public election in 2007 for Hong Kong's chief executive in 2007 and declared that there would be no universal suffrage for the Legislative Council election slated for 2008. Hong Kong's pro-democracy leaders responded that Hong Kong's autonomy had been violated, with the core principals of the Basic Law and the 1984 Sino-British Joint Declaration—that Hong Kong would be ruled by the people of Hong Kong—replaced by a Beijing dictatorship. In September 2004, elections for the 60-member Legislative Council allowed an increase in the number of elected members from 24 to 30, where it will apparently now stay until Beijing decides otherwise.

Of course, the biggest news to garner international attention was not Hong Kong's struggle for autonomy, but rather its role in the eruption of a mysterious, flu-like illness in the spring of 2003. Spreading from a Hong Kong hotel, severe acute respiratory syndrome, or SARS, infected more than 8,000 people in 29 countries over the next few months, killing more than 700 of them. In Hong Kong, which together with China suffered the most, the illness sickened 1,775 people and claimed almost 300 lives. Needless to say, SARS was a major blow to Hong Kong's economy, reducing the city to a tourist ghost town and costing the city $4 to $6 billion in retail trade and business. Unemployment hit 8.7%, the highest since the statistic was first recorded in 1981. To encourage tourism and boost the local economy, Hong Kong turned to action film star Jackie Chan as its international spokesperson.

2 Hong Kong Today

Ever since the 1997 handover, foremost in almost every visitor's mind today is, "How much has Hong Kong changed?" To the casual observer, not much. In fact, if it hadn't dominated the news, I doubt the average tourist would even notice there'd *been* a handover. Entry formalities for most other nationalities remain unchanged. English remains an official language, and the English names of buildings, streets, and attractions have stayed the same. The Hong Kong dollar, pegged to the U.S. dollar, remains legal tender, and in most hotels, restaurants, and shops that cater to tourists, it's business as usual.

There are, however, discernable differences. Most visible was the replacement of the Union Jack and colonial Hong Kong flag with China's starred flag and the new Hong Kong Special Administrative Region's flag emblazoned with the bauhinia flower. In addition, new coins bearing the bauhinia were minted (the old coins with the queen's head remain valid but are being snapped up by collectors) and new stamps were issued. The words "Royal" and "ER" (Elizabeth Regina) disappeared throughout Hong Kong, along with royal crests, crowns, and coats of arms. The police sport new badges.

Of course, the British population also noticeably declined after the handover, due primarily to the completion of large construction projects such as the new airport, the departure of the British military, and stricter regulations making it more difficult for casual workers to remain in the SAR. Although the number of U.K. residents was never huge (less than 2% before the handover), British presence loomed understandably larger when Hong Kong was a colony. Today the SAR seems increasingly more Chinese, with more in common with Shenzhen across the Chinese border than with its former colonizer. Of course, Hong Kong has more links now—financially and emotionally—with mainland China than it ever had in the past. Tourism from Europe, North America, and Japan, once a major market but down since the September 11 terrorist attacks in the United States and taking another hit with the SARS epidemic, is now greatly eclipsed by visitors from mainland China, especially since the 2003 introduction of relaxed travel laws that exempted mainland Chinese of certain geographic areas (mostly wealthy areas like Shanghai, Beijing, and so on) from the requirement that they visit Hong Kong only in tour groups, thereby allowing them to travel to Hong Kong on their own. Today, mainland Chinese make up more than half of all visitor arrivals into Hong Kong, followed by Taiwanese, who account for more than 10%.

Naturally, another question that looms large in the minds of visitors to Hong Kong is, "What about SARS?" While no one can be certain that another outbreak will never happen and a vaccination against the illness has yet to be developed, there was a collective sigh of relief when 2004 passed without a repeat of the 2003 catastrophe. But Hong Kong is ready. The temperatures of all passengers passing through border controls—at the Hong Kong airport, the border checkpoint between Hong Kong and mainland China, and ferry terminals serving Macau and beyond—are thermally scanned for fever. There are hand sanitizers throughout Hong Kong, and one positive result of the SARS epidemic is that the city cleaned up its trash and refuse, making it cleaner than it has ever been.

Yet most striking about Hong Kong since the handover is that it suffers from an identity crisis: What should be its role in a greater China? Long serving as the manufacturing liaison between China and the rest of the world, Hong Kong is now challenged by a dazzling, dynamic, confident Shanghai. Hong Kong manufacturers have moved across the border to Shenzhen to take advantage of lower production costs. Guangzhou threatens to take over Hong Kong's role as a transportation hub with a new airport and a proposed deep-water port. Other woes include fears that rights guaranteed by Hong Kong's constitution are being eroded by authorities in mainland China; every sign of hostility between Taiwan and Beijing sends shivers up the collective Hong Kong spine. Pollution, primarily from Hong Kong's increasing vehicular traffic and from regional diesel pollution in the Pearl River Delta, has reached an all-time high, threatening not only the health of its citizens but its status as a major tourist destination.

Yet if you ask me, Hong Kong seems poised for a tourism renaissance, due in no small part to increased tourism from the mainland. Many new projects are in the works, including a Disneyland scheduled to open by 2006 and, for the first time in a decade, new first-class hotels in the Central District. New restaurants are blossoming all over the city, and the nightlife scene has never been more robust. Many hotels, particularly those offering reasonable rates, are often full, due largely to individual tourism from the mainland and Hong Kong's reputation as a convention destination. Although unemployment (now around 7.2%) remains high, economic indicators hint at an economic recovery.

Still, no one can predict the future, as Hong Kong has always been a city in transformation. The Hong Kong I am writing about now is not the same city that existed just a few short years ago and is not the Hong Kong you'll probably experience when you go there. Changes occur at a dizzying pace here: Relatively new buildings are torn down to make way for even newer, shinier skyscrapers; whole neighborhoods are obliterated in the name of progress; reclaimed land is taken from an ever-shrinking harbor; and traditional villages are replaced with satellite towns. Hong Kong's city skyline has surged upward and outward so dramatically since my first visit in 1983, it sometimes seems like decades rather than a year must have elapsed each time I see it anew. Change is commonplace, and yet it's hard not to lament the loss of familiar things that suddenly vanish; it's harder still not to brood over what's likely to come.

But don't worry. If this is your first trip to Hong Kong, you're much more likely to notice its Chinese aspects than its Westernized appearance as ducks hanging by their necks in restaurant windows, bamboo scaffolding, herbal- medicine shops, street-side markets, Chinese characters on huge neon signs, wooden fishing boats, shrines to the kitchen god, fortune-tellers, temples, laundry fluttering from bamboo poles, dim sum trolleys, and the clicking of mahjong tiles all conspire to create an atmosphere that is overwhelmingly Chinese.

In short, Hong Kong is a place like no other, with an energy and irresistible draw that will surely captivate travelers for generations to come.

3 Life in Hong Kong

THE PEOPLE

With a population of approximately 6.8 million, Hong Kong is overwhelmingly Chinese—some 95% of its residents are Chinese, more than half of whom were born in Hong Kong. But the Chinese themselves are a diverse people and they hail from different parts of China. Most are Cantonese from southern China, the area just beyond Hong Kong's border—hence, Cantonese is the most widely spoken language of the region. Other Chinese include the Hakka, traditionally farmers whose women are easily recognizable by their hats with a black fringe, and the Tanka, the majority of Hong Kong's shrinking boat population. Hong Kong's many Chinese restaurants specializing in Cantonese, Sichuan, Chiu Chow, Pekingese, Shanghainese, and other regional foods are testaments of the city's diversity.

Hong Kong, with a total land area of approximately 1,100 sq. km (425 sq. miles; about half the size of Rhode Island), is one of the most densely populated areas in the world. The best place to appreciate this is atop Victoria Peak, where you can feast your eyes on Hong Kong's famous harbor, and as far as the eye can see, mile upon mile of high-rise apartments. If Hong Kong were a vast plain, it would be as ugly as Tokyo. But it's saved by undulating mountain peaks, which cover virtually all of Hong Kong and provide dramatic background to the cityscape and coastal areas. Because of its dense population and limited land space, with more than 16,000 people per square mile, Hong Kong has long been saddled with acute housing deficiencies. Just a few decades ago, in an area called Mong Kok in northwestern Kowloon, there were an astounding 652,910 people per square mile. One house designed for 12 people had 459 living in it, including 104 people who shared one room and four people who lived on the roof.

Since 1953, when a huge fire left more than 50,000 squatters homeless, Hong Kong has pursued one of the world's most ambitious housing projects, with the aim of providing every Hong Kong family with a home of its own. By 1993, half of Hong Kong's population lived in government-subsidized public housing, a higher proportion than anywhere else in the world.

Tips for the Business Traveler to Hong Kong

- **Bring plenty of business cards.** They are exchanged constantly, and you'll be highly suspect without them (if you run out, hotel business centers can arrange to have new ones printed within 24 hr.). When presenting your card, hold it out with both hands, turned so that the receiver can read it. Chinese names are written with the family name first, followed by the given name and then the middle name.
- **Use formal names for addressing business associates** unless told to do otherwise; you'll find that many Hong Kong Chinese used to dealing with foreigners have adopted a Western first name.
- **Shaking hands is appropriate** for greetings and introductions.
- **Business attire**—a suit and tie for men; blazers/jackets and skirts for women—is worn throughout the year, even in summer (though women can get away with just blouses in the summer).
- **Avoid the Chinese New Year,** as all of Hong Kong shuts down for at least 3 days; based on the lunar calendar, it falls between late January and mid-February.
- **Entertainment** is an integral part of conducting business in Hong Kong, whether it's a meal in which the host orders the food and serves his or her guests, an evening at the racetracks, or a round of golf.
- If an invitation is extended, it is understood that **the host will treat.** Do not insist on paying; this will only embarrass your host. Accept graciously, and promise to pick up the tab next time around.
- Contact the **Hong Kong Trade Development Council,** Hong Kong Convention & Exhibition Centre, 1 Expo Dr., Wan Chai (© **852/1830 668;** www.tdctrade.com), for more information on conducting business in Hong Kong.

Most public housing is clustered in the New Territories, in a forest of high-rises that leaves foreign visitors aghast. Each apartment building is approximately 30 stories tall, containing about 1,000 apartments and 3,000 to 4,000 residents. Seven or eight apartment buildings comprise an estate, which is like a small town with its own name, shopping center, recreational and sports facilities, playgrounds, schools, and social services. A typical apartment is indescribably small by Western standards—approximately 250 square feet, with a single window. It consists of a combination living room/bedroom, a kitchen nook, and bathroom, and is typically shared by a couple with one or two children. According to government figures, every household in Hong Kong has at least one TV; many have one for each member of the household, even if the house consists of only one or two rooms. But as cramped, unimaginative, and sterile as these housing projects may seem, they're a vast improvement over the way much of the population used to live. They also account for most of Hong Kong's construction growth in the past 2 decades, especially in the New Territories.

And where are these people coming from? Many are newly arrived from mainland China, more than 54,000 a year. Many Hong Kong Chinese look down on these newcomers as provincial, rude, and uneducated, and indeed, many of them now occupy the lowest rung on the economic ladder, accepting squalid living conditions in hopes of forging a better life, just as other Hong Kong Chinese did before them. There are also many young mainland Chinese wives in Hong Kong, since eligible Hong Kong bachelors often return to their parents' or ancestors' homeland in China in search of a bride. "Hong Kong girls are considered too materialistic," one Hong Kong resident told me, "and mainland Chinese will work harder." And, for those in mainland China, Hong Kong has long been the promised land.

ARCHITECTURE

If you never ventured much beyond the waterfronts of Victoria Harbour, you might easily believe that Hong Kong is nothing more than chrome-and-glass skyscrapers, huge housing projects, shopping malls, and miles of glowing neon signs heralding countless open-fronted shops.

But Hong Kong was inhabited long before the British arrived, and some pre-colonial Chinese architecture still survives in the hinterlands. Several rural villages boast buildings and temples with fine woodcarving, and are examples of centuries-old Chinese craftsmanship. Especially fascinating are the walled villages in the New Territories, a few of which are still inhabited, and one of which has been meticulously restored and turned into a museum of traditional lifestyles (see chapter 10). These villages were built from the 14th through the 17th centuries by clan families to protect themselves from roving bandits, invaders, and even wild tigers. A few of the clans' ancestral halls, homes, and mansions also survive.

Also surviving are some of Hong Kong's temples. One of the oldest is a Tin Hau temple in Causeway Bay, dedicated to the seafarers' patron goddess. Hong Kong's most famous temple, however, is Man Mo, built in the 1840s and dedicated to the gods of literature and war. See p. 250 and 169, respectively.

Some colonial architecture also remains. One of Hong Kong's most familiar landmarks is the clock tower next to the Star Ferry terminus at Tsim Sha Tsui; it is all that remains of the old railway station that once linked the colony with China and beyond. On the Hong Kong Island side, the former Supreme Court in Central features Greco-Victorian columns and Chinese wood beam eaves. Today it houses the Legislative Council chamber. Nearby, in Hong Kong Park, is the Flagstaff House, Hong Kong's oldest surviving colonial-style building and now home to a museum of tea ware (p. 165).

Construction in Hong Kong has been going on at such a frenzied pace that if you haven't been here in 20 years (or even 10), you probably won't recognize the skylines of Central and Wan Chai. Among the most dramatic buildings are the extension of the Hong Kong Convention and Exhibition Centre on reclaimed land on the Wan Chai waterfront, boasting the world's largest plate-glass window and a three-tiered roof said to resemble a gull's wings in flight; the 78-story Central Plaza, located near the Wan Chai waterfront and boasting an Art Deco style with eye-catching nighttime lighting that changes color with each quarter hour, thereby giving the time; and the Hongkong and Shanghai Bank, designed by British architect Norman Foster and featuring entire floors suspended from steel masts and a 48m-tall (160-ft.) sun scoop on the roof that uses 480 mirrors to reflect sunlight down into the bank's atrium and public plaza. Atop Victoria Peak is the Peak Tower, topped by a crescent-shaped bowl not unlike a wok. But Hong Kong's tallest building is the Two IFC (International Finance Centre) tower, standing 420m (1,378 ft.) high beside Hong Kong Station.

Even though Hong Kong's structures are Western, they were built using bamboo scaffolding and constructed according to ancient Chinese beliefs, especially the 3,000-year-old Taoist principle of *feng shui* (geomancy) that allows humankind to live in peace with the environment and nature, ensuring good luck, prosperity, wealth, health, and happiness. Even today, most office and apartment buildings in Hong Kong have been laid out in accordance to *feng shui* principles (see the "*Feng Shui*—Restoring a Balance with Nature" box below).

CULTURAL LIFE

If you want to see Hong Kong's Chinese cultural life, simply step outside. Much of Hong Kong's drama is played in its streets, whether it's amateur Chinese opera singers at the famous Temple Street Night Market or a fortune-teller who has set up a chair and table at the side of the road or a Taoist temple. Virtually everything the Chinese consider vital still thrives in Hong Kong, including ancient religious beliefs, superstitions, wedding customs, and festivals.

The first sign that Hong Kong's cultural life is not confined to its stages and concert halls can be observed if you get up early and stroll through a city park, where you'll see people practicing tai chi (Chinese shadow boxing), which looks like dance in slow motion. Originally a martial art developed about 1,000 years ago, tai chi today is a form of exercise that restores harmony in the body through 200 individual movements designed to use every muscle in the body. Good places to observe the art include Kowloon Park in Tsim Sha Tsui as well as Victoria Park, Hong Kong Park, and the Zoological and Botanical Gardens on Hong Kong Island. If you wish, you can even partake in a free tai chi session held 3 mornings a week on the Tsim Sha Tsui waterfront (see p. 179).

Hong Kong's many festivals are the most obvious expression of cultural life, most of which feature parades, dances, and observances of local customs. Lion dances, for example, may be performed to the accompaniment of drums, while in the evenings, there may be puppet shows or Chinese opera performances.

Of the various Chinese performing arts, Chinese opera is the most popular and widely loved. Dating back to the Mongol period, it has always appealed to both the ruling class and the masses. Virtue, corruption, violence, and lust are common themes, and performances feature elaborate costumes and makeup, haunting atonal orchestrations, and crashing cymbals. The actor-singers train for many years. The costumes signify specific stage personalities; yellow is reserved for emperors, while purple is the color worn by barbarians. Unlike Western performances, Chinese operas are noisy affairs, with families coming and going during long performances, chatting with friends, and eating.

In Hong Kong, you can also attend concerts of Western classical music, jazz, and pop, and performances of ballet, modern dance, and theater (see chapter 9).

CHINESE MEDICINE

For most minor ailments, many Chinese are more likely to pay a visit to their neighborhood medicine store than see a doctor. Most traditional medicine stores cater solely to the practice of Chinese herbal medicine, with some cures dating back 2,000 years. The medicinal stock, however, includes much more than roots and plants—take a look inside one of Hong Kong's many medicinal shops and you'll find a bewildering array of jars and drawers containing everything from ginseng and deer's horn to fossilized bones and animal teeth. Deer's horn is said to be effective against fever; bones, teeth, and seashells are used as tranquilizers and cures for insomnia. In prescribing treatment, herbalists take into account the patient's overall mental and physical well-being in the belief that disease and illness are caused by an imbalance in bodily forces. In contrast to Western medicine, treatment is often preventive rather than remedial. Visitors particularly interested in traditional Chinese medicine will want to visit the Hong Kong Museum of Medical Sciences (see p. 169).

Acupuncture is also alive and well in Hong Kong, with approximately 400 acupuncturists offering their services. With a history that goes back 4,000 years, acupuncture is based on 365 pressure points, which in turn act upon certain organs; slender, stainless-steel needles are used, which vary in length from ½ inch to 10 inches. Most acupuncturists also use moxa (dried mugwort), a slow-burning herb that applies gentle heat.

RELIGION, MYTH & FOLKLORE

Most Hong Kong Chinese worship both Buddhist and Taoist deities, something they do not find at all incongruous. They also worship their family ancestors. There are ancestral altars in homes, and certain days are set aside for visiting ancestral graves. Many temples have large tablet halls, where Hong Kong families can worship the memorialized photographs of their dead. There are about 360 temples scattered throughout Hong Kong; some embody a mixture of both Buddhist and Taoist principles.

Feng Shui—Restoring a Balance with Nature

Feng shui, which translates literally as "wind water," is an ancient method of divination in which harmony is achieved with the spirits of nature. Virtually every Hong Kong Chinese believes that before a house or building can be erected, a tree chopped down, or a boulder moved, a geomancer must be called in to make certain that the spirits inhabiting the place aren't disturbed. The geomancer, who uses a compasslike device as an aid, determines the alignment of walls, doors, desks, and even beds, so as not to provoke the anger of the spirits residing there. He does this by achieving a balance among the eight elements of nature—heaven, earth, hills, wind, fire, thunder, rain, and ocean. Also considered are the spirits of yin (male-active) and yang (female-passive) forces that control our world.

Even non-Chinese-owned companies in Hong Kong comply with *feng shui* principles, if only to appease their Chinese employees. But it doesn't hurt to be safe; tales abound of ill luck befalling those working or living inside buildings that ignored the needs of resident spirits.

Since facing the water is considered excellent *feng shui,* when the Regent Hotel (now the InterContinental) was constructed, it incorporated a huge glass window overlooking the harbor. The next best thing, if you can't look out over water, is to bring the water inside, which is why many offices, shops, and restaurants have aquariums. Another way to deflect evil influences is to hang a small, eight-sided mirror outside your window. Other Chinese touches are incorporated into modern architecture—the Hongkong and Shanghai Bank, for example, is guarded by a pair of bronze lions, protecting its occupants.

If you wish to learn more about the principles of *feng shui,* see whether a lecture is being offered through the HKTB's Meet the People program (see chapter 6 for more details). Also note that *feng shui,* the transliteration used by the HKTB, is also transliterated as *fung shui.*

While Buddhism is concerned with the afterlife, Taoism is a folk faith whose devotees believe in luck and in currying its favor. Fortune-tellers, therefore, are usually found only at Taoist temples. Tao, essentially, is the way of the universe, the spirit of all things, and cannot be perceived. However, Taoist gods must be worshipped and Taoist spirits appeased. Most popular is Tin Hau, goddess of the sea and protectress of fishermen. Hong Kong has at least 24 temples that were erected in her honor. But each profession or trade has its own god—ironically, policemen and gangsters have the same one.

If you look for them, you'll find shrines dedicated to the earth god, Tou Ti, at the entrance to almost every store or restaurant in Hong Kong. They're usually below knee level, so that everyone pays homage upon entering and departing. Restaurants also have shrines dedicated to the kitchen god, Kwan Kung, to protect workers from knives and other sharp objects.

Although not a religion as such, another guiding principle in Chinese thought is Confucianism. Confucius, who lived in the 5th century B.C., devised a strict set of rules designed to create the perfect human being. Kindness, selflessness, obedience, and courtesy were preached, with carefully prescribed rules of how people should interact with one another. Since the masses were largely illiterate, Confucius communicated by means of easy-to-remember proverbs.

But despite the fact that many Hong Kong Chinese are both Buddhist and Taoist, they are not a particularly religious people in the Western sense of the word. There is no special day for worship, so devotees simply visit a temple whenever they want to pay their respects or feel the need for spiritual guidance. Otherwise, religion in Hong Kong plays a subtle role and is evident more in philosophy and action than in pious ceremony. To the Chinese, religion is a way of life and thus affects everyday living.

Almost every home has a small shrine, where lighted joss sticks are thought to bring good luck. In New Year celebrations, door gods are placed on the front door for good luck, and all lights are switched on to discourage monster spirits. On New Year's Day, homes are not swept for fear of whisking away good luck. And during a full moon or major festival, housewives will often set fire to paper creations of homes, cars, or fake money to bring good luck.

But since no one can ever have too much good luck, superstitions abound in Hong Kong. Certain numbers, for example, have connotations. The most auspicious number is 8, because its pronunciation (baht) is similar to the word for wealth (faht). Likewise, the most inauspicious number is 4, since it sounds almost exactly like the Chinese word for death. Thirteen is also an unlucky number, so many Hong Kong buildings simply skip it in their floor-numbering scheme.

To be on the safe side, Hong Kong Chinese will also visit fortune-tellers. Some read palms, while others study facial features, consult astrological birth charts, or let a little bird select a fortune card from a deck.

Index

See also Accommodations index, below.

FROMMER'S® COMPLETE TRAVEL GUIDES

Alaska
Alaska Cruises & Ports of Call
American Southwest
Amsterdam
Argentina & Chile
Arizona
Atlanta
Australia
Austria
Bahamas
Barcelona, Madrid & Seville
Beijing
Belgium, Holland & Luxembourg
Bermuda
Boston
Brazil
British Columbia & the Canadian
  Rockies
Brussels & Bruges
Budapest & the Best of Hungary
Calgary
California
Canada
Cancún, Cozumel & the Yucatán
Cape Cod, Nantucket & Martha's
  Vineyard
Caribbean
Caribbean Ports of Call
Carolinas & Georgia
Chicago
China
Colorado
Costa Rica
Cruises & Ports of Call
Cuba
Denmark
Denver, Boulder & Colorado
  Springs
England
Europe
Europe by Rail
European Cruises & Ports of Call

Florence, Tuscany & Umbria
Florida
France
Germany
Great Britain
Greece
Greek Islands
Halifax
Hawaii
Hong Kong
Honolulu, Waikiki & Oahu
India
Ireland
Italy
Jamaica
Japan
Kauai
Las Vegas
London
Los Angeles
Maryland & Delaware
Maui
Mexico
Montana & Wyoming
Montréal & Québec City
Munich & the Bavarian Alps
Nashville & Memphis
New England
Newfoundland & Labrador
New Mexico
New Orleans
New York City
New York State
New Zealand
Northern Italy
Norway
Nova Scotia, New Brunswick &
  Prince Edward Island
Oregon
Ottawa
Paris
Peru

Philadelphia & the Amish
  Country
Portugal
Prague & the Best of the Czech
  Republic
Provence & the Riviera
Puerto Rico
Rome
San Antonio & Austin
San Diego
San Francisco
Santa Fe, Taos & Albuquerque
Scandinavia
Scotland
Seattle
Shanghai
Sicily
Singapore & Malaysia
South Africa
South America
South Florida
South Pacific
Southeast Asia
Spain
Sweden
Switzerland
Texas
Thailand
Tokyo
Toronto
Turkey
USA
Utah
Vancouver & Victoria
Vermont, New Hampshire &
  Maine
Vienna & the Danube Valley
Virgin Islands
Virginia
Walt Disney World® & Orlando
Washington, D.C.
Washington State

FROMMER'S® DOLLAR-A-DAY GUIDES

Australia from $50 a Day
California from $70 a Day
England from $75 a Day
Europe from $85 a Day
Florida from $70 a Day
Hawaii from $80 a Day

Ireland from $80 a Day
Italy from $70 a Day
London from $90 a Day
New York City from $90 a Day
Paris from $90 a Day
San Francisco from $70 a Day

Washington, D.C. from $80 a
  Day
Portable London from $90 a Day
Portable New York City from $90
  a Day
Portable Paris from $90 a Day

FROMMER'S® PORTABLE GUIDES

Acapulco, Ixtapa & Zihuatanejo
Amsterdam
Aruba
Australia's Great Barrier Reef
Bahamas
Berlin
Big Island of Hawaii
Boston
California Wine Country
Cancún
Cayman Islands
Charleston
Chicago
Disneyland®
Dominican Republic
Dublin

Florence
Frankfurt
Hong Kong
Las Vegas
Las Vegas for Non-Gamblers
London
Los Angeles
Los Cabos & Baja
Maine Coast
Maui
Miami
Nantucket & Martha's Vineyard
New Orleans
New York City
Paris

Phoenix & Scottsdale
Portland
Puerto Rico
Puerto Vallarta, Manzanillo &
  Guadalajara
Rio de Janeiro
San Diego
San Francisco
Savannah
Vancouver
Vancouver Island
Venice
Virgin Islands
Washington, D.C.
Whistler

FROMMER'S® NATIONAL PARK GUIDES

Algonquin Provincial Park
Banff & Jasper
Family Vacations in the National
  Parks

Grand Canyon
National Parks of the American
  West
Rocky Mountain

Yellowstone & Grand Teton
Yosemite & Sequoia/Kings
  Canyon
Zion & Bryce Canyon

FROMMER'S® MEMORABLE WALKS

Chicago
London

New York
Paris

San Francisco

FROMMER'S® WITH KIDS GUIDES

Chicago
Las Vegas
New York City

Ottawa
San Francisco
Toronto

Vancouver
Walt Disney World® & Orlando
Washington, D.C.

SUZY GERSHMAN'S BORN TO SHOP GUIDES

Born to Shop: France
Born to Shop: Hong Kong,
  Shanghai & Beijing

Born to Shop: Italy
Born to Shop: London

Born to Shop: New York
Born to Shop: Paris

FROMMER'S® IRREVERENT GUIDES

Amsterdam
Boston
Chicago
Las Vegas
London

Los Angeles
Manhattan
New Orleans
Paris
Rome

San Francisco
Seattle & Portland
Vancouver
Walt Disney World®
Washington, D.C.

FROMMER'S® BEST-LOVED DRIVING TOURS

Austria
Britain
California
France

Germany
Ireland
Italy
New England

Northern Italy
Scotland
Spain
Tuscany & Umbria

THE UNOFFICIAL GUIDES®

Beyond Disney
California with Kids
Central Italy
Chicago
Cruises
Disneyland®
England
Florida
Florida with Kids
Inside Disney

Hawaii
Las Vegas
London
Maui
Mexico's Best Beach Resorts
Mini Las Vegas
Mini Mickey
New Orleans
New York City
Paris

San Francisco
Skiing & Snowboarding in the
  West
South Florida including Miami &
  the Keys
Walt Disney World®
Walt Disney World® for
  Grown-ups
Walt Disney World® with Kids
Washington, D.C.

SPECIAL-INTEREST TITLES

Athens Past & Present
Cities Ranked & Rated
Frommer's Best Day Trips from London
Frommer's Best RV & Tent Campgrounds
  in the U.S.A.
Frommer's Caribbean Hideaways
Frommer's China: The 50 Most Memorable Trips
Frommer's Exploring America by RV
Frommer's Gay & Lesbian Europe
Frommer's NYC Free & Dirt Cheap

Frommer's Road Atlas Europe
Frommer's Road Atlas France
Frommer's Road Atlas Ireland
Frommer's Wonderful Weekends from
  New York City
The New York Times' Guide to Unforgettable
  Weekends
Retirement Places Rated
Rome Past & Present

Travel Tip: He who finds the best hotel deal has more to spend on facials involving knobbly vegetables.

Hello, the Roaming Gnome here. I've been nabbed from the garden and taken round the world. The people who took me are so terribly clever. They find the best offerings on Travelocity. For very little cha-ching. And that means I get to be pampered and exfoliated till I'm pink as a bunny's doodah.

travelocity®

1-888-TRAVELOCITY / travelocity.com / America Online Keyword: Travel

Travel Tip: Make sure there's customer service for any change of plans — involving friendly natives, for example.

One can plan and plan, but if you don't book with the right people you can't seize le moment and canoodle with the poodle named Pansy. I, for one, am all for fraternizing with the locals. Better yet, if I need to extend my stay and my gnome nappers are willing, it can all be arranged through the 800 number at, oh look, how convenient, the lovely company coat of arms.

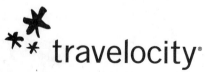
travelocity®

1-888-TRAVELOCITY / travelocity.com / America Online Keyword: Travel